PHILO

VI

THE LOEB CLASSICAL LIBRARY

FOUNDED BY JAMES LOEB, LL.D.

EDITED BY

†T. E. PAGE, C.H., LITT.D.

†E. CAPPS, PH.D., LL.D.   †W. H. D. ROUSE, LITT.D.

L. A. POST, L.H.D.   E. H. WARMINGTON, M.A., F.R.HIST.SOC.

PHILO

VI

PHILO *Judaeus*

WITH AN ENGLISH TRANSLATION BY

F. H. COLSON, M.A.

LATE FELLOW OF ST. JOHN'S COLLEGE, CAMBRIDGE

IN TEN VOLUMES
(AND TWO SUPPLEMENTARY VOLUMES)

VI

CAMBRIDGE, MASSACHUSETTS
HARVARD UNIVERSITY PRESS
LONDON
WILLIAM HEINEMANN LTD
MCMLXVI

First printed 1935
Reprinted 1950, 1959, 1966

CONTENTS OF VOLUME VI

PREFACE TO VOLUME VI

Mr. Whitaker left no work of any kind bearing on the contents of this volume, and it therefore appears in my name only.

The great difference of subject matter from the five previous volumes has made the long detailed analytical introductions less necessary and where the narrative runs on continuously for a considerable length almost useless. I have accordingly retained them only in a very modified form. I have continued to divide the annotation into footnotes which seemed needed for the comprehension of the passages and appendix notes mainly for illustration, but both footnotes and appendix are considerably diminished.

One point perhaps requires apology or at least justification. What appears here as the Second Book of the Life of Moses was before the publication of Cohn's edition divided into two, a Second Book of twelve Chapters, and a Third Book of thirty-nine. Cohn who has demonstrated the erroneousness of this division,[a] takes the middle course of numbering the Chapters as of two books, but the sections as of one. Since Cohn originated the arrangement by sections this was probably the wiser course. But now that citation by sections is superseding the old citation by

See note on p. 274.

chapters this difference of arrangement between sections and chapters seemed to me confusing and I have accordingly numbered the chapters continuously from 1 to 50; and therefore in tracing a reference to a particular chapter of *De Vita Mosis*, iii. my readers will have to subtract twelve. I hope any inconvenience caused by this will be diminished by the fact that most, if not all, references to Philo in earlier writers cite not only the chapters of a treatise but the Mangey pages, which of course remain unchanged.

I may add that Dr. Rouse's help, which has been generously given throughout, has been particularly useful in this volume.

F. H. C.

April 1935.

GENERAL INTRODUCTION

In this volume we enter [a] upon the second main division of Philo's works. The preceding five volumes have been occupied with what is usually called the commentary or allegorical commentary. We now pass on to his Exposition of the Laws to which the biographical treatises in this volume serve as an introduction. Philo starts with the assumption that the Pentateuch as a whole is a law-book written by the lawgiver himself. But this law-book obviously opens and continues with a large amount of material which is not, strictly speaking, legislative but narrative. Hence the theory is developed that Moses began with describing the foundation of the world-commonwealth or cosmopolis which was to be governed by the laws, and followed it by describing the lives of those who had observed those laws while still unwritten and were therefore themselves " living laws," as well as

---

[a] Or perhaps I shall rather say " re-enter," as *De Abr.* assumes that the *De Opificio* is the opening book of the " Exposition." And so the German translators begin with the *De Op.* and proceed at once to *De Abr.* In this translation we have followed the traditional arrangement, which is also that adopted by Cohn and Wendland, not perhaps without justification. It must be noted that if *De Op.* begins the Exposition, it serves the same purpose for the Commentary which begins with Gen. ii. 1, and seems to assume that the story of Creation has been adequately dealt with.

the rewards which obedience, and the punishments which disobedience, in the past had incurred. He has already in the *De Opificio* expounded Moses' story of the cosmogony. In the four treatises contained in this volume and two others which have not been preserved he deals with the rest of what he calls the historical part of the legislation.

The general plan of the first three of these six treatises, namely the extant *Abraham* and the lost *Isaac* and *Jacob*, was to shew that Moses set before us the history of the soul in two triads. The first triad, Enos, Enoch and Noah, represent respectively Hope, Repentance or Improvement, and Justice. These three are the imperfectly wise, for though Justice is the Queen of virtues and indeed Noah is called perfect, he is only perfect in his generation—that is, relatively only—and therefore falls below the second triad of the truly wise. This triad, Abraham, Isaac and Jacob, represent respectively Wisdom or Virtue as acquired by teaching, nature and practice. The first triad is disposed of in §§ 7-47 of *De Abrahamo*; the second forms the subject of the rest of that treatise, and no doubt of the two that have been lost.

The formula Nature (natural ability), Teaching, Practice as covering the necessary requirements for education is a commonplace in ancient scholastic literature. Philo is the first, so far as I know, to apply it to spiritual life, and we have met with this application frequently in the Allegorical Commentary.[a] But though it is one of his leading ideas, he takes little pains to show how it fits the three great Patriarchs. The chequered career of Jacob, " long

---

[a] Cf. *De Sac.* 5 f., *De Cong.* 35 f., *De Mut.* 12 and note, *De Som.* i. 160, 167, 173.

trained in the athletics of adversity," [a] qualifies him no doubt for the name of the Practiser so regularly applied to him, but it is difficult to see how Abraham pre-eminently represents wisdom acquired by teaching. True, he receives and obeys the Divine instructions, but so do Isaac and Jacob, though perhaps in a lesser degree, and Isaac's name of the Self-Taught does not exclude discipleship to God. What, if anything, Philo found in the life of Isaac to justify this epithet applied to him almost as often as Practiser is to Jacob he never tells us.[b] I imagine that the idea rests chiefly on the meaning of the name. Isaac is "laughter" and therefore "joy," and joy is the result, or as he calls it, the reward when the mind finds what it seeks instinctively and without labour.[c]

The *De Abrahamo* after the first 47 sections gives the main incidents of Abraham's life, not in chronological order, but to illustrate his piety, hospitality, tact and kindness, courage and self-control. In every case except the last, which describes Abraham's resignation at the death of Sarah, the narrative is followed by an allegorical interpretation. The general principles of these allegories is much the same as in the Commentary, but the method is in one respect very different. No knowledge of the Pentateuch beyond the passage under discussion is supposed to be possessed by the reader, and consequently there is

---

[a] *De Ios.* 26.

[b] Though Stanley discovered in Isaac a gentleness and meditativeness which distinguishes him from the other two. See, for "the gentle Isaac," *Jewish Church*, i. p. 32.

[c] See, particularly *De Praemiis* 50, where also faith is said to be the "reward" of the soul which learns by teaching, since instruction requires the readiness of the instructed to believe. This passage perhaps gives us the best clue to the meaning which Philo attaches to the formula.

none of the rambling from text to text or of the insetting in the main allegory of minor allegories suggested by casual phrases, which constitutes the most striking characteristic and the chief difficulty of the other set of treatises.

The *De Iosepho* is something of an excrescence in the scheme. The qualities of the ideal "politician" or "statesman" might serve as an effective supplement to those of the contemplative and philosophical life, but they do not bear much relation to the three types of Nature, Teaching and Practice, and when Philo in the *De Praemiis* [a] gives a sort of recapitulatory survey of the historical part of the law-book, while Abraham, Isaac, Jacob and Moses are all discussed again, there is no word of Joseph. I should imagine that he felt, what of course is true, that in the Joseph chapters of Genesis he had a fine dramatic story which could not be without undue compression worked into the life of Jacob, a story rich in incidents which offer themselves for epic narrative, and in situations which gave full scope for the rhetorical exhibitions in which his age delighted. If in view of contemporary misgovernment he felt a pleasure in showing how justly Egypt had once been governed by a Jew, the feeling was only natural.

The treatment of the life of Joseph in the *De Iosepho* makes a startling contrast to the persistent depreciation to which his character has been subjected throughout the Allegorical Commentary. There he is the man wise in his own conceit,[b] the philosopher of statecraft rather than truth,[c] the honourer of spurious goods,[d] whose study is of the body and vain imaginations,[e]

---

[a] §§ 22-56.　　　　[b] *Leg. All.* iii. 179.
[c] *Quod Det.* 7　　[d] *De Sob.* 14.　　　　*De Agr.* 56.

xii

the many-sided vanity of life.[a] One explanation given is that the two opposing views belong to different periods and stages in Philo's life. Professor Goodenough [b] ascribes it to the difference of audiences addressed in the Exposition and the Commentary, or to a chronic vacillation in Philo's own temperament, or to both together. I am inclined to think that the " chronic vacillation of character " is enough in itself, though I should prefer to call it a chronic tendency to see both sides of a question alternately or even simultaneously. Philo undoubtedly looks upon the philosophical life as the highest, and the practical life which includes the political as a necessary evil. But he is as firm upon the necessity of the latter as on the superiority of the former, and further the lower may be conceived of as a discipline or stepping-stone to the higher. If this is realized, the twofold representation of Joseph will not present insuperable difficulties. The main fact in the life of Joseph was that he lived in Egypt and was Pharaoh's viceroy. Since Egypt spiritually is the body and the King of Egypt the body-loving mind, Joseph may represent the agent which that king employs for his baser purposes. He is not from this point of view a historical person, but a τρόπος or temperament [c] and Philo has no difficulty in finding isolated facts and passages which can be made to

[a] *De Conf.* 71. Besides these and many others note especially the sustained depreciation in *De Som.* ii. 10-16 and often later in the same treatise.

[b] " Philo's Exposition of the Law and his De Vita Mosis," *Harvard Theological Review*, April 1933.

[c] Or " one of the traits or feelings existing in every man's soul," as he is definitely stated to be in *De Som.* ii. 98. From this point of view we are told to forget the actual cruelty of the brothers.

bear this out. His coat of many colours, his name of " addition " signifying adventitious goods, his mounting the second chariot, his swearing by the health of Pharaoh, the arrogant claims of his dreams, can all be pressed into service, while anything that does not fit can, if needed, be ignored.[a] On the other hand, political life is also capable of bringing out higher qualities, and of those the historical Joseph is the obvious exemplar. In fact, Philo's treatment of Joseph gives us the clearest example of his belief that the spiritual truths which may " break out of the Word " are manifold, not only different, but even at first sight contradictory.[b]

On the whole, these two treatises proceed on the same general method, though in *De Iosepho* the rhetorical element is far more and the allegorical less conspicuous. But the two books on the life of Moses stand to some extent by themselves. The opening of the first book does not suggest that it is a sequel to the four that have preceded, but assigns a different reason for its composition, viz. that its object is to make the story and character of the great legislator

[a] Not but that opposing facts are sometimes too strong and numerous to be ignored. Thus in *De Mig.* 16-24, when the allegory is based on the carrying of Joseph's bones to Canaan, these " bones " or memorable actions are catalogued, and even in *De Som.* ii., where the representation of him as the impersonation of vanity is most developed, the hope is held out that ultimately he will be reconciled with his brethren (§ 108). Again, when the allegory demands a more favourable view, as when the point is that he *finds* his brethren, he becomes the man who mixes in public life, but has no thirst for fame (πολιτικὸς μὲν ἥκιστα δὲ δοξομανής, *De Fuga* 126).

[b] For instance, the coat of many colours, which has served in *De Som.* i. 219 to represent the falseness of the mere politician, stands in *De Ios.* 32 for the resourcefulness in peace and war of the true statesman.

known to the outer world. The constitution of the book is also very different. Allegory is almost entirely banished from the narrative and confined to explanation of the priest's vestments and the form and apparatus of the Tabernacle. Regarded as biography, they are not so satisfactory as the *De Abrahamo* and the *De Iosepho*. Philo's arrangement of the life of Moses under the four heads of king, lawgiver, priest and prophet does, no doubt, serve for a logical basis to the work, but it leads him into many oddities. While the story of Moses as king or leader is carried on consistently to the end of Exodus xviii., what next to the deliverance itself is the central point of the story, the theophany on Sinai, is entirely omitted ; the account of Balaam and Balak, which has little to do with Moses himself, is given at disproportionate length, while the stories of the Red Sea and the Manna and the Golden Calf are given twice over.

These and other considerations have led what is probably the great majority of scholars to think that the two books are not an integral part of the Exposition, but a work composed on a separate occasion, and (at least in the eyes of those who consider the Exposition to be intended primarily for Jewish readers) [a]

---

[a] Any discussion of this disputed question may be left till we come to the Laws themselves in the next volume. Meanwhile I find it difficult to resist the general impression that Philo in writing the *De Abrahamo* and *De Iosepho* as well as the *De Vita Mosis*, in which the fact is admitted, had Gentiles rather than Jews in view. Observe, for instance (unless it is to be put down as a mere mannerism), the strict economy of names in all four books. Just as neither Balaam nor even Aaron in the third and fourth is ever mentioned by name, so too Lot in the first and the brothers in the second (even when they act or speak individually) are only indicated by their relationship to Abraham or Jacob.

for a different audience. While not venturing to hold the contrary I do not feel enough confidence in Philo's consistency of method to regard this as certain. Anyhow, the fact is clear that, however and for whomsoever composed, the two books effect what indeed is implied in the recapitulatory survey in the *De Praemiis*, where Moses is joined with Abraham, Isaac and Jacob as the recipient of the rewards of obedience which the Pentateuch in Philo's view is intended to preach. Without them his survey of the lessons of the history which is begun in the *De Abrahamo* and his portrait of the " Living Laws "[a] would be hopelessly incomplete, and their right place in the series is that which has been given them in all editions and is retained in this translation.

Taking the four books as a whole I would make two comments. One is that the separate stories are admirably told with much fire, vigour and lucidity. The "stilted and frigid"[b] speeches repel us, but to Greek readers living in the age of Epideictic oratory they would be congenial enough. As for the narratives themselves, none of us would wish to exchange them for the sacred simplicity of our own version. But the Gentile readers who had no such associations must have found them a pleasant contrast to the harsh Greek of the Septuagint.

[a] Moses is of course primarily the lawgiver, rather than himself the law, and Philo may possibly have shrunk from saying that Moses the biographer *intended* his own biography to serve the same purpose as the biographies of the patriarchs. Still the title of " Living Law " is applied to him in *De Mos.* i. 162.

[b] The epithets are quoted from my own judgement of them as given in the General Introduction to Vol. I. p xxii. I am inclined now to modify them with regard to some of the speeches.

GENERAL INTRODUCTION

The second point is the essential fidelity with which Philo adheres to the narrative of Scripture. Though he professes to draw also from the Tradition of the Elders, there is little or none of the legendary accretions with which the Book of Jubilees, the so-called " Antiquities of Philo " and even Josephus, to say nothing of later Rabbinical tradition, endeavour to embellish the history of the Patriarchs and of Moses.[a] There is of course any amount of amplification : that is according to the practice of many if not most ancient historians, who consider it their business not merely to state but to interpret facts—to infer what the actors probably would have felt, said, or done in the given circumstances. A good example is the description of the battle of Abraham and 318 men against the four kings,[b] where the LXX " he came upon them by night and smote them " is expanded into " he attacked the enemy by night when they had supped and were preparing to go to sleep. Some fell helpless victims to him in their beds, others who took arms against him were completely annihilated," with a few more words about the extinction of the whole army. As Josephus, *Ant.* i. 177,[c] gives similar details,

[a] The closest approach to this is the account of Moses' education in *Mos.* i. 21 ff., but even this is merely a statement of what an Egyptian prince would, in Philo's view, have naturally been taught.   [b] *De Abr.* 233 f.

[c] As the relation of Josephus's narrative to Philo's may be of interest to some readers, I may remark here that Cohn in the introduction to his fourth volume, p. xxv, considers that Josephus did make use of Philo, particularly of *Mos.* i. and ii. He quotes ten examples of similar thought and phrases, mainly the former. Thackeray, in his notes to the Loeb translation of *Ant.* i. and ii., cites some five instances of the kind from the *De Abr.* and *De Ios.* The resemblance of thought in *Ant.* i. 18 f. to the opening of *De Op.* is far more striking, but clearly Josephus may have read that work or

this is quoted as a " striking parallel," but surely it merely describes what is naturally to be expected in a successful night attack by a small force against a larger.

As for the text, we find nothing corresponding to the difficulties and corruptions which we found in the first five volumes. In the first place the MSS., at least those which are used by Cohn, are far more numerous. They vary from thirteen in number to eleven, whereas in the other set of treatises the maximum was seven, and in three cases the editor was forced to rely on one or two codices, none of them remarkable for accuracy. Secondly, the straightforward narrative as opposed to the tortuous argument of the Allegorical Commentary was apparently handled by the scribes with greater ease and accuracy. Consequently, though there are plenty of the minor differences certain to be found in this larger number of MSS. so that the Apparatus Criticus is no shorter, the emendations adopted by Cohn are few and in only one case has the present translator ventured to add any to the list.

its opening, without reading or at least making systematic use of the other treatises. I think this last should be regarded as somewhat uncertain, but see note on pp. 608 f.

LIST OF PHILO'S WORKS

SHOWING THEIR DIVISION INTO VOLUMES IN THIS EDITION

LIST OF PHILO'S WORKS

[1] Only two fragments extant.
[2] Extant only in an Armenian version.

ON ABRAHAM

(DE ABRAHAMO)

INTRODUCTION TO *DE ABRAHAMO*

AFTER stating his intention to follow Moses in describing the " living " before proceeding to the written Laws (1-6) Philo deals with the first and less perfect triad. First Enos the hoper, whose name equivalent to " Man " shows that hope is the first mark of a true man (7-10). Secondly repentance represented by Enoch, who was " transferred " *i.e.* to a better life and was " not found," for the good are rare and solitary (17-26). Thirdly, Noah, who was " just " in comparison with the wicked generation destroyed by the Flood (27-46).

The higher triad of the three great Patriarchs are not only typical of the trinity, Teaching, Nature and Practice, but are also the parents of Israel, the soul which attains to the sight of God (48-59). To come to Abraham himself, the literal story of his migrations shows his self-sacrifice (60-67) ; allegorically it denotes the soul's journey from godless astronomy first to self-knowledge (Haran), then to the knowledge of God (68-88). His adventures in Egypt (89-98) suggest that the tortures which plagued Pharaoh represent what the sensual mind suffers from the virtues which, while it professes to love them, are incompatible with it (99-106). Next comes the story of the three Angelic Visitors (107-118). Allegorically they represent the Self-existent and the beneficent and sovereign potencies apprehended according as the soul can rise to the full conception or is moved by hope of benefits or fear, and Philo points out that while men distrust these last motives, God does not hold them worthless (119-132). In fact the tale of the destruction of the Cities of the Plain represents the Self-existent as leaving these tasks to His subordinates

(133-146). This leads him to an allegory in which the five cities are the five senses, the noblest of which, sight, is figured by Zoar (147-166).

Next comes the sacrifice of Isaac (167-177). The greatness of Abraham is vindicated against hostile criticisms based on the frequency of similar stories of child immolation (178-199). Allegorically the story means that a devout soul often feels a duty of surrendering its " Isaac," Joy, which nevertheless through God's mercy it is allowed to retain (200-207).

These narratives have illustrated Abraham's piety. Next comes his kindness to men as shewn in his settlement of the dispute with Lot (208-216). This dispute may be taken to represent allegorically the incompatibility of love for the goods of the soul with love for bodily or external things (217-224). Then his courage appears in his victory over the four kings who had routed the armies of the five cities (225-235), and this conflict is allegorized as one between the four passions and the five senses, in which the intervention of reason turns the scale against the former (236-244). Philo now goes on to say something of the virtues of Sarah, particularly as shewn by her advocacy of the mating with Hagar (245-254) and this leads on to an account of the grief coupled with resignation shown by Abraham at her death (255-261). The treatise concludes with an eloquent praise of Abraham's faith and of his right to the title of " Elder " and the crowning tribute that he both did the law and was himself the Law (262-end).

ΒΙΟΣ ΣΟΦΟΥ ΤΟΥ ΚΑΤΑ ΔΙΔΑΣΚΑΛΙΑΝ ΤΕΛΕΙΩΘΕΝΤΟΣ Η ΝΟΜΩΝ ΑΓΡΑΦΩΝ ⟨ΤΟ ΠΡΩΤΟΝ⟩ Ο ΕΣΤΙ ΠΕΡΙ ΑΒΡΑΑΜ

[1]
1 I. Τῶν ἱερῶν νόμων ἐν πέντε βίβλοις ἀναγραφέν-
των ἡ πρώτη καλεῖται καὶ ἐπιγράφεται Γένεσις ἀπὸ
τῆς τοῦ κόσμου γενέσεως, ἣν ἐν ἀρχῇ περιέχει,
λαβοῦσα τὴν πρόσρησιν, καίτοι μυρίων ἄλλων
ἐμφερομένων πραγμάτων, ὅσα κατ᾽ εἰρήνην ἢ πόλεμον ἢ φορὰς καὶ ἀφορίας ἢ λιμὸν καὶ εὐθηνίαν
ἢ τὰς μεγίστας τῶν ἐπὶ γῆς φθορὰς διὰ πυρὸς καὶ
ὕδατος ἢ τοὐναντίον γενέσεις καὶ εὐτροφίας ζῴων
καὶ φυτῶν κατὰ τὴν ἀέρος καὶ τῶν ἐτησίων ὡρῶν
εὐκρασίαν καὶ ἀνδρῶν τῶν μὲν ἀρετῇ τῶν δὲ κακίᾳ
2 συμβιωσάντων· ἀλλ᾽ ἐπεὶ τούτων τὰ μέν ἐστι τοῦ
κόσμου μέρη, τὰ δὲ παθήματα, τελειότατον δὲ καὶ
πληρέστατον ὁ κόσμος, αὐτῷ τὴν ὅλην βίβλον
ἀνέθηκεν. ὃν μὲν οὖν τρόπον ἡ κοσμοποιία διατέτακται, διὰ τῆς προτέρας συντάξεως,
2]
3 ὡς οἷόν τε | ἦν, ἠκριβώσαμεν. ἐπεὶ δὲ τοὺς νόμους
κατὰ τὸ ἑξῆς ⟨καὶ⟩ ἀκόλουθον ἀναγκαῖον διερευνᾶσθαι, τῶν ἐπὶ μέρους καὶ ὡς ἂν εἰκόνων ὑπέρ-
θεσιν ποιησάμενοι τοὺς καθολικωτέρους καὶ ὡς ἂν

---

a *i.e.* the Deluge and the destruction of Sodom and
Gomorrah. Philo classes these two together, ignoring the
purely local character of the latter. Compare his treatment
of the two in *Mos.* ii. 52-65, and *cf. ib.* 263.

4

ON ABRAHAM

THAT IS, THE LIFE OF THE WISE MAN MADE PERFECT THROUGH TEACHING, OR THE FIRST BOOK ON UNWRITTEN LAWS

I. The first of the five books in which the holy 1
laws are written bears the name and inscription of
Genesis, from the genesis or creation of the world,
an account of which it contains at its beginning. It
has received this title in spite of its embracing
numberless other matters ; for it tells of peace and
war, of fruitfulness and barrenness, of dearth and
plenty ; how fire and water wrought great destruction of what is on earth ;[a] how on the other hand
plants and animals were born and throve through the
kindly tempering of the air and the yearly seasons,
and so too men, some of whom lived a life of virtue,
others of vice. But since some of these things are 2
parts of the world, and others events which befall it,
and the world is the complete consummation which
contains them all, he dedicated the whole book to it.

The story of the order in which the world was
made has been set forth in detail by us as well as
was possible in the preceding treatise [b] ; but, since 3
it is necessary to carry out our examination of the
law in regular sequence, let us postpone consideration of particular laws, which are, so to speak, copies,
and examine first those which are more general and

[b] *i.e.* the *De Opificio.* See General Introduction to this
volume, p. ix, note *a.*

4 ἀρχετύπους προτέρους διερευνήσωμεν. οὗτοι δέ
εἰσιν ἀνδρῶν οἱ ἀνεπιλήπτως καὶ καλῶς βιώσαντες,
ὧν τὰς ἀρετὰς ἐν ταῖς ἱερωτάταις ἐστηλιτεῦσθαι
γραφαῖς συμβέβηκεν, οὐ πρὸς τὸν ἐκείνων ἔπαινον
αὐτὸ μόνον, ἀλλὰ καὶ ὑπὲρ τοῦ τοὺς ἐντυγχάνοντας
προτρέψασθαι καὶ ἐπὶ τὸν ὅμοιον ζῆλον ἀγαγεῖν.
5 οἱ γὰρ ἔμψυχοι καὶ λογικοὶ νόμοι ἄνδρες ἐκεῖνοι
γεγόνασιν, οὓς δυοῖν χάριν ἐσέμνυνεν· ἑνὸς μὲν
βουλόμενος ἐπιδεῖξαι, ὅτι τὰ τεθειμένα διατάγματα
τῆς φύσεως οὐκ ἀπᾴδει, δευτέρου δὲ ὅτι οὐ πολὺς
πόνος τοῖς ἐθέλουσι κατὰ τοὺς κειμένους νόμους
ζῆν, ὁπότε καὶ ἀγράφῳ τῇ νομοθεσίᾳ, πρίν τι τὴν
ἀρχὴν ἀναγραφῆναι τῶν ἐν μέρει, ῥᾳδίως καὶ εὐ-
πετῶς ἐχρήσαντο οἱ πρῶτοι· ὡς δεόντως ἄν τινα
φάναι, τοὺς τεθέντας νόμους μηδὲν ἄλλ' ἢ ὑπομνήματα εἶναι βίου τῶν παλαιῶν, ἀρχαιολογοῦντας
6 ἔργα καὶ λόγους, οἷς ἐχρήσαντο. ἐκεῖνοι γὰρ οὔτε
γνώριμοι καὶ φοιτηταὶ γενόμενοί τινων οὔτε παρὰ
διδασκάλοις ἃ χρὴ πράττειν καὶ λέγειν ἀναδιδαχθέντες, αὐτήκοοι δὲ καὶ αὐτομαθεῖς, ἀκολουθίαν
φύσεως ἀσπασάμενοι, τὴν φύσιν αὐτήν, ὅπερ ἐστὶ
πρὸς ἀλήθειαν, πρεσβύτατον θεσμὸν εἶναι ὑπολαβόντες ἅπαντα τὸν βίον ηὐνομήθησαν, ὑπαίτιον
μὲν οὐδὲν γνώμαις ἑκουσίοις ἐργασάμενοι, περὶ δὲ
τῶν ἐκ τύχης ποτνιώμενοι τὸν θεὸν καὶ λιταῖς καὶ
ἱκεσίαις ἐξευμενιζόμενοι πρὸς ὁλοκλήρου μετουσίαν
ζωῆς δι' ἀμφοτέρων κατορθουμένης τῶν τε ἐκ
προνοίας καὶ τῶν ἄνευ ἑκουσίου γνώμης.
7 ΙΙ. Ἐπειδὴ τοίνυν ἀρχὴ μετουσίας ἀγαθῶν ἐστιν
ἐλπὶς καὶ ταύτην οἷα λεωφόρον ὁδὸν ἡ φιλάρετος

ᵃ See App. p. 597.

may be called the originals of those copies. These 4 are such men as lived good and blameless lives, whose virtues stand permanently recorded in the most holy scriptures, not merely to sound their praises but for the instruction of the reader and as an inducement to him to aspire to the same ; for in 5 these men we have laws endowed with life and reason,[a] and Moses extolled them for two reasons. First he wished to shew that the enacted ordinances are not inconsistent with nature ; and secondly that those who wish to live in accordance with the laws as they stand have no difficult task, seeing that the first generations before any at all of the particular statutes was set in writing followed the unwritten law with perfect ease, so that one might properly say that the enacted laws are nothing else than memorials of the life of the ancients, preserving to a later generation their actual words and deeds. For they were not scholars or pupils of others, nor 6 did they learn under teachers what was right to say or do : they listened to no voice or instruction but their own : they gladly accepted conformity with nature, holding that nature itself was, as indeed it is, the most venerable of statutes, and thus their whole life was one of happy obedience to law. They committed no guilty action of their own free will or purpose, and where chance led them wrong they besought God's mercy and propitiated Him with prayers and supplications, and thus secured a perfect life guided aright in both fields, both in their premeditated actions and in such as were not of freely-willed purpose.

II. Since, then, the first step towards the possession 7 of blessings is hope, and hope like a high road is

ἀνατέμνει καὶ ἀνοίγει ψυχὴ σπουδάζουσα τυχεῖν
τοῦ πρὸς ἀλήθειαν καλοῦ, τὸν πρῶτον ἐλπίδος
ἐραστὴν προσεῖπεν "ἄνθρωπον" τὸ κοινὸν τοῦ
γένους ὄνομα κατ' ἐξαίρετον χάριν δωρησάμενος
8 αὐτῷ—Χαλδαῖοι γὰρ τὸν ἄνθρωπον Ἐνὼς καλοῦσιν
—ὡς μόνου πρὸς ἀλήθειαν ὄντος ἀνθρώπου τοῦ τὰ
ἀγαθὰ προσδοκῶντος καὶ ἐλπίσι χρησταῖς ἐφιδρυ-
μένου· ἐξ οὗ δῆλον, ὅτι τὸν δύσελπιν οὐκ ἄνθρωπον
ἀλλ' ἀνθρωποειδὲς ἡγεῖται θηρίον τὸ οἰκειότατον
9 ἀνθρωπίνης ψυχῆς, ἐλπίδα, ἀφῃρημένον. ὅθεν καὶ
παγκάλως ὑμνῆσαι βουλόμενος τὸν εὔελπιν προ-
ειπών, ὅτι οὗτος ἤλπισεν ἐπὶ τὸν τῶν ὅλων πατέρα
[3] καὶ ποιητήν, ἐπιλέγει· "αὕτη ἡ βίβλος | γενέσεως
ἀνθρώπων," καίτοι πατέρων καὶ πάππων ἤδη
γεγονότων· ἀλλὰ τοὺς μὲν ἀρχηγέτας τοῦ μικτοῦ
γένους ὑπέλαβεν εἶναι, τουτονὶ δὲ τοῦ καθαρωτάτου
10 καὶ διηθημένου, ὅπερ ὄντως ἐστὶ λογικόν. καθάπερ
γὰρ ποιητὴς Ὅμηρος, μυρίων ποιητῶν ὄντων, κατ'
ἐξοχὴν λέγεται, καὶ τὸ μέλαν ᾧ γράφομεν, καίτοι
παντὸς ὃ μὴ λευκόν ἐστι μέλανος ὄντος, καὶ ἄρχων
Ἀθήνησιν ὁ ἐπώνυμος καὶ τῶν ἐννέα ἀρχόντων
ἄριστος, ἀφ' οὗ οἱ χρόνοι καταριθμοῦνται, τὸν αὐτὸν
τρόπον καὶ τὸν ἐλπίδι χρώμενον "ἄνθρωπον" κατ'
ἐξοχὴν ὠνόμασε τὰ πλήθη τῶν ἄλλων ἀφησυχάσας

---

[a] Philo uses "Chaldaean" as a synonym for Hebrew
frequently in these works, though not in the treatises contained in Vols. I.-V.

[b] This argument, founded on Gen. iv. 26, LXX "He called
his name Enos; he hoped to call on the name of the Lord
God" (E.V. "then began men to call upon the name of the
Lord") and on the fact that Enos is a poetical Hebrew term
for "man," has already been given in substantially the same
form in *Quod Det.* 138.

constructed and opened up by the virtue-loving soul in its eagerness to gain true excellence, Moses called the first lover of hope " Man," thus bestowing on him as a special favour the name which is common to the race (for the Chaldean[a] name for Man is Enos), **8** on the grounds that he alone is a true man who expects good things and rests firmly on comfortable hopes.[b] This plainly shows that he regards a despondent person as no man but a beast in human shape, since he has been robbed of the nearest and dearest possession of the human soul, namely hope. And, therefore, in his wish to give the highest praise **9** to the hoper, after first stating that he set his hope on the Father and Maker of all, he adds, " this is the book of the coming into being of men," though fathers and grandfathers had already come into being. But he held that they were the founders of the mixed race, but Enos of that from which all impurity had been strained, in fact of the race which is truly reasonable. For just as we give the title of **10** " *the* poet " to Homer in virtue of his pre-eminence, though there are multitudes of poets besides him, and " *the* black "[c] to the material with which we write, though everything is black which is not white, and " *the* Archon "[d] at Athens to the chief of the nine archons, the Archon Eponymos, from whose year of office dates are calculated, so too Moses gave the name of man in pre-eminence to him who cherished hope and left unnoticed the many others as un-

---

[c] μέλαν being the regular word for " ink."

[d] The 1st Archon was called simply ὁ ἄρχων, the 2nd ἄρχων βασιλεύς, the 3rd ἄρχων πολέμαρχος, the other nine θεσμοθέται. The addition of ἐπώνυμος (" who gives his name to dates," etc.) seems to be a later use.

ὡς οὐκ ἀξίων τῆς αὐτῆς προσρήσεως ἐπιλαχεῖν.

11 εὖ μέντοι καὶ τὴν βίβλον γενέσεως τοῦ
πρὸς ἀλήθειαν ἀνθρώπου προσεῖπεν, οὐκ ἀπὸ σκοποῦ, διότι γραφῆς καὶ μνήμης ἄξιος ὁ εὔελπις, οὐ
τῆς ἐν χαρτιδίοις ὑπὸ σητῶν διαφθαρησομένοις,
ἀλλὰ τῆς ἐν ἀθανάτῳ τῇ φύσει, παρ' ᾗ τὰς σπου-
δαίας πράξεις ἀναγράπτους εἶναι συμβέβηκεν.

12 εἰ μέντοι καταριθμήσειέ τις ἀπὸ τοῦ
πρώτου καὶ γηγενοῦς, τὸν ὑπὸ μὲν Χαλδαίων Ἐνὼς
Ἑλλάδι δὲ διαλέκτῳ προσαγορευόμενον '' ἄνθρω-
13 πον '' εὑρήσει τέταρτον. ἐν ἀριθμοῖς δὲ ἡ τετρὰς
τετίμηται παρά τε τοῖς ἄλλοις φιλοσόφοις, ὅσοι τὰς
ἀσωμάτους οὐσίας καὶ νοητὰς ἠσπάσαντο, καὶ
μάλιστα παρὰ Μωυσεῖ τῷ πανσόφῳ, ὃς σεμνύνων
τὸν τέταρτον ἀριθμόν φησιν ὅτι '' ἅγιός ἐστι καὶ
αἰνετός''· δι' ἃς δ' αἰτίας ἐλέχθη, διὰ τῆς προτέρας
14 συντάξεως εἴρηται. ἅγιος δὲ καὶ ἐπαινετὸς ὁ
εὔελπις, ὡς τοὐναντίον ἄναγνος καὶ ψεκτὸς ὁ
δύσελπις, φόβῳ πρὸς ἅπαντα συμβούλῳ κακῷ
χρώμενος· οὐδὲν γὰρ οὕτως ἐχθρὸν ἄλλο ἄλλῳ
φασίν, ὡς ἐλπίδα φόβῳ καὶ φόβον ἐλπίδι· καὶ
μήποτ' εἰκότως· προσδοκία μὲν γὰρ ἑκάτερον, ἀλλ'
ἡ μὲν ἀγαθῶν, ἡ δ' ἔμπαλιν κακῶν, ἀκατάλλακτοι
δ' αἱ φύσεις τούτων καὶ ἀσύμβατοι.

15 III. τοσαῦτα μὲν ἀπόχρη περὶ ἐλπίδος εἰπεῖν, ἣν

---

[a] So in *Quod Det.* 139 that "the hoper is written in the
book of God" is deduced from "this is the book of the
generation of men" following on Gen. iv. 26. Of course the
phrase introduces what is coming and begins a fresh para-
graph. For a similar misunderstanding *cf.* the treatment of
Gen. ii. 4, in *Leg. All.* i. 19, and of Gen. vi. 9 in § 31 below.

[b] Enos as Adam's grandson would naturally be third, or,
if Abel and Cain are reckoned, fifth. Philo may obtain the

worthy to receive the same title. He did **11**
well, too, in speaking of the *book* of the coming into
being of the true man.[a] The word was appropriate
because the hoper deserves a memorial written not
on pieces of paper which moths shall destroy but in
the undying book of nature where good actions are
registered. Further, if we reckon the **12**
generations from the first, the earth-born man, we
shall find that he, who is called by the Chaldeans
Enos and in our tongue Man, is fourth.[b] Now the **13**
number four has been held in high honour by the
other philosophers who devoted themselves to the
study of immaterial and conceptual realities, and
especially by the all-wise Moses who when glorifying
that number speaks of it as "holy and for praise,"[c]
and why he so called it has been shewn in the former
treatise.[d] Holy, too, and praiseworthy is the hopeful **14**
man, just as on the contrary the despondent is unholy
and blameworthy, since in all things he takes fear
for his evil counsellor; for no two things are more at
enmity with each other, men say, than fear and hope,
and surely that is natural, for each is an expectation,
hope of good, fear on the other hand of evil, and
their natures are irreconcilable and incapable of
agreement. III. No more need be said about **15**

---

number he requires by omitting either Abel, because in Gen.
iv. 25 Seth is spoken of as a substitute for him, or Cain as
accursed. See App. p. 597.

[c] Or "praiseworthy." See Lev. xix. 24 "In the fourth
year the fruit shall be holy and αἰνετός to the Lord." In *De
Plant.* 119, Philo takes αἰνετός (probably rightly) as meaning
something for which we may praise the Lord. So, too, in
De Som. i. 33, though there it is the fourth year which is
αἰνετός. Here the adjective is applied to the number itself
and, as the sequel shews, means worthy of praise.

[d] *De Op.* 47 ff.

ἐπὶ θύραις οἷα πυλωρὸν ἡ φύσις ἱδρύσατο βασιλίδων
τῶν ἔνδον ἀρετῶν, αἷς οὐκ ἔστιν ἐντυχεῖν μὴ ταύτην
16 προθεραπεύσαντας. πολλὰ μὲν οὖν οἱ νομοθέται,
πολλὰ δὲ οἱ πανταχοῦ νόμοι πραγματεύονται περὶ
τοῦ τὰς ψυχὰς τῶν ἐλευθέρων ἐλπίδων χρηστῶν
ἀναπλῆσαι· ὁ δ' ἄνευ παραινέσεως δίχα τοῦ κελευσθῆναι γενόμενος εὔελπις ἀγράφῳ μὲν νόμῳ δὲ
πάλιν αὐτομαθεῖ τὴν ἀρετὴν ταύτην πεπαίδευται,
ὃν ἡ φύσις ἔθηκε.

17 Δευτέραν δ' ἔλαχε τάξιν μετὰ τὴν ἐλπίδα ἡ ἐπὶ
τοῖς ἁμαρτανομένοις μετάνοια καὶ βελτίωσις· ὅθεν
ἑξῆς ἀναγράφει τὸν ἀπὸ χείρονος βίου πρὸς
τὸν ἀμείνω μεταβαλόντα, ὃς καλεῖται παρὰ μὲν
Ἑβραίοις Ἐνώχ, ὡς δ' ἂν Ἕλληνες εἴποιεν " κε-
χαρισμένος," ἐφ' οὗ καὶ ταυτὶ λέλεκται, ὡς ἄρα
[4] | " εὐηρέστησεν Ἐνὼχ τῷ θεῷ καὶ οὐχ ηὑρίσκετο,
18 ὅτι μετέθηκεν αὐτὸν ὁ θεός." ἡ γὰρ μετάθεσις
τροπὴν ἐμφαίνει καὶ μεταβολήν· πρὸς δὲ τὸ βέλτιον
ἡ μεταβολή, διότι προμηθείᾳ γίνεται θεοῦ· πᾶν γὰρ
τὸ σὺν θεῷ καλὸν καὶ συμφέρον πάντως, ἐπεὶ καὶ
τὸ ἄνευ θείας ἐπιφροσύνης ἀλυσιτελές.

19 εὖ δ' εἴρηται τὸ " οὐχ ηὑρίσκετο " ἐπὶ τοῦ μετα-
τεθειμένου, τῷ τὸν ἀρχαῖον καὶ ἐπίληπτον ἀπαλη-
λίφθαι βίον καὶ ἠφανίσθαι καὶ μηκέθ' εὑρίσκεσθαι,
καθάπερ εἰ μηδὲ τὴν ἀρχὴν ἐγένετο, ἢ τῷ τὸν
μετατιθέμενον καὶ ἐν τῇ βελτίονι ταχθέντα τάξει
δυσεύρετον εἶναι φύσει· πολύχουν μὲν γὰρ ἡ κακία,
διὸ καὶ πολλοῖς γνώριμον, σπάνιον δ' ἡ ἀρετή, ὡς
20 μηδ' ὑπ' ὀλίγων καταλαμβάνεσθαι. καὶ ἄλλως ὁ

---

[a] Gen. v. 24. The lxx version " Enoch was well-pleasing
to God, and he was not found because God translated him "

the subject of hope, set by nature as a door-keeper at the portals of the royal virtues within, to which access cannot be gained unless we have first paid our respects to her. Great indeed are the efforts 16 expended both by lawgivers and by laws in every nation in filling the souls of free men with comfortable hopes; but he who gains this virtue of hopefulness without being led to it by exhortation or command has been educated into it by a law which nature has laid down, a law unwritten yet intuitively learnt.

The second place after hope is given to repentance 17 for sins and to improvement, and, therefore, Moses mentions next in order him who changed from the worse life to the better, called by the Hebrews Enoch but in our language "recipient of grace." We are told of him that he proved "to be pleasing to God and was not found because God transferred him,[a]" for 18 transference implies turning and changing, and the change is to the better because it is brought about by the forethought of God. For all that is done with God's help is excellent and truly profitable, as also all that has not His directing care is unprofitable.

And the expression used of the trans- 19 ferred person, that he was not found, is well said, either because the old reprehensible life is blotted out and disappears and is no more found, as though it had never been at all, or because he who is thus transferred and takes his place in the better class is naturally hard to find. For evil is widely spread and therefore known to many, while virtue is rare, so that even the few cannot comprehend it. Besides, 20

(E.V. "Enoch walked with God: and he was not; for God took him") is familiar from Hebrews xi. 5. See App. p. 597).

μὲν φαῦλος ἀγορὰν καὶ θέατρα καὶ δικαστήρια
βουλευτήριά τε καὶ ἐκκλησίας καὶ πάντα σύλλογον
καὶ θίασον ἀνθρώπων ἅτε φιλοπραγμοσύνη συζῶν
μετατρέχει, τὴν μὲν γλῶτταν ἀνιεὶς πρὸς ἄμετρον
καὶ ἀπέραντον καὶ ἄκριτον διήγησιν, συγχέων
ἅπαντα καὶ φύρων, ἀληθέσι ψευδῆ καὶ ῥητοῖς
ἄρρητα καὶ ἴδια κοινοῖς καὶ ἱεροῖς βέβηλα καὶ
σπουδαίοις γελοῖα ἀναμιγνύς, διὰ τὸ μὴ πεπαι-
δεῦσθαι τὸ ἐν καιρῷ κάλλιστον, ἡσυχίαν, τὰ δὲ ὦτα
21 ἐπουρίσας[1] ἕνεκα πολυπράγμονος περιεργίας· τὰ γὰρ
ἑτέρων εἴτε ἀγαθὰ εἴτ' αὖ κακὰ γλίχεται μανθάνειν,
ὡς αὐτίκα τοῖς μὲν φθονεῖν, ἐφ' οἷς δὲ ἥδεσθαι·
βάσκανον γὰρ καὶ μισόκαλον καὶ φιλοπόνηρον ὁ
22 φαῦλος φύσει. IV. ὁ δ' ἀστεῖος ἔμπαλιν ἀπράγ-
μονος ζηλωτὴς βίου γεγονὼς ὑποχωρεῖ καὶ μόνωσιν
ἀγαπᾷ, λανθάνειν τοὺς πολλοὺς ἀξιῶν, οὐ διὰ
μισανθρωπίαν—φιλάνθρωπος γάρ, εἰ καί τις ἄλλος,
—ἀλλὰ διὰ τὸ προβεβλῆσθαι κακίαν, ἣν ὁ πολὺς
ὄχλος ἀσπάζεται, χαίρων μὲν ἐφ' οἷς στένειν ἄξιον,
23 λυπούμενος δὲ ἐφ' οἷς γεγηθέναι καλόν. ὧν ἕνεκα
συγκλεισάμενος οἴκοι τὰ πολλὰ καταμένει μόλις τὰς
κλισιάδας ὑπερβαίνων ἢ διὰ τοὺς ἐπιφοιτῶντας
συνεχέστερον ἔξω πόλεως προελθὼν ἐν μοναγρίᾳ
ποιεῖται τὰς διατριβὰς ἥδιον συμβιωταῖς χρώμενος
τοῖς ἅπαντος τοῦ γένους ἀνθρώπων ἀρίστοις, ὧν τὰ
μὲν σώματα διέλυσεν ὁ χρόνος, τὰς δ' ἀρετὰς αἱ
ἀπολειφθεῖσαι γραφαὶ ζωπυροῦσι διά τε ποιημάτων
καὶ τῶν καταλογάδην συγγραμμάτων, οἷς ἡ ψυχὴ

---

[1] ἐπουρίσας] so Cohn, but the text is very doubtful. Some
MSS. have ἐπορθιάσας εὐπορίας (with variations of order and
spelling), others ἐπουριάσας or ἐπουριάς. The natural sense of
ἐπουρίζω (lit. "direct with a favouring wind") seems by itself

the worthless man whose life is one long restlessness haunts market-places, theatres, law-courts, council-halls, assemblies, and every group and gathering of men; his tongue he lets loose for unmeasured, end-less, indiscriminate talk, bringing chaos and confusion into everything, mixing true with false, fit with unfit, public with private, holy with profane, sensible with absurd, because he has not been trained to that silence which in season is most excellent. His ears 21 he keeps alert in meddlesome curiosity, ever eager to learn his neighbour's affairs, whether good or bad, and ready with envy for the former and joy at the latter ; for the worthless man is a creature naturally malicious, a hater of good and lover of evil. IV. The man of worth on the other hand, having acquired 22 a desire for a quiet life, withdraws from the public and loves solitude, and his choice is to be unnoticed by the many, not because he is misanthropical, for he is eminently a philanthropist, but because he has rejected vice which is welcomed by the multitude who rejoice at what calls for mourning and grieve where it is well to be glad. And therefore he mostly 23 secludes himself at home and scarcely ever crosses his threshold, or else because of the frequency of visitors he leaves the town and spends his days in some lonely farm, finding pleasanter society in those noblest of the whole human race whose bodies time has turned into dust but the flame of their virtues is kept alive by the written records which have survived them in poetry or in prose and serve

---

strange in this context. I should prefer to read ἐπορθιάσας ἐπ' οὐρίας (" pricked up and ready to catch any chance "). It is true that ἐπορθιάζω is not used elsewhere with ὦτα, but ἀνορθιάζω is several times so used by Philo. See further on *Mos.* i. 283.

PHILO

24 πέφυκε βελτιοῦσθαι. διὰ τοῦτο εἶπεν ὅτι ὁ μετα-
τεθεὶς " οὐχ εὑρίσκετο " δυσεύρετος καὶ δυσθήρατος
ὤν. μεθορμίζεται οὖν εἰς παιδείαν ἐξ ἀμαθίας καὶ
ἐξ ἀφροσύνης εἰς φρόνησιν ἔκ τε δειλίας εἰς |
[5] ἀνδρείαν καὶ ἐξ ἀσεβείας εἰς εὐσέβειαν, καὶ πάλιν
ἐκ μὲν φιληδονίας εἰς ἐγκράτειαν, ἐκ δὲ φιλοδοξίας
εἰς ἀτυφίαν· ὧν τίς ἢ πλοῦτος ἐπάξιος ἢ βασιλείας
25 καὶ δυναστείας κτῆσις ὠφελιμωτέρα; εἰ γὰρ χρὴ
τἀληθὲς εἰπεῖν, ὁ μὴ τυφλὸς ἀλλ' ὀξὺ βλέπων
πλοῦτος ἢ τῶν ἀρετῶν ἐστι περιουσία, ἣν εὐθὺς
γνήσιον καὶ εὔνομον παρὰ τὰς νόθους καὶ ψευδωνύμους ἀρχὰς ὑποληπτέον ἡγεμονίαν ἐνδίκως ἅπαντα
26 πρυτανεύουσαν.   οὐ δεῖ δὲ ἀγνοεῖν, ὅτι
τὰ δευτερεῖα φέρεται μετάνοια τελειότητος, ὥσπερ
καὶ ἀνόσου σώματος ἡ πρὸς ὑγείαν ἐξ ἀσθενείας
μεταβολή. τὸ μὲν οὖν διηνεκὲς καὶ τέλειον ἐν
ἀρεταῖς ἐγγυτάτω θείας ἵσταται δυνάμεως, ἡ δ' ἀπό
τινος χρόνου βελτίωσις ἴδιον ἀγαθὸν εὐφυοῦς ψυχῆς
ἐστι μὴ τοῖς παιδικοῖς ἐπιμενούσης ἀλλ' ἁδροτέροις
καὶ ἀνδρὸς ὄντως φρονήμασιν ἐπιζητούσης εὔδιον
κατάστασιν [ψυχῆς] καὶ τῇ φαντασίᾳ τῶν καλῶν
ἐπιτρεχούσης.
27 V. Ὅθεν εἰκότως τῷ μετανενοηκότι τάττει κατὰ
τὸ ἑξῆς τὸν θεοφιλῆ καὶ φιλάρετον, ὃς Ἑβραίων
μὲν τῇ γλώττῃ καλεῖται Νῶε, τῇ δὲ Ἑλλήνων
" ἀνάπαυσις " ἢ " δίκαιος," οἰκειόταται προσρήσεις
σοφῷ· ἐμφανῶς μὲν ὁ δίκαιος, ἄμεινον γὰρ οὐδὲν
δικαιοσύνης, τῆς ἐν ἀρεταῖς ἡγεμονίδος, ἢ καθάπερ
ἐν χορῷ καλλιστεύουσα πρεσβεύει· ἡ δ' ἀνάπαυσις,
ἐπεὶ καὶ τοὐναντίον τὴν παρὰ φύσιν κίνησιν ταραχῶν

---

[a] " Unnatural movement of the soul " is a phrase used
by the Stoics to define πάθος S. V.F. iii. 462 and 476.

to promote the growth of goodness in the soul. That 24 was why he said that the "transferred" was not found, being hard to find and hard to seek. So he passes across from ignorance to instruction, from folly to sound sense, from cowardice to courage, from impiety to piety, and again from voluptuousness to self-control, from vaingloriousness to simplicity. And what wealth is equal in worth to these, or what possession of royalty or dominion more profitable? For in very truth the wealth which is not blind 25 but keen of sight is abundance of virtues, which consequently we must needs hold to be, in contrast to the bastard governments falsely so-called, genuine and equitable sovereignty ruling in justice over all.

But we must not forget that repentance 26 holds the second place to perfection, just as a change from sickness to health is second to a body free from disease ; so, then, unbroken perfection of virtues stands nearest to divine power, but improvement in the course of time is the peculiar treasure of a soul gifted by nature, which does not stay in childish thoughts but by such as are more robust and truly manly seeks to gain a condition of serenity and pursues the vision of the excellent.

V. Naturally, therefore, next to the repentant he 27 sets the lover of virtue and beloved by God, who in the Hebrew language is called Noah but in ours "rest" or "just," both very suitable titles for the Sage. "Just" is obviously so, for nothing is better than justice, the chief among the virtues, who like the fairest maiden of the dance holds the highest place. But "rest" is appropriate also, since its opposite, unnatural movement,[a] proves to be the cause

17

καὶ θορύβων στάσεών τε καὶ πολέμων αἰτίαν εἶναι
συμβέβηκεν, ἣν μετίασιν οἱ φαῦλοι, ἠρεμαῖον δὲ καὶ
ἡσυχάζοντα καὶ σταθερὸν ἔτι δὲ καὶ εἰρηνικὸν βίον
28 οἱ καλοκἀγαθίαν τετιμηκότες.   ἑπόμενος
δ' αὐτὸς αὑτῷ καὶ τὴν ἑβδόμην, ἣν Ἑβραῖοι
σάββατα καλοῦσιν, ἀνάπαυσιν ὀνομάζει, οὐχ, ὡς
οἴονταί τινες, ὅτι δι' ἓξ ἡμερῶν τῶν συνήθων ἔργων
ἀπείχετο τὸ πλῆθος, ἀλλ' ὅτι τῷ ὄντι ὁ ἕβδομος
ἀριθμὸς ἔν τε τῷ κόσμῳ καὶ ἐν ἡμῖν αὐτοῖς ἀεὶ
ἀστασίαστος καὶ ἀπόλεμος καὶ ἀφιλόνεικος καὶ
29 εἰρηνικώτατος ἁπάντων ἀριθμῶν ἐστι.   μάρτυρες
δὲ τοῦ λεχθέντος αἱ ἐν ἡμῖν δυνάμεις· αἱ μὲν γὰρ
ἓξ τὸν ἄπαυστον καὶ συνεχῆ πόλεμον ἐν γῇ καὶ
θαλάττῃ συγκροτοῦσιν, αἵ τε πέντε αἰσθήσεις καὶ
ὁ προφορικὸς λόγος, αἱ μὲν πόθῳ τῶν αἰσθητῶν,
ὧν ἐὰν μὴ τυγχάνωσιν, ἀνιῶνται, ὁ δ' ἀχαλίνῳ
30 στόματι μυρία τῶν ἡσυχαστέων ἐκλαλῶν· ἡ δ'
ἑβδόμη δύναμις ἡ περὶ τὸν ἡγεμόνα νοῦν, ὃς ὅταν
ἐπικυδέστερος γένηται τῶν ἓξ καὶ δυνατωτέρᾳ
ῥώμῃ κατακρατήσας ἀναχωρήσῃ, μόνωσιν ἀσπασά-
μενος καὶ ταῖς ἑαυτοῦ πρὸς ἑαυτὸν ⟨χαίρων⟩[1]
ὁμιλίαις ὡς ἀπροσδεὴς ὢν ἑτέρου καὶ αὐταρκέ-
στατος ἑαυτῷ, τηνικαῦτα φροντίδων καὶ πραγμα-
[6] τειῶν | ἀπαλλαγεὶς τῶν ἐν τῷ θνητῷ γένει βίον
εὔδιον καὶ γαληνὸν ἀσπάζεται.
31 VI. Οὕτως δ' ἀποσεμνύνει τὸν φιλάρετον, ὥστε
καὶ γενεαλογῶν αὐτὸν οὐ, καθάπερ ἔθος ἐπὶ τῶν
ἄλλων, πάππων ἢ προπάππων ἢ προγόνων ποιεῖται
κατάλογον, ὅσοι πρὸς ἀνδρῶν ἢ πρὸς γυναικῶν
εἰσιν, ἀλλά τινων ἀρετῶν, μόνον οὐχὶ βοῶν ἀντι-

---

[1] Or read τὰς . . . ὁμιλίας omitting χαίρων.

of turmoil and confusion and factions and wars. Such movement is sought by the worthless, while a life which is calm, serene, tranquil and peaceful to boot is the object of those who have valued nobility of conduct. He shews consistency, too, when he 28 gives to the seventh day, which the Hebrews call sabbath, the name of rest; not, as some think, because the multitude abstained after six days from their usual tasks, but because in truth the number seven, both in the world and in ourselves, is always free from factions and war and quarrelling and is of all numbers the most peaceful. This statement is attested by 29 the faculties within us, for six [a] of them wage ceaseless and continuous war on land and sea, namely the five senses and speech, the former in their craving for the objects of sense, deprivation of which is painful to them, speech because with unbridled mouth it perpetually gives utterance where silence is due. But the seventh faculty is that of the 30 dominant mind, which, after triumphing over the six and returning victorious through its superior strength, welcomes solitude and rejoices in its own society, feeling that it needs no other and is completely sufficient for itself, and then released from the cares and concerns of mortal kind gladly accepts a life of calmness and serenity.

VI. So highly does Moses extol the lover of virtue 31 that when he gives his genealogy he does not, as he usually does in other cases, make a list of his grandfathers, great-grandfathers and ancestors in the male and female line, but of certain virtues, and this is

---

[a] Elsewhere, when Philo's argument requires it, the faculties, excluding mind, are seven by the addition of reproduction (τὸ γόνιμον), *De Op.* 117, *De Mut.* 111.

PHILO

κρυς, ὅτι οἰκία καὶ συγγένεια καὶ πατρὶς οὐδεμία
ἐστὶν ἑτέρα σοφῷ ὅτι μὴ ἀρεταὶ καὶ αἱ κατ᾽ ἀρετὰς
πράξεις· " αὗται " γάρ φησιν " αἱ γενέσεις Νῶε·
Νῶε ἄνθρωπος δίκαιος, τέλειος ἐν τῇ γενεᾷ αὐτοῦ,
32 τῷ θεῷ εὐηρέστησεν." οὐ δεῖ δὲ ἀγνοεῖν, ὅτι νῦν
" ἄνθρωπον " οὐ κοινῷ τύπῳ τὸ λογικὸν θνητὸν
ζῷον καλεῖ, τὸν μέντοι κατ᾽ ἐξοχήν, ὃς ἐπαληθεύει
τοὔνομα τὰ ἀτίθασα καὶ λελυττηκότα πάθη καὶ τὰς
θηριωδεστάτας κακίας τῆς ψυχῆς ἀπεληλακώς.
33 σημεῖον δέ· μετὰ τὸν " ἄνθρωπον " ἐπιλέγει τὸν
" δίκαιον " εἰπὼν " ἄνθρωπος δίκαιος," ὡς ἀδίκου
μὲν οὐδενὸς ὄντος ἀνθρώπου (κυριώτερον δ᾽ εἰπεῖν
ἀνθρωπομόρφου θηρίου), μόνου δὲ ὃς ἂν ζηλωτὴς ᾖ
34 δικαιοσύνης.   φησὶ δ᾽ αὐτὸν καὶ " τέλειον " γεγονέναι διὰ τούτου παριστάς, ὡς οὐ μίαν
ἀρετὴν ἀλλὰ πάσας ἐκτήσατο καὶ κτησάμενος
ἑκάστῃ κατὰ τὸ ἐπιβάλλον χρώμενος διετέλεσεν.
35   ἐπιστεφανῶν δ᾽ αὐτὸν ὡς ἀγωνιστὴν
ἐκνενικηκότα κηρύγματι λαμπροτάτῳ προσεπικοσμεῖ
φάσκων, ὅτι " τῷ θεῷ εὐηρέστησεν "· οὗ τί γένοιτ᾽
ἂν ἐν τῇ φύσει κρεῖττον; τίς καλοκἀγαθίας ἐν-
αργέστερος[1] ἔλεγχος; εἰ γὰρ οἱ δυσαρεστήσαντες τῷ
θεῷ κακοδαίμονες, οἷς εὐαρεστῆσαι συνέβη πάντως
36 εὐδαίμονες.   VII. οὐκ ἀπὸ σκοποῦ μέντοι ταῖς τοσαύταις ἀρεταῖς ὑμνήσας τὸν ἄνθρωπον
ἐπεῖπεν, ὅτι " τέλειος ἦν ἐν τῇ γενεᾷ αὐτοῦ," δηλῶν
ὅτι οὐ καθάπαξ ἀλλὰ κατὰ σύγκρισιν τῶν κατ᾽
37 ἐκεῖνον τὸν χρόνον γεγονότων ἀγαθὸς ἦν. ἤδη γὰρ

[1] mss. τῆς κ. ἐναργέστατος.

---

[a] Gen. vi. 9, cf. Quod Deus 117.
[b] i.e. "a man, a just one." As the Greek adjective needs
no substantive expressed, ἄνθρωπος, which would be otherwise

little less than a direct assertion that a sage has no house or kinsfolk or country save virtues and virtuous actions; "for these," he says, "are the generations of Noah. Noah, a man just and perfect in his generation, was well-pleasing to God."[a] But we must not 32 fail to note that in this passage he gives the name of man not according to the common form of speech, to the mortal animal endowed with reason, but to the man who is man pre-eminently, who verifies the name by having expelled from the soul the untamed and frantic passions and the truly beast-like vices. Here 33 is a proof. After "man" he adds "just," implying by the combination[b] that the unjust is no man, or more properly speaking a beast in human form, and that the follower after righteousness alone is man.

He says, too, that Noah became "perfect," thereby 34 shewing that he acquired not one virtue but all, and having acquired them continued to exercise each as opportunities allowed. And as he crowns him 35 as victor in the contest, he gives him further distinction by a proclamation couched in words of splendid praise, "he was well-pleasing to God." What better thing than this has nature to give? What clearer proof can there be of nobility of life? For, if those who have been ill-pleasing to God are ill-fated, happy most surely are those whose lot it is to be well-pleasing to God. VII. But Moses makes 36 a good point when, after praising him as possessed of all these virtues, he adds that he was perfect in his generation, thus shewing he was not good absolutely but in comparison with the men of that time. For 37

---

superfluous, must have a special emphasis. Assuming, as Philo does, that the LXX follows the usage of classical Greek, the argument has some weight.

οὐκ εἰς μακρὰν ἐπιμνησθήσεται σοφῶν ἑτέρων, οἳ
τὴν ἀρετὴν ἀνανταγώνιστον ἔσχον, οὐ πονηροῖς
ἀντεξετασθέντες οὐδ' ὅτι βελτίους ἐγένοντο τῶν
κατ' αὐτοὺς ἀποδοχῆς καὶ προνομίας ἀξιωθέντες,
ἀλλ' ὅτι φύσιν εὔμοιρον κτησάμενοι διετήρησαν
αὐτὴν ἀδιάστροφον, οὐ φυγόντες μοχθηρὰ ἐπιτηδεύ-
ματα, ἀλλ' οὐδὲ τὴν ἀρχὴν αὐτοῖς περιπεσόντες,
προηγουμένως δὲ καλῶν ἔργων καὶ λόγων ἀσκηταὶ
38 γενόμενοι τὸν βίον ἐπεκόσμουν. θαυμασιώτατοι
μὲν οὖν ἄνδρες ἐκεῖνοι γεγόνασιν, οἳ ταῖς ὁρμαῖς
ἐλευθέραις καὶ εὐγενέσιν ἐχρήσαντο, μὴ κατὰ
μίμησιν ἢ ἐναντίωσιν ἑτέρων, ἀλλ' αὐτὸ τὸ καλὸν
καὶ τὸ δίκαιον ἀποδεξάμενοι, θαυμάσιος δὲ καὶ ὁ
τῆς καθ' αὑτὸν γενεᾶς διενηνοχὼς καὶ μηδενὶ
συνενεχθεὶς ὧν ἐζήλωσαν οἱ πολλοί· δευτερείων μὲν
οὗτος ἐφίξεται, τὰ δὲ πρῶτα τῶν ἄθλων ἐκείνοις
39 ἀναδώσει ἡ φύσις. τὰ μέντοι δευτερεῖα καὶ αὐτὰ
[7] μεγάλα· τί | δ' οὐχὶ μέγα καὶ περιμάχητον ὧν
ὀρέγει καὶ δωρεῖται θεός;   σαφεστάτη δὲ
πίστις αἱ τῶν χαρίτων ὑπερβολαί, ὧν οὗτος ἔτυχεν.
40 ἐπεὶ γὰρ ἀδικημάτων φορὰν ἤνεγκεν ὁ χρόνος
ἐκεῖνος καὶ πᾶσα χώρα καὶ ἔθνος καὶ πόλις καὶ
οἰκία καὶ ἕκαστος ἰδίᾳ πονηρῶν ἐπιτηδευμάτων
ἀνεπέπληστο, πάντων ἑκουσίως καὶ ἐκ προνοίας ὡς
ἐν ἀγῶνι περὶ τῶν ἐν τῷ διαμαρτάνειν πρωτείων
ἁμιλλωμένων—μετὰ σπουδῆς γὰρ ἁπάσης ἐφιλο-
νείκουν, ἑκάστου τὸν πλησίον μεγέθει κακίας ὑπερ-
βαλεῖν ἐπειγομένου καὶ μηδὲν παραλείποντος τῶν
41 πρὸς ἐπίληπτον καὶ ἐπάρατον βίον. VIII. ἐφ' οἷς
ὁ θεὸς εἰκότως δυσχεράνας, εἰ τὸ ζῷον τὸ ἄριστον

22

we shall shortly find him mentioning other sages
whose virtue was unchallenged, who are not contrasted with the bad, who are adjudged worthy of
approval and precedence, not because they were
better than their contemporaries but because they
possessed a happily-gifted nature and kept it un-
perverted, who did not have to shun evil courses or
indeed come into contact with them at all, but
attained pre-eminence in practising that excellence
of words and deeds with which they adorned their
lives. The highest admiration, then, is due to those 38
in whom the ruling impulses were of free and noble
birth, who accepted the excellent and just for their
own selves and not in imitation of or in opposition to
others. But admiration is also due to him who stood
apart from his own generation and conformed himself to none of the aims and aspirations of the many.
He will win the second prize, though the first will be
awarded by nature to those others. Yet great also is 39
the second prize in itself, for how could anything fail to
be great and worthy of our efforts which God offers and
gives ? And the clearest proof of this is
the exceeding magnitude of the bounties which Noah
obtained. That time bore its harvest of iniquities, and 40
every country and nation and city and household and
every private individual was filled with evil practices ;
one and all, as though in a race, engaged in rivalry
pre-willed and premeditated for the first places in
sinfulness, and put all possible zeal into the contention, each one pressing on to exceed his neighbour in
magnitude of vice and leaving nothing undone which
could lead to a guilty and accursed life. VIII.
Naturally this roused the wrath of God, to think that 41
man, who seemed the best of all living creatures,

εἶναι δοκοῦν καὶ συγγενείας ἀξιωθὲν τῆς πρὸς αὐτὸν
ἕνεκα τῆς ἐν τῷ λόγῳ κοινωνίας, δέον ἀρετὴν
ἐπιτηδεύειν, ἐζήλωσε κακίαν καὶ τὰ εἴδη πάντα
κακίας, δίκην ὁρίζει τὴν προσήκουσαν, ἀφανίσαι
τοὺς τότε ὄντας κατακλυσμῷ διανοηθείς, οὐ μόνον
τοὺς ἐν τῇ πεδιάδι καὶ τοῖς χθαμαλωτέροις ἀλλὰ
καὶ τοὺς ἐν τοῖς ὑψηλοτάτοις ὄρεσι κατοικοῦντας.
42 ἡ μὲν γὰρ μεγάλη θάλαττα μετέωρος ὡς οὐδέπω
πρότερον ἀρθεῖσα διὰ τῶν στομάτων ἀθρόα ῥύμῃ
τοῖς καθ' ἡμᾶς εἰσερρύη πελάγεσι, τὰ δὲ πλημ-
μύραντα νήσους καὶ ἠπείρους ἐπέκλυσε, πηγῶν δ'
ἀενάων καὶ ποταμῶν αὐθιγενῶν τε καὶ χειμάρρων
ἐπάλληλοι φοραὶ συνῆπτον ἀλλήλαις ἀναχεόμεναι
43 καὶ πρὸς ὕψος ἐπαιρόμεναι ἐπέβαινον. οὐ μὴν
οὐδὲ ὁ ἀὴρ ἠρέμει· πάντα γὰρ τὸν οὐρανὸν βαθὺ
καὶ συνεχὲς νέφος ἐπεῖχε καὶ πνεύματα ἦν ἐξαίσια
πάταγοί τε βροντῶν καὶ ἐπιλάμψεις ἀστραπῶν καὶ
κεραυνῶν φοραί, καταρρηγνυμένων ὄμβρων ἀπαύσ-
των, ὡς νομίσαι τὰ μέρη τοῦ παντὸς εἰς μίαν φύσιν
τὴν ὕδατος ἀναστοιχειούμενα σπεύδειν, ἕως τοῦ μὲν
ἄνωθεν καταράττοντος τοῦ δὲ κάτωθεν ἐπανιόντος
μετάρσια ἤρθη τὰ ῥεῖθρα, οἷς οὐ μόνον ἡ πεδιὰς καὶ
ὅση χθαμαλὴ κατακλυσθεῖσα ἠφανίσθη, ἀλλὰ καὶ
44 τῶν ὑψηλοτάτων ὀρῶν αἱ κορυφαί. πάντα γὰρ τὰ
μέρη τῆς γῆς ἔδυ καθ' ὕδατος, ὡς πᾶσαν καθ-
ηρπάσθαι καὶ τὸν κόσμον ἀκρωτηριασθέντα μεγάλῳ
τμήματι τὸν παντελῆ καὶ ὁλόκληρον, ὃ μήτε εἰπεῖν

---

a LXX Gen. vii. 11 "the fountains of the abyss were broken
up." By the Hebrew word translated in the LXX by ἄβυσσος
is understood the "ocean which both encircled the world,
and occupied the vast hollows beneath the earth" (Driver).
Philo seems to represent the first part of this conception by

who had been judged worthy of kinship with Him because he shared the gift of reason, had, instead of practising virtue as he should, shewn zeal for vice and for every particular form of it. Accordingly He appointed the penalty which fitted their wickedness. He determined to destroy all those who were then alive by a deluge, not only those who dwelt in the plains and lower lands, but also the inhabitants of the highest mountains. For the great deep[a] rose on 42 high as it had never risen before, and gathering its force rushed through its outlets into the seas of our parts, and the rising tides of these flooded the islands and continents, while in quick succession the streams from the perennial fountains and from the rivers spring-fed or winter-torrents pressed on to join each other and mounted upwards to a vast height. Nor 43 was the air still, for a deep unbroken cloud covered the heaven, and there were monstrous blasts of wind and crashings of thunder and flashings of lightning and downfall of thunderbolts, while the rainstorms dashed down ceaselessly, so that one might think that the different parts of the universe were hurrying to be resolved into the single element of water, until, as in one form it rushed down from above and in another rose up from below, the streams were lifted on high, and thus not only the plains and lowlands were submerged and lost to sight, but even the peaks of the highest mountains. For all parts of the 44 earth sank below the water, so that it was entirely carried away as though by violence, and the world seemed mutilated by the loss of a great section, its completeness and perfection destroyed and defaced,

"the great sea or deep," and the second by the "perennial fountains."

PHILO

μήτε νοῆσαι θέμις, λελωβῆσθαι δοκεῖν. ἀλλὰ γὰρ
καὶ ὁ ἀήρ, ἔξω μέρους βραχέος τοῦ κατὰ σελήνην,
ἅπας ἀνήλωτο νικηθεὶς ὑπὸ τῆς τοῦ ὕδατος φορᾶς
καὶ βίας, ὅπερ ἀνὰ κράτος τὴν ἐκείνου χώραν
45 ἐπέσχε. τότε δὴ τότε εὐθὺς ἐφθείρετο ὅσα σπαρτὰ
καὶ δένδρα—φθείρει γὰρ ὡς ἔνδεια καὶ πλῆθος
ἄμετρον,—ἔθνησκον δ' αἱ μυρίαι τῶν ζῴων ἀγέλαι
ἡμέρων ὁμοῦ καὶ ἀγρίων· ἦν γὰρ εἰκός, τοῦ κρατίστου γένους ἀνθρώπων ἀφανιζομένου, μηδὲν ὑπολειφθῆναι τῶν χειρόνων, ἐπεὶ καὶ πρὸς τὰς ἐκείνου
χρείας ἐγένετο δοῦλα τρόπον τινὰ δεσποτικαῖς
46 προστάξεσιν ὑπηρετήσοντα.   τοσούτων |

[8] δὴ καὶ τηλικούτων ἐπιρραξάντων κακῶν, ἅπερ
ἐκεῖνος ὁ καιρὸς ὤμβρησε—πάντα γὰρ τὰ τοῦ
κόσμου μέρη, δίχα τῶν κατὰ τὸν οὐρανόν, ἐκινήθη
παρὰ φύσιν, ὡς ἂν βαρεῖαν καὶ θανατώδη νόσον
νοσήσαντα,—μόνος δὲ εἷς οἶκος ὁ τοῦ λεχθέντος
ἀνδρὸς δικαίου καὶ θεοφιλοῦς διασῴζεται δύο
λαβόντος τὰς ἀνωτάτω δωρεάς, μίαν μέν, ἣν εἶπον,
τὸ μὴ πᾶσι τούτοις συναπολέσθαι, ἑτέραν δὲ τὸ
πάλιν ἀρχηγέτην αὐτὸν ὑπάρξαι νέας ἀνθρώπων
σπορᾶς· ἠξίωσε γὰρ αὐτὸν ὁ θεὸς καὶ τέλος τοῦ
γένους ἡμῶν καὶ ἀρχὴν γενέσθαι, τέλος μὲν τῶν
πρὸ τοῦ κατακλυσμοῦ, τῶν δὲ μετὰ τὸν κατακλυσμὸν ἀρχήν.

47 IX. Τοιοῦτος μὲν ὁ τῶν καθ' αὑτὸν ἄριστος,
τοιαῦτα δὲ καὶ τὰ τεθειμένα ἆθλα αὐτῷ, ὁποῖα
δεδήλωκεν ὁ ἱερὸς λόγος. τῶν δ' εἰρημένων τριῶν
εἴτε ἀνδρῶν εἴτε ψυχῆς τρόπων ἐναρμόνιος ἡ τάξις·
ὁ μὲν γὰρ τέλειος ὁλόκληρος ἐξ ἀρχῆς, ὁ δὲ μετα-
τεθειμένος ἡμίεργος, τοῦ βίου τὸν μὲν πρότερον
χρόνον ἀναθεὶς κακίᾳ, τὸν δ' ὕστερον ἀρετῇ, πρὸς

26

a thing too terrible for words or even for thoughts. Indeed even the air, except a small portion belonging to the moon, had been completely made away with, vanquished by the rush and violence of the water which perforce occupied its place. Then 45 indeed at once all crops and trees perished, for excessive quantity of water is as destructive as the lack of it, and the numberless herds of animals died, tame and wild alike ; for it was to be expected that if the highest kind, the human, was annihilated none of the inferior kinds would be left, since they were made for man's needs, as slaves in a sense meant to obey their masters' orders.   When all these 46 evils, so many and so vast, had burst upon the world in the downpour which that occasion brought, and the unnatural convulsion had shaken all its parts save the heavenly as with a grievous and deadly plague, one house alone, that of the man called just and dear to God, was preserved. Thus he received two gifts of the highest kind—one that, as I have said, he did not perish with the rest, the other that he should be in his turn the founder of a new race of men. For God deemed him worthy to be both the last and the first of our kind—last of those who lived before the flood and first of those who lived after it.

IX. Such was he who was best of his contem- 47 poraries, and such were the prizes awarded to him, the nature of which is made clear in holy writ. Now the three mentioned above, whether we think of them as men or types of soul, form a series of regular gradation : the perfect man is complete from the first ; the transferred stands half-way, since he devoted the earlier part of his life to vice but the latter to

ἣν μετανέστη καὶ μετῳκίσατο, ὁ δὲ ἐλπίζων, ὡς
αὐτὸ δηλοῖ τοὔνομα, ἐλλιπής, ἐφιέμενος μὲν ἀεὶ τοῦ
καλοῦ, μήπω δ' ἐφικέσθαι τούτου δεδυνημένος,
ἀλλ' ἐοικὼς τοῖς πλέουσιν, οἳ σπεύδοντες εἰς λιμένας
καταίρειν θαλαττεύουσιν ἐνορμίσασθαι μὴ δυνάμενοι.

48   X. Ἡ μὲν οὖν προτέρα τριὰς τῶν ἀρετὴν ἐπι-
ποθησάντων δεδήλωται. μείζων δέ ἐστιν ἡ ἑτέρα,
περὶ ἧς νυνὶ λεκτέον. ἐκείνη μὲν γὰρ τοῖς ἐν
ἡλικίᾳ παιδικῇ μαθήμασιν ἔοικεν, αὕτη δὲ τοῖς
ἀνδρῶν ἀθλητικῶν γυμνάσμασιν ἐπὶ τοὺς ἱεροὺς
ὄντως ἀλειφομένων ἀγῶνας, οἳ σωμασκίας κατα-
φρονοῦντες τὴν ἐν τῇ ψυχῇ κατασκευάζουσιν
εὐεξίαν ἐφιέμενοι τῆς κατὰ τῶν ἀντιπάλων παθῶν
49 νίκης. οἷς μὲν οὖν διενήνοχεν ἕκαστος ἐφ' ἓν καὶ
τὸ αὐτὸ τέλος ἐπειγόμενος, αὖθις ἀκριβέστερον
ἐροῦμεν· ἃ δὲ χρὴ περὶ τῶν τριῶν συλλήβδην
50 προειπεῖν, ἀναγκαῖον μὴ παρασιωπῆσαι. τούτους
τοίνυν συμβέβηκε μιᾶς οἰκίας καὶ ἑνὸς γένους εἶναι
—ὁ γὰρ τελευταῖος υἱὸς μέν ἐστι τοῦ μέσου, υἱωνὸς
δὲ τοῦ πρώτου—καὶ πάντας φιλοθέους ὁμοῦ καὶ
θεοφιλεῖς, ἀγαπήσαντας τὸν ἀληθῆ θεὸν καὶ ἀντ-
αγαπηθέντας πρὸς αὐτοῦ, ὃς ἠξίωσε, καθάπερ
δηλοῦσιν οἱ χρησμοί, διὰ τὰς ὑπερβολὰς τῶν
ἀρετῶν αἷς συνεβίουν κοινωνῆσαι τῆς προσρήσεως
51 αὐτοῖς.¹ τὸ γὰρ ἴδιον ὄνομα τοῖς ἐκείνων ἐν-
αρμοσάμενος ἥνωσε, τὴν ἐκ τῶν τριῶν σύνθετον
κλῆσιν ἐπιφημίσας ἑαυτῷ· "τοῦτο γάρ μου" φησίν
"ὄνομά ἐστιν αἰώνιον, θεὸς Ἀβραὰμ καὶ θεὸς
[9] Ἰσαὰκ καὶ θεὸς Ἰακώβ"—ἀντὶ τοῦ | καθάπαξ τὸ

---

¹ So most mss.: Cohn prints αὐτοῦ, but suggests the
insertion of αὐτούς.

virtue to which he passed over and migrated; the hoper, as his very name shews, is defective inasmuch as though he always desired the excellent he has not yet been able to attain to it, but resembles sailors eager to put into port, who yet remain at sea unable to reach their haven.

X. So now we have explained the first trinity of those who yearn for virtue; but greater is the second trinity of which we have now to speak. The first we may compare to the studies of children, but the latter to the exercises of athletes who are preparing for games which are really sacred,[a] men who despise bodily training but foster robustness of soul in their desire for victory over their antagonists, the passions. How each of these differed from the others while pressing on to one and the same goal will be described in detail later; but there is something to be said about them taken as a whole which must not be omitted. We find that these three are all of one house and one family. The last is the son of the second and grandson to the first. All alike are God-lovers and God-beloved, and their affection for the true God was returned by Him, Who deigned, as His utterances shew, in recognition of their high and life-long virtues to make them partners in the title which He took, for He united them by joining His special name to theirs and calling Himself by one combined of the three. "For this," He said, "is my eternal name[b]— the God of Abraham, the God of Isaac and the God of Jacob," relative instead of absolute,[c] and surely that

---

[a] In contrast to the falsely called "holy" games of the Greeks; cf. *De Agr.* 116 f.
[b] Ex iii. 15, cf. *De Mut.* 12 f.
[c] See App. p. 597.

πρός τι· καὶ μήποτ᾽ εἰκότως· ὀνόματος γὰρ ὁ θεὸς
οὐ δεῖται, μὴ δεόμενος δ᾽ ὅμως ἐχαρίζετο τῷ
γένει τῶν ἀνθρώπων κλῆσιν οἰκείαν, ἵν᾽ ἔχοντες
καταφυγὴν πρὸς ἱκεσίας καὶ λιτὰς μὴ ἀμοιρῶσιν
52 ἐλπίδος χρηστῆς.   XI. ταῦτα μὲν οὖν
ἐπ᾽ ἀνδρῶν ὁσίων εἰρῆσθαι δοκεῖ, μηνύματα δ᾽
ἐστὶ φύσεως ἀδηλοτέρας καὶ πολὺ βελτίονος τῆς ἐν
αἰσθητοῖς. τρόπους γὰρ ψυχῆς ἔοικεν ὁ ἱερὸς
διερευνᾶσθαι λόγος, ἀστείους ἅπαντας, τὸν μὲν ἐκ
διδασκαλίας, τὸν δ᾽ ἐκ φύσεως, τὸν δ᾽ ἐξ ἀσκήσεως
ἐφιέμενον τοῦ καλοῦ. ὁ μὲν γὰρ πρῶτος, ἐπίκλησιν
Ἀβραάμ, σύμβολον διδασκαλικῆς ἀρετῆς ἐστιν, ὁ
δὲ μέσος, Ἰσαάκ, φυσικῆς, ὁ δὲ τρίτος, Ἰακώβ,
53 ἀσκητικῆς. ἀλλὰ γὰρ οὐκ ἀγνοητέον, ὅτι μετεποιεῖτο τῶν τριῶν ἕκαστος δυνάμεων, ὠνομάσθη
δὲ ἀπὸ τῆς πλεοναζούσης κατ᾽ ἐπικράτειαν· οὔτε
γὰρ διδασκαλίαν ἄνευ φύσεως ἢ ἀσκήσεως τελειω-
θῆναι δυνατὸν οὔτε φύσις ἐπὶ πέρας ἐστὶν ἐλθεῖν
ἱκανὴ δίχα τοῦ μαθεῖν καὶ ἀσκῆσαι οὔτε ἄσκησις,
εἰ μὴ προθεμελιωθείη φύσει τε καὶ διδασκαλίᾳ.
54 προσηκόντως οὖν καὶ τὴν τῶν τριῶν λόγῳ μὲν
ἀνδρῶν ἔργῳ δ᾽ ὡς εἶπον ἀρετῶν οἰκειότητα
συνῆψε, φύσεως, μαθήσεως, ἀσκήσεως,[1] ἃς ἑτέρῳ
ὀνόματι Χάριτας ἰσαρίθμους ἄνθρωποι καλοῦσιν, ἢ
τῷ κεχαρίσθαι τὸν θεὸν τῷ ἡμετέρῳ γένει τὰς τρεῖς
δυνάμεις πρὸς τελειότητα τοῦ βίου ἢ παρόσον αὗται
δεδώρηνται ψυχῇ λογικῇ ἑαυτάς, δώρημα τέλειον
καὶ κάλλιστον, ἵνα καὶ τὸ αἰώνιον ὄνομα τὸ δηλούμενον ἐν τοῖς χρησμοῖς ἐπὶ τριῶν μὴ ἐπ᾽ ἀνθρώπων
55 μᾶλλον ἢ τῶν εἰρημένων δυνάμεων λέγηται. ἀνθρώπων μὲν γὰρ φθαρτὴ φύσις, ἄφθαρτος δ᾽ ἡ τῶν

[1] MSS. φύσις μάθησις ἄσκησις.

30

is natural. God indeed needs no name; yet, though He needed it not, He nevertheless vouchsafed to give to humankind a name of Himself suited to them, that so men might be able to take refuge in prayers and supplications and not be deprived of comforting hopes.

XI. These words do indeed appear to 52 apply to men of holy life, but they are also statements about an order of things which is not so apparent but is far superior to the order which is perceived by the senses. For the holy word seems to be searching into types of soul, all of them of high worth, one which pursues the good through teaching, one through nature and one through practice. The first called Abraham, the second Isaac and the third Jacob, are symbols of virtue acquired respectively by teaching, nature and practice. But indeed we must not fail 53 to note that each possesses the three qualities, but gets his name from that which chiefly predominates in him; for teaching cannot be consummated without nature or practice, nor is nature capable of reaching its zenith without learning and practising, nor practice either unless the foundation of nature and teaching has first been laid. Very properly, then, 54 Moses thus associated these three together, nominally men, but really, as I have said, virtues—teaching, nature, practice. Another name is given to them by men, who call them the Graces, also three in number; either because these values are a gift of God's grace to our kind for perfecting its life, or because they have given themselves to the reasonable soul as a perfect and most excellent gift. Thus the eternal name revealed in his words is meant to indicate the three said values rather than actual men. For the nature of man is perishable, but that of 55

31

ἀρετῶν· εὐλογώτερον δὲ ἐπιφημίζεσθαι τὸ[1] ἀίδιον
ἀφθάρτοις πρὸ θνητῶν, ἐπεὶ συγγενὲς μὲν ἀιδιότη-
τος ἀφθαρσία, ἐχθρὸν δὲ θάνατος.

56 XII. Χρὴ μέντοι μηδ' ἐκεῖνο ἀγνοεῖν, ὅτι τὸν μὲν
πρῶτον ἄνθρωπον τὸν γηγενῆ πατέρα τῶν ἄχρι τοῦ
κατακλυσμοῦ φύντων εἰσήγαγε, τὸν δὲ μόνον ἐκ
τῆς τοσαύτης φθορᾶς ὑπολειφθέντα πανοίκιον ἕνεκα
δικαιοσύνης καὶ τῆς ἄλλης καλοκἀγαθίας τοῦ νεά-
σοντος αὖθις καινοῦ γένους ἀνθρώπων, τὴν δὲ
περίσεμνον τριάδα καὶ περιμάχητον ἑνὸς εἴδους
ἐπιλεγομένου " βασίλειον καὶ ἱεράτευμα καὶ ἔθνος
57 ἅγιον "[a] οἱ χρησμοὶ καλοῦσι. μηνύει δὲ τοὔνομα
τὴν δύναμιν αὐτοῦ· προσονομάζεται γὰρ Ἑβραίων
γλώττῃ τὸ ἔθνος Ἰσραήλ, ὅπερ ἑρμηνευθέν ἐστιν
" ὁρῶν θεόν."[b] ὅρασις δ' ἡ μὲν δι' ὀφθαλμῶν ἐν
ἁπάσαις καλλιστεύει ταῖς αἰσθήσεσιν, ἐπεὶ καὶ διὰ
μόνης καταλαμβάνεται τὰ κάλλιστα τῶν ὄντων,
ἥλιος καὶ σελήνη καὶ ὁ σύμπας οὐρανός τε καὶ
κόσμος, ἡ δὲ διὰ τοῦ τῆς ψυχῆς ἡγεμονικοῦ προ-
[10] φέρει τὰς ἄλλας ὅσαι περὶ αὐτὸ δυνάμεις· αὕτη | δέ
58 ἐστι φρόνησις ὄψις οὖσα διανοίας. ὅτῳ δὲ μὴ
μόνον ἐξεγένετο τἆλλα ὅσα ἐν τῇ φύσει δι' ἐπι-
στήμης καταλαμβάνειν, ἀλλὰ καὶ τὸν πατέρα καὶ
ποιητὴν τῶν συμπάντων ὁρᾶν, ἐπ' ἄκρον εὐδαιμονίας ἴστω προεληλυθώς· οὐδὲν γὰρ ἀνωτέρω
θεοῦ, πρὸς ὃν εἴ τις τὸ τῆς ψυχῆς ὄμμα τείνας
59 ἔφθακε, μονὴν εὐχέσθω καὶ στάσιν. αἱ μὲν γὰρ
ἀνάντεις ὁδοὶ καματηραὶ καὶ βραδεῖαι, ἡ δὲ κατὰ
πρανοῦς φορά, συρμὸν ἔχουσα τὸ πλέον ἢ κάθοδον,

---

[1] MSS. τὸν ἀίδιον.

[a] Ex. xix. 6.
[b] Cf. note on Quod Deus 46.

virtue is imperishable. And it is more reasonable that what is eternal should be predicated of the imperishable than of the mortal, since imperishableness is akin to eternality, while death is at enmity with it.

XII. There is another thing which we must not fail 56 to know : while Moses represented the first man, the earth-born, as father of all that were born up to the deluge, and Noah who with all his house alone survived that great destruction because of his justice and excellent character in other ways as the father of the new race which would spring up afresh, the oracles speak of this august and precious trinity as parent of one species of that race, which species is called "royal" and "priesthood" and "holy nation."[a] Its high position is shewn by the name ; 57 for the nation is called in the Hebrew tongue Israel, which, being interpreted, is "He who sees God." Now the sight of the eyes is the most excellent of all the senses, since by it alone we apprehend the most excellent of existing things, the sun and the moon and the whole heaven and world ; but the sight of the mind, the dominant element in the soul, surpasses all the other faculties of the mind, and this is wisdom which is the sight of the understanding.[b] But he to 58 whom it is given not only to apprehend by means of knowledge all else that nature has to shew, but also to see the Father and Maker of all, may rest assured that he is advanced to the crowning point of happiness ; for nothing is higher than God, and whoso has stretched the eyesight of the soul to reach Him should pray that he may there abide and stand firm ; for 59 journeys uphill are toilsome and slow, but the downhill course where one is swept along rather than

ταχεῖα καὶ ῥᾴστη. πολλὰ δὲ τὰ κάτω βιαζόμενα,
ὧν οὐδὲν ὄφελος, ὅταν ἐκ τῶν αὑτοῦ δυνάμεων
ἀνακρεμάσας τὴν ψυχὴν ὁ θεὸς ὁλκῇ δυνατωτέρᾳ
πρὸς ἑαυτὸν ἐπισπάσηται.

60 XIII. Ταῦτα μὲν οὖν κοινῇ περὶ τῶν τριῶν
ἀναγκαίως προειρήσθω. λεκτέον δ' ἑξῆς, ἐν οἷς
ἕκαστος ἰδίᾳ προήνεγκεν, ἀπὸ τοῦ πρώτου τὴν
ἀρχὴν λαβόντας. ἐκεῖνος τοίνυν εὐσεβείας, ἀρετῆς
τῆς ἀνωτάτω καὶ μεγίστης, ζηλωτὴς γενόμενος
ἐσπούδασεν ἕπεσθαι θεῷ καὶ καταπειθὴς εἶναι τοῖς
προσταττομένοις ὑπ' αὐτοῦ, προστάξεις ὑπολαμβάνων οὐ τὰς διὰ φωνῆς καὶ γραμμάτων μηνυο-
μένας αὐτὸ μόνον, ἀλλὰ καὶ τὰς διὰ τῆς φύσεως
τρανοτέροις σημείοις δηλουμένας, ἃς ἡ ἀληθεστάτη
τῶν αἰσθήσεων πρὸ ἀκοῆς τῆς ἀπίστου καὶ ἀβεβαίου
61 καταλαμβάνει. θεώμενος γάρ τις τὴν ἐν τῇ φύσει
τάξιν καὶ τὴν παντὸς λόγου κρείττονα πολιτείαν, ᾗ
χρῆται ὁ κόσμος, ἀναδιδάσκεται, φθεγγομένου
μηδενός, εὔνομον καὶ εἰρηνικὸν βίον ἐπιτηδεύειν εἰς
τὴν τῶν καλῶν ἐξομοίωσιν ἀποβλέποντα. ἐναργέστατα δὲ τῆς εὐσεβείας ἀποδείξεις εἰσίν, ἃς
περιέχουσιν αἱ ἱεραὶ γραφαί· πρώτην δὲ λεκτέον, ἣ
62 καὶ πρώτη τέτακται. XIV. λογίῳ πληχθεὶς περὶ
τοῦ πατρίδα καὶ συγγένειαν καὶ πατρῷον οἶκον
καταλιπεῖν καὶ μεταναστῆναι, καθάπερ ἀπὸ τῆς
ξένης εἰς τὴν οἰκείαν ἐπανιὼν ἀλλ' οὐκ ἀπὸ τῆς
οἰκείας εἰς τὴν ξένην μέλλων ἀπαίρειν, ἐπέσπευδε
συντείνων, νομίζων ἰσότιμον εἶναι τῷ τελειῶσαι τὸ
63 ταχέως τὸ προσταχθὲν ἀνύσαι. καίτοι τίνα ἕτερον

ᵃ Philo seems to assume that the command to leave
country and kindred, cf. Gen. xii. 1, was given to Abraham
in Chaldaea and not in Haran. So perhaps the A.V. "the

34

descends is swift and most easy. And many are the forces which would bear us down, yet none of them avail when God sets the soul suspended to His potencies and with a mightier attraction draws it to Himself.

XIII. So much for what was needed by way of 60 preliminary discussion on the three in common. We must now speak of the superior merits shewn by each separately, beginning with the first. Abraham, then, filled with zeal for piety, the highest and greatest of virtues, was eager to follow God and to be obedient to His commands ; understanding by commands not only those conveyed in speech and writing but also those made manifest by nature with clearer signs, and apprehended by the sense which is the most truthful of all and superior to hearing, on which no certain reliance can be placed. For anyone who 61 contemplates the order in nature and the constitution enjoyed by the world-city whose excellence no words can describe, needs no speaker to teach him to practise a law-abiding and peaceful life and to aim at assimilating himself to its beauties. But the clearest proofs of his piety are those which the holy scriptures contain, and the first which should be mentioned is that which comes first in order. XIV. Under the force of an oracle [a] which bade him leave 62 his country and kinsfolk and seek a new home, thinking that quickness in executing the command was as good as full accomplishment, he hastened eagerly to obey, not as though he were leaving home for a strange land but rather as returning from amid strangers to his home. Yet who else would be likely 63

Lord had said," as against the R.V. "the Lord said." Philo may have implied the same from Gen. xv. 7. *Cf.* Acts vii. 2.

εἰκὸς οὕτως ἀκλινῆ καὶ ἄτρεπτον γενέσθαι, ὡς μὴ
φίλτροις ὑπαχθῆναι καὶ ὑπενδοῦναι συγγενῶν καὶ
πατρίδος, ὧν ὁ πόθος ἑκάστῳ τρόπον τινὰ συγ-
γεγένηται καὶ συνηύξηται καὶ μᾶλλον ἢ οὐχ ἧττον
64 τῶν ἡνωμένων μερῶν συμπέφυκε; μάρτυρες δὲ
οἱ νομοθέται τὴν δευτερεύουσαν θανάτου τιμωρίαν
κατὰ τῶν ἐπὶ τοῖς μεγίστοις ἑαλωκότων ὁρίσαντες
φυγήν, οὐ δευτερεύουσαν, ὥς γ' ἐμοὶ δοκεῖ, παρ'
ἀληθείᾳ δικαζούσῃ, πολὺ δὲ ἀργαλεωτέραν, εἴ γε
πέρας μὲν κακοπραγιῶν ὁ θάνατος, ἀρχὴ δ', οὐ
πέρας, ἡ φυγὴ καινοτέρων συμφορῶν, ἀνθ' ἑνὸς τοῦ
χωρὶς ἀλγηδόνων μυρίους ἐπάγουσα θανάτους τοὺς
[11] σὺν αἰσθήσει. | κατ' ἐμπορίαν ἔνιοι πόθῳ χρηματι-
65 σμοῦ πλέοντες ἢ κατὰ πρεσβείαν ἢ κατὰ θέαν τῶν
ἐπὶ τῆς ἀλλοδαπῆς δι' ἔρωτα παιδείας, ὁλκοὺς
ἔχοντες δυνάμεις τῆς ἔξω μονῆς οἱ μὲν τὰς ἐπι-
κερδείας, οἱ δὲ τὸ τὴν πόλιν ἐπὶ καιρῶν ἐν τοῖς
ἀναγκαιοτάτοις καὶ μεγίστοις ὀνῆσαι, οἱ δὲ ἱστορίαν
ὧν πρότερον ἠγνόουν τέρψιν ἅμα καὶ ὠφέλειαν τῇ
ψυχῇ παρασκευάζουσαν—τυφλοὶ γὰρ παρ' ὀξὺ
βλέποντας ἀναποδήμητοι παρ' ἐκδεδημηκότας—,
ὅμως ἐπείγονται τὸ πατρῷον ἔδαφος ἰδεῖν καὶ
προσκυνῆσαι καὶ συνήθεις ἀσπάσασθαι συγγενῶν τε
καὶ φίλων ἡδίστης καὶ ποθεινοτάτης ὄψεως ἀπολαῦσαι καὶ πολλάκις τὰς πράξεις, ὧν ἕνεκα ἐξεδή-
μησαν, μηκυνομένας ὁρῶντες κατέλιπον ἱμέρῳ τῶν
66 προσηκόντων ἑλχθέντες βιαιοτάτῳ.   μετ'

to be so firm and unmoved of purpose as not to yield and succumb to the charms of kinsfolk and country? The desire of these may be said to be born and grow with each of us and is a part of our nature as much as or even more than the parts which unite to make the whole. And this is attested by the 64 legislators who have appointed banishment as the penalty second only to death for those who have been convicted of the greatest crimes, though indeed, in my opinion, it is not second to death, if truth gives its verdict, but rather a far heavier punishment, since death ends our troubles but banishment is not the end but the beginning of other new misfortunes and entails in place of the one death which puts an end to pains a thousand deaths in which we do not lose sensation. Some men go on voyages for trading 65 purposes in their desire for making money or on embassies or in their love of culture to see the sights of a foreign land. These are subject to influences driving them to stay abroad, in some cases financial gains, in others the chance of benefiting their country, when occasion offers, in its most vital and important interests, in others acquiring knowledge of things which they did not know before and thus providing at once pleasure and profit to the soul, for the stay-at-home is to the travelled as the blind are to the keen-sighted. Yet all these are eager to see and salute their native soil, and to greet their familiars and to have the sweet and most desired enjoyment of beholding their kinsfolk and friends. And often when they find the business for which they left home protracting itself they abandon it, drawn by the constraining desire for their own belongings.

But Abraham, the moment he was 66

ὀλίγων δὲ οὗτος ἢ καὶ μόνος ἅμα τῷ κελευσθῆναι
μετανίστατο καὶ τῇ ψυχῇ πρὸ τοῦ σώματος τὴν
ἀποικίαν ἐστέλλετο, τὸν ἐπὶ τοῖς θνητοῖς ἵμερον
67 παρευημεροῦντος ἔρωτος οὐρανίου. οὐδενὸς οὖν
φροντίσας, οὐ φυλετῶν, οὐ δημοτῶν, οὐ συμφοιτη-
τῶν, οὐχ ἑταίρων, οὐ τῶν ἀφ' αἵματος ὅσοι πρὸς
πατρὸς ἢ μητρὸς ἦσαν, οὐ πατρίδος, οὐκ ἀρχαίων
ἐθῶν, οὐ συντροφίας, οὐ συνδιαιτήσεως, ὧν ἕκαστον
ἀγωγόν τε καὶ δυσαπόσπαστον ὁλκὸν ἔχον δύναμιν,
ἐλευθέραις καὶ ἀφέτοις ὁρμαῖς ᾗ τάχιστα μετανίσταται, τὸ μὲν πρῶτον ἀπὸ τῆς Χαλδαίων γῆς,
εὐδαίμονος χώρας καὶ κατ' ἐκεῖνον ἀκμαζούσης τὸν
χρόνον, εἰς τὴν Χαρραίων γῆν, ἔπειτα οὐ μακρὰν
ὕστερον καὶ ἀπὸ ταύτης εἰς ἕτερον τόπον, περὶ οὗ
λέξομεν ἐκεῖνο πρότερον εἰπόντες.

68   XV. Αἱ δηλωθεῖσαι ἀποικίαι τῷ μὲν ῥητῷ τῆς
γραφῆς ὑπ' ἀνδρὸς σοφοῦ γεγόνασι, κατὰ δὲ τοὺς
ἐν ἀλληγορίᾳ νόμους ὑπὸ φιλαρέτου ψυχῆς τὸν
69 ἀληθῆ ζητούσης θεόν. Χαλδαῖοι γὰρ ἐν τοῖς
μάλιστα διαπονήσαντες ἀστρονομίαν καὶ πάντα ταῖς
κινήσεσι τῶν ἀστέρων ἀναθέντες ὑπέλαβον οἰκο-
νομεῖσθαι τὰ ἐν κόσμῳ δυνάμεσιν, ἃς περιέχουσιν
ἀριθμοὶ καὶ ἀριθμῶν ἀναλογίαι, ⟨καὶ⟩ τὴν ὁρατὴν
οὐσίαν ἐσέμνυνον τῆς ἀοράτου καὶ νοητῆς οὐ
λαβόντες ἔννοιαν, ἀλλὰ τὴν ἐν ἐκείνοις τάξιν δι-
ερευνώμενοι κατά τε τὰς ἡλίου καὶ σελήνης καὶ τῶν
ἄλλων πλανήτων καὶ ἀπλανῶν περιόδους καὶ κατὰ
τὰς τῶν ἐτησίων ὡρῶν μεταβολὰς καὶ κατὰ τὴν
τῶν οὐρανίων πρὸς τὰ ἐπίγεια συμπάθειαν τὸν
κόσμον αὐτὸν ὑπέλαβον εἶναι θεόν, οὐκ εὐαγῶς τὸ

bidden, departed with a few or even alone, and his emigration was one of soul rather than body, for the heavenly love overpowered his desire for mortal things. And so taking no thought for anything, 67 either for his fellow-clansmen, or wardsmen, or schoolmates, or comrades, or blood relations on father's or mother's side, or country, or ancestral customs, or community of nurture or home life, all of them ties possessing a power to allure and attract which it is hard to throw off, he followed a free and unfettered impulse and departed with all speed first from Chaldea, a land at that time blessed by fortune and at the height of its prosperity, and migrated to Haran; then not long afterwards he left this too for another place, about which we shall speak after dealing with something else to which I now proceed.[a]

XV. The migrations as set forth by the literal text 68 of the scriptures are made by a man of wisdom, but according to the laws of allegory by a virtue-loving soul in its search for the true God. For the 69 Chaldeans were especially active in the elaboration of astrology and ascribed everything to the movements of the stars. They supposed that the course of the phenomena of the world is guided by influences contained in numbers and numerical proportions. Thus they glorified visible existence, leaving out of consideration the intelligible and invisible. But while exploring numerical order as applied to the revolution of the sun, moon and other planets and fixed stars, and the changes of the yearly seasons and the interdependence of phenomena in heaven and on earth, they concluded that the world itself

[a] Gen. xi. 31 and xii. 5. For the meaning of "another place" see on § 85.

70 γενόμενον ἐξομοιώσαντες τῷ πεποιηκότι. ταύτῃ
τοι τῇ δόξῃ συντραφεὶς καὶ χαλδαΐσας μακρόν τινα
[12] χρόνον, ὥσπερ ἐκ βαθέος ὕπνου | διοίξας τὸ τῆς
ψυχῆς ὄμμα καὶ καθαρὰν αὐγὴν ἀντὶ σκότους
βαθέος βλέπειν ἀρξάμενος ἠκολούθησε τῷ φέγγει
καὶ κατεῖδεν, ὃ μὴ πρότερον ἐθεάσατο, τοῦ κόσμου
τινὰ ἡνίοχον καὶ κυβερνήτην ἐφεστῶτα καὶ σωτηρίως εὐθύνοντα τὸ οἰκεῖον ἔργον, ἐπιμέλειάν τε καὶ
προστασίαν καὶ τῶν ἐν αὐτῷ μερῶν ὅσα θείας
71 ἐπάξια φροντίδος ποιούμενον. ὅπως οὖν βεβαιώ-
σηται τὴν φανεῖσαν ὄψιν ἐν τῇ διανοίᾳ παγιώτερον,
αὖθίς φησιν ὁ ἱερὸς λόγος αὐτῷ· "τὰ μεγάλα, ὦ
οὗτος, ὑποτυπώσει βραχυτέρων πολλάκις γνωρί-
ζηται, πρὸς ἅ τις ἀπιδὼν ηὔξησε τὴν φαντασίαν
ἀπεριγράφοις μεγέθεσι. παραπεμψάμενος οὖν τούς
τε κατ᾿ οὐρανὸν περιπολοῦντας καὶ τὴν Χαλδαϊκὴν
ἐπιστήμην μετανάστηθι πρὸς ὀλίγον χρόνον ἀπὸ
τῆς μεγίστης πόλεως, τοῦδε τοῦ κόσμου, πρὸς
βραχυτέραν, δι᾿ ἧς δυνήσῃ μᾶλλον καταλαβεῖν τὸν
72 ἔφορον τοῦ παντός."   διὰ τοῦτο τὴν
πρώτην ἀποικίαν ἀπὸ τῆς Χαλδαίων γῆς εἰς τὴν
Χαρραίων λέγεται ποιήσασθαι. XVI. Χαρρὰν δὲ
Ἑλληνιστὶ "τρῶγλαι" λέγονται, κατὰ σύμβολον
αἱ τῶν ἡμετέρων αἰσθήσεων χῶραι, δι᾿ ὧν ὥσπερ
ὀπῶν ἑκάστη διακύπτειν πέφυκε πρὸς τὴν τῶν
73 οἰκείων ἀντίληψιν. ἀλλὰ τί τούτων, εἴποι τις ἄν,
ὄφελος ἦν, εἰ μὴ νοῦς ἀόρατος καθάπερ θαυματο-
ποιὸς ἔνδοθεν ὑπήχει ταῖς ἑαυτοῦ δυνάμεσιν, ἃς

---

[a] The allegorical meaning of Haran is given more fully
and clearly in *De Mig.* 176 ff. and *De Som.* i. 41 ff. Haran

40

was God, thus profanely likening the created to the Creator. In this creed Abraham had been reared, 70 and for a long time remained a Chaldean. Then opening the soul's eye as though after profound sleep, and beginning to see the pure beam instead of the deep darkness, he followed the ray and discerned what he had not beheld before, a charioteer and pilot presiding over the world and directing in safety his own work, assuming the charge and superintendence of that work and of all such parts of it as are worthy of the divine care. And so to establish more firmly 71 in his understanding the sight which had been revealed to him the Holy Word follows it up by saying to him, "Friend, the great is often known by its outlines as shown in the smaller, and by looking at them the observer finds the scope of his vision infinitely enlarged. Dismiss, then, the rangers of the heavens and the science of Chaldea, and depart for a short time from the greatest of cities, this world, to the lesser, and thus you will be better able to apprehend the overseer of the All."

This is why he is said to emigrate first from the land of 72 Chaldea to that of Haran.[a] XVI. Now Haran in our language means "holes," a symbol for the seats of our senses through which each of them naturally peers as through orifices to apprehend what belongs to it. Yet what use, we might ask, would they be if 73 the invisible mind were not there like a juggler to prompt its faculties, sometimes relaxing and giving

being the place of sense-perception is the bodily tenement of the mind (*De Mig.* 187), and therefore stands for Socratic self-knowledge as a whole in contrast to astrological speculation. It thus gives the conviction that there is a higher power than mind and thus leads to the second migration from self-knowledge to knowledge of God.

τοτὲ μὲν ἀνιεὶς καὶ ἐπιχαλῶν τοτὲ δὲ ἀντισπῶν καὶ
ἀνθέλκων βίᾳ κίνησιν ἐμμελῆ καὶ πάλιν ἡσυχίαν
ἐμπαρεῖχε τοῖς θαυμασίοις; τοῦτο ἔχων παρὰ
σεαυτῷ τὸ παράδειγμα ῥᾳδίως οὗ σφόδρα ποθεῖς
74 λαβεῖν τὴν ἐπιστήμην κατανοήσεις. οὐ γὰρ ἐν σοὶ
μὲν νοῦς ἐστιν ἡγεμὼν ἐπιτεταγμένος, ᾧ καὶ τοῦ
σώματος ἅπασα κοινωνία πειθαρχεῖ καὶ ἑκάστη τῶν
αἰσθήσεων ἕπεται, ὁ δὲ κόσμος, τὸ κάλλιστον καὶ
μέγιστον καὶ τελεώτατον ἔργον, οὗ πάντα τὰ ἄλλα
συμβέβηκεν εἶναι μέρη, βασιλέως ἀμοιρεῖ τοῦ
συνέχοντος[1] καὶ ἐνδίκως ἐπιτροπεύοντος. εἰ δ᾽
ἀόρατος ὁ βασιλεύς, μὴ θαυμάσῃς· οὐδὲ γὰρ ὁ ἐν
75 σοὶ νοῦς ὁρατός. ταῦτά τις ἐπιλογιζόμενος καὶ οὐ
πόρρωθεν ἀλλ᾽ ἐγγύθεν ἀναδιδασκόμενος ἔκ τε
ἑαυτοῦ καὶ τῶν περὶ αὐτὸν εἴσεται σαφῶς, ὅτι ὁ
κόσμος οὐκ ἔστιν ὁ πρῶτος θεός, ἀλλ᾽ ἔργον τοῦ
πρώτου θεοῦ καὶ τοῦ συμπάντων πατρός, ὃς ἀειδὴς
ὢν πάντα φαίνει μικρῶν τε αὖ καὶ μεγάλων δια-
76 δεικνὺς τὰς φύσεις. σώματος γὰρ ὀφθαλμοῖς οὐκ
ἠξίωσε καταλαμβάνεσθαι, τάχα μὲν ἐπειδὴ θνητὸν
ἀιδίου ψαύειν οὐχ ὅσιον ἦν, τάχα δὲ καὶ δι᾽ ἀσθένειαν τῆς ἡμετέρας ὄψεως· οὐ γὰρ ἂν ἐχώρησε
τὰς ἀπὸ τοῦ ὄντος ἐκχεομένας αὐγάς, ὁπότε οὐδὲ
ταῖς ἀφ᾽ ἡλίου προσβλέπειν ἀκτῖσιν οἷά τέ ἐστι.
[13]
77 XVII. | τεκμήριον δὲ ἐναργέστατον τῆς ἀποικίας,
ἣν ἀπ᾽ ἀστρονομίας καὶ τῆς χαλδαϊζούσης δόξης
ἡ διάνοια ἐστείλατο· λέγεται γὰρ εὐθὺς ἅμα τῇ
μεταναστάσει τοῦ σοφοῦ· " ὤφθη δὲ ὁ θεὸς τῷ
Ἀβραάμ " ᾧ δῆλον ὅτι πρότερον οὐκ ἦν ἐμφανής,

---

[1] MSS. συνέχοντος.

---

[a] Gen. xii. 7. But this " appearance " comes when Abraham
is in Canaan. If Philo is following Genesis carefully the

them a free rein, sometimes forcibly pulling and jerking them back, and thus causing its puppets at one time to move in harmony, at another to rest? With this example in yourself you will easily apprehend that which you so earnestly desire to know. For it cannot be that while in yourself there is a mind 74 appointed as your ruler which all the community of the body obeys and each of the senses follows, the world, the fairest, and greatest and most perfect work of all, of which everything else is a part, is without a king who holds it together and directs it with justice. That the king is invisible need not cause you to wonder, for neither is the mind in yourself visible. Anyone who reflects on these things and 75 learns from no distant source, but from one near at hand, namely himself and what makes him what he is, will know for certain that the world is not the primal God but a work of the primal God and Father of all Who, though invisible, yet brings all things to light, revealing the natures of great and small. For 76 He did not deem it right to be apprehended by the eyes of the body, perhaps because it was contrary to holiness that the mortal should touch the eternal, perhaps too because of the weakness of our sight. For our sight could not have borne the rays that pour from Him that is, since it is not even able to look upon the beams of the sun. XVII. We have a very 77 clear proof of the mind's migration from astrology and the Chaldean creed in the words which follow at once the story of the departure of the Sage. " God," it says, " was seen by Abraham." [a] This shews that God was not manifested to him before, when in his

μετανάστασις must embrace both migrations. But the sequel suggests that he mistakenly assigns it to the Haran period.

ὅτε χαλδαΐζων τῇ τῶν ἀστέρων χορείᾳ προσεῖχεν
ἔξω τοῦ κόσμου καὶ τῆς αἰσθητῆς οὐσίας εὐ-
άρμοστον καὶ νοητὴν φύσιν οὐδεμίαν ἁπλῶς κατα-
78 λαμβάνων. ἐπεὶ δὲ μετεχώρησε καὶ μεθωρμίσατο,
κατὰ τἀναγκαῖον ἔγνω τὸν κόσμον ὑπήκοον ἀλλ'
οὐκ αὐτοκράτορα, οὐ πρυτανεύοντα ἀλλὰ πρυτα-
νευόμενον ὑπ' αἰτίου τοῦ πεποιηκότος, ὅπερ ἡ
79 διάνοια τότε πρῶτον ἀναβλέψασα εἶδε. πολλὴ γὰρ
αὐτῆς πρότερον ἀχλὺς ὑπὸ τῶν αἰσθητῶν κατ-
εκέχυτο, ἣν ἐνθέρμοις καὶ διαπύροις δόγμασιν
ἀνασκεδάσασα μόλις ἴσχυσεν ὡς ἐν αἰθρίᾳ καθαρᾷ
τοῦ πάλαι κρυπτομένου καὶ ἀειδοῦς φαντασίαν
λαβεῖν· ὃς ἕνεκα φιλανθρωπίας ἀφικνουμένην τὴν
ψυχὴν ὡς ἑαυτὸν οὐκ ἀπεστράφη, προϋπαντήσας
δὲ τὴν ἑαυτοῦ φύσιν ἔδειξε, καθ' ὅσον οἷόν τε ἦν
80 ἰδεῖν τὸν βλέποντα. διὸ λέγεται, οὐχ ὅτι ὁ σοφὸς
εἶδε θεόν, ἀλλ' ὅτι " ὁ θεὸς ὤφθη " τῷ σοφῷ· καὶ
γὰρ ἦν ἀδύνατον καταλαβεῖν τινα δι' αὑτοῦ τὸ πρὸς
ἀλήθειαν ὄν, μὴ παραφήναντος ἐκείνου ἑαυτὸν καὶ
ἐπιδείξαντος.
81 XVIII. Μαρτυρεῖ δὲ τοῖς εἰρημένοις καὶ ἡ τοῦ
ὀνόματος ὑπαλλαγὴ καὶ μετάθεσις. ἐκαλεῖτο γὰρ
Ἄβραμ τὸ ἀρχαῖον ὄνομα, προσερρήθη δ' ὕστερον
Ἀβραάμ, φωνῇ μὲν ἑνὸς στοιχείου τοῦ ἄλφα
διπλασιασθέντος, δυνάμει δὲ μεγάλου πράγματος
82 καὶ δόγματος ἐνδειξαμένου τὴν μεταβολήν. Ἄβραμ
μὲν γὰρ ἑρμηνευθέν ἐστι " πατὴρ μετέωρος,"
Ἀβραὰμ δὲ " πατὴρ ἐκλεκτὸς ἠχοῦς," τὸ μὲν
πρότερον ἐμφαῖνον τὸν ἀστρολογικὸν καὶ μετεωρο-
λογικὸν ἐπικαλούμενον, οὕτως τῶν Χαλδαϊκῶν

Chaldean way he was fixing his thoughts on the choric movement of the stars with no apprehension at all of an harmonious and intelligible order of things outside the world and the sphere of sense. But when he had departed and changed his habita- 78 tion he could not help but know that the world is not sovereign but dependent, not governing but governed by its Maker and First Cause. And this his mind then saw for the first time with its re- covered sight. For before a great mist had been 79 shed upon it by the things of sense, and only with difficulty could it dispel this mist under the warmth and fervour of higher verities and so be able as in clear open sky to receive the vision of Him Who so long lay hidden and invisible. He in His love for mankind, when the soul came into His presence, did not turn away His face, but came forward to meet him and revealed His nature, so far as the beholder's power of sight allowed. That is why we are told not 80 that the Sage saw God, but that God was seen by him. For it were impossible that anyone should by himself apprehend the truly Existent, did not He reveal and manifest Himself.

XVIII. What has been said is attested by the altera- 81 tion and change in his name, for his original name was Abram, but afterwards he was addressed as Abraham.[a] To the ear there was but a duplication of one letter, alpha, but in fact and in the truth con- veyed this duplication shewed a change of great importance. Abram is by interpretation "uplifted 82 father"; Abraham, "elect father of sound." The former signifies one called astrologer and meteoro-

[a] Gen. xvii. 5. For the interpretation of Abram and Abraham (Greek Abraam) *cf. De Cher.* 4, 7, *De Gig.* 62, 64, *De Mut.* 66.

PHILO

δογμάτων ἐπιμελούμενον, ὡς ἄν τις πατὴρ ἐγγόνων
83 ἐπιμεληθείη, τὸ δ' ὕστερον τὸν σοφόν. διὰ μὲν γὰρ
τῆς ἠχοῦς τὸν προφορικὸν λόγον αἰνίττεται, διὰ τοῦ
πατρὸς δὲ τὸν ἡγεμόνα νοῦν—πατὴρ γὰρ ὁ ἐνδιάθετος φύσει τοῦ γεγωνοῦ πρεσβύτερός γε ὢν καὶ
τὰ λεκτέα ὑποσπείρων—, διὰ δὲ τοῦ ἐπιλέκτου τὸν
ἀστεῖον· εἰκαῖος μὲν γὰρ καὶ πεφυρμένος ὁ φαῦλος τρόπος, ἐκλεκτὸς δὲ ὁ ἀγαθός, ἐπικριθεὶς ἐξ
84 ἁπάντων ἀριστίνδην. τῷ μὲν οὖν μετεωρολογικῷ
μεῖζον οὐδὲν τοῦ κόσμου τὸ παράπαν εἶναι δοκεῖ, ᾧ
καὶ τὰς τῶν γινομένων αἰτίας ἀνατίθησιν· ὁ δὲ
σοφὸς ἀκριβεστέροις ὄμμασιν ἰδών τι τελεώτερον
νοητὸν ἄρχον τε καὶ ἡγεμονεῦον, ὑφ' οὗ τἆλλα |
[14] δεσπόζεται καὶ κυβερνᾶται, πολλὰ κατεμέμψατο
τῆς προτέρας ζωῆς ἑαυτὸν ὡς τυφλὸν βίον δι-
εξεληλυθότα, σκηριπτόμενον ἐπὶ τοῖς αἰσθητοῖς,
ἀβεβαίῳ καὶ ἀνιδρύτῳ φύσει πράγματι.

δευτέραν δ' ἀποικίαν στέλλεται λογίῳ πάλιν πεισ-
85 θεὶς ὁ ἀστεῖος οὐκέτ' ἐκ πόλεως εἰς πόλιν, ἀλλ' εἰς
χώραν ἐρήμην, ἐν ᾗ πλαζόμενος διετέλει μὴ δυσ-
αρεστῶν τῇ πλάνῃ καὶ τῷ δι' αὐτὴν ἀνιδρύτῳ.
86 καίτοι τίς ἕτερος οὐκ ἂν ἠχθέσθη μὴ μόνον τῆς
οἰκείας ἀπανιστάμενος, ἀλλὰ καὶ ἐξ ἁπάσης πόλεως
ἐλαυνόμενος εἰς δυσβάτους καὶ δυσπορεύτους ἀνοδίας; τίς δ' οὐκ ἂν μετατραπόμενος ἐπαλινδρόμη-
σεν οἴκαδε, βραχέα μὲν φροντίσας τῶν μελλουσῶν
ἐλπίδων, τὴν δὲ παροῦσαν ἀπορίαν σπεύδων ἐκφυγεῖν, εὐήθειαν ὑπολαβὼν ἀδήλων χάριν ἀγαθῶν

---

[a] Gen. xii. 9. lxx "And Abram departed and having
journeyed encamped in the wilderness." E.V. "And Abram
journeyed going on still towards the south." Philo con-
veniently ignores the earlier movements of Abraham in

46

logist, one who takes care of the Chaldean tenets as a father would of his children. The latter signifies 83 the Sage, for he uses "sound" as a figure for spoken thought and "father" for the ruling mind, since the inward thought is by its nature father of the uttered, being senior to it, the secret begetter of what it has to say. "Elect" signifies the man of worth, for the worthless character is random and confused, while the good is elect, chosen out of all for his merits. Now to the meteorologist nothing at all seems 84 greater than the universe, and he credits it with the causation of what comes into being. But the wise man with more discerning eyes sees something more perfect perceived by mind, something which rules and governs, the master and pilot of all else. And therefore he blames himself severely for his former life, feeling that all his years have been passed in blindness with no staff to support him but the world of sense, which is by its nature an insecure and unstable thing.   The second migration 85 which the man of worth undertakes, again in obedience to an oracle, is not as before from state to state but into a desert country in which he continued to wander, never complaining of the wandering or the insecurity which it caused.[a]   Yet who else would not 86 have felt it a burden not only to be severed from his own country, but also to be driven out of all city life into pathless tracts where the traveller could hardly find a way ? Who would not have turned his course and hurried back homeward, paying little regard to future hopes, but eager to escape his present hardships, and thinking it folly to choose admitted evil

Canaan and fastens on the ultimate goal—the wilderness, as a symbol of the solitude of the mystic.

87 ὁμολογούμενα αἱρεῖσθαι κακά; μόνος δ᾽ οὑτοσὶ
τοὐναντίον πεπονθέναι φαίνεται, βίον ἥδιστον
νομίζων τὸν ἄνευ συνδιαιτήσεως τῆς τῶν πολλῶν.
καὶ πέφυκεν οὕτως ἔχειν· οἱ γὰρ ζητοῦντες καὶ
ἐπιποθοῦντες θεὸν ἀνευρεῖν τὴν φίλην αὐτῷ μόνωσιν
ἀγαπῶσι, κατ᾽ αὐτὸ τοῦτο σπεύδοντες πρῶτον
ἐξομοιοῦσθαι τῇ μακαρίᾳ καὶ εὐδαίμονι φύσει.

88 ἑκατέραν οὖν ἀπόδοσιν πεποιημένοι,
τήν τε ῥητὴν ὡς ἐπ᾽ ἀνδρὸς καὶ τὴν δι᾽ ὑπονοιῶν
ὡς ἐπὶ ψυχῆς, ἀξιέραστον καὶ τὸν ἄνδρα καὶ τὸν
νοῦν ἀπεφήναμεν, τὸν μὲν πεισθέντα λογίοις ἐκ
δυσαποσπάστων ἀφελκυσθέντα, τὸν δὲ νοῦν, ὅτι οὐ
μέχρι παντὸς ἀπατηθεὶς ἐπὶ τῆς αἰσθητῆς οὐσίας
ἔστη τὸν ὁρατὸν κόσμον ὑπολαβὼν μέγιστον καὶ
πρῶτον εἶναι θεόν, ἀλλὰ ἀναδραμὼν τῷ λογισμῷ
φύσιν ἑτέραν ἀμείνω τῆς ὁρατῆς νοητὴν ἐθεάσατο
καὶ τὸν ἀμφοῖν ποιητὴν ὁμοῦ καὶ ἡγεμόνα.

89 XIX. Ταῦτα τοῦ θεοφιλοῦς τὰ προτέλεια, οἷς
ἕπονται πράξεις οὐκ εὐκαταφρόνητοι. τὸ δὲ μέγεθος αὐτῶν οὐ παντί τῳ δῆλον, ἀλλὰ μόνον τοῖς
γευσαμένοις ἀρετῆς, οἳ τὰ θαυμαζόμενα παρὰ τοῖς
πολλοῖς εἰώθασι χλευάζειν ἕνεκα μεγέθους τῶν περὶ

90 ψυχὴν ἀγαθῶν. ἀποδεξάμενος οὖν ὁ θεὸς τὴν
εἰρημένην πρᾶξιν αὐτίκα τὸν ἀστεῖον ἀμείβεται
μεγάλῃ δωρεᾷ, τὸν γάμον αὐτῷ κινδυνεύσαντα πρὸς
δυνατοῦ καὶ ἀκρατοῦς ἀνδρὸς ἐπιβουλευθῆναι

91 διατηρήσας ἄψαυστόν τε καὶ σῶον. ἡ δ᾽ αἰτία τῆς
ἐπιθέσεως ἀρχὴν ἔλαβε τοιάνδε. καρπῶν ἀφορίας

ᵃ For §§ 91-98 see Gen. xii. 10-20.

for the sake of uncertain good? Yet he alone ap- 87
pears to have had feelings the opposite of these, and
to have thought that no life was so pleasant as one
lived without association with the multitude. And
that is natural, for those who seek God and yearn
to find Him love the solitude which is dear to Him,
and in this way first of all hasten to make themselves
like His blessed and happy nature.   So in 88
both our expositions, the literal as applied to the man
and the allegorical as applied to the soul, we have
shewn both man and soul to be worthy of our affection. We have shewn how the man in obedience to
divine commands was drawn away from the stubborn
hold of his associations and how the mind did not
remain for ever deceived nor stand rooted in the
realm of sense, nor suppose that the visible world was
the Almighty and Primal God, but using its reason
sped upwards and turned its gaze upon the intelligible order which is superior to the visible and upon
Him who is maker and ruler of both alike.

XIX. This is the opening of the story of the friend 89
of God, and it is followed by actions which call for
anything but contempt. But their greatness is not
clear to everyone, but only to those who have tasted
virtue and who recognize the greatness of the good
things which belong to the soul and therefore are wont
to deride those which win the admiration of the multitude. God, then, approving of the action just re- 90
lated, at once rewards the man of worth with a great
gift; for when his marriage was threatened through
the designs of a licentious potentate, God kept it
safe and unharmed. *a* The occasion which led up to 91
the attempted outrage originated in the following
way. There had been a failure of the crops for a

49

ἐπὶ συχνὸν χρόνον γενομένης, τοτὲ μὲν διὰ πολλὴν
καὶ ἄμετρον ἐπομβρίαν τοτὲ δὲ δι' αὐχμὸν καὶ
ζάλην, αἱ κατὰ Συρίαν πόλεις συνεχεῖ λιμῷ πιε-
σθεῖσαι κεναὶ τῶν οἰκητόρων ἦσαν, ἄλλων ἀλλαχόσε
σκιδναμένων κατὰ ζήτησιν τροφῆς καὶ πορισμὸν
92 τῶν ἀναγκαίων. πυθόμενος οὖν Ἀβραὰμ ἄφθονον
εὐθηνίαν καὶ εὐετηρίαν ἐν Αἰγύπτῳ, τοῦ μὲν ποταμοῦ ταῖς πλημμύραις λιμνάσαντος ἐν καιρῷ τὰ
πεδία, τῶν δὲ τὸν σπόρον εὔσταχυν ἐνεγκόντων καὶ
[15] ἀναθρεψαμένων | εὐκρασίαις πνευμάτων, ἀπαίρει
93 πᾶσαν τὴν οἰκίαν ἐπαγόμενος. ἦν δ' αὐτῷ γυνὴ τήν τε
ψυχὴν ἀρίστη καὶ τὸ σῶμα τῶν καθ' αὑτὴν περικαλ-
λεστάτη· ταύτην ἰδόντες τῶν Αἰγυπτίων οἱ ἐν τέλει
καὶ τῆς εὐμορφίας ἀγάμενοι—λανθάνει γὰρ τοὺς ἐν
94 ἐξοχαῖς οὐδέν—μηνύουσι τῷ βασιλεῖ. μεταπεμψάμενος δὲ τὴν ἄνθρωπον καὶ θεασάμενος ἐκπρεπε-
στάτην ὄψιν, βραχὺ φροντίσας αἰδοῦς καὶ νόμων τῶν
ἐπὶ τιμῇ ξένων ὁρισθέντων, ἐνδοὺς ἀκρασίᾳ διενοεῖτο λόγῳ μὲν αὐτὴν ἀγαγέσθαι πρὸς γάμον, τὸ
95 δ' ἀληθὲς αἰσχύνειν. ἡ δ' ἅτε ἐν ἀλλοτρίᾳ γῇ παρ'
ἀκρατεῖ τε καὶ ὠμοθύμῳ δυνάστῃ τοῦ βοηθήσοντος
ἀποροῦσα—οὐδὲ γὰρ ὁ ἀνὴρ ἔσθενεν ἀρήγειν τὸν
ἐπικρεμάμενον ἐκ τῶν δυνατωτέρων φόβον δεδιώς
—ἐπὶ τὴν τελευταίαν ἅμ' ἐκείνῳ καταφεύγει
96 συμμαχίαν τὴν ἐκ θεοῦ. λαβὼν δὲ τῶν ξένων
οἶκτον ὁ εὐμενὴς καὶ ἵλεως καὶ ὑπέρμαχος τῶν
ἀδικουμένων ἀλγηδόνας δυσκαρτερήτους καὶ χαλε-
πὰς τιμωρίας ἐπάγει τῷ βασιλεῖ, παντοίων κακῶν
ἀναπλήσας αὐτοῦ σῶμα καὶ ψυχὴν δυσιάτων, ὡς τὰς
μὲν ἐφ' ἡδονὴν ἀγούσας ὀρέξεις ἁπάσας ἐκκεκόφ-
θαι, τὰς δ' ἐναντίας παρεισεληλυθέναι φροντίδας

considerable period, at one time through a great and excessive rainfall, at another through drought and stormy weather; and the cities of Syria, hard pressed through continual famine, were stripped of their inhabitants who scattered in different directions to seek for food and to procure necessities. Abraham, then, 92 learning that there was a rich and abundant supply of corn in Egypt, where the river by its seasonal flooding had turned the plains into pools, and well-tempered winds had produced and fostered a fine growth of corn, set off thither with his whole household. He had a wife distinguished greatly for her 93 goodness of soul and beauty of body, in which she surpassed all the women of her time. When the chief people of Egypt saw her and admired her beauty, since the highly placed leave nothing unobserved, they told the king. He sent for the 94 woman, and, marking her surpassing comeliness, paid little regard to decency or the laws enacted to shew respect to strangers, but gave rein to his licence and determined nominally to take her in marriage, but in reality to bring her to shame. She who in a 95 foreign country was at the mercy of a licentious and cruel-hearted despot and had no one to protect her, for her husband was helpless, menaced as he was by the terror of stronger powers, joined him in fleeing for refuge to the last remaining championship, that of God. And God, Who is kindly and merciful and 96 shields the wronged, had pity for the strangers and plied the king with almost intolerable pains and grievous penalties. He filled him body and soul with all manner of scarce curable plagues. All appetite for pleasure was eradicated and replaced by visitations of the opposite kind, by cravings for release

περὶ ἀπαλλαγῆς ἀνηνύτων βασάνων, ὑφ' ὧν γυμναζόμενος μεθ' ἡμέραν καὶ νύκτωρ ἐξετραχηλίζετο.
97 παραπέλαυσε δὲ τῆς τιμωρίας καὶ σύμπας ὁ οἶκος
αὐτῷ, μηδενὸς ἐπὶ τῇ παρανομίᾳ δυσχεράναντος,
ἀλλὰ πάντων ἕνεκα τοῦ συναινεῖν μόνον οὐ συγ-
98 χειρουργησάντων τὸ ἀδίκημα. τοῦτον τὸν τρόπον ἡ
μὲν ἁγνεία τῆς γυναικὸς διασώζεται, τοῦ δὲ ἀνδρὸς
τὴν καλοκἀγαθίαν καὶ εὐσέβειαν ὁ θεὸς ἠξίωσεν
ἐπιδείξασθαι γέρας αὐτῷ μέγιστον παρασχών,
ἀσινῆ καὶ ἀνύβριστον ὅσον οὔπω κινδυνεύσαντα
διαφθαρῆναι τὸν γάμον, ὃς οὐκ ἔμελλεν ὀλίγων
ἀριθμὸν υἱῶν ἢ θυγατέρων γεννᾶν, ἀλλ' ὅλον ἔθνος
καὶ ἐθνῶν τὸ θεοφιλέστατον, ὅ μοι δοκεῖ τὴν ὑπὲρ
παντὸς ἀνθρώπων γένους ἱερωσύνην καὶ προφητείαν
λαχεῖν.
99 XX. Ἤκουσα μέντοι καὶ φυσικῶν ἀνδρῶν οὐκ
ἀπὸ σκοποῦ τὰ περὶ τὸν τόπον ἀλληγορούντων, οἳ
τὸν μὲν ἄνδρα συμβολικῶς ἔφασκον σπουδαῖον
εἶναι νοῦν ἐκ τῆς περὶ τοὔνομα ἑρμηνευθείσης
δυνάμεως τεκμαιρόμενοι τρόπον ἀστεῖον ἐν ψυχῇ,
τὴν δὲ τούτου γυναῖκα ἀρετήν, ἧς τοὔνομά ἐστι
Χαλδαϊστὶ μὲν Σάρρα, Ἑλληνιστὶ δὲ " ἄρχουσα,"
διὰ τὸ μηδὲν ἀρετῆς ἀρχικώτερον εἶναι καὶ ἡγεμο-
100 νικώτερον. γάμος δέ, ὃν μὲν ἁρμόζεται ἡδονή,
σωμάτων κοινωνίαν ἔλαχεν, ὃν δὲ σοφία, λογισμῶν
καθάρσεως ἐφιεμένων καὶ τελείων ἀρετῶν. ἐναντιώτατοι δὲ ἀλλήλοις εἰσὶν οἱ λεχθέντες γάμοι.
101 κατὰ μὲν γὰρ τὸν τῶν σωμάτων σπείρει μὲν τὸ

ᵃ Or " students of the (higher) truths of Nature," almost in
some contexts (e.g. Mos. ii. 216) = " theologians." Nature is
so closely akin to the divine (see note on De Sac. 98) that
allegorical truths such as these especially belong to its study,

from the endless tortures which night and day haunted and racked him almost to death. The whole 97 household, too, shared the punishment with him, since none had shewn indignation at the outrage, but all by consenting were almost accomplices in the misdeed. Thus the chastity of the woman was pre- 98 served, while the nobility and piety of the man was evidenced by God, Who deigned to grant him this signal boon, that his marriage, which would have been in almost immediate danger of violation, should remain free from harm and outrage, that marriage from which was to issue not a family of a few sons and daughters, but a whole nation, and that the nation dearest of all to God, which, as I hold, has received the gift of priesthood and prophecy on behalf of all mankind.

XX. I have also heard some natural philosophers [a] 99 who took the passage allegorically, not without good reason. They said that the husband was a figure for the good mind, judging by the meaning given for interpretation of this name that it stood for a good disposition of soul. The wife, they said, was virtue, her name being in Chaldean Sarah but in our language a sovereign lady,[b] because nothing is more sovereign or dominant than virtue. Now in a marriage where 100 the union is brought about by pleasure, the partnership is between body and body, but in the marriage made by wisdom it is between thoughts which seek purification and perfect virtues. Now the two kinds of marriage are directly opposed to each other. For 101 in the bodily marriage the male sows the seed and the

cf. De Post. 7 τὴν δι' ἀλληγορίας ὁδὸν φυσικοῖς φίλην ἀνδράσι, and De Mut. 62 φυσιολογοῦντες. See further App. p. 597.
  b Cf. De Cher. 8, De Mut. 77.

ἄρρεν, γονὴν δ᾽ ὑποδέχεται τὸ θῆλυ, κατὰ δὲ τὴν |
[16] ἐν ψυχαῖς σύνοδον ἔμπαλιν ἡ μὲν ἀρετὴ τάξιν
γυναικὸς ἔχειν δοκοῦσα σπείρειν πέφυκε βουλὰς
ἀγαθὰς καὶ λόγους σπουδαίους καὶ βιωφελεστάτων
εἰσηγήσεις δογμάτων, ὁ δὲ λογισμὸς εἰς τὴν ἀνδρὸς
χώραν τάττεσθαι νομισθεὶς τὰς ἱεροπρεπεῖς καὶ
θείας ὑποδέχεται σποράς· ἢ μήποτε τὸ λεχθὲν
ἔψευσται δι᾽ ἀπάτην ὀνομάτων, ἐπειδήπερ ὁ μὲν
νοῦς ἄρρενος ἡ δ᾽ ἀρετὴ θήλεος μετέχει χαρακτῆρος
102 ἐν φωναῖς. εἰ δέ τις τὰς ἐπισκιαζούσας κλήσεις
ἀπαμφιάσας γυμνὰ τὰ πράγματα βουληθείη καθαρῶς ἰδεῖν εἴσεται διότι ἄρρεν μέν ἐστιν ἡ ἀρετὴ
φύσει, παρόσον κινεῖ καὶ διατίθησι καὶ καλὰς
ἐννοίας καλῶν πράξεων καὶ λόγων ὑπηχεῖ, θῆλυ
δὲ ὁ λογισμὸς κινούμενος καὶ παιδευόμενος καὶ
ὠφελούμενος καὶ συνόλως ἐν τῷ πάσχειν ἐξεταζό-
μενος, καὶ τὸ πάθος αὐτῷ τοῦτο μόνον ἐστὶ σωτή-
103 ριον. XXI. ἅπαντες μὲν οὖν καὶ οἱ φαυλότατοι
τῷ λόγῳ τιμῶσι καὶ θαυμάζουσιν ἀρετὴν ὅσα τῷ
δοκεῖν, χρῶνται δ᾽ αὐτῆς τοῖς παραγγέλμασιν οἱ
ἀστεῖοι μόνοι. διὸ καὶ ὁ τῆς Αἰγύπτου βασιλεύς,
ὅπερ ἐστὶ συμβολικῶς νοῦς φιλοσώματος, καθυποκρινόμενος ὡς ἐν θεάτρῳ προσποίητον ἐπιμορφάζει
κοινωνίαν, πρὸς ἐγκράτειαν ὁ ἀκρατὴς καὶ πρὸς
σωφροσύνην ὁ ἀκόλαστος καὶ πρὸς δικαιοσύνην
ὁ ἄδικος, καὶ καλεῖ τὴν ἀρετὴν ὡς ἑαυτὸν τῆς παρὰ
104 τοῖς πολλοῖς εὐφημίας γλιχόμενος. ὅπερ κατιδὼν
ὁ ἔφορος—μόνῳ γὰρ ἔξεστι θεῷ ψυχὴν ἰδεῖν—
ἐμίσησε καὶ προὔβαλετο καὶ βασάνοις ἤλεγξεν
ἀργαλεωτάταις ἦθος κατεψευσμένον. αἱ δὲ βάσανοι
διὰ τίνων ὀργάνων; ἢ πάντως διὰ τῶν τῆς ἀρετῆς
μερῶι ἅπερ ἐπεισιόντα χαλεπῶς αἰκίζεται καὶ
54

female receives it; on the other hand in the matings within the soul, though virtue seemingly ranks as wife, her natural function is to sow good counsels and excellent words and to inculcate tenets truly profitable to life, while thought, though held to take the place of the husband, receives the holy and divine sowings. Perhaps however the statement [a] above is a mistake due to the deceptiveness of the nouns, since in the actual words employed $νοῦς$ has the masculine, and $ἀρετή$ the feminine form. And if anyone is willing to divest 102 facts of the terms which obscure them and observe them in their nakedness in a clear light he will understand that virtue is male, since it causes movement and affects conditions and suggests noble conceptions of noble deeds and words, while thought is female, being moved and trained and helped, and in general belonging to the passive category, which passivity is its sole means of preservation. XXI. All men, then, 103 even the most worthless, professedly honour and admire virtue so far as outward appearance goes, but only the worthy practise its injunctions. And so the king of Egypt, under which figure is symbolized the mind which loves the body, acts a part as in a theatre and assumes a counterfeited fellowship, he, the licentious with chastity, the profligate with self-control, the unjust with justice, and in his desire to earn a good repute with the multitude invites virtue to join him. Seeing this, God the surveyor, since He alone 104 can scan the soul, hates and rejects the sham character and submits it to the test of most painful tortures. What are the instruments of these tortures? Surely the different parts of virtue which enter in and plague

[a] *i.e.* that virtue is wife, and mind husband; but see App. pp. 597–598.

τιτρώσκει; βάσανος μὲν γάρ ἐστιν ἀπληστίας
ὀλιγοδεΐα, βάσανος δὲ λαγνείας ἐγκράτεια· στρε-
βλοῦται δὲ καὶ ὁ φιλόδοξος ἀτυφίας εὐημερούσης καὶ
105 ὁ ἄδικος δικαιοσύνης ἐπαινουμένης. μίαν γὰρ
ἀμήχανον ψυχὴν κατοικεῖν δύο τὰς ἐχθρὰς φύσεις,
κακίαν καὶ ἀρετήν· οὗ χάριν, ἐπειδὰν συνενεχθῶσιν,
ἀσύμβατοι καὶ ἀκατάλλακτοι στάσεις καὶ πόλεμοι
συγκροτοῦνται, καίτοι τῆς ἀρετῆς εἰρηνικωτάτην
φύσιν ἐχούσης, ἣ φασιν ἐπιμελὲς εἶναι, ὅταν εἰς
χειρῶν ἅμιλλαν ἰέναι μέλλῃ, τῆς ἰδίας δυνάμεως
ἀποπειρᾶσθαι πρότερον, ἵν᾽, εἰ μὲν ἰσχύοι κατ-
αγωνίσασθαι, συνιστῆται, εἰ δ᾽ ἀσθενεστέρα χρῷτο
τῇ δυνάμει, μηδὲ συγκαταβῆναι τὴν ἀρχὴν εἰς τὸν
106 ἀγῶνα θαρρήσῃ· κακίαν μὲν γὰρ ἡττᾶσθαι οὐκ
αἰσχρόν, ᾗ συγγενὲς ἀδοξία, ἀρετὴν δὲ ὄνειδος, ᾗ
πάντων οἰκειότατον εὔκλεια, δι᾽ ἣν πέφυκε νικᾶν ἢ
διατηρεῖν αὐτὴν ἀήττητον.

107 XXII. Τὸ μὲν οὖν Αἰγυπτίων ἄξενον καὶ ἀκό-
λαστον εἴρηται. τοῦ δὲ τοιαῦτα πεπονθότος ἄξιον
θαυμάσαι τὴν φιλανθρωπίαν, ὃς μεσημβρίας |
[17] θεασάμενος τρεῖς ὡς ἄνδρας ὁδοιποροῦντας—οἱ δὲ
θειοτέρας ὄντες φύσεως ἐλελήθεσαν—προσδραμὼν
ἱκέτευε λιπαρῶς μὴ παρελθεῖν αὐτοῦ τὴν σκηνήν,
ἀλλ᾽ ὡς πρέπον εἰσεληλυθότας ξενίων μετασχεῖν· οἱ
δ᾽ οὐκ ἐκ τῶν λεγομένων μᾶλλον ἢ τῆς διανοίας
εἰδότες ἀληθεύοντα μηδὲν ἐνδοιάσαντες ἐπινεύουσι.
108 πληρωθεὶς δὲ τὴν ψυχὴν χαρᾶς πάντ᾽ ἐσπούδαζεν
εἰς τὸ ἀνυπέρθετον τῆς ὑποδοχῆς καὶ τῇ μὲν γυναικί
φησι " σπεῦσον καὶ τρία μέτρα ποίησον ἐγκρυφιῶν,"
αὐτὸς δὲ εἰς τὰ βουκόλια συντείνας, ἁπαλὸν καὶ
109 εὔσαρκον ἀγαγὼν μόσχον, οἰκέτῃ παραδίδωσιν. ὁ

ᵃ For §§ 107-118 see Gen. xviii.

and wound him grievously? For greediness is tortured by frugal contentment and lewdness by continence. And so the vainglorious is racked when simplicity prevails, and the unjust when justice is praised. For 105 it is impossible for the single soul to have for its tenant two hostile natures, vice and virtue, and therefore when they meet factions and wars are set on foot incapable of truce or reconciliation. And yet virtue's nature is most peaceable, and she is careful, so they say, to test her own strength before the conflict, so that if she is able to contend to the end she may take the field, but if she finds her strength too weak she may shrink from entering the contest at all. For vice 106 feels no disgrace in defeat, since ill-repute is congenital to her, but to virtue it is a reproach, for nearest and dearest to her is good fame which makes it natural for her to be victorious or at least to keep herself undefeated.

XXII. *a* I have described the inhospitality and 107 licentiousness of the Egyptians. Turning to the victim of this outrage, we may well admire his kindness of heart. When at noon he saw three travellers in the form of men, for their diviner nature was not apparent to him, he ran to them and earnestly begged of them not to pass his tent but to enter as was fitting and partake of hospitality. But they, knowing, not so much by his words as by the feeling he showed, that he spoke the truth, assented without hesitation. And he, his soul full of joy, was eager to carry out 108 the reception without delay, and said to his wife: "Hasten and bake three measures of cakes in the ashes." Meanwhile he himself hurried to the stalls and brought a tender and well-fed calf which he gave to the servant who killed it and dressed it with all 109

δὲ καταθύσας σκευάζει τάχιστα· βραδὺς γὰρ οὐδεὶς
πρὸς φιλανθρωπίαν ἐν οἴκῳ σοφοῦ, ἀλλὰ καὶ γυναῖκες καὶ ἄνδρες καὶ δοῦλοι καὶ ἐλεύθεροι προ-
θυμότατοι πρὸς τὰς τῶν ξενιζομένων ὑπηρεσίας.
110 ἑστιαθέντες δ' οὐ τοῖς εὐτρεπισθεῖσι μᾶλλον ἢ τῇ
τοῦ ξενοδόχου γνώμῃ καὶ πολλῇ τινι καὶ ἀπεράντῳ
φιλοτιμίᾳ παρέχουσιν ἆθλον ἐλπίδος μεῖζον αὐτῷ,
υἱοῦ γνησίου γένεσιν εἰς νέωτα βεβαιωθησομένην
ὑποσχόμενοι δι' ἑνὸς τοῦ τῶν τριῶν ἀρίστου—
λέγειν γὰρ ἐν ταὐτῷ πάντας ἀθρόους ἦν ἀφιλό-
σοφον, ἑνὶ δὲ λέγοντι τοὺς ἄλλους συνεπινεύειν
111 ἐμπρεπές—. ἀλλὰ γὰρ οὐδ' ὑπισχνουμένοις ἕνεκα
τοῦ περὶ τὸ πρᾶγμα ἀπίστου βεβαίως προσεῖχον·
ἤδη γὰρ ὑπερήλικες γεγονότες διὰ μακρὸν γῆρας
112 ἀπεγνώκεσαν παιδὸς σπορᾶν. ἀκούσασαν οὖν τὴν
γυναῖκα ἐν ἀρχῇ φησι γελάσαι καὶ μετὰ ταῦτα,
εἰπόντων " μὴ ἀδυνατεῖ παρὰ τῷ θεῷ πᾶν ῥῆμα; "
καταιδεσθεῖσαν ἠρνῆσθαι τὸν γέλωτα· πάντα γὰρ
ᾔδει θεῷ δυνατὰ σχεδὸν ἐξ ἔτι σπαργάνων τουτὶ τὸ
113 δόγμα προμαθοῦσα. τότε μοι δοκεῖ πρῶτον οὐκέθ'
ὁμοίαν τῶν ὁρωμένων λαβεῖν φαντασίαν, ἀλλὰ
σεμνοτέραν ἢ προφητῶν ἢ ἀγγέλων μεταβαλόντων
ἀπὸ πνευματικῆς καὶ ψυχοειδοῦς οὐσίας εἰς ἀν-
θρωπόμορφον ἰδέαν.
114 XXIII. Τὸ μὲν οὖν φιλόξενον τοῦ ἀνδρὸς εἴρηται,
πάρεργον ὂν ἀρετῆς μείζονος· ἡ δ' ἀρετὴ θεοσέβεια,
περὶ ἧς καὶ πρότερον εἴπομεν, ἧς δεῖγμα σαφέσ-
τατον τὰ νῦν λεχθέντα ἐστὶν ὡς ἐπὶ ξένων ἀνδρῶν.

ᵃ *i.e.* Sarah's denial of her laughter is ascribed to a
recognition that the Visitor was divine, rather than as in
58

speed. For in a wise man's house no one is slow in showing kindness ; but women and men, slaves and free, are full of zeal to do service to their guests. After 110 feasting not so much on the viands prepared for them as on the goodwill of their host, and on this example of a great and unbounded generosity, they presented him with a reward surpassing his hopes, by promising him the birth of a son born in wedlock. And this promise, which was to be made good in the next year, was given through one, and that the highest, of the three. For wise refinement demanded that all should not speak together at once but rather that one should speak and the others shew assent. But to Abraham 111 and Sarah the thing seemed incredible, and therefore they did not pay serious regard even to the promises of the three. For as they had passed the years of parenthood their great age had made them despair of the birth of a son. So the scripture says that the 112 wife first laughed at the words and afterwards when they said, " Is anything impossible with God ? " was ashamed and denied her laughter, for she knew that all things were possible with God, a truth which she had learnt long ago, and even from the cradle. It 113 was then, I think, that she first saw in the strangers before her a different and grander aspect, that of prophets or angels, transformed from their spiritual and soul-like nature into human shape.[a]

XXIII. We have described Abraham's hospitality 114 which was but a by-product of a greater virtue. That virtue is piety, of which we have spoken before, and it is quite clearly seen in this story, even if we think of the strangers as men. Some may feel that the 115

Genesis to fear. Otherwise Philo here gives the natural interpretation of the incident. See note on § 206.

PHILO

115 εἰ δ᾽ εὐδαίμονα καὶ μακάριον οἶκον ὑπέλαβόν εἶναί
τινες, ἐν ᾧ συνέβη καταχθῆναι καὶ ἐνδιατρῖψαι
σοφούς, οὐκ ἂν ἀξιώσαντας ἀλλ᾽ οὐδ᾽ ὅσον διακῦψαι
μόνον, εἴ τι πάθος ἐνεώρων ταῖς ψυχαῖς τῶν ἔνδον
ὄντων ἀνίατον, ἐγὼ δὲ οὐκ οἶδα, τίνα ὑπερβολὴν
εὐδαιμονίας καὶ μακαριότητος εἶναι φῶ περὶ τὴν
οἰκίαν, ἐν ᾗ καταχθῆναι καὶ ξενίων λαχεῖν ὑπέμειναν ἄγγελοι πρὸς ἀνθρώπων,[1] ἱεραὶ καὶ θεῖαι
φύσεις, ὑποδιάκονοι καὶ ὕπαρχοι τοῦ πρώτου θεοῦ,
[18] | δι᾽ ὧν οἷα πρεσβευτῶν ὅσα ἂν θελήσῃ τῷ γένει
116 ἡμῶν προθεσπίσαι διαγγέλλει. πῶς γὰρ ἂν τὴν
ἀρχὴν εἰσελθεῖν ὑπέμειναν, εἰ μὴ καθάπερ νεὼς εὖ
συντεταγμένον πλήρωμα τοὺς ἔνδον ἅπαντας ᾔδεσαν
ἑνὶ πειθαρχοῦντας κελεύσματι τῷ τοῦ προεστηκότος
ὡσανεὶ κυβερνήτου; πῶς δ᾽ ἂν ἑστιωμένων καὶ
ξενιζομένων παρέσχον ὑπόληψιν, εἰ μὴ τὸν ἑστιάτορα συγγενῆ καὶ ὁμόδουλον ἡγοῦντο τῷ αὐτῶν
προσπεφευγότα δεσπότῃ; νομιστέον μέντοι καὶ
κατὰ τὴν εἴσοδον αὐτῶν ἔτι μᾶλλον ἐπιδοῦναι
πάντα τὰ μέρη τῆς οἰκίας πρὸς τὸ βέλτιον αὔρᾳ
117 τινὶ τελειοτάτης ἀρετῆς ἐπιπνευσθέντα. τὸ δὲ συμ-
πόσιον οἷον εἰκὸς γενέσθαι, τὴν ἐν εὐωχίαις
ἀφέλειαν ἐπιδεικνυμένων πρὸς τὸν ἑστιάτορα τῶν
ἑστιωμένων καὶ γυμνοῖς ἤθεσι προσαγορευόντων
καὶ ὁμιλίας τὰς ἁρμοττούσας τῷ καιρῷ ποιου-
118 μένων. τεράστιον δὲ καὶ τὸ μὴ πίνοντας πινόντων
καὶ τὸ μὴ ἐσθίοντας ἐσθιόντων παρέχειν φαντασίαν.
ἀλλὰ ταυτί γε ὡς ἀκόλουθα· τὸ δὲ πρῶτον ἐκεῖνο
τερατωδέστατον, ἀσωμάτους ὄντας [τοῦδε σώματος]

---

[1] So one ms. The others ἀνθρώπους, which Cohn prints in
the text, but later declared for -ων. The accusative, however
= " in relation with men " is not impossible.

house must have been happy and blessed in which such an event as this took place, that wise men halted there and made a stay who would not have deigned even to look inside if they saw anything hopelessly wrong in the souls of the inmates. And, if this is so, I do not know how to express the vast happiness and blessedness of that house where angels did not shrink from halting and receiving hospitality from men— angels, those holy and divine beings, the servitors and lieutenants of the primal God whom He employs as ambassadors to announce the predictions which He wills to make to our race. For how could they have 116 brought themselves to enter at all if they had not known that all the household, like a well ordered crew, was obedient to a single call from him who steered them like a pilot ? And how should they have given ground for the idea that they feasted and received hospitality unless they thought that the giver of the feast was their kinsman and fellow-servant who had sought refuge with their master ? Indeed we must suppose that at their entrance all parts of the house advanced still further in goodness and felt some breath of the inspiration of perfect virtue. The 117 conduct of the meal was such as it should be. The guests showed to their entertainer the frank simplicity of a festive gathering. Their manner in addressing him was unreserved, and their converse suited to the occasion. It is a marvel indeed that 118 though they neither ate nor drank they gave the appearance of both eating and drinking.[a] But that is a secondary matter ; the first and greatest wonder is that, though incorporeal, they assumed human

[a] See App. p. 598.

εἰς ἰδέαν ἀνθρώπων μεμορφῶσθαι χάριτι τῇ πρὸς
τὸν ἀστεῖον· τίνος γὰρ ἕνεκα ταῦτα ἐθαυματουργεῖτο ἢ τοῦ παρασχεῖν αἴσθησιν τῷ σοφῷ διὰ
τρανοτέρας ὄψεως, ὅτι οὐ λέληθε τὸν πατέρα
τοιοῦτος ὤν;

119 XXIV. Τὰ μὲν οὖν τῆς ῥητῆς ἀποδόσεως ὡδὶ
λελέχθω· τῆς δὲ δι' ὑπονοιῶν ἀρκτέον. σύμβολα τὰ
ἐν φωναῖς τῶν διανοίᾳ μόνῃ καταλαμβανομένων
ἐστίν· ἐπειδὰν οὖν ἡ ψυχὴ καθάπερ ἐν μεσημβρίᾳ
θεῷ περιλαμφθῇ καὶ ὅλη δι' ὅλων νοητοῦ φωτὸς
ἀναπλησθεῖσα ταῖς ἐν κύκλῳ κεχυμέναις αὐγαῖς¹
ἄσκιος γένηται, τριττὴν φαντασίαν ἑνὸς ὑποκειμένου καταλαμβάνει, τοῦ μὲν ὡς ὄντος, τῶν δ'
ἄλλων δυοῖν ὡς ἂν ἀπαυγαζομένων ἀπὸ τούτου
σκιῶν· ὁποῖόν τι συμβαίνει καὶ τοῖς ἐν αἰσθητῷ
φωτὶ διατρίβουσιν· ἢ γὰρ ἑστώτων ἢ κινουμένων
120 διτταὶ σκιαὶ πολλάκις συνεμπίπτουσι. μὴ μέντοι
νομισάτω τις ἐπὶ θεοῦ τὰς σκιὰς κυριολογεῖσθαι·
κατάχρησις ὀνόματός ἐστι μόνον πρὸς ἐναργεστέραν
ἔμφασιν τοῦ δηλουμένου πράγματος, ἐπεὶ τό γε
121 ἀληθὲς οὐχ ὧδε ἔχει· ἀλλ' ἔστιν, ὡς ἄν τις ἐγγύτατα
τῆς ἀληθείας ἱστάμενος εἴποι, πατὴρ μὲν τῶν ὅλων
[19] ὁ μέσος, ὃς ἐν ταῖς | ἱεραῖς γραφαῖς κυρίῳ ὀνόματι
καλεῖται ὁ ὤν, αἱ δὲ παρ' ἑκάτερα αἱ πρεσβύταται
καὶ ἐγγυτάτω τοῦ ὄντος δυνάμεις, ἡ μὲν ποιητική,
ἡ δ' αὖ βασιλική· προσαγορεύεται δὲ ἡ μὲν ποιητικὴ
θεός, ταύτῃ γὰρ ἔθηκέ τε καὶ διεκόσμησε τὸ πᾶν,
ἡ δὲ βασιλικὴ κύριος, θέμις γὰρ ἄρχειν καὶ κρατεῖν
122 τὸ πεποιηκὸς τοῦ γενομένου. δορυφορούμενος οὖν

¹ mss. (with the exception of H²) τὰς . . κεχυμένας αὐγὰς,
which perhaps might be kept, as Cohn suggests, by correcting
ἄσκιος γένηται to ἀσκίους δέχηται or ἀσπάσηται.

form to do kindness to the man of worth. For why was this miracle worked save to cause the Sage to perceive with clearer vision that the Father did not fail to recognize his wisdom?

XXIV. Here we may leave the literal exposition 119 and begin the allegorical. Spoken words contain symbols of things apprehended by the understanding only. When, then, as at noon-tide God shines around the soul, and the light of the mind fills it through and through and the shadows are driven from it by the rays which pour all around it, the single object presents to it a triple vision, one representing the reality, the other two the shadows reflected from it. Our life in the light which our senses perceive gives us a somewhat similar experience, for objects standing or moving often cast two shadows at once. No 120 one, however, should think that the shadows can be properly spoken of as God. To call them so is loose speaking, serving merely to give a clearer view of the fact which we are explaining, since the real truth is otherwise. Rather, as anyone who has approached 121 nearest to the truth would say, the central place is held by the Father of the Universe, Who in the sacred scriptures is called He that is as His proper name, while on either side of Him are the senior potencies, the nearest to Him, the creative and the kingly. The title of the former is God,[a] since it made and ordered the All; the title of the latter is Lord, since it is the fundamental right of the maker to rule and control what he has brought into being. So the central Being with each of His pot- 122

---

[a] Evidently an allusion to the accepted derivation of θεός from τίθημι. Cf. De Conf. 137 δύναμις καθ' ἥν ἔθηκε καὶ διετάξατο τὰ πάντα κέκληται ἐτύμως θεός, where ἐτύμως shews that an etymology is intended (see note). Cf. also De Mut. 29.

ὁ μέσος ὑφ' ἑκατέρας τῶν δυνάμεων παρέχει τῇ
ὁρατικῇ διανοίᾳ τοτὲ μὲν ἑνὸς τοτὲ δὲ τριῶν φαντασίαν, ἑνὸς μὲν ὅταν ἄκρως τύχῃ καθαρθεῖσα καὶ
μὴ μόνον τὰ πλήθη τῶν ἀριθμῶν ἀλλὰ καὶ τὴν
γείτονα μονάδος δυάδα ὑπερβᾶσα πρὸς τὴν ἀμιγῆ
καὶ ἀσύμπλοκον καὶ καθ' αὑτὴν οὐδενὸς ἐπιδεᾶ τὸ
παράπαν ἰδέαν ἐπείγηται, τριῶν δὲ ὅταν μήπω τὰς
μεγάλας τελεσθεῖσα τελετὰς ἔτι ἐν ταῖς βραχυ-
τέραις ὀργιάζηται καὶ μὴ δύνηται τὸ ὂν ἄνευ ἑτέρου
τινὸς ἐξ αὐτοῦ μόνου καταλαβεῖν, ἀλλὰ διὰ τῶν
123 δρωμένων, ἢ κτίζον ἢ ἄρχον. δεύτερος μὲν οὖν,
ὥς φασι, πλοῦς οὗτος, μετέχει δ' οὐδὲν ἧττον δόξης
θεοφιλοῦς· ὁ δὲ πρότερος τρόπος οὐ μετέχει, ἀλλ'
αὐτός ἐστι θεοφιλὴς δόξα, μᾶλλον δὲ καὶ δόξης
πρεσβυτέρα καὶ παντὸς τιμιωτέρα τοῦ δοκεῖν ἀλήθεια.   γνωριμώτερον δὲ τὸ δηλούμενον
124 παραστατέον. XXV. τρεῖς εἰσιν ἠθῶν ἀνθρωπίνων τάξεις, ὧν ἑκάστη διακεκλήρωται μίαν τῶν
εἰρημένων φαντασιῶν ἡ μὲν ἀρίστη τὴν μέσην τοῦ
ὄντως ὄντος, ἡ δὲ μετ' ἐκείνην τὴν ἐπὶ δεξιά, τὴν
εὐεργέτιν, ᾗ θεὸς ὄνομα, ἡ δὲ τρίτη τὴν ἐπὶ θάτερα,
125 τὴν ἀρχικήν, ἣ καλεῖται κύριος. τὰ μὲν οὖν ἄριστα
τῶν ἠθῶν τὸν καθ' αὑτὸν ἄνευ τινὸς ὄντα θεραπεύει
πρὸς μηδενὸς ἑτέρου μεθελκόμενα, τῷ τετάσθαι
μοναδικῶς πρὸς τὴν ἑνὸς τιμήν· τῶν δ' ἄλλων τὰ
μὲν διὰ τῆς εὐεργέτιδος συνίσταται καὶ γνωρίζεται

ᵃ For this proverbial phrase see note on De Som. i. 44.

encies as His squire presents to the mind which has vision the appearance sometimes of one, sometimes of three : of one, when that mind is highly purified and, passing beyond not merely the multiplicity of other numbers, but even the dyad which is next to the unit, presses on to the ideal form which is free from mixture and complexity, and being self-contained needs nothing more ; of three, when, as yet uninitiated into the highest mysteries, it is still a votary only of the minor rites and unable to apprehend the Existent alone by Itself and apart from all else, but only through Its actions, as either creative or ruling. This is, as they say, a " second best 123 voyage[a] " ; yet all the same there is in it an element of a way of thinking such as God approves. But the former state of mind has not merely an element. It is in itself the divinely-approved way, or rather it is the truth, higher than a way of thinking, more precious than anything which is merely thought.   But it would be well to state the point in a more familiar guise. XXV. There are three classes of human 124 temperaments, each of them so constituted that the vision presents itself in one of the three ways abovementioned. To the best class it presents itself in the middle form, that of the essentially existent ; to the next best, in that which stands on the right, the beneficent, which bears the name of God ; to the third, in that on the left, the governing, which is called Lord. Temperaments of the last kind 125 worship the solely Self-existent and nothing can make them swerve from this, because they are subject to the single attraction which leads them to honour the one. Of the other two types, one is introduced and made known to the Father by

δυνάμεως τῷ πατρί, τὰ δὲ διὰ τῆς βασιλικῆς.

126 ὃ δὲ λέγω, τοιοῦτόν ἐστιν. ἄνθρωποι μὲν ἐπειδὰν αἴσθωνται κατὰ πρόφασιν ἑταιρείας προσιόντας αὑτοῖς τινας ἐπὶ θήρᾳ πλεονεξιῶν, ὑποβλέπονταί τε καὶ ἀποστρέφονται τὴν προσποίητον κολακείαν καὶ τιθασείαν αὐτῶν δεδιότες ὡς

127 σφόδρα ἐπιζήμιον· ὁ δὲ θεὸς ἅτε βλάβην οὐκ ἐπιδεχόμενος ἅπαντας τοὺς καθ' ἡντινοῦν ἰδέαν προαιρουμένους τιμᾶν αὐτὸν ἄσμενος προσκαλεῖται, μηδένα σκορακίζειν ἀξιῶν τὸ παράπαν, ἀλλὰ μόνον οὐκ ἄντικρυς τοῖς ἀκοὰς ἔχουσιν ἐν τῇ ψυχῇ θεσ-

128 πίζει τάδε· "τὰ μὲν πρῶτα τῶν ἄθλων κείσεται τοῖς ἐμὲ θεραπεύουσι δι' ἐμὲ αὐτόν, τὰ δὲ δεύτερα τοῖς δι' ἑαυτούς, ἢ τυχεῖν ἀγαθῶν ἐλπίζουσιν ἢ τιμωριῶν ἀπαλλαγὴν εὑρήσεσθαι προσδοκῶσι· καὶ γὰρ εἰ ἔμμισθος ἡ τῶνδε θεραπεία καὶ μὴ ἀδέκαστος, ἀλλ' οὐδὲν ἧττον ἐντὸς εἰλεῖται θείων περι-

129 βόλων καὶ οὐκ ἔξω πλάζεται. τὰ δὲ ἆθλα τοῖς
[20] μὲν ἐμὲ τιμῶσι δι' ἐμὲ κείσεται φίλια, τοῖς δὲ διὰ τὰς χρείας φίλια μὲν οὔ, τὸ δὲ μὴ ἀλλοτρίοις νομίζεσθαι· δέχομαι γὰρ καὶ τὸν τῆς εὐεργέτιδός μου δυνάμεως βουλόμενον μεταλαχεῖν εἰς μετουσίαν ἀγαθῶν καὶ τὸν φόβῳ τὴν ἡγεμονικὴν καὶ δεσποτικὴν ἱλασκόμενον ἐξουσίαν εἰς ἀποτροπὴν κολάσεως· οὐ γὰρ ἀγνοῶ, διότι πρὸς τῷ χείρους μὴ γίγνεσθαι καὶ βελτίους ἔσονται τῷ συνεχεῖ τῆς θεραπείας εἰλικρινῆ καὶ καθαρὰν εὐσέβειαν ἀσκή-

130 σαντες. εἰ γὰρ καὶ μάλιστα οἱ τρόποι διαφέρουσιν, ἀφ' ὧν ποιοῦνται τὰς πρὸς τὴν ἀρέσκειαν ὁρμάς, οὐκ αἰτιατέον, ὅτι σκοπὸς εἷς καὶ τέλος ἕν ἐστιν

131 αὐτοῖς, τὸ θεραπεύειν ἐμέ." ὅτι δ' ἡ

the beneficial, the other by the kingly potency.
My meaning is something as follows : 126
men, when they see others approaching them under
profession of friendship, in quest of advantages to
be gained from them, look askance and turn away ;
they fear that counterfeited adulation and suavity
which they regard as exceedingly pernicious. But 127
God cannot suffer injury, and therefore He gladly
invites all who set themselves to honour Him under
any form whatsoever, and in His eyes none such
deserves rejection. Indeed one might almost say
that to those whose souls have ears God speaks
plainly as follows : " My first prizes will be set apart 128
for those who honour Me for Myself alone, the
second to those who honour Me for their own sakes,
either hoping to win blessings or expecting to obtain
remission of punishments, since, though their worship
is for reward and not disinterested, yet all the same
its range lies within the divine precincts and does not
stray outside. But the prizes set aside for those 129
who honour Me for Myself will be gifts of friendship ; to those whose motive is self-interest they do
not show friendship but that I do not count them as
aliens. For I accept both him who wishes to enjoy
My beneficial power and thus partake of blessings
and him who propitiates the dominance and authority
of the master to avoid chastisement. For I know well
that they will not only not be worsened, but actually
bettered, through the persistence of their worship
and through practising piety pure and undefiled.
For, however different are the characters which pro- 130
duce in them the impulses to do My pleasure, no
charge shall be brought against them, since they
have one aim and object, to serve Me."

τριττὴ φαντασία δυνάμει[1] ἑνός ἐστιν ὑποκειμένου,
φανερὸν οὐ μόνον ἐκ τῆς ἐν ἀλληγορίᾳ θεωρίας,
ἀλλὰ καὶ τῆς ῥητῆς γραφῆς τάδε περιεχούσης·
132 ἡνίκα μὲν γὰρ ὁ σοφὸς ἱκετεύει τοὺς ἐοικότας
ὁδοιπόροις τρεῖς ξενισθῆναι παρ' αὐτῷ, διαλέγεται
τούτοις οὐχ ὡς τρισίν, ἀλλ' ὡς ἑνί, καί φησι·
" κύριε, εἰ ἄρα εὗρον χάριν παρὰ σοί, μὴ παρέλθῃς
τὸν παῖδά σου·" τὸ γὰρ " κύριε " καὶ τὸ " παρὰ
σοί " καὶ τὸ " μὴ παρέλθῃς " καὶ ὅσα τοιαῦτα πρὸς
ἕνα πέφυκεν ἀλλ' οὐ πρὸς πλείους λέγεσθαι· ἡνίκα
δὲ ξενιζόμενοι φιλοφρονοῦνται τὸν ξενοδόχον, πάλιν
εἷς ὑπισχνεῖται ὡς μόνος αὐτὸς παρὼν γνησίου
παιδὸς σπορὰν διὰ τῶνδε· " ἐπανιὼν ἥξω πρὸς σὲ
κατὰ τὸν καιρὸν τοῦτον εἰς νέωτα, καὶ ἕξει υἱὸν
Σάρρα ἡ γυνή σου."
133 XXVI. Φανερώτατα μέντοι καὶ διαπονητότατα[2]
μηνύει διὰ τῶν ἑξῆς τὸ δηλούμενον. ἡ Σοδομιτῶν
χώρα, μοῖρα τῆς Χανανίτιδος γῆς, ἣν ὕστερον
ὠνόμασαν Συρίαν Παλαιστίνην, ἀδικημάτων μυρίων ὅσων γεμισθεῖσα καὶ μάλιστα τῶν ἐκ γαστρι-
μαργίας καὶ λαγνείας ὅσα τε μεγέθη καὶ πλήθη τῶν
ἄλλων ἡδονῶν ἐπιτειχίσασα ἤδη παρὰ τῷ δικαστῇ
134 τῶν ὅλων κατέγνωστο. αἴτιον δὲ τῆς περὶ τὸ
ἀκολασταίνειν ἀμετρίας ἐγένετο τοῖς οἰκήτορσιν ἡ
τῶν χορηγιῶν ἐπάλληλος ἀφθονία· βαθύγειος γὰρ
καὶ εὔυδρος οὖσα ἡ χώρα παντοίων ἀνὰ πᾶν ἔτος
εὐφορίᾳ καρπῶν ἐχρῆτο· " μεγίστη δ' ἀρχὴ κακῶν "

---

[1] Cohn suspects δυνάμει, needlessly, I think. No doubt
δυνάμει is properly opposed to οὐσίᾳ or ἐντελεχείᾳ. Cf. De Op.
47, Leg. All. i. 61. But the statement here is that the vision
of one is the reality which lies behind the vision of three.
Actually a φαντασία can only be of that which appears.

That the triple vision is in reality *a* a vision of a single 131
object is clear not merely from the principles of
allegory but from the literal text which contains the
following account. When the Sage supplicates the 132
three seeming travellers to accept his hospitality,
he discourses with them as though they were one
and not three. He says, " Sir, if indeed I have found
favour with thee, do not thou pass thy servant by."
Here " Sir " and " with thee " and " do not thou
pass " and the other like phrases must be addressed
to one and not to more than one ; and during their
entertainment, when they show courtesy to their
host, we find one only, as though no other was present, promising the birth of a son born in wedlock
in the following words : " I will return and come to
thee at this season next year, and Sarah, thy wife,
shall have a son." *b*

XXVI. *c* He brings out the point most clearly and 133
elaborately in what follows. The land of the Sodomites, a part of the land of Canaan afterwards called
Palestinian Syria, was brimful of innumerable
iniquities, particularly such as arise from gluttony
and lewdness, and multiplied and enlarged every
other possible pleasure with so formidable a menace
that it had at last been condemned by the Judge of
All. The inhabitants owed this extreme licence to the 134
never-failing lavishness of their sources of wealth, for,
deep-soiled and well-watered as it was, the land had
every year a prolific harvest of all manner of fruits,

---

a Or " virtually." See critical note.
b See Gen. xviii. 3 and 10.
c For §§ 133-141 see Gen. xix.

---

² Some MSS. ἀδιαπονητότατα or ἀδιαπόνητα : Cohn suggests
ἀδιαπορητότατα.

ὡς εἶπέ τις οὐκ ἀπὸ σκοποῦ " τὰ λίαν ἀγαθά."
135 ὧν ἀδυνατοῦντες φέρειν τὸν κόρον ὥσπερ τὰ θρέμματα σκιρτῶντες ἀπαυχενίζουσι τὸν τῆς φύσεως
νόμον, ἄκρατον πολὺν καὶ ὀψοφαγίας καὶ ὀχείας
ἐκθέσμους μεταδιώκοντες· οὐ γὰρ μόνον θηλυμα-
νοῦντες ἀλλοτρίους γάμους διέφθειρον, ἀλλὰ καὶ
ἄνδρες ὄντες ἄρρεσιν ἐπιβαίνοντες, τὴν κοινὴν πρὸς
τοὺς πάσχοντας οἱ δρῶντες φύσιν οὐκ αἰδούμενοι,
παιδοσποροῦντες ἠλέγχοντο μὲν ἀτελῆ γονὴν σπεί-
ροντες, ὁ δ' ἔλεγχος πρὸς οὐδὲν ἦν ὄφελος, ὑπὸ
136 βιαιοτέρας νικωμένων ἐπιθυμίας. εἶτ' ἐκ τοῦ κατ'
[21] | ὀλίγον ἐθίζοντες τὰ γυναικῶν ὑπομένειν τοὺς
ἄνδρας γεννηθέντας θήλειαν κατεσκεύασαν αὑτοῖς
νόσον, κακὸν δύσμαχον, οὐ μόνον τὰ σώματα
μαλακότητι καὶ θρύψει γυναικοῦντες, ἀλλὰ καὶ τὰς
ψυχὰς ἀγεννεστέρας ἀπεργαζόμενοι, καὶ τό γε ἐπ'
αὐτούς[1] ἧκον μέρος τὸ σύμπαν ἀνθρώπων γένος
διέφθειρον· εἰ γοῦν Ἕλληνες ὁμοῦ καὶ βάρβαροι
συμφωνήσαντες ἐζήλωσαν τὰς τοιαύτας ὁμιλίας,
ἠρήμωντο ἂν ἑξῆς αἱ πόλεις ὥσπερ λοιμώδει νόσῳ
137 κενωθεῖσαι. XXVII. λαβὼν δὲ ὁ θεὸς οἶκτον ἅτε
σωτὴρ καὶ φιλάνθρωπος τὰς μὲν κατὰ φύσιν ἀνδρῶν
καὶ γυναικῶν συνόδους γινομένας ἕνεκα παίδων
σπορᾶς ηὔξησεν ὡς ἔνι μάλιστα, τὰς δ' ἐκφύλους
καὶ ἐκθέσμους διαμισήσας ἔσβεσε καὶ τοὺς ὀργῶντας ἐπὶ ταύτας προβαλόμενος οὐχὶ τὰς ἐν ἔθει
καινουργήσας δ' ἐκτόπους καὶ παρηλλαγμένας
138 τιμωρίας ἐτιμωρήσατο. κελεύει γὰρ ἐξαίφνης τὸν
ἀέρα νεφωθέντα πολὺν ὄμβρον οὐχ ὕδατος ἀλλὰ

---

[1] MSS. ἐφ' αὑτοῖς or ἐπ' αὑτοῖς.

[a] ἀρχὴ μεγίστη τῶν ἐν ἀνθρώποις κακῶν, | ὠγαθέ, τὰ λίαν
ἀγαθά. Menander.

and the chief beginning of evils, as one has aptly said, is goods in excess.[a] Incapable of bearing such satiety, 135 plunging like cattle, they threw off from their necks the law of nature and applied themselves to deep drinking of strong liquor and dainty feeding and for-bidden forms of intercourse. Not only in their mad lust for women did they violate the marriages of their neighbours, but also men mounted males without respect for the sex nature which the active partner shares with the passive ; and so when they tried to beget children they were discovered to be incapable of any but a sterile seed. Yet the discovery availed them not, so much stronger was the force of the lust which mastered them. Then, as little by little they accus- 136 tomed those who were by nature men to submit to play the part of women, they saddled them with the formidable curse of a female disease. For not only did they emasculate their bodies by luxury and voluptuousness but they worked a further degenera-tion in their souls and, as far as in them lay, were corrupting the whole of mankind. Certainly, had Greeks and barbarians joined together in affecting such unions, city after city would have become a desert, as though depopulated by a pestilential sickness. XXVII. But God, moved by pity for mankind whose 137 Saviour and Lover He was, gave increase in the greatest possible degree to the unions which men and women naturally make for begetting children, but abominated and extinguished this unnatural and for-bidden intercourse, and those who lusted for such He cast forth and chastised with punishments not of the usual kind but startling and extraordinary, newly-created for this purpose. He bade the air grow sud- 138 denly overclouded and pour forth a great rain, not of

πυρὸς ὕειν· ἀθρόας δὲ νιφούσης ἀδιαστάτῳ καὶ
ἀπαύστῳ ῥύμῃ φλογός, ἐκαίοντο μὲν ἀγροὶ καὶ
λειμῶνες καὶ λάσια ἄλση καὶ ἕλη δασύτατα καὶ
δρυμοὶ βαθεῖς, ἐκαίετο δ' ἡ πεδιὰς καὶ ὁ τοῦ σίτου
καὶ τῶν ἄλλων σπαρτῶν ἅπας καρπός, ἐκαίετο δὲ
καὶ τῆς ὀρεινῆς ἡ δενδροφόρος, στελεχῶν ῥίζαις
139 αὐταῖς ἐμπιπραμένων· ἐπαύλεις δὲ καὶ οἰκίαι καὶ
τείχη καὶ ὅσα ἐν οἰκοδομαῖς ἰδιωτικὰ καὶ δημόσια
πάντα συγκατεπίμπραντο καὶ ἡμέρᾳ μιᾷ αἱ μὲν
εὐανδροῦσαι πόλεις τάφος τῶν οἰκητόρων ἐγεγένηντο, αἱ δ' ἐκ λίθων καὶ ξύλων κατασκευαὶ τέφρα
140 καὶ λεπτὴ κόνις. ἐπεὶ δὲ τὰ ἐν φανερῷ καὶ ὑπὲρ
γῆς ἅπαντα κατανάλωσεν ἡ φλόξ, ἤδη καὶ τὴν γῆν
αὐτὴν ἔκαιε κατωτάτω διαδῦσα καὶ τὴν ἐν-
υπάρχουσαν ζωτικὴν δύναμιν ἔφθειρεν εἰς ἀγονίαν
παντελῆ, ὑπὲρ τοῦ μηδ' αὖθίς ποτε καρπὸν ἐνεγκεῖν
ἢ χλοηφορῆσαι τὸ παράπαν δυνηθῆναι· καὶ μέχρι νῦν
καίεται, τὸ γὰρ κεραύνιον πῦρ ἥκιστα σβεννύμενον
141 ἢ νέμεται ἢ ἐντύφεται. πίστις δὲ σαφεστάτη τὰ
ὁρώμενα· τοῦ γὰρ συμβεβηκότος πάθους μνημεῖόν
ἐστιν ὅ τε ἀναδιδόμενος ἀεὶ καπνὸς καὶ ὃ μεταλ-
λεύουσι θεῖον· τῆς δὲ περὶ τὴν χώραν παλαιᾶς
εὐδαιμονίας ἐναργέστατον ὑπολείπεται δεῖγμα πόλις
μία τῶν ὁμόρων καὶ ἡ ἐν κύκλῳ γῆ, πολυάνθρωπος
μὲν ἡ πόλις, εὔχορτος δὲ καὶ εὔσταχυς καὶ συνόλως
καρποφόρος ἡ γῆ, πρὸς ἔλεγχον δίκης γνώμῃ θείᾳ
δικασθείσης.
142 XXVIII. Ἀλλὰ γὰρ οὐχ ἕνεκα τοῦ δηλῶσαί με
τὰς μεγαλουργηθείσας συμφορὰς καινὰς ταῦτα
διεξῆλθον, ἀλλ' ἐκεῖνο βουλόμενος παραστῆσαι, ὅτι
τῶν τριῶν ὡς ἀνδρῶν ἐπιφανέντων τῷ σοφῷ δύο

water but fire. And when the flames streamed down
massed in one constant and perpetual rush, they
burnt up the fields and meadows, the leafy groves, the
overgrowths of the marshland and the dense thickets.
They burnt the plainland and all the fruit of the corn
and other crops. They burnt the forest-land on the
mountains, where trunks and roots alike were consumed. The conflagration reached to byres and 139
houses and walls and all public and private property
contained in buildings ; and in one day populous
cities had become the grave of the inhabitants and
fabrics of stone and timber had turned into ashes and
fine dust. And when the flame had utterly consumed 140
all that was visible and above ground it penetrated
right down into the earth itself, destroyed its inherent
life-power and reduced it to complete sterility to prevent it from ever bearing fruit and herbage at all.
And to this day it goes on burning, for the fire of the
thunderbolt is never quenched. but either continues
its ravages or else smoulders. And the clearest proof 141
is what is still visible, for a monument of the disastrous
event remains in the smoke which rises ceaselessly
and the brimstone which the miners obtain ; while
the ancient prosperity of the country is most plainly
attested by the survival of one of the cities of the
neighbourhood and the land round it ; for the city is
thickly populated and the land rich in corn and pasturage and fertile in general, thus providing a standing evidence to the sentence decreed by the divine
judgement.

XXVIII. However, I have given these details not in 142
order to describe the unprecedented calamity of God's
mighty working, but in my wish to shew something
else. Scripture tells us that of the three who appeared

PHILO

[22] μόνους εἰς τὴν | ἀφανισθεῖσαν χώραν τὰ λόγιά φησιν
ἐλθεῖν ἐπ’ ὀλέθρῳ τῶν οἰκητόρων, τοῦ τρίτου μὴ
143 δικαιώσαντος ἥκειν· ὃς κατά γε τὴν ἐμὴν ἔννοιαν
ἦν ὁ πρὸς ἀλήθειαν ὤν, ἁρμόττον ὑπολαβὼν εἶναι
τὰ μὲν ἀγαθὰ παρὼν δι’ αὑτοῦ χαρίζεσθαι, μόναις
δ’ ἐπιτρέπειν ταῖς δυνάμεσι καθ’ ὑπηρεσίαν τὰ
ἐναντία χειρουργεῖν, ἵνα μόνων ἀγαθῶν αἴτιος,
144 κακοῦ δὲ μηδενὸς προηγουμένως νομίζηται. τοῦτό
μοι δοκοῦσι καὶ τῶν βασιλέων οἱ μιμούμενοι τὴν
θείαν φύσιν πράττειν, τὰς μὲν χάριτας δι’ ἑαυτῶν
προτείνοντες, τὰς δὲ τιμωρίας δι’ ἑτέρων βεβαιοῦν-
145 τες. ἀλλ’ ἐπειδὴ τῶν δυεῖν δυνάμεων ἡ μὲν εὐ-
εργέτις ἐστίν, ἡ δὲ κολαστήριος, ἑκατέρα κατὰ τὸ
εἰκὸς ἐπιφαίνεται τῇ Σοδομιτῶν γῇ, διότι τῶν
ἀρίστων ἐν αὐτῇ πέντε πόλεων τέτταρες μὲν ἔμελ
λον ἐμπίπρασθαι, μία δὲ ἀπαθὴς παντὸς κακοῦ
σῷος ὑπολείπεσθαι. ἐχρῆν γὰρ διὰ μὲν τῆς κολα-
στηρίου γίνεσθαι τὴν φθοράν, σῴζεσθαι δὲ διὰ τῆς
146 εὐεργέτιδος. ἀλλ’ ἐπειδὴ καὶ τὸ σῳζόμενον μέρος
οὐχ ὁλοκλήρους καὶ παντελεῖς εἶχεν ἀρετάς, δυνάμει
μὲν τοῦ ὄντος εὐεργετεῖτο, προηγουμένως δὲ τῆς
ἐκείνου φαντασίας ἀνάξιον ἐνομίσθη τυχεῖν.
147 XXIX. Ἡ μὲν οὖν ἐν φανερῷ καὶ πρὸς τοὺς
πολλοὺς ἀπόδοσις ἥδ’ ἐστίν· ἡ δ’ ἐν ἀποκρύφῳ καὶ
πρὸς ὀλίγους, ὅσοι τρόπους ψυχῆς ἐρευνῶσιν ἀλλ’
οὐ σωμάτων μορφάς, αὐτίκα λεχθήσεται. συμβολικῶς ἡ πεντάπολις αἱ ἐν ἡμῖν πέντε αἰσθήσεις
εἰσί, τὰ τῶν ἡδονῶν ὄργανα, δι’ ὧν ἅπασαι μικραὶ

---

[a] Or "primarily."

[b] The idea that God's direct agency appears only in doing
good and that He leaves punishment to His subordinates has
been already worked out in *De Conf.* 168 ff. on the text "let

to the Sage in the guise of men two only went on to the land whose existence was blotted out to destroy the inhabitants, but the third thought good not to accompany them. In my opinion that one was the 143 truly Existent, who held it fitting that He should be present to give good gifts by His own agency, but should leave the execution of the opposite of good entirely in the hands of His potencies acting as His ministers, that so He might appear to be the cause of good only, but not directly[a] the cause of anything evil.[b] This is the practice, I think, of kings also, who 144 imitate the divine nature. They are their own agents in granting boons, but employ others to enforce punishment. But since of the two potencies 145 one is beneficial and the other punitive it was natural that each should make his appearance in the land of the Sodomites, since of the five most flourishing cities in it four were to be burnt but one was to be left, preserved from all evil that could harm it. It was right that the punitive should be employed for destruction, but the beneficial for preservation. Yet since the 146 virtues of the part preserved were not complete and perfect, while it received benefits through a potency of the Existent, it was not thought worthy to be granted the vision of Him directly.

XXIX. Such is the natural and obvious rendering 147 of the story as suited for the multitude. We will proceed at once to the hidden and inward meaning which appeals to the few who study soul characteristics rather than bodily forms. Symbolically the group of five cities is the five senses in us, the instruments of the pleasures which, whether great or small, are

us go down and confuse their tongue," and so, too, in *De Fuga* 68 ff. *Cf.* also *De Op.* 72 ff.

PHILO

148 τε αὖ καὶ μεγάλαι τελεσιουργοῦνται. ἢ γὰρ
ὁρῶντες χρωμάτων καὶ σχημάτων ποικιλίας ἔν τε
ἀψύχοις καὶ ψυχὴν ἔχουσιν ἡδόμεθα ἢ φωνῶν
ἐμμελεστάτων ἀκούοντες ἢ κατὰ γεῦσιν ἐν τοῖς
περὶ ἐδωδὴν καὶ πόσιν ἢ κατ᾽ ὄσφρησιν ἐν εὐωδίαις
ἀτμῶν ἢ ἐν μαλακοῖς καὶ θερμοῖς ἔτι δὲ λείοις κατὰ
149 τὴν ἁφήν. ζωωδέσταται μὲν οὖν καὶ ἀνδραποδω-
δέσταται τῶν πέντε τρεῖς εἰσιν αἰσθήσεις, γεῦσις,
ὄσφρησις, ἁφή, περὶ ἃς τῶν θρεμμάτων καὶ τῶν
θηρίων τὰ γαστριμαργότατα καὶ συνουσιαστικώ-
τατα μάλιστα ἐπτόηται· δι᾽ ὅλης γὰρ ἡμέρας καὶ
νυκτὸς ἢ τροφῶν ἀπλήστως ἐμφορεῖται ἢ πρὸς τὰς
150 ὀχείας ὁρμᾷ. δύο δ᾽ εἰσὶν ἐμφιλόσοφοι καὶ ἡγε-
μονίδες, ἀκοὴ καὶ ὅρασις· βραδύτερα δέ πως καὶ
θηλύτερα ὦτα ὀφθαλμῶν ἐπὶ τὰ ὁρατὰ φθανόντων
ὑπὸ εὐτολμίας καὶ οὐκ ἀναμενόντων, ἄχρις ἂν
ἐκεῖνα κινήσῃ, προϋπαντιαζόντων δὲ καὶ ἀντικινῆ-
σαι γλιχομένων. ἀκοὴ μὲν οὖν, διότι βραδεῖα καὶ
[23] θηλυτέρα, δευτερεύουσαν τάξιν τετάχθω, | προνομία
δ᾽ ἔστω τις ἐξαίρετος ὁράσει· ταύτην γὰρ ὁ θεὸς
βασιλίδα τῶν ἄλλων ἀπέφηνεν ἐπάνω θεὶς ἀπασῶν
καὶ ὥσπερ ἐπ᾽ ἀκροπόλεως ἱδρυσάμενος οἰκειοτάτην
151 ἀπειργάσατο ψυχῇ.   τεκμηριώσαιτο δ᾽
ἄν τις ἐκ τοῦ συμμεταβάλλειν ταῖς ἐκείνης τροπαῖς·
λύπης μὲν γὰρ ἐγγινομένης, ὀφθαλμοὶ συννοίας
γέμουσι καὶ κατηφείας, χαρᾶς δ᾽ ἔμπαλιν, ὑπομει-
διῶσι καὶ γεγήθασι, φόβου δὲ κρατήσαντος, ταρα-
χώδους γέμουσιν ἀταξίας, κινήσεις καὶ παλμοὺς
152 καὶ περιστροφὰς ἀτάκτους ἐνδεχόμενοι· εἰ δ᾽ ὀργὴ
κατάσχοι, τραχυτέρα πως καὶ ὕφαιμος ἡ ὄψις, καὶ
ἐν μὲν τῷ λογίζεσθαι καὶ φροντίζειν τινὸς ἠρεμεῖ
καὶ ἐκνένευκε, μόνον οὐ συνεκτείνουσα τῇ διανοίᾳ
76

brought to their accomplishment by the senses. For **148**
we get pleasure either by seeing varieties of colours
and shapes in objects, whether possessed of physical
life or not, or by hearing very melodious sounds or
through taste in matters of food and drink, or through
smell in fragrant perfumes or through touch in soft
and warm and also in smooth substances. Now of the **149**
five, the three most animal and servile are taste, smell,
and touch, which cause particular excitation in the
cattle and wild beasts most given to gluttony and
sexual passion. For all day and night they fill themselves with food insatiably or are at rut. The other **150**
two have a link with philosophy and hold the leading
place—hearing and sight. But the ears are in a way
more sluggish and womanish than eyes. The eyes
have the courage to reach out to the visible objects
and do not wait to be acted on by them, but anticipate
the meeting, and seek to act upon them instead.
Hearing, then, sluggish and more womanish as it is,
must be put in the second place and a special precedence must be given to sight, for God has made it the
queen of the other senses and set it above them all,
and, establishing it as it were on a citadel, has
associated it most closely with the soul.

We may find a proof of this in the way in which it **151**
changes with the soul's phases. When the soul feels
grief, the eyes are full of anxiety and depression.
When on the other hand it feels joy, they smile and
rejoice. When fear is supreme, they are full of turbulent confusion, and move and quiver and roll con-
fusedly. If anger prevails, the organ of sight is **152**
harsher and bloodshot, and during reflection and careful consideration of any question it has a quiet and
distant appearance, almost as though it was accommo-

ἑαυτήν, ἐν δὲ ταῖς ἀναψύξεσι καὶ ἀνέσεσι συνανίεται
153 καὶ χαλᾶται· καὶ προσιόντι μὲν φίλῳ προευαγ-
γελίζεται τὸ τῆς εὐνοίας πάθος εὐδίῳ καὶ γαληνῷ
βλέμματι, εἰ δ' ἐχθρὸς τύχοι, τὸ δυσάρεστον τῆς
ψυχῆς πάθος προμηνύει· καὶ θρασύτητι μὲν προπη-
δῶσι καὶ προεκτρέχουσιν ὀφθαλμοί, αἰδοῖ δὲ πράως
ἠρεμοῦσι· [καὶ] ὡς συνελόντι φράσαι ψυχῆς εἰκόνα
δεδημιουργῆσθαι τὴν ὅρασιν ἀκρότητι τέχνης εὖ
μεμιμημένης ἐναργὲς ἐμφαίνουσαν εἴδωλον οἷα διὰ
κατόπτρου τὴν φύσιν ὁρατὴν ἐξ αὑτῆς οὐκ ἐχούσης.
154　　　　ἀλλὰ γὰρ οὐ ταύτῃ μόνον τὰς ἄλλας
αἰσθήσεις ὑπερβάλλει τὸ κάλλος ὀφθαλμῶν, ἀλλὰ
καὶ διότι τῶν ἄλλων ἐν ταῖς ἐγρηγόρσεσι—τὴν γὰρ
καθ' ὕπνον ἀπραξίαν οὐ παραληπτέον—ἐπιλείπουσιν
αἱ χρήσεις· ὁπότε γὰρ μὴ κινήσειέ τι τῶν ἐκτός,
ἡσυχάζουσιν, αἱ δὲ τῶν ὀφθαλμῶν ἀναπεπταμένων
ἐνέργειαι συνεχεῖς καὶ ἀδιάστατοι μηδέποτε πληρου-
μένων εἰσὶ καὶ ταύτῃ παριστάντων, ἣν ἔχουσι πρὸς
155 ψυχὴν συγγένειαν. ἀλλ' ἐκείνη μὲν ἀεικίνητος
οὖσα μεθ' ἡμέραν καὶ νύκτωρ διανίσταται, τοῖς δ'
ἅτε σαρκὸς πλεῖστον μετέχουσιν αὐτάρκης ἐδόθη
δωρεά, μέρος ἥμισυ τοῦ παντὸς χρόνου καὶ βίου
διατελεῖν ἐνεργοῦντας τὰς ἁρμοττούσας ἐνεργείας.
156　　XXX. ὃ δ' ἐστὶν ἀναγκαιότατον τῆς
ἀπὸ τῶν ὀμμάτων ὠφελείας, ἤδη λεκτέον. μόνῃ
γὰρ ὁράσει τῶν αἰσθήσεων ὁ θεὸς ἀνέτειλε φῶς, ὃ
καὶ τῶν ὄντων ἐστὶ κάλλιστον καὶ πρῶτον ἐν ἱεραῖς
157 βίβλοις ὠνομάσθη καλόν. διττὴ δὲ φωτὸς φύσις·
τὸ μὲν γὰρ ἀπὸ τοῦ χρειώδους πυρός, φθαρτοῦ
φθαρτόν, ἐκλάμπει σβέσιν ἐνδεχόμενον, τὸ δὲ

ᵃ For the distinction between the "useful" and the
"heavenly" fire cf. Quis Rerum 136 and note.

dating itself to the outlook of the mind. In times of
mental refreshment and relaxation it relaxes also and
is at its ease. When a friend approaches, its peaceful 153
and sunny look is the happy herald of the kindly
feeling within, while in the case of an enemy it gives
a warning of the soul's displeasure. Courage makes
the eyes dart swiftly forward. Modesty makes them
gentle and reposeful. In short, one may say that
sight has been created as an image of the soul, and
through the perfection of the art which has produced
so faithful a copy presents a clear and mirror-like
reflection of the original whose nature is in itself invisible.   But indeed it is not only in this 154
way that the excellence of the eyes exceeds the
other senses, but also because in waking moments,
since we need not consider their inaction in sleep,
they cease to function. For when no outward
object moves them they are still, whilst the eyes
when open are constant and unceasing in their
activities ; they have always room for more, and
in this way they shew their kinship with the soul.
But, while the soul is always in motion and wakeful 155
day and night, the eyes in which the fleshly is the
principal ingredient must rest satisfied with the gift
of continuing to exercise the activities which befit
them for half the whole span of time and human life.

XXX. But the most vital part of the 156
benefit we gain from sight remains now to be told.
God made the light to shine upon sight alone of the
senses, and light is the best of existing things and was
the first to be called good in the sacred books. Now 157
light has a double nature : one is the effulgence of
the fire of common use,[a] perishable as that which
produces it and liable to extinction, the other, the

ἄσβεστον καὶ ἀδιάφθορόν ἐστιν, ἄνωθεν ἀπὸ τοῦ
οὐρανοῦ πρὸς ἡμᾶς φερόμενον, ὥσπερ ἀπ' ἀενάων
πηγῶν ἑκάστου τῶν ἀστέρων αὐγὰς ἐκχέοντος·
ἑκατέρῳ δ' ἡ ὄψις ἐνομιλεῖ καὶ δι' ἀμφοτέρων
προσβάλλει τοῖς ὁρατοῖς εἰς ἀκριβεστάτην ἀντί-
158 ληψιν. ἔτι τοίνυν ἐπιχειρῶμεν ὀφθαλμοὺς λόγοις
ἐγκωμιάζειν, τοῦ θεοῦ τοὺς ἀληθεῖς ἐπαίνους αὐτῶν
[24] | στηλιτεύσαντος ἐν οὐρανῷ, τοὺς ἀστέρας; ἡλίου
γὰρ αὐγαὶ καὶ σελήνης καὶ τῶν ἄλλων πλανήτων
καὶ ἀπλανῶν τοῦ χάριν γεγόνασιν ὅτι μὴ τῆς
ὀφθαλμῶν ἐνεργείας εἰς τὴν τοῦ ὁρᾶν ὑπηρεσίαν;
159 διὸ καὶ προσχρώμενοι τῇ πασῶν ἀρίστῃ δωρεᾷ
φωτὶ καταθεῶνται τὰ ἐν κόσμῳ, γῆν, φυτά, ζῷα,
καρπούς, πελαγῶν ἀναχύσεις ποταμοὺς αὐθιγενεῖς
τε καὶ χειμάρρους πηγῶν τε διαφοράς, ὧν αἱ
μὲν ψυχρὸν αἱ δὲ θερμὸν νᾶμα προχέουσι, πάντων
τῶν κατὰ τὸν ἀέρα συνισταμένων τὰς φύσεις
—ἀμύθητοι δέ εἰσιν ἰδέαι καὶ ἀπερίληπτοι λόγῳ,—
καὶ ἐπὶ πᾶσι τὸν οὐρανόν, ὃς ἀληθείᾳ κόσμος
ἐν κόσμῳ δεδημιούργηται, καὶ τὰ κατ' οὐρανὸν
κάλλη καὶ θεῖα ἀγάλματα. τίς οὖν τῶν ἄλλων
αἰσθήσεων ἐπαυχήσει διαβῆναί ποτε τοσοῦτον;
160 XXXI. ἀλλ' ἐάσαντες τὰς ἐπὶ ταῖς φάτναις τὸ
σύμφυτον ἡμῖν θρέμμα πιαινούσας, τὴν ἐπιθυμίαν, ἐξετάσωμεν τὴν τοῦ λόγου μεταποιουμένην ἀκοήν·
ἧς ὁ σύντονος καὶ τελειότατος δρόμος ἵσταται κατὰ
ἀέρα τὸν περίγειον, ὅταν βίᾳ πνευμάτων καὶ κτύποι
βροντῶν συρμὸν πολὺν καὶ χαλεπὸν πάταγον
161 ἐξηχῶσιν. ὀφθαλμοὶ δὲ ἀπὸ γῆς ἐν ἀκαρεῖ φθάνου-
σιν εἰς οὐρανὸν καὶ τὰ πέρατα τοῦ παντός, ἐπ' ἀνατολὰς ὁμοῦ καὶ δύσεις ἄρκτον τε καὶ μεσημβρίαν,

unquenchable and imperishable, brought to us from heaven above, where each of the stars pours forth its rays as though from perennial fountains. With each of these the sight is conversant, and through both it strikes upon visible objects so as to apprehend them with all exactness. Need we still try to expend words 158 in extolling the eyes, when God has set graven in the heaven their true praises, the stars? For with what purpose have the rays of the sun and moon and the other stars, planets or fixed, been made save to serve the action of the eyes and to minister to sight? And 159 so it is, by using light, the best of gifts, that men contemplate the world's contents, earth, plants, living creatures, fruits, seas with their tides, rivers spring-fed or winter torrents, various kinds of fountains, some sending up a cold, others a warm, stream, and all the phenomena of the air with their several natures, the different forms of which are so countless that speech can never include them all; above all, heaven, which in truth has been framed as a world within a world, and the divine and hallowed forms which beautify it. Which of the other senses, then, can boast that it ever traverses so great a span? XXXI. Let us leave out of consideration those senses 160 which do but fatten in its manger the beast which shares our nature, lust, and examine the one which does lay claim to reason, hearing. When its travelling is tense and at its fullest, that is when the violent winds with their long, sweeping sound or the loud thunders with their terrific claps make themselves heard, it halts within the air that surrounds the earth. But the eyes leave earth and in an instant 161 reach heaven, and the boundaries of the universe, east, west, north and south alike, and when they

⟨καὶ⟩ ἀφικνούμενοι πρὸς τὸ θεωρεῖν ἕλκουσιν ἐπὶ
162 τὰ φανέντα τὴν διάνοιαν.   ἡ δὲ τὸ παραπλήσιον ἐνδεξαμένη πάθος οὐκ ἠρεμεῖ, ἀλλ' ἅτε
ἀκοίμητος καὶ ἀεικίνητος οὖσα, παρὰ τῆς ὄψεως
τοῦ δύνασθαι τὰ νοητὰ θεωρεῖν τὰς ἀφορμὰς λαβοῦσα, εἰς σκέψιν ἦλθε, πότερον τὰ φανέντα ταῦτ'
ἐστὶν ἀγένητα ἢ γενέσεως ἔλαβεν ἀρχὴν καὶ πότερον
ἄπειρα ἢ πεπερασμένα καὶ πότερον εἷς ἢ πλείονές
εἰσι κόσμοι καὶ πότερον τὰ τέτταρα στοιχεῖα τῶν
ἁπάντων ἐστὶν ἢ φύσιν ἐξαίρετον οὐρανὸς καὶ τὰ
ἐν αὐτῷ κεκλήρωται θειοτέρας καὶ οὐχὶ τοῖς ἄλλοις
163 τῆς αὐτῆς οὐσίας ἐπιλαχόντα· εἰ δὲ δὴ καὶ γέγονεν
ὁ κόσμος, ὑπὸ τίνος γέγονε καὶ τίς ὁ δημιουργὸς
κατ' οὐσίαν ἢ ποιότητα καὶ τί διανοηθεὶς ἐποίει καὶ
τί νῦν πράττει καὶ τίς αὐτῷ διαγωγὴ καὶ βίος καὶ
ὅσα ἄλλα περιττὸς νοῦς φρονήσει συμβιῶν εἴωθε
164 διερευνᾶσθαι. ταῦτα δὲ καὶ τὰ τοιαῦτα ἀνάκειται
τῷ φιλοσοφεῖν· ἐξ οὗ δῆλόν ἐστιν, ὅτι σοφία καὶ
φιλοσοφία τὴν ἀρχὴν ἀπ' οὐδενὸς εἴληφεν ἑτέρου
τῶν ἐν ἡμῖν ἢ τῆς ἡγεμονίδος τῶν αἰσθήσεων ὁράσεως, ἣν καὶ μόνην ἐκ τῆς σωματικῆς χώρας
διέσωσεν ὁ θεὸς τὰς τέσσαρας φθείρας, ὅτι αἱ μὲν
σαρκὶ καὶ τοῖς σαρκὸς πάθεσιν ἐδούλευσαν, ἡ δὲ
ἴσχυσεν ἀνατεῖναι τὸν αὐχένα καὶ βλέψαι καὶ |
[25] τέρψεις ἑτέρας ἀνευρεῖν πολὺ βελτίους τῶν σωμα-
τικῶν ἡδονῶν ἐκ τῆς περὶ τὸν κόσμον θεωρίας καὶ
165 τῶν ἐν αὐτῷ. μίαν οὖν ὥσπερ ἐκ πενταπόλεως τῶν
πέντε αἰσθήσεων τὴν ὅρασιν ἐξαιρέτου γέρως τυχεῖν
ἁρμόττον ἦν καὶ φθειρομένων τῶν ἄλλων διαμένειν,

---

a For the thought cf. Timaeus 47A "whence," i.e. from
the knowledge which sight gives us, "we have derived

82

arrive draw the understanding to the observation of what they have seen.   162 And the understanding affected in like manner is not quiescent, but, unsleeping and constantly in motion as it is, takes the sight as the starting-point for its power of observing the things of the mind, and proceeds to investigate whether these phenomena are un-created or had some beginning of creation, whether they are infinite or finite, whether there is one world or more than one, whether the four elements make up all things, or on the other hand heaven and its contents enjoy a special nature of their own and have been given a substance which differs from the others and is more divine. Further, if the world has been 163 created, who is the Creator ? What is His essence and quality ? What was His purpose in making it ? What does He do now and what is His occupation and way of life? And all the other questions which the curious mind with good sense ever at its side is wont to ex-plore. But these and the like belong to philosophy, 164 whence it is clear that wisdom and philosophy owe their origin to no other of our faculties but to the princess of the senses, sight.[a] And this alone of all the bodily region did God preserve when He destroyed the four, because they were in slavery to flesh and the passions of flesh, while the sight had the strength to stretch its neck upwards, and to look, and to find in the contemplation of the world and its contents plea-sures far better than those of the body. It was fitting, 165 then, that the one of the five senses which form, so to speak, a group of five cities, should receive a special privilege and continue to exist when the others were

philosophy." A similar adaptation of the same passage was made in *De Op.* 54, where see note.

ὅτι οὐ περὶ τὰ θνητὰ εἰλεῖται μόνον ὡς ἐκεῖναι,
μετανίστασθαι δὲ πρὸς τὰς ἀφθάρτους φύσεις ἀξιοῖ
166 χαίρουσα τῇ θέᾳ τούτων. διὸ καὶ παγκάλως " μι-
κράν " τε καὶ " οὐ μικρὰν " τὴν πόλιν ταύτην οἱ
χρησμοὶ διασυνιστᾶσιν αἰνιττόμενοι τὴν ὅρασιν·
μικρὰ μὲν γὰρ λέγεται εἶναι, διότι βραχὺ μέρος
τῶν ἐν ἡμῖν ἐστι, μεγάλη δέ, διότι μεγάλων ἐφίεται
τὸν σύμπαντα οὐρανὸν καὶ κόσμον γλιχομένη
καταθεάσασθαι.
167   XXXII. Περὶ μὲν οὖν τῆς ἐπιφανείσης ὄψεως
καὶ τῶν ἀοιδίμων καὶ παγκάλων ξενίων, ἐν οἷς
δοκῶν ἑστιᾶν ὁ ξενοδόχος εἱστιᾶτο, καθ᾽ ὅσον
ἐφικτὸν ἦν, ἀκριβοῦσιν ἡμῖν τὰ περὶ τὸν τόπον
δεδήλωται. μεγίστην δὲ πρᾶξιν ἀξίαν ἀκοῆς οὐχ
ἡσυχαστέον· ὀλίγου γὰρ δέω φάναι πάσας ὅσαι θεοφιλεῖς ὑπερβάλλει. λεκτέον δὲ τὰ καίρια περὶ
168 αὐτῆς. υἱὸς ἐκ τῆς γαμετῆς γίνεται τῷ σοφῷ
γνήσιος, ἀγαπητὸς καὶ μόνος, τό τε σῶμα κάλ-
λιστος καὶ τὴν ψυχὴν ἄριστος· ἤδη γὰρ τελειοτέρας
τῆς ἡλικίας ἐξέφαινεν ἀρετάς, ὡς τὸν πατέρα μὴ
πάθει μόνον εὐνοίας φυσικῆς ἀλλὰ καὶ γνώμῃ
καθάπερ ἠθῶν δικαστὴν ἰσχυρᾷ τινι κεχρῆσθαι
169 φιλοστοργίᾳ. διακειμένῳ δ᾽ οὕτως ἐξαπιναίως
θεσπίζεται λόγιον οὔποτ᾽ ἐλπισθέν, σφαγιάσαι τὸν
υἱὸν ἐπί τινος ὑψηλοτάτου κολωνοῦ πορρωτάτω
170 πόλεως ἀποστάντα τριῶν ὁδὸν ἡμερῶν. ὁ δὲ καίτοι

ᵃ Gen. xix. 20 πόλις αὕτη ἐγγὺς . . . ἢ ἐστι μικρά. . . . οὐ
μικρά ἐστι; R.V. "This city is near . . . and it is a little one.
. . . Is it not a little one?" Philo either fails to see that the
last three words are a question, or more probably thinks
that the grammatical possibility of treating them as a statement is a sufficient ground for extracting an allegorical
lesson.

destroyed, because its range is not confined to mortal things, as theirs is, but it aspires to find a new home amid imperishable beings and rejoice in their contemplation. And therefore it is excellently said, 166 when the oracles represent this city first as small and then as not small, figuring thereby sight.[a] For sight is said to be small in that it is a little part of all we contain, but great in that great are its desires, since it is the whole world and heaven which it yearns to survey.

XXXII. [b] I have now told with all the care that lay 167 within my powers the story of the vision which was manifested to Abraham and of that splendid and magnificent exchange of hospitality, where the host who seemed to give the feast was himself the feasted. But his greatest action which deserves reporting must not be passed over in silence. For I might almost say that all the other actions which won the favour of God are surpassed by this ; and on this subject I must say what is needed. The wife of the 168 Sage bore to him in full wedlock his only and dearly-cherished son, a child of great bodily beauty and excellence of soul. For already he was showing a perfection of virtues beyond his years, so that his father, moved not merely by a feeling of natural affection but also by such deliberate judgement as a censor of character might make, cherished for him a great tenderness. Such were his feelings when 169 suddenly to his surprise there came a divine message that he should sacrifice his son on a certain lofty hill at a very considerable distance,[c] as much as three days' journey, from the city. He, though devoted to 170

[b] For §§ 167-177 see Gen. xxii. 1-19.

[c] Strictly speaking ἀποστάντα agrees with υἱόν. Perhaps we should read ἀποστάντος.

ἀλέκτῳ πόθῳ τοῦ παιδὸς ἐκκρεμάμενος οὔτε τὴν
χρόαν μετέβαλεν οὔτε τὴν ψυχὴν ἐγνάμφθη, γνώμῃ
δ᾽ ἀνενδότῳ καὶ ἀρρεπεῖ διέμεινεν ἀκλινής, οἷος καὶ
πρόσθεν ἦν· ἔρωτι δὲ θείῳ δεδαμασμένος ἀνὰ κράτος
ἐνίκα πάντα ὅσα συγγενείας ὀνόματα καὶ φίλτρα[a]
καὶ μηδενὶ τῶν ἔνδον ἐξειπὼν τὸ λόγιον, ἐκ πολυ-
ανθρώπου θεραπείας οἰκετῶν δύο μόνους τοὺς πρε-
σβυτάτους καὶ μάλιστα φιλοδεσπότους παραλαβών,
ὡς ἕνεκά τινος ἱερουργίας τῶν ἐν ἔθει τέταρτος
171 ἐξῄει σὺν τῷ παιδί. τὸν δὲ προσταχθέντα χῶρον
ὥσπερ ἀπὸ σκοπιᾶς ἰδὼν ἐκ μακροῦ τοῖς μὲν
θεράπουσι κελεύει καταμένειν, τῷ δὲ παιδὶ πῦρ καὶ
ξύλα δίδωσι κομίζειν, αὐτὸ δικαιώσας τὸ ἱερεῖον[b]
τὰ πρὸς τὴν θυσίαν ἐπηχθίσθαι, κουφότατον βάρος·
172 οὐδὲν γὰρ εὐσεβείας ἀπονώτερον. βαδίζοντες δ᾽
ἰσοταχῶς οὐ τοῖς σώμασι μᾶλλον ἢ ταῖς διανοίαις
[26] ὁδὸν τὴν ἐπίτομον, ἧς ὁσιότης τὸ τέλος, ἐπὶ τὸν |
173 προσταχθέντα τόπον ἀφικνοῦνται. κἄπειθ᾽ ὁ μὲν
πατὴρ συνεκόμιζε λίθους, ἵνα δείμαιτο βωμόν, ὁ δὲ
υἱὸς τὰ μὲν ἄλλα ὁρῶν ὅσα πρὸς ἱερουργίαν εὐτρεπῆ,
ζῷον δὲ μηδέν, ἀπιδὼν εἰς τὸν πατέρα '' ἰδοὺ τὸ
πῦρ '' ἔφη '' καὶ τὰ ξύλα, πάτερ, ποῦ τὸ ἱερεῖον;''
174 ἕτερος μὲν οὖν ἃ δρᾶν ἔμελλεν εἰδὼς καὶ τῇ ψυχῇ
συσκιάζων ὑπὸ τοῦ λεχθέντος κἂν συνεχύθη καὶ
δακρύων πληρωθεὶς ἔμφασιν τοῦ γενησομένου παρ-
175 έσχεν ἐκ τῆς περιπαθήσεως ἡσυχάζων. ὁ δ᾽
οὐδεμίαν ἐνδεξάμενος τροπὴν οὔτε κατὰ τὸ σῶμα
οὔτε κατὰ τὴν διάνοιαν σταθερῷ μὲν τῷ βλέμματι
σταθερῷ δὲ τῷ λογισμῷ φησι πρὸς τὴν πεῦσιν
ἀποκρινόμενος· '' ὦ τέκνον, ὁ θεὸς ὄψεται ἱερεῖον

---

[a] Literally "the names and love-charms of kinship."
[b] In Genesis Isaac does not carry the fire.

his son with a fondness which no words can express, shewed no change of colour nor weakening of soul, but remained steadfast as ever with a judgement that never bent nor wavered. Mastered by his love for God, he mightily overcame all the fascination expressed in the fond terms of family affection,[a] and told the divine call to none of his household, but taking out of his numerous following two only, the oldest and most loyal, he went forth with his son, four in all, as though to perform one of the ordinary rites. But, when, like **171** a scout on some commanding point, he saw the appointed place afar off, he bade his servants stay there, but gave his son the fire[b] and wood to carry ; for he thought it good that the victim himself should bear the load of the instruments of sacrifice, a light burden indeed, for nothing is less toilsome than piety. They walked with equal speed of mind rather **172** than body along the short straight road at the end of which is holiness and came to the appointed place.[c] And then, while the father was collecting stones to **173** build the altar, the son, seeing everything else ready for sacrifice but no animal, looked at his father and said : " My father, behold the fire and the wood, but where is the victim ? " To anyone else who **174** knew what he was about to do, and was hiding it in his heart, these words would have brought confusion and tearfulness and he would have remained silent through extreme emotion, and thus given an indica- tion of what was going to happen. But Abraham **175** admitted no swerving of body or mind, and with visage and thought alike unmoved he said in answer to the question, " Child, God will provide Himself a

---

[c] LXX Gen. xxii. 8 καὶ ἐπορεύθησαν οἱ δύο ἅμα. Philo has gained from this phrase a fuller spiritual lesson in *De Mig.* 166 f.

PHILO

ἑαυτῷ καὶ ἐν ἐρημίᾳ πολλῇ, δι' ἣν ἴσως ἀπογινώ-
σκεις εὑρεθήσεσθαι· πάντα δ' ἴσθι θεῷ δυνατὰ καὶ
ὅσα ἐν ἀμηχάνῳ καὶ ἀπόρῳ κεῖται παρ' ἀνθρώ-
176 ποις." καὶ ταῦθ' ἅμα λέγων ᾗ τάχιστα τὸν υἱὸν
ἐξαρπάσας ἐπιτίθησι τῷ βωμῷ καὶ σπασάμενος τῇ
δεξιᾷ τὸ ξίφος ἐπέφερεν ὡς ἀναιρήσων· φθάνει δ'
ὁ σωτὴρ θεὸς ἀπ' ἀέρος φωνῇ μεσολαβήσας τὸ
ἔργον, ᾗ προσέταττεν ἀνέχειν καὶ μὴ ψαῦσαι τοῦ
παιδός, ὀνομαστὶ καλέσας δὶς τὸν πατέρα, ἵν'
ἐπιστρέψας καὶ ἀντισπάσας διακωλύσῃ τὴν σφαγὴν
177 ἐργάσασθαι. XXXIII. καὶ ὁ μὲν διασῴζεται, τὸ
δῶρον ἀντιχαρισαμένου τοῦ θεοῦ καὶ τὸν φέροντα
ἐν οἷς εὐσεβεῖτο ἀντιτιμήσαντος· τῷ δ' ἤδη καὶ ἡ
πρᾶξις, εἰ καὶ μὴ τὸ τέλος ἐπηκολούθησεν, ὁλόκληρος καὶ παντελὴς οὐ μόνον ἐν ταῖς ἱεραῖς βίβλοις
ἀλλὰ καὶ ἐν ταῖς τῶν ἀναγινωσκόντων διανοίαις
ἀνάγραπτος ἐστηλίτευται.

178 Ἀλλὰ τοῖς φιλαπεχθήμοσι καὶ πάντα διαβάλ-
λουσιν, οἳ ψόγον πρὸ ἐπαίνου τιμᾶν ἐθίζονται, τὸ
πραχθὲν ἔργον οὐ δοκεῖ μέγα καὶ θαυμαστόν, ὡς
179 ἡμεῖς ὑπολαμβάνομεν εἶναι. πολλοὺς γὰρ καὶ
ἄλλους φασὶ τῶν πάνυ φιλοικείων καὶ φιλοτέκνων
ἐπιδοῦναι τοὺς ἑαυτῶν παῖδας, τοὺς μὲν ὑπὲρ
πατρίδων σφαγιασθησομένους, λυτήρια ἢ πολέμων ἢ
αὐχμῶν ἢ ἐπομβρίας ἢ νοσημάτων λοιμικῶν γενη-
σομένους, τοὺς δ' ὑπὲρ νενομισμένης εὐσεβείας, εἰ
180 καὶ μὴ πρὸς ἀλήθειαν οὔσης· Ἑλλήνων μέν γε τοὺς
δοκιμωτάτους, οὐκ ἰδιώτας μόνον ἀλλὰ καὶ βασιλεῖς, ὀλίγα φροντίσαντας ὧν ἐγέννησαν διὰ τῆς
τούτων ἀναιρέσεως δυνάμεις στρατευμάτων μεγάλας καὶ πολυανθρώπους ἐν μὲν τῇ συμμαχίᾳ τεταγ-

victim, even in this wide desert, which perhaps makes
you give up hope of finding it; but know that to
God all things are possible, including those that are
impossible or insuperable to men." And, as he said 176
this, he hastily seized his son, laid him on the altar
and with his drawn knife in his right hand was preparing with it to deal the death blow. But ere he
did so, God the Saviour stopped the deed half-way
with a voice from the air, in which He ordered him
to stay and not touch the lad. And twice He called
the father by name to turn him and draw him back
from his purpose and thus prevent his carrying out
the slaughter. XXXIII. So Isaac was saved, since 177
God returned the gift of him and used the offering
which piety rendered to Him to repay the offerer,
while for Abraham the action, though not followed
by the intended ending, was complete and perfect,
and the record of it as such stands graven not only
in the sacred books but in the minds of the readers.

But quarrelsome critics who misconstrue every- 178
thing and have a way of valuing censure above praise
do not think Abraham's action great or wonderful,
as we suppose it to be. They say that many other 179
persons, full of love for their kinsfolk and offspring,
have given their children, some to be sacrificed for
their country to serve as a price to redeem it from
wars or drought or excessive rainfall or pestilence,
others for the sake of what was held to be piety
though it is not really so. Indeed they say that 180
among the Greeks men of the highest reputation,
not only private individuals but kings, have with
little thought of their offspring put them to death,
and thereby saved armed forces of great strength
and magnitude when enlisted as their allies, and

μένας διασῶσαι, ἐν δὲ τῇ μερίδι τῶν ἐχθρῶν αὐτο-
181 βοεῖ διαφθεῖραι· βαρβαρικὰ δὲ ἔθνη μέχρι πολλοῦ
παιδοκτονίαν ὡς ὅσιον ἔργον καὶ θεοφιλὲς προσέσ-
θαι, ὧν μεμνῆσθαι τοῦ ἄγους καὶ τὸν ἱερώτατον
Μωυσῆν· αἰτιώμενος γὰρ αὐτοὺς τοῦ μιάσματος
φάσκει, ὅτι " τοὺς υἱοὺς αὐτῶν καὶ τὰς θυγατέρας
182 κατακαίουσι τοῖς θεοῖς αὐτῶν"· Ἰνδῶν δὲ | τοὺς
[27] γυμνοσοφιστὰς ἄχρι νῦν, ἐπειδὰν ἄρχηται καταλαμβάνειν ἡ μακρὰ καὶ ἀνίατος νόσος, τὸ γῆρας, πρὶν
βεβαίως κρατηθῆναι, πυρὰν νήσαντας ἑαυτοὺς ἐμ-
πιπράναι, δυναμένους ἔτι πρὸς πολυετίαν ἴσως
ἀντισχεῖν· ἤδη δὲ καὶ γύναια προαποθανόντων
ἀνδρῶν ὁρμῆσαι γεγηθότα πρὸς τὴν αὐτὴν πυρὰν
καὶ ζῶντα τοῖς ἐκείνων σώμασιν ὑπομεῖναι συγ-
183 καταφλεχθῆναι· ταῦτα μὲν εἰκότως ἄν τις τῆς
εὐτολμίας θαυμάσειεν ἐκ πολλοῦ τοῦ περιόντος
καταφρονητικῶς ἔχοντα θανάτου καὶ ὡς ἐπ'
ἀθανασίαν αὐτὸν ἱέμενα καὶ ἀπνευστὶ θέοντα·
XXXIV. τὸν δὲ τί προσῆκεν ἐπαινεῖν ὡς ἐγχειρη-
τὴν κεκαινουργημένης πράξεως, ἣν καὶ ἰδιῶται καὶ
βασιλεῖς καὶ ὅλα ἔθνη δρῶσιν ἐν καιροῖς;
184 ἐγὼ δὲ πρὸς τὴν τούτων βασκανίαν καὶ πικρίαν
ἐκεῖνα λέξω· τῶν καταθυόντων παῖδας οἱ μὲν ἔθει
τοῦτο δρῶσιν, ὥσπερ ἐνίους ἔφασκον τῶν βαρβάρων, οἱ δὲ δι' ἀβουλήτους καὶ μεγάλας ὑποθέσεις
πόλεών τε καὶ χωρῶν ἑτέρως κατορθοῦσθαι μὴ
δυναμένων, ὧν οἱ μὲν ἀνάγκῃ τοὺς αὑτῶν ἐπι-

---

[a] Philo may be thinking of Iphigeneia and Macaria in
Euripides' *Heracleidae*, though neither exactly fits the circumstances.   [b] Deut. xii. 31.

destroyed them without striking a blow when arrayed
as enemies.[a] Barbarian nations, they add, have for 181
long admitted child sacrifice as a holy deed and
acceptable to God, and this practice of theirs is
mentioned by the holy Moses as an abomination,
for, charging them with this pollution, he says that
" they burn their sons and daughters to their gods." [b]
Again they point out that in India the gymno- 182
sophists even now when the long incurable disease
of old age begins to take hold of them, even before
they are completely in its clutches, make up a
funeral pile and burn themselves on it, though they
might possibly last out many years more. And the
womenfolk when the husbands die before them have
been known to hasten rejoicing to share their pyre,
and allow themselves to be burned alive with the
corpses of the men.[c] These women might reasonably, 183
no doubt, be praised for their courage, so great and
more than great is their contempt for death, and
the breathless eagerness with which they rush to
it as though it were immortality. XXXIV. Why,
then, they ask, should we praise Abraham, as though
the deed which he undertook was unprecedented,
when private individuals and kings and whole nations
do it when occasion calls? To their 184
malignity and bitterness I reply as follows. Some of
those who sacrifice their children follow custom in
so doing, as was the case according to the critics with
some of the barbarians. Others have important and
painful reasons for their action because their cities
and countries cannot but fail otherwise. These give
their children partly under compulsion and the

[c] For Philo's knowledge of the Indian custom see App.
p. 598.

διδόασιν ὑπὸ δυνατωτέρων βιασθέντες, οἱ δὲ δόξης
καὶ τιμῆς ἐφιέμενοι καὶ εὐκλείας μὲν τῆς ἐν τῷ
185 παρόντι, εὐφημίας δὲ τῆς εἰς ὕστερον. οἱ μὲν οὖν
ἔθει σφαγιάζοντες οὐδὲν ὡς ἔοικε μέγα δρῶσιν·
ἐγχρονίζον γὰρ ἔθος ἐξισοῦται φύσει πολλάκις, ὡς
καὶ τὰ δυσυπομόνητα καὶ δυσκαρτέρητα ῥᾳδίως
ἐπελαφρίζειν, τὰς ὑπερβολὰς τῶν φοβερῶν ἐξευ-
186 μαρίζον. τῶν δ' ἕνεκα δέους ἐπιδιδόντων ἔπαινος
οὐδείς· ὁ γὰρ ἔπαινος ἐν ἑκουσίοις κατορθώμασι
γράφεται, τὰ δ' ἀβούλητα ἑτέροις ἀνάκειται πράγμασιν, ἢ καιροῖς ἢ τύχαις ἢ ταῖς ἀπ' ἀνθρώπων
187 ἀνάγκαις. εἰ δέ τις δόξης ὀρεγόμενος υἱὸν ἢ
θυγατέρα προΐεται, ψέγοιτ' ἂν ἐνδίκως μᾶλλον ἢ
ἐπαινοῖτο, θανάτῳ τῶν φιλτάτων ὠνούμενος τιμήν,
ἣν καὶ κεκτημένος ὤφειλεν ὑπὲρ σωτηρίας τῶν
188 τέκνων ἀπορρίπτειν.   ἐρευνητέον οὖν, εἰ
ὑπό τινος τῶν λεχθέντων ἡττηθεὶς ἐκεῖνος ἔμελλε
σφαγιάζειν τὸν υἱόν, ἔθους ἢ τιμῆς ἢ δέους. ἔθος
μὲν οὖν τὸ ἐπὶ παιδοκτονίᾳ Βαβυλὼν καὶ Μεσο-
ποταμία καὶ τὸ Χαλδαίων ἔθνος οὐ παραδέχεται, ἐν
οἷς ἐτράφη καὶ ἐπεβίωσε τὸν πλείονα χρόνον, ὡς τῇ
συνεχείᾳ τῶν δρωμένων ἀμβλυτέραις ταῖς τῶν δει-
189 νῶν φαντασίαις κεκρατῆσθαι¹ δοκεῖν. καὶ μὴν οὐδὲ
φόβος τις ἦν ἀπ' ἀνθρώπων—οὐδὲ γὰρ τὸ χρησθὲν
αὐτῷ μόνῳ λόγιον ᾔδει τις—, οὐδέ τις συμφορὰ
κοινὴ κατείληφεν, ἧς ἔδει τὴν θεραπείαν ἀναιρέσει
190 γενέσθαι τοῦ δοκιμωτάτου παιδός. ἀλλὰ θηρώ-
[28] μενος | ἔπαινον τῶν πολλῶν ἐπὶ τὴν πρᾶξιν ὥρμησε;

---

¹ Perhaps, as Mangey suggests, κεχρῆσθαι.

pressure of higher powers, partly through desire for glory and honour, to win fame at the time and a good name in the future. Now those who are led 185 by custom to make the sacrifice would not seem to be doing anything great, for long-standing custom often becomes equal to nature, so that in matters where patience and resolution are difficult to attain it gives ease and relief by reducing their terrors to moderate dimensions. Where the gift is made 186 through fear no praise is due, for praise is recorded for voluntary good deeds, while for those which are involuntary other things are responsible, favourable occasions, chances or force brought to bear by men. And if anyone throws away a son or a daughter 187 through desire for glory he will be justly blamed rather than praised, for with the life of his dearest he is purchasing an honour which he ought to cast aside, if he possessed it, to ensure the safety of his children.　　　　We must therefore examine 188 whether Abraham, when he intended to sacrifice his son, was mastered by any of these motives, custom or love of honour or fear. Now in Babylonia and Mesopotamia and with the nation of the Chaldeans with whom he was brought up and lived the greater part of his life the custom of child slaughter does not obtain, so as to suggest that his realization of its horrors was rendered less powerful by the regularity of such a practice. Surely, too, he had nothing to 189 fear from man, since no one knew of the oracular message which he alone had received ; nor was he under the pressure of any public misfortune which could be remedied only by the immolation of a child of special worth. Or was the quest of praise from the 190 multitude the motive which urged him to the deed ?

καὶ τίς ἔπαινος ἐν ἐρημίᾳ, μηδενὸς τοῦ μέλλοντος
ἐπευφημήσειν παρόντος, ἀλλὰ καὶ τῶν δυεῖν οἰκετῶν
μακρὰν ἐπίτηδες ἀπολειφθέντων, ἵνα μὴ ἐγκαλ-
λωπίζεσθαι καὶ ἐνεπιδείκνυσθαι δοκῇ μάρτυρας
191 ἐπαγόμενος ὧν εὐσέβει; XXXV. στόμασιν οὖν
ἀχαλίνοις καὶ κακηγόροις θύρας ἐπιθέντες μετρια-
ζέτωσαν τὸν ἐν αὐτοῖς μισόκαλον φθόνον καὶ
ἀρετὰς ἀνδρῶν εὖ βεβιωκότων μὴ σινέσθωσαν, ἃς
ἁρμόττον ἦν εὐφημίᾳ συνεπικοσμεῖν.

ὅτι δὲ τῷ ὄντι ἐπαινετὴ καὶ ἀξιέραστος ἡ πρᾶξις, ἐκ
192 πολλῶν εὐμαρὲς ἰδεῖν. πρῶτον μὲν τοίνυν τὸ
πείθεσθαι θεῷ παρὰ πᾶσι τοῖς εὖ φρονοῦσι σεμνὸν
καὶ περιμάχητον εἶναι νομιζόμενον ἐν τοῖς μάλιστα
ἐπετήδευεν, ὡς μηδενὸς πώποτε τῶν προστεταγ-
μένων ἀλογῆσαι, ἄνευ δυσκολίας καὶ ἀηδίας, κἂν
πόνων τε καὶ ἀλγηδόνων μεστὸν ᾖ· παρὸ καὶ τὸ
χρησθὲν ἐπὶ τῷ υἱῷ γενναιότατα καὶ στερρότατα
193 ἤνεγκεν. ἔπειτ᾽ οὐκ ὄντος ἔθους ἐν τῇ χώρᾳ,
καθάπερ ἴσως παρ᾽ ἐνίοις ἐστίν, ἀνθρωποθυτεῖν, ὃ
τῇ συνεχείᾳ τὰς τῶν δεινῶν φαντασίας εἴωθεν
ἐκλύειν, αὐτὸς ἔμελλε πρῶτος ἄρχεσθαι καινοτάτου
καὶ παρηλλαγμένου πράγματος, ὅ μοι δοκεῖ μηδεὶς
ἂν ὑπομεῖναι, καὶ εἰ σιδήρου τὴν ψυχὴν ἢ ἀδάμαντος
κατεσκεύαστο· "φύσει" γὰρ ὡς εἶπέ τις "ἔργον
194 μάχεσθαι." γνήσιόν τε υἱὸν πεποιημένος μόνον
τοῦτον εὐθὺς εἶχε καὶ τὸ πάθος ἐπ᾽ αὐτῷ τῆς εὐνοίας γνήσιον, ὑπερβάλλον τοὺς σώφρονας ἔρωτας
195 καὶ τὰς φιλίας, ὅσαι δι᾽ ὀνόματος γεγόνασι. προσῆν
94

What praise could there be in a solitude where no one was present to report his fame afterwards, but even the two servants had been purposely left afar off lest he should appear to be making a boastful parade by bringing witnesses to his pious conduct ? XXXV. Let them, therefore, set bolt and bar to 191 their unbridled evil-speaking mouths, control their envy and hatred of excellence and not mar the virtues of men who have lived a good life, virtues which they should rather help to glorify by their good report.   That the deed really deserves our praise and love can easily be seen in many ways. First, 192 then, he made a special practice of obedience to God, a duty which every right-minded person holds to be worthy of all respect and effort. Hitherto he had not neglected any of God's commands, nor ever met them with repining or discontent, however charged with toils and pains they might be, and therefore he bore the sentence pronounced on his son with all nobleness and firmness. Secondly, since 193 human sacrifice was not in that country, as it was perhaps in some, sanctioned by custom which is so apt through constant repetition to weaken the realization of the terrible, he would have been the first himself to initiate a totally new and extraordinary procedure, and this, to my mind, is a thing which no one could have brought himself to do even if his soul had been made of iron or adamant, for, as it has been said, it is hard work to fight against nature. And, 194 as he had begotten no son in the truest sense but Isaac, his feeling of affection for him was necessarily on the same high level of truth, higher even than the chaste forms of love and also the much talked-of ties of friendship. Further, he had a most potent 195

PHILO

δέ τι καὶ βιαστικώτατον φίλτρον, τὸ μὴ καθ'
ἡλικίαν ἀλλ' ἐν γήρᾳ γεγεννηκέναι τὸν παῖδα· τοῖς
γὰρ ὀψιγόνοις ἐπιμεμήνασί πως οἱ τοκεῖς, ἢ τῷ
μακρὸν ἐπιποθῆσαι χρόνον τὴν γένεσιν αὐτῶν ἢ τῷ
μηκέθ' ἑτέρους ἐλπίζειν ἔσεσθαι, τῆς φύσεως
ἐνταῦθα ἱσταμένης ὡς ἐπὶ τελευταῖον καὶ ὕστατον
196 ὅρον. ἐκ πολυπαιδίας μὲν οὖν ἕνα προέσθαι θεῷ
καθάπερ ἀπαρχήν τινα τέκνων παράδοξον οὐδέν,
ἔχοντα τὰς ἐπὶ τοῖς ζῶσιν ἡδονὰς οὐ μικρὰ παραμύ-
θια καὶ μειλίγματα τῆς ἐπὶ τῷ σφαγιασθέντι λύπης·
ὃν δὲ μόνον τις ἔσχεν ἀγαπητὸν διδοὺς λόγου
παντὸς μεῖζον ἔργον διαπράττεται, μηδὲν οἰκειότητι
χαριζόμενος, ἀλλ' ὅλῃ τῇ ῥοπῇ πρὸς τὸ θεοφιλὲς
197 ταλαντεύων. ἐκεῖνο μὲν δὴ ἐξαίρετον καὶ μόνῳ
σχεδόν τι τούτῳ πεπραγμένον· οἱ μὲν γὰρ ἄλλοι,
κἂν ὑπὲρ σωτηρίας πατρίδων ἢ στρατευμάτων
ἐπιδιδῶσι σφαγιασθησομένους τοὺς ἑαυτῶν, ἢ οἴκοι
καταμένουσιν ἢ μακρὰν ἀφίστανται τῶν βωμῶν ἤ,
κἂν παρατυγχάνωσι, τὰς ὄψεις ἀποστρέφονται θεά-
198 σασθαι μὴ ὑπομένοντες, ἄλλων ἀναιρούντων· ὁ δ'
[29] ὥσπερ ἱερεὺς | αὐτὸς κατήρχετο τῆς ἱερουργίας, ἐφ'
υἱῷ τὰ πάντα ἀρίστῳ φιλοστοργότατος πατήρ·
ἐμέλισε δ' ἂν ἴσως καὶ νόμῳ τῶν ὁλοκαυτωμάτων
κατὰ μέλη τὸν υἱὸν ἱερουργῶν. οὕτως οὐ τὸ μέν τι
μέρος ἀπέκλινε πρὸς τὸν παῖδα, τὸ δέ τι πρὸς
εὐσέβειαν, ἀλλ' ὅλην τὴν ψυχὴν δι' ὅλων ὁσιότητι
προσεκλήρωσεν ὀλίγα φροντίσας συγγενικοῦ αἵ-
199 ματος. τί δὴ τῶν εἰρημένων πρὸς ἑτέρους κοινόν;
τί δ' οὐκ ἐξαίρετον καὶ παντὸς λόγου κρεῖττον;
96

incentive to love in that he had begotten the boy
in his old age and not in his years of vigour. For
parents somehow dote on their late-born children,
either because they have longed for their birth for
so many years or because they do not hope to have
any more, since nature comes to a halt at this point
as its final and furthermost boundary. For a father 196
to surrender one of a numerous family as a tithe to
God is nothing extraordinary, since each of the
survivors continues to give him pleasure, and this is
no small solace and mitigation of his grief for the
one who has been sacrificed. But one who gives his
only darling son performs an action for which no
language is adequate, since he concedes nothing to
the tie of relationship, but his whole weight is thrown
into the scale on the side of acceptability with God.
The following point is exceptional, and his conduct 197
in it is practically unique. Other fathers, even if
they give their children to be sacrificed for the safety
of their country or armies, either stay at home or
stand far away from the altars, or, if they are present,
turn away their eyes, since they cannot bear the
sight, and leave others to kill the victim. But here 198
we have the most affectionate of fathers himself
beginning the sacrificial rite as priest with the very
best of sons for victim. Perhaps too, following the law
of burnt offering, he would have dismembered his
son and offered him limb by limb. Thus we see that
he did not incline partly to the boy and partly to
piety, but devoted his whole soul through and
through to holiness and disregarded the claims of
their common blood. Which of all the points men- 199
tioned is shared by others ? Which does not stand
by itself and defy description ? Thus everyone who

ὡς τόν γε μὴ φύσει βάσκανον καὶ φιλοπόνηρον
καταπλαγῆναι καὶ θαυμάσαι τῆς περιττῆς ἄγαν
εὐσεβείας, οὐχ ἅπαντα ὅσα εἶπον ἀθρόα εἰς νοῦν
βαλλόμενον, ἀλλὰ κἂν ἕν τι τῶν πάντων· ἱκανὴ γὰρ
καὶ ἡ ἑνὸς φαντασία τύπῳ τινὶ βραχεῖ—βραχὺ δ'
οὐδὲν ἔργον σοφοῦ—μέγεθος ψυχῆς καὶ ὕψος
ἐμφῆναι.

200 XXXVI. Ἀλλὰ γὰρ οὐκ ἐπὶ τῆς ῥητῆς καὶ
φανερᾶς ἀποδόσεως ἵσταται τὰ λεχθέντα, φύσιν δὲ
τοῖς πολλοῖς ἀδηλοτέραν ἔοικε παρεμφαίνειν, ἣν οἱ
τὰ νοητὰ πρὸ τῶν αἰσθητῶν ἀποδεχόμενοι καὶ ὁρᾶν
201 δυνάμενοι γνωρίζουσιν. ἔστι δὲ τοιάδε· ὁ μελλήσας
σφαγιάζεσθαι καλεῖται Χαλδαϊστὶ μὲν Ἰσαάκ, Ἑλληνιστὶ δὲ μεταληφθέντος τοῦ ὀνόματος "γέλως"·
γέλως δ' οὐχ ὁ κατὰ παιδιὰν ἐγγινόμενος
σώματι παραλαμβάνεται τὰ νῦν, ἀλλ' ἡ κατὰ
202 διάνοιαν εὐπάθεια καὶ χαρά. ταύτην ὁ σοφὸς
ἱερουργεῖν λέγεται δεόντως θεῷ διὰ συμβόλου
παριστάς, ὅτι τὸ χαίρειν μόνῳ θεῷ οἰκειότατόν
ἐστιν· ἐπίλυπον μὲν γὰρ τὸ ἀνθρώπινον γένος καὶ
περιδεές, ἢ παρόντων κακῶν ἢ προσδοκωμένων, ὡς
ἢ ἐπὶ τοῖς ἐν χερσὶν ἀβουλήτοις ἀνιᾶσθαι ἢ ἐπὶ τοῖς
μέλλουσι ταραχῇ καὶ φόβῳ κραδαίνεσθαι· ἄλυπος
δὲ καὶ ἄφοβος καὶ παντὸς πάθους ἀμέτοχος ἡ τοῦ
θεοῦ φύσις εὐδαιμονίας καὶ μακαριότητος παντελοῦς
203 μόνη μετέχουσα. τῷ δὴ τὴν ἀληθῆ ταύτην ὁμολο-
γίαν ὡμολογηκότι τρόπῳ χρηστὸς ὢν καὶ φιλάνθρωπος ὁ θεός, φθόνον ἐληλακὼς ἀφ' ἑαυτοῦ, προσηκόντως ἀντιχαρίζεται τὸ δῶρον, καθ' ὅσον ἔχει
δυνάμεως ὁ ληψόμενος, καὶ μόνον οὐ ταῦτα θεσπίζει

ᵃ In the strict Stoic sense of the word, for reasonable forms
of πάθος. See note on De Mut. 1 and references there given.
98

is not malignant or a lover of evil must be overwhelmed with admiration for his extraordinary piety ;
and he need not take into consideration at once all
the points which I have mentioned, for any single
one of them would be enough. For to picture in
the mind one of these, however small the form which
the picture takes, though no action of the Sage is
small, is enough to show the greatness and loftiness
of his soul.

XXXVI. But the story here told is not confined to 200
the literal and obvious explanation, but seems to
have in it the elements of a further suggestion,
obscure to the many but recognized by those who
prefer the mental to the sensible and have the power
to see it. It is as follows. The proposed victim is 201
called in Chaldaean Isaac, but, if the word is translated into our language, Laughter. But the laughter
here understood is not the laughter which amuse-
ment arouses in the body, but the good emotion ^a of
the understanding, that is joy. This the Sage is 202
said to sacrifice as his duty to God, thus showing in
a figure that rejoicing is most closely associated with
God alone. For mankind is subject to grief and very
fearful of evils either present or expected, so that
men are either distressed by disagreeables close at
hand or are agitated by troublous fear of those which
are still to come. But the nature of God is without
grief or fear and wholly exempt from passion of any
kind, and alone partakes of perfect happiness and
bliss. The frame of mind which has made this true 203
acknowledgement God, Who has banished jealousy
from His presence in His kindness and love for mankind, fitly rewards by returning the gift in so far as
the recipient's capacity allows. And indeed we may

204 λέγων· " τὸ μὲν τῆς χαρᾶς γένος καὶ τὸ χαίρειν ὅτι
οὐκ ἔστιν ἑτέρου πλὴν ἐμοῦ τοῦ πατρὸς τῶν ὅλων
κτῆμα, σαφῶς οἶδα, κεκτημένος δ' ὅμως οὐ φθονῶ
τοῖς ἀξίοις χρῆσθαι· ἄξιος δὲ τίς ἂν εἴη, πλὴν εἴ
τις ἐμοὶ καὶ τοῖς ἐμοῖς βουλήμασιν ἕποιτο; τούτῳ
γὰρ ἥκιστα μὲν ἀνιᾶσθαι ἥκιστα δὲ φοβεῖσθαι συμ-
βήσεται πορευομένῳ ταύτην τὴν ὁδόν, ἣ πάθεσι μὲν
καὶ κακίαις ἐστὶν ἄβατος, εὐπαθείαις δὲ καὶ ἀρεταῖς
205 ἐμπεριπατεῖται."   μηδεὶς δ' ὑπολαβέτω
τὴν ἄκρατον καὶ ἀμιγῆ λύπης χαρὰν ἀπ' οὐρανοῦ
[30] καταβαίνειν ἐπὶ τὴν γῆν, ἀλλὰ | κέκραται¹ ἐξ ἀμφοῖν,
περιττεύοντος τοῦ κρείττονος· ὅνπερ τρόπον καὶ τὸ
φῶς ἐν οὐρανῷ μὲν ἄκρατον καὶ ἀμιγὲς σκότους
ἐστίν, ἐν δὲ τοῖς ὑπὸ σελήνην ἀέρι ζοφερῷ κεκρα-
206 μένον φαίνεται. ταύτης ἔνεκα τῆς αἰτίας δοκεῖ μοι
καὶ πρότερον γελάσασα ἡ ἀρετῆς ἐπώνυμος Σάρρα
πρὸς τὸν πυνθανόμενον ἀρνήσασθαι τὸν γέλωτα,
καταδείσασα μή ποτε ἄρα τὸ χαίρειν οὐδενὸς ὂν
γενητοῦ, μόνου δὲ τοῦ θεοῦ, σφετερίζηται· διόπερ
θαρσύνων αὐτὴν ὁ ἱερὸς λόγος φησί· μηδὲν εὐλαβη-
207 θῇς, ὄντως ἐγέλασας καὶ μέτεστί σοι χαρᾶς. οὐ
γὰρ εἴασεν ὁ πατὴρ τῶν ἀνθρώπων τὸ γένος λύπαις
καὶ ὀδύναις καὶ ἄχθεσιν ἀνιάτοις ἐμφέρεσθαι, παρ-
έμιξε δὲ καὶ τῆς ἀμείνονος φύσεως, εὐδιάσαι καὶ
γαληνιάσαι ποτὲ τὴν ψυχὴν δικαιώσας· τὴν δὲ τῶν

¹ MSS. ἀλλ' ἐγκέκραται or ἀλλὰ κρέμαται et alia. Perhaps
ἀλλά κρᾶμά τι.

ᵃ Gen. xviii. 12 and 15. Sarah's laughter has been explained in the obvious way in § 112. Here we have a more

almost hear His voice saying : " All joy and rejoicing 204
I know well is the possession of none other save Me
alone, the Father of All.   Yet I do not grudge that
this My possession should be used by such as are
worthy, and who should be worthy save one who
should follow Me and My will, for he will prove to
be most exempt from distress and fear if he travels
by this road which passion and vice cannot tread,
but good feelings and virtue can walk therein."

But let no one suppose that joy de- 205
scends from heaven to earth pure and free from any
mixture of grief.   No, it is a mixture of both, though
the better element is the stronger, just as light too
in heaven is pure from any mixture of darkness but
in regions below the moon is clearly mixed with
dusky air.   This was the reason, I think, why Sarah 206
who bears the name of virtue first laughs, and then,
in reply to her questioner, denies the laughter.[a]
She feared lest she should be grasping for herself
the joy which belongs not to created being but to
God alone.   Therefore, the holy word bids her be of
good cheer and says : " Be not afraid : thou didst
indeed laugh and dost participate in joy."   For the 207
Father did not suffer the whole course of the human
race to move amid griefs and pains and burdens which
admit no remedy, but mixed with them something
of the better nature and judged it well that the soul
should at times dwell in sunshine and calm ; and as

spiritual interpretation.   That the laughter signified joy, not
incredulity, has already been suggested in *Leg. All.* iii. 217 f.
and *De Mut.* 166.   In neither of these places, however, has
the subsequent denial been dealt with.   The interpretation
here suggested that the soul begins to doubt whether joy is
not more than humanity can expect appears again in *Spec.
Leg.* ii. 54.

PHILO

σοφῶν καὶ τὸν πλείω χρόνον τοῦ βίου γήθειν καὶ
εὐφραίνεσθαι τοῖς τοῦ κόσμου θεωρήμασιν ἐβουλήθη.

208 XXXVII. Τοσαῦτα μὲν περὶ τῆς τοῦ ἀνδρὸς
εὐσεβείας, εἰ καὶ πολλῶν ἄλλων ἐστὶν ἀφθονία,
λελέχθω. διερευνητέον δὲ καὶ τὴν πρὸς ἀνθρώπους
αὐτοῦ δεξιότητα· τῆς γὰρ αὐτῆς φύσεώς ἐστιν
εὐσεβῆ τε εἶναι καὶ φιλάνθρωπον, καὶ περὶ τὸν
αὐτὸν ἑκάτερον, ὁσιότης μὲν πρὸς θεόν, δικαιοσύνη
δὲ πρὸς ἀνθρώπους, θεωρεῖται. πάντα μὲν οὖν τὰ
πεπραγμένα μακρὸν ἂν εἴη διεξιέναι, δυεῖν δὲ ἢ
209 τριῶν οὐκ ἄτοπον ἐπιμνησθῆναι. πολυάργυρος καὶ
πολύχρυσος ἐν τοῖς μάλιστα ὢν καὶ θρεμμάτων
πολυζῴους ἔχων ἀγέλας καὶ τῶν ἐγχωρίων καὶ
αὐτοχθόνων τοῖς ἱκανὰ κεκτημένοις ἐν τῷ περι-
ουσιάζειν ἁμιλλώμενος καὶ πλουσιώτερος γεγονὼς
ἢ κατὰ μέτοικον ὑπ' οὐδενὸς ἐμέμφθη τῶν ὑπο-
δεξαμένων, ἀλλ' ὑπὸ πάντων τῶν εἰς πεῖραν ἐλθόντων
210 ἐπαινούμενος διετέλεσεν. εἰ δὲ καί τις, οἷα φιλεῖ
πολλάκις, ἐκ θεραπόντων καὶ τῶν συνδιατριβόντων
ἅμιλλα καὶ διαφορὰ πρὸς ἑτέρους ἐγένετο, ταύτην
ἐπειρᾶτο διαλύειν ἡσυχῇ βαρυτέρῳ ἤθει τὰ φιλό-
νεικα καὶ ταραχώδη καὶ στασιαστικὰ πάντα προβε-
211 βλημένος καὶ τῆς ψυχῆς ἀπεληλακώς. καὶ θαυμαστὸν οὐδέν, εἰ πρὸς τοὺς ἀλλοτρίους τοιοῦτος ἦν,
οἳ βαρυτέρᾳ καὶ δυνατωτέρᾳ χειρὶ συμφωνήσαντες
ἠμύναντο ἂν ἄρχοντα χειρῶν ἀδίκων, ὁπότε καὶ
πρὸς τοὺς γένει μὲν οἰκείους, γνώμῃ δ' ἠλλοτριω-

---

[a] Or "kindness and courtesy." See note on *De Fuga* 31.
[b] For Abraham's wealth *cf.* Gen. xiii. 2 and xxiv. 35.
[c] Or "seriousness." But the word seems strange.

for the soul of the wise He willed that it should pass the chief part of its life in glad-hearted contemplation of what the world has to show.

XXXVII. These examples must suffice for our treatment of Abraham's piety, though others might be found in great plenty. But we must also examine the good and wise behaviour [a] shown in his dealings with men. For the nature which is pious is also kindly, and the same person will exhibit both qualities, holiness to God and justice to men. It would be too long, indeed, to describe all his actions, but it would not be out of place to mention two or three. Though he was exceedingly rich [b] in silver and gold and possessed many herds of numerous live-stock and in abundance of wealth rivalled those of the natives and original inhabitants who possessed good means, and became more opulent than would be expected of an immigrant, he incurred no censure from those who received him into their midst but continued to be praised by all who had experience of him. But, if, as often happens, any of his servants or regular associates had a quarrel or difference with his neighbours, he would try to put an end to it quietly, banishing and expelling from the soul by means of his greater dignity [c] of character all that tended to strife and confusion and faction. And we need not wonder that he so bore himself to strangers who could have united to repel him with their superior weight of strength if he was the aggressor in injustice, when we see what moderation he showed to those who, connected with him by birth but estranged from him in moral principles, stood

Mangey wished to read πρᾳοτέρῳ. Cohn notes that the Armenian seems to have read πρᾳοτέρῳ τὰ βαρύτερα.

μένους, ἐρήμους καὶ μόνους καὶ πολλῷ καταδεέστερα κεκτημένους ἐμετρίαζεν, ἐλαττούμενος ἑκὼν
212 ἐν οἷς πλεονεκτεῖν ἐδύνατο. ἦν γὰρ ἀδελφιδοῦς
αὐτῷ, τῆς πατρίδος ὅτε μετανίστατο, συνεξεληλυθώς, ἀβέβαιος, ὑπαμφίβολος, ἀντιρρέπων ὧδε
[31] κἀκεῖσε, τοτὲ μὲν προσσαίνων | φιλικοῖς ἀσπάσμασι, τοτὲ δὲ ἀφηνιάζων καὶ ἀπαυχενίζων διὰ τὴν
213 τῶν τρόπων ἀνωμαλίαν. ὅθεν καὶ τὸ οἰκετικὸν
αὐτῷ δύσερι καὶ ταραχῶδες ἦν σωφρονιστὴν οὐκ
ἔχον καὶ μάλιστα τὸ ποιμενικὸν μακρὰν τοῦ δεσπότου διεζευγμένον· ἀπελευθεριάζοντες γοῦν ὑπ'
αὐθαδείας ἀεὶ διεφέροντο τοῖς προεστηκόσι τῶν
θρεμμάτων τοῦ σοφοῦ τὰ πολλὰ εἴκουσι διὰ τὴν τοῦ
δεσπότου πραϋπάθειαν· ὑφ' οὗ πρὸς ἀπόνοιαν
ἐπιδόντες καὶ θράσος ἀναίσχυντον ὤργων, μηνιῶντες ἤδη καὶ τὸ ἀκατάλλακτον ἐν αὐτοῖς ζωπυροῦντες, ἕως ἀπηνάγκασαν τοὺς ἀδικουμένους εἰς
214 ἄμυναν ὁρμῆσαι. μάχης δὲ ἐμβριθεστάτης γενομένης, ἀκούσας ὁ ἀστεῖος τὴν ἀντεφόρμησιν, εἰδὼς
ἐπικυδεστέραν οὖσαν τὴν αὑτοῦ μερίδα πλήθει τε
καὶ δυνάμει, τὴν διαφορὰν οὐκ εἴασεν ἄχρι νίκης
ἐλθεῖν, ὑπὲρ τοῦ μὴ ἀνιᾶσαι τὸν ἀδελφιδοῦν ἐφ'
ἥττῃ τῶν ἰδίων, ἀλλ' ἐν μεθορίῳ στὰς συμβατηρίοις λόγοις τοὺς διαφερομένους κατήλλαξεν, οὐ
πρὸς τὸ παρὸν μόνον ἀλλὰ καὶ τὸν μέλλοντα χρόνον.
215 εἰδὼς γὰρ ὅτι συνοικοῦντες μὲν καὶ ἐν ταὐτῷ
διαιτώμενοι γνωσιμαχοῦντες φιλονεικήσουσι στάσεις ἀεὶ καὶ πολέμους κατ' ἀλλήλων ἐγείροντες, ἵνα

---

^a For §§ 212-216 see Gen. xiii. 5-11.

alone and unsupported and with possessions far inferior to his, and how he willingly accepted to be at a disadvantage when he might have taken advantage of them. *For he had a nephew who had 212 accompanied him when he migrated from his native land, an unreliable and hesitating person, ever inclining this way and that, sometimes fawning on him with loving greetings, sometimes rebellious and refractory through the inconsistency of his different moods. Therefore his servants too were quarrel- 213 some and turbulent, as they had no one to control them, and this was particularly the case with the shepherds who were stationed at a distance from their master; thus breaking out of control in their wilfulness they were ever quarrelling with the Sage's herdsmen who many times gave way to them because of their master's gentleness. Then, advancing to a senseless audacity which knew no shame, they grew rampant and fostered in their hearts the flame of a passion beyond hope of conciliation until they compelled their opponents to begin defending themselves against the injustice. When the fight had 214 become very serious, the man of worth, hearing how the aggressors had been countered, and knowing that his own party was more distinguished in strength and number, did not allow the quarrel to be terminated by a victory, as he did not wish to distress his nephew through seeing his own party defeated. So he took up his stand between them and reconciled the disputants by proposals of agreement, good not only for the present but for the future. For he 215 knew that if they lived together and shared the same dwelling-place they would engage in obstinate contention, for ever stirring up wars and factions against

μὴ τοῦτο γένοιτο, συμφέρον ὑπέλαβεν εἶναι παραι-
τήσασθαι τὸ ὁμοδίαιτον καὶ τὴν οἴκησιν διαζεῦξαι·
καὶ μεταπεμψάμενος τὸν ἀδελφιδοῦν αἵρεσιν αὐτῷ
δίδωσι τῆς ἀμείνονος χώρας, ἄσμενος ὁμολογῶν ἣν
ἂν ἐπιλέξηται μερίδα λήψεσθαι· κερδανεῖν γὰρ
216 κέρδος μέγιστον, τὴν εἰρήνην. καίτοι τίς ἂν ἕτερος
ἀσθενεστέρῳ παραχωρήσειεν οὑτινοσοῦν ἰσχυρό-
τερος ὤν; τίς δὲ νικᾶν δυνάμενος βούλοιτ' ἂν
ἡττᾶσθαι, μὴ συγχρώμενος τῷ δύνασθαι; μόνος
δὲ οὗτος τὸ ἄριστον οὐκ ἐν ῥώμῃ καὶ πλεονεξίᾳ
τιθέμενος ἀλλ' ἐν ἀστασιάστῳ βίῳ καὶ τό γε ἐπ'
αὐτὸν ἧκον μέρος ἡσυχάζοντι πάντων ἔδοξεν εἶναι
θαυμασιώτατος.

217 XXXVIII. Ἐπειδὴ τοίνυν ὡς ἐπ' ἀνθρώπου ἡ
λέξις ἐγκωμιαστικὴ λέλεκται, μηνύονται δὲ καὶ
τρόποι ψυχῆς κατὰ τοὺς ἀπὸ τῶν ῥητῶν ἐπὶ τὰ
νοητὰ μετιόντας, ἁρμόττον ἂν εἴη καὶ τούτους
218 ἀνερευνῆσαι. μυρίοι μὲν οὖν εἰσιν ἀπὸ μυρίων
ἀφορμῶν κατὰ παντοδαπὰς ἰδέας πραγμάτων συν-
ιστάμενοι, δύο δ' οἱ νυνὶ μέλλοντες ἐπικρίνεσθαι
τρόποι, ὧν ὁ μὲν πρεσβύτερος, ὁ δὲ νεώτερος,
πρεσβύτερος μὲν ὁ τὰ πρῶτα καὶ ἡγεμονικὰ τῇ
φύσει τιμῶν, νεώτερος δὲ ὁ τὰ ὑπήκοα καὶ ἐν
219 ἐσχατιαῖς ἐξεταζόμενα. πρεσβύτερα μὲν οὖν καὶ
ἡγεμονικὰ φρόνησις καὶ σωφροσύνη καὶ δικαιοσύνη
[32] καὶ ἀνδρεία καὶ πᾶν ὅ τι περὶ ἀρετὴν | καὶ αἱ κατ'
ἀρετὴν πράξεις· νεώτερα δὲ πλοῦτος καὶ δόξα καὶ
ἀρχὴ καὶ εὐγένεια, οὐχ ἡ ἀληθής, ἀλλ' ἣν οἱ πολλοὶ
νομίζουσι, καὶ ὅσα ἄλλα τὴν τρίτην μετὰ τὰ ψυχικὰ

each other. To prevent this, he thought it expedient to refuse to continue their living together and to arrange for their dwelling at a distance from each other. So, sending for his nephew, he gave him a choice of the better district, gladly agreeing that he should take whatever part he chose; for he considered that he would thereby get peace, the greatest of gains. And yet who else would give 216 way in any single point to the weaker if he were the stronger? Who, when he could conquer, would be willing to be defeated and not avail himself of his power? He alone took for his ideal not the exercise of strength and self-aggrandizement but a life free from strife and so far as lay with him of tranquillity, and thereby he showed himself the most admirable of men.

XXXVIII. The actual words of the story are an 217 encomium on Abraham as a man; but, according to those who proceed from the literal to the spiritual, characters of soul are indicated also, and therefore it will be well to investigate them too. Such char- 218 acters are numberless, proceeding from numberless starting-points and arising from every kind and variety of circumstance; but those now to be examined are two only, one higher and senior and one lower and junior. The senior is that character which honours things primal and dominant in their nature, the junior that which honours things subject and lowest in the list. Now the senior and dominant 219 are wisdom and temperance and justice and courage and virtue regarded as a whole and actions inspired by virtue, but the junior are wealth and reputation and office and good birth, good not in the true sense but in the sense which the multitude give to it, and everything else which coming after the things of

καὶ σωματικὰ τάξιν εἴληχεν, ἥτις εὐθύς ἐστι καὶ
220 τελευταία. τούτων οὖν τῶν τρόπων ἑκάτερος ἔχει
καθάπερ τινὰς ποίμνας καὶ ἀγέλας, ὁ μὲν τῶν ἐκτὸς
ὀρεγόμενος ἄργυρον, χρυσόν, ἐσθῆτας, πάντα ὅσα
τοῦ πλουτεῖν ὗλαι καὶ παρασκευαί, καὶ πάλιν ὅπλα,
μηχανήματα, τριήρεις, ἱππικὴν καὶ πεζικὴν καὶ
ναυτικὴν δύναμιν, τὰς πρὸς ἡγεμονίαν ἀφορμάς,
ἐξ ὧν περιγίνεται τὸ βεβαίως κρατεῖν, ὁ δὲ καλοκἀγαθίας ἐραστὴς τὰ καθ' ἑκάστην ἀρετὴν δόγματα
221 καὶ τὰ σοφίας αὐτῆς θεωρήματα.   προ-
στάται δὲ καὶ ἐπιμεληταὶ τούτων ἑκατέρων εἰσί
τινες οἷα θρεμμάτων ποιμένες, τῶν μὲν ἐκτὸς οἱ φιλο-
χρήματοι καὶ φιλόδοξοι καὶ στρατηγιῶντες καὶ ὅσοι
τὴν ἐπὶ τοῖς πλήθεσι δυναστείαν ἀγαπῶσι, τῶν δὲ
περὶ ψυχὴν ὅσοι φιλόκαλοι καὶ φιλάρετοι, μὴ τὰ
νόθα πρὸ τῶν γνησίων ἀλλὰ τὰ γνήσια πρὸ τῶν
222 νόθων ἀγαθὰ αἱρούμενοι. γίνεται οὖν φυσική τις
αὐτοῖς ἡ διαμάχη μηδὲν ἐγνωκόσι τῶν αὐτῶν, ἀλλ'
ἀπᾴδουσι καὶ διαφερομένοις ἀεὶ περὶ πράγματος
συνεκτικωτάτου τῶν ἐν βίῳ, τοῦτο δ' ἐστὶν ἡ κρίσις
223 τῶν πρὸς ἀλήθειαν ἀγαθῶν. ἄχρι μὲν οὖν τινος
ἐπολεμεῖτο ἡ ψυχὴ καὶ τὴν στάσιν ταύτην ἐχώρει
μήπω κεκαθαρμένη παντελῶς, ἀλλ' ἔτι τῶν παθῶν
καὶ νοσημάτων παρευημερούντων τοὺς ὑγιαίνοντας
λόγους· ἀφ' οὗ δὲ ἤρξατο δυνατωτέρα γίνεσθαι καὶ
ῥώμῃ κραταιοτέρᾳ τὸν ἐπιτειχισμὸν τῶν ἐναντίων
δοξῶν καθαιρεῖν, πτερυξαμένη καὶ φρονήματος
ὑποπλησθεῖσα τὸν τὰς ἐκτὸς ὗλας τεθαυμακότα
τρόπον ἐν αὑτῇ διατειχίζει καὶ διαζεύγνυσι καὶ ὡς

---

^a Or "was the subject of attack, and allowed the revolt to

soul and body takes the third place which is neces- 220
sarily also the last. Each of the two characters possesses what we may call flocks and herds. The
devotee of things external has silver, gold, raiment,
all the materials of wealth and the means for procuring them, and again arms, engines, triremes,
cavalry, infantry and naval forces, the foundations
of sovereignty which produce security of power.
The lover of moral excellence has the principles of
each separate virtue and the truths discovered by
wisdom itself.   Now those who preside 221
and have charge over each of these two are, as it
were, herdsmen of cattle. The externals are cared for
by lovers of wealth or glory, the would-be generals and
all who hanker for power over multitudes, the things
of the soul by lovers of moral excellence and virtue,
who prefer the genuine goods to the spurious and not
the spurious to the genuine. So there is a natural 222
conflict between them since they have no common
principle but are for ever jangling and quarrelling
about the most important thing in life, and that is the
decision what are the true goods. For a time the soul 223
was in a state of war, and was the scene of this conflict,[a]
for as yet it was not perfectly purified, but its passions
and distempers still prevailed over its healthy principles. But from the time when it began to grow
more powerful and demolish by superior strength
the works with which the opposing doctrines threatened it, it spreads its wings, and, its spirit grown to
fullness, sets a wall and barrier between it and that side
of its character which has given its admiration to the
gear of external things. And it talks with it as with

proceed," *i.e.* the soul is here identified, as it certainly is
below, with its own better side.

224 ἀνθρώπῳ διαλεγομένῃ φησίν· ἀμήχανον ὁμοδίαιτον
εἶναί σε καὶ ὁμόσπονδον ἐραστῇ σοφίας καὶ ἀρετῆς,
ἴθι δὴ καὶ μετοικισάμενος μακρὰν ἀποζεύχθητι,
μηδεμίαν ἔχων κοινωνίαν, ἀλλὰ μηδὲ σχεῖν δυνά-
μενος· ὅσα γὰρ ὑπολαμβάνεις εἶναι δεξιά, ταῦτ'
οἴεται ἐκεῖνος εὐώνυμα, καὶ ὅσα τοὐναντίον σκαιά,
ταῦτα παρ' ἐκείνῳ νενόμισται δεξιά.

225 XXXIX. Οὐ τοίνυν εἰρηνικὸς καὶ φιλοδίκαιος
αὐτὸ μόνον ἦν ὁ ἀστεῖος, ἀλλὰ καὶ ἀνδρεῖος καὶ
πολεμικός· οὐχ ἕνεκα τοῦ πολεμεῖν—οὐ γὰρ δύσερις
[33] ἦν[1] καὶ φιλόνεικος,—ἀλλ' ὑπὲρ βεβαίου τῆς πρὸς τὸ
226 μέλλον εἰρήνης, ἣν οἱ ἀντίπαλοι καθῄρουν. | σαφε-
στάτη δὲ πίστις τὰ πραχθέντα. τὴν πρὸς ἀνατολὰς
μοῖραν τῆς οἰκουμένης τέτταρες μεγάλοι βασιλεῖς
εἰλήχεσαν, οἷς ὑπήκουεν ἔθνη τὰ ἑῷα, τά τε ἐκτὸς
καὶ ἐντὸς Εὐφράτου. τὰ μὲν οὖν ἄλλα διέμενεν
ἀστασίαστα πειθαρχοῦντα τοῖς τῶν βασιλέων ἐπι-
τάγμασι καὶ τοὺς ἐτησίους δασμοὺς ἀποφασίστως
εἰσφέροντα· μόνη δὲ ἡ Σοδομιτῶν χώρα, πρὶν κατα-
φλεχθῆναι, παραλύειν ἤρξατο τὴν εἰρήνην ἀπό-
227 στασιν ἐκ πολλοῦ διανοουμένη. πάνυ γὰρ οὔσης
εὐδαίμονος πέντε βασιλεῖς ἐπεκράτουν τάς τε πόλεις
καὶ τὴν γῆν δασάμενοι πολλὴν μὲν οὐκ οὖσαν,
εὔσταχυν δὲ καὶ εὔδενδρον καὶ καρπῶν περίπλεων·
ὃ γὰρ ταῖς ἄλλαις τὸ μέγεθος, τοῦθ' ἡ ἀρετὴ Σοδό-
μοις παρέσχεν, ὅθεν καὶ πλείους ἐραστὰς ἔσχεν
228 ἡγεμόνας τὸ κάλλος αὐτῆς καταπλαγέντας. οὗτοι
τὸν ἄλλον χρόνον τοὺς ἐπιταχθέντας φόρους ἀπε-

---

[1] mss. ὧν or omit.

[a] This evidently gives an allegorical interpretation to Gen.

110

a man and says : " It is impossible that thou and 224
the lover of wisdom and virtue should have a common
home and common ties. Away, change thy dwelling
and betake thyself afar off, for thou hast not, or
rather canst not have, fellowship with him. For all
that thou holdest to be on the right he thinks to be
on the left, and conversely what to thee is on the
wrong side in his judgement stands on the right." [a]

XXIX. So, then, the man of worth was not merely 225
peaceable and a lover of justice but courageous and
warlike, not for the sake of warring, for he was not
quarrelsome or cantankerous, but to secure peace
for the future, the peace which the opponents were
destroying. The clearest proof of this is his actions. [b] 226
That part of the inhabited world which lies towards
the east was in the hands of four great kings who held
in subjection the nations of the Orient on both sides
of the Euphrates. Now the other nations continued
to be free from sedition, obeying the orders of the
king, and paying their taxes without demur. Only
the country of the Sodomites, before it was consumed
by fire, began to undermine this peaceful condition
by a long-standing plan of revolt. For, as it was 227
exceedingly prosperous, it was ruled by five kings
who taxed the cities and the land, which though not
large was rich in corn and well wooded and teeming
with fruits, for the position which size gave to other
countries, was given to Sodom by its goodliness, and
hence it had a plurality of rulers who loved it and were
fascinated by its charm. These hitherto rendered 228
the appointed tributes to the collectors of revenue

xiii. 9 " if thou wilt take the left hand, then I will go to
the right; or if thou wilt take the right hand, then I will go
to the left."

[b] For §§ 225-235 see Gen. xiv.

δίδοσαν τοῖς ἐκλογεῦσι τῶν χρημάτων, τοὺς δυνατω
τέρους ὧν ἦσαν ὕπαρχοι τιμῶντες ἅμα καὶ δεδιότες·
ἐπεὶ δὲ ἐκορέσθησαν ἀγαθῶν καί, ὅπερ φιλεῖ, κόρος
ὕβριν ἐγέννησε, πλέον τῆς δυνάμεως φρονήσαντες
ἀπαυχενίζουσι τὸ πρῶτον, εἶθ᾽ οἷα κακοὶ δοῦλοι
δεσπόταις τοῖς ἑαυτῶν ἐπιτίθενται στάσει πιστεύ
229 σαντες ἢ ῥώμῃ.ᵃ οἱ δὲ τῆς ἑαυτῶν εὐγενείας ὑπο
μνησθέντες καὶ φραξάμενοι δυνατωτέρᾳ χειρὶ μάλα
καταφρονητικῶς ᾔεσαν ὡς αὐτοβοεὶ περιεσόμενοι
καὶ συμπλακέντες τοὺς μὲν εὐθὺς εἰς φυγὴν ἀνε
σκέδασαν, τοὺς δὲ ἐπιστροφάδην κτείνοντες ἡβηδὸν
διαφθείρουσιν, αἰχμαλώτων δὲ πολὺν ὄχλον ἀγα
γόντες μετὰ τῆς ἄλλης λείας διενέμοντο· προσαπ
άγουσι μέντοι καὶ τοῦ σοφοῦ τὸν ἀδελφιδοῦν εἰς μίαν
τῆς πενταπόλεως οὐκ ἐκ πολλοῦ μετῳκηκότα.

230   XL. τοῦτο μηνυθὲν ὑπό τινος τῶν ἐκ
τῆς τροπῆς διασωθέντων χαλεπῶς αὐτὸν ἠνίασε
καὶ οὐκέτ᾽ ἠρέμει διὰ τοῦτο συγκεχυμένος καὶ
ζῶντα πενθῶν τὸ ἀργαλεώτερον ἢ εἰ τεθνεῶτα
ἐπύθετο· τέλος μὲν γάρ, ὡς αὐτό που δηλοῖ τοῦ
νομα, τῶν κατὰ τὸν βίον ἀπάντων καὶ μάλιστα
κακῶν ᾔδει τὴν τελευτήν, μυρία δὲ τῶν ἀβουλήτων
231 ἐφεδρεύοντα τοῖς ζῶσι. διώκειν δ᾽ εὐτρεπιζόμενος
ἐπὶ τῷ ῥύσασθαι τὸν ἀδελφιδοῦν ἠπόρει συμμάχων,
ἅτε ξένος ὢν καὶ μέτοικος καὶ μηδενὸς τολμῶντος
ἀμάχοις δυνάμεσι τοσούτων βασιλέων καὶ ἄρτι
232 νενικηκότων ἐναντιοῦσθαι. καινοτάτην δ᾽ ἐξεῦρε
συμμαχίαν—πόρος γὰρ ἐν ἀπόροις, ὅταν δικαίων
καὶ φιλανθρώπων ἔργων ἐφιῆταί τις, εὑρίσκεται—·

ᵃ Or "to the strength" (which they wrongly supposed
themselves to have). But this is awkward. I should like
to read ⟨μᾶλλον⟩ ἤ.

out of both respect for and fear of the higher potentates whose satraps they were. But, when they had been surfeited with good things, and as so often happens satiety had begotten insolence, they grew ambitious beyond their powers and first shook off the yoke and then, like bad slaves, attacked their masters, trusting to sedition or violence.[a] But these 229 masters, mindful of their higher birth and armed with more powerful force, advanced in great disdain to the attack, expecting to conquer them with the utmost ease. And, when they engaged, some they sent flying helter-skelter at once, others they mowed down in wholesale massacre, while a great number were taken prisoners and distributed with the rest of the booty. Among these they took the nephew of the Sage, who had migrated not long before into one of the five cities. XL. When 230 this was reported to Abraham by one of those who escaped from the rout, it distressed him exceedingly. He could no longer rest, so severe was the shock, and mourned for the living with greater sorrow than if he had heard of his death. For he knew that death or decease, as the name itself shows, is the end of everything in life, and particularly of its ills, while the troubles which lie in wait for the living are numberless. But, when he made ready to pursue 231 the enemy to rescue his nephew, he was at a loss for allies, since he was a stranger and an immigrant, and no one dared to oppose the invincible forces of the kings, considering their number and their recent victory. But he obtained allies in quite a new 232 quarter, for resource is found where resource is none, when one is set on deeds of justice and kindness. He

συναγαγὼν γὰρ τοὺς οἰκέτας καὶ τοῖς ἀργυρωνήτοις προστάξας οἴκοι καταμένειν—ἔδεισε γὰρ ἐξ αὐτῶν αὐτομολίαν—τοὺς οἰκότριβας καταλέγει καὶ διανείμας εἰς ἑκατονταρχίας τρισὶν ἐπῄει τάξεσιν,[a] οὐ ταύταις πεποιθώς—πολλοστὴ γὰρ ἦν μοῖρα τῶν παρὰ τοῖς βασιλεῦσιν—, ἀλλὰ τῷ ὑπερμάχῳ καὶ

[34]
233 προαγωνιστῇ τοῦ | δικαίου θεῷ. συντείνων οὖν ἔσπευδε μηδὲν τάχους ἀνιείς, ἕως καιροφυλακήσας νυκτὸς ἐπιπίπτει τοῖς πολεμίοις δεδειπνοποιημένοις ἤδη καὶ πρὸς ὕπνον μέλλουσι τρέπεσθαι· καὶ τοὺς μὲν ἐν εὐναῖς ἱέρευε, τοὺς δ' ἀντιταχθέντας ἄρδην ἀνῄρει, πάντων δ' ἐρρωμένως ἐπεκράτει τῷ θαρ-
234 ραλέῳ τῆς ψυχῆς μᾶλλον ἢ ταῖς παρασκευαῖς. καὶ οὐ πρότερον ἀνῆκεν, ἕως τὴν μὲν ἀντίπαλον στρατιὰν βασιλεῦσιν αὐτοῖς ἡβηδὸν ἀνελὼν πρὸ τοῦ στρατοπέδου κατεστόρεσε, τὸν δὲ ἀδελφιδοῦν ἀνήγαγε μετὰ λαμπρᾶς καὶ ἐπιφανεστάτης νίκης ἅπασαν τὴν ἵππον καὶ τὴν τῶν ἄλλων πληθὺν ὑπο-
235 ζυγίων καὶ λείαν ἀφθονωτάτην προσπαραλαβών. ὃν θεασάμενος ὁ μέγας ἱερεὺς τοῦ μεγίστου θεοῦ ἐπανιόντα καὶ τροπαιοφοροῦντα σῶον μετὰ σῴου τῆς ἰδίας δυνάμεως—οὐδένα γὰρ τῶν συνόντων ἀπέβαλε—, καταπλαγεὶς τὸ μέγεθος τῆς πράξεως καὶ ὅπερ εἰκὸς ἐννοηθείς, ὡς οὐκ ἄνευ θείας ἐπιφροσύνης καὶ συμμαχίας κατωρθώθη, τὰς χεῖρας ἀνατείνας εἰς τὸν οὐρανὸν εὐχαῖς αὐτὸν γεραίρει καὶ ἐπινίκια ἔθυε καὶ πάντας τοὺς συναραμένους τῷ ἀγῶνι λαμπρῶς εἱστία, γεγηθὼς καὶ συνηδόμενος ὡς ἐπ' οἰκείῳ κατορθώματι· καὶ ἦν τῷ ὄντι οἰκεῖον

---

[a] So LXX (ἠρίθμησε).   E.V. " led forth."

114

collected his servants and, after bidding those who
had been acquired by purchase to remain at home,
since he feared that they might desert, he made a
roll-call[a] of those who were home-bred, distributed
them into centuries and advanced with three battalions. Yet he did not trust in these, for they were
but a small fraction of the kings' forces, but in God,
the champion and defender of the just. So he 233
pressed forward eagerly and never abated his speed
until, watching for his chance, he attacked the enemy
by night when they had supped and were preparing
to go to sleep. Some fell helpless victims to him in
their beds, others who took arms against him were
completely annihilated, and all were mightily overcome more by his courage of soul than by the resources at his command. Nor did he stay his hand 234
until he had completely slaughtered the opposing
army with their kings as well and left them lying
in front of the camp. His nephew he brought back
in the triumph of his brilliant and magnificent victory, taking too with him all the horses of the cavalry
and the whole multitude of the other beasts and
spoil in vast plenty. When the high priest of the 235
most high God saw him approaching with his trophies,
leader and army alike unhurt, for he had lost none
of his own company, he was astonished by the feat,
and, thinking, as indeed was natural, that such success
was not won without God's directing care and help
to their arms, he stretched his hands to heaven and
honoured him with prayers on his behalf and offered
sacrifices of thanksgiving for the victory and feasted
handsomely those who had taken part in the contest,
rejoicing and sharing their gladness as though the
success were his own ; and so indeed it was, for " the

αὐτῷ· " κοινὰ " γὰρ κατὰ τὴν παροιμίαν " τὰ
φίλων," πολὺ δὲ πλέον τὰ τῶν ἀγαθῶν, οἷς ἓν τέλος
εὐαρεστεῖν θεῷ.

236 XLI. Ταῦτα μὲν οὖν αἱ ῥηταὶ γραφαὶ περιέχουσιν. ἀσώματα δὲ ὅσοι καὶ γυμνὰ θεωρεῖν τὰ
πράγματα δύνανται, οἱ ψυχῇ μᾶλλον ἢ σώματι
ζῶντες, φήσουσι τῶν ἐννέα βασιλέων τοὺς μὲν
τέτταρας εἶναι τὰς ἐν ἡμῖν τῶν τεττάρων παθῶν
δυνάμεις, ἡδονῆς, ἐπιθυμίας, φόβου, λύπης, τοὺς
δὲ πέντε τὰς ἰσαρίθμους αἰσθήσεις, ὅρασιν, ἀκοήν,
237 γεῦσιν, ὄσφρησιν, ἀφήν. τρόπον γάρ τινα βασι-
λεύουσι καὶ ἄρχουσιν ἡμῶν ἀνημμέναι τὸ κράτος,
ἀλλ' οὐχ ὁμοίως· ὑπήκοοι γὰρ αἱ πέντε τῶν τεττάρων εἰσὶ καὶ φόρους αὐταῖς καὶ δασμοὺς ἀναγ-
238 καίους φέρουσιν ὑπὸ φύσεως ὁρισθέντας. ἐξ ὧν
γὰρ ἂν ἴδωμεν ἢ ἀκούσωμεν ἢ ὀσφρανθῶμεν ἢ
γευσώμεθα ἢ ἁψώμεθα, λῦπαι καὶ ἡδοναὶ καὶ φόβοι
καὶ ἐπιθυμίαι συνίστανται, μηδενὸς τῶν παθῶν
καθ' αὑτὸ σθένοντος, εἰ μὴ ἐχορηγεῖτο ταῖς διὰ τῶν
239 αἰσθήσεων παρασκευαῖς. αὗται γὰρ ἐκείνων δυνάμεις εἰσίν, ἢ διὰ χρωμάτων καὶ σχημάτων ἢ διὰ
φωνῆς τῆς ἐν τῷ λέγειν ἢ ἀκούειν ἢ διὰ χυλῶν ἢ
δι' ἀτμῶν ἢ τῶν ἐν ἁπτοῖς, ἃ μαλακὰ καὶ σκληρὰ
[35] ἢ τραχέα | καὶ λεῖα ἢ θερμὰ καὶ ψυχρά· ταῦτα γὰρ
πάντα διὰ τῶν αἰσθήσεων ἑκάστῳ τῶν παθῶν
240 χορηγεῖται. καὶ μέχρι μὲν οἱ λεχθέντες ἀποδίδον-
ται φόροι, μένει τοῖς βασιλεῦσιν ἡ ὁμαιχμία, ὅταν
δὲ μηκέθ' ὁμοίως συντελῶνται, στάσεις εὐθὺς καὶ
πόλεμοι συνίστανται· τοῦτο δὲ συμβαίνειν ἔοικεν,
ὅταν ἀφικνῆται τὸ ἐπώδυνον γῆρας, ἐν ᾧ τῶν μὲν
παθῶν ἀσθενέστερον οὐδὲν γίνεται, τάχα δὲ καὶ τῆς
παλαιᾶς δυνάμεως κραταιότερον, ἀμυδραὶ δὲ ὄψεις

belongings of friends are held in common," as the proverb says, and this is far more true of the belongings of the good whose one end is to be well-pleasing to God.

XLI. This is what we find in the scriptures read 236 literally ; but those who can contemplate facts stripped of the body and in naked reality, those who live with the soul rather than with the body, will say that of these nine kings, four are the power exercised within us by the four passions, pleasure, desire, fear and grief, and that the five are the five senses, sight, hearing, taste, smell and touch. For these 237 nine are in a sense invested with sovereignty and are our kings and rulers but not all in the same way. For the five are subject to the four, and are forced to pay them the tolls and tributes determined by nature. Griefs and pleasures and fears and desires 238 arise out of what we see or hear or smell or taste or touch, and none of the passions would have any strength of itself if it were not furnished with what the senses supply ; for these supplies constitute 239 the forces of the passions, taking the form of colours and shapes, or sounds spoken or heard, or flavours, or scents, or the qualities attached to things tangible, soft and hard or rough and smooth or warm and cold, all of which are supplied through the senses to each of the passions. And while the said tributes are 240 rendered the alliance between the kings holds good, but when they are no longer paid discord and wars at once arise, and this obviously happens when old age with its pains arrives. For then, while none of the passions is weaker, and perhaps is even stronger than of old, yet the eyes are dim and the ears dull of

PHILO

καὶ ὦτα δυσήκοα καὶ ἑκάστη τῶν ἄλλων αἰσθήσεων
ἀμβλυτέρα, μηκέθ' ὁμοίως ἕκαστα ἀκριβοῦν καὶ
δικάζειν δυναμένη μηδ' ἴσα τῷ πλήθει[1] ὑποτελεῖν·
εἰκότως οὖν ἐξασθενήσασαι πάντα τρόπον καὶ κλι-
θεῖσαι δι' αὐτῶν ὑπὸ τῶν ἀντιπάλων παθῶν ῥᾳδίως
241 ἀνατρέπονται.   φυσικώτατα δὲ ἐκεῖνο
εἴρηται, ὅτι τῶν πέντε βασιλέων δύο μὲν εἰς φρέατα
ἐμπίπτουσι, τρεῖς δὲ πρὸς φυγὴν ὥρμησαν· ἁφὴ μὲν
γὰρ καὶ γεῦσις ἄχρι τῶν τοῦ σώματος βαθυτάτων
ἀφικνοῦνται σπλάγχνοις παραπέμπουσαι τὰ οἰκεῖα
πρὸς διοίκησιν, ὀφθαλμοὶ δὲ καὶ ὦτα καὶ ὄσφρησις
ἔξω τὰ πολλὰ βαίνουσαι ἀποδιδράσκουσι τὴν δου-
242 λείαν τοῦ σώματος.   οἷς ἅπασιν ἐφ-
εδρεύων ὁ ἀστεῖος, ἐπειδὴ κατεῖδε τὰ σύμμαχα καὶ
φίλα πρὸ μικροῦ νοσοῦντα καὶ πόλεμον ἀντ' εἰρήνης
ταῖς ἐννέα βασιλείαις γενόμενον, πρὸς τὰς πέντε
τῶν τεττάρων περὶ κράτους ἀρχῆς ἁμιλλωμένων,
ἐξαπιναίως καιροφυλακήσας ἐπιτίθεται, φιλοτιμού-
μενος δημοκρατίαν, τὴν ἀρίστην τῶν πολιτειῶν,
ἀντὶ τυραννίδων καὶ δυναστειῶν ἐν τῇ ψυχῇ κατα-
στήσασθαι καὶ τὸ ἔννομον καὶ τὸ δίκαιον ἀντὶ
παρανομίας καὶ ἀδικίας, αἳ τέως ἐπεκράτουν.
243   ἔστι δ' οὐ πλάσμα μύθου τὸ λεχθέν,
ἀλλὰ πρᾶγμα τῶν ἀψευδεστάτων ἐν ἡμῖν αὐτοῖς
θεωρούμενον· πολλάκις μὲν γὰρ ὁμόνοιαν τὴν πρὸς
τὰ πάθη διατηροῦσιν αἱ αἰσθήσεις χορηγοῦσαι τὰ

[1] I suggest πλήρει ("equal to the full quota"): Mangey
πάθει or πάθεσι.

---

[a] See note on § 99 above.

[b] For Philo's admiration for democracy, by which he seems
to mean each part of the state possessing its proper amount
of power, see note on *Quod Deus* 176.

[c] The happy coincidence of the number of the kings with

hearing and each of the other senses blunted, so
that it cannot in the same way judge each thing
with accuracy or make the same contribution in
amount as before. And so, weakened all round as
they are and already giving way of themselves, it is
natural that they should be easily routed by the
opposing passions.   There is much philo- 241
sophical truth[a] in the saying that of the five kings
two fell into the wells and three took to flight.
For touch and taste descend to the lowest recesses
of the body and transmit to its inward parts what may
properly be dealt with by them ; but eyes and ears
and smell for the most part pass outside and escape
enslavement by the body.   All this the 242
man of worth was watching from his lair, and when
he saw trouble festering, where but now was alliance
and friendship, and war instead of peace arising
between the nine kingdoms, with the four com-
peting against the five for the sovereign power, he
seized his opportunity and suddenly made the
attack, ambitious to establish in the soul democracy,[b]
the best of constitutions, instead of the rule of
tyrants and overlords, and legality and justice
instead of lawlessness and injustice which hitherto
prevailed.   All this is no fable of my in- 243
vention, but a fact, and that one of the surest which
we may observe in ourselves.[c] For the senses, though
often they may maintain concord with the passions
and provide them with the objects which they per-

the accepted four passions and five senses naturally attracts
Philo to this ingenious allegory. The weak point seems to
be that in the story the rebellion of the five against the four
is not due to the influence of Abraham, as in the allegory
the refusal of the senses to minister to the passions is due to
reason.

PHILO

αἰσθητὰ αὐτοῖς, πολλάκις δὲ καὶ στασιάζουσι μηκέτ᾽
ἀξιοῦσαι τὰ ἴσα τελεῖν ἢ μὴ δυνάμεναι διὰ τὸ παρεῖναι τὸν σωφρονιστὴν λόγον· ὃς ἐπειδὰν ἀναλάβῃ
τὴν αὑτοῦ παντευχίαν, τὰς ἀρετὰς καὶ τὰ τούτων
δόγματα καὶ θεωρήματα, δύναμιν ἀνανταγώνιστον,
ἐρρωμενέστατα κρατεῖ· φθαρτὰ γὰρ ἀφθάρτῳ συν-
244 οικεῖν οὐ θέμις. αἱ μὲν οὖν ἐννέα δυναστεῖαι
τεττάρων παθῶν καὶ πέντε αἰσθήσεων φθαρταί τε
καὶ φθορᾶς αἴτιαι, ὁ δ᾽ ὁρμητηρίῳ χρώμενος ταῖς
ἀρεταῖς λόγος ἱερὸς καὶ θεῖος ὄντως, ἐν ἀριθμῷ
ταττόμενος δεκάδι τῇ παντελείᾳ, πρὸς ἅμιλλαν
ἐλθών, ἐρρωμενεστέρᾳ δυνάμει τῇ κατὰ θεὸν χρώμενος ἀνὰ κράτος νικᾷ τὰς εἰρημένας δυναστείας.

[36]
245   XLII. | Χρόνῳ δ᾽ ὕστερον αὐτῷ τελευτᾷ ἡ γυνὴ
θυμηρεστάτη καὶ τὰ πάντα ἀρίστη, μυρία δείγματα
τῆς φιλανδρίας ἐνεγκαμένη, τὴν σὺν αὐτῷ τῶν
συγγενῶν ἀπόλειψιν, τὴν ἐκ τῆς οἰκείας ἀνενδοίαστον μετάστασιν, τὰς ἐπὶ τῆς ἀλλοδαπῆς συνεχεῖς
καὶ ἐπαλλήλους πλάνας, τὰς κατὰ λιμὸν ἐνδείας,
246 τὰς ἐν πολέμοις συστρατείας. ἀεὶ γὰρ καὶ πανταχοῦ παρῆν οὐδένα τόπον ἢ καιρὸν ἀπολείπουσα,
κοινωνὸς ὄντως βίου καὶ τῶν κατὰ τὸν βίον πραγμάτων, ἐξ ἴσου δικαιοῦσα μετέχειν ἀγαθῶν ὁμοῦ
καὶ κακῶν· οὐ γὰρ ὥσπερ ἔνιαι τὰς μὲν κακοπραγίας ἀπεδίδρασκε, ταῖς δ᾽ εὐτυχίαις ἐφήδρευεν,
ἀλλὰ τὸν ἐν ἀμφοτέραις κλῆρον ὡς ἐπιβάλλοντα
καὶ ἁρμόττοντα γαμετῇ μετὰ προθυμίας πάσης ἀν-
247 εδέχετο.   XLIII. πολλὰ δὲ ἔχων ἐγκώ-

ᵃ For the perfection of ten as used in Scripture, *cf. De
Cong.* 89 ff. (where Gen. xiv. is quoted among other ex-

ceive, often too revolt and are unwilling any longer
to pay the same dues or unable to do so because of
the presence of reason, the chastener. For when
reason puts on its panoply of the virtues and the
doctrines and the lore which embody them, armed
with this irresistible power it mightily overcomes.
For corruptible and incorruptible may not live
together. Now the nine overlords, the four passions 244
and the five senses, are corruptible and the sources
of corruption, but the truly divine and holy Word,
whose stronghold is in the virtues, whose place in the
order of number is tenth, the supremely perfect
number,[a] comes to the contest and with the help of
the mightier power of God wins an easy victory over
the said overlords.

XLII. After this in the course of time he lost the 245
wife who was the darling of his heart and gifted with
every excellence. She showed her wifely love by
numberless proofs, by sharing with him the severance
from his kinsfolk, by bearing without hesitation the
departure from her homeland, the continual and
unceasing wanderings on a foreign soil and privation
in famine, and by the campaigns in which she accompanied him. Everywhere and always she was at his 246
side, no place or occasion omitted, his true partner in
life and life's events, resolved to share alike the good
and ill. She did not, like some other women, run
away from mishaps and lie ready to pounce on pieces
of good luck, but accepted her portion of both with
all alacrity as the fit and proper test of a wedded wife.

XLIII. [b] Many a story I could relate in 247

amples). For its arithmetical virtues *cf. De Dec.* 20 ff. See
App. p. 598.
    [b] For §§ 247-254 see Gen. xvi. 1-6.

μια τῆς ἀνθρώπου διεξιέναι, ἑνὸς ὑπομνησθήσομαι,
ὃ γενήσεται καὶ τῶν ἄλλων σαφεστάτη πίστις.
ἄγονος γὰρ οὖσα καὶ στεῖρα, δείσασα μὴ κατὰ τὸ
παντελὲς ἔρημος γενεᾶς ὁ θεοφιλὴς οἶκος ἀπο-
248 λειφθῇ, προσελθοῦσα τῷ ἀνδρί φησι τάδε· " πολὺν
μὲν ἤδη χρόνον συμβιοῦμεν ἀλλήλοις εὐαρεστοῦντες,
οὗ δὲ χάριν καὶ αὐτοὶ συνεληλύθαμεν καὶ ἡ φύσις
τὴν ἀνδρὸς καὶ γυναικὸς ἡρμόσατο κοινωνίαν,
τέκνων γένεσις οὐκ ἔστιν, ἀλλ' οὐδ' εἰσαῦθις ἐξ
249 ἐμοῦ γε ὑπερήλικος ἤδη γεγονυίας ἐλπίζεται. μὴ
δὴ παραπόλαυε τῆς ἐμῆς ἀγονίας μηδ' ἕνεκα τῆς
πρὸς ἐμὲ εὐνοίας αὐτὸς δυνάμενος εἶναι πατὴρ
κεκώλυσο· ζηλοτυπία γὰρ οὐκ ἂν γένοιτό μοι πρὸς
ἑτέραν, ἣν οὐ δι' ἐπιθυμίαν ἄλογον ἄξῃ, νόμον δὲ
250 φύσεως ἐκπιμπλὰς ἀναγκαῖον. οὗ χάριν οὐχ ὑπερ-
θήσομαι νυμφοστολεῖν ὡς τὸ ἐνδέον ἐμοὶ μέλλουσαν
ἐκπληροῦν· καὶ εἴ γε ἀπαντήσειαν αἱ περὶ σπορᾶς
τέκνων εὐχαί, σὰ μὲν ἔσται τὰ γεννώμενα γνήσια,
251 θέσει δὲ πάντως ἐμά. πρὸς δὲ τὸ ἀνύποπτον τῆς
ζηλοτυπίας ἐμήν, εἰ βούλει, θεράπαιναν ἀγαγοῦ, τὸ
μὲν σῶμα δούλην, ἐλευθέραν δὲ καὶ εὐγενῆ τὴν
διάνοιαν, ἧς ἐκ πολλῶν χρόνων πεῖραν ἔλαβον καὶ
βάσανον, ἀφ' ἧς ἡμέρας τὸ πρῶτον εἰς τὴν ἐμὴν
οἰκίαν ἤχθη, γένος μὲν Αἰγυπτίαν, τὴν δὲ προ-
252 αίρεσιν Ἑβραίαν. ἔστι μὲν ἡμῖν οὐσία πολλὴ καὶ
ἄφθονος πλοῦτος, οὐχ ὡς μετοίκοις—ἤδη γὰρ τῶν
αὐτοχθόνων τοὺς ἐν εὐτυχίαις λαμπραῖς ὑπερβάλ-
λομεν—, κληρονόμος δ' οὐδεὶς ἀποδέδεικται καὶ
διάδοχος, καίτοι γε εἶναι δυνάμενος, ἂν ταῖς ἐμαῖς
253 παραινέσεσι πεισθῇς." ὁ δὲ θαυμάσας τῆς γυναικὸς ἔτι μᾶλλον τὴν ἀεὶ καινουμένην φιλανδρίαν καὶ
νεάζουσαν καὶ τὸ περὶ τοῦ μέλλοντος ἐξεταστικὸν

praise of this woman, but one I will mention which will be the clearest proof that the others are true. Being childless and barren and fearing lest the house beloved of God should be left entirely desolate, she 248 came to her husband and said : " Long have we lived together in mutual goodwill. But the purpose for which we ourselves came together and for which nature formed the union of man and wife, the birth of children, has not been fulfilled, nor is there any future hope of it, through me at least who am now past the age. But do not let the trouble of my 249 barrenness extend to you, or kind feeling to me keep you from becoming what you can become, a father, for I shall have no jealousy of another woman, whom you will take not for unreasoning lust but in fulfilment of nature's inevitable law. And therefore I 250 shall not be backward to lead to you a bride who will supply what is lacking in myself. And if our prayers for the birth of children are answered the offspring will be yours in full parenthood, but surely mine also by adoption. But to avoid any suspicion of 251 jealousy on my part take if you will my handmaiden, outwardly a slave, inwardly of free and noble race, proved and tested by me for many years from the day when she was first brought to my house, an Egyptian by birth, but a Hebrew by her rule of life. We have 252 much substance and abundance of wealth, not on the usual scale of immigrants, for in this we now outshine those of the native inhabitants who are noted for their prosperity, but no heir or successor has appeared, though there may be if you follow my advice." Abraham with increased admiration 253 for the wifely love, which never grew old and was ever showing itself anew, and her careful forethought

PHILO

καὶ προμηθὲς ἄγεται τὴν ὑπ᾿ αὐτῆς δοκιμασθεῖσαν
[37] ἄχρι τοῦ παιδοποιήσασθαι, | ὡς δ᾿ οἱ σαφέστατα
διηγούμενοί φασιν, ἄχρι τοῦ μόνον ἐγκύμονα γενέ-
σθαι· γενομένης δ᾿ οὐκ εἰς μακράν, ἀποσχέσθαι διά
τε φυσικὴν ἐγκράτειαν καὶ τὴν τιμήν, ἣν ἀπένεμε
254 τῇ γαμετῇ. γίνεται μὲν οὖν υἱὸς ἐκ τῆς θεραπαι-
νίδος εὐθὺς τότε, γίνεται δὲ καὶ μακροῖς χρόνοις
ὕστερον γνήσιος ἀπεγνωκόσι τὴν ἐξ ἀλλήλων γένεσιν, ἆθλον καλοκἀγαθίας ἐλπίδος πάσης τελειότερον
τοῦ φιλοδώρου θεοῦ παρασχόντος.

255 XLIV. Τοσαῦτα μὲν ἀπόχρη δείγματα περὶ τῆς
γυναικὸς εἰρῆσθαι, πλείω δ᾿ ἐστὶν ἐγκώμια τοῦ
σοφοῦ, ὧν ὀλίγῳ πρότερον ἔνια διεξῆλθον. λέξω δὲ
καὶ τὸ περὶ τὴν τελευτὴν τῆς γυναικὸς οὐκ ἄξιον
256 ἔργον ἡσυχασθῆναι. τοιαύτην γὰρ ἀποβαλὼν κοινωνὸν τοῦ σύμπαντος βίου, οἵαν ἔδειξεν ὁ λόγος καὶ
μηνύουσιν οἱ χρησμοί, τῆς λύπης ἐπαποδυομένης
ἤδη καὶ κατὰ τῆς ψυχῆς κονιομένης ὥσπερ ἀθλητὴς
ἐπεκράτησε ῥώσας καὶ θαρσύνας εὖ μάλα τὸν
ἀντίπαλον φύσει τῶν παθῶν λογισμόν, ᾧ συμβούλῳ
παρὰ πάντα τὸν βίον χρώμενος τότε διαφερόντως
ἠξίωσε πείθεσθαι τὰ βέλτιστα παραινοῦντι καὶ
257 συμφέροντα. ἦν δὲ ταυτί· μήτε πλέον τοῦ μετρίου
σφαδάζειν ὡς ἐπὶ καινοτάτῃ καὶ ἀγενήτῳ συμφορᾷ
μήτε ἀπαθείᾳ καθάπερ μηδενὸς ὀδυνηροῦ συμβεβηκότος χρῆσθαι, τὸ δὲ μέσον πρὸ τῶν ἄκρων ἑλό-
μενον μετριοπαθεῖν πειρᾶσθαι, τῇ μὲν φύσει τὸ
οἰκεῖον χρέος ἀπολαβούσῃ μὴ δυσχεραίνοντα, τὸ

---

a Presumably as related in the traditions of which Philo
speaks in *Mos.* i. 4. Naturally they credited Abraham with
all the continence possible, and, indeed, it might fairly be
inferred from Gen. xvi. 6.

124

for the future, took the mate whom she had approved
and kept her till she had borne a child, or, as the
surest version of the story runs,[a] only till she became
pregnant, and when this occurred not long after he
abstained from her through his natural continence
and the honour which he paid to his lawful spouse.
So a son was born just at that time to the hand- 254
maiden, but long afterwards the wedded pair, who
had despaired of the procreation of children, had a
son of their own, a reward for their high excellence,
a gift from God the bountiful, surpassing all their
hopes.

XLIV. [b] We need give no further proofs of the 255
merits of this wife. More numerous are those of
the Sage, some of which I have praised in detail a
little earlier. But I will speak of one which concerns
the death of his wife, in which his conduct should
not be passed over in silence. When he had lost 256
his life-long partner, whose qualities have been described in our discourse and are related in the oracles,
when sorrow was making itself ready to wrestle with
his soul, he grappled with it, as in the arena, and
prevailed. He gave strength and high courage to
the natural antagonist of passion, reason, which he
had taken as his counsellor throughout his life and
now particularly was determined to obey, so excellent and profitable were its exhortations. The 257
advice was that he should not grieve over-bitterly
as at an utterly new and unheard-of misfortune, nor
yet assume an indifference as though nothing painful
had occurred, but choose the mean rather than the
extremes and aim at moderation of feeling, not resent
that nature should be paid the debt which is its due,

[b] For §§ 255–261 see Gen. xxiii.

δὲ συμβεβηκὸς ἡσυχῇ καὶ πράως ἐπελαφρίζοντα.
258 μαρτυρίαι δὲ τούτων ἐν ταῖς ἱεραῖς
βίβλοις κατάκεινται, ἃς οὐ θέμις ψευδομαρτυριῶν
ἁλῶναι, μηνύουσαι ὅτι βραχέα τῷ σώματι ἐπιδακρύσας θᾶττον ἀπανέστη τοῦ νεκροῦ, τὸ πενθεῖν
ἐπὶ πλέον, ὡς ἔοικεν, ἀλλότριον ἡγησάμενος σοφίας,
ὑφ' ἧς ἀνεδιδάχθη τὸν θάνατον νομίζειν μὴ σβέσιν
ψυχῆς, ἀλλὰ χωρισμὸν καὶ διάζευξιν ἀπὸ σώματος,
ὅθεν ἦλθεν ἀπιούσης· ἦλθε δέ, ὡς ἐν τῇ κοσμοποιίᾳ
259 δεδήλωται, παρὰ θεοῦ. καθάπερ δὲ οὐδεὶς ἂν
ἄχθοιτο τῶν μετρίων χρέος ἢ παρακαταθήκην
ἀποτίνων τῷ προεμένῳ, τὸν αὐτὸν τρόπον οὐδὲ τῆς
φύσεως ἀπολαμβανούσης τὰ οἰκεῖα χαλεπαίνειν
260 ᾤετο δεῖν, ἀλλὰ τοῖς ἀναγκαίοις ἀσμενίζειν. ὡς δ'
ἧκον οἱ ἐν τέλει τῶν κατὰ τὴν χώραν συναλγή-
σοντες, ἰδόντες οὐδὲν τῶν ἐν ἔθει παρ' αὐτοῖς
γινομένων ἐπὶ τοῖς πενθοῦσιν,[1] οὐκ ὀλόφυρσιν, οὐ
θρῆνον, οὐ κοπετόν, οὐκ ἀνδρῶν, οὐ γυναικῶν, ἀλλὰ
τῆς συμπάσης οἰκίας εὐσταθῆ καὶ νηφάλιον κατ-
ήφειαν, ἐθαύμαζον οὐ μετρίως καὶ τὸν ἄλλον βίον
261 προκαταπεπληγμένοι τοῦ ἀνδρός. εἶτ' οὐ στέγοντες
ἐν ἑαυτοῖς τὰ τῆς ἀρετῆς αὐτοῦ μεγέθη καὶ κάλλη—
πάντα γὰρ ἦν ἐξαίρετα—προσελθόντες ἐξεφώνησαν
[38] | "βασιλεὺς παρὰ θεοῦ εἶ σὺ ἐν ἡμῖν," ἀληθέστατα
λέγοντες· αἱ μὲν γὰρ ἄλλαι βασιλεῖαι πρὸς ἀνθρώπων καθίστανται, πολέμοις καὶ στρατείαις καὶ
κακοῖς ἀμυθήτοις, ἅπερ ἀντεπιφέρουσιν ἀλληλο-
κτονοῦντες οἱ δυναστειῶν ἐφιέμενοι, πεζὰς καὶ
ἱππικὰς καὶ ναυτικὰς δυνάμεις ἐπιτειχίζοντες· τὴν
δὲ τοῦ σοφοῦ βασιλείαν ὀρέγει θεός, ἣν παραλαβὼν
ὁ σπουδαῖος οὐδενὶ μὲν αἴτιος γίνεται κακοῦ, πᾶσι

[1] Perhaps read πένθεσιν as Cohn suggests.

but quietly and gently lighten the blow.[a]

The testimonies for this are to be found in the holy 258 books which may never be convicted of false witness. They show that after weeping for a little over the corpse he quickly rose up from it, holding further mourning, it appears, to be out of keeping with wisdom, which taught him that death is not the extinction of the soul but its separation and detachment from the body and its return to the place whence it came ; and it came, as was shown in the story of creation, from God.[b]   And, as no reasonable 259 person would chafe at repaying a debt or deposit to him who had proffered it, so too he must not fret when nature took back her own, but accept the inevitable with equanimity.   Now, when the chief 260 men of the country came to sympathize and saw nothing of the sort of mourning which was customary with themselves, no wailing, no chanting of dirges, no beating of breasts either of men or of women, but a quiet sober air of sorrow pervading the whole house, they were profoundly amazed, though indeed the rest of his life had struck them with admiration. Then, as the greatness and glory of his virtue in all 261 its pre-eminence were more than they could keep to themselves, they approached him and exclaimed : "Thou art a king from God among us."   The words were indeed true, for other kingdoms are established among men with wars and campaigns and numberless ills which the ambitious for power inflict on each other in mutual slaughter, with forces of foot and horse and ships which they raise for the strife.   But the kingdom of the Sage comes by the gift of God, and the virtuous man who receives it brings no harm

---

[a] See App. pp. 598-599.   [b] *i.e.* in *De Op.* 135.

δὲ τοῖς ὑπηκόοις ἀγαθῶν κτήσεως ὁμοῦ καὶ χρήσεως, εἰρήνην καὶ εὐνομίαν καταγγέλλων.

262　XLV. Ἔστι δὲ καὶ ἀνάγραπτος ἔπαινος αὐτῷ
χρησμοῖς μαρτυρηθείς, οὓς Μωυσῆς ἐθεσπίσθη,[1] δι'
οὗ μηνύεται ὅτι " ἐπίστευσε τῷ θεῷ," ὅπερ λεχθῆναι μὲν βραχύτατόν ἐστιν, ἔργῳ δὲ βεβαιωθῆναι
263　μέγιστον. τίνι γὰρ ἄλλῳ πιστευτέον; ἆρά γε
ἡγεμονίαις ἢ δόξαις καὶ τιμαῖς ἢ περιουσίᾳ πλούτου
καὶ εὐγενείᾳ ἢ ὑγείᾳ καὶ εὐαισθησίᾳ ἢ ῥώμῃ καὶ
κάλλει σώματος; ἀλλὰ ἀρχὴ μὲν πᾶσα σφαλερὸν
μυρίους ἔχουσα τοὺς λοχῶντας ἐφέδρους· εἰ δέ που
καὶ βεβαιωθείη, μετὰ μυρίων ὅσων κακῶν, ἃ δρῶσι
καὶ πάσχουσιν οἱ ἐν ταῖς ἡγεμονίαις, βεβαιοῦται.
264　δόξαι δὲ καὶ τιμαὶ κτῆμα σφαλερώτατον, ἐν ἀκρί-
τοις ἤθεσι καὶ πτηνοῖς λόγοις ἀνεξετάστων ἀνθρώπων σαλεῦον· κἂν εἰ παραμένοι, γνήσιον ἀγαθὸν
265　ἔχειν οὐ πέφυκε. πλοῦτοι δὲ καὶ εὐγένειαι προσ-
ορίζονται[2] μὲν καὶ τοῖς φαυλοτάτοις· εἰ δὲ καὶ
μόνοις σπουδαίοις, ἐγκώμια προγόνων καὶ τύχης
266　ἀλλ' οὐ τῶν ἐχόντων εἰσίν.　　　ἀλλ' οὐδ'
ἐπὶ τοῖς περὶ τὸ σῶμα μέγα φρονεῖν ἄξιον, ἐν οἷς
τὰ ἄλογα ζῷα πλεονεκτεῖ· τίς γὰρ ἀνθρώπων ἰσχυ-
ρότερος ἢ ῥωμαλεώτερος ταύρου μὲν ἐν ἡμέροις, ἐν
δ' ἀγρίοις λέοντος; τίς δ' ὀξυωπέστερος ἱέρακος ἢ
ἀετοῦ; τίς δὲ περὶ ἀκοὴν εὐτυχὴς οὕτως, ὡς τῶν
ζῴων τὸ νωθέστατον, ὄνος; τίς δὲ περὶ τὰς ὀσφρή-
σεις κυνὸς ἀκριβέστερος, ὅν φασιν οἱ κυνηγετικοὶ

---

[1] This use of θεσπίζω in the passive with the person prophesying as subject is very unusual. This passage is the
only example given in L. & S. revised. I should prefer to
read ἐθέσπισε.　　　[2] MSS. προσορμίζονται.

to anyone, but the acquisition and enjoyment of good things to all his subjects, to whom he is the herald of peace and order.[a]

XLV. There is another record of praise attested 262 by words from Moses' prophetic lips. In these it is stated that he " trusted in God." Now that is a little thing if measured in words, but a very great thing if made good by action. For in what else should one 263 trust ? In high offices or fame and honours or abundance of wealth and noble birth or health and efficacy of the senses or strength and beauty of body ? But office is wholly precarious, beset by countless foes who lie in wait for it, and if by chance it is secured the security is accompanied by countless ills in which those in high positions are either the agents or the victims. Fame and honour are a most precarious 264 possession, tossed about on the reckless tempers and flighty words of careless men : and, when it abides, it cannot of its own nature contain genuine good. As for wealth and high birth, they attach themselves 265 even to the most worthless of men, and even if they were confined to the virtuous they would be a compliment not to the actual possessors but to their ancestors and to fortune.   Again, neither 266 should we pride ourselves greatly on bodily endowments in which the unreasoning animals have the advantage over us ; for what man is stronger or more muscular than the bull among domestic and the lion among wild beasts ? Who has a keener sight than the hawk or the eagle ? or who is so favoured in powers of hearing as that stupidest of animals, the ass ? And as for smell, who has more accurate discernment than the hound, which, as the huntsmen

[a] See App. p. 599.

ρινηλατοῦντα τοῖς μακρὰν πτώμασιν εὐσκόπως ἐπι-
τρέχειν οὐ προϊδόμενον; ὅπερ γὰρ ὄψις ἑτέροις,
τοῦτο μυκτῆρες κυσὶ θηρευτικοῖς καὶ ἰχνευτικοῖς.
267 ὑγιεινότατά γε μὴν καὶ ὡς ἔνι μάλιστα ἄνοσα
πλεῖστα τῶν ἀλόγων ζῴων ἐστίν. ἐν δὲ τῷ περὶ
κάλλους ἀγῶνι καὶ τῶν ἀψύχων ἔνιά μοι δοκεῖ νικᾶν
δύνασθαι τὰς ἀνδρῶν ὁμοῦ καὶ γυναικῶν εὐμορφίας
καὶ ὑπερβάλλειν, ἀγάλματα καὶ ξόανα καὶ ζωγρα-
φήματα καὶ συνόλως ὅσα γραφικῆς ἔργα καὶ πλασ-
τικῆς ἐν ἑκατέρα τέχνῃ κατορθούμενα, περὶ ἃ
σπουδάζουσιν Ἕλληνες ὁμοῦ καὶ βάρβαροι πρὸς
κόσμον τῶν πόλεων ἐν τοῖς ἐπιφανεστάτοις χωρίοις
268 ἀνατιθέντες.   XLVI. μόνον οὖν ἀψευδὲς
[39] | καὶ βέβαιον ἀγαθὸν ἡ πρὸς θεὸν πίστις, παρ-
ηγόρημα βίου, πλήρωμα χρηστῶν ἐλπίδων, ἀφορία
μὲν κακῶν, ἀγαθῶν δὲ φορά, κακοδαιμονίας ἀπόγνωσις, γνῶσις εὐσεβείας, κλῆρος εὐδαιμονίας,
ψυχῆς ἐν ἅπασι βελτίωσις ἐπερηρεισμένης καὶ
ἐφιδρυμένης τῷ πάντων αἰτίῳ καὶ δυναμένῳ μὲν
269 πάντα, βουλομένῳ δὲ τὰ ἄριστα. καθάπερ γὰρ οἱ
μὲν δι' ὀλισθηρᾶς ὁδοῦ βαδίζοντες ὑποσκελίζονται
καὶ πίπτουσιν, οἱ δὲ διὰ ξηρᾶς καὶ λεωφόρου ἀ-
πταίστῳ χρῶνται πορείᾳ, οὕτως οἱ διὰ τῶν σω-
ματικῶν μὲν καὶ τῶν ἐκτὸς τὴν ψυχὴν ἄγοντες
οὐδὲν ἀλλ' ἢ πίπτειν αὐτὴν ἐθίζουσιν—ὀλισθηρὰ
γὰρ ταῦτά γε καὶ πάντων ἀβεβαιότατα—οἱ δὲ διὰ
τῶν κατὰ τὰς ἀρετὰς θεωρημάτων ἐπὶ θεὸν σπεύδοντες ἀσφαλῆ καὶ ἀκράδαντον ὁδὸν εὐθύνουσιν, ὡς
ἀψευδέστατα φάναι, ὅτι ὁ μὲν ἐκείνοις πεπιστευκὼς
ἀπιστεῖ θεῷ, ὁ δ' ἀπιστῶν ἐκείνοις πεπίστευκε θεῷ.

ᵃ Or " plenitude."
ᵇ A somewhat inadequate rendering for ἀπόγνωσις, which

tell us, led unerringly by the scent, races to the distant
quarry which it has not seen; for what sight is to
other animals the nostrils are to the hounds used for
hunting or tracking. Health? Why, most of the un- 267
reasoning animals are exceedingly healthy and as far
as possible free from disease. Beauty? In the competition for this, I should say that some lifeless
objects can beat and surpass the comeliness both of
men and women. Such are the images and statues
and pictures and in general all the creations of the
painters and the sculptors which achieve success in
either art and rouse the enthusiasm of Greeks and
barbarians alike, who set them up in the most conspicuous places to adorn their cities.

XLVI. Faith in God, then, is the one sure and in- 268
fallible good, consolation of life, fulfilment[a] of bright
hopes, dearth of ills, harvest of goods, inacquaintance[b]
with misery, acquaintance with piety, heritage of
happiness, all-round betterment of the soul which is
firmly stayed on Him Who is the cause of all things
and can do all things yet only wills the best. For, 269
just as those who walk on a slippery road are tripped
up and fall, while others on a dry highway tread without stumbling, so those who set the soul travelling
along the path of the bodily and the external are but
learning it to fall, so slippery and utterly insecure are
all such things; while those who press onward to God
along the doctrines of virtue walk straight upon a
path which is safe and unshaken, so that we may say
with all truth that belief in the former things is disbelief in God, and disbelief in them belief in God.

generally means "despair," and, in connexion with κακοδαι
μονίας, "confidence of the absence." Philo, however, evidently intends an antithesis of form as well as of sense.

270 ἀλλ' οὐ μόνον τὴν πρὸς τὸ ὂν πίστιν αὐτῷ μαρτυ-
ροῦσιν οἱ χρησμοί, τὴν βασιλίδα τῶν ἀρετῶν, ἀλλὰ
καὶ πρῶτον αὐτὸν ἀπεφήναντο '' πρεσβύτερον,'' τῶν
πρὸ αὐτοῦ τριπλάσια καὶ πολλαπλάσια ἔτη βιω-
σάντων, ὧν οὐδένα παρειλήφαμεν ἀξιωθέντα ταύτης
271 τῆς προσρήσεως.   καὶ μήποτ' εἰκότως· ὁ γὰρ
ἀληθείᾳ πρεσβύτερος οὐκ ἐν μήκει χρόνων ἀλλ' ἐν
ἐπαινετῷ καὶ τελείῳ βίῳ θεωρεῖται. τοὺς μὲν οὖν
αἰῶνα πολὺν τρίψαντας ἐν τῇ μετὰ σώματος ζωῇ
δίχα καλοκαγαθίας πολυχρονίους παῖδας λεκτέον,
μαθήματα πολιᾶς ἄξια μηδέποτε παιδευθέντας, τὸν
δὲ φρονήσεως καὶ σοφίας καὶ τῆς πρὸς θεὸν πίστεως
ἐρασθέντα λέγοι τις ἂν ἐνδίκως εἶναι πρεσβύτερον,
272 παρωνυμοῦντα τῷ πρώτῳ. τῷ γὰρ ὄντι πρῶτος ὁ
σοφὸς τοῦ ἀνθρώπων γένους, ὡς κυβερνήτης μὲν
ἐν νηΐ, ἄρχων δ' ἐν πόλει, στρατηγὸς δ' ἐν πολέμῳ,
καὶ ψυχὴ μὲν ἐν σώματι, νοῦς δ' ἐν ψυχῇ, καὶ πάλιν
οὐρανὸς μὲν ἐν κόσμῳ, θεὸς δ' ἐν οὐρανῷ.
273 ὃς τῆς πρὸς αὐτὸν πίστεως ἀγάμενος τὸν ἄνδρα
πίστιν ἀντιδίδωσιν αὐτῷ, τὴν δι' ὅρκου βεβαίωσιν
ὧν ὑπέσχετο δωρεῶν, οὐκέτι μόνον ὡς ἀνθρώπῳ
θεός, ἀλλὰ καὶ ὡς φίλος γνωρίμῳ διαλεγόμενος·
φησὶ γὰρ '' κατ' ἐμαυτοῦ ὤμοσα,'' παρ' ᾧ ὁ λόγος
ὅρκος ἐστίν, ἕνεκα τοῦ τὴν διάνοιαν ἀκλινῶς καὶ
274 παγίως ἔτι μᾶλλον ἢ πρότερον ἐρηρεῖσθαι. πρεσβύτερος μὲν οὖν καὶ πρῶτος ἔστι τε καὶ λεγέσθω
ὁ ἀστεῖος, νεώτερος δὲ καὶ ἔσχατος πᾶς ἄφρων,
τὰ νεωτεροποιὰ καὶ ἐν ἐσχατιαῖς ταττόμενα
275 μετιών.
[40]   Ταῦτα | μὲν οὖν ἐπὶ τοσοῦτον εἰρήσθω. τῷ δὲ
πλήθει καὶ μεγέθει τῶν ἐπαίνων ἐπιτιθεὶς ὥσπερ
τινὰ κεφαλὴν τοῦ σοφοῦ φησιν, ὅτι τὸν θεῖον νόμον

But not only do the oracles attest his possession of 270
the queen of virtues, faith in the existent, but he is
also the first whom they speak of as elder,[a] though
those who lived before him tripled or many times
multiplied his years. Yet of none of them do we hear
that he was held worthy of the title and rightly, for the
true elder is shown as such not by his length of days
but by a laudable and perfect life. Those who have 271
passed a long span of years in the existence of the
body without goodness or beauty of life must be
called long-lived children who have never been
schooled in the learning worthy of grey hairs ; but he
who is enamoured of sound sense and wisdom and
faith in God may be justly called elder, a name of
like significance to " first." For indeed the wise man 272
is the first of the human race, as a pilot in a ship or a
ruler in a city or a general in war, or again as a soul
in a body and a mind in a soul, or once more heaven
in the world or God in heaven. That God 273
marvelling at Abraham's faith in Him repaid him with
faithfulness by confirming with an oath the gifts which
He had promised, and here He no longer talked with
him as God with man but as a friend with a familiar.
For He, with Whom a word is an oath, yet says " By
Myself have I sworn," [b] so that his mind might be
established more securely and firmly even than it was
before. So, then, the man of worth is elder and first, 274
and so must he be called ; but younger and last is
every fool who pursues the ways which belong to
rebellious youth and stand lowest in the list.

So much for all this, but to these praises of the Sage, 275
so many and so great, Moses adds this crowning saying " that this man did the divine law and the divine

[a] Gen. xxiv. 1 ; LXX. πρεσβύτερος, E.V. "old." [b] Gen. xxii. 16.

καὶ τὰ θεῖα προστάγματα πάντα ἐποίησεν ὁ ἀνὴρ
οὗτος, οὐ γράμμασιν ἀναδιδαχθείς, ἀλλ' ἀγράφῳ τῇ
φύσει σπουδάσας ὑγιαινούσαις καὶ ἀνόσοις ὁρμαῖς
ἐπακολουθῆσαι· περὶ δὲ ὧν ὁ θεὸς ὁμολογεῖ, τί
προσῆκεν ἀνθρώπους ἢ βεβαιότατα πιστεύειν;
276 τοιοῦτος ὁ βίος τοῦ πρώτου καὶ ἀρχηγέτου τοῦ
ἔθνους ἐστίν, ὡς μὲν ἔνιοι φήσουσι, νόμιμος, ὡς
δ' ὁ παρ' ἐμοῦ λόγος ἔδειξε, νόμος αὐτὸς ὢν καὶ
θεσμὸς ἄγραφος.

commands." [a] He did them, not taught by written words, but unwritten nature gave him the zeal to follow where wholesome and untainted impulse led him. And when they have God's promises before them what should men do but trust in them most firmly? Such was the life of the first, the founder 276 of the nation, one who obeyed the law, some will say, but rather, as our discourse has shown, himself a law and an unwritten statute.

[a] Gen. xxvi. 5.

ON JOSEPH

(DE IOSEPHO)

INTRODUCTION TO *DE IOSEPHO*

THE place of this treatise in the series, as well as the remarkable contrast between the character of Joseph as here represented and the Joseph of the allegorical commentary, have been discussed in the General Introduction to this volume. The treatise after a few words about the preparation given by the shepherd's craft for government tells the story of Joseph's dream, his brothers' jealousy, their sale of him to the merchants who in turn sold him to Potiphar and the false report which they made to Jacob (1-27). It contains the first two of the set speeches which are a distinguishing feature of the treatise, viz. Reuben's remonstrance (17-21) and Jacob's lamentation (23-27). The allegorization which follows treats a few scattered points and not the story as a whole. That politicians have to deal with institutions which are conventional rather than natural is indicated by Joseph's name of " Addition " (to Nature), that they must be resourceful by his coat of many colours, that they are often a prey to vanity by the false story that wild beasts had devoured him, that they are often bought and sold by the two sales (28-36) ; and it is to be noted that though the main purpose of the treatise is to show the ideal statesman, these mostly deal with the baser side of political life. When the story is resumed it relates his history in Potiphar's house till his imprisonment, in the course of which we have the eloquent but rather absurd remonstrance of Joseph to Potiphar's wife (37-53). The subjoined allegories are much more relevant than the earlier ones to the substance of the story and to the higher side of the politician. We may see the spiritual barrenness of the multitude and its tendency to

ON JOSEPH

cater for pleasure in Potiphar, the eunuch and cook, its demands on the statesman in Potiphar's wife and the refusal of the true statesman to cringe in Joseph's rejections of her overtures (54-79). In 80-124 the story is carried on through Joseph's life in prison, his interpretation of the dreams and his release and exaltation. Then from 125-147 follows what is not so much an allegory in the proper sense as a meditation on the thought that all life is a dream and the task of a true statesman is to discover and set forth the truths which lie behind this dream. After this we have a few more definitely allegorical interpretations of some of the incidents of Joseph's exaltation as illustrating the attitude of the democracy to the politician, and an attempt to show that the different treatment by Pharaoh of the cook (Potiphar), the butler and the baker represent the different ways in which the body-loving mind regards luxuries and necessities (148-156). From this point onwards to the end the story runs on continuously through the adventures of Joseph and his brethren as it appears in Genesis with, of course, much amplification both of incidents and speeches.

ΒΙΟΣ ΠΟΛΙΤΙΚΟΥ ΟΠΕΡ ΕΣΤΙ ΠΕΡΙ
ΙΩΣΗΦ

I. Τρεῖς μέν εἰσιν ἰδέαι, δι' ὧν τὸ ἄριστον τέλος,
μάθησις, φύσις, ἄσκησις, τρεῖς δὲ καὶ σοφῶν οἱ
πρεσβύτατοι κατὰ Μωυσῆν ἐπώνυμοι τούτων· ὧν
τοὺς βίους ἀναγεγραφώς, τόν τε ἐκ διδασκαλίας καὶ
τὸν αὐτομαθῆ καὶ τὸν ἀσκητικόν, τέταρτον κατὰ τὸ
ἑξῆς ἀναγράψω τὸν πολιτικόν, οὗ πάλιν ἐπώνυμον
ἕνα τῶν φυλάρχων διασυνίστησιν ἐκ πρώτης ἡλικίας
2 συγκροτηθέντα. ἤρξατο μέντοι συγκροτεῖσθαι περὶ
ἔτη γεγονὼς ἑπτακαίδεκα τοῖς κατὰ ποιμενικὴν
θεωρήμασιν, ἃ συνᾴδει τοῖς περὶ πόλιν· ὅθεν οἶμαι
καὶ τὸ ποιητικὸν γένος "ποιμένας λαῶν" τοὺς
βασιλεῖς εἴωθεν ὀνομάζειν· ὁ γὰρ τὴν ποιμενικὴν
κατωρθωκὼς ἄριστος ἂν εἴη καὶ βασιλεύς, τῆς
καλλίστης ζῴων ἀγέλης, ἀνθρώπων, τὴν ἐπιμέλειαν
123 ἐν ταῖς ἐλάττονος σπουδῆς ἀξίαις ἀναδιδαχθείς· καὶ
καθάπερ τῷ μέλλοντι πολεμαρχεῖν καὶ στρατηγεῖν
ἀναγκαιότατον αἱ περὶ τὰ κυνηγέσια μελέται, τὸν |
[42] αὐτὸν τρόπον καὶ οἷς ἐλπὶς ἐπιτροπεῦσαι πόλεως
οἰκειότατον ποιμενικὴ προάγων τις οὖσα ἐπιστα-

---

[a] Gen. xxxvii. 2.   [b] *Il.* i. 263 and often elsewhere

ON JOSEPH

THAT IS, THE LIFE OF THE STATESMAN

I. The factors which produce consummate excel- 1
lence are three in number: learning, nature, practice. And these names are represented in three
of the wise men to whom Moses gives the senior
place. Since I have described the lives of these
three, the life which results from teaching, the life of
the self-taught and the life of practice, I will carry
on the series by describing a fourth life, that of
the statesman. This name again has its representation in one of the patriarchs who, as Moses shews,
was trained to his calling from his earliest youth.
This training was first given to him at about the age 2
of seventeen by the lore of the shepherd's craft,[a]
which corresponds closely to the lore of statesmanship. And therefore I think the order of poets
often speaks of kings as shepherds of peoples,[b] for
success in shepherding will produce the best king,
since through the charge of flocks which deserve
less thought and care he has been taught the charge
of the noblest flock of living creatures—mankind.
And, just as to the future leaders in wars, or in com- 3
manding armies, practice in the hunting-field is most
necessary, so to those who hope to superintend a
state nothing is so suitable as shepherding, which
gives practice in the exercise of authority and

4 σίας καὶ στρατηγίας.ᵃ ἐνορῶν οὖν ὁ πατὴρ αὐτῷ
φρόνημα εὐγενὲς καὶ μεῖζον ἢ κατ' ἰδιώτην ἐθαύ-
μαζε καὶ περιεῖπε καὶ τῶν ἄλλων υἱῶν μᾶλλον
ἔστεργεν, ἐπειδὴ ὀψίγονος ἦν, ὅπερ οὐδενὸς ἧττον
ἀγωγόν ἐστιν εἰς εὔνοιαν· καὶ ἅτε φιλόκαλος ὢν
ἐζωπύρει τὴν τοῦ παιδὸς φύσιν ἐξαιρέτοις καὶ
περιτταῖς ἐπιμελείαις, ἵνα μὴ ἐντύφηται μόνον,
5 ἀλλὰ καὶ θᾶττον ἐκλάμψῃ. II. φθόνος
δὲ ὁ ἀεὶ ταῖς μεγάλαις εὐπραγίαις ἀντίπαλος καὶ
τότε πᾶσι τοῖς μέρεσιν οἰκίαν κατορθοῦσαν ἐπι-
θέμενος διέστησε καθ' ἑνὸς πολλοὺς ἀδελφοὺς
ἀλείψας, οἳ τῇ πρὸς ἐκεῖνον εὐνοίᾳ τοῦ πατρὸς
ἰσόρροπον δύσνοιαν ἐπεδείκνυντο μισοῦντες ὅσον
ἐστέργετο· τὸ δὲ μῖσος οὐκ ἐξελάλουν, ἀλλ' ἐν
ἑαυτοῖς ἐταμίευον, ὅθεν εἰκότως ἀργαλεώτερον
ἐφύετο· τὰ γὰρ στεγόμενα πάθη μὴ διαπνέοντα τοῖς
6 ἐπισχοῦσι λόγοις βαρύτερα. χρώμενος οὖν ἀκάκοις
τοῖς ἤθεσι καὶ τὴν ὑποικουροῦσαν ἔχθραν ἐκ τῶν
ἀδελφῶν οὐ συνιείς, ὄναρ ἰδὼν αἴσιον, ὡς δὴ εὔνοις
διηγεῖται· " ἔδοξα " γάρ φησιν " ἀμήτου καιρὸν
ἐφεστάναι καὶ πάντας ἡμᾶς ἀφικομένους εἰς τὸ
πεδίον ἐπὶ τὴν τοῦ καρποῦ συλλογὴν δρέπανα
λαβόντας θερίζειν, αἰφνίδιον δὲ τὸ μὲν ἐμὸν δράγμα
ὑπανίστασθαι καὶ μετεωρισθὲν ὀρθοῦσθαι, τὰ δὲ
ὑμέτερα ὥσπερ ἀπὸ συνθήματος ἐπιδραμόντα τεθηπέναι καὶ μετὰ τιμῆς τῆς πάσης προσκυνεῖν."

ᵃ This can hardly be right: though στρατηγία is sometimes
used in the civic sense of the praetorship, Philo is not likely
to have used so predominantly military a word where the civic
is in antithesis to the military. Two mss. have δημαγωγίας,
but neither is this a very suitable word. What is wanted is
ἡγεμονίας, or its equivalent. See also App. p. 600.

generalship.[a] So his father, observing in him a noble 4
spirit which rose above ordinary conditions, rendered to him high admiration and respect, while his
love for this child of his later years—and nothing
conduces to affection more than this—exceeded his
love for his other sons. And being himself a lover
of excellence, by special and exceptional attentions
he fostered the fire of the boy's nature, in the hope
that it would not merely smoulder but burst rapidly
into flame. II. [b]But envy, which is ever 5
the enemy of high success, in this case too set to
work and created division in a household where every
part had been happily flourishing, and stirred up
the many brethren against the one. They displayed
ill-will to Joseph as a counterpoise to his father's
goodwill, and equalled his love with their hatred.[c]
They did not, however, proclaim that hatred aloud,
but kept it a secret among themselves, and thus it
naturally grew to greater bitterness. For emotions
which are cooped up and find no vent become more
violent because expression is stifled. Joseph in the 6
simple innocence of his nature had no notion of the
enmity which was lurking in his brothers' hearts, and,
believing them to be friendly, told them a significant
dream which he had seen. " I thought," he said,
" that harvest-time was with us, and that we had all
come to the plain to gather in the crops. We had
taken our sickles and were reaping, when suddenly
my sheaf rose and stood bolt upright, while yours,
as though at a signal, rushed up in astonishment and
did homage to mine with every mark of honour."

[b] §§ 5–27 follow fairly closely the narrative of Gen. xxxvii.
[c] Literally " hating him as much as he was loved " (by his
father).

7 οἱ δὲ εἰς σύνεσιν ἀκριβεῖς καὶ δεινοὶ διὰ συμβόλων ἰχνηλατῆσαι πρᾶγμ᾽ ἀδηλούμενον¹ εἰκόσι στοχασμοῖς "μὴ νομίζεις" ἔφασαν "ἔσεσθαι βασιλεὺς
ἡμῶν καὶ κύριος; ταῦτα γὰρ διὰ τῆς κατεψευσμένης
φαντασίας ὑπαινίττῃ." τὸ δὲ μῖσος ἔτι μᾶλλον
ἐζωπυρεῖτο προσλαμβάνον ἀεί τινα καινὴν πρόφασιν
8 εἰς συναύξησιν. ὁ δὲ οὐδὲν ὑπιδόμενος ὀλίγαις
ὕστερον ἡμέραις ὄναρ ἰδὼν ἕτερον καταπληκτικώ-
τερον τοῦ προτέρου τοῖς ἀδελφοῖς ἀνέφερεν· ᾤετο
γὰρ ἥλιον καὶ σελήνην καὶ ἕνδεκα ἀστέρας ἥκοντας προσκυνεῖν αὐτόν, ὡς τὸν πατέρα θαυμάσαντα
τὸ γεγονὸς ἐναποθέσθαι τῇ διανοίᾳ ταμιεύοντα καὶ
9 σκοπούμενον τὸ ἐσόμενον. ἐμβριθῶς δ᾽ ἐνουθέτει
τὸν παῖδα κατὰ δέος τοῦ μή τι διαμαρτεῖν καὶ
φησιν· "ἆρα δυνησόμεθα ἐγὼ καὶ ἡ μήτηρ καὶ
οἱ ἀδελφοὶ προσκυνῆσαί σε;—διὰ μὲν γὰρ ἡλίου
τὸν πατέρα, διὰ δὲ σελήνης τὴν μητέρα, διὰ δὲ
[43] τῶν ἕνδεκα ἀστέρων τοὺς | ἕνδεκα ἀδελφοὺς ὑπο-
σημαίνειν ἔοικας—ὃ μηδὲ εἰς νοῦν ποτε ἔλθοι τὸν
σόν, ὦ παῖ, λαθοῦσα δὲ καὶ ἡ μνήμη τῶν φανέν-
των ὑπεξέλθοι· τὸ γὰρ τὴν ἐπὶ τοῖς οἰκείοις ἐλπίζειν
καὶ καραδοκεῖν ἡγεμονίαν ἀπευκτὸν ἄγαν παρ᾽ ἐμοὶ
κριτῇ, νομίζω δὲ καὶ παρὰ πᾶσιν, ὅσοις ἰσότητος
10 μέλει καὶ συγγενικῶν δικαίων." εὐλαβηθεὶς δ᾽ ὁ πατήρ, μή τις ἐκ τῆς συνδιαιτήσεως ἐπι-
γένηται ταραχὴ καὶ στάσις τοῖς ἀδελφοῖς μνησικα-
κοῦσιν ὑπὲρ τῶν ὀνειράτων τῷ θεασαμένῳ, τοὺς μὲν
ἐκπέμπει ποιμανοῦντας, τὸν δὲ οἴκοι παρεφύλαττεν
ἄχρι καιροῦ τοῦ προσήκοντος, εἰδὼς ὅτι τῶν τῆς

¹ Most mss. πρᾶγμα δηλούμενον which Cohn in his translation adopted (taking it with διὰ συμβόλων). The order of
words seems to me to favour his earlier view.

His brothers, being men of keen intelligence, skil- 7
ful at interpreting symbols and thus by probable
conjectures discovering the obscure, replied : " Do
you think that you will be our lord and king ? For
that is what you hint at in this lying vision." And
their hatred, ever finding some new ground to aug-
ment it, was still more kindled against him. He, 8
suspecting nothing, a few days after saw and told
his brothers another dream even more astounding
than the former. In this he dreamt that the sun
and moon and eleven stars came and did him homage.
This caused surprise to his father, who laid up the
matter in his mind and carefully watched to see what
the outcome would be. But, fearing that the boy 9
had made a serious mistake,[a] he chid him severely,
saying, " You seem to mean by the sun your father
and by the moon your mother and by the eleven
stars your eleven brothers. Can it be that I and
your mother and your brothers shall do you homage ?
Let no such thought ever enter your mind, my son,
and let the memory of what you saw insensibly fade
away. For the idea of hoping and eagerly expecting
to gain dominion over your family is very odious in
my judgement, and I think that all who care for
equality and justice between kinsfolk must agree."

Then, dreading lest continued associa- 10
tion should breed disturbance and broils among the
brothers through the grudge which they bore against
the dreamer for his visions, Jacob sent them away
to tend the sheep, but kept him at home for such
season as should prove needed. He knew that time

[a] Or " fearing that he himself had made a mistake " (in
setting store upon the dream).

PHILO

ψυχῆς παθῶν καὶ νοσημάτων λέγεται εἶναι χρόνος
ἰατρός, ἱκανὸς καὶ πένθος ἀνελεῖν καὶ θυμὸν σβέσαι
καὶ φόβον θεραπεῦσαι· πάντα γὰρ ἐξευμαρίζει καὶ
11 ὅσα κατὰ τὴν φύσιν δυσίατα. ὡς δ' ἐτόπασε μηδὲν
ἔτι ταῖς διανοίαις αὐτῶν ἔχθος ὑποικουροῦν, ἐκπέμπει τὸν υἱὸν ἅμα μὲν τοὺς ἀδελφοὺς ἀσπασόμενον,
ἅμα δὲ καὶ δηλώσοντα, πῶς ἔχουσιν αὐτοί τε καὶ αἱ
τῶν θρεμμάτων ἀγέλαι.
12 III. Ταύτην τὴν ὁδὸν ἀρχὴν συνέβη γενέσθαι
μεγάλων κακῶν τε αὖ καὶ ἀγαθῶν παρ' ἐλπίδας
ἑκατέρων. ὁ μὲν γὰρ ταῖς ἐπισκήψεσι πειθαρχῶν
τοῦ πατρὸς ᾔει πρὸς τοὺς ἀδελφούς, οἱ δὲ μακρόθεν
ἀφικνούμενον ἰδόντες ἄλλος ἄλλῳ διελάλουν οὐδὲν
εὔφημον, ὁπότε οὐδ' ὀνομαστὶ προσαγορεύειν ἠξίουν
αὐτόν, ἀλλ' ὀνειροπλῆγα καὶ " ἐνυπνιαστὴν " καὶ
τοιαῦτα ἐπεφήμιζον καὶ ἐπὶ τοσοῦτον προῆγον
ὀργῆς, ὥστε καὶ τὸν ἐπ' αὐτῷ φόνον οὐ πάντες ἀλλ'
οἱ πλείους ἐβούλευον καὶ ὑπὲρ τοῦ μὴ καταφωρα-
θῆναι ῥιπτεῖν ἀνελόντες ἐγνώκεσαν εἰς ὄρυγμα γῆς
βαθύτατον· πολλαὶ δέ εἰσι περὶ τὸν τόπον ὕδατος
13 ὀμβρίου δεξαμεναί. καὶ μικροῦ τὸ μέγιστον ἄγος,
ἀδελφοκτονίαν, εἰργάσαντο, εἰ μὴ παρηγορίαις τοῦ
πρεσβυτάτου μόλις ἐπείσθησαν, ὃς παρῄνει μὴ
ἐφάψασθαι τοῦ μιάσματος, ἀλλ' αὐτὸ μόνον εἰς ἓν
τῶν ὀρυγμάτων ῥῖψαι, διανοούμενός τι σωτήριον,
ἵνα λαβὼν μετὰ τὴν ἀναχώρησιν ἀπαθῆ παντὸς
14 κακοῦ παραπέμψῃ τῷ πατρί. συναινεσάντων δέ, ὁ
μὲν προσιὼν ἠσπάζετο, οἱ δὲ ὡς πολέμιον συλ-

146

is said to be the physician of the distempers and ailments of the soul and is able to remove grief, to quench anger and to heal fear, for time relieves everything, even what is naturally hard to cure. But when he guessed that they would have ceased 11 to harbour enmity in their hearts, he sent him partly to salute his brothers and partly to bring him word how it fared with themselves and the flocks under their charge.

III. This journey proved to be the source of great 12 evil and great good, both exceeding anything that could have been expected. For Joseph, in obedience to his father's commands, went to his brethren, but they, when they saw him coming afar off, talked to each other, and their language was very sinister. They did not even deign to speak of him by his name, but called him the dream-driveller and the vision-monger and similar terms. Their anger reached such a pitch that they plotted by a majority, though not unanimously, to murder him, and in order to avoid detection they determined to throw his dead body into a very deep pit in the ground. In that region there are many such, made to hold the rain-water. And they were only deterred from 13 committing that most accursed of deeds, fratricide, by the exhortation of the eldest among them, to which they reluctantly yielded. He urged them to keep their souls clear from the abominable act, and merely to throw him into one of the deep pits, thinking to contrive some means for saving him and hoping when they had gone away to take him up and send him to their father quite unharmed. When 14 they had agreed to this, Joseph approached and saluted them, but they caught hold of him as though

PHILO

λαβόντες ἀπαμπίσχουσι τὴν ἐσθῆτα καὶ τὸν μὲν
καθιμῶσιν εἰς βαθεῖς βόθρους, τὴν δ' ἐρίφου αἵματι
φοινίξαντες διαπέμπονται τῷ πατρὶ πρόφασιν ὡς
ὑπὸ θηρίων δαπανηθέντος.

15 IV. Ἐκείνῃ δὲ τῇ ἡμέρᾳ κατά τινα συντυχίαν
ἔμποροί τινες ὡδοιπόρουν τῶν ἔθος ἐχόντων ἀπ'
Ἀραβίας εἰς Αἴγυπτον κομίζειν φόρτον· οἷς ἀνελκύ-
σαντες τὸν ἀδελφὸν πιπράσκουσιν, ἡγησαμένου τὴν
γνώμην τοῦ καθ' ἡλικίαν τετάρτου· καὶ γὰρ οὗτός
μοι δοκῶ δείσας, μή ποθ' ὑπὸ τῶν ὀργὴν ἀμείλικτον
ἐπ' αὐτῷ ζωπυρούντων δολοφονηθῇ, συνεβούλευ-
[44] σεν ἀποδόσθαι δουλείαν ὑπαλλαττόμενος | θανάτου,
16 κουφότερον κακὸν μείζονος. ὁ δὲ πρεσβύτατος—
οὐ γὰρ παρῆν πιπρασκομένου—διακύψας καὶ μὴ
κατιδών, ὃν ἀπολελοίπει πρὸ μικροῦ, ἐβόα καὶ
ἐκεκράγει καὶ τὰς ἐσθῆτας περιρρηξάμενος ἄνω καὶ
κάτω καθάπερ ἐμμανὴς ἐφέρετο τὰς χεῖρας κροτῶν
καὶ τὰς τρίχας τίλλων, "τί πέπονθε;" λέγων·
17 "εἴπατε, ζῇ ἢ τέθνηκεν; εἰ μὲν οὐκ ἔστι, δείξατέ
μοι τὸν νεκρόν, ἵν' ἐπιδακρύσας τῷ πτώματι λω-
φήσω τῆς συμφορᾶς· ἰδὼν κείμενον παρηγορηθήσο-
μαι. τί καὶ νεκρῷ μνησικακοῦμεν; πρὸς τοὺς
ἐκποδὼν φθόνος οὐδεὶς φύεται. εἰ δὲ ζῇ, ποῖ γῆς
ἀπελήλυθε; φυλάττεται παρὰ τίσιν; οὐ γὰρ δὴ
κἀγὼ καθάπερ ἐκεῖνος ἐν ὑποψίαις εἰμί, ὡς ἀπι-
18 στεῖσθαι." εἰπόντων δ' ὅτι πέπραται καὶ τὴν τιμὴν
ἐπιδεικνυμένων, "καλὴν ἐμπορίαν" εἶπεν "ἐστεί-
λασθε· τὰ κέρδη διανειμώμεθα· τοῖς ἀνδραποδισταῖς
περὶ κακίας ἄθλων ἁμιλλησάμενοι στεφανηφορῶμεν,

---

^a Or "a fine business you have embarked on."

148

he were an enemy in battle and stripped him of his coat. They then let him down by ropes into the open depths. His coat they dyed red in the blood of a kid, and sent it to his father with the story that wild beasts had made away with him.

IV. Now it chanced that day that some merchants 15 belonging to a caravan which was wont to carry wares from Arabia to Egypt were travelling that way. To these they sold their brother, after hauling him up, the leader in this plan being the fourth eldest brother. He, I imagine, feared that Joseph might be treacherously murdered by the others who were inflamed with such merciless wrath against him, and therefore advised them to sell him and thus substitute the 16 lesser evil of slavery for the greater evil of death. The eldest brother had not been present at the sale. When he looked down into the pit and did not see the boy whom he had left there a short time before, he cried aloud and shouted, rent his garments and rushed up and down like a madman, beating his hands together and tearing his hair. "Tell me," he cried, "what 17 has become of him. Is he alive or dead? If he is no more, shew me his dead body, that I may weep over the corpse and thus make the calamity seem lighter. If I see him lying here I shall be comforted. Why do we still bear a grudge to the dead? Envy cannot fasten on the departed. But if he is alive where on earth has he gone? In whose charge is he kept? Tell me, for you cannot suspect me as well as him that 18 you should refuse me your confidence." When they said that he had been sold, and shewed the price that had been paid, "A fine bargain you have made,"[a] he said. "Let us divide the profits. We have competed with slave-dealers for the prize of wickedness;

PHILO

προσυπερβάλλοντες αὐτοὺς ὠμότητι σεμνυνώμεθα·
κατὰ ἀλλοτρίων ἐκεῖνοι συντίθενται, κατὰ δ᾽ οἰκειο-
19 τάτων καὶ φιλτάτων ἡμεῖς. κεκαινούργηται μέγα
ὄνειδος, περιβόητος αἰσχύνη. μνημεῖα καλοκἀγαθίας οἱ πατέρες ἡμῶν πανταχοῦ τῆς οἰκουμένης
ἀπέλιπον, ἀπολείψομεν καὶ ἡμεῖς ἀπιστίας καὶ
μισανθρωπίας ἀθεραπεύτους διαβολάς· φθάνουσι
γὰρ αἱ τῶν μεγαλουργηθέντων φῆμαι πανταχόσε,
τῶν μὲν ἐπαινετῶν θαυμαζόμεναι, τῶν δ᾽ ὑπαιτίων
20 ψόγου καὶ κατηγορίας τυγχάνουσαι. τίνα ἄρα
τρόπον ὁ πατὴρ ἡμῶν τὴν περὶ τῶν συμβεβηκότων
ἀκοὴν δέξεται; τρισμακαρίῳ καὶ τρισευδαίμονι
τὸν καθ᾽ ἡμᾶς βίον ἀβίωτον παρέσχησθε. τὸν
πραθέντα τῆς δουλείας ἢ τοὺς πεπρακότας τῆς
ὠμότητος οἰκτιεῖται; πολὺ μᾶλλον εὖ οἶδα ἡμᾶς,
ἐπεὶ καὶ τοῦ ἀδικεῖσθαι τὸ ἀδικεῖν χαλεπώτερον·
τὸ μὲν γὰρ δυσὶ βοηθεῖται τοῖς μεγίστοις, ἐλέῳ καὶ
ἐλπίδι, τὸ δ᾽ οὐδετέρου μετέχον ἅπασιν ἥττάται
21 τοῖς κριταῖς. ἀλλὰ τί ταῦτα θρηνῶν ἀπηχῶ; βέλτιον ἡσυχάζειν, μὴ καὶ αὐτὸς παραπολαύσω τινὸς
ἀπευκτοῦ· τραχύτατοι γάρ ⟨ἐστε⟩ εἰς ὀργὴν καὶ
ἀπαραίτητοι καὶ πνεῖ λαμπρὸς ἔτι ὁ ἐν ἑκάστῳ
θυμός.''

22 V. Ὡς δ᾽ ἤκουσεν ὁ πατὴρ οὐ τἀληθές, ὅτι
πέπραται ὁ υἱὸς αὐτοῦ, τὸ δὲ ψεῦδος, ὅτι τέθνηκε
καὶ ὡς ὑπὸ θηρίων ἐξανάλωται, πληχθεὶς τὰ μὲν
ὦτα διὰ τῶν λεγομένων, τοὺς δ᾽ ὀφθαλμοὺς διὰ
τοῦ φανέντος—ὁ γὰρ χιτὼν αὐτοῦ κατεσχισμένος |
[45] καὶ κατῃκισμένος καὶ πολλῷ αἵματι πεφοινιγμένος
ἐκεκόμιστο—, συγχυθεὶς ὑπὸ τῆς περιπαθήσεως

---

[a] Or '' his life under the conditions which we have created.''

150

let us wear the crown, and glory that we surpass them in cruelty, for their designs are aimed against aliens, ours against our nearest and dearest. A great and **19** novel reproach has been brought about, a far-famed disgrace. Our fathers left behind in every part of the world records of their noble conduct; we shall leave behind us beyond all retrieving the scandal of our faithlessness and inhumanity. For, when deeds of grave import are done, the rumours of them reach everywhere, causing admiration where they are praiseworthy, censure and contumely when they are guilty. How will our father receive the report of the **20** event? Thrice blessed he was and thrice happy, and ye have made his life with us*a* intolerable. Which will he pity most, the sold for his enslavement or the sellers for their cruelty? Surely us far more than him, since it is less grievous to suffer wrong than to do it.*b* The former is assisted by two mighty forces, pity and hope; the latter has no part in either, and in the judgement of all comes off the worst. But why **21** do I lament thus wildly? It were better to hold my peace, lest I too come in for a share in some horrible fate. For ye are exceedingly savage of temper and merciless, and the fierceness in each heart is still in full blast."

V. When his father heard, not the truth that his **22** son had been sold, but the lie that he was dead and had seemingly been devoured by wild beasts, the words that he heard and the sight that he saw fell like a blow on his ears and eyes. For Joseph's tunic had been brought to him rent and marred and stained scarlet with much blood. Collapsing under his great

---

But I should prefer to read as Mangey suggests τὸ καθ' ἡμᾶς = "as far as we can do it."   *b* See App. p. 600.

PHILO

ἀχανὴς ἐπὶ πλεῖστον χρόνον ἔκειτο, μηδ' ὅσον τὴν
κεφαλὴν ἐπᾶραι δυνάμενος, θλιβούσης καὶ ἐκτραχη-
23 λιζούσης τῆς συμφορᾶς. εἶθ' ὥσπερ τινὰ πηγὴν
δακρύων ἐξαίφνης ἀνιεὶς μετ' οἰμωγῆς πικρᾶς
παρειὰς καὶ γένεια καὶ στέρνα κατένιπτε καὶ τὰς
περὶ αὐτὸν ἐσθῆτας ἅμα τοιαῦτ' ἐπιλέγων· " οὐχ ὁ
θάνατός με λυπεῖ, τέκνον, ἀλλ' ὁ τούτου τρόπος[1]· εἰ
ἐπὶ γῆς ἐτάφης τῆς σῆς, παρηγορούμην, ἐθερά-
πευσα, ἐνοσήλευσα πρότερον, ἀποθνήσκοντι τε-
λευταίων ἀσπασμῶν ἐκοινώνησα, τοὺς ὀφθαλμοὺς
συνέκλεισα, ἐπεδάκρυσα κειμένῳ τῷ νεκρῷ, πολυ-
τελῶς ἐκήδευσα, τῶν νομιζομένων οὐδὲν παρ-
24 έλιπον. ἀλλ' εἰ καὶ ἐπὶ τῆς ξένης, εἶπον ἄν· τὸ
οἰκεῖον ὄφλημα τῆς φύσεως ἀπολαβούσης, ὦ οὗτος,
μὴ κατήφει· πρὸς ζῶντας αἱ πατρίδες, ἀποθανόντων
δὲ πᾶσα γῆ τάφος· ὠκύμορος οὐδεὶς ἢ πάντες
ἄνθρωποι, καὶ γὰρ ὁ μακροβιώτατος ὀλιγοχρόνιος
25 ἀντεξεταζόμενος αἰῶνι. εἰ δὲ δὴ καὶ βιαίως καὶ
ἐξ ἐπιβουλῆς ἔδει θνήσκειν, ἢν ἄν μοι κουφότερον
κακόν, ὑπ' ἀνθρώπων ἀναιρεθέντος, οἳ κτείναντες
νεκρὸν ἂν ἠλέησαν, ὡς ἐπαμήσασθαι κόνιν καὶ τὸ
σῶμα συγκρύψαι· εἰ δὲ καὶ πάντων ἐγεγένηντο
ὠμότατοι, τί πλέον εἶχον ἢ ῥίψαντες ἄταφον ἀπ-
αλλάττεσθαι; τῶν δ' ἐν ὁδῷ παριόντων ἴσως τις
ἐπιστὰς καὶ θεασάμενος, οἶκτον τῆς κοινῆς λαβὼν
φύσεως, ἐπιμελείας καὶ ταφῆς ἠξίωσε. νυνὶ δ',
ὡς λόγος, ἀτιθάσοις καὶ σαρκοβόροις θηρσὶν εὐωχία
καὶ θοίνη γέγονας γευσαμένοις καὶ ἑστιαθεῖσι τῶν

---

[1] mss. τάφος.

[a] Cf. De Abr. 257.
[b] Perhaps a somewhat distorted reminiscence of ἀνδρῶν
γὰρ ἐπιφανῶν πᾶσα γῆ τάφος Thuc. ii. 43.

emotion, he lay for a great while with closed lips, not even able to lift his head, so utterly did the calamity afflict and break him down. Then, suddenly pouring 23 forth tears like a fountain, he watered his cheeks and chin and breast and his own raiment, while bitterly wailing, and uttered such words as these : " Child, it is not your death which grieves me, but the manner of it. If you had been buried in your own land, I should have comforted and watched and nursed your sick-bed, exchanged the last farewells as you died, closed your eyes, wept over the body as it lay there, given it a costly funeral and left none of the customary rites undone. Nay, even if it had been on foreign 24 soil, I should have said to myself : ' Man, be not downcast that nature has recovered the forfeit that was her due.'ᵃ Separate countries concern the living : every land is the tomb of the dead.ᵇ Death comes early to none, or rather it comes early to all, for few are the years of the longest-lived compared with eternity. And, indeed, if you needs must have died 25 by violence or through premeditation, it would have been a lighter ill to me, slain as you would have been by human beings, who would have pitied their dead victim, gathered some dust and covered the corpse. And then if they had been the cruellest of men, what more could they have done but cast it out unburied and go their way, and then perhaps some passer-by would have stayed his steps, and, as he looked, felt pity for our common nature and deemed the tendance of burial to be its due. But, as it is, you have become, in common phrase, a rich banquet for savage carnivorous beasts who have found my own flesh and blood to their taste, and feasted thereon. I am long 26

PHILO

26 ἐμῶν σπλάγχνων. ἀθλητής εἰμι τῶν ἀβουλήτων, εἰκῆ γεγύμνασμαι πολλαῖς κακοπαθείαις, ἀλώμενος, ξενιτεύων, θητεύων, ἀναγκαζόμενος, ἄχρι καὶ ψυχῆς ἐπιβουλευόμενος ὑφ' ὧν ἥκιστ' ἐχρῆν· καὶ πολλὰ μὲν εἶδον, πολλὰ δ' ἤκουσα, μυρία δ' αὐτὸς ἔπαθον τῶν ἀνηκέστων, ἐφ' οἷς παιδευθεὶς μετριοπαθεῖν οὐκ ἐγνάμφθην· ἀλλ' οὐδὲν τοῦ συμβεβηκότος ἀφορητότερον, ὅ μου τὴν ῥώμην τῆς ψυχῆς ἀνατέ-
27 τροφε καὶ καθῄρηκε. τί γὰρ μεῖζον ἢ οἰκτρότερον πένθος; ἡ μὲν ἐσθὴς τοῦ παιδὸς διακεκόμισταί μοι τῷ πατρί, τοῦ δὲ οὐ μέρος, οὐ μέλος, οὐ βραχὺ λείψανον· ἀλλ' ὁ μὲν ὅλος δι' ὅλων δεδαπάνηται μηδὲ ταφῆς δυνηθεὶς μεταλαχεῖν, ἡ δ' οὐδ' ἂν εἰσπεμφθῆναί μοι δοκεῖ τὸ παράπαν, εἰ μὴ πρὸς ἀνίας ὑπόμνησιν καὶ ὧν ὑπέμεινε καίνωσιν, εἰς ἀλήστους καὶ συνεχεῖς ἐμοὶ συμφοράς.'' καὶ ὁ μὲν
[46] τοιαῦτ' ἀπωδύρετο. οἱ δ' ἔμποροι | πιπράσκουσι τὸν παῖδα ἐν Αἰγύπτῳ τῶν εὐνούχων τινὶ τοῦ βασιλέως, ὅς ἐστιν ἀρχιμάγειρος.

28 VI. Ἄξιον μέντοι μετὰ τὴν ῥητὴν διήγησιν καὶ τὰ ἐν ὑπονοίαις προσαποδοῦναι· σχεδὸν γὰρ τὰ πάντα ἢ τὰ πλεῖστα τῆς νομοθεσίας ἀλληγορεῖται. ὁ τοίνυν ἐπικρινόμενος τρόπος παρὰ μὲν Ἑβραίοις Ἰωσὴφ καλεῖται, παρὰ δ' Ἕλλησι '' κυρίου πρόσθεσις,'' εὐθυβολώτατον ⟨ὄνομα⟩ καὶ τῷ δηλουμένῳ πράγματι οἰκειότατον· προσθήκη γάρ ἐστι τῆς τὸ κῦρος ἁπάντων ἀνημμένης φύσεως ἡ κατὰ δήμους

---

[a] So lxx. E.V. "An officer of Pharaoh's, the captain of the guard."

154

trained in the athletics of adversity, drilled by many a random stroke of misfortune, a wanderer, a stranger, a serf, a thrall, my very life and soul a mark for the malice of those by whom I should least have been so treated. Many desperate calamities I have seen and heard : thousands of them have I experienced myself, but trained to moderate my feelings at such I remained unmoved. But none was more unbearable than this event which has overturned and destroyed the strength of my soul. For what sorrow could be 27 greater or more pitiful ? My son's raiment has been conveyed to me, his father, but not a part of him, not a limb, not a tiny fragment. But, while he has been utterly made away with beyond even any possibility of burial, his raiment too would not have been sent to me at all save to remind me of my sorrow, and to make his sufferings live again as calamities constant and indelible to myself." Thus did he bewail. But the merchants sold the boy in Egypt to one of the king's eunuchs who was his chief cook.[a]

VI. After this literal account of the story, it will 28 be well to explain the underlying meaning, for, broadly speaking, all or most of the law-book is an allegory. The kind of character then here under discussion is called in the Hebrew "Joseph," but in our language is "addition of a lord," a most significant title well suited to the thing which it indicates, since polity as seen in the various peoples is an addition to nature who is invested with a universal lordship.[b]

[b] The interpretation of Joseph as = "Addition" has appeared in *De Mut.* 89 and *De Som.* ii. 47 without any appendage. There, however, it is applied to adventitious wealth, luxuries and the like. Here the appendage "of a lord" helps Philo in the political interpretation which he gives. See further App. p. 600.

PHILO

29 πολιτεία. ἡ μὲν γὰρ μεγαλόπολις ὅδε ὁ κόσμος
ἐστὶ καὶ μιᾷ χρῆται πολιτείᾳ καὶ νόμῳ ἑνί· λόγος
δέ ἐστι φύσεως προστακτικὸς μὲν ὧν πρακτέον,
ἀπαγορευτικὸς δὲ ὧν οὐ ποιητέον· αἱ δὲ κατὰ
τόπους αὗται πόλεις ἀπερίγραφοί τέ εἰσιν ἀριθμῷ
καὶ πολιτείαις χρῶνται διαφερούσαις καὶ νόμοις
οὐχὶ τοῖς αὐτοῖς, ἄλλα γὰρ παρ' ἄλλοις ἔθη καὶ
30 νόμιμα παρεξευρημένα καὶ προστεθειμένα. αἴτιον
δὲ τὸ ἄμικτον καὶ ἀκοινώνητον οὐ μόνον Ἑλλήνων
πρὸς βαρβάρους ἢ βαρβάρων πρὸς Ἕλληνας, ἀλλὰ
καὶ τὸ ἑκατέρου γένους ἰδίᾳ πρὸς τὸ ὁμόφυλον· εἶθ'
ὡς ἔοικε τὰ ἀναίτια αἰτιώμενοι, καιροὺς ἀβουλήτους, ἀγονίαν καρπῶν, τὸ λυπρόγεων, τὴν θέσιν ὅτι
παράλιος ἢ μεσόγειος ἢ κατὰ νῆσον ἢ κατὰ ἤπειρον
ἢ ὅσα τούτοις ὁμοιότροπα, τἀληθὲς ἡσυχάζουσιν·
ἔστι δ' ἡ πλεονεξία καὶ ἡ πρὸς ἀλλήλους ἀπιστία, δι'
ἃς οὐκ ἀρκεσθέντες τοῖς τῆς φύσεως θεσμοῖς τὰ
δόξαντα συμφέρειν κοινῇ τοῖς ὁμογνώμοσιν ὁμίλοις
31 ταῦτα νόμους ἐπεφήμισαν. ὥστε εἰκότως προσθῆκαι μᾶλλον αἱ κατὰ μέρος πολιτεῖαι μιᾶς τῆς
κατὰ τὴν φύσιν· προσθῆκαι μὲν γὰρ οἱ κατὰ πόλεις
νόμοι τοῦ τῆς φύσεως ὀρθοῦ λόγου, προσθήκη
δέ ἐστι πολιτικὸς ἀνὴρ τοῦ βιοῦντος κατὰ φύσιν.

32   VII. οὐκ ἀπὸ σκοποῦ μέντοι καὶ
χιτῶνα ποικίλον ἀναλαμβάνειν λέγεται· ποικίλον
γὰρ πολιτεία καὶ πολύτροπον, μυρίας ὅσας ἐνδεχο-
μένη μεταβολάς, προσώποις, πράγμασιν, αἰτίαις,

ᵃ This term for the Stoic ideal of the world conceived of as
a state and expressed in the name κοσμοπολίτης has been used
in De Op. 19 and appears again in Mos. ii. 51. It is not
quoted from any other writer than Philo in this sense. Cf.
also μεγαλοπολίτης De Op. 143.

For this world is the Megalopolis or "great city," [a] 29 and it has a single polity and a single law, and this is the word or reason of nature, commanding what should be done and forbidding what should not be done. But the local cities which we see are unlimited in number and subject to diverse polities and laws by no means identical, for different peoples have different customs and regulations which are extra inventions and additions. The cause of this is the reluctance to 30 combine or have fellowship with each other, shewn not only by Greeks to barbarians and barbarians to Greeks, but also within each of them separately in dealing with their own kin. And then we find them alleging causes for this which are no real causes, such as unfavourable seasons, want of fertility, poverty of soil or how the state is situated, whether it is maritime or inland or whether it is on an island or on the mainland and the like. The true cause they never mention, and that is their covetousness and mutual mistrusts, which keep them from being satisfied with the ordinances of nature, and lead them to give the name of laws to whatever approves itself as advantageous to the communities which hold the same views. Thus naturally particular polities are rather 31 an addition to the single polity of nature, for the laws of the different states are additions to the right reason of nature, and the politician is an addition to the man whose life accords with nature.

VII. Further, he is quite properly said to assume a 32 coat of varied colours,[b] for political life is a thing varied and multiple, liable to innumerable changes brought about by personalities, circumstances,

---

[b] Gen. xxxvii. 3. Observe that the point has not been mentioned in the narrative.

πράξεων ἰδιότησι, καιρῶν καὶ τόπων διαφοραῖς.
33 ὥσπερ γὰρ κυβερνήτης ταῖς τῶν πνευμάτων μεταβολαῖς συμμεταβάλλει τὰς πρὸς εὔπλοιαν βοηθείας,
εὐθύνων τὸ σκάφος οὐχ ἑνὶ τρόπῳ, καὶ ἰατρὸς οὐ
μιᾷ χρῆται θεραπείᾳ πρὸς ἅπαντας τοὺς κάμνοντας,
ἀλλ’ οὐδὲ πρὸς ἕνα, τοῦ πάθους μὴ ἐπιμένοντος,
ἀλλ’ ἐπιτηρῶν ἀνέσεις, ἐπιτάσεις, πληρώσεις, κενώσεις, αἰτίων μεταβολὰς ποικίλλει ταῦτα¹ πρὸς
[47] σωτηρίαν ποτὲ μὲν ταυτὶ ποτὲ δὲ ταυτὶ | προσ-
34 φέρων, οὕτως, οἶμαι, καὶ τὸν πολιτικὸν ἀναγκαῖον
εἶναί τινα πολυειδῆ καὶ πολύμορφον, ἕτερον μὲν
κατ’ εἰρήνην, ἕτερον δ’ ἐν πολέμῳ, ἄλλον δὲ ἐπι-
συνισταμένων ὀλίγων ἢ πολλῶν, τῶν μὲν ὀλίγων
εὐτόνως κατεξανιστάμενον, μετὰ δὲ πειθοῦς τοῖς
πολλοῖς ὁμιλοῦντα, καὶ ὅπου μὲν μετὰ κινδύνου τὸ
εἶναι,² διὰ τὸ κοινωφελὲς φθάνοντα τοὺς ἄλλους
αὐτουργίᾳ, ὅπου δὲ πόνων ἡ σκέψις, ἑτέροις ὑπ-
35 ηρετεῖν ἐξιστάμενον. εὖ μέντοι τὸ φάναι πιπρά-
σκεσθαι τὸν ἄνθρωπον· ὁ μὲν γὰρ δημοκόπος καὶ
δημηγόρος ἀναβὰς ἐπὶ τὸ βῆμα, καθάπερ τὰ πι-
πρασκόμενα τῶν ἀνδραπόδων, δοῦλος ἀντ’ ἐλευθέρου
γίνεται διὰ τῶν τιμῶν, ἃς δοκεῖ λαμβάνειν, ἀπ-
36 αχθεὶς ὑπὸ μυρίων δεσποτῶν. ὁ δ’ αὐτὸς καὶ
θηριάλωτος εἰσάγεται· θηρίον δὲ ἀτίθασον ἡ
λοχῶσα κενοδοξία συναρπάζουσα καὶ διαφθείρουσα

---

¹ Unless ἀνέσεις etc. can represent processes rather than
symptoms, in which case we should have to change, as
Mangey suggested, αἰτίων into σιτίων, ταῦτα is quite illogical.
Cohn suggests πάντα or τά. The latter is adopted in the
translation.

² This τὸ εἶναι seems quite impossible and the reading of
some mss. τοῦ εἶναι (" danger to existence "), though thought
possible by Cohn, does not commend itself. I suggest for

motives, individualities of conduct, differences in occasions and places. The pilot is helped to a success- 33 ful voyage by means which change with the changes of the wind, and does not confine his guidance of the ship to one method. The physician does not use a single form of treatment for all his patients, nor even for an individual if the physical condition does not remain unaltered, but he watches the lowering and the heightening of the strain, its alternations of fullness and emptiness and all the changes of symptoms,[a] and varies his salutary processes, sometimes using one kind and sometimes another. And 34 so too the politician must needs be a man of many sides and many forms. He must be a different man in peace from what he is in war, another man as those who venture to oppose him are few or many, resisting the few with vigorous action but using persuasion in his dealings with the many, and when danger is involved he will, to effect the common good, outstrip all others in his personal activity, but when the prospect is one of labour merely he will stand aside and leave others to serve him. Again it 35 is rightly said that this person is sold, for when the would-be popular orator mounts the platform, like a slave in the market, he becomes a bond-servant instead of a free man, and, through the seeming honours which he receives, the captive of a thousand masters. Again, he is also represented as the prey 36 of wild beasts, and indeed the vainglory which lies in ambush and then seizes and destroys those who

<hr />

[a] Lit. "causes."

consideration τὸ ἰέναι διὰ τοῦ κοινωφελοῦς (according to the common idiom of ἰέναι διά). "When the path of serving the commonweal involves danger," etc.

τοὺς χρωμένους. οἱ δ' ὠνησάμενοι καὶ πιπράσκου-
σιν· οὐ γὰρ εἷς δεσπότης τῶν πολιτευομένων, ἀλλ'
ὄχλος, ἐξ ἑτέρων ἕτεροι κατά τινας ἐφεδρείας καὶ
διαδοχάς· οἱ δὲ τρίπρατοι κακῶν θεραπόντων
τρόπον ἀλλάττουσι τοὺς κυρίους οὐχ ὑπομένοντες
τοὺς προτέρους διὰ τὴν ἀψίκορον καὶ φιλόκαινον
τῶν ἠθῶν ἀνωμαλίαν.

37 VIII. Τοσαῦτα καὶ περὶ τούτων. ὁ μέντοι
νεανίας εἰς Αἴγυπτον ἀχθεὶς καὶ γενόμενος, ὡς
ἐλέχθη, παρ' εὐνούχῳ δεσπότῃ, τῆς καλοκἀγαθίας
καὶ εὐγενείας πεῖραν ὀλίγαις ἡμέραις δοὺς τὴν ἐπὶ
τοῖς ὁμοδούλοις ἀρχὴν παραλαμβάνει καὶ συμπάσης
τῆς οἰκίας τὴν ἐπιμέλειαν· ἤδη γὰρ ὁ κτησάμενος
ἐτεκμηριοῦτο διὰ πολλῶν, ὡς οὐκ ἄνευ θείας ἐπιφροσύνης ἐκεῖνος ἕκαστα λέγει τε καὶ πράττει.
38 τῷ μὲν οὖν δοκεῖν ὑπὸ τοῦ πριαμένου καθίστατο
τῆς οἰκίας ἐπίτροπος, ἔργῳ δὲ καὶ ταῖς ἀληθείαις
ὑπὸ φύσεως μνωμένης αὐτῷ πόλεων καὶ ἔθνους καὶ
χώρας μεγάλης ἡγεμονίαν· ἔδει γὰρ τὸν μέλλοντα
ἔσεσθαι πολιτικὸν ἐγγυμνάσασθαι καὶ ἐνασκηθῆναι
πρότερον τοῖς κατ' οἰκονομίαν· οἰκία τε γὰρ πόλις
ἐστὶν ἐσταλμένη καὶ βραχεῖα καὶ οἰκονομία συν-
ηγμένη τις πολιτεία, ὡς καὶ πόλις μὲν οἶκος μέγας,
39 πολιτεία δὲ κοινή τις οἰκονομία. δι' ὧν μάλιστα
παρίσταται τὸν αὐτὸν οἰκονομικόν τε εἶναι καὶ
πολιτικόν, κἂν τὰ πλήθη καὶ μεγέθη τῶν ὑπο-
κειμένων διαλλάττῃ· καθάπερ ἐπὶ ζωγραφίας ἔχει

---

^a The false statement, as in *De Som.* ii. 65, is treated as
true for the purposes of allegory. *Cf. De Mig.* 21.
^b §§ 37-53 follow the narrative of Gen. xxxix.
^c See note on *De Abr.* 99.

indulge it is a savage beast.[a] Once more his purchasers sell him again, for politicians have not one but a multitude of masters who buy them one from another, each waiting to take his turn in the succession, and those who are thus sold again and again like bad servants change their masters, because, capricious and fitful in character as they are and ever hankering after novelty, they cannot endure their old lords.

VIII. [b] Enough on this subject also. To resume the 37 story, when the youth had been brought to Egypt and as I have said placed with the eunuch as his master, he gave proof in a few days of his nobility of character and nature, and therefore he received authority over his fellow-servants and the charge of the whole household; for his owner had already observed many signs that everything which he said or did was under God's directing care. So, while in outward 38 appearance it was his purchaser who appointed him steward of his household, in fact and reality it was nature's [c] doing, who was taking steps to procure for him the command of whole cities and a nation and a great country. For the future statesman needed first to be trained and practised in house management; for a house is a city compressed into small dimensions, and household management may be called a kind of state management, just as a city too is a great house and statesmanship the household management of the general public.[d] All this shews 39 clearly that the household manager is identical with the statesman, however much what is under the purview of the two may differ in number and size. The same holds with sculpture and painting, for the

♦ See App. p. 600.

καὶ πλαστικῆς· ὁ γὰρ ἀγαθὸς ἀνδριαντοποιὸς ἢ ζω-
γράφος, ἐάν τε πολλὰ καὶ κολοσσιαῖα μεγέθη
κατασκευάζῃ, ἐάν τε ὀλίγα καὶ βραχύτερα, τὴν
αὐτὴν ἐπιδεικνύμενος τέχνην ὁ αὐτός ἐστι.

40 IX. Σφόδρα δὲ εὐδοκιμῶν ἐν τοῖς κατὰ τὴν
οἰκουρίαν ἐπιβουλεύεται πρὸς τῆς τοῦ δεσπότου
[48] γυναικὸς ἐπιβουλὴν τὴν ἐξ ἔρωτος | ἀκολάστου.
τῇ γὰρ εὐμορφίᾳ ἐπιμανεῖσα τοῦ νεανίσκου καὶ
ἀκαθέκτως περὶ τὸ πάθος λυττῶσα τοὺς περὶ
μίξεως λόγους προσέφερεν ἐρρωμένως ἐναντιουμένῳ
καὶ μηδ' ὅλως προσίεσθαι ὑπομένοντι διὰ τὴν ἐκ
φύσεως καὶ μελέτης ἐνυπάρξασαν κοσμιότητα καὶ
41 σωφροσύνην. ἐπεὶ δὲ ζωπυροῦσα καὶ ἀναφλέγουσα
τὴν ἔκνομον ἐπιθυμίαν ἀεὶ μὲν ἀπεπειρᾶτο, ἀεὶ δ'
ἀπετύγχανε, βίᾳ λοιπὸν προσπαθοῦσα ἐχρῆτο καὶ
λαβομένη τῆς ἀμπεχόνης εὐτόνως ἄχρι τῆς εὐνῆς
ἐπεσπάσατο ῥώμῃ κραταιοτέρᾳ, τοῦ πάθους ἰσχὺν
ἐπιδιδόντος, ὃ καὶ τοὺς ἀσθενεστάτους εἴωθε νευ-
42 ροῦν. ὁ δὲ τῆς παρούσης ἀκαιρίας γενόμενος δυ-
νατώτερος τὰς ἐλευθερίους καὶ ἀξίας τοῦ γένους
ἔρρηξε φωνάς, "τί βιάζῃ;" λέγων· "ἐξαιρέτοις
ἔθεσι καὶ νομίμοις χρώμεθα ἡμεῖς οἱ Ἑβραίων
43 ἀπόγονοι. τοῖς ἄλλοις ἐφεῖται μετὰ τὴν τεσσαρεσκαιδεκάτην ἡλικίαν πόρναις καὶ χαμαιτύπαις καὶ
ταῖς ὅσαι μισθαρνοῦσιν ἐπὶ τοῖς σώμασι μετὰ πολλῆς ἀδείας χρῆσθαι, παρ' ἡμῖν δὲ οὐδ' ἑταίρᾳ ζῆν
ἔξεστιν, ἀλλὰ κατὰ τῆς ἑταιρούσης ὥρισται δίκη
θάνατος. πρὸ δὴ συνόδων νομίμων ὁμιλίαν ἑτέρας
γυναικὸς οὐκ ἴσμεν, ἀλλ' ἁγνοὶ γάμων ἁγναῖς

---

a Cf. Deut. xxiii. 17. The passage hardly suggests this

good statuary or painter, whether the works which he produces are many and of colossal size or few and smaller, is the same man exhibiting the same skill.

IX. But while he was winning a high reputation 40 in household affairs, his master's wife made him the object of her designs, which were prompted by licentious love ; for wrought up to madness by the beauty of the youth, and putting no restraint upon the frenzy of her passion, she made proposals of intercourse to him which he stoutly resisted and utterly refused to accept, so strong was the sense of decency and temperance which nature and the exercise of control had implanted in him. And, 41 since, as she fed the fire of lawless lust till it burst into a blaze, her constant efforts to gain him as constantly failed, at last in an accession of passion she was fain to employ violence. She caught hold of his outer garment and powerfully drew him to her bed by superior force, since passion which often braces even the weakest gave her new vigour. But 42 he shewed power which was more than a match for the untoward situation and burst into speech with a frankness worthy of his race. " What," he said, "are you forcing me to ? We children of the Hebrews follow laws and customs which are especially our own. Other nations are permitted after the fourteenth 43 year to deal without interference with harlots and strumpets and all those who make a traffic of their bodies, but with us a courtesan is not even permitted to live, and death is the penalty appointed for women who ply this trade.[a] Before the lawful union we know no mating with other women, but come as virgin men

extreme interpretation, but Philo repeats it n *De Spec. Leg.* iii. 51.

παρθένοις προσερχόμεθα προτεθειμένοι τέλος οὐχ
44 ἡδονὴν ἀλλὰ γνησίων παίδων σποράν. εἰς δὴ
ταύτην καθαρεύσας τὴν ἡμέραν οὐκ ἄρξομαι παρανομεῖν ἀπὸ μοιχείας, τοῦ μεγίστου τῶν ἀδικημάτων, ὀφείλων, εἰ καὶ τὸν ἄλλον χρόνον ὑπῆρχον
ἐκδεδιῃτημένος καὶ νεότητος ὁρμαῖς ἠγμένος καὶ
τὴν ἐγχώριον ἐζηλωκὼς τρυφήν, ὅμως ἀλλότριον μὴ
θηρᾶν γάμον· ἐφ' ᾧ τίς ἀνθρώπων οὐ φονᾷ; περὶ
γὰρ τῶν ἄλλων εἰωθότες διαφέρεσθαι μόνον τοῦθ'
ὁμογνωμονοῦντες πανταχοῦ πάντες ἄξιον θανάτων
μυρίων ἐνόμισαν ἀκρίτους ἐκδιδόντες τοὺς ἁλόντας
45 τοῖς πεφωρακόσι. σὺ δ' ἐπιδαψιλευομένη καὶ
τρίτον[1] προστίθῃς μοι μίασμα κελεύουσα μὴ μοι-
χεύειν μόνον, ἀλλὰ καὶ δέσποιναν καὶ δεσπότου
γυναῖκα διαφθείρειν· εἰ μὴ ἄρα τούτου χάριν παρ-
ῆλθον εἰς τὴν ὑμετέραν οἰκίαν, ἵν' ἀποστὰς τῶν
ὑπηρεσιῶν, ἃς δεῖ θεράποντα παρέχειν, μεθύω
καὶ ἐμπαροινῶ ταῖς ἐλπίσι τοῦ πριαμένου νοθεύων
46 αὐτοῦ γάμον, οἰκίαν, συγγένειαν. ἀλλὰ γὰρ οὐχ
ὡς δεσπότην μόνον ἀλλὰ καὶ ὡς εὐεργέτην ἤδη
τιμᾶν προάγομαι· πάντ' ἐπιτέτροφέ μοι τὰ οἰκεῖα,
οὐδὲν οὐ μικρὸν οὐ μέγα ὑπεξῄρηται τὸ παράπαν
δίχα σοῦ τῆς γυναικός· ἀνθ' ὧν ἄξιον αὐτὸν ἐν οἷς
[49] παραινεῖς ἀμείψασθαι; καλὰς | ὡς ἔοικεν ἀντιπαρ-
έξω δωρεὰς ταῖς προϋπηργμέναις χάρισιν οἰκείας.
47 ὁ μὲν δεσπότης αἰχμάλωτον ὄντα με καὶ ξένον ταῖς
εὐεργεσίαις ἐλεύθερον καὶ ἀστὸν τὸ γοῦν ἐπ' αὐτὸν

---

[1] So mss.: Cohn τριττόν. If τρίτον is kept the three μιάσματα
will be (1) harlotry, (2) adultery, (3) adultery with a master's
wife. With τριττόν they will presumably be (1) adultery,
(2) adultery with a mistress, (3) adultery with a master's

to virgin maidens. The end we seek in wedlock is not pleasure but the begetting of lawful children. To this day I have remained pure, and I will not take 44 the first step in transgression by committing adultery, the greatest of crimes. For even if I had always hitherto lived an irregular life, drawn by the appetites of youth and following after the luxury of this land, I ought not to make the wedded wife of another my prey. Who does not thirst for the blood of the adulterer? For while men are accustomed to differ on other matters they are all and everywhere of one mind on this; they count the culprits worthy of a multitude of deaths, and deliver them unjudged into the hands of those who have discovered their guilt. But you in your extravagance would impose upon 45 me a third pollution when you bid me not only commit adultery but also defile my mistress and my master's wife. You cannot think that for this purpose I came into your house, to decline the duties which a servant should render and play like a drunkard and a sot with the hopes of the master who bought me by debasing his bed, his household and his kin. Indeed I am called on to honour him not 46 only as a master but further as a benefactor. He has entrusted to me all his belongings and nothing at all great or small has been withdrawn from me save you, his wife. Is it well that I should requite him for this by doing what you urge me to do? A fine gift this would seem to be, a suitable return for preceding favours! The master found me a captive 47 and an alien, and has made me by his kindnesses a free man and a citizen as far as he can do it. Shall

---

wife. But no stress is laid on any distinction between these two in the sequel.

ἦκον μέρος ἀπειργάσατο, ἐγὼ δ' ὁ δοῦλος ὡς ξένῳ
καὶ αἰχμαλώτῳ προσενεχθήσομαι τῷ δεσπότῃ;
τίνι ψυχῇ παραδεξάμενος τὸ ἀνοσιούργημα τοῦτο;
προσβλέψω δὲ τίσιν ὀφθαλμοῖς ὁ σιδηροῦς ἐγώ;
τὸ συνειδὸς ἐλλαμβανόμενον ὀρθοῖς ὄμμασιν οὐκ
ἐάσει προσβλέπειν, κἂν δυνηθῶ λανθάνειν· λήσομαι
δ' οὐδαμῶς· εἰσὶ γὰρ ἐξετασταὶ μυρίοι τῶν λάθρα
48 δρωμένων, οἷς οὐ θέμις ἡσυχάζειν. ἐῶ λέγειν ὅτι,
κἂν μηδεὶς ἕτερος αἴσθηται ἢ συναισθόμενος μὴ
κατείπῃ, μηνυτὴς οὐδὲν ἧττον αὐτὸς γενήσομαι κατ'
ἐμαυτοῦ τῷ χρώματι, τῷ βλέμματι, τῇ φωνῇ,
καθάπερ μικρῷ πρότερον εἶπον, ὑπὸ τοῦ συνειδότος
ἐλεγχόμενος· εἰ δὲ καὶ μηδεὶς κατερεῖ, τὴν πάρεδρον
τοῦ θεοῦ δίκην καὶ τῶν πραγμάτων ἔφορον οὔτε
δέδιμεν οὔτ' αἰδούμεθα; ''

49 X. Πολλὰ τοιαῦτα συνείροντος καὶ φιλοσο-
φοῦντος, ἐκεκώφητο πρὸς ἅπαντα· δειναὶ γὰρ αἱ
ἐπιθυμίαι καὶ τὰς ἀκριβεστάτας τῶν αἰσθήσεων
ἐπισκιάσαι· ὅπερ συνιδὼν ἀποδιδράσκει τὰ ἱμάτια
καταλιπὼν ἐν ταῖς χερσὶν αὐτῆς, ὧν ἐπείληπτο.
50 τοῦτο παρέσχεν αὐτῇ τὸ ἔργον εὑρεσιλογεῖν προφάσεις σκεπτομένῃ κατὰ τοῦ νεανίσκου, αἷς αὐτὸν
ἀμυνεῖται· παραγενομένῳ γὰρ ἐξ ἀγορᾶς τῷ αὐτῆς
ἀνδρὶ καθυποκρινομένη τὴν σώφρονα καὶ κοσμίαν
καὶ τοῖς ἀκολάστοις ἐπιτηδεύμασι πάνυ δυσχεραί-
νουσαν ''ἤγαγες'' ἔφη ''θεράποντα ἡμῖν παῖδα
Ἑβραῖον, ὃς οὐ μόνον ἤδη τὴν σὴν ψυχὴν διέφθαρ-
κεν εὐχερῶς καὶ ἀνεξετάστως ἐπιτρέψαντος αὐτῷ
τὴν οἰκίαν, ἀλλὰ καὶ ἐμοῦ ἀπετόλμησεν αἰσχῦναι
51 τὸ σῶμα. ταῖς γὰρ ὁμοδούλοις οὐκ ἐξήρκεσεν
αὐτῷ χρῆσθαι μόναις ἀσελγεστάτῳ καὶ λαγνιστάτῳ
γενομένῳ, πειρᾶν δὲ καὶ τὴν δέσποιναν ἐπεχείρησεν

I, the slave, deal with the master as though he were an alien and a captive ? What would be my inward feelings if I agreed to this unholy act ? What my looks when I face him, iron-hearted though I be ? No, conscience will take hold of me and not suffer me to look him straight in the face [a] even if I can escape detection. And that cannot be, for there are thousands to sit in judgement on my secret doings who must not remain silent; not to mention that, 48 even if no other knows of it or reports the knowledge which he shares with me, all the same I shall turn informer against myself through my colour, my look, my voice, convicted as I said just now by my conscience. And even if no one denounce me, have we no fear or respect for justice, the assessor of God, justice who surveys all our doings ? " [b]

X. Thus he spoke long and wisely, but she re- 49 mained deaf to it all. For lust is powerful to becloud even the keenest of the senses. And seeing this he fled leaving in her hands the garments which she had grasped. This action of his gave her the op- 50 portunity to invent a story and devise charges against the youth to punish him. When her husband came in from the market she put on the air of a chaste and modest woman who regards licentious practices with the utmost indignation. " You brought to us," she said, "a Hebrew lad as servant, who has not only corrupted your soul when you lightly and thoughtlessly entrusted your household to him, but has had the audacity to dishonour my body. For not content 51 with taking merely the women who were his fellow-servants, so utterly lewd and lascivious has he shown himself, he has attempted to violate me by force,

[a] Or " with unchanged eyes."   [b] See App. pp. 600-601.

ἐμὲ καὶ βιάζεσθαι. καὶ τὰ δείγματα τῆς φρενοβλαβείας ἐναργῆ καὶ δῆλά ἐστι· περιπαθήσασα γὰρ ὡς ἐξεφώνησα τοὺς ἔνδον βοηθοὺς ἐπικαλοῦσα, πτοηθεὶς διὰ τὸ ἀπερίσκεπτον τὴν ἐσθῆτα καταλιπὼν ἀποδιδράσκει φόβῳ συλλήψεως.'' ἦν καὶ ἐπιδεικνυμένη πίστιν ἐδόκει προσφέρειν τῶν λεγομένων.

52 ἅπερ ἀληθῆ νομίσας ὁ δεσπότης εἶναι κελεύει τὸν ἄνθρωπον εἰς εἱρκτὴν ἀπαγαγεῖν δυσὶ τοῖς μεγίστοις ἁμαρτών, ἑνὶ μὲν ὅτι μὴ μεταδοὺς ἀπολογίας ἀκρίτως κατέγνω τοῦ μηδὲν ἠδικηκότος ὡς τὰ μέγιστα παρανομήσαντος, ἑτέρῳ δὲ ὅτι ἡ ἐσθής, ἣν προύφερεν ἡ γυνὴ ὡς ἀπολειφθεῖσαν ὑπὸ τοῦ νεανίσκου, πίστις ἦν βίας, οὐχ ἣν ἐκεῖνος εἰργάζετο, ἀλλὰ τὴν ὑπομονὴν[1] ἣν ὑπέμεινεν ἐκ τῆς γυναικός· βιαζομένου μὲν γὰρ ἔργον ἦν τὴν ἀμπεχόνην τῆς δεσποίνης κατέχειν, βιασθέντος δὲ τὴν ἰδίαν ἀφαιρε-
53
[50] θῆναι. συγγνωστὸς | δ' ἴσως τῆς ἄγαν ἀπαιδευσίας, ἅτε τὴν δίαιταν ἐν μαγειρείῳ ποιούμενος αἵματος καὶ καπνοῦ καὶ τέφρας ἀνάπλεω,[2] τοῦ λογισμοῦ καιρὸν οὐκ ἔχοντος ἐνηρεμεῖν καὶ σχολάζειν ἑαυτῷ διὰ τὸ πεφύρθαι μᾶλλον ἢ οὐχ ἧττον τοῦ σώματος.

54 XI. Τρεῖς ἤδη χαρακτῆρας τοῦ πολιτικοῦ διετύπωσε, τόν τε ποιμενικὸν καὶ τὸν οἰκονομικὸν καὶ τὸν καρτερικόν. περὶ μὲν οὖν τῶν προτέρων εἴρηται δυεῖν, ὁ δ' ἐγκρατὴς οὐχ ἧττον ἐκείνων πρὸς
55 πολιτείαν συντείνει. πρὸς μὲν οὖν ἅπαντα τὰ τοῦ βίου πράγματα λυσιτελὲς ἐγκράτεια καὶ σωτήριον,

---

[1] Not only awkward, but ungrammatical. It would be simpler with Mangey to expunge τὴν ὑπ. than, as Wendland suggests, to substitute τῆς ἐπιβουλῆς.
[2] mss. ἀνάπλεως or -ων.

me his mistress. The proofs of his insane depravity are clear and evident, for when in my great agitation I cried aloud and called those who were indoors to my aid, he was so scared at my unexpected action[a] that he left his garment behind and fled in fear of arrest." This garment she showed and made as though she were proffering a proof of her tale. Joseph's master, believing this to be true, ordered 52 him to be carried away to prison, and in this he committed two great errors. First he gave him no opportunity of defence, and convicted unheard this entirely innocent person as guilty of the greatest misconduct. Secondly, the raiment which his wife produced as left by the youth was a proof of violence not employed by him but suffered at her hands. For if force were used by him he would retain his mistress's robe, if against him he would lose his own. But his master may perhaps be pardoned for his 53 gross ignorance, since his days were spent in a kitchen full of blood and smoke and cinders, where the reason even more, or at least no less, than the body lives amid confusion and has no chance of quietly retiring into itself.

XI. Moses has now set before us three character- 54 istics of the statesman, his shepherd-craft, his household-management, his self-control. We have dealt with the two first, but the last-named has quite as much bearing on statesmanship. While in all the 55 affairs of life self-mastery is a source of profit and

---

[a] This is an unusual sense for ἀπερίσκεπτος which regularly means with Philo "reckless" or "inconsiderate." It is possible, though less likely, that it may mean here "in his thoughtlessness," *i.e.* he did not consider what evidence he would leave behind him.

πρὸς δὲ τὰ πόλεως καὶ διαφερόντως, ὡς ἀφθόνως
τοῖς βουλομένοις μανθάνειν πάρεστι καὶ προχειρό-
56 τατα. τίς γὰρ ἀγνοεῖ τὰς ἐξ ἀκρασίας ἔθνεσι καὶ
χώραις καὶ ὅλοις κλίμασι τῆς οἰκουμένης ἐν γῇ καὶ
θαλάττῃ γινομένας συμφοράς; τῶν γὰρ πολέμων
οἱ πλείους καὶ μέγιστοι δι' ἔρωτας καὶ μοιχείας καὶ
γυναικῶν ἀπάτας συνέστησαν, ὑφ' ὧν τὸ πλεῖστον
καὶ ἄριστον ἐξαναλώθη τοῦ τε Ἑλληνικοῦ καὶ
βαρβαρικοῦ γένους καὶ τῶν πόλεων ἡ νεότης
57 ἐφθάρη. εἰ δὲ τὰ ἐξ ἀκρασίας στάσεις ἐμφύλιοι
καὶ πόλεμοι καὶ κακὰ ἐπὶ κακοῖς ἀμύθητα, δῆλον
ὅτι τὰ ἐκ σωφροσύνης εὐστάθεια καὶ εἰρήνη καὶ
τελείων κτῆσις ἀγαθῶν καὶ ἀπόλαυσις.

58 XII. Ἄξιον μέντοι καὶ τὰ διὰ τούτων ἐμφαινό-
μενα κατὰ τὸ ἀκόλουθον παραστῆσαι. ὁ πριάμενος
τὸν ἐπικρινόμενον εὐνοῦχος εἶναι λέγεται· δεόντως·
ὁ γὰρ ὠνούμενος τὸν πολιτικὸν ὄχλος ἐστὶ πρὸς
ἀλήθειαν εὐνοῦχος, ὅσα μὲν τῷ δοκεῖν ἔχων τὰ
γεννητικά, τὰς δ' εἰς τὸ γεννᾶν δυνάμεις ἀφηρη-
μένος, καθάπερ καὶ οἱ τὰς ὄψεις ὑποχυθέντες ὀφθαλμοὺς ἔχοντες τῆς δι' ὀφθαλμῶν ἐνεργείας στέρονται
59 βλέπειν οὐ δυνάμενοι. τίς οὖν ἡ πρὸς ὄχλον εὐνούχων ὁμοιότης; ὅτι ἄγονός ἐστι σοφίας δοκῶν
ἐπιτηδεύειν ἀρετήν· ὅταν γὰρ μιγάδων καὶ συγκλύδων πλῆθος ἀνθρώπων εἰς ταὐτὸν συνέλθῃ, λέγει
μὲν τὰ δέοντα, φρονεῖ δὲ καὶ πράττει τἀναντία, τὰ
νόθα πρὸ τῶν γνησίων ἀποδεχόμενος, ἕνεκα τοῦ
δόξῃς μὲν ἡττᾶσθαι, τὸ δ' ἀληθείᾳ καλὸν μὴ ἐπι-
60 τηδεύειν. ὅθεν καὶ—τὸ παραλογώτατον—γυνὴ τῷ

---

[a] Philo is no doubt thinking primarily of the Trojan War,
and it is not unlike him to magnify this into a plural. Still

safety, it is particularly so in affairs of state, as those who will may learn from plentiful and obvious examples. Who does not know the misfortunes which 56 licentiousness brings to nations and countries and whole latitudes of the civilized world on land and sea ? For the majority of wars, and those the greatest, have arisen through amours and adulteries and the deceits of women, which have consumed the greatest and choicest part of the Greek race and the barbarian also, and destroyed the youth of their cities.[a] And, if the results of licentiousness are civil strife and 57 war, and ill upon ill without number, clearly the results of continence are stability and peace and the acquisition and enjoyment of perfect blessings.

XII. We should now, however, in due course 58 show the lessons revealed to us by this story. The purchaser of the subject of our examination is said to be a eunuch; rightly so, for the multitude which purchases the statesman is in very truth a eunuch, possessing to all appearance the organs of generation but deprived of the power of using them, just as those who suffer from cataract have eyes but lack the active use of them and cannot see. How then 59 does the multitude resemble eunuchs ? It is because the multitude is unproductive of wisdom, though it seems to practise virtue. For when a mixed crowd of heterogeneous persons comes together, it says what is right, but it thinks and does the opposite. It prefers the spurious to the genuine, because it is under the dominion of appearances and does not practise what is truly excellent. And, therefore, also, paradoxical though it be, this 60

he can hardly have failed to have Antony and Cleopatra also in mind.

εὐνούχῳ τούτῳ συνοικεῖ· μνᾶται γὰρ ὄχλος ἐπιθυμίαν, ὥσπερ ἀνὴρ γυναῖκα, δι᾽ ἧς ἕκαστα καὶ λέγει καὶ πράττει σύμβουλον αὐτὴν ποιούμενος ἁπάντων ῥητῶν καὶ ἀπορρήτων μικρῶν τε αὖ καὶ μεγάλων, ἥκιστα προσέχειν εἰωθὼς τοῖς ἐκ λογι-

61 σμοῦ.   προσφυέστατα μέντοι καὶ ἀρχιμάγειρον αὐτὸν καλεῖ· καθάπερ γὰρ οὐδὲν ἕτερον ἐπιτηδεύει μάγειρος ἢ τὰς ἀνηνύτους καὶ περιττὰς γαστρὸς ἡδονάς, τὸν αὐτὸν τρόπον καὶ ὁ πολιτικὸς ὄχλος τὰς δι᾽ ἀκοῆς τέρψεις τε καὶ θρύψεις, ὑφ᾽ ὧν

[51]   οἱ τόνοι τῆς διανοίας χαλῶνται καὶ τρόπον τινὰ |
62   τὰ νεῦρα τῆς ψυχῆς ἐκλύεται. τὴν δὲ πρὸς ἰατροὺς μαγείρων διαφορὰν τίς οὐκ οἶδεν; οἱ μὲν τὰ ὑγιεινά, κἂν μὴ προσηνῆ τυγχάνῃ, μόνα διὰ σπουδῆς τῆς πάσης εὐτρεπίζονται, οἱ δ᾽ ἔμπαλιν

63 μόνα τὰ ἡδέα τοῦ συμφέροντος ἀλογοῦντες. ἰατροῖς μὲν οὖν ἐοίκασιν ἐν δήμῳ νόμοι καὶ οἱ κατὰ νόμους ἄρχοντες βουλευταί τε καὶ δικασταὶ φροντίζοντες τῆς τῶν κοινῶν σωτηρίας καὶ ἀσφαλείας ἀκολάκευτοι, ὀψαρτυταῖς δὲ οἱ πολυάνθρωποι τῶν νεωτέρων ὅμιλοι· μέλει γὰρ αὐτοῖς οὐ τὰ συνοίσοντα, ἀλλὰ πῶς τὴν ἐν τῷ παρόντι καρπώσονται

64 μόνον ἡδονήν. XIII. ἐρᾷ δ᾽ ὡς ἀκόλαστος γυνὴ καὶ ἡ τῶν ὄχλων ἐπιθυμία τοῦ πολιτικοῦ καί φησιν αὐτῷ· "παρελθών, ὦ οὗτος, εἰς ὄχλον, ᾧ συνοικῶ, πάντων ἐκλαθοῦ τῶν ἰδίων ἠθῶν, ἐπιτηδευμάτων, λόγων, ἔργων, ἐν οἷς ἐτράφης· ἐμοὶ δὲ πειθάρχει καὶ ἐμὲ θεράπευε καὶ ὅσα δι᾽ ἡδονῆς ἐστί μοι

65 πρᾶττε. αὐστηρὸν γὰρ καὶ αὐθέκαστον καὶ ἀληθείας ἑταῖρον καὶ ἀκριβοδίκαιον, ὄγκῳ καὶ σεμ-

---

ᵃ See App. p. 601.

eunuch is mated with a wife. For the multitude woos desire as a man woos a woman, and makes her his medium in all that he says and does, and takes her as his counsellor in all things great and small, whether decency sanctions them or not, and is wont to pay little heed to the promptings of reason.

Very aptly too does Moses call him a chief cook ; 61 for, just as the cook is solely occupied in endlessly providing superfluous pleasures for the belly, so is the multitude, considered as politicians, in choosing what charms and pleases the ears, and thus the tension of the understanding is relaxed and the sinews of the soul, so to speak, unstrung. As for 62 the difference between cooks and physicians, it is a matter of common knowledge.[a] The physician devotes all his energies solely to preparing what is wholesome, even if it is unpalatable, while the cook deals with the pleasant only and has no thought of what is beneficial. Now in a democracy, physi- 63 cians are represented by laws, and those who rule in accordance with the law, members of councils and juries who consider the safety and security of the common weal and are proof against flattery ; cooks by the swarming crowd of younger spirits, for they do not care what will be beneficial but only how they may reap pleasure for the moment. XIII. And like a licentious woman the desire of the multi- 64 tudes makes love to the statesman. " Forward,[b] lad," she says, " forward, to my mate, the multitude. Forget your own old ways, the habits, the words, the actions in which you were bred. Obey me, wait on me and do all that gives me pleasure. The stern, 65 strict, uncompromising friend of truth, stiff and solemn

[b] Or " when you address . . . forget."

νότητι πρὸς ἅπαντα χρώμενον καὶ πρὸς μηδὲν
εἴκοντα, μόνου περιεχόμενον ἀεὶ τοῦ συμφέροντος
ἄνευ θεραπείας τῶν ἀκροωμένων, οὐκ ἀνέχομαι.
66 διαβολὰς δ' ἐρανιῶ κατὰ σοῦ μυρίας καὶ[1] πρὸς τὸν
ἐμὸν ἄνδρα τὸν ὄχλον, τὸν σὸν δεσπότην· ἄχρι
γὰρ νῦν ἀπελευθεριάζειν δοκεῖς μοι καὶ ὅτι δοῦλος
τυραννικοῦ γέγονας δεσπότου λίαν ἀγνοεῖς. εἰ δὲ
ᾔδεις, ὅτι αὐτοπραγία μὲν οἰκειότατον ἐλευθέρῳ,
οἰκέτῃ δ' ἀλλότριον, ἐπεπαίδευσο ἂν αὐθάδειαν μεθ-
έμενος εἰς ἐμὲ βλέπειν τὴν ἐκείνου γυναῖκα, ἐπιθυμίαν, καὶ δρᾶν τὰ πρὸς ἀρέσκειαν τὴν ἐμήν,
67 δι' ὧν μάλιστα εὐαρεστήσεις.   XIV. ὁ
δὲ πολιτικὸς ὄντως οὐκ ἀγνοεῖ μέν, ὅτι δεσποτικὴν
ἐξουσίαν ἔχει ὁ δῆμος, αὐτὸν δ' οὐχ ὁμολογήσει
δοῦλον ἀλλ' ἐλεύθερον καὶ . . .[2] τὴν τῆς ψυχῆς
ἀρέσκειαν. ἀλλ' ἄντικρυς ἐρεῖ· "δημοκοπεῖν οὔτ'
ἔμαθον οὔτ' ἐπιτηδεύσω ποτέ, πόλεως δὲ προστασίαν καὶ ἐπιμέλειαν ἔχειν ἐγχειρισθείς, ὡς
ἀγαθὸς ἐπίτροπος ἢ πατὴρ εὔνους[3] ἀδόλως καὶ
68 καθαρῶς ἄνευ τῆς ἐχθρᾶς ὑποκρίσεως. ταῦτα
φρονῶν ἐξετασθήσομαι μηδὲν ὑποστέλλων μηδὲ
συγκρύπτων φωρὸς τρόπον, ἀλλὰ τὸ συνειδὸς
αὐγάζων ὡς ἐν ἡλίῳ καὶ φωτί· φῶς γὰρ ἡ ἀλήθεια·
φοβηθήσομαι δ' οὐδὲν ὧν ἂν ἐπανατείνηται, κἂν
θάνατον ἀπειλῇ· θανάτου γὰρ ἐμοὶ κακὸν ἀργαλεώ-

[1] Cohn, who prints καὶ, notes "*excludendum videtur*." It
certainly seems pointless. If retained, it must mean that
the charges are disseminated in general as well as made
to the master in particular.
[2] Something is clearly lost; Mangey's πάντα δρῶντα κατὰ
will make good sense.
[3] Here, too, Cohn indicates a lacuna and suggests δράσω

and inflexible in all his dealings, who clings to the beneficial only and pays no court to his audience, is to me intolerable. And I will collect any number 66 of charges against you to produce before my husband, the multitude, your master. For hitherto you have seemed to me to act as if at liberty and you are quite unaware that you have become the slave of a despotic master. But if you had known that independence may be quite properly possessed by the free man, but is denied to the slave, you would have schooled yourself to abandon your self-will and to look to me, Desire, his wife, and do what may please me as the best way to secure his favour."

XIV. Now the true statesman knows 67 quite well that the people has the power of a master, yet he will not admit that he is a slave, but regards himself as a free man and shapes his activities to please his own soul. He will frankly say, " I have never learned to cringe to the people, and I will never practise it. But since the leadership and charge of the state is put into my hands I will know how to hold it as a good guardian or an affectionate father, guilelessly and sincerely without the dissimulation which I hate. Being thus minded, I 68 will not be found cloaking and hiding anything as a thief might do, but I will keep my conscience clear as in the light of the sun, for truth is light. I will fear none of the tyrant's menaces, even though he threaten me with death, for death is a less evil than

---

or χρηματιῶ. It does not seem to me necessary. It is not difficult to understand ἔμαθον καὶ ἐπιτηδεύσω. To understand an affirmative out of a negative is a looseness which may be found in good writers. A good example occurs in the opening lines of Horace's *Satires.*

PHILO

69 τερον ὑπόκρισις. ἦν ὑπομενῶ τοῦ χάριν; καὶ γὰρ
εἰ δεσπότης ὁ δῆμος, ἀλλ᾽ οὐκ ἐγὼ δοῦλος, εὐπατρίδης δ᾽ εἰ καί τις ἄλλος ἐφιέμενος ἐγγραφῆς
τῆς ἐν τῷ μεγίστῳ καὶ ἀρίστῳ πολιτεύματι τοῦδε
70 τοῦ κόσμου. ὅταν | γὰρ μὴ δῶρα, μὴ παρα-
[52] κλήσεις, μὴ τιμῶν ἔρως, μὴ ἀρχῆς ἐπιθυμία, μὴ
ἀλαζονεία, μὴ ὁ τοῦ δοκεῖν ἵμερος, μὴ ἀκολασία,
μὴ ἀνανδρία, μὴ ἀδικία, μηδὲν ἄλλο τῶν ὅσα ἐκ
πάθους ἢ κακίας ὑπάγηται, τίνος ἔτι φοβηθήσομαι
71 δεσποτείαν; ἢ δῆλον ὅτι τὴν ἀπ᾽ ἀνθρώπων; ἀλλ᾽
οὗτοί γε τὴν σώματος ἐπιγράφονται κυρείαν, οὐ τὴν
κατ᾽ ἐμέ· ἐγὼ γὰρ ἀπὸ τοῦ κρείττονος, τῆς ἐν
ἐμαυτῷ διανοίας, χρηματίζω, καθ᾽ ἣν παρεσκεύ-
ασμαι βιοῦν ὀλίγα φροντίζων τοῦ θνητοῦ σώματος,
ὃ κἂν ὀστρέου δίκην περιπεφυκὸς ἐπηρεάζηται πρός
τινων, ἀφειμένος[1] τῶν ἔνδον δεσποτῶν τε χαλε-
πῶν καὶ δεσποινῶν, οὐκ ἀνάσομαι τὴν βαρυτάτην
72 ἀνάγκην ἐκπεφευγώς. ἐὰν οὖν δικάζειν δέῃ, δι-
κάσω μήτε πλουσίῳ προσθέμενος διὰ τὴν περιουσίαν μήτε πένητι διὰ τὸν ἐπὶ ταῖς ἀτυχίαις ἔλεον,
ἀλλὰ τὰ τῶν κρινομένων ἀξιώματα καὶ σχήματα
παρακαλυψάμενος ἀδόλως βραβεύσω τὸ φανησό-
73 μενον δίκαιον. ἐάν τε βουλεύω, γνώμας εἰσηγή-
σομαι τὰς κοινωφελεῖς, κἂν μὴ πρὸς ἡδονὴν ὦσιν·
ἐάν τε ἐκκλησιάζω, τοὺς θῶπας λόγους ἑτέροις
καταλιπὼν τοῖς σωτηρίοις χρήσομαι καὶ συμ-
φέρουσιν, ἐπιτιμῶν, νουθετῶν, σωφρονίζων, οὐκ
αὐθάδειαν μανιώδη καὶ παράφορον ἀλλὰ νήφουσαν
74 παρρησίαν ἐπιτετηδευκώς. εἰ δὲ μὴ χαίρει τις ταῖς
βελτιώσεσιν, ἐπιτιμάτω καὶ γονεῦσι καὶ ἐπιτρόποις

---

[1] So Mangey: most mss. ἀφειμένον, which Cohn retains,
others -ων. The masculine seems to me necessary for the sense.

176

dissimulation. And why should I submit to it ? **69**
For, though the people be a master, I am not a
slave, but as highly-born as any, one who claims
enrolment among the citizens of that best and
greatest state, this world. For when neither presents **70**
nor appeals nor craving for honours nor desire for
office nor spirit of pretentiousness nor longing for
reputation, nor incontinence, nor unmanliness, nor
injustice, nor any other creation of passion and vice
can subdue me, what domination is still left for me
to fear ? Clearly, it can only be that of men, but **71**
men, while they assume the sovereignty of my body,
are not sovereigns of the real I. For I take my
title from the better part, the understanding within
me, and by that I am prepared to live with little
thought of the mortal body, the shell-like growth
which encases me. And, though some may mal-
treat it, yet, if I be free from the hard masters and
mistresses within, I shall suffer no affliction, since I
have escaped the cruellest tyranny of all. If then **72**
I have to serve on a jury, I will give my verdict
without favouring the rich because of his abundant
wealth, or the poor through pity of his misfortunes,
but drawing a veil over the dignity or the outward appearance of the litigants I will in all honesty
award what shall appear just. If I act as a councillor **73**
I will introduce such proposals as are for the common
good, even if they be not agreeable. If I speak in
the general assembly I will leave all talk of flattery
to others and resort only to such as is salutary and
beneficial, reproving, warning, correcting in words
studied to shew a sober frankness without foolish and
frantic arrogance. He who does not gladly receive **74**
improving advice must to be consistent censure

καὶ διδασκάλοις καὶ πᾶσι τοῖς κηδεμόσιν, ὅτι τέκνα
γνήσια καὶ ὀρφανοὺς παῖδας καὶ φοιτητὰς κακη-
γοροῦσιν, ἔστι δ' ὅτε καὶ τύπτουσιν, οἷς οὔτε
βλασφημίαν οὔθ' ὕβριν ὅσιον ἐπιφημίζειν, ἀλλὰ
75 τοὐναντίον τὰ φιλίας καὶ εὐνοίας ὀνόματα. πάνυ
γὰρ ἀνάξιον τὸν πολιτικὸν ἐμὲ καὶ τὰ τοῦ δήμου
πάντα ἐπιτετραμμένον ἐν τοῖς περὶ τοῦ συμφέροντος λογισμοῖς χείρονα γενέσθαι τινὸς τὴν ἰατρικὴν
76 τέχνην ἐπιτηδεύοντος. ἐκεῖνος γὰρ οὐδὲν τῆς περὶ
τὸν θεραπευόμενον λαμπρότητος ἐν ταῖς νομιζο-
μέναις εὐτυχίαις φροντίσας, οὔθ' ὅτι εὐγενὴς ἦν ἢ
πολυχρήματος οὔθ' ὅτι τῶν κατ' αὐτὸν ἐνδοξότατος
βασιλεὺς ἢ τύραννος, ἑνὸς περιέχεται μόνου τοῦ
σῶσαι κατὰ δύναμιν, κἂν δέῃ τομαῖς ἢ καύσεσι
χρῆσθαι, καίει τε καὶ τέμνει τὸν ἄρχοντα καὶ
77 δεσπότην ὁ ὑπήκοος καὶ λεγόμενος δοῦλος. ἐγὼ δ'
οὐχ ἕνα ἄνδρα πόλιν δ' ὅλην κάμνουσαν παραλαβὼν
ὑπ' ἀργαλεωτέρων νόσων, ἃς κατεσκεύασαν αἱ
συγγενεῖς ἐπιθυμίαι, τί πράσσειν ὀφείλω; προέμενος
τὰ συνοίσοντα πᾶσι κοινῇ τὰ τοῦ δεῖνος ἢ τοῦ δεῖνος
ὦτα θεραπεύειν ἀνελευθέρῳ καὶ σφόδρα δουλοπρεπεῖ
κολακείᾳ; τεθνάναι μᾶλλον ἂν ἑλοίμην ἢ πρὸς
[53] ἡδονήν τι φθεγξάμενος | ἐπικρύψαι τὴν ἀλήθειαν
καὶ τοῦ συμφέροντος ἀμελῆσαι.

78   '' πρὸς ταῦθ' ''

ὡς ὁ τραγικός φησιν

     '' ἴτω μὲν πῦρ, ἴτω δὲ φάσγανον.''—
'' πίμπρα, κάταιθε σάρκας, ἐμπλήσθητί μου
πίνων κελαινὸν αἷμα· πρόσθε γὰρ κάτω
γῆς εἶσιν ἄστρα, γῆ δ' ἄνεισ' εἰς αἰθέρα,
πρὶν ἐξ ἐμοῦ σοι θῶπ' ἀπαντῆσαι λόγον.''

178

parents and guardians and teachers and all persons
in charge, because they reprimand and sometimes
even beat their own children or orphan-wards or
pupils, though really it is against all morality to call
such treatment evil-speaking or outrage instead of
friendliness and benevolence. For it were a quite 75
unworthy thing that I, the statesman, to whom are
committed all the interests of the people, should,
in planning for their benefit, shew myself inferior to
anyone who practises the physician's art. He cares 76
not how brilliant is the good fortune, as men hold
it, which attends his patient or that he is high-born
or wealthy or the most glorious king or despot of
his time, but devotes himself to one object only, to
save him to the best of his ability, even if he must
use cautery or surgery, and he applies the fire or
the knife, he the subject to his ruler, he the so-
called slave to his master. And I, who am called 77
to attend not on a single person but on the whole
state afflicted by the more powerful distempers
which its inbred lusts have produced, what ought
I to do ? Shall I sacrifice the future welfare of all
and minister to the cares of this man and that man
with flattery utterly slave-like and unworthy of the
free ? I would rather lie dead than with some
pleasant words conceal the truth and disregard real
welfare. As the tragedian says : 78

> So then come fire, come sword.[a]
> Burn me, consume my flesh, drink my dark blood,
> Take fill of me; for sooner shall the stars
> Go 'neath the earth, and earth go up to sky
> Than thou shalt from these lips hear fawning word.

[a] The first line is from Eur. *Phoenissae* 521. The others
also from Eur. Quoted *Leg. All.* iii. 202 and *Quod Probus* 99,
where the speaker is given as Heracles.

79 οὕτως οὖν ἠρρενωμένον τὸ φρόνημα καὶ ἐκτὸς
πάντων παθῶν ἱστάμενον, ἡδονῆς, φόβου, λύπης,
ἐπιθυμίας, ἄνδρα πολιτικὸν ὁ δεσπότης δῆμος οὐκ
ἀνέχεται, συλλαβὼν δ' ὡς ἐχθρὸν κολάζει τὸν εὔ-
νουν καὶ φίλον, πρὸ ἐκείνου τιμωρούμενος ἑαυτὸν
τῇ μεγίστῃ τῶν τιμωριῶν, ἀπαιδευσίᾳ, δι' ἣν οὐκ
ἔμαθεν ἄρχεσθαι, τὸ κάλλιστον καὶ βιωφελέστατον,
ἐξ οὗ περιγίνεται καὶ τὸ ἄρχειν.

80   XV. Ἀποχρώντως δὴ καὶ περὶ τούτων διειλεγ-
μένοι τὰ ἑξῆς ἴδωμεν. ὁ διαβληθεὶς νεανίας ὑπὸ
τῆς ἐρωμένης γυναικὸς τῷ δεσπότῃ πλασαμένης
ἀντιστρόφους αἰτίας, αἷς ἦν ἔνοχος αὐτή, μηδ'
ἀπολογίας τυχὼν εἰς εἱρκτὴν ἀπάγεται· καὶ γενόμενος ἐν τῷ δεσμωτηρίῳ τοσοῦτον ἀρετῆς μέγεθος
ἐπεδείξατο, ὡς καὶ τοὺς πονηροτάτους τῶν ἐκεῖ
τεθηπέναι καὶ καταπλήττεσθαι καὶ παρηγόρημα
τῶν συμφορῶν ὑπολαμβάνειν ἀλεξίκακον εὑρηκέναι
81 τὸν ἄνθρωπον. ὅσης δ' ἀπανθρωπίας οἱ εἱρκτο-
φύλακες γέμουσι καὶ ὠμότητος, οὐδεὶς ἀγνοεῖ· φύσει
τε γὰρ ἀνηλεεῖς εἰσι καὶ μελέτῃ συγκροτοῦνται
θηριούμενοι καθ' ἑκάστην ἡμέραν πρὸς ἀγριότητα,
χρηστὸν μὲν οὐδὲν ἀλλ' οὐδ' ἐκ τύχης ὁρῶντες ἢ
λέγοντες ἢ δρῶντες, ὅσα δὲ βιαιότατα καὶ χαλεπώ-
82 τατα. καθάπερ γὰρ οἱ τὰ σώματα εὐπαγεῖς, ὅταν
τὴν ἐξ ἀθλητικῆς ἄσκησιν προσλάβωσι, νευροῦνται
δύναμιν ἀνανταγώνιστον καὶ εὐεξίαν ὑπερβάλλουσαν κτώμενοι, τὸν αὐτὸν τρόπον, ὅταν ἀτίθασος
καὶ ἀμείλικτος φύσις ἄσκησιν εἰς τὸ ἀνήμερον
προσλάβῃ, διχόθεν ἄβατος καὶ ἀπρόσιτος οἴκτῳ

180

When the statesman stands thus aloof from all 79
passions, from pleasure, from fear, from pain, from
desire, with the spirit of a true man, the despot-
people cannot away with him, but takes him and
chastises as an enemy its friend and well-wisher.
And thus it lays upon itself rather than on its
victim the greatest of punishments, indiscipline,
whereby it fails to learn the lesson of submission to
government, that lesson most excellent and of life-
long profit, which he who learns learns also how to
govern.

XV. *a* Having sufficiently discussed these matters, 80
let us proceed to the next. The youth who had
been brought into disgrace with his master by the
false charges of a lovesick woman, charges which
were the counterpart of those to which she was
liable herself, was carried away to gaol without even
any opportunity of making his defence. In the prison
he displayed such a wealth of virtue that even the
vilest of the inmates were astounded and over-
awed, and considered that they had found in him
a consolation for misfortunes and a defence against
future ills. Everyone knows how full of inhumanity 81
and cruelty gaolers are ; pitiless by nature and case-
hardened by practice, they are brutalized day by
day towards savagery, because they never even by
chance see or say or do any kindness, but only the
extremes of violence and cruelty. Just as men 82
of well-built physique, if they add to this athletic
training, grow sinewy and gain irresistible strength
and unequalled robustness, so, whenever any un-
civilized and unsoftened nature adds practice to its
harshness, it becomes doubly impervious and in-

---

a For §§ 80-124 see Gen. xxxix. 20-xli. 45.

83 γίνεται, χρηστῷ πάθει καὶ φιλανθρώπῳ. ὥσπερ
γὰρ οἱ τῶν ἀγαθῶν ὁμιληταὶ βελτιοῦνται τοὺς
τρόπους χαίροντες τοῖς συνοῦσιν, οὕτω καὶ οἱ τοῖς
πονηροῖς συζῶντες ἀπομάττονταί τι τῆς ἐκείνων
κακίας· δεινὸν γὰρ τὸ ἔθος ἐξομοιῶσαι καὶ βιάσα-
84 σθαι πρὸς φύσιν. συνδιατρίβουσιν οὖν οἱ εἰρκτο-
φύλακες λωποδύταις, κλέπταις, τοιχωρύχοις, ὑβρι-
σταῖς, βιαίοις, φθορεῦσιν, ἀνδροφόνοις, μοιχοῖς, ἱερο-
σύλοις, ὧν ἀφ' ἑκάστου σπῶνταί τι μοχθηρίας
καὶ συνερανίζουσι καὶ ἐκ τῆς πολυμιγοῦς κράσεως
85 ἓν ἀποτελοῦσι πάμφυρτον καὶ παμμίαρον κακόν.
[54] XVI. ἀλλ' ὅμως ὁ τοιοῦτος | ἡμερωθεὶς ὑπὸ τῆς
τοῦ νεανίσκου καλοκἀγαθίας οὐ μόνον ἀδείας καὶ
ἐκεχειρίας μετέδωκεν, ἀλλὰ καὶ ἀρχῆς τῆς ἐφ'
ἅπασι τοῖς δεσμώταις, ὡς λόγῳ μὲν ἕνεκα προσχή-
ματος ἐμμένειν εἰρκτοφύλαξ, τὴν δ' ἐν ἔργοις τάξιν
παρακεχωρηκέναι τῷ νεανίᾳ, δι' ἧς οὐκ ὀλίγα
86 συνέβαινε τοὺς ἀπαχθέντας ὠφελεῖσθαι. τὸ γοῦν
χωρίον οὐδ' ὀνομάζειν ἔτ' ἠξίουν εἰρκτήν, ἀλλὰ
σωφρονιστήριον· ἀντὶ γὰρ βασάνων καὶ τιμωριῶν,
ἃς νύκτωρ καὶ μεθ' ἡμέραν ὑπέμενον τυπτόμενοι
καὶ καταδούμενοι καὶ τί κακὸν οὐ πάσχοντες,
λόγοις καὶ δόγμασι τοῖς φιλοσοφίας ἐνουθετοῦντο
καὶ ταῖς ἀνυσιμωτέραις παντὸς λόγου πράξεσι τοῦ
87 διδάσκοντος. τὸν γὰρ αὑτοῦ βίον σωφροσύνης καὶ
πάσης ἀρετῆς οἷα γραφὴν ἀρχέτυπον εὖ δεδημιουργημένην ἐν μέσῳ θεὶς ἐπέστρεψε καὶ τοὺς πάνυ
δοκοῦντας ἀνιάτως ἔχειν, οἷς μακραὶ νόσοι τῆς
ψυχῆς ἐλώφησαν ἤδη κακίζουσιν ἐπὶ τοῖς πεπραγ-
182

accessible to the kindly and humane emotion of pity. For, even as those who consort with the good are 83 improved in character by the pleasure they take in their associates, so those who live with the bad take on some impression of their vice. Custom has a wonderful power of forcing everything into the likeness of nature. Gaolers then spend their days 84 with footpads, thieves, burglars, men of violence and outrage, who commit rape, murder, adultery and sacrilege, and from each of these they imbibe and accumulate something of their villainy, out of which miscellaneous amalgam they produce a single body of evil, a fusion of every sort of pollution. XVI. But nevertheless one of this kind, tamed by 85 the nobility of the youth, not only allowed him some security from violence and hardship, but gave him the command of all the prisoners ; and thus while he remained nominally and for the sake of appearance the keeper of the gaol, he resigned to Joseph the actual office, which thus became the source of no small benefit to those who were in confinement. Thus even the place, as they felt, could 86 not rightly be called a prison, but a house of correction. For instead of the tortures and punishments which they used to endure night and day under the lash or in manacles or in every possible affliction, they were rebuked by his wise words and doctrines of philosophy, while the conduct of their teacher effected more than any words. For by setting before 87 them his life of temperance and every virtue, like an original picture of skilled workmanship, he converted even those who seemed to be quite incurable, who as the long-standing distempers of their soul abated reproached themselves for their past

PHILO

μένοις αὐτοὺς καὶ μετανοοῦσι καὶ τοιαῦτ' ἐπιφθεγ-
γομένοις· '' ποῦ ποτ' ἄρ' ἦν πάλαι τοσοῦτον ἀγαθόν,
οὗ τὴν ἀρχὴν ἐσφάλμεν; ἰδοὺ γὰρ ἐπιλάμψαντος
αὐτοῦ, ὡς πρὸς κάτοπτρον τὴν ἀκοσμίαν ὁρῶντες
αὑτῶν αἰσχυνόμεθα.''

88 XVII. Τοῦτον τὸν τρόπον βελτιουμένων εἰσ-
άγονται δύο εὐνοῦχοι τοῦ βασιλέως, ὁ μὲν ἀρχιοινοχόος, ὁ δὲ ἀρχισιτοποιός, ἐν οἷς ἐπετράπησαν
κατηγορηθέντες καὶ καταγνωσθέντες. ὁ δὲ καὶ
τούτων τὴν ἐπιμέλειαν ἣν καὶ τῶν ἄλλων ἐποιεῖτο,
εὐχόμενος ὅπως οἷός τε ᾖ μηδὲν χείρους τῶν ἀν-
89 επιλήπτων ἀπεργάσασθαι τοὺς ὑφ' ἑαυτῷ. χρόνου
δ' οὐ μακροῦ διελθόντος, ἐπιὼν τοὺς δεσμώτας ὁρᾷ
συννοίας καὶ κατηφείας γέμοντας μᾶλλον ἢ πρότερον τοὺς εὐνούχους καὶ στοχασάμενος ἐκ τῆς
σφοδρᾶς λύπης προσπεπτωκέναι τι νεώτερον ἐπυν-
90 θάνετο τὴν αἰτίαν. ἀποκριναμένων δέ, ὡς ὀνείρους
ἰδόντες ἄσης καὶ ἀδημονίας πεπλήρωνται, μηδενὸς
ὄντος τοῦ διακρινοῦντος, '' θαρσεῖτε '' ἔφη '' καὶ δι-
ηγεῖσθε, γνώριμοι γὰρ ἔσονται βουλομένου θεοῦ·
βούλεται δὲ τὰ συνεσκιασμένα τῶν πραγμάτων
ἀνακαλύπτειν τοῖς ἀλήθειαν ποθοῦσιν.''

91 εἶτα πρότερος ὁ ἀρχιοινοχόος φησίν· '' ἔδοξα
μεγάλην ἄμπελον ἐκπεφυκέναι τριῶν πυθμένων
ἓν εὐερνέστατον στέλεχος, τεθηλυῖαν καὶ βοτρυη-
φοροῦσαν ὡς ἐν ἀκμῇ τῆς ὀπώρας, ὑποπερκαζούσης
δὲ τῆς σταφυλῆς δρέψασθαι τῶν βοτρύων καὶ εἰς
ἔκπωμα βασιλικὸν ἀποθλίβειν, ὅπερ ἱκανῶς ἔχον
92 ἀκράτου προσενεγκεῖν τῷ βασιλεῖ.'' ὁ δὲ μικρὸν
ἐπισχὼν '' εὐτυχίαν '' εἶπεν '' ἡ φαντασία σοι κατ-
αγγέλλει καὶ τῆς προτέρας ἀνάληψιν ἀρχῆς· αἱ
γὰρ τρεῖς ῥίζαι τῆς ἀμπέλου τρεῖς ἡμέρας ὑπο-

and repented with such utterances as these : " Ah, where in old days was this great blessing which at first we failed to find ? See, when it shines on us we behold as in a mirror our misbehaviour and are ashamed."

XVII. While they were thus growing in goodness, 88 two eunuchs of the king were brought in, the chief butler and the chief baker, both of them accused and condemned for dereliction of duties. Joseph paid the same attention to them as to the others, in his earnest wish to raise if possible those under him to the level of those who were innocent of offence. And 89 after no long time on visiting the prisoners he saw that they were full of depression and dejection, even more than before, and, guessing from their extreme sadness that something unusual had befallen them, he asked the reason. When they answered that they 90 had had dreams which filled them with sore trouble and distress because there was no one to interpret them, he said to them : " Cheer up, and tell me these dreams, for their meaning will be known, if God wills, and He does will to unveil what is hidden to those who desire the truth." Then the chief butler 91 spoke first and said : " I dreamt that I saw a great vine, an exceedingly fine stalk growing from three roots. It was thriving and covered with grapes as in the height of the vintage season, and from a cluster which was turning ripe black I plucked some grapes and squeezed them into the royal cup, and when it had plenty of liquor I brought it to the king." Joseph 92 paused for a little, and then said : " Your vision is an announcement to you of good fortune and the recovery of your former office. The three roots of

185

γράφουσι, μεθ' ἃς ὑπομνησθήσεταί σου ὁ βασιλεὺς
καὶ μεταπεμψάμενος ἐνθένδε παρέξει μὲν ἀμνηστίαν,
ἐπιτρέψει δὲ τῆς αὐτῆς μεταποιεῖσθαι τάξεως, καὶ
ὑπὲρ βεβαιώσεως τῆς ἀρχῆς οἰνοχοήσεις ἀναδοὺς
ἔκπωμα τῷ δεσπότῃ." καὶ ὁ μὲν ἐγεγήθει ταῦτ'
93 ἀκούσας.   XVIII. ὁ δ' ἀρχισιτοποιὸς |
[55] ἀποδεξάμενος τὴν διάκρισιν, ὡς καὶ αὐτὸς εὐτυχὲς
ὄναρ ἰδών—ἦν δ' οὐ μετρίως παλίμφημον—, ἀπατηθεὶς ταῖς ἑτέρου χρησταῖς ἐλπίσι φησίν· "ἀλλὰ
κἀγὼ κανηφορεῖν ἔδοξα καὶ τρία πλήρη κανᾶ πεμ-
μάτων κομίζειν ἐπὶ τῆς κεφαλῆς, τὸ δ' ἀνωτάτω
πλῆρες εἶναι παντοίων γενῶν, οἷς ἔθος ἐστὶ χρῆσθαι τὸν βασιλέα—ποικίλας δ' εἶναι τὰς πρὸς δίαιταν
βασιλικὴν σιτοπόνων περιεργίας—, ὄρνεις δὲ καθ-
ιπταμένους ἁρπάζειν ἀπὸ τῆς κεφαλῆς καὶ ἀπλήστως
ἐμφορεῖσθαι, μέχρις οὗ πάντ' ἀναλῶσαι καὶ μηδὲν
94 τῶν εὐτρεπισθέντων ὑπολιπέσθαι." ὁ δὲ "ἐβου-
λόμην μὲν" εἶπε "μὴ παραστῆναί σοι τὴν φαντασίαν ἢ φανεῖσαν ἡσυχασθῆναι ἤ, εἰ καὶ διηγεῖτό
τις, μακρὰν γοῦν, ἵνα μὴ κατακούσαιμι, τῶν ἐμῶν
ὤτων γενέσθαι τὴν διήγησιν· ὀκνῶ τε γάρ, εἰ καί
τις ἄλλος, εἶναι κακῶν ἄγγελος συναλγῶ τε τοῖς
ἐν συμφοραῖς, ἕνεκα φιλανθρωπίας οὐχ ἥκιστα τῶν
95 ὑπομενόντων ὀδυνώμενος. ἀλλ' ἐπειδὴ τοῖς ὀνείρων
κριταῖς ἀληθεύειν ἀναγκαῖον θεῖα λόγια διερμη-
νεύουσι καὶ προφητεύουσι, λέξω μηδὲν ὑποστειλά-
μενος· ἀψευδεῖν γὰρ ἐπὶ μὲν πάντων ἄριστον, ἐπὶ
96 δὲ τῶν θείων ἀποφθεγμάτων καὶ ὁσιώτατον. τὰ
τοῖα κανᾶ σύμβολον τριῶν ἡμερῶν ἐστιν· ἐπισχὼν

the vine denote three days, after which the king will
remember you and send for you from this place. He
will then grant you free pardon, and allow you to take
your old post, and to confirm you in the office you will
act as butler and offer the cup to your master." The
chief butler rejoiced on hearing this.

XVIII. The chief baker, for his part, approved the 93
interpretation, and, thinking that he himself had had
a lucky dream, though in reality it was very much the
reverse, and misled by the comforting hopes of the
other, proceeded as follows : " I too had a dream. I
thought I was carrying three baskets—full of bake-
meats—on my head, the uppermost full of all the
different kinds which are regularly provided for
the use of the king, for the delicacies produced by
the caterers for the king's table are varied and elaborate. Then birds flew down and snatched them from
my head, and gobbled them insatiably until all was
consumed and nothing of the provisions was left."
Joseph replied : " I could have wished that this 94
vision had never been seen by you, or, if seen, had
remained unmentioned, or, if its story were told, that
at least it should have been told far away from my
ears to prevent my hearing it. For no one shrinks
more than I from being a messenger of ill-tidings.
I sympathize with those in misfortune, and kindly
affection makes me feel as much pain as the actual
sufferers. But the interpreters of dreams must needs 95
tell the truth, since they are prophets expounding
divine oracles, and I will therefore speak without
reserve ; for, while veracity is best in all matters, in
dealing with God's messages, anything else is pro-
fanity.[a] The three baskets are symbols of three days. 96

---

[a] ὅσιον here in the sense of what is demanded by religion.

ταύτας ὁ βασιλεὺς ἀνασκολοπισθῆναί σε καὶ τὴν
κεφαλὴν ἀποτμηθῆναι κελεύσει καὶ καταπτάμενα
ὄρνεα τῶν σῶν εὐωχηθήσεται σαρκῶν, ἄχρις ἂν
97 ὅλος ἐξαναλωθῇς.'' καὶ ὁ μὲν ὥσπερ εἰκὸς συγχυθεὶς ἀνατέτραπτο, καραδοκῶν τὴν ὁρισθεῖσαν
προθεσμίαν καὶ τῇ διανοίᾳ τὰς ἀνίας προσδεχό-
μενος. ὡς δ' αἱ τρεῖς ἡμέραι διῆλθον, γενέθλιος
ἐπέστη τοῦ βασιλέως, ἐν ᾗ πάντες οἱ κατὰ τὴν
χώραν ἐπανηγύριζον, διαφερόντως δ' οἱ περὶ τὰ
98 βασίλεια. ἑστιωμένων οὖν τῶν ἐν τέλει καὶ τῆς
θεραπείας εὐωχουμένης ὥσπερ ἐν δημοθοινίᾳ, τῶν
κατὰ τὸ δεσμωτήριον εὐνούχων ὑπομνησθεὶς ἀχθῆναι κελεύει καὶ θεασάμενος τἀκ τῆς τῶν ὀνείρων
διακρίσεως ἐπισφραγίζεται, προστάξας τὸν μὲν ἀνα-
σκολοπισθῆναι τὴν κεφαλὴν ἀποτμηθέντα, τῷ δὲ
τὴν ἀρχὴν ἣν διεῖπε πρότερον ἀπονεῖμαι.

99 XIX. Καταλλαγεὶς δὲ ὁ ἀρχιοινοχόος ἐκλαν-
θάνεται τοῦ τὰς καταλλαγὰς προειπόντος καὶ
ἕκαστα τῶν συμπεσόντων ἀτυχημάτων ἐπικουφί-
σαντος, ἴσως μὲν ἐπειδὴ πᾶς ἀχάριστος ἀμνήμων
ἐστὶν εὐεργετῶν, ἴσως δὲ καὶ κατὰ πρόνοιαν θεοῦ
βουληθέντος τὰς εὐπραγίας τῷ νεανίᾳ μὴ δι' ἀν-
100 θρώπου γενέσθαι μᾶλλον ἢ δι' ἑαυτοῦ. μετὰ γὰρ
διετῆ χρόνον τῷ βασιλεῖ τὰ μέλλοντα τῇ χώρᾳ
συμβαίνειν ἀγαθὰ καὶ κακὰ διτταῖς φαντασίαις δι'
ὀνείρου θεσπίζεται ταὐτὸν ὑποσημαινούσαις ἕνεκα
101 βεβαιοτέρας πίστεως. ἔδοξε γὰρ ἑπτὰ βόας ἀνέρ-
πειν ἐκ τοῦ ποταμοῦ, πίονας καὶ σφόδρα εὐσάρκους
καὶ καλὰς ὀφθῆναι, καὶ παρὰ ταῖς ὄχθαις νέμεσθαι·
[56] μεθ' ἃς ἑτέρας ἀριθμὸν ἴσας, | ἀσάρκους τρόπον
τινὰ καὶ κατεσκελετευμένας καὶ εἰδεχθεστάτας,
ἀνελθεῖν καὶ συννέμεσθαι ταῖς προτέραις· εἶτ'
188

When these have passed, the king will order you to be impaled and beheaded, and the birds will feast upon your flesh until you are entirely devoured." The baker, as might be expected, was confounded 97 and upset, having the appointed day before his eyes and mentally anticipating its pangs. But, when the three days had passed, came the king's birthday, when all the inhabitants of the country held festive gatherings, and particularly those of the palace. So, 98 while the dignitaries were banqueting, and the servants were regaling themselves as at a public feast, the king remembered the eunuchs in the prison and bade them be brought to him. And, when he saw them, he ratified what had been forecast in the interpretation of the dreams, by ordering one to be beheaded and impaled and the other to be restored to his former office.

XIX. But, when he was reconciled to his master, 99 the chief butler forgot him who had predicted the reconciliation and alleviated all the misfortunes which befell him ; perhaps because the ungrateful are always forgetful of their benefactors, perhaps also in the providence of God Who willed that the happy events which befell the youth should be due to God rather than to man. For after two years the future 100 of his country for both good and ill was revealed to the king when dreaming, in two visions with the same significance, repeated in order to carry stronger conviction. He dreamt that seven oxen came up from 101 the river, fat and well covered with flesh and fair to look upon, and browsed beside the banks. After them seven others, mere skeletons, and fleshless, so to speak, and loathsome in appearance, came up and browsed with the former seven. Then suddenly

189

ἐξαπιναίως ὑπὸ τῶν χειρόνων καταβρωθῆναι τὰς
ἀμείνους καὶ μηδὲν ἀλλὰ μηδὲ τὸ βραχύτατον ταῖς
ἐμφορηθείσαις πρὸς ὄγκον ἐπιδοῦναι τὰς γαστέρας,
102 ἀλλ' ἢ μᾶλλον ἢ οὐχ ἧττον ἐστάλθαι. περιαναστὰς
δὲ καὶ κοιμηθεὶς πάλιν ἑτέρᾳ πληχθῆναι φαντασίᾳ·
νομίσαι γὰρ ἑπτὰ πυροῦ στάχυς ἐκπεφυκότας ἑνὸς
πυθμένος, ἰσαιτάτους τοῖς μεγέθεσιν, αὐξομένους
καὶ τεθηλότας αἴρεσθαι πρὸς ὕψος μάλ' εὐρώστους·
εἶθ' ἑτέρους ἑπτὰ λεπτοὺς καὶ ἀσθενεῖς ἀναπεφυ-
κέναι πλησίον, ὑφ' ὧν ἐπιδραμόντων καταποθῆναι
103 τὸν εὔσταχυν πυθμένα. ταύτην ἰδὼν τὴν ὄψιν, τὸ
λειπόμενον τῆς νυκτὸς ἄυπνος διατελέσας—ἤγειρον
γὰρ αἱ φροντίδες κεντοῦσαι καὶ τιτρώσκουσαι—,
μεταπέμπεται τοὺς σοφιστὰς ἅμα τῇ ἕῳ καὶ τὴν
104 φαντασίαν διηγεῖται. μηδενὸς δὲ στοχασμοῖς εἰκόσι
τἀληθὲς ἰχνηλατῆσαι δυναμένου, παρελθὼν ὁ ἀρχιοινοχόος φησίν· " ὦ δέσποτα, τὸν ἄνδρα ὃν ζητεῖς
ἐλπίς ἐστιν εὑρήσειν· ἁμαρτόντας ἐμὲ καὶ τὸν ἀρχισιτοποιὸν ἐκέλευσας εἰς τὸ δεσμωτήριον ἀπαχθῆ-
ναι, ἐν ᾧ τοῦ ἀρχιμαγείρου θεράπων ἦν Ἑβραῖος,
ᾧτινι διηγησάμεθα ἐγώ τε κἀκεῖνος ὀνείρατα τὰ
φανέντα ἡμῖν· ὁ δ' οὕτως εὐθυβόλως καὶ εὐσκόπως
διέκρινεν, ὡς ὅσα προεῖπεν ἑκατέρῳ συμβῆναι, τῷ
μὲν ἣν ὑπέμεινε τιμωρίαν, ἐμοὶ δὲ τὸ σοῦ τυχεῖν
105 ἵλεω καὶ εὐμενοῦς." XX. ὁ μὲν οὖν
βασιλεὺς ἀκούσας προστάττει συντείναντας ἀνα-
καλεῖν τὸν νεανίαν. οἱ δ' ἀποκείραντες—βαθεῖαι
γὰρ ἦσαν αὐτῷ χαῖται καθειργμένῳ κεφαλῆς καὶ
γενείου—καὶ ἀντὶ ῥυπώσης λαμπρὰν ἐσθῆτα ἀντι-
δόντες καὶ τἄλλα φαιδρύναντες εἰσάγουσιν αὐτὸν
106 πρὸς τὸν βασιλέα· ὃς ἐκ τῆς ὄψεως τεκμηράμενος

the better seven were devoured by the worse, and yet these after swallowing the others shewed not the smallest increase in bulk of belly but were even more, or at least not less, shrunken. The king awoke and 102 then slept again, and was beset by another vision. He thought that seven ears of wheat had sprung out of a single stalk. They were very equal in size and grew and throve and rose to a considerable height, fine and strong. Then seven others sprang up near them, thin and feeble, which overran and swallowed up the stalk which bore the good ears. After seeing 103 this the king remained sleepless for the rest of the night, kept awake by the thoughts which pricked and stung him. At dawn he sent for his wise men and told them the vision, and when no one could make any 104 likely conjecture which could give a clue to the truth, the chief butler came forward and said : " Master, we may hope to find the man whom you seek. When I and the chief baker had offended, we were by your orders cast into prison where there was a Hebrew servant of the chief cook, to whom we two told the dreams which we had seen, and he interpreted them so exactly and skilfully that all that he had predicted happened to each of us, to him the penalty which he suffered, to me my admission to your clemency and favour." XX. The king on hearing this 105 bade them hasten and summon the youth. They obeyed, but first they had him shaven and shorn, for in his confinement the hair had grown long and thick on his head and chin. Then they put on him a bright and clean raiment instead of his filthy prison clothes, and smartened him in other ways and thus brought him to the king. The king, judging him by his ap- 106 pearance to be a man of free and noble birth, for the

ἄνδρα ἐλεύθερον καὶ εὐγενῆ—χαρακτῆρες γὰρ ἐπιφαίνονταί τινες τῷ σώματι τῶν ὁρωμένων οὐχ ὁρατοὶ πᾶσιν, ἀλλ᾽ οἷς τὸ τῆς διανοίας ὄμμα ὀξυδορκεῖ—" μαντεύεται " εἶπεν " ἡ ψυχή μου περὶ τοῦ μὴ εἰς ἅπαν ἀσαφείᾳ τοὺς ὀνείρους ἐπισκιασθήσεσθαι· δεῖγμα γὰρ σοφίας ὁ νεανίας οὗτος ὑποφαίνει, διακαλύψει τὴν ἀλήθειαν, οἷα φωτὶ σκότος ἐπιστήμη τὴν ἀμαθίαν τῶν παρ᾽ ἡμῖν σοφιστῶν ἀποσκεδάσει." καὶ τοὺς ὀνείρους δι-
107 ηγεῖτο.   ὁ δὲ τἀξίωμα τοῦ λέγοντος οὐδὲν καταπλαγεὶς ὥσπερ ὑπηκόῳ βασιλεύς, ἀλλ᾽ οὐχ ὑπήκοος βασιλεῖ, παρρησίᾳ σὺν αἰδοῖ χρώμενος διελέγετο καί φησιν· " ὅσα μέλλει ποιεῖν ὁ θεὸς ἐν τῇ χώρᾳ, προμεμήνυκέ σοι. τὰς μέντοι διττὰς φαντασίας μὴ ὑπολάβῃς εἶναι διττοὺς ὀνείρους· εἷς ἐστι, τὴν ἀναδίπλωσιν ἔχων οὐ περιττήν, ἀλλὰ πρὸς
108 ἔλεγχον βεβαιοτέρας πίστεως. αἵ τε γὰρ πίονες ἑπτὰ βόες καὶ οἱ εὔβλαστοι καὶ εὐθαλεῖς ἑπτὰ |
[57] στάχυες ἐνιαυτοὺς ἑπτὰ δηλοῦσιν εὐθηνίας καὶ εὐετηρίας καὶ ἑπτὰ ἑτέρους λιμοῦ αἱ ἐπανιοῦσαι ἑπτὰ βόες λεπταὶ καὶ εἰδεχθεῖς καὶ οἱ παρεφθαρ-
109 μένοι καὶ μεμυκότες ἑπτὰ στάχυες. ἥξει μὲν οὖν ἑπταετία προτέρα πολλὴν καὶ ἄφθονον ἔχουσα εὐκαρπίαν, πλημμύραις μὲν ἀνὰ πᾶν ἔτος τοῦ ποταμοῦ λιμνάζοντος τὰς ἀρούρας, τῶν δὲ πεδίων ὡς οὔπω πρότερον εὐτοκία χρωμένων· ἥξει δὲ μετὰ ταῦτα ἑπταετία πάλιν ἐναντία χαλεπὴν ἔνδειαν καὶ σπάνιν τῶν ἀναγκαίων ἐπιφέρουσα, μήτ᾽ ἀναχεομένου τοῦ ποταμοῦ μήτε τῆς γῆς λιπαινομένης, ὡς τῆς προτέρας εὐθηνίας ἐκλαθέσθαι καὶ εἴ τι λεί-
110 ψανον παλαιᾶς εὐετηρίας ἦν ἀναλωθῆναι. τὰ μὲν οὖν ἐκ τῆς διακρίσεως τοιαῦτ᾽ ἐστίν. ὑπηχεῖ δὲ
192

persons of those whom we see exhibit characteristics which are not visible to all, but only to those in whom the eye of the understanding is quick to discern, said : " My soul has a prophetic inkling that my dreams will not for ever remain veiled in obscurity, for in this youth there are signs and indications of wisdom. He will reveal the truth, and as light disperses darkness his knowledge will disperse the ignorance of our wizards." So he told him the dreams.

Joseph, nothing awed by the high dignity of the 107 speaker, spoke to him with frankness combined with modesty, rather as a king to a subject than as a subject to the king. " God has given you," he said, " warning of all that He is about to do in the land. But do not suppose that the two visions are two dreams. There is one dream repeated, though the repeating is not superfluous, but given to convince you more firmly of its trustworthiness. For both the 108 seven fat oxen and the seven well-grown and flourishing ears indicate seven years of abundance and prosperity, while the seven oxen that came up after, thin and loathly, and the seven blasted and shrunken ears mean seven other years of famine. The first period 109 of seven years, then, will come bringing a large and plentiful wealth of crops, while the river each year, with its rising waters, turns the fields into pools and the plains have a fertility never known before. But after this will come in its turn another period of seven years of the opposite kind, bringing severe dearth and lack of the means of living, with the river ceasing to overflow and the fields to get their fatness, so that men will forget the former prosperity and every trace of the old abundance will be blotted out. Such are 110 the facts which appear from the interpretation, but

PHILO

μοι καὶ ἐκλαλεῖ τὸ θεῖον ὑποβάλλον τὰ ὡς ἐν νόσῳ
σωτήρια· νόσος δὲ πόλεων καὶ χωρίων ἡ βαρυτάτη
λιμός, ᾗ κατασκευαστέον ἀσθένειαν, ἵνα μὴ τε-
111 λείως ῥωσθεῖσα τοὺς οἰκήτορας ἐκφάγῃ. πῶς οὖν
ἀσθενήσει; τοῦ καρποῦ τῶν ἑπτὰ ἐτῶν, ἐν οἷς ἡ
εὐφορία, τὸ πλεονάζον μετὰ τὰς αὐτάρκεις τοῖς
πλήθεσι τροφὰς—ἔσται δ' ἴσως μέρος πέμπτον—
θησαυριστέον ἐν πόλει καὶ κώμαις, μὴ μετακομί-
ζοντας τὰ θέρη μακρόθεν, ἀλλ' ἐξ ὧν ἂν ᾖ χωρίων,
ἐν ἐκείνοις φυλάττοντας πρὸς τὴν τῶν οἰκούν-
112 των παρηγορίαν· συγκομίζειν δὲ τὸν καρπὸν αὐτοῖς
δράγμασι μήτε ἀλοῶντας μήτε συνόλως καθαίροντας,
τεττάρων ἕνεκα· ἑνὸς μὲν τοῦ σκέπῃ χρώμενον
πρὸς πλείω χρόνον διαμένειν ἀδιάφθορον· ἑτέρου δὲ
τοῦ καθ' ἕκαστον ἐνιαυτὸν γίνεσθαι τῆς εὐθηνίας
ὑπόμνησιν, ἀλοώντων καὶ λικμώντων· ἡ γὰρ μίμη-
σις τῶν πρὸς ἀλήθειαν ἀγαθῶν δευτέραν ἔμελ-
113 λεν ἡδονὴν ἀπεργάζεσθαι· τρίτου δὲ τοῦ μηδ' εἰς
ἀριθμὸν ἐλθεῖν, ἐν στάχυσι καὶ δράγμασιν ἀδήλου
καὶ ἀπεριγράφου τοῦ καρποῦ ὑπάρχοντος, ἵνα μὴ
προαναπέσωσιν αἱ διάνοιαι τῶν ἐγχωρίων ἐν ταῖς
ἀναλώσεσι τοῦ συλλογισθέντος, ἀλλ' εὐθυμίᾳ χρώμενοι τῇ σιτίων ἀμείνονι τροφῇ—τρέφει γὰρ ἐν τοῖς
μάλιστα ἐλπίς—ἐπικουφίζωσι τὴν ἐκ τῆς ἐνδείας
βαρεῖαν νόσον· τετάρτου δὲ τοῦ καὶ τοῖς θρέμ-

---

[a] For this regular use of ὑπηχεῖν in Philo for a voice heard
inwardly see note on *De Som.* i. 164.

[b] Or " country districts "; *cf.* the common use of the word
for farms or estates.

[c] There is no authority for this statement in Genesis, or the
arguments adduced for it. But Philo may well have heard
or read of precedents.

[d] *i.e.* when we thresh the annual allowance from the store

194

I also hear the promptings ^{a} of the divine voice, devising safeguards for the disease, as we may call it ; and famine in cities and localities ^{b} is the severest of diseases, and we must provide means of weakening it lest it grow to full strength and devour the inhabitants. How, then, shall it be weakened ? What 111 is left over from the harvest of the seven years of abundance after the necessary allowance for feeding the multitudes, which perhaps will be a fifth, should be stored in the city and villages, without transporting the crops to a distance, but keeping them in the places where they have been produced, to encourage the inhabitants. And the crops should be brought 112 in just as they are in the sheaves, without threshing them or purging them in any way, ^{c} for four reasons. First, that being thus under shelter they will last longer without spoiling ; secondly, that every year when they are threshed and winnowed they will serve as a reminder of the prosperous time, for we always find that imitation ^{d} of our real blessings has brought a repetition of the pleasure ; thirdly, the grain cannot 113 even be reckoned when it is contained in ears and sheaves, and therefore is an uncertain and incalculable quantity. This will prevent the minds of the inhabitants from being prematurely depressed, when they see that the grain, which is a known quantity, ^{e} is being gradually consumed. On the contrary, they will have courage, nourished on a food which is better than corn, since hope is the best of nourishments, and take more lightly the heavy scourge of want. Fourthly, to provide a store of fodder for the cattle

we copy what we do in the ordinary harvest and therefore are reminded of it. But Cohn in his translation adopts Mangey's ὑπόμνησις.

^{e} Lit. " which has been calculated."

μασι χιλὸν τεταμιεῦσθαι, τῶν ἀχύρων καὶ ἀθέρων
114 ἐκ τῆς τοῦ καρποῦ καθάρσεως διακρινομένων. ἐπι-
μελητὴν δὲ τούτων χειροτονητέον ἄνδρα φρονιμώ-
τατον καὶ συνετώτατον καὶ ἐν πᾶσι δόκιμον, ὃς
γένοιτ' ἂν ἱκανὸς ἀμισῶς καὶ ἀνεπάφως εὐτρεπῆ
τὰ λεχθέντα ποιεῖν μηδεμίαν αἴσθησιν τοῖς πλή-
θεσιν ἐνδιδοὺς περὶ τοῦ γενησομένου λιμοῦ· χαλεπὸν
γὰρ τὸ προκάμνοντας ταῖς ψυχαῖς ἀναπεσεῖν δυσ-
115 ελπιστίᾳ. ἐὰν δέ τις ἐπιζητῇ τὴν αἰτίαν, φήσει
δεῖν, καθάπερ ἐν εἰρήνῃ προνοεῖν τῶν ἐν τῷ
[58] πολέμῳ παρασκευῶν, καὶ ἐν | εὐπορίαις τῶν κατ'
ἔνδειαν· ἀδήλους δὲ εἶναι πολέμους καὶ λιμοὺς
καὶ συνόλως τοὺς καιροὺς τῶν ἀβουλήτων, εἰς
οὓς ἀναγκαῖον εἶναι παρεσκευάσθαι, ἀλλὰ μὴ
γενομένων τότε τὴν θεραπείαν ζητεῖν, ὅτ' οὐδὲν
ὄφελος."

116 XXI. Ἀκούσας δὲ ὁ βασιλεὺς καὶ τὴν τῶν
ὀνείρων διάκρισιν εὐθυβόλως καὶ εὐσκόπως στοχα-
ζομένην τῆς ἀληθείας καὶ τὴν συμβουλίαν ὅσα τῷ
δοκεῖν ὠφελιμωτάτην κατὰ τὴν τοῦ μέλλοντος
ἀδήλου πρόνοιαν, τοὺς συνόντας ἐγγυτέρω προσελθεῖν κελεύσας, ἵνα μὴ κατακούοι, "ἆρ'" εἶπεν,
"ἄνδρες, εὑρήσομεν τοιοῦτον ἄνθρωπον, ὃς ἔχει
117 πνεῦμα θεῖον ἐν ἑαυτῷ;" συνεπαινούντων δὲ καὶ
συνευφημούντων, ἀπιδὼν εἰς τὸν παρεστῶτα "ἐγγὺς" εἶπεν "ἐστὶν ὃν παραινεῖς ἀναζητεῖν, οὐ
μακρὰν ἀφέστηκεν ὁ φρόνιμος καὶ συνετός, ὃν ἔδει
κατὰ τὰς σὰς ὑφηγήσεις σκοπεῖν, αὐτὸς ὢν τυγ-
χάνεις· οὐ γὰρ ἄνευ θεοῦ ταῦτ' ἀποφθέγγεσθαί μοι
δοκεῖς. ἴθι δὴ καὶ παραλάμβανε τήν τ' ἐπιμέλειαν
τῆς ἐμῆς οἰκίας καὶ τὴν Αἰγύπτου πάσης ἐπι-
118 τροπήν. εὐχέρειαν δ' οὐδείς μου καταγνώσεται
196

when the bran and chaff are separated through the purging of the grain. And to take charge of all this 114 you must appoint a man of the utmost prudence and good sense and well-approved all round, one who will be competent, without exciting hatred or open resistance, to make the preparations here described without giving the multitude any idea of the coming famine. For it would be a grievous thing if they should faint in anticipation and lose heart through lack of hope. And, if anyone asks the reason for 115 these measures, he should be told that, just as in peace we must exercise forethought in preparing for war, so, too, in years of plenty must we provide against dearth. Wars and famines and times of adversity in general are uncertain, and we must stand ready to meet them, not wait till they have come and look for the remedy when nothing is available."

XXI. The king having heard both his interpreta- 116 tion of the dreams, so exactly and skilfully divining the truth, and his advice to all appearance most profitable in its foresight for the uncertainties of the future, bade his companions come closer to him so that Joseph might not hear, and said : " Sirs, shall we find another man such as this, who has in him the spirit of God ? " When they with one accord praised 117 and applauded his words, he looked at Joseph who was standing by, and said : "He whom you bid us seek is near at hand, the man of prudence and sense is not far distant. He for whom according to your advice we should look is yourself, for I think that God is with you in the words you speak. Come, then, and take the charge of my house, and the superintendence of all Egypt. And no one will 118 condemn me for hastiness, for I am not actuated by

μὴ φιλαυτίᾳ χρωμένου, πάθει δυσιάτῳ· αἵ τε
γὰρ μεγάλαι τῶν φύσεων χρόνοις οὐ δοκιμάζονται
μακροῖς, ὄγκῳ δυνάμεως βιαζόμεναι φθάνειν εἰς
ἀποδοχὴν αὐτῶν ἀνυπέρθετον, τά τε πράγματα
μέλλησιν καὶ διατριβὴν οὐκ ἀνέχεται, τῶν καιρῶν
119 ἐπειγόντων εἰς τὰς ἀναγκαίας παρασκευάς." εἶτ'
αὐτὸν καθίστησι τῆς βασιλείας διάδοχον, μᾶλλον δ',
εἰ χρὴ τἀληθὲς εἰπεῖν, βασιλέα, τὸ μὲν ὄνομα τῆς
ἀρχῆς ὑπολειπόμενος αὐτῷ, τῆς δ' ἐν ἔργοις
ἡγεμονίας ἐκστὰς ἐκείνῳ καὶ τἆλλα πράττων ὅσα
120 ἐπὶ τιμῇ τοῦ νεανίου. δίδωσιν οὖν αὐτῷ σφραγῖδα
βασιλικὴν καὶ ἱερὰν ἐσθῆτα καὶ κύκλον χρυσοῦν
περιδέραιον καὶ ἐπὶ δευτερεῖον τῶν ἁρμάτων ἀνα-
βιβάσας κελεύει περιελθεῖν τὴν πόλιν, προερχομένου
κήρυκος καὶ δηλοῦντος τοῖς ἀγνοοῦσι τὴν χειρο-
121 τονίαν. μετονομάζει δ' αὐτὸν ἀπὸ τῆς ὀνειροκρι-
τικῆς ἐγχωρίῳ γλώττῃ προσαγορεύσας καὶ ἐγγυᾷ
πρὸς γάμον αὐτῷ τὴν ἐπιφανεστάτην τῶν κατ'
Αἴγυπτον ἱερέως Ἡλίου θυγατέρα. ταῦτ' ἐγένετο,
περὶ ἔτη γεγονότος ἤδη τριάκοντα.
122 τοιαῦτα τῶν εὐσεβῶν τὰ τέλη· κἂν γὰρ κλιθῶσιν,
οὐκ εἰς ἅπαν πίπτουσιν, ἀλλὰ διαναστάντες ὀρθοῦν-
ται παγίως καὶ βεβαίως, ὡς μηκέθ' ὑποσκελι-
123 σθῆναι. τίς γὰρ ἂν προσεδόκησε μιᾷ ἡμέρᾳ τὸν
αὐτὸν ἀντὶ μὲν δούλου δεσπότην, ἀντὶ δὲ δεσμώτου
[59] πάντων ἀξιονικότατον, | καὶ τὸν ὑποδιάκονον
εἱρκτοφύλακος ὕπαρχον βασιλέως ἔσεσθαι καὶ ἀντὶ
τῆς εἱρκτῆς τὰ βασίλεια οἰκήσειν, τὰ πρῶτα τῶν
ἐπὶ τιμαῖς φερόμενον ἀντὶ τῶν εἰς ἀτιμίαν ἐσχάτων;
124 ἀλλ' ὅμως καὶ γέγονε ταῦτα καὶ γενήσεται πολλάκις, ὅταν δοκῇ τῷ θεῷ· μόνον ἐντυφέσθω τι

self-confidence, that passion so hard to cure. Great natures take no long time to prove themselves, but by the massiveness of their power force others to give them a rapid and immediate acceptance ; and the facts of the case do not admit of delay and procrastination, since the needs of the time urge us on to make the necessary preparations." He then ap- 119 pointed him viceroy of the kingdom, or rather, if the truth be said, king, reserving indeed to himself the name of the office, but resigning to him the actual sovereignty and doing everything else that might give the young man honour. So, then, he bestowed 120 on him the royal seal and put upon him a sacred robe and a golden necklace, and setting him on his second chariot bade him go the round of the city with a crier walking in front who proclaimed the appointment to those who did not know of it. He 121 also gave him another name in the language of the country, based on his art of dream interpretation, and betrothed him to the most distinguished of the ladies of Egypt, the daughter of the priest of the Sun. These events happened when he was about thirty years old. Such is the latter end 122 of the pious ; though they be bent they do not altogether fall, but arise and stand upright firm and strong, never to be brought low any more. For 123 who would have expected that in a single day the same man would turn from slave to master, from a prisoner to the highest of dignitaries, that the gaoler's underling would be the king's vice-regent and lodge in the palace instead of the gaol, thus winning the foremost place of honour instead of the lowest of dishonour ? But nevertheless these things have 124 happened and will often happen when God so wills.

καλοκἀγαθίας ἐμπύρευμα ταῖς ψυχαῖς ὅπερ ἀναγ-
καῖόν ποτε ῥιπιζόμενον ἐκλάμψαι.

125 XXII. Ἐπεὶ δὲ πρόκειται μετὰ τὴν ῥητὴν
ἀπόδοσιν καὶ τὴν τροπικωτέραν ἐξετάζειν, λεκτέον
ἃ χρὴ καὶ περὶ αὐτῆς. ἴσως μὲν οὖν γελάσονταί
τινες τῶν εἰκαιοτέρων ἀκούσαντες· ἐγὼ δ' ἐρῶ
μηδὲν ὑποστειλάμενος, ὅτι ὁ πολιτικὸς πάντως
ὀνειροκριτικός ἐστιν, οὐχὶ τῶν βωμολόχων οὐδὲ
τῶν ἐναδολεσχούντων καὶ ἐνσοφιστευόντων ἐπὶ
μισθῷ καὶ τὴν τῶν καθ' ὕπνον φαντασιῶν διάκρισιν
ἀργυρισμοῦ πρόβλημα πεποιημένων, ἀλλὰ τὸν
κοινὸν καὶ πάνδημον καὶ μέγαν ὄνειρον οὐ κοιμωμένων μόνον ἀλλὰ καὶ ἐγρηγορότων εἰωθὼς ἀκρι-
126 βοῦν. ὁ δὲ ὄνειρος οὗτος, ὡς ἀψευδέστατα φάναι,
ὁ τῶν ἀνθρώπων ἐστὶ βίος· ὡς γὰρ ἐν ταῖς καθ'
ὕπνον φαντασίαις βλέποντες οὐ βλέπομεν καὶ
ἀκούοντες οὐκ ἀκούομεν καὶ γευόμενοι ἢ ἁπτόμενοι
οὔτε γευόμεθα οὔτε ἁπτόμεθα λέγοντές τε οὐ
λέγομεν καὶ περιπατοῦντες οὐ περιπατοῦμεν καὶ
ταῖς ἄλλαις κινήσεσι καὶ σχέσεσι χρῆσθαι δοκοῦντες
οὐδεμιᾷ τὸ παράπαν χρώμεθα—κεναὶ δ' εἰσὶ τῆς
διανοίας πρὸς οὐδὲν ὑποκείμενον ἀληθείᾳ μόνον
ἀναζωγραφούσης καὶ ἀνειδωλοποιούσης τὰ μὴ ὄντα
ὡς ὄντα,—οὕτω καὶ τῶν παρ' ἡμῖν ἐγρηγορότων αἱ
φαντασίαι τοῖς ἐνυπνίοις ἐοίκασιν· ἦλθον, ἀπῆλθον,
ἐφάνησαν, ἀπεπήδησαν, πρὶν καταληφθῆναι βε-
127 βαίως ἀπέπτησαν. ἐρευνησάτω δ' ἕκαστος αὑτὸν
καὶ τὸν ἔλεγχον οἴκοθεν ἄνευ τῶν παρ' ἐμοῦ πί-
στεων εἴσεται, καὶ μάλιστ' εἴ τις πρεσβύτερος ἤδη
γεγονὼς τυγχάνοι· οὗτος ἦν ὁ ποτὲ βρέφος καὶ
μετὰ ταῦτα παῖς, εἶτ' ἔφηβος, εἶτα μειράκιον, καὶ
128 νεανίας αὖθις, εἶτ' ἀνήρ, καὶ γέρων ὕστατον. ἀλλὰ

Only there must be some live coal of nobility smouldering in the soul, which is sure, if it be fanned into flame, to blaze into light.

XXII. But since it is our purpose to examine the 125 more allegorical meaning after the literal, I must say what is needful on that also. Perhaps some of the more thoughtless will laugh at my words ; but I will say quite plainly that the statesman is most certainly an interpreter of dreams, not one of the parasites, nor one of the praters who shew off their cleverness for hire and use their art of interpreting the visions given in sleep as a pretext for making money ; but one who is accustomed to judge with exactness that great general universal dream which is dreamt not only by the sleeping but also by the waking.ᵃ This dream in veriest truth is human life : 126 for, just as in the visions of sleep, seeing we see not, hearing we hear not, tasting and touching we neither taste nor touch, speaking we speak not, walking we walk not, and the other motions which we make or postures we adopt we do not make or adopt at all, but they are empty creations of the mind which without any basis of reality produces pictures and images of things which are not, as though they were, so, too, the visions and imaginations of our waking hours resemble dreams. They come ; they go ; they appear ; they speed away ; they fly off before we can securely grasp them ; let every man search into his own heart and 127 he will test the truth of this at first hand, with no need of proof from me, especially if he is now advanced in years. This is he who was once a babe, after this a boy, then a lad, then a stripling, then a young man, then a grown man and last an old man. But where 128

ᵃ For some discussion of §§ 125–147 see App. pp. 601–602.

ποῦ πάντ' ἐκεῖνα; οὐκ ἐν μὲν παιδὶ τὸ βρέφος
ὑπεξῆλθεν, ὁ δὲ παῖς ἐν παρήβῳ, ὁ δ' ἔφηβος ἐν
μειρακίῳ, τὸ δὲ μειράκιον ἐν νεανίᾳ, ἐν ἀνδρὶ δ' ὁ
νεανίας, ἀνὴρ δ' ἐν γέροντι, γήρᾳ δ' ἕπεται τε-
129 λευτή; τάχα μέντοι τάχα καὶ τῶν ἡλικιῶν ἑκάστη
παραχωροῦσα τοῦ κράτους τῇ μεθ' ἑαυτὴν προαπο-
θνῄσκει, τῆς φύσεως ἡμᾶς ἀναδιδασκούσης ἡσυχῇ
μὴ δεδιέναι τὸν ἐπὶ πᾶσι θάνατον, ἐπειδὴ τοὺς προτέρους εὐμαρῶς ἠνέγκαμεν, τὸν βρέφους, τὸν
παιδός, τὸν ἐφήβου, τὸν μειρακίου, τὸν νεανίου, τὸν
ἀνδρός, ὧν οὐδεὶς ἔτ' ἐστὶ γήρως ἐπιστάντος.

130   XXIII. τὰ δ' ἄλλα ὅσα περὶ τὸ σῶμα
οὐκ ἐνύπνια; οὐ κάλλος μὲν ἐφήμερον, πρὶν ἀν-
[60] θῆσαι μαραινόμενον; ὑγεία δὲ | ἀβέβαιον διὰ τὰς
ἐφέδρους ἀσθενείας; ἰσχὺς δ' εὐάλωτον νόσοις ἐκ
μυρίων προφάσεων; ἥ τ' ἀκρίβεια τῶν αἰσθήσεων
οὐ παγία ῥεύματος ἐνστάσει βραχέος ἀνατρέπεται;
131   τὴν δὲ τῶν ἐκτὸς ἀσάφειαν τίς οὐκ
οἶδε; μιᾷ ἡμέρᾳ πλοῦτοι μεγάλοι πολλάκις ἀπερ-
ρύησαν· τὰ πρωτεῖα τῶν ἐν ταῖς ἀνωτάτω τιμαῖς
ἐνεγκάμενοι μυρίοι πρὸς ἡμελημένων καὶ ἀφανῶν
ἀδοξίαν μετέβαλον· ἀρχαὶ βασιλέων αἱ μέγισται
132 καθῃρέθησαν βραχείᾳ καιροῦ ῥοπῇ. ἐγγυαταί μου
τὸν λόγον Διονύσιος ὁ ἐν Κορίνθῳ, ὃς Σικελίας
μὲν τύραννος ἦν, ἐκπεσὼν δὲ τῆς ἡγεμονίας εἰς
Κόρινθον καταφεύγει καὶ γραμματιστὴς ὁ τοσοῦτος
133 ἡγεμὼν γίνεται. συνεγγυᾶται καὶ Κροῖσος ὁ
Λυδίας βασιλεύς, πλουσιώτατος βασιλέων, ὃς ἐλ-
πίσας τὴν Περσῶν καθελεῖν ἀρχὴν οὐ μόνον τὴν

─────────

[a] Cf. De Cher. 114.
[b] The γραμματιστής is lower than the γραμματικός, cf. the

are all these gone ? Has not the baby vanished in the boy, the boy in the lad, the lad in the stripling, the stripling in the youth, the youth in the man, the man in the old man, while on old age follows death ? [a] Perhaps, indeed, each of the stages, as it resigns its 129 rule to its successor, dies an anticipatory death, nature thus silently teaching us not to fear the death which ends all, since we have borne so easily the earlier deaths :—that of the babe, of the boy, of the lad, of the stripling, of the man, who are all no more when old age has come.   XXIII. And the other 130 things of the body are they not dreams ? Is not beauty but for a day, withering before it flowers ; health insecure because of the infirmities that lie ready to attack it ; strength an easy victim of the diseases which arise from numberless causes ; accuracy of senses unstable and easily upset by the onset of some little humour ?   As for the 131 external goods, who does not know their uncertainty ? Magnificent fortunes have often been dissolved in a single day. Multitudes who have won the first place with the highest honour have passed over to the unglorious lot of the unmeritable and obscure. The greatest kings have seen their empires overthrown when occasion gives a slight turn to the scale. What 132 I say is vouched for by Dionysius of Corinth, who was the tyrant of Sicily, but when he fell from power fled to Corinth and there this great sovereign became a teacher of the rudiments.[b] Another witness is 133 Croesus, the king of Lydia, wealthiest of monarchs, who hoped to overthrow the empire of the Persians,

definition of γραμματιστική as γραμματικὴ ἀτελεστέρα, De Cong. 148. Cicero, Tusc. iii. 27, merely says of Dionysius " docebat pueros."

οἰκείαν προσαπέβαλεν, ἀλλὰ καὶ ζωγρηθεὶς ἐμέλ-
134 λησε καταπίμπρασθαι. μάρτυρες τῶν ἐνυπνίων
οὐκ ἄνδρες μόνον, ἀλλὰ καὶ πόλεις, ἔθνη, χῶραι, ἡ
Ἑλλάς, ἡ βάρβαρος, ἠπειρῶται, νησιῶται, ἡ
Εὐρώπη, ἡ Ἀσία, δύσις, ἀνατολή. μεμένηκε
γὰρ οὐδὲν οὐδαμοῦ τὸ παράπαν ἐν ὁμοίῳ, τροπαῖς
δὲ καὶ μεταβολαῖς ἐχρήσατο πάντα διὰ πάντων.
135 Αἴγυπτός ποτε πολλῶν ἐθνῶν ἡγεμονίαν εἶχεν,
ἀλλὰ νῦν ἐστι δούλη. Μακεδόνες οὕτως ἐπὶ καιρῶν
ἤκμασαν, ὡς ἁπάσης ἀνάψασθαι τῆς οἰκουμένης
τὸ κράτος, ἀλλὰ νῦν τοῖς ἐκλογεῦσι τῶν χρημάτων
τοὺς ἐπιταχθέντας ὑπὸ τῶν κυρίων δασμοὺς ἐτη-
136 σίους εἰσφέρουσι. ποῦ δὲ ἡ τῶν Πτολεμαίων οἰκία
καὶ ἡ καθ' ἕκαστον τῶν διαδόχων ἐπιφάνεια μέχρι
γῆς καὶ θαλάττης περάτων ἐκλάμψασα; ποῦ δ' αἱ
τῶν αὐτονόμων ἐθνῶν καὶ πόλεων ἐλευθερίαι; ποῦ
δ' ἔμπαλιν αἱ δουλεῖαι τῶν ὑπηκόων; οὐ Πέρσαι
μὲν Παρθυαίων ἐπεκράτουν, νυνὶ δὲ Περσῶν Παρ-
θυαῖοι διὰ τὰς τῶν ἀνθρωπείων πραγμάτων στροφὰς
καὶ τὰς ἄνω καὶ κάτω πεττείας καὶ μεταθέσεις
137 αὐτῶν; ἀναπλάττουσιν ἔνιοι μακράς τινας καὶ
ἀπεράτους εὐτυχίας ἑαυτοῖς, αἱ δ' ἀρχαὶ μεγάλων
κακῶν εἰσι· καὶ σπεύδοντες ὡς ἐπ' ἀγαθῶν κληρο-
νομίαν εὑρίσκουσι δεινὰς κακοπραγίας, καὶ τοὐναντίον κακὸν προσδοκήσαντες ἀγαθοῖς ἐνέτυχον.
138 ἀθληταὶ δυνάμεσι καὶ ῥώμαις καὶ εὐεξίαις σωμάτων
μέγα φρονοῦντες, ἀνενδοίαστον νίκην ἐλπίσαντες,
ἐξαγώνιοι πολλάκις ἐγένοντο μὴ δοκιμασθέντες ἢ
καταστάντες εἰς τὸν ἀγῶνα ἡττήθησαν, οἱ δ'
ἀπογνόντες καὶ δευτερείων ἐφίξεσθαι τὰ πρῶτα

---

[a] Cf. *Quod Deus* 173 f.　　　　[b] *i.e.* of Alexander.

and not only lost his own as well but was taken
prisoner and on the point of being burnt alive. That 134
these are dreams is attested not only by single men,
but by cities, nations, countries, by Greeks, by the
world of the barbarians, by dwellers on the mainland,
by dwellers on islands, by Europe, by Asia, by West,
by East.ᵃ For nothing at all anywhere has remained
in the same condition ; everywhere all has been
subject to changes and vicissitudes. Egypt once 135
held the sovereignty over many nations, but now is
in slavery. The Macedonians in their day of success
flourished so greatly that they held dominion over
all the habitable world, but now they pay to the tax-
collectors the yearly tributes imposed by their
masters. Where is the house of the Ptolemies, and 136
the fame of the several Successors ᵇ whose light once
shone to the utmost boundaries of land and sea ?
Where are the liberties of the independent nations
and cities, where again the servitude of the vassals ?
Did not the Persians once rule the Parthians, and
now the Parthians rule the Persians ? So much do
human affairs twist and change, go backward and
forward as on the draught-board. Some picture for 137
their future a long and unlimited run of luck, and
the outcome is great calamity, and when they press
eagerly to secure what they think to be their heritage
of good they find terrible misfortunes, while on the
contrary when they expect evil what they meet
with is good. Athletes mightily proud of the 138
strength and muscle and robustness of their bodies,
hoping for undoubted victory, have often failed to
pass the test and been excluded from the arena, or
if admitted, have been vanquished, while others who
despaired of taking even the second place have won

139 τῶν ἄθλων στεφανηφοροῦντες ἤραντο. θέρους ἀναχ-
θέντες τινές—ὁ γὰρ καιρὸς εὐπλοίας—ἐναυάγησαν,
ἕτεροι δὲ χειμῶνος ἀνατραπήσεσθαι προσδοκῶντες
ἀκινδύνως ἄχρι λιμένων παρεπέμφθησαν. ὡς ἐφ'
ὁμολογούμενα κέρδη συντείνουσιν ἔνιοι τῶν ἐμ-
πόρων ἀγνοοῦντες τὰς ἐφέδρους ζημίας, ἔμπαλιν
λογιζόμενοι βλαβήσεσθαι μεγάλων ἀπέλαυσαν |
[61] ὠφελειῶν. οὕτως ἄδηλοι μὲν αἱ τύχαι πρὸς ἑκά-
140 τερα, τὰ δ' ἀνθρώπεια ὡς ἐπὶ ζυγοῦ ταλαντεύεται
βάρεσιν ἀνίσοις ἐπικουφιζόμενα καὶ καθέλκοντα·
δεινὴ δ' ἀσάφεια καὶ πολὺ σκότος κατακέχυται τῶν
πραγμάτων· ὡς δ' ἐν βαθεῖ ὕπνῳ πλαζόμεθα μηδὲν
ἐμπεριελθεῖν ἀκριβείᾳ λογισμοῦ δυνάμενοι μηδ'
εὐτόνως καὶ παγίως ἐπιδράξασθαί τινος, σκιαῖς γὰρ
141 ἔοικε καὶ φάσμασι. καὶ ὥσπερ ἐν ταῖς πομπαῖς τὰ
πρῶτα παρέρχεται φεύγοντα τὰς ὄψεις κἂν τοῖς
χειμάρροις τὸ φερόμενον ῥεῦμα φθάνει παραδραμὸν
ὀξύτητι τάχους τὴν κατάληψιν, οὕτω καὶ τὰ ἐν τῷ
βίῳ πράγματα φερόμενα καὶ παρεξιόντα φαντάζε-
ται μὲν ὡς ὑπομένοντα, μένει δ' οὐδ' ἐπ' ἀκαρές,
142 ἀλλ' ἀεὶ ὑποσύρεται.   καὶ οἱ ἐγρηγορότες,
ὅσα γε πρὸς τὸ ἐν ταῖς καταλήψεσιν ἀβέβαιον
οὐδὲν τῶν κοιμωμένων διαφέροντες, ἀπατῶντες
ἑαυτοὺς ἱκανοὶ νομίζουσιν εἶναι τὰς φύσεις τῶν
πραγμάτων ἀπλανέσι λογισμοῖς ὁρᾶν· οἷς ἑκάστη
τῶν αἰσθήσεων εἰς ἐπιστήμην ἐμπόδιος, δεκαζομένη
θεάμασιν, ἀκούσμασι, χυλῶν ποιότησιν, ἀτμῶν
ἰδιότησι, πρὸς ἅπερ ἀποκλίνουσα συνεφέλκεται καὶ
τὴν ὅλην ψυχὴν οὐκ ἐῶσα ὀρθοῦσθαι καὶ ἀπταίστως
οἷα διὰ λεωφόρων ὁδῶν προέρχεσθαι· τὸ δ' ὑψηλο-

the first prize and worn the crown. Some who 139
embarked in summer, the safe sailing season, have
been shipwrecked; others who sailed in winter,
expecting to be capsized, have reached the harbour
in security. Of merchants, some hurry to what seems
certain gain, and little know the disasters that await
them. Again, when they reckon that they will
suffer loss, they win great profits. Thus fortunes 140
are uncertain either way, and human affairs swing
as on a scale with unequal weights, carried lightly
up or pressing the balance down, and terrible is the
uncertainty and vast the darkness which envelops
the events of life. We flounder as though in deep
sleep, unable to compass anything by accurate
reasoning or to grasp it vigorously and firmly, for
all are like shadows and phantoms. And as in 141
processions the front part passes on and is lost to
sight, and in the winter torrents the stream in its
course speeds past us and by its violence and rapidity
outstrips our observation, so too the events of life
rush along past us, and though they make a show of
remaining do not stay even for a moment, but are
ever swept away.   And those who 142
are awake, who in the uncertainty of apprehension
differ nothing from the sleeping, deceive themselves
and think that they are capable of discerning differences in the nature of things by incontrovertible
processes of reason. Each sense impedes their attainment of knowledge, seduced whether by the sights
it sees or by the sounds it hears, or by varieties of
flavours, or by scents of different quality, to which
it turns aside and is dragged along with them, and
prevents the soul as a whole from standing erect
and advancing without stumbling as along a high

τάπεινον καὶ μεγαλόμικρον καὶ πᾶν ὅσον ἀνισό-
τητι καὶ ἀνωμαλίᾳ συγγενὲς ἀπεργάζεται καὶ σκοτο-
δινιᾶν ἀναγκάζει καὶ πολὺν ἐμποιεῖ ἴλιγγον.

143   XXIV. τοσαύτης οὖν ταραχῆς καὶ
ἀταξίας ἔτι δὲ ἀσαφείας γέμοντος τοῦ βίου, παρ-
ελθόντα δεῖ τὸν πολιτικὸν ὥσπερ τινὰ σοφὸν τὴν
ὀνειροκριτικὴν τὰ μεθημερινὰ ἐνύπνια καὶ φάσμα-
τα τῶν ἐγρηγορέναι δοκούντων διακρίνειν εἰκόσι
στοχασμοῖς καὶ εὐλόγοις πιθανότησι περὶ ἑκάστου
ἀναδιδάσκοντα, ὅτι τοῦτο καλόν, ἐκεῖνο αἰσχρόν,
τοῦτο ἀγαθόν, κακὸν ἐκεῖνο, τουτὶ δίκαιον, ἄδικον
τοὐναντίον, καὶ τἆλλα ταύτῃ, τὸ φρόνιμον, τὸ
ἀνδρεῖον, τὸ εὐσεβές, τὸ ὅσιον, τὸ συμφέρον, τὸ
ὠφέλιμον, καὶ πάλιν τὸ ἀνωφελές, τὸ ἀλόγιστον,
τὸ ἀγεννές, τὸ ἀσεβές, τὸ ἀνόσιον, τὸ ἀσύμφορον,
144 τὸ βλαβερόν, τὸ φίλαυτον.[1]   καὶ ἔτι πρὸς τούτοις[2]
ἀλλότριον τοῦτο, μὴ ἐπιθύμει· ἴδιον τοῦτο, χρῶ μὴ
παραχρώμενος· περιουσιάζεις, μεταδίδου· πλούτου
γὰρ τὸ κάλλος οὐκ ἐν βαλαντίοις, ἀλλ' ἐν τῇ τῶν
χρῃζόντων ἐπικουρίᾳ· ὀλίγα κέκτησαι, μὴ φθόνει
τοῖς ἔχουσι· πένητα γὰρ βάσκανον οὐδεὶς ἂν ἐλεή-
σαι· εὐδοξεῖς καὶ τετίμησαι, μὴ καταλαζονεύου·
ταπεινὸς εἶ ταῖς τύχαις, ἀλλὰ τὸ φρόνημα μὴ κατα-
πιπτέτω· πάντα σοι κατὰ νοῦν χωρεῖ, μεταβολὴν
εὐλαβοῦ· πταίεις πολλάκις, χρηστὰ ἔλπιζε· πρὸς

---

[1] The two lists balance so closely that one may be tempted
to make the balance complete, and Cohn suggests the omission of τὸ ἀνωφελές at the beginning of the second and the
insertion of τὸ φιλάνθρωπον. The argument does not seem
to me convincing. Perhaps, too, φιλόθεον rather than φιλάνθρωπον is the reverse of Philo's φίλαυτον. *Cf. Quod
Det.* 32.

[2] The transition to a totally different kind of question

road. And thus the senses produce the confusion of high with low and great with small, and all that is akin to inequality and irregularity, and the soul's sight swims perforce in the great dizziness which they create. XXIV. Since, then, human life 143 is full of this vast confusion and disorder and uncertainty also, the statesman must come forward, and, like some wise expounder of dreams, interpret the day-time visions and phantoms of those who think themselves awake, and with suggestions commended by reason and probability shew them the truth about each of these visions : that this is beautiful, that ugly, this just, that unjust, and so with all the rest ; what is prudent, courageous, pious, religious, beneficial, profitable, and conversely what is unprofitable, unreasonable, ignoble, impious, irreligious, deleterious, harmful, selfish.[a] And he will 144 give other lessons, such as, This is another's, do not covet it ; This is your own, use it but do not misuse it ; You have abundance of wealth, give a share to others, for the excellence of wealth consists not in a full purse but in succouring the needy ; Your possessions are small, be not jealous of the rich, for envious poverty gets pity from none ; You have high reputation and have received honour, be not arrogant ; Your fortunes are lowly, let not your spirits sink also ; All goes with you as you would have it, be prepared for change ; You have made many a trip, hope for a better time, for with men

---

[a] Or perhaps better " self-assertive."

---

seems a little abrupt. It may be observed that what we might expect, viz. ἄλλα οἷον, would very easily be lost before ἀλλότριον.

145 γὰρ τἀναντία τῶν ἀνθρώπων αἱ τροπαί. σελήνη
μὲν γὰρ καὶ ἥλιος καὶ ὁ σύμπας οὐρανὸς σαφεῖς καὶ
ἀριδήλους ἔχει τὰς τρανότητας, ἅτε πάντων τῶν |

[62] κατ᾽ αὐτὸν ὁμοίων μενόντων καὶ τοῖς τῆς ἀληθείας
αὐτῆς μετρουμένων κανόσιν ἐν τάξεσιν ἐναρμονίοις
καὶ συμφωνιῶν ταῖς ἀρίσταις, τὰ δ᾽ ἐπίγεια πολλῆς ἀταξίας γέμοντα καὶ ταραχῆς ἀσύμφωνα καὶ
ἀνάρμοστα, ὡς κυριώτατα φάναι, ὅτι ταῦτα μὲν
βαθὺ σκότος κατείληφεν, ἐκεῖνα δ᾽ ἐμφέρεται τηλ-
αυγεστάτῳ φωτί, μᾶλλον δ᾽ αὐτὸ φῶς ἐστιν εἰλι-
146 κρινέστατον καὶ καθαρώτατον. εἰ γοῦν βουληθείη
διακύπτειν εἴσω τις τῶν πραγμάτων, εὑρήσει τὸν
οὐρανὸν ἡμέραν αἰώνιον, νυκτὸς καὶ πάσης σκιᾶς
ἀμέτοχον, ἅτε περιλαμπόμενον ἀσβέστοις καὶ
147 ἀκηράτοις ἀδιαστάτως φέγγεσιν. ὅσῳ τε διαφέρουσιν οἱ παρ᾽ ἡμῖν ἐγρηγορότες τῶν κοιμωμένων, τοσούτῳ καὶ ἐν ἅπαντι τῷ κόσμῳ τὰ οὐράνια
τῶν ἐπιγείων, τὰ μὲν ἐγρηγόρσει χρώμενα ἀκοι-
μήτῳ διὰ τὰς ἀπλανεῖς καὶ ἀπταίστους καὶ ἐν
ἅπασι κατορθούσας ἐνεργείας, τὰ δ᾽ ὕπνῳ κατεχό-
μενα, κἂν εἰ πρὸς βραχὺ διαναστάη, πάλιν καθελκό-
μενα καὶ καταδαρθάνοντα διὰ τὸ μηδὲν εὐθυτενῶς
δύνασθαι τῇ ψυχῇ βλέπειν, ἀλλὰ πλάζεσθαι καὶ
περιπταίειν· ἐπισκοτεῖται γὰρ ψευδέσι δόξαις, ὑφ᾽
ὧν ὀνειρώττειν ἀναγκαζόμενα καὶ τῶν πραγμάτων
ὑστερίζοντα οὐδὲν παγίως καὶ βεβαίως ἱκανὰ
148 καταλαμβάνειν ἐστί.   XXV. συμβολικῶς μέντοι καὶ ἐπὶ τὸ δευτερεῖον τῶν βασιλικῶν
ἁρμάτων ἀναβαίνειν λέγεται δι᾽ αἰτίαν τοιάνδε· ὁ
πολιτικὸς τὰ δευτερεῖα φέρεται βασιλέως· οὔτε γὰρ
ἰδιώτης ἐστὶν οὔτε βασιλεύς, ἀλλ᾽ ἀμφοῖν μεθόριος,
ἰδιώτου μὲν ὢν κρείττων, ἐλάττων δ᾽ εἰς ἀρχὴν

things turn to their opposite ; The sun and moon and 145
the whole heaven stand out in such clear and plain
distinctness because everything there remains the
same and regulated by the standards of truth itself
moves in harmonious order and with the grandest
of symphonies ; while earthly things are brimful of
disorder and confusion and in the fullest sense of the
words discordant and inharmonious, because in them
deep darkness reigns while in heaven all moves in
most radiant light, or rather heaven is light itself
most pure and unalloyed. And indeed if one be 146
willing to look into the inner realities he will find
that heaven is an eternal day, wherein there is no
night or any shadow, because around it shine without
ceasing unquenchable and undefiled beams of light.
And the same difference that there is here in people 147
when asleep and when awake exists in the universe
as a whole between the heavenly and the earthly,
for the former is kept in unsleeping wakefulness by
active forces which do not err or stumble and go
always aright, but the earthly life is sunk in sleep,
and even if it wake up for a little is dragged down
again and falls asleep, because it can see nothing
steadily with its soul but wanders and stumbles about
darkened as it is by false opinions which compel it
to dream, and thus never catching up with realities
it is incapable of apprehending anything firmly and
securely.   XXV. Again there is a sym- 148
bolic meaning in saying that Joseph mounts on the
king's second chariot, and the reason is this. The
statesman takes a second place to the king, for he is
neither a private person nor a king, but something
between the two. He is greater than a private
person but less than a king in absolute power, since

αὐτεξούσιον βασιλέως, τῷ δήμῳ βασιλεῖ χρώμενος,
ὑπὲρ οὗ πάντα πράττειν προῄρηται καθαρᾷ καὶ
149 ἀδολωτάτῃ πίστει.   φέρεται δὲ ὡς ἐφ᾽
ἁρματείου δίφρου μετέωρος ὑπό τε τῶν πραγμάτων
καὶ τῶν ὄχλων εἰς ὕψος αἰρόμενος, καὶ μάλισθ᾽
ὅταν κατὰ νοῦν ἕκαστα μικρὰ καὶ μεγάλα χωρῇ,
μηδενὸς ἀντιπνέοντος μηδ᾽ ἀντιστατοῦντος, ἀλλ᾽ ὡς
ἐν εὐπλοίᾳ πάντων σωτηρίως ὑπὸ θεοῦ κυβερνω-
μένων.   ὅν τε δίδωσιν ὁ βασιλεὺς δακτύ-
λιον, ἐναργέστατον δεῖγμα πίστεώς ἐστιν, ἣν πεπί-
στευκεν ὅ τε βασιλεὺς δῆμος τῷ πολιτικῷ καὶ ὁ
πολιτικὸς τῷ βασιλεύοντι δήμῳ.

150 ὁ δὲ περὶ τὸν τράχηλον χρυσοῦς κύκλος εὐδοξίαν
ὁμοῦ καὶ κόλασιν ἔοικεν ὑποσημαίνειν· ἕως μὲν
γὰρ τὰ κατὰ τὴν πολιτείαν εὐοδεῖ πράγματα αὐτῷ,
γαῦρός ἐστι καὶ σεμνὸς ὑπὸ τῶν ὄχλων τιμώμενος·
ἐπειδὰν δὲ πταῖσμα συμβῇ, μὴ κατὰ προαίρεσιν
—τοῦτο γὰρ ὑπαίτιον—, ἀλλὰ τυχηρόν, ὅπερ ἐστὶ
συγγνωστόν, οὐδὲν ἧττον ἕλκεται κάτω διὰ τοῦ
περιαυχενίου κόσμου καὶ ταπεινοῦται, μόνον οὐκ
ἐπιλέγοντος τοῦ δεσπότου· "τὸν περιαυχένιον τοῦτον κύκλον ἐδωρησάμην σοι καὶ κόσμον κατορθου-
μένων τῶν ἐμῶν καὶ ἀγχόνην ἀποτυγχανομένων."

151
[63]   XXVI. | Ἤκουσα μέντοι καθ᾽ ἑτέραν ἰδέαν
τροπικώτερον τὰ περὶ τὸν τόπον ἀκριβούντων. ἦν
δὲ τοιάδε· τὸν βασιλέα τῆς Αἰγύπτου τὸν ἡμέτερον
νοῦν ἔλεγον εἶναι, τὸν τῆς καθ᾽ ἕκαστον σωματικῆς
χώρας ἡγεμόνα, ὃς οἷα βασιλεὺς ἀνῆπται τὸ κράτος.
152 ᾧ γενομένῳ φιλοσωμάτῳ τρία τὰ πλείστης ἀξιού-
μενα σπουδῆς διαπονεῖται, σιτία καὶ ὄψα καὶ ποτά,

he has the people for his king, and to serve that king with pure and guileless good faith is the task he has set before him.   He rides, too, aloft seated 149 on a chariot, raised on high both by the affairs he handles and the multitude around him, especially when everything great and small goes as he would have it, when from none comes any counterblast or opposition, and under the safe pilotage of God all is well with the voyage.   And the ring which the king gives is the clearest sign of the good faith which the king-people places in the statesman and the statesman in the king-people.

The golden chain around his neck seems to indicate 150 both high fame and punishment, for while affairs of state fare well in his hands he is proud and dignified and honoured by the multitude, but when disaster befalls him, not indeed of his set purpose which would imply guilt, but by chance which is a venial matter, he is all the same dragged down to the dust by the decoration round his neck, and as he falls you may almost hear his master say : " I gave you this neck circlet both as a decoration when my business prospers and as a halter when it goes amiss." [a]

XXVI. I have heard, however, some scholars give 151 an allegorical exposition of this part of the story in a different form. It was as follows. The king of Egypt, they said, was our mind, the ruler of the land of the body in each of us over which he is invested with kingly power. When this mind 152 becomes enamoured of the body, its efforts are expended on three things which it deems most worthy of its care and trouble, bread, meat and drink ; and,

[a] The incidents of Joseph's exaltation discussed in these sections are treated somewhat differently in *De Som.* ii. 43-47.

PHILO

παρὸ καὶ τρισὶ χρῆται τοῖς τῶν λεγομένων ἐπιμελη
ταῖς, ἀρχισιτοποιῷ καὶ ἀρχιοινοχόῳ καὶ ἀρχι
μαγείρῳ· πρυτανεύει γὰρ ὁ μὲν τὰ περὶ ἐδωδήν, ὁ
δὲ τὰ περὶ πόσιν, ὁ δ' ἐπιτέτακται τοῖς περὶ αὐτὰ
153 τὰ ὄψα ἡδύσμασιν. πάντες δέ εἰσιν εὐνοῦχοι, ἐπει
δὴ ὁ φιλήδονος ἄγονός ἐστι τῶν ἀναγκαιοτάτων,
σωφροσύνης, αἰδοῦς, ἐγκρατείας, δικαιοσύνης, ἀπά
σης ἀρετῆς· οὐδὲν γὰρ οὕτως ἐχθρὸν ἄλλο ἄλλῳ, ὡς
ἀρετῇ ἡδονή, δι' ἣν ἀλογοῦσιν οἱ πολλοὶ ὧν μόνον
ἄξιον πεφροντικέναι, ταῖς ἀκαθέκτοις ἐπιθυμίαις
154 χαριζόμενοι καὶ οἷς ἂν προστάττωσιν εἴκοντες. ὁ
μὲν οὖν ἀρχιμάγειρος οὔτ' εἰς δεσμωτήριον ἀπ
άγεται οὔτε τινὶ περιπίπτει λύμῃ διὰ τὸ μὴ σφόδρα
τῶν ἀναγκαίων εἶναι τὰς παραρτύσεις οὐχ ἡδονὰς
οὔσας ἀλλ' εὔσβεστα ἡδονῶν ὑπεκκαύματα, δύο
δὲ τῶν περὶ τὴν ἄθλιον γαστέρα πραγματευομένων,
ἀρχισιτοποιὸς καὶ ἀρχιοινοχόος, ἐπειδὴ τὰ συνεκ
τικώτατα τῶν εἰς τὸ ζῆν χρησίμων ἐστὶ βρῶσις καὶ
πόσις, ὧν ἐπιμελείας μὲν ἀξιουμένων οἱ προεστῶτες
εἰκότως ἐπαίνων τυγχάνουσιν, ὀλιγωρουμένων δὲ
155 ὀργῆς καὶ κολάσεως ἀξιοῦνται. διαφορὰ δὲ κἂν
ταῖς κολάσεσιν, ὅτι διάφορος ἡ χρεία, σιτίων μὲν
ἀναγκαιοτάτη, οἴνου δὲ οὐ πάνυ χρησίμη· καὶ γὰρ
ἀκράτου δίχα ζῶσιν ἄνθρωποι ναματιαίῳ ὕδατι
156 ποτῷ χρώμενοι. δι' ἣν αἰτίαν πρὸς μὲν τὸν ἀρχι
οινοχόον γίνονται καταλλαγαὶ καὶ συμβάσεις ὡς
ἂν ἁμαρτόντα περὶ τὸ ἔλαττον μέρος, ἀσύμβατα
δὲ καὶ ἀκατάλλακτα τὰ πρὸς τὸν ἀρχισιτοποιὸν
ἐστιν ἄχρι θανάτου λαμβάνοντα τὴν ὀργὴν ὡς ἂν
περὶ τὸ μέγιστον ἀδικήσαντα· τελευτὴ γὰρ ἕπεται
σιτίων σπάνει· οὗ χάριν καὶ ὁ περὶ ταῦτ' ἐξαμαρ
τὼν εἰκότως θνήσκει κρεμασθείς, ὅμοιον κακὸν

214

therefore, it provides three offices to provide for these, a chief baker, a chief butler and a chief cook, for the first presides over the food, the second over the drink, the third over the seasoning which adds relish to the actual meat. All are eunuchs, since 153 the lover of pleasure is barren of all the chief necessities, temperance, modesty, self-restraint, justice and every virtue; for no two things can be more hostile to each other than virtue is to pleasure, which makes the many disregard what alone deserves their care, satisfy their unbridled lusts and submit to whatever those lusts command. So, then, the chief cook is not haled 154 to prison and meets with no maltreatment, because the extra seasonings he prepares are not of the most indispensable kind and are not pleasure, but incitements to pleasure, which kindle only to be quenched. Not so with the other two whose business lies with the miserable belly, namely the chief baker and the chief butler. For the most essential of the needs of life are food and drink, and those who take charge of them are naturally held to deserve praise if they treat the charge as worthy of their care, but anger and punishment if they neglect it. The punishment 155 also differs in the two cases because the usefulness of the two differs, being absolutely vital in regard to bread-food, less so in regard to wine, for men can live without strong liquor by drinking fresh water, and 156 therefore it is possible to make terms of reconciliation with the chief butler as an offender in a less important matter. Not so with the chief baker who, being guilty in what is all-important, is the object of an anger which demands his life. For death is the consequence of lack of bread-food, and therefore the offender in this is properly put to death by hanging,

215

ᾧ διέθηκε παθών· καὶ γὰρ αὐτὸς ἀνεκρέμασε καὶ παρέτεινε τὸν πεινῶντα λιμῷ.

157 XXVII. Τοσαῦτα καὶ περὶ τούτου. ὁ μέντοι βασιλέως ὕπαρχος κατασταθεὶς καὶ τῆς Αἰγύπτου τὴν ἐπιμέλειαν καὶ προστασίαν λαβὼν ἐξῄει γνωρισθησόμενος ἅπασι τοῖς ἐγχωρίοις καὶ τοὺς λεγομένους νομοὺς ἐπιὼν κατὰ πόλεις πολὺν αὐτοῦ πόθον ἐνειργάζετο τοῖς ὁρῶσιν, οὐ μόνον ταῖς ὠφελείαις, ἃς ἑκάστοις παρεῖχεν, ἀλλὰ καὶ ταῖς περὶ τὴν ὄψιν τε καὶ τὴν ἄλλην ὁμιλίαν ἀλέκτοις 158 καὶ ἐξαιρέτοις χάρισιν. ἐπεὶ δὲ κατὰ τὴν τῶν ὀνειράτων σύγκρισιν[1] ἐνέστη προτέρα τῆς εὐθηνίας [64] ἡ ἑπταετία, τὸ πέμπτον | τῶν καρπῶν ἀνὰ πᾶν ἔτος συνάγων διά τε τῶν ὑπάρχων[2] καὶ τῶν ἄλλων, οἳ πρὸς τὰς δημοσίας χρείας ὑπηρέτουν αὐτῷ, τοσαύτην ἤθροισε πληθὺν δραγμάτων, ὅσην οὐδείς πω πρότερον γενομένην ἐμέμνητο· πίστις δὲ σαφεστάτη τὸ μηδ᾽ ἀριθμηθῆναι δύνασθαι, καίτοι μυρία τινῶν πονηθέντων, οἷς ἐπιμελές, περιεργίᾳ διαριθμήσα-159 σθαι. διεξελθόντων δὲ τῶν ἑπτὰ ἐτῶν, ἐν οἷς εὐφόρησεν ἡ πεδιάς, ἀρχὴν ἐλάμβανεν ὁ λιμός, ὃν ἐπιβαίνοντα καὶ συναυξόμενον οὐκ ἐχώρησεν Αἴγυπτος· ἀναχεόμενος γὰρ καὶ τὰς ἑξῆς ἀεὶ πόλεις καὶ χώρας ἐπικαταλαμβάνων ἄχρι περάτων καὶ τῶν πρὸς ἔω καὶ τῶν πρὸς δυσμὰς ἔφθασε τὴν οἰ-160 κουμένην ἐν κύκλῳ πᾶσαν κατασχών. λέγεται γοῦν

---

[1] Cohn would read διάκρισιν, but cf. De Mig. 19 τὰς ἀληθεῖς καὶ σαφεῖς τῶν πραγμάτων συγκρίσεις (referring also to Joseph's dreams) εἶναι κατὰ θεόν.

[2] Perhaps read τοπάρχων, the word used (in the form τοπάρχης) in Gen. xli. 34.

suffering what he has made others to suffer, for indeed he has hanged and racked the starving man with hunger.

XXVII. So much for this.[a] To continue the story, 157 Joseph, thus appointed viceroy to the king and promoted to the superintendence of Egypt, took a journey to make himself known to all the people of the country. He visited the nomes,[b] as they are called, city by city, and made his presence very welcome to those who saw him, not only through the benefits which they received from him, but through the remarkable and exceptional charm of his appearance and his general deportment. When the 158 first seven years of plenty came, as his reading of the dreams had predicted, he employed the ⟨local⟩ prefects and others who served him in providing for the public needs to collect a fifth part of the fruits every year, and the quantity of sheaves which he amassed surpassed anything within the memory of men. The clearest proof of this is that it was impossible even to count them, though some persons who were interested in it spent a vast amount of labour in making elaborate calculations. But when 159 the seven years during which the plains bore plentifully were ended, the famine began and spread and grew till Egypt could not hold it. It overran successively the cities and countries which lay in its path to the utmost limits of east and west, and rapidly made itself master of the whole civilized world round Egypt. In fact, it is said that never did so great a 160

---

[a] From this point on to § 257 Philo's narrative follows Gen. xli. 46-xlvii. 12 without serious interruption.

[b] The name regularly given to the districts of Egypt. See L. & S.

μηδέποτε κοινὴ νόσος κατασκῆψαι τοσαύτη, καθάπερ ἣν ἰατρῶν παῖδες ὀνομάζουσιν ἑρπῆνα· καὶ γὰρ
αὕτη πᾶσι τοῖς μέρεσιν ἐπιφοιτῶσα τὴν κοινωνίαν
τῶν ἡλκωμένων σωμάτων ὅλην δι' ὅλων στοιχηδὸν
161 πυρὸς τρόπον ἐπινέμεται. τοὺς οὖν ἀφ' ἑκάστης
δοκιμωτάτους αἱρούμενοι σιτώνας ἐξέπεμπον εἰς
Αἴγυπτον· ἤδη γὰρ ἡ πρόνοια τοῦ νεανίσκου πανταχόσε διηγγέλλετο ταμιευσαμένου τροφὰς ἀφθόνους
162 εἰς καιρὸν ἐνδείας. ὁ δὲ τὸ μὲν πρῶτον κελεύει
ἀνοιχθῆναι τοὺς σωροὺς ἅπαντας, ὑπολαμβάνων εὐ-
θυμοτέρους παρασκευάσειν τοὺς ἰδόντας καὶ τρόπον
τινὰ τὰς ψυχὰς ἀναθρέψειν πρὸ τῶν σωμάτων
ἐλπίσι χρησταῖς, ἔπειτα διὰ τῶν ἐπιτραπέντων τὰς
σιταρχίας ἐπώλει τοῖς ἔχουσιν ὠνητικῶς, στοχαζό-
μενος τοῦ μέλλοντος ἀεὶ καὶ τὸ ἐπιὸν ὁρῶν τοῦ
παρόντος ἀκριβέστερον.
163 XXVIII. Ἐν δὲ τούτῳ καὶ ὁ πατήρ, ὑποσπανιζόντων ἤδη τῶν ἀναγκαίων, ἀγνοῶν τὴν τοῦ παιδὸς
εὐτυχίαν ἐκπέμπει δέκα τῶν υἱῶν ἐπὶ σιτωνίαν τὸν
νεώτατον οἴκοι κατασχών, ὃς ἦν ὁμομήτριος ἀδελ-
164 φὸς τῷ βασιλέως ὑπάρχῳ. καὶ οἱ μὲν εἰς Αἴγυπτον
ἐλθόντες ἐντυγχάνουσιν ὡς ἀλλοτρίῳ τἀδελφῷ καὶ
τὴν περὶ αὐτὸν ἀξίωσιν καταπλαγέντες ἔθει παλαιῷ
προσκυνοῦσιν, ἤδη καὶ τῶν ὀνειράτων αὐτοῦ λαμβα-
165 νόντων βεβαίωσιν. ὁ δὲ τοὺς πεπρακότας θεασάμενος εὐθὺς ἐγνώρισεν ἅπαντας ὑπὸ μηδενὸς αὐτὸς
γνωρισθεὶς τὸ παράπαν, μὴ βουληθέντος πω τοῦ
θεοῦ τἀληθὲς ἀναφῆναι διά τινας ἀναγκαίας αἰτίας,
ἃς τότε βέλτιον ἦν ἡσυχάζεσθαι, ἀλλ' ἢ τὴν ὄψιν
218

scourge fall upon the whole community. In this it resembled what the medical schools call herpes, which attacks every part and spreads in successive stages like a fire over the whole framework of the festering body. Accordingly from each city the most ap- 161 proved persons were chosen and sent to Egypt, for already the story of Joseph's foresight in storing up abundance of food against a time of dearth had penetrated to every quarter. He first ordered all 162 the stores to be thrown open, thinking that he would thus increase the courage of those who saw them, and, so to speak, feed their souls with comforting hopes before he fed their bodies. Afterwards, through the commissioners of victualling he sold to those who wished to buy, still always forecasting the after-time and keeping a keener eye on the future than on the present.

XXVIII. In these circumstances, his father, too, 163 as the necessities of life were now growing scarce, little knowing his boy's good fortune, sent ten of his sons to buy corn, but kept at home the youngest, the uterine brother of the king's viceroy. The ten came 164 to Egypt and had an interview with their brother, thinking him to be a stranger, and awestruck at his dignified position bowed to him in the old-fashioned way, and thus at the very outset brought his dreams to fulfilment.[a] He, seeing those who had sold him, 165 immediately recognized them all, though none of them recognized him. It was not God's will to reveal the truth as yet, for cogent reasons which were best at the time kept secret, and therefore He

---

[a] Philo is probably thinking of Gen. xlii. 9 " Joseph remembered the dreams which he dreamed of them, and said unto them, Ye are spies."

ἀλλάξαντος εἰς σεμνότερον εἶδος τοῦ τὴν χώραν
ἐπιτραπέντος ἢ παρατρέψαντος τὰς ἀκριβεῖς κατα-
166 λήψεις τῆς διανοίας τῶν ὁρώντων. εἶτ' οὐχ ὥσπερ
νέος καὶ τοσαύτης ἡγεμονίας διάδοχος ἀρχὴν τὴν
μετὰ βασιλέα πρώτην ἀναψάμενος, εἰς ὃν ἀνατολαὶ
[65] καὶ δύσεις ἀπέβλεπον, | ἡλικίας ἀκμῇ καὶ μεγέθει
τῆς ἐξουσίας ἐπαρθείς, καιρὸν ἔχων ἀμύνης ἐμνησι-
κάκησεν, ἀλλ' ἐγκρατῶς τὸ πάθος ἐνεγκὼν καὶ
ταμιευσάμενος αὐτοῦ τῇ ψυχῇ μετὰ πολλοῦ τοῦ
προμηθοῦς ἐπεμόρφαζεν ἀλλοτρίωσιν καὶ βλέμμασι
καὶ φωνῇ καὶ τοῖς ἄλλοις καθυποκρινόμενος τὸν
δυσχεραίνοντα " οὐδέν " εἶπεν, " ὦ οὗτοι, φρονεῖτε
εἰρηνικόν, ἀλλά τις τῶν βασιλέως ἐχθρῶν κατασκόπους ὑμᾶς ἐξέπεμψεν, ᾧ κακὰς ὑπηρεσίας ὁμο-
λογήσαντες ὑπηρετήσειν λήσεσθαι μὲν ᾠήθητε,
λανθάνει δ' οὐδὲν τῶν δρωμένων ἐπ' ἐνέδρᾳ, κἂν
167 βαθεῖ σκότῳ συσκιάζηται."   πειρωμένων
δ' ἀπολογεῖσθαι καὶ διεξιόντων, ὡς ἐπ' ἀγενήτοις
κατηγοροῦνται, μήτε γὰρ παρὰ δυσμενῶν ἥκειν
μήτ' αὐτοὶ τοῖς ἐγχωρίοις ἀπέχθεσθαι μηδ' ἂν
ὑπομεῖναί ποτε τοιαύτην διακονίαν, εἶναι γὰρ τὰς
φύσεις εἰρηνικοὶ καὶ μεμαθηκέναι σχεδὸν ἐξ ἔτι
νηπίων παίδων τιμᾶν εὐστάθειαν παρ' ὁσιωτάτῳ
καὶ θεοφιλεστάτῳ πατρί, ᾧ δώδεκα γενομένων
υἱῶν ἕνα μὲν τὸν νεώτατον οὐκ ἔχοντά πω ἡλικίαν
ἀποδημίας οἴκοι καταμεῖναι, δέκα δὲ τοὺς ὁρω-
μένους ἡμᾶς ἐνταῦθα ὑπάρχειν, τὸν δὲ λοιπὸν
ἐκποδὼν γεγενῆσθαι—,   XXIX. ταῦτ'

either changed and added grandeur to the appearance of the regent or else perverted the understanding of the brothers from properly apprehending what they saw. Then, though, young as he was, promoted **166** to so high a command, invested with the first office after the king, looked up to by east and west, flushed with the vigour of his prime and the greatness of his power, with the opportunity of revenge in his hands, he might well have shewn vindictiveness, he did not do so. He bore up firmly against his feelings, and, keeping them under the management of his soul, with a carefully considered purpose, he feigned disfavour and with looks and voice and the rest of his demeanour counterfeited indignation. "Sirs," he said, "your intentions are not peaceful. You have been sent as spies by one of the king's enemies, to whom you have agreed to render this base service thinking that you would escape detection. But no treacherous action passes undetected, however profound the obscurity in which it is shrouded." The brothers attempted **167** to defend themselves, and maintained that the charges had no foundation of fact. They had not been sent, they said, by ill-disposed persons, and they themselves had no hostility to the people of the country and could never have brought themselves to undertake such employment, being men of peaceful nature who had learned almost from infancy to value a steady and quiet life under a father of scrupulous conduct and highly favoured by God. "This father has had twelve sons, the youngest of whom has stayed at home, being not of an age to travel. Ten are we whom you see before you here, and the twelfth has passed away."

ἀκούσας ὡς ἐπὶ τεθνεῶτι ἑαυτῷ παρὰ τῶν ἀπο-
168 δομένων τί τὴν ψυχὴν ἆρα ἐπεπόνθει; καὶ γὰρ
εἰ μὴ ἐξελάλησε τότε τὸ παραστὰν πάθος, ἀλλὰ
τούτοις ὑποτυφομένῳ καὶ ζωπυρουμένῳ πάντως τὰ
ἐντὸς ἐκαίετο, βαθεῖ δ᾽ ὅμως ᾔει φησὶν αὐτοῖς·
" εἰ τῷ ὄντι μὴ κατασκεψόμενοι τὴν γῆν ἀφίχθε,
πρὸς πίστιν τὴν ἐμὴν ὑμεῖς μὲν ἐνταυθοῖ διατρίψατε
βραχύν τινα χρόνον, ὁ δὲ νεώτατος ἀδελφὸς ὑμῶν
ἀφικέσθω μετακληθεὶς ἐπιστολιμαίοις γράμμασιν.
169 ἐὰν δ᾽ ἕνεκα τοῦ πατρὸς ἐπείγησθε ἀπιέναι φοβη-
σομένου τάχα τὴν μακρὰν ὑμῶν διάζευξιν, οἱ μὲν
ἄλλοι πάντες ἀπάρατε, καταμεινάτω δ᾽ εἷς ὁμηρεύ-
σων, ἄχρις ἂν ἐπανέλθητε σὺν τῷ νεωτάτῳ· τιμωρία
δὲ κατὰ τῶν μὴ πειθαρχούντων ἡ ἀνωτάτω προ-
170 κείσεται θάνατος." καὶ ὁ μὲν τοιαῦτ᾽ ἀπειλήσας
ὑποβλεπόμενος καὶ βαρείας ὀργῆς δείγματα παρα-
σχὼν ὅσα τῷ δοκεῖν ἀπηλλάττετο· οἱ δὲ συννοίας
καὶ κατηφείας γεμισθέντες ἐκάκιζον ἑαυτοὺς ἕνεκα
τῆς πρὸς τὸν ἀδελφὸν ἐπιβουλῆς " ἐκεῖνο " λέγοντες
" τἀδίκημα τῶν παρόντων ἐστὶ κακῶν αἴτιον, τῆς
ἐφόρου δίκης τῶν ἀνθρωπείων πραγμάτων ἤδη τι
μηχανωμένης καθ᾽ ἡμῶν· βραχὺν γὰρ ἡσυχάσασα
χρόνον διανίσταται τὴν ἀμείλικτον καὶ ἀπαραίτητον
αὐτῆς ἐπιδεικνυμένη φύσιν τοῖς ἀξίοις κολάσεως.
171 πῶς γὰρ οὐκ ἄξιοι; οἳ δεόμενον καὶ ποτνιώμενον
τὸν ἀδελφὸν οἱ ἀνηλεεῖς ὑπερείδομεν οὐδὲν μὲν
ἐξαμαρτόντα, φαντασίας δὲ τὰς καθ᾽ ὕπνον διὰ τὸ
φιλοίκειον ὡς συνήθεσιν ἀνενεγκόντα, ὑπὲρ ὧν οἱ
θηριωδέστατοι καὶ πάντων ἀγριώτατοι δυσχεραί-
[66] νοντες ἡμεῖς οὐχ ὅσια—δεῖ γὰρ | ἀψευδεῖν—εἰργα-
172 σάμεθα. τοιγαροῦν καὶ ταῦτα καὶ ἔτι χείρω τού-

―――――――――

[a] Or "with consummate acting." See App. p. 602.

XXIX. When he heard this and found himself spoken of as dead by those who had sold him, what do we suppose were the sensations of his soul? Though he gave no utterance to the emotion which 168 he felt, yet inwardly he was consumed by the secret fire which their words had kindled. In spite of this, he said, assuming a very impressive air,*a* "If it is true that you have not come to spy out the land, do you as a proof of good faith to me abide here for a short time and let your youngest brother be summoned hither by letter. But, if you are anxious 169 to depart for the sake of your father who will perhaps be alarmed at his long separation from you, let all the rest set off but one remain to serve as a hostage until you return with the youngest. And any disobedience in this will entail the extreme penalty of death." Thus he threatened with grim 170 looks, and giving to all appearance signs of great anger took his departure. But they, filled with gloom and depression, began to reproach themselves for their plot against their brother. "That wrong we did," they said, "is the cause of our present evil plight. Justice, the surveyor of human affairs, is now devising our downfall. For a little while she kept quiet, but now is awake and shews her implacable and inexorable nature to those who deserve punishment. And who deserves it more than we, 171 who mercilessly disregarded the prayers and supplications of our brother, though he had committed no offence, but merely in family affection recounted to us as his intimates the visions of his sleep, in resentment for which, with unparalleled brutality and savagery, we wrought what truth forces us to admit were unholy deeds? And, therefore, let us 172

223

PHILO

τῶν πείσεσθαι προσδοκῶμεν, οἵτινες μόνοι σχεδὸν
ἐξ ἁπάντων ἀνθρώπων εὐπατρίδαι λεγόμενοι διὰ
τὰς πατέρων καὶ πάππων καὶ προγόνων ὑπερβαλλούσας ἀρετὰς ἠσχύναμεν τὴν συγγένειαν ἐπιφανὲς
173 ὄνειδος κτήσασθαι σπουδάσαντες.'' ὁ δὲ πρεσβύτατος τῶν ἀδελφῶν, ὃς καὶ ἐν ἀρχῇ, συντιθεμένων
τὴν ἐπιβουλήν, ἠναντιοῦτο, '' ἐπὶ δὴ πεπραγμένοις ''
εἶπεν '' ἀνωφελεῖς αἱ μεταμέλειαι· παρεκάλουν,
ἱκέτευον, ἐξετάζων ὅσον ἐστὶ τὸ ἀνοσιούργημα, μὴ
θυμῷ χαρίζεσθαι· συναινεῖν δέον, ταῖς ἀβουλίαις
174 ἑαυτῶν εἴξατε. τοιγαροῦν καρπούμεθα τῆς αὐθαδείας καὶ ἀσεβείας τἀπίχειρα· ζητεῖται μὲν ἡ ἐπ'
ἐκείνῳ τυρευθεῖσα ἐπιβουλή, ὁ δὲ ζητῶν οὐκ ἔστιν
ἄνθρωπος, ἀλλ' ἢ θεὸς ἢ λόγος ἢ νόμος θεῖος.''

175   XXX. ταῦτα δ' ἤκουεν ὁ πραθεὶς
ἀδελφὸς ἡσυχῇ διαλαλούντων, ἑρμηνέως μεταξὺ
ὄντος· καὶ νικηθεὶς ὑπὸ τοῦ πάθους, μέλλων δα-
κρύειν, ὡς μὴ γένοιτο καταφανής, ἀποστρέφεται καὶ
προχέας θερμὰ καὶ ἐπάλληλα δάκρυα καὶ πρὸς
ὀλίγον ἐπικουφισθείς, τὴν ὄψιν ἀπομαξάμενος, ἐπι-
στρέφει καὶ κελεύει τὸν ἡλικίᾳ δεύτερον τῶν
ἀδελφῶν ἐν ὄψεσι ταῖς ἁπάντων δεθῆναι, τὸν αὐτῷ
κατάλληλον—ὁ γὰρ ἐν πλείοσι δεύτερος τῷ παρε-
σχάτῳ κατάλληλος, ἐπεὶ καὶ τῷ τελευταίῳ ὁ πρῶτος
176 —· ἴσως μέντοι καὶ διότι τὴν πλείστην μοῖραν ἔδοξε
τῶν ἁμαρτηθέντων εἰσενεγκεῖν μόνον οὐ συνταγματ-
αρχῶν καὶ τοὺς ἄλλους ἀλείφων ἐπὶ δυσμένειαν·
εἰ γὰρ συνετάχθη τῷ πρεσβυτάτῳ χρηστὰ καὶ

ª Gen. xlii. 23 '' they knew not that Joseph understood, for
there was an interpreter between them.'' By missing out
the first half of this Philo obscures the point. Presumably
he means the same as Genesis, viz. that they ventured on

224

expect to suffer this, and even more than this, we who though almost alone among men we owe our title of nobly-born to the surpassing virtues of father, grandfather and ancestors, have shamed our kin and hastened to load ourselves with infamy and disgrace." The eldest of the brothers, who origin- 173 ally opposed them when they were forming their plot, said : " Remorse for what is done is useless. I proved to you the enormity of the crime and begged and exhorted you not to give way to your wrath, but when you should have accepted my advice you let your evil counsels have their way. And so we are 174 reaping the rewards of our self-will and impiety. The plot we hatched for him is under inquisition, but the inquisitor is no man but God or the word or law of God." XXX. As they talked 175 thus quietly, since an interpreter was acting for them,[a] the brother whom they had sold heard what they said, and, overcome by his emotion and on the point to weep, turned aside to avoid discovery and let the tears stream warm and fast. Then, some- what relieved, he wiped them from his face, turned round and bade the second eldest of the brothers to be bound in the sight of them all. This brother corresponded to himself, for the second of a large number corresponds to the last but one as the eldest does to the last. But perhaps too he thought that 176 that brother had the greatest responsibility for the wickedness, since he might be almost called the officer of the company and the ringleader of their spite. For if he had ranged himself with the eldest when

this quiet conversation, because they supposed that he would not understand them in the absence of the interpreter, who had acted before.

φιλάνθρωπα βουλευομένῳ, νεώτερος μὲν ἐκείνου,
τῶν δ' ἄλλων πρεσβύτερος ὤν, ἴσως ἂν ἴσως ἐπ-
εσχέθη τἀδίκημα, τῶν τὴν ἀνωτάτω τάξιν καὶ τιμὴν
ἐχόντων συμπνεόντων καὶ ὁμογνωμονούντων περὶ
πράγματος, ὃ κἂν[1] καθ' αὑτὸ πολλὴν ῥοπὴν συνεφ-
177 είλκετο· νυνὶ δ' ἀποστὰς τῆς ἡμέρου καὶ ἀμείνονος
τάξεως πρὸς τὴν ἀνήμερον καὶ χαλεπὴν ηὐτομόλησε
καὶ ταύτης ἀποδειχθεὶς ἡγεμὼν οὕτως ἐθάρσυνε
τοὺς συνεφαπτομένους τοῦ παρανομήματος, ὡς
ἀνενδότως τὸν ἐπίληπτον ἆθλον διαθλῆσαι. διὰ
ταῦτ' ἐξ ἁπάντων μόνος οὗτος δεθῆναί μοι δοκεῖ.
178 οἱ δ' ἄλλοι τὴν οἴκαδε ἐπάνοδον ἤδη παρευτρεπί-
ζονται, κελεύσαντος τοῦ τῆς χώρας ἐπιτρόπου τοῖς
πυροπωλοῦσι τὰ ἀγγεῖα τῶν ἀδελφῶν ὡς ξένων
ἅπαντα πληρῶσαι καὶ ἣν ἔλαβον τιμὴν ἐπὶ τῶν
στομίων λάθρα καταθεῖναι μὴ προειπόντας οἷς
ἀπεδίδοσαν καὶ τρίτον τι προσεπιδαψιλεύεσθαι
τροφάς, αἳ γένοιντ' ἂν ἱκαναὶ κατὰ τὴν ὁδόν,
ἐξαιρέτους ὑπὲρ τοῦ παραπεμφθῆναι τὴν σιτωνίαν
179 ἀμείωτον. ὁδοιπορούντων δὲ καὶ τὸν ἐν δεσμοῖς
ἀδελφὸν ὡς εἰκὸς οἰκτιζομένων, οὐχ ἧττον δ' ἐπὶ
τῷ πατρὶ κατηφούντων, εἰ πάλιν ἀκούσεται συμ-
[67] φορᾶς, καθ' ἑκάστην ὁδὸν | ἐλαττουμένης καὶ
ἀποκειρομένης αὐτοῦ τῆς εὐπαιδίας, καὶ λεγόντων
" ἀλλ' οὐδὲ πιστεύσει δεδέσθαι, πρόφασιν δ' εἶναι
τὰ δεσμὰ τελευτῆς ὑπολήψεται διὰ τὸ τοὺς ἅπαξ
πληγέντας εἰς τὰ αὐτὰ προσπταίειν," ἑσπέρα καταλαμβάνει καὶ τῶν ὑποζυγίων καθελόντες τὰ ἄχθη
τὰ μὲν ἐπεκούφιζον, αὐτοὶ δὲ βαρυτέρας ταῖς ψυχαῖς

---

[1] My correction: mss. and Cohn καί. Mangey ἂν ἐφείλκετο
for συνεφείλκετο.

he counselled kindness and humanity, being, though younger than he, older than the others, the wrong-doing might well have been stopped. For the two highest in position and honour would have been united in sentiment and purpose on the question, and this of itself would have had great weight to turn the scale. As it was, he left the mild, the better, side, and 177 deserted to the cruel and savage side, and being appointed their leader so encouraged his fellow-malefactors that they played out without flinching the criminal contest. It was for this reason, I think, that he alone of them all was put in bonds.

As the others were now preparing for their journey 178 homewards, the regent ordered the corn-factors to fill all their sacks, thus treating them as guests, and secondly to place secretly in the mouth of each sack the price which had been paid, without giving information of this repayment to the recipients, and thirdly to bestow an additional bounty, namely a special stock of provisions sufficient for the journey, so that the corn purchased might be brought to its destination undiminished. The brothers journeyed 179 on, pitying as was natural the one whom they left in bonds, and no less depressed at the thought of their father, how he would again hear of misfortune and feel that every journey diminished and curtailed his wealth of children. "Indeed," they said, "he will not even believe that he has been put in bonds, but think that bonds are a pretext to cloak death, since those who have once received a blow often find themselves brought up against the same calamity." As they thus talked, evening overtook them, and when they had unloaded their beasts, though these were relieved, they themselves felt the burden of their

PHILO

φροντίδας ἐδέχοντο· φιλεῖ γὰρ ἐν ταῖς ἀνα-
παύλαις τῶν σωμάτων ἐναργεστέρας τῶν ἀβουλήτων
ἡ διάνοια λαμβάνουσα φαντασίας χαλεπῶς ἄγαν
180 θλίβεσθαι καὶ πιέζεσθαι. XXXI. λύσας δέ τις ἓν
ἀγγεῖον ὁρᾷ παρὰ τῷ στομίῳ βαλάντιον ὑπόμεστον
ἀργυρίου καὶ διαριθμησάμενος εὕρισκεν ὅσην τοῦ
σίτου καθῆκε τιμὴν ἀποδεδομένην αὐτῷ καὶ κατα-
181 πλαγεὶς τοῖς ἀδελφοῖς ἀνέφερεν. οἱ δ' οὐ χάριν
ἀλλ' ἐνέδραν ὑποτοπήσαντες ἠθύμουν καὶ βουλό-
μενοι πάντα τὰ ἀγγεῖα διερευνήσασθαι φόβῳ
διώξεως ἄραντες ᾗ τάχιστα συνέτεινον καὶ μόνον
οὐκ ἀπνευστὶ θέοντες πολυήμερον ὁδὸν ἐπιτεμόντες
182 ἀνύουσιν. εἶτ' ἀλλαχόθεν ἄλλοι τὸν πατέρα οὐκ
ἀδακρυτὶ περιλαβόντες ἐφίλουν ἑκάστῳ περιπλεκό-
μενον καὶ περιχεόμενον ἐκθύμως, καίτοι τῆς ψυχῆς
ἤδη τι μαντευομένης ἀβούλητον· καὶ γὰρ προσιόντας
καὶ δεξιουμένους κατενόει καὶ τὸν ὑπολειφθέντα
υἱὸν ὡς ὑστερηκότα τῆς βραδυτῆτος ᾐτιᾶτο καὶ
πρὸς τὰς εἰσόδους ἀπέβλεπε σπεύδων τὸν ἀριθμὸν
183 τῶν τέκνων πλήρη θεάσασθαι. μηδενὸς δ' ἔξωθεν
ἔτι προσεπιφοιτῶντος, διεπτοημένον ἰδόντες " τῶν
ἀβουλήτων " ἔφασαν, " ὦ πάτερ, ἀνιαρότερος τῆς
μαθήσεως ὁ ἐνδοιασμός ἐστι· μαθὼν μὲν γάρ τις
ὁδὸν εὗρεν εἰς σωτηρίαν, ἡ δ' ἀμφίβολος ἄγνοια
δυσοδίας καὶ ἀπορίας αἴτιον· ἄκουε δὴ σφόδρα μὲν
184 ἀνιαροῦ διηγήματος, ἀναγκαίου δὲ λεχθῆναι. ὁ
συμπεμφθεὶς ἡμῖν ἀδελφὸς ἐπὶ σιτωνίαν καὶ μὴ
ἐπανεληλυθὼς ζῇ μέν—δεῖ γὰρ τὸν ὡς ἐπὶ τεθνεῶτι
ἀπαλλάξαι σου μείζονα φόβον—, ζῶν δ' ἐν Αἰγύπτῳ

---

[a] More literally "from different sides," or perhaps "taking
hold of different parts."

228

cares weigh heavier on their souls. For when the
body takes rest the mind receives clearer visions of
adversities and is grievously afflicted and oppressed
thereby. XXXI. One of them, loosing a particular 180
sack, saw at its mouth a purse nearly full of silver,
and, counting it, found that the exact price which
he had paid for the corn had been restored to him.
Filled with astonishment, he told his brothers, who,
suspecting that it was not a gift but a trap, were dis-
mayed. And though they fain would have examined 181
all the sacks, so great was their fear of pursuit that
they started off and hurried on with all speed, and
racing along with hardly a pause for breath made a
short matter of accomplishing a journey of many days.
Then grouped around *a* their father they embraced 182
him, weeping the while, and kissed him as he clung
to each and folded them passionately in his arms,
though his soul already had a boding of some calamity.
For he took note of them as they approached and
greeted him, and, thinking that the son who was
actually left behind was playing the laggard, he
blamed him for his slowness and kept looking to
the different approaches in his eagerness to see the
number of his children complete. And, seeing his 183
agitation when no one else appeared from outside,
they said : " In calamity, to learn the truth is less
painful than to doubt. He who has learned the truth
may find the way to safety ; the ignorance of doubt
produces the perplexity which finds no path. Listen,
then, to a story, which, painful though it be, must
needs be told. The brother who was sent with us to 184
buy corn and has not returned is alive—you must cast
from your mind the worse fear of his death—but,
though alive, he remains in Egypt with the regent

καταμένει παρὰ τῷ τῆς χώρας ἐπιτρόπῳ, ὃς εἴτ' ἐκ
διαβολῆς εἴτε καὶ ὑποτοπήσας αὐτὸς αἰτίαν ἡμῖν
185 ὡς κατασκόποις ἐπέφερεν. ἀπολογουμένων[1] δὲ ὅσα
ὁ καιρὸς καὶ περί τε σοῦ τοῦ πατρὸς διεξιόντων[1] καὶ
τῶν ἀπολειπομένων ἀδελφῶν, ἑνὸς μὲν τοῦ τεθνεῶ-
τος, ἑτέρου δὲ τοῦ παρὰ σοὶ διατρίβοντος, ὃν ἔφαμεν
ἔτι νέον ὄντα διὰ τὴν ἡλικίαν οἴκοι[2] καταμεῖναι,
πάντα ἀπαμπίσχοντες καὶ ἀπογυμνοῦντες τὰ τῆς
συγγενείας εἰς τὸ ἀνύποπτον οὐδὲν ἠνύσαμεν, ἀλλ'
ἔφη μόνην ἂν αὐτῷ πίστιν ἀψευδοῦς ὁμολογίας
γενέσθαι τὴν ὡς αὐτὸν ἄφιξιν τοῦ νεωτάτου παιδός,
οὗ χάριν καὶ τὸν δεύτερον κατεσχηκέναι ῥύσιόν τε
186 καὶ ἐνέχυρον ἐκείνου. τὸ μὲν οὖν ἐπίταγμα πάντων
ἀνιαρότατον, ὁ δὲ καιρὸς αὐτὸ προστάττει μᾶλλον
[68] τοῦ κελεύοντος, ᾧ | πειστέον ἐξ ἀνάγκης διὰ
τἀπιτήδεια, μόνης Αἰγύπτου χορηγούσης αὐτὰ
187 τοῖς λιμῷ πιεσθεῖσιν." XXXII. ὁ δὲ
βαρύτατον ἀναστενάξας "τίνα πρῶτον" εἶπεν " ὀλο-
φύρωμαι; τὸν παρέσχατον, ὃς οὐ τελευταῖος ἀλλὰ
πρῶτος ἔλαχε τὴν τῶν συμφορῶν τάξιν; ἢ τὸν
δεύτερον, ὃς τὰ δευτερεῖα τῶν κακῶν ἤρατο, πρὸ
θανάτου δεσμά; ἢ τὸν νεώτατον, ὃς ἀπευκταιο-
τάτην ὁδὸν ἀφίξεται, ἐὰν ἄρα ἀπίῃ, ταῖς τῶν
ἀδελφῶν κακοπραγίαις οὐ σωφρονισθείς; ἐγὼ δὲ
κατὰ μέλη καὶ μέρη διαρτώμενος—μέρη γὰρ τέκνα
γονέων—εἰς ἀπαιδίαν κινδυνεύω περιελθεῖν ὁ πολύ-
188 παις καὶ εὔπαις ἄχρι πρὸ μικροῦ νομισθείς." ὁ δὲ
πρεσβύτατος " εἰς ὁμηρείαν" ἔφη " σοὶ δύο υἱοὺς
δίδωμι, οὓς καὶ μόνους ἐγέννησα· τούτους ἀπό-
κτεινον, ἐὰν μὴ σῶον ἀποδῶ τὸν ἐγχειρισθησόμενον

---

[1] The ungrammatical genitives should perhaps be corrected
to nominatives. [2] MSS. οἴκαδε.

of the land, who, either on some accusations laid by others, or on his own suspicions, charged us with being spies. We made all the defence which the occasion called for. We told him of you, our father, 185 and the brothers who were absent from our company, how one of them was dead and the other was abiding with you, who, as we said, was still quite young and therefore on account of his age kept at home. But when we thus laid bare without concealment all the facts about our family we made no headway in removing his suspicion. He told us that the only proof which he would accept of the truth of our assertions was that the youngest son should be sent to him, and that to ensure this he detained the second son as pledge and security for the other. This command 186 is painful beyond everything, but is laid upon us less by him who issued it than by the needs of the time, which we must perforce obey to get those provisions which Egypt alone supplies to people who are hard pressed by famine." XXXII. Their 187 father gave a deep groan, and said : " Whom should I lament for first ? My youngest but one, who was not the last but the first to be placed on the list of unfortunates, or the second eldest who won the second prize of evils, bonds in place of death, or the youngest who, if he does go, will go on a journey of truly evil omen, unlessoned by the misfortunes of his brothers? While I, divided limb by limb and part by part, since the child is part of its parent, am like to survive childless, I who but lately was held to be the father of a fine and numerous family." His eldest son then 188 said : " I give you my two sons, my only children, as hostages. Slay them if I do not restore to you in safety the brother whom you will entrust to my hand,

PHILO

ἀδελφοί, ὃς ἀφικόμενος εἰς Αἴγυπτον δύο περιποιή-
σει τὰ μέγιστα ἡμῖν, ἓν μὲν πίστιν σαφῆ τοῦ μὴ
κατασκόπους μηδὲ πολεμίους εἶναι, ἕτερον δὲ τὸ
τὸν ἀδελφὸν τὸν ἐν δεσμοῖς ἀπολαβεῖν δυνηθῆναι."
189 σφόδρα δ' ἀχθομένου τοῦ πατρὸς καὶ λέγοντος
ἀγνοεῖν,[1] ὅτι δυεῖν ὄντων ὁμομητρίων ὁ μὲν ἤδη
τέθνηκεν, ὁ δ' ἔρημος καὶ μόνος ἀπολειφθεὶς
εὐλαβήσεται τὴν ὁδὸν καὶ ζῶν προαποθανεῖται τῷ
δέει κατὰ τὴν φοβερῶν ἐκείνων ὑπόμνησιν, ἃ
συνέβη τὸν πρότερον παθεῖν, ταῦτα λέγοντος, τὸν
εὐτολμότατον καὶ ἀρχικὸν φύσει καὶ δυνατὸν
εἰπεῖν—ἦν δὲ καθ' ἡλικίαν ἀπὸ τοῦ πρώτου τέταρτος—προστησάμενοι διερμηνεύειν ἔπεισαν τὰ δο-
190 κοῦντα πᾶσιν. ἐδόκει δὲ τῶν μὲν ἀναγκαίων
ὑστεριζόντων—ὁ γὰρ κομισθεὶς πρότερος σῖτος
ἐπιλελοίπει—, κρατοῦντος δὲ τοῦ λιμοῦ καὶ πιέ-
ζοντος, ὠνησομένους ἀπιέναι, μὴ βαδιεῖσθαι δὲ τοῦ
νεωτάτου καταμένοντος· τὸν γὰρ τῆς χώρας ἐπίτροπον ἀπηγορευκέναι δίχα τούτου παραγενέσθαι.
191   λογισάμενος δὲ ἅτε σοφὸς ἀνήρ, ὡς
ἔστιν ἄμεινον ἕνα προέσθαι τῷ τοῦ μέλλοντος
ἀδήλῳ καὶ ἀμφιβόλῳ πρὸ τῆς ὁμολογουμένης τῶν
τοσούτων ἀπωλείας, ἣν ὑπομενεῖ πᾶς οἶκος ἐνδείᾳ
192 πιεσθείς, ἀνιάτῳ νόσῳ, φησὶν αὐτοῖς· " ἀλλ' εἰ τῆς
ἐμῆς βουλήσεως ἐπικρατέστερα τὰ τῆς ἀνάγκης
ἐστίν, εἰκτέον· ἴσως γὰρ ἴσως ἡ φύσις οἰκονομεῖ τι
βέλτιον, ὃ μήπω ταῖς διανοίαις ἡμῶν παραφαίνειν
193 ἀξιοῖ. λαβόντες οὖν καὶ τὸν νεώτατον, ὡς προ-
ῄρησθε, ἄπιτε, μὴ μέντοι τὸν αὐτὸν ὃν καὶ πρόσθεν
τρόπον· πάλαι μὲν γὰρ ἀργυρίου μόνον ἔδει πρὸς

---

[1] ἀγνοεῖν in this sense is strange: Cohn suggests ἀποκνεῖν,
Mangey (better) ἀμφιγνοεῖν: I would also suggest as nearer

232

whose coming to Egypt will procure us two very great gains, first the clear proof that we are not spies or enemies, secondly the power to recover our brother from bondage." The father was much distressed, and 189 said that he knew not what to do, since of the two full brothers one was already dead and the other left desolate and alone would dread the journey and suffer a living death through fright recalling the horrors which had befallen his precursor. When he thus spoke, they put forward the fourth in age, the most courageous of them all, a man princely in nature and powerful of speech, and persuaded him to act as spokesman of what they all thought. This was, that, since the 190 necessaries of life were running short, as the first stock of corn which they had brought was exhausted and the stress of the famine pressed hard upon them, they should set out to buy more corn but would not do so if their youngest brother stayed behind, since the ruler of the land had forbidden them to appear without him.   Their father, reckoning in 191 his wisdom that it was better to surrender one to the mercy of an obscure and dubious future than that many should suffer the undoubted destruction which the stress of famine, that fatal scourge, would inflict upon the whole household, said: "Nay, if the call of necessity 192 is stronger than my wishes, I must yield, for haply it may be that nature has some better gift in store, which as yet she refuses to reveal to our mind. Take, 193 then, the youngest as you propose, and depart, but not in the same fashion as before, for on the former occasion when you were unknown and had not met

---

to the MSS. ἃ ἐνόει, "what was in his mind." The ταῦτα λέγοντος is anacoluthic in any case.

σιτωνίαν ἀγνοουμένοις ἀνθρώποις καὶ μηδέν πω
πεπονθόσιν ἀνήκεστον, νυνὶ δὲ καὶ δώρων, τριῶν
[69] ἕνεκα, τῆς τε | πρὸς τὸν ἡγεμόνα καὶ σιτάρχην
ἀρεσκείας, ὑφ' οὗ γνωρίζεσθαί φατε, καὶ τοῦ τὸν
ἐν δεσμοῖς ἀπολαβεῖν θᾶττον πολλὰ καταθέντας
αὐτοῦ λύτρα καὶ τοῦ τὴν ὑπόνοιαν τῆς κατασκοπῆς
194 ὡς ἔνι μάλιστα ἰάσασθαι. πάντων οὖν ὅσων ἡ
ἡμετέρα γῆ φέρει λαβόντες ὥσπερ τινὰς ἀπαρχὰς
κομίζετε τῷ ἀνθρώπῳ καὶ δισσὸν ἀργύριον, τό τε
ἀποδοθὲν πρότερον, ὃ ἴσως ἀγνοίᾳ τινὸς ἀπεδόθη,
195 καὶ ἕτερον αὔταρκες εἰς σιτωνίαν. ἐπιφέρεσθε μέντοι καὶ τὰς ἡμετέρας εὐχάς, ἃς πρὸς τὸν σωτῆρα
ποιούμεθα θεόν, ἵνα καὶ εὐάρεστοι τοῖς ἐγχωρίοις
ξενιτεύοντες ἦτε καὶ ἐπανέρχησθε σῷοι τὰς ἀναγκαίας παρακαταθήκας, υἱούς, ἀποδιδόντες πατρί,
τόν τε καταλειφθέντα πρότερον ἐν δεσμοῖς καὶ
ὃν συνεπάγεσθε νυνὶ νεώτατον καὶ πραγμάτων
ἄπειρον.'' ἄραντες δὲ συνέτεινον εἰς Αἴγυπτον.
196 XXXIII. Εἶτ' ὀλίγαις ὕστερον ἡμέραις ἀφικομένους ἰδὼν ὁ τῆς χώρας ἐπίτροπος ἤσθη πάνυ καὶ
κελεύει τῷ τῆς οἰκίας ἐπιμελουμένῳ πολυτελὲς
ἄριστον εὐτρεπίζειν καὶ τοὺς ἄνδρας εἰσάγειν ἁλῶν
197 καὶ τραπέζης μεθέξοντας. εἰσαχθέντες δὲ καὶ ἐφ'
ὅτῳ μὴ συναισθόμενοι διεπτόηντο καὶ συγχυθέντες
ἐτόπαζον ἐπὶ κλοπῇ μέλλειν συκοφαντεῖσθαι ὡς
ὑφελόμενοι τὴν τοῦ σίτου τιμήν, ἣν πρότερον ἐν
τοῖς ἀγγείοις ἀνεῦρον· εἶτα τῷ τῆς οἰκίας ἐπι-
μελητῇ προσελθόντες ἀπελογοῦντο περὶ οὗ μηδεὶς
ἐτόλμα κατηγορεῖν τὸ συνειδὸς ἰώμενοι καὶ ἅμα
προφέροντες ἐπεδείκνυον τὸ ἀργύριον εἰς ἀπόδοσιν.

with any fatal disaster you only needed money to pay
for the corn, but now you must take presents also for
three reasons, to propitiate the governor and chief
victualler to whom you say you are known, to hasten
the delivery of the prisoner with a considerable ran-
som, and to remedy the suspicion that you are spies
as much as you can. Take, then, samples of all 194
the products of our land, firstfruits, as it were, and
a double sum of money, to make good what was restored to you on your former visit, perhaps through
someone's oversight, and also enough for purchasing
the corn. Carry with you, further, my own prayers 195
which I offer to the God of our salvation that you, as
strangers in the land, may be well-pleasing to the
inhabitants, and also may return in safety and restore
to your father the sureties which he has been forced
to pledge, even his sons, both him who before was
left behind in bondage and the one whom you now
take with you, the youngest so inexperienced in
life."

XXXIII. They set off, and hastened to Egypt. 196
On their arrival a few days afterwards the governor
saw them and was greatly pleased. He bade the
steward of his household prepare a sumptuous meal
and bring them in to partake of his salt and board.
Conducted thus, with no knowledge of what was 197
intended, they were scared and perturbed, guessing
that they were to be libelled as thieves for having
filched the price of the corn which they had found in
the sacks on the first occasion. Then they approached
the steward and made their defence, clearing their
consciences of a matter on which no one was venturing to charge them, and at the same time they produced and shewed him the money which they had

235

198 ὃ δὲ χρηστοῖς καὶ φιλανθρώποις λόγοις εὐθυμο-
τέρους αὐτοὺς ἐποίει φάσκων· " οὐδεὶς ἀσεβής
ἐστιν οὕτως, ὡς τὰς τοῦ θεοῦ χάριτας συκοφαντεῖν,
ὃς ἵλεως εἴη· θησαυροὺς γὰρ ἐν τοῖς ὑμετέροις
ὤμβρησεν ἀγγείοις οὐ μόνον τροφὰς ἀλλὰ καὶ
199 πλοῦτον ἐξ ἑτοίμου διδούς." οἱ δὲ παρηγορηθέντες
ἐν τάξει διετίθεσαν ἃ οἴκοθεν ἐπηνέγκαντο δῶρα
καὶ παραγενομένῳ τῷ δεσπότῃ τῆς οἰκίας προσ-
έφερον· πυνθανομένῳ δέ, πῶς ἔχοιεν καὶ εἰ ὁ πατὴρ
ζῇ, περὶ οὗ πρόσθεν ἔλεγον, ἀποκρίνονται περὶ μὲν
αὐτῶν οὐδέν, περὶ δὲ τοῦ πατρὸς ὅτι ζῇ καὶ ὑγιαί-
200 νει. κατευξάμενος δ' ἐκείνῳ καὶ θεοφιλέστατον προσ-
ειπών, τὸν ὁμομήτριον περιβλεψάμενος ἀδελφὸν
ὡς εἶδεν, οὐ κατασχὼν ἀλλ' ἤδη νικώμενος ὑπὸ τοῦ
πάθους, πρὶν γενέσθαι καταφανής, ἐπιστρέφεται
καὶ δραμὼν πρόφασιν ἐπί τι τῶν κατεπειγόντων—
ἐκλαλῆσαι γὰρ τἀληθὲς καιρὸς οὐκ ἦν—ἐν μυχῷ τινι
τῆς οἰκίας ἀνακλαυσάμενος ἀποχεῖ τὴν τῶν δακρύων
201 φοράν. XXXIV. εἶτ' ἀπονιψάμενος λογισμῷ τῆς
ἀνίας ἐπεκράτησε καὶ προσελθὼν εἱστία τοὺς ξένους
ἀποδοὺς πρότερον καὶ τὸν ἀντὶ τοῦ νεωτάτου
κατασχεθέντα εἰς ὁμηρείαν· συνε101ιστιῶντο δὲ καὶ
202 ἄλλοι τῶν παρ' Αἰγυπτίοις δοκίμων.   αἱ
δ' ὑποδοχαὶ κατὰ τὰ πάτρια ἑκάστοις ἐγίνοντο,
χαλεπὸν ἡγουμένου παλαιοὺς νόμους παριδεῖν, καὶ
ταῦτα ἐν εὐωχίᾳ τινί, ἔνθα τῶν ἀηδιῶν αἱ ἡδοναὶ
203 πλείους. | ἑξῆς δὲ προστάξαντος κατὰ τὰς ἡλικίας
[70] καθέζεσθαι, μήπω τῶν ἀνθρώπων ἐν ταῖς συμ-
ποτικαῖς συνουσίαις κατακλίσει χρωμένων, ἐθαύ-

---

[a] Perhaps based on Gen. xliii. 32 " they set on for him by
himself, and them by themselves, and for the Egyptians by
themselves."

brought for repayment. But he raised their courage 198
with kind and friendly words. " No one," he said,
" is so impious as to libel the bounties of God Whose
mercy I invoke. For He has poured treasure into
your sacks, thereby providing not only sustenance
but wealth to spend as you need it." Thus en- 199
couraged, they proceeded to set out in order the gifts
they had brought from home, and when the master
of the house arrived they offered them to him. He
asked them how they were, and whether the father
of whom they spoke before still lived, in answer to
which they said nothing about themselves but told
him that their father was alive and well. Joseph 200
invoked a blessing on him and pronounced him most
favoured by God, and then, when, looking round, he
saw Benjamin, his own mother's son, he could not
contain himself, but, overcome by emotion, turned
aside before he could be observed, and hastened,
nominally on some pressing business, as the time for
disclosure had not come, into a corner of the house
and there burst into weeping and let the tears stream
forth. XXXIV. Then he washed his face, and, reason 201
prevailing over his troubled feelings, approached his
guests and led them to the feast, having first restored
the prisoner who had been detained as hostage for the
youngest. Other Egyptian dignitaries feasted with
them. The method of entertainment 202
followed in each case ancestral practice,[a] since he
strongly disapproved of neglecting old customs,
particularly at a festivity where the pleasures out-
number the disagreeables. When the guests were 203
seated, arranged by his commands in order of age, as
at that date it was not the custom to recline at con-

μαζον, εἰ Αἰγύπτιοι ζηλωταὶ τῶν αὐτῶν Ἑβραίοις
εἰσὶ τάξεώς τε πεφροντικότες καὶ τὰς πρεσβυτέρων
204 καὶ νεωτέρων τιμὰς διακρίνειν ἐπιστάμενοι. τάχα
μέντοι καὶ τὸν ἄλλον χρόνον, ἔφασκον, τῆς χώρας
ἀμαθέστερον τὰ περὶ δίαιταν ἀγούσης, ὁ ἀνὴρ οὗτος
τοῖς κοινοῖς ἐπιστὰς οὐ μόνον τοῖς μεγάλοις πράγμασιν ἥρμοσεν εὐταξίαν, δι᾽ ὧν τὰ εἰρήνης καὶ
πολέμου κατορθοῦσθαι πέφυκεν, ἀλλὰ καὶ τοῖς
εὐτελεστέροις εἶναι δοκοῦσιν, ὧν τὰ πλεῖστα ἐν
παιδιαῖς· ἱλαρότητα γὰρ ἐπιζητοῦσιν εὐωχίαι
σεμνὸν ἄγαν καὶ αὐστηρὸν συμπότην ἥκιστα παρα-
205 δεχόμεναι. τοιούτους ἐπαίνους ἠρέμα συνειρόντων,
τράπεζαι μὲν οὐ σφόδρα πολυτελεῖς εἰσκομίζονται,
διὰ τὸν λιμὸν οὐκ ἀξιώσαντος τοῦ ξενοδόχου ταῖς
ἑτέρων ἀτυχίαις ἐντρυφᾶν· αὐτοὶ δ᾽ ἅτε σύνεσιν
ἀκριβεῖς καὶ τοῦτ᾽ εἰς τὰ ἐγκώμια παρελάμβανον,
ὡς ἀπειροκαλίαν, πρᾶγμα ἐπίφθονον, ἀπέστραπται,
λέγοντες· ὡς καὶ τὸ τοῦ συναλγοῦντος τοῖς δεο-
μένοις καὶ τὸ τοῦ ἑστιάτορος σχῆμα διασῴζει
μεθόριον ἀμφοῖν τιθεὶς αὐτὸν καὶ τὴν ἐν ἑκατέρῳ
206 μέμψιν ἐκφεύγων. αἱ μὲν οὖν παρασκευαὶ τὸ
ἀμισὲς εἶχον πρόσφοροι τῷ καιρῷ γεγονυῖαι· τὸ δ᾽
ἐλλιπὲς ἀνεπλήρουν αἱ συνεχεῖς φιλοφροσύναι προ-
πόσεσιν, εὐχαῖς, παραινέσεσι ταῖς εἰς ἀνάληψιν, ἃ
τοῖς ἐλευθέροις καὶ μὴ ἀμούσοις τὸ ἦθος ἡδίω τῶν
ὅσα περὶ ἐδωδὴν καὶ πόσιν εὐτρεπίζουσιν οἱ φιλ-

---

[a] See Gen. xliii. 33, where the statement that they were
placed in order of seniority is followed by " the men marvelled
one with another."

[b] Philo may have found a ground for this in the phrase

vivial gatherings, they were surprised to find that
the Egyptians affected the same fashions as the
Hebrews, and were careful of order of precedence,
and knew how to discriminate between younger and
older in the honours which they paid them.[a] "It may 204
be," they said, "that in other times the style of life
in this country was less civilized, until this man, when
put over the state, introduced good order not only
in the important matters which give rise to success
in peace and war, but in those regarded as less
important which mainly belong to the lighter side
of life. For festivities demand cheerfulness and
have no room for the over-grave and austere guest."
While they thus quietly descanted in his praise the 205
tables were brought in, not over-sumptuously laden,[b]
because their host, on account of the famine, dis-
liked the thought of luxury while others were suffering want; and they themselves had the sound sense
to include in their eulogies this also, that he had
shunned the odious fault of tasteless display. He
had preserved, they said, the attitude both of a
sympathizer with the needy and of the host at a feast,
had set himself in the mean between the two and
escaped censure on either count. The arrangements, 206
then, did not offend good taste, but were suitable to
the occasion, and any deficiency was made good by
the constant signs of kind feeling shewn in toasts
and good wishes and invitations to take refreshment,
things which to liberal and cultured temperaments
give more pleasure than all the preparations of food
and drink provided by the lovers of high feasting for

"set on bread" in contrast to the more elaborate preparations of Gen. xviii. He apparently forgets that the steward
had been ordered to provide a sumptuous meal (§ 196).

ἐστιάτορες καὶ φιλόδειπνοι τὰ μηδεμιᾶς ἄξια σπουδῆς εἰς ὀλιγοφρόνων ἐπίδειξιν πομποστολοῦντες.

207 XXXV. Τῇ δ᾽ ὑστεραίᾳ ἅμα τῇ ἕῳ μεταπεμψάμενος τὸν ἐπίτροπον τῆς οἰκίας κελεύει τὰ ἀγγεῖα
τῶν ἀνδρῶν ὅσα ἐπηνέγκαντο γεμίσαι σίτου καὶ
πάλιν ἐπὶ τῶν στομίων τὴν τιμὴν ἐν βαλαντίοις
καταθεῖναι, εἰς δὲ τὸ τοῦ νεωτάτου καὶ τὸ κάλλιστον τῶν ἀργυρῶν ἔκπωμα, ᾧ πίνειν ἔθος εἶχεν
208 αὐτός. καὶ ὁ μὲν τὰ προσταχθέντα προθύμως ἐπ-
ετέλει μηδένα μάρτυρα παραλαμβάνων, οἱ δ᾽ οὐδὲν
τῶν κρύφα γεγονότων εἰδότες ἀνεζεύγνυσαν ἐπὶ τοῖς
209 παρ᾽ ἐλπίδας ἀγαθοῖς ἅπασι χαίροντες. ἃ μὲν γὰρ
προσεδόκησαν, ταῦτα ἦν· ἐπὶ κλοπῇ τοῦ ἀπο-
δοθέντος ἀργυρίου συκοφαντίαν ἕξειν, ἀδελφὸν τὸν
ὁμηρεύοντα μὴ ἀπολήψεσθαι, προσαποβαλεῖν καὶ
τὸν νεώτατον ἴσως ὑπὸ τοῦ σπουδάσαντος αὐτὸν
210 ἀχθῆναι βίᾳ κατασχεθέντα. τὰ δ᾽ ἀποβάντα αἰσίων
[71] τελειότερα εὐχῶν· τὸ πρὸς | τῷ μὴ συκοφαντηθῆναι
τραπέζης καὶ ἁλῶν, ἃ σύμβολα γνησίου φιλίας
ἀνθρώποις ἀνεύρηται, μεταλαχεῖν, τὸ κομίσασθαι
τὸν ἀδελφὸν ἀνύβριστον, μηδενὸς ἐντυχόντος καὶ
δεηθέντος, τὸ καὶ τὸν νεώτατον ἀγαγεῖν πρὸς τὸν
πατέρα σῶον, ἐκπεφευγότας μὲν τὰς ἐπὶ κατασκόπων ὑπονοίας, ἄφθονον δὲ τροφῶν πλῆθος ἐπι-
φερομένους, χρηστὰ δὲ καὶ περὶ τοῦ μέλλοντος
λογιζομένους· εἰ γὰρ ἐπιλίποι τἀπιτήδεια πολλάκις,
ἔφασκον, οὐκέθ᾽ ὡς πρότερον περιδεεῖς ἀλλὰ γεγη-
θότες ὡς πρὸς ἴδιον ἀλλ᾽ οὐ ξένον τὸν τῆς χώρας

themselves and others, who make a parade of what is unworthy of care and attention with the ostentation natural to men of little mind.

XXXV. On the next day at dawn he sent for the 207 steward of the house and bade him fill with corn all the sacks which the men had brought, and again put the purchase-money in purses at the mouths of the sacks, and also to place in that of the youngest his finest piece of silver, the cup out of which he was accustomed to drink himself. The steward readily 208 carried out his orders without anyone else being present, and they, knowing nothing of these secret doings, set off in high spirits at all their good fortune so far beyond their hopes. What they had expected 209 was to find themselves the victims of a false charge of stealing the money which had been restored to them, to fail to recover their brother who was left as hostage and perhaps also in addition to lose the youngest who might be forcibly detained by the governor who had urged his coming. What had 210 happened surpassed their most sanguine wishes. Instead of being subjected to accusation, they had been made partners in the board and salt which men have devised as the symbols of true friendship. They had recovered their brother inviolate without any intervention or entreaty. They were bringing, too, the youngest safe and sound to his father, and while they had escaped the suspicion of being spies they were taking with them a rich abundance of food and moreover had comfortable prospects for the future. " For if provisions should chance to fail," they reasoned, " we shall leave home not in extreme fear as before but with joyful hearts, knowing that we shall find in the governor of the country not a stranger but a per-

211 ἐπίτροπον ἀποδημήσομεν.　　　XXXVI. ἀλλὰ
γὰρ οὕτω διακειμένων καὶ τοιαῦτα ταῖς ψυχαῖς
ἀναπολούντων, αἰφνίδιος καὶ ἀπροσδόκητος ταραχὴ
καταλαμβάνει. προσταχθεὶς γὰρ ὁ τῆς οἰκίας
ἐπιμελητής, ἐπαγόμενος θεραπόντων πλῆθος οὐκ
ὀλίγον, κατασείων τὰς χεῖρας καὶ μένειν ὑποσημαί-
212 νων ἐβοηδρόμει. καὶ συντείνας ἄσθματος πλήρης
" ἐπεσφράγισθε " εἶπε " καὶ τὰς προτέρας καθ᾽
αὑτῶν αἰτίας· ἀγαθὰ κακοῖς ἀμειψάμενοι πάλιν τὴν
αὐτὴν ὁδὸν τῶν ἀδικημάτων ἐτράπεσθε· τὴν τοῦ
σίτου τιμὴν ὑπεξελόμενοι καὶ μεῖζον ἔτι προσεξ-
ειργάσασθε· πονηρία γὰρ τυχοῦσα ἀμνηστίας ἐπι-
213 δίδωσι. τὸ κάλλιστον καὶ τιμιώτατον ἔκπωμα τοῦ
δεσπότου, ἐν ᾧ προπόσεις προὔπινεν ὑμῖν, κεκλό-
φατε οἱ λίαν εὐχάριστοι, οἱ λίαν εἰρηνικοί, οἱ μηδ᾽
ὄνομα κατασκοπῆς εἰδότες, οἱ διττὸν ἀργύριον εἰς
ἀπόδοσιν τοῦ προτέρου κεκομικότες, ἐνέδραν ὡς
ἔοικε καὶ δέλεαρ ἐπὶ θήραν καὶ ἁρπαγὴν πλειόνων. ἀλλ᾽ οὐκ εἰς ἅπαν εὐοδεῖ κακία, λανθάνειν δ᾽
214 ἀεὶ τεχνάζουσα καταφωρᾶται." ταῦτα συνείροντος,
ἀχανεῖς ἐπάγησαν, λύπης καὶ φόβου, τῶν ἀργα-
λεωτάτων κακῶν, ἐξαίφνης ἐπιπεσόντων, ὡς μηδὲ
διᾶραι τὸ στόμα δύνασθαι· τῶν γὰρ ἀπροσδοκήτων
κακῶν αἱ προσβολαὶ καὶ τοῖς δεινοῖς περὶ λόγους
215 ἀφωνίαν ἐμποιοῦσι. παρειμένοι δ᾽ ὅμως ὑπὲρ τοῦ
μὴ δοκεῖν ἁλισκόμενοι τῷ συνειδότι καθησυχάζειν
" πῶς " ἔφασαν " ἀπολογησόμεθα καὶ πρὸς τίνα;
σὺ γὰρ μέλλεις ἔσεσθαι καὶ δικαστὴς ὁ κατήγορος,
ὃς ὤφειλες καὶ ἑτέρων αἰτιωμένων ἡμῖν συν-
αγορεύειν ἐξ ὧν ἐπειράθης· ἢ τὸ μὲν ἀργύριον τὸ

sonal friend."　　　　　　　XXXVI. While they were **211**
in this mood, and their souls occupied with these reflections, a sudden and unexpected discomfiture overtook them.　For the steward, by order of his master,
with a considerable body of servants, appeared in
pursuit waving his hands and beckoning to them to
halt.　And when he arrived, all eagerness and panting **212**
hard, " You have set the seal," he said, " to the
earlier charges made against you.　You have returned evil for good and once more set your feet
in the same path of iniquity.　You have filched the
price of the corn and committed in addition a still
worse crime, for villainy grows if it receives condona-
tion.　You have stolen the finest and most valuable **213**
of my master's cups in which he pledged you, you,
who were so exceedingly grateful, so exceedingly
peace-loving, you who did not so much as know the
meaning of ' spy,' you who brought double money
to pay what was due before, apparently as a trap and
snare to serve you in your quest for still more plunder.
But wickedness does not prosper in the long run ;
it is ever scheming to remain hid but is detected in
the end."　While he continued in this strain, they **214**
stood paralysed and speechless, suddenly seized by
those most painful inflictions, grief and fear, so that
they could not even open their mouths.　For the
onset of unexpected ills can render even eloquent
speakers mute.　Yet, unnerved as they were, they **215**
did not wish their silence to be construed as a sign
that their conscience convicted them, and therefore
they replied : " How shall we defend ourselves, and
to whom ?　You will be our judge, you who are also
our accuser, who from your experience of us should
rather be the advocate did others arraign us.　Could

εὑρεθὲν ἐν τοῖς ἀγγείοις πρότερον οὐδενὸς ἐλέγ-
χοντος ἐκομίσαμεν ἀποδώσοντες, τοσαύτῃ δ' ἐχρη-
σάμεθα τῶν τρόπων μεταβολῇ, ὡς τὸν ξενοδόχον
ἀμείψασθαι ζημίαις καὶ κλοπαῖς· ἀλλ' οὔτε γέγονε
216 τοῦτο μήτ' εἰς νοῦν ἔλθοι ποτὲ τὸν ἡμέτερον. ὃς
δ' ἂν ἔχων ἁλῷ τὸ ἔκπωμα τῶν ἀδελφῶν, θνη-
σκέτω· θανάτου γὰρ τἀδίκημα, εἰ γέγονεν ὄντως,
τιμώμεθα διὰ πολλά· πρῶτον μὲν ὅτι πλεονεξία
καὶ τὸ τῶν ἀλλοτρίων ἐπιθυμεῖν παρανομώτατον,
δεύτερον ὅτι τοὺς ὠφεληκότας βλάπτειν ἐπιχειρεῖν
ἀνοσιώτατον, τρίτον δὲ ὅτι τοὺς μέγα φρονοῦντας
[72] ἐπ' εὐγενείᾳ τὸ τῶν προγόνων ἀξίωμα | καθαιρεῖν
ἔργοις ὑπαιτίοις τολμᾶν ὄνειδος αἴσχιστον· οἷς
ἅπασιν ἔνοχος ὤν, εἴ τις ἡμῶν ὑφῄρηται, θανάτων
217 μυρίων ἄξια πεπραχὼς τελευτάτω." XXXVII. καὶ
ἅμα λέγοντες τὰ ἄχθη τῶν ὑποζυγίων καθαιροῦσι
καὶ προτρέπονται μετὰ πάσης ἐπιμελείας ἐρευνᾶν.
ὁ δὲ οὐκ ἀγνοῶν ἐν τῷ τοῦ νεωτάτου κατακείμενον
ἅτε αὐτὸς λάθρα θεὶς ἐσοφίζετο καὶ τὴν ἀρχὴν ἀπὸ
τοῦ πρεσβυτάτου ποιησάμενος ἑξῆς κατὰ στοῖχον
ἐπακολουθῶν ταῖς ἡλικίαις ἐσκόπει, προφέροντος
ἑκάστου καὶ ἐπιδεικνυμένου τὰ ἀγγεῖα, μέχρι τοῦ
τελευταίου, παρ' ᾧ καὶ τὸ ζητούμενον ἀνευρέθη,
ὡς ἰδόντας ἀθρόους ἀνοιμῶξαι καὶ τὰς ἐσθῆτας
διαρρήξαντας ἐκδακρύειν ἐπιστένοντας καὶ ζῶντα
τὸν ἀδελφὸν ἔτι προθρηνοῦντας καὶ οὐχ ἧττον
αὐτοὺς καὶ τὸν πατέρα, ὃς προὔλεγε τὰς συμ-
βησομένας τῷ υἱῷ κακοπραγίας, δι' ἃς βουλομένοις
218 συναποδημεῖν τὸν ἀδελφὸν οὐκ ἐπέτρεπε. κατ-

it be that after bringing in repayment the money we found in our sacks though no one challenged us, we completely changed our characters, so as to require our entertainer by mulcting and robbing him ? No, we have not done so, and may no such thought ever enter our mind. Let whoever of the brothers is 216 proved to have the cup be put to death, for death is the penalty at which we assess the crime if it really has been committed, for several reasons. First, because covetousness and the desire for what is another's is against all law ; secondly, because to attempt to injure benefactors is a most unholy deed ; thirdly, because to those who pride themselves on their high lineage it is a most shameful reproach if they do not shrink from ruining the prestige of their ancestors by deeds of guilt. And since, if any one of us has committed this theft, he is liable on all these counts, let him die since his deed deserves a thousand deaths."
XXXVII. With these words they pulled the packs 217 from off their beasts, and bade him search with all diligence. He, who knew well that the cup was lying in the sack of the youngest son, since he had secretly put it there himself, tricked them by beginning his examination with the eldest, and continued in regular order according to their age, as each produced and shewed his sack, until he reached the last. When the object of the search was actually found in his possession, a wail arose from the whole body at the sight. They rent their clothes and wept and groaned, mourning for the death which awaited the brother who was still alive, and no less for themselves and their father who foretold the misfortunes which would befall his son and had therefore for a time refused to consent to their wish that their brother should travel

ηφοῦντες δὲ καὶ συγκεχυμένοι τὴν αὐτὴν ὑπέστρεφον
ὁδὸν εἰς τὴν πόλιν ἐκπεπληγμένοι τῷ συμβεβηκότι
καὶ τὸ πρᾶγμα ἐπιβουλὴν ἀλλ' οὐ φιλαργυρίαν
ἀδελφοῦ νομίζοντες· εἶτα τῷ τῆς χώρας ἐπιτρόπῳ
προσαχθέντες φιλάδελφον εὔνοιαν ἀπὸ γνησίου πά-
219 θους ἐπιδείκνυνται. προσπεσόντες γὰρ ἀθρόοι τοῖς
ἐκείνου γόνασιν ὡς κλοπῇ πάντες ἔνοχοι, ὃ μηδ'
εἰπεῖν θέμις ἐπ' αὐτῶν,[1] ἐδακρυρρόουν, ἱκέτευον,
ἑαυτοὺς ἐξεδίδοσαν, ἑκούσιον δουλείαν ὑπισχνοῦντο,
δεσπότην προσηγόρευον ἐκεῖνον, προβλήτους,[2] οἰκότριβας, ἀργυρωνήτους, οὐδὲν παραλείποντες τῶν
οἰκετικῶν ὀνομάτων, ἀνεκάλουν ἑαυτούς.
220 ὁ δ' ἔτι μᾶλλον ἀποπειρώμενος ἤθει βαρυτάτῳ
φησὶν αὐτοῖς· " μηδέποτε τοῦτο ἐργασαίμην, ὡς
τοσούτους ἀπάγειν ἑνὸς ἁμαρτόντος· τί γὰρ εἰς
μετουσίαν ἄξιον καλεῖν τιμωριῶν τοὺς μὴ τῶν
ἀδικημάτων κοινοπραγήσαντας; ἐκεῖνος μόνος,
221 ἐπεὶ καὶ μόνος ἔπραξε, κολαζέσθω. πυνθάνομαι
μὲν οὖν, ὅτι πρὸ τῆς πόλεως καὶ θάνατον ὡρίζετε
κατὰ τοῦ ἁλόντος· ἐγὼ δ' ἕκαστα πρὸς τὸ ἐπιεικὲς
ἄγων καὶ ἡμερώτερον ἐπικουφίζω τὴν τιμωρίαν
222 δουλείαν ὁρίσας ἀντὶ θανάτου." XXXVIII. χαλεπῶς δὲ τὴν ἀπειλὴν φερόντων καὶ ἐφ' οἷς ἐσυκοφαν-
τοῦντο καταδυομένων ὁ τέταρτος καθ' ἡλικίαν—ἦν

---

[1] mss. ἐπ' αὐτῷ.
[2] So Cohn and Mangey with some mss. authority. Most
mss. have προσηλύτους or προσβλήτους. See note a.

---

[a] Assuming that προβλήτους is to be read, its place in the
series as a "servile name," followed by οἰκότριβας and ἀργυρωνήτους, suggests that it also describes a special type of
slave. If so, it may perhaps refer to children who had been
exposed in infancy and then annexed by persons who
brought them up as their own slaves. Thus they would

with them.   Downcast and confounded they returned **218**
by the same road to the city, appalled at the event
and attributing it to a malicious plot and not to the
covetousness of their brother.   Then, when brought
before the governor, they shewed their brotherly
good feeling by their genuine emotion.   For, falling **219**
in a body at his knees, as though they were all guilty
of the theft, a charge the mere mention of which
was an outrage, they wept, they besought him, they
put themselves at his disposal, they volunteered to
submit to enslavement, they called him their master
and themselves his slaves of any and every kind, outcasts,[a] household bred or purchased in the market ;
no servile name did they leave unsaid.   But **220**
he, to try them still further, assumed a very severe [b]
air and said : " I trust that I may never act thus, and
send so many to captivity for the sin of one.   For
what good reason is there for including in the penalties
those who had no share in the offence ?   He yonder,
who alone did the deed, let him suffer for it.   Now, I **221**
am told that before you entered the city [c] death was
the sentence you too approved for the guilty person,
but as I am ever inclined for the moderate and humaner
course I reduce the punishment and sentence him to
slavery instead of death."   XXXVIII. This stern **222**
decision had greatly distressed them, utterly dejected as they were by the false accusations made
against them, when the fourth in age, who combined

naturally form a third class to οἰκότριβας (taken as = οἰκογένεις)
and ἀργυρωνήτους.   I have not been able to find in Greek or
Roman legislation any allusion to such a status, but see
App. p. 602.
  [b] Or perhaps " dignified," " impressive," *cf. De Abr.* 210.
Possibly, as Mangey suggested, read βαθυτέρῳ, *cf.* § 168 above.
  [c] Lit. " in front of the city."

PHILO

δὲ τολμητὴς μετ' αἰδοῦς καὶ θαρραλέος, παρρησίαν
τὴν ἄνευ ἀναισχυντίας ἐπιτετηδευκώς—προσελθών
φησι· '' δέομαι, δέσποτα, μὴ θυμῷ χαρίσασθαι μηδ'
ὅτι τέταξαι τὴν μετὰ βασιλέα τάξιν προκαταγνῶναι
223 πρὸ τῆς ἀπολογίας ἡμῶν. πυνθανομένῳ σοι κατὰ
τὴν προτέραν ἐπιδημίαν περί τε ἀδελφοῦ καὶ πα-
[73] τρὸς ἀπεκρινάμεθα· πατὴρ μέν | ἐστι πρεσβύτης,
οὐ χρόνῳ μᾶλλον γεγηρακὼς ἢ ταῖς ἐπαλλήλοις
δυστυχίαις, ὑφ' ὧν γυμναζόμενος ἀθλητοῦ τρόπον
ἐν πόνοις καὶ δυσκαρτερήτοις κακοπαθείαις δι-
ετέλεσεν· ἀδελφὸς δὲ κομιδῇ νέος ἐστίν, ἐκτόπως
στεργόμενος ὑπὸ τοῦ πατρός, ἐπειδὴ καὶ ὀψίγονός
ἐστι καὶ δυεῖν γενομένων ὁμομητρίων ἀπελείφθη
μόνος, τοῦ πρεσβυτέρου βιαίως ἀποθανόντος.
224 κελεύοντος δὲ σοῦ ἐνθάδε τὸν ἀδελφὸν ἀγαγεῖν καὶ
ἀπειλοῦντος, εἰ μὴ παραγένοιτο, μηδ' ἡμῖν εἰς ὄψιν
ἐλθεῖν ἔτι τὴν σὴν ἐπιτραπήσεσθαι, κατηφοῦντες
ἀπηλλαττόμεθα καὶ μόλις οἴκαδε ἐπανελθόντες
225 ἐδηλοῦμεν τὰ ἀπὸ σοῦ τῷ πατρί. ὁ δὲ κατ' ἀρχὰς
μὲν ἀντέλεγε δεδιὼς σφόδρα περὶ τῷ παιδί, τῶν
δ' ἀναγκαίων ὑποσπανιζόντων καὶ μηδενὸς ἡμῶν
τολμῶντος ἐπὶ σιτωνίαν ἥκειν δίχα τοῦ νεωτάτου
διὰ τὰς σὰς ἐπανατάσεις, μόλις πείθεται τοῦτον
συνεκπέμψαι μυρία μὲν αἰτιώμενος, ὅτι ἀδελφὸν
ἄλλον ἔχειν ὡμολογήσαμεν, μυρία δ' οἰκτιζόμενος,
εἰ μελλήσει διαζεύγνυσθαι· νήπιος γάρ ἐστι καὶ
πραγμάτων ἄπειρος, οὐ μόνον τῶν κατὰ τὴν ἀλ-
226 λοδαπήν, ἀλλὰ καὶ τῶν κατὰ τὴν πόλιν.[1] πρὸς οὖν

---

[1] The singular seems strange. Mangey wished to correct
either to τὴν ⟨ἰδίαν⟩ πόλιν or τὰς πόλεις. The latter is accepted

boldness and courage with modesty and practised
frankness of speech without effrontery, approached
him and said : " My lord, I pray you not to give way
to wrath, nor, because you have been appointed to
the second post after the king, to condemn before you
have heard our defence. When you asked us at our 223
first visit of our brother and father, we answered,
' Our father is an old man, aged not so much by years
as by repeated misfortunes, whereby as in a training-
school he has been continually exercised amid labours
and sufferings which have tried him sore. But our
brother is quite young, the idol and darling of his
father, because he is the child of his later years, the
only one left of the two that their mother bore, since
the elder has died a violent death. Now when you 224
bade us bring that brother here, and threatened that
if he did not arrive we should not even be admitted
again to your presence, we departed in dejection,
and, when we got home, only with reluctance told
your orders to our father. He at first opposed them in 225
his great fear for the boy, but, when necessaries grew
scarce and yet none of us dared to come and buy corn
without the youngest because of the stern warning
you had given, he was with difficulty persuaded to
send the boy with us. Many a time did he blame us
for admitting that we had another brother. Many
a time did he pity himself for the coming separation
from the boy, for he is but a child and without experience, not only of life in a foreign land, but of city [a] life

---

[a] Cohn translates " einheimischen," which would seem to
represent Mangey's τὴν ἰδίαν πόλιν (see critical note).

by Cohn in a similar passage in *De Decal.* 13, where the mss.
have κατὰ πόλιν. (The absence of the article perhaps makes
a difference, and κατὰ πόλιν might be read in both passages.)

οὕτω διακείμενον τὸν πατέρα πῶς ἂν ἀφικοίμεθα;
τίσι δ᾽ ὀφθαλμοῖς αὐτὸν θεάσασθαι δίχα τούτου
δυνησόμεθα; τελευτὴν οἰκτίστην ὑπομενεῖ μόνον
ἀκούσας, ὡς οὐκ ἐπανελήλυθεν· εἶθ᾽ ἡμᾶς ἀνδρο-
φόνους καὶ πατροκτόνους ἕκαστος ἐρεῖ τῶν φιλ-
απεχθημόνων καὶ ἐπὶ ταῖς τοιαύταις συμφοραῖς
227 ἐθελοκακούντων. τὸ δὲ πλεῖστον τῆς κατηγορίας
ῥυήσεται κατ᾽ ἐμοῦ· πολλὰ γὰρ ὑπεσχόμην τῷ πατρὶ
προέσθαι παρακαταθήκην λαμβάνειν ὁμολογῶν, ἣν
ἀποδώσειν, ὅταν ἀπαιτηθῶ· πῶς δ᾽ ἄν, εἰ μὴ ἐξ-
ευμενισθείης αὐτός, ἀποδοῦναι δυναίμην; οἶκτον
δέομαι τοῦ πρεσβύτου λαβεῖν καὶ εἰς ἔννοιαν ἐλθεῖν
τῶν κακῶν οἷσπερ ἀνιαθήσεται μὴ κομισάμενος ὃν
228 ἀβουλῶν ἐνεχείρισεν. ἀλλὰ σὺ μὲν ὑπὲρ ὧν ἔδοξας
ἠδικῆσθαι δίκας λάμβανε. δώσω δ᾽ ἐθελοντὴς ἐγώ·
δοῦλον ἀπὸ ταύτης ἀνάγραφε τῆς ἡμέρας, ἄσμενος
ὑπομενῶ τὰ τῶν νεωνήτων, ἐὰν τὸ παιδίον ἐθελήσῃς
229 ἐᾶσαι. λήψεται¹ δ᾽ οὐκ αὐτὸς τὴν χάριν, ἐὰν ἄρα
διδῷς, ἀλλ᾽ ὁ μὴ παρὼν ἐπικουφισθεὶς τῶν φροντίδων, ὁ τῶν τοσούτων πατὴρ ἱκετῶν ἁπάντων·
ἱκέται γάρ ἐσμεν καταπεφευγότες ἐπὶ τὴν σὴν
230 ἱερωτάτην δεξιάν, ἧς μηδέποτε διαμάρτοιμεν. ἔλεος
οὖν εἰσελθέτω σε γήρως ἀνδρὸς τοὺς ἀρετῆς ἄθλους
κατὰ πᾶσαν ἡλικίαν διαπονήσαντος· τὰς κατὰ
Συρίαν πόλεις εἰς ἀποδοχὴν αὐτοῦ καὶ τιμὴν ἐπέστρεψε, καίτοι ξενικωτέροις ἔθεσι καὶ νομίμοις καὶ
πολὺ διεστῶσι χρώμενος, οὐ βραχεῖ τινι τῶν ἐγχωρίων ἠλλοτριωμένος· ἀλλ᾽ ἡ τοῦ βίου καλοκἀγαθία
καὶ τὸ σύμφωνον καὶ ὁμολογούμενον πρὸς ἔργα
λόγων καὶ πρὸς λόγους ἔργων ἐξενίκησεν, ὡς καὶ
[74] τοὺς ἕνεκα | τῶν πατρίων μὴ εὐγνώμονας μεθ-

¹ MSS. λήψῃ.

in general. Then, since such are our father's feelings, 226
how can we return to him ? How can we look him
in the face without the boy ? He will suffer the
saddest of deaths on merely hearing that he has not
returned, and we shall be called murderers and parri-
cides by all the spiteful people who gloat over such
misfortunes. And the chief stream of obloquy will 227
be directed against me, for I pledged myself with
many forfeits to my father, and declared that I received the boy as a deposit which I would restore
when it was demanded from me. But how can I restore
it, unless you yourself are propitiated ? I pray you
to take pity on the old man, and realize the miseries
which he will suffer if he does not recover him whom
he unwillingly entrusted to my hand. But do you 228
exact the penalty for the wrongs which you believe
yourself to have received. I will willingly pay it.
Write me down your slave from this day onwards. I
will gladly endure what the newly-bought endure
if you will spare the child. This boon, if indeed you 229
grant it, will be a boon not to the boy himself but to
one who is not here present, whom you will relieve
of his cares, the father of all these many suppliants.
For suppliants we are who have fled for refuge to
your most august right hand, which we pray may
never fail us. Take pity, then, on the old age of one 230
who has spent all his years labouring in the arena of
virtue. The cities of Syria he won over to receive and
honour him, though his customs and usages were
strange to them and very different, and those of the
country alien to him in no small degree. But the
nobility of his life, and his acknowledged harmony of
words with deeds and deeds with words, prevailed so
that even those whom national feelings prejudiced

231 ἁρμόσασθαι. τοιαύτην μέλλεις κατατίθεσθαι χάριν,
ἧς οὐκ ἂν δύναιτό τις μείζονα λαβεῖν· τίς γὰρ ἂν
γένοιτο πατρὶ δωρεὰ μείζων ἢ υἱὸν ἀπογνωσθέντα
κομίσασθαι; "

232 XXXIX. Πάντα δ' ἦσαν ἀπόπειρα καὶ ταῦτα
καὶ τὰ πρότερα, πῶς ἔχουσι τοῦ τῆς χώρας ἐπιτρόπου σκοποῦντος εὐνοίας πρὸς τὸν ὁμομήτριον
ἀδελφόν· ἐδεδίει γάρ, μὴ φυσικῇ τινι ἀλλοτριώσει
κέχρηνται, καθάπερ οἱ ἐκ μητρυιῶν γεγονότες πρὸς

233 τὸν ἐξ ἑτέρας ἰσοτίμου γυναικὸς οἶκον. διὰ τοῦτο
καὶ ὡς κατασκόπους ᾐτιᾶτο καὶ περὶ τοῦ γένους
ἐπυνθάνετο πρόφασιν τοῦ γνῶναι, εἰ περίεστιν ὁ
ἀδελφός, ἀλλὰ μὴ ἐξ ἐπιβουλῆς ἀνῄρηται, καὶ ἕνα
κατέσχε τοὺς ἄλλους ἐάσας ἀπαίρειν ὁμολογή-
σαντας ἀγαγεῖν τὸν νεώτατον, ὃν ἰδεῖν μάλιστ'
ἐπόθει καὶ τῆς ἐπ' αὐτῷ χαλεπῆς καὶ βαρυτάτης

234 ἀνίας ἀπαλλαγῆναι,[1] καὶ ἐπειδὴ παρεγένετο καὶ τὸν
ἀδελφὸν ἐθεάσατο, μικρὸν ὅσον ἀνεθεὶς τῆς φροντίδος, καλέσας ἐπὶ ξενίαν καὶ ἑστιῶν πολυτελεσ-
τέραις εὐώχει τὸν ὁμομήτριον παρασκευαῖς, ἀπο-
βλέπων εἰς ἕκαστον καὶ τεκμαιρόμενος ἐκ τῆς

235 ὄψεως, εἴ τις αὐτοῖς ὑποικουρεῖ φθόνος, καὶ ὡς
ἀσμενίζοντας ἑώρα καὶ ἀναχεομένους ἐπὶ τῇ τοῦ
νεωτάτου τιμῇ, δυσὶν ἤδη μαρτυρίαις σημειω-
σάμενος τὸ μηδὲν ἔχθος ὑποτύφεσθαι καὶ τρίτην
ἐπενόησε, τὴν τοῦ κεκλέφθαι δοκοῦντος ἐκπώματος

---

[1] Cohn and Mangey's punctuation seems to me faulty in
this sentence. They place full stops after ἀπαλλαγῆναι and
φθόνος (Mangey also after ἀνῄρηται). But surely it is all one
sentence introduced by διὰ τοῦτο and stating that all these
steps were taken as a test.

---

[a] Benjamin's "mess" was five times as much as any of

against him were brought over to his ways. Such **231**
is the gratitude which you will earn, and what greater
could be earned? For what greater boon could a
father have than the recovery of a son of whose safety
he has despaired?"

XXXIX. All this and what had gone before was **232**
intended to test what feeling they shewed under
the eyes of the governor to his own mother's son.
For he feared that they might have had that natural
estrangement which the children of a stepmother
often shew to the family of another wife who was no
less esteemed than their own mother. This was the **233**
reason why he accused them of spying, and questioned them on their kin in order to know whether
that brother was alive and had not been the victim
of a plot, and also why he detained one when he
let the others depart after agreeing to bring the
youngest, whom he greatly yearned to see and thus
shake off the trouble which weighed on him so
heavily. This again was why, though when he **234**
came to join them and seeing his brother felt just a
little relieved, he after inviting them to the hospitality of his board entertained his mother's son on
a richer scale than the rest,[a] but meanwhile observed
each of them to judge from their looks whether they
still cherished some secret envy. Finally it was for **235**
the same reason that when he saw how pleased and
overjoyed they were at the honour paid to that
brother and thus had established by two testimonies
that there was no smouldering enmity, he devised
this third testimony, namely to pretend that the

theirs, Gen. xliii. 34. Philo has rather strangely omitted
to mention this in his account of the feast. Josephus, *Ant.*
ii. 125, gives the same reason for the action.

αἰτίαν ἀναθεὶς τῷ νεωτάτῳ· σαφέστατος γὰρ
ἔμελλεν ἔλεγχος οὑτοσὶ γενέσθαι τῆς ἑκάστου
διανοίας καὶ οἰκειότητος τῆς πρὸς τὸν συκοφαν-
236 τούμενον ἀδελφόν. ἐξ ὧν ἁπάντων ἤδη συνεπεί-
θετο περὶ τοῦ μὴ καταστασιάζεσθαι μηδ᾽ ἐπι-
βουλεύεσθαι τὸν μητρῷον οἶκον λογισμόν τε εἰκότα
καὶ περὶ τῶν αὐτῷ συμβεβηκότων ἐλάμβανεν, ὡς
οὐκ ἐπιβουλαῖς ἀδελφῶν αὐτὰ μᾶλλον εἴη πεπονθὼς
ἢ κατὰ πρόνοιαν θεοῦ τὰ μακρὰν ἐμβλέποντος καὶ
τὰ μέλλοντα οὐχ ἧττον τῶν παρόντων ὁρῶντος.

237 XL. Εἶτ᾽ ἐπὶ συμβάσεις καὶ καταλλαγὰς ἵετο
νικώμενος ὑπὸ φιλοικείου πάθους καὶ ὑπὲρ τοῦ
μηδὲν ὄνειδος προσβαλεῖν τοῖς ἀδελφοῖς ἕνεκα τῆς
πράξεως οὐδένα τῶν Αἰγυπτίων ἐδικαίωσε παρεῖναι
238 κατὰ τὴν πρώτην ἀναγνώρισιν· ἀλλὰ κελεύσας
ἅπασαν τὴν θεραπείαν μεταστῆναι, πηγήν τινα
δακρύων ἐξαίφνης ἀνεὶς καὶ τῇ δεξιᾷ προσελθεῖν
ἐγγυτέρω σημήνας, ἵνα μηδ᾽ ἐκ τύχης ἐπακοῦσαί
τις ἄλλος δυνηθῇ, φησὶν αὐτοῖς· '' ἐπεσκιασμένον
πρᾶγμα καὶ χρόνῳ μακρῷ συγκεκρύφθαι δοκοῦν
μέλλων ἀνακαλύπτειν μόνος μόνοις ὑμῖν ἀπαμ-
πίσχω· ἀδελφὸν ὃν ἀπέδοσθε εἰς Αἴγυπτον, ἐκεῖνος
239 ὃν ὁρᾶτε νῦν παρεστῶτα αὐτός εἰμι ἐγώ.'' κατα-
πλαγέντων δ᾽ αὐτῶν παρ᾽ ἐλπίδα καὶ διεπτοημένων
καὶ ὥσπερ ὁλκῇ τινι βιαίῳ τὰς ὄψεις ἐπὶ γῆν κατα-
βεβληκότων καὶ πεπηγότων ἀφώνων καὶ ἀχανῶν,
[75] '' μὴ κατηφεῖτε '' | εἶπεν, '' ἀμνηστίαν ἁπάντων
παρέχω τῶν εἰς ἐμὲ πεπραγμένων, μηδενὸς ἑτέρου
240 δεῖσθε παρακλήτου· αὐτοκελεύστῳ καὶ ἑκουσίῳ
γνώμῃ πρὸς συμβάσεις ἐθελοντὴς ἀφῖγμαι συμβού-
λοις[1] χρησάμενος δυσί, τῇ τε πρὸς τὸν πατέρα

---

[1] MSS. συμβόλοις.

cup had been stolen, and charge the theft to the youngest. For this would be the clearest way of testing the real feeling of each, and their attachment to the brother thus falsely accused. On all these 236 grounds he was now convinced that there was no factious conspiracy to undo his mother's family, and also considering what had happened to himself he came to the conclusion that his experiences were probably due not so much to their conspiring as to the providence of God Who beholds distant events and sees the future no less than the present.

XL. So then, overcome by family affection, he 237 hastened to conclude his reconciliation. And that no reproach might attach to the brothers for their action he judged it best that no Egyptian should be present at the first recognition. Instead he bade all 238 the staff to withdraw, and then suddenly shedding a flood of tears and beckoning to them with his right hand to approach nearer so that no one else could by chance hear him, he said : " I am going to reveal to you a matter which has been shrouded in darkness and long time hidden, and I do so while you and I are all alone. The brother whom you sold into Egypt is I myself, whom you see standing beside you." When, astonished and staggered at the un- 239 expected news, they stood rooted to the spot mute and speechless with eyes cast to the ground as though drawn by some compelling force, " Be not downcast," he continued, "I forgive and forget all what you did to me. Do not ask for any other advocate. Of my own free, unbidden judgement I 240 have voluntarily come to make my peace with you. In this I have two fellow-counsellors, my reverence

PHILO

εὐσεβείᾳ, ᾧ τὸ πλεῖστον τῆς χάριτος ἀνατίθημι, καὶ
τῇ φυσικῇ φιλανθρωπίᾳ, ᾗ πρὸς ἅπαντας δια-
241 φερόντως δὲ πρὸς τοὺς ἀφ' αἵματος χρῶμαι. καὶ
νομίζω τῶν συμβεβηκότων οὐχ ὑμᾶς ἀλλὰ θεὸν
αἴτιον γεγενῆσθαι βουληθέντα με τῶν αὐτοῦ χαρίτων καὶ δωρεῶν, ἃς ἐν τοῖς ἀναγκαιοτάτοις καιροῖς
ἠξίωσε τῷ γένει τῶν ἀνθρώπων παρασχεῖν, ὑπη-
242 ρέτην γενέσθαι καὶ διάκονον. ἐναργῆ δὲ πίστιν
δύνασθε λαβεῖν ἐξ ὧν ὁρᾶτε· πᾶσαν μὲν Αἴγυπτον
ἐπιτέτραμμαι, τιμὴν δὲ ἔχω τὴν πρώτην παρὰ τῷ
βασιλεῖ καὶ μὲ νέον ὄντα πρεσβύτερος ὢν ὡς πατέρα
τιμᾷ· θεραπεύομαί τε οὐχ ὑπὸ τῶν ἐγχωρίων μόνον
ἀλλὰ καὶ ὑπὸ πλείστων ἄλλων ἐθνῶν, ὅσα καὶ
ὑπήκοα καὶ αὐτόνομα· χρεία γὰρ πάντα διὰ τὴν
243 ἔνδειαν προεστῶτος. ἄργυρός τε καὶ χρυσὸς καί,
τὸ τούτων ἀναγκαιότερον, αἱ τροφαὶ παρ' ἐμοὶ μόνῳ
ταμιεύονται διανέμοντι καὶ κατακερματίζοντι πρὸς
τὰς ἀναγκαίας χρείας ἑκάστοις τῶν δεομένων, ὡς
μήτε τι τῶν εἰς τρυφὴν περιττεῦσαι μήτε τι τῶν
244 εἰς ἐκπλήρωσιν ἐνδείας ἐπιλιπεῖν. ἀλλ' οὐκ ἐναβρυ-
νόμενος καὶ σεμνυνόμενος ταυτὶ διεξῆλθον, ἀλλ'
ἵν' αἴσθησθε, ὅτι τῶν τηλικούτων οὐδεὶς ἔμελλεν
ἀνθρώπων αἴτιος ἔσεσθαι δούλῳ καὶ μετὰ ταῦτα
δεσμώτῃ γενομένῳ—καὶ γὰρ ἐδέθην ποτὲ συκο-
φαντηθείς—, ἀλλ' ὁ τὰς ἐσχάτας συμφοράς τε καὶ
δυσπραγίας μεθαρμοσάμενος εἰς τὰς ἀνωτάτω καὶ
245 πρώτας εὐτυχίας θεὸς ἦν, ᾧ πάντα δυνατά. ταῦτα
ἐμοῦ διανοουμένου, μηκέτι εὐλαβῶς ἔχετε τὰς δυσ-
φροσύνας ἐκποδὼν ποιησάμενοι καὶ πρὸς ἱλαρὰν
μεταβαλόντες εὐθυμίαν. εὖ δ' ἂν ἔχοι καὶ πρὸς τὸν
πατέρα συντεῖναι καὶ πρῶτον αὐτῷ τὰ περὶ τῆς

for our father, which is chiefly responsible for the
favour I shew you, and the natural humanity which
I feel to all men, and particularly to those of my
blood. And I consider that the cause of what has 241
happened is not you but God, Who willed to use me
as His servant, to administer the boons and gifts
which He deigns to grant to the human race in the
time of their greatest need. You can have a clear 242
proof of this in what you see. All Egypt is committed to my hands, and I hold the first place of
honour with the king, and though I am young, and he
my elder, he honours me as a father. I have waiting
on my will not only the inhabitants of the land, but
most of the other nations, whether subject or independent, for because of the dearth they all need
me at the head. Silver and gold are stored in my 243
keeping alone, and, what is more necessary than
these, the means of sustenance, which I distribute
and parcel out to those who ask, according to their
necessary requirements, so that they have no superfluities which might serve for luxury nor lack of what
may satisfy actual want. But I have told you all 244
this, not because I plume and pride myself thereon,
but that you may perceive that no man could have
caused such greatness to come to one who was a
slave and afterwards a prisoner—for I was once in
bonds under a false charge—but He Who turned
my condition of extreme calamity into one of unequalled and exalted good fortune was God to
Whom all things are possible. Since I am so dis- 245
posed, fear no more, but cast aside your heaviness of
heart and take a cheerful courage in its stead. It
would be well that you should hasten to our father,
and first of all give him the good tidings that you

ἐμῆς εὑρέσεως εὐαγγελίσασθαι· φθάνουσι γὰρ αἱ
246 φῆμαι πανταχόσε.''   XLI. οἱ δὲ κατὰ
διαδοχὴν τοὺς ἐπαίνους αὐτοῦ συνείροντες ἀπαύστως ἀχαλίνοις στόμασιν ἐξύμνουν ἄλλος ἄλλο τι
διεξιών, ὁ μὲν τὸ ἀμνησίκακον, ὁ δὲ τὸ φιλοίκειον,
ὁ δὲ τὴν σύνεσιν, ἅπαντες δ' ἀθρόοι τὴν εὐσέβειαν
ἐπὶ τὸν θεὸν ἀναφέροντος τὰ τέλη τῶν κατορθου-
μένων καὶ μηκέτι ταῖς ἀβουλήτοις ἀρχαῖς καὶ
πρώταις ἐνστάσεσι τῶν μὴ κατὰ γνώμην δυσχεράναντος καὶ τὴν ὑπερβάλλουσαν μετ' αἰδοῦς καρ-
247 τερίαν· ὃς ἐν τοσαύταις γεγονὼς ἀνωμαλίαις οὔτε
δουλεύων βλάσφημον οὐδὲν εἶπε κατὰ τῶν ἀδελφῶν
ὡς πεπρακότων οὔτ' εἰς εἱρκτὴν ἀπαγόμενος ὑπ'
ἀθυμίας ἐξελάλησέ τι τῶν ἀπορρήτων οὔτε πολὺν
[76] χρόνον ἐκεῖ καταμένων, οἷα | φιλεῖ, τοῖς δεσμώταις
ἔθους ὄντος τὰς ἰδίας ἀτυχίας ἀναμετρεῖσθαι, ἀπ-
248 εγύμνωσεν· ἀλλ' ὡς μηδὲν εἰδὼς τῶν αὐτῷ συμβεβηκότων, ἀλλ' οὐδ' ὅτε τὰ ὀνείρατα διέκρινεν ἢ τοῖς
εὐνούχοις ἢ τῷ βασιλεῖ, καιρὸν ἔχων εἰς μήνυσιν
ἐπιτήδειον, ἐφθέγξατό τι περὶ τῆς ἰδίας εὐγενείας,
οὐδ' ὅτε βασιλέως ὕπαρχος ἐχειροτονεῖτο καὶ τῆς
Αἰγύπτου πάσης τὴν ἐπιμέλειαν καὶ προστασίαν
παρελάμβανεν, ἵνα μὴ δόξῃ τις εἶναι τῶν ἠμελημένων καὶ ἀφανῶν, ἀλλὰ τῷ ὄντι εὐπατρίδης, οὐ
φύσει δοῦλος, ἀλλ' ἐπιβουλὰς ὑφ' ὧν ἥκιστ' ἐχρῆν
249 ἀνηκέστους ὑπομεμενηκὼς καὶ συμφοράς. ἔτι δὲ
πρὸς τούτοις ἐρρύη πολὺς ἔπαινος ἰσότητος αὐτοῦ
καὶ δεξιότητος· τὰς γὰρ τῶν ἄλλων ἀλαζονείας καὶ

---

[a] §§ 246–249 have no basis in Genesis. The nearest corresponding text is xlv. 15 " and after that his brethren talked

258

have found me, for rumours travel fast in all directions." XLI. *The brothers, letting their 246
tongues run freely, ceased not to sound his praises
point by point. Each one had a different theme,
one his readiness to forgive, one his family affection,
one his prudence, while all united in praising his
piety in attributing to God the success which crowned
his career and abandoning all resentment at the
unwelcome experiences which had attended its dis-
tressing opening and earliest stages. They praised
also the pre-eminent self-restraint of his modest
reticence. He had passed through all these vicissi- 247
tudes, yet neither while in slavery did he denounce
his brothers for selling him nor when he was haled
to prison did he in his despondency disclose any
secret, nor during his long stay there make any
revelations of the usual kind, since prisoners are
apt to descant upon their personal misfortunes. He 248
behaved as though he knew nothing of his past experiences, and not even when he was interpreting
their dreams to the eunuchs or the king, though he
had a suitable opportunity for disclosing the facts,
did he say a word about his own high lineage. Nor
yet, when he was appointed to be the king's viceroy
and was charged with the superintendence and head-
ship over all Egypt, did he say anything to prevent
the belief that he was of obscure and ignoble station,
whereas he was really a noble, no slave by birth, but
the unfortunate victim of the ruthless conspiracy of
those who should have been the last to treat him so.
In addition there was a great outflow of praise of 249
his fairness and kind behaviour, for they knew the

with him." Did Philo read or think he read περὶ for πρὸs
αὐτόν?

ἀπαιδευσίας ἡγεμόνων εἰδότες ἐθαύμαζον τὸ ἀνεπί-
φαντον καὶ ἀτραγῴδητον καὶ ὡς εὐθὺς ἰδὼν κατὰ
τὴν προτέραν ὁδὸν ἀποκτεῖναι δυνάμενος ἢ τὸ γοῦν
τελευταῖον λιμώττουσι τροφὰς μὴ παρασχεῖν πρὸς
τῷ μὴ τιμωρήσασθαι καὶ ὡς χάριτος ἀξίοις δωρεὰν
ἔδωκε τἀπιτήδεια τὴν τιμὴν αὐτῶν ἀποδοθῆναι
250 κελεύσας. οὕτω μέντοι τὰ τῆς ἐπιβουλῆς καὶ
πράσεως εἰς ἅπαν ἠγνοήθη καὶ διέλαθεν, ὥσθ' οἱ ἐν
τέλει τῶν Αἰγυπτίων συνήδοντο, ὡς πρῶτον ἄρτι
τῶν ἀδελφῶν τοῦ προεστῶτος ἡκόντων, καὶ ἐπὶ
ξενίαν ἐκάλουν καὶ φθάνοντες εὐηγγελίζοντο τῷ
βασιλεῖ, καὶ πάντα διὰ πάντων ἔγεμε χαρᾶς οὐκ
ἔλαττον ἢ εἴπερ εὐφόρησεν ἡ πεδιὰς καὶ ὁ λιμὸς εἰς
251 εὐθηνίαν μετέβαλε. XLII. γνοὺς δ' ὁ βασιλεύς,
ὅτι καὶ πατήρ ἐστιν αὐτῷ καὶ ἡ γενεὰ πολυάνθρωπος, προτρέπει μεταναστῆναι πανοικὶ τὴν
βαθυγειοτάτην Αἰγύπτου μοῖραν ὁμολογήσας δε-
δωρῆσθαι τοῖς ἀφιξομένοις. ἀπήνας οὖν καὶ ἁρμα-
μάξας καὶ πλῆθος ὑποζυγίων ἐπηχθισμένων τἀπιτήδεια δίδωσι τοῖς ἀδελφοῖς καὶ θεραπείαν ἱκανήν,
ἵνα μετ' ἀσφαλείας ἀγάγωσι τὸν πατέρα.
252 Παραγενομένων δὲ καὶ τὰ περὶ τὸν ἀδελφὸν
ἄπιστα καὶ μείζονα ἐλπίδων διηγουμένων, οὐ πάνυ
προσεῖχε· κἂν γὰρ οἱ λέγοντες ἀξιοπιστότατοι, ἀλλ'
ἥ γε τοῦ πράγματος ὑπερβολὴ ῥᾳδίως συναινεῖν οὐκ
253 ἐπέτρεπεν. ἰδὼν δὲ ὁ πρεσβύτης τὰς ἐν τοιούτῳ

---

a Lit. "the last thing at any rate," *i.e.* the extreme of
clemency which could be expected. Cohn takes it with
λιμώττουσι—" in the extremity of famine." The position of
γοῦν seems to me to be against this. Mangey *postea certe*,
presumably meaning " at the conclusion of the interview."

arrogance and gross rudeness of other governors, and admired the absence of obtrusiveness and blustering. They remembered how directly he saw them on their former expedition, though he might have put them to death or at the very least ^a refused to provide them with food against the famine, so far from taking vengeance he treated them as worthy of his favour and gave them the victuals for nothing by bidding the price to be restored to them. In 250 fact the story of their conspiracy and selling of him to slavery was so completely unknown and remained so secret that the chiefs of the Egyptians rejoiced to hear that the brothers of the governor had now for the first time come to visit him. They invited them to share their hospitality and hastened to bring the good news to the king, and universal joy reigned everywhere, no less than if the fields had borne fruit and the famine had been changed into abundance. XLII. When the king learned that his 251 viceroy had a father and that his family was very numerous, he urged that the whole household should leave its present home, and promised to give the most fertile part of Egypt to the expected settlers. He therefore gave the brothers carts and wagons and a great number of beasts laden with provisions, and an adequate body of servants, that they might bring their father safely.

When they arrived home and told the story of 252 their brother, so incredible and beyond anything he could have hoped for, he gave no heed to them at all, for, however worthy of credit the speakers might be, the extravagance of the tale did not allow him to assent to it readily. But, when the old man saw 253 the equipments suited for an occasion of the kind,

καιρῷ παρασκευὰς καὶ χορηγίας τῶν ἀναγκαίων
ἀφθόνους τοῖς περὶ τούτου λεγομένοις εὐτυχήμασι
συναδούσας ὕμνει τὸν θεόν, ὅτι τὸ δοκοῦν ἐκλελοι-
254 πέναι μέρος τῆς οἰκίας ἀπεπλήρωσεν. ἡ δὲ χαρὰ
καὶ φόβον εὐθὺς ἐγέννησε τῇ ψυχῇ περὶ τῆς τῶν
πατρίων ἐκδιαιτήσεως· ᾔδει γὰρ καὶ νεότητα
εὐόλισθον φύσει καὶ ξενιτείας τὴν εἰς τὸ ἁμαρτάνειν
ἐκεχειρίαν καὶ μάλιστα τῆς ἐν Αἰγύπτῳ χώρας
[77] τυφλωττούσης περὶ τὸν ἀληθῆ θεὸν ἕνεκα | τοῦ
γενητὰ καὶ θνητὰ θεοπλαστεῖν καὶ προσέτι πλούτου
καὶ δόξης ἐπιθέσεις ⟨ἃς⟩[1] ὀλιγόφροσι διανοίαις ἐπιτίθενται καὶ διότι ἀπολειφθείς, μηδενὸς τῶν ἐκ
τῆς πατρῴας οἰκίας συνεξεληλυθότος[2] σωφρονιστοῦ,
μόνος ὢν καὶ ἔρημος διδασκάλων ἀγαθῶν ἕτοιμος
255 ἔσται πρὸς τὴν τῶν ὀθνείων μεταβολήν. οὕτως
οὖν διακείμενον ἰδὼν ᾧ μόνῳ δυνατὸν ἀόρατον
ψυχὴν ὁρᾶν ἔλεον λαμβάνει καὶ κοιμωμένῳ νύκτωρ
ἐπιφανείς φησι· " μηδὲν εὐλαβοῦ περὶ τῆς εἰς
Αἴγυπτον ἀφίξεως· αὐτὸς ἡγεμονεύσω τῆς ὁδοῦ
παρέχων τὴν ἀποδημίαν ἀσφαλῆ καὶ εὐάρεστον·
ἀποδώσω μέντοι καὶ τὸν τριπόθητον υἱόν, ὃς ποτε
τεθνάναι νομισθεὶς ἐκ πολυετίας οὐ ζῶν μόνον ἀλλὰ
καὶ χώρας τοσαύτης ἡγεμὼν ἀναφαίνεται." πληρωθεὶς δ' εὐελπιστίας ἅμα τῇ ἕῳ γεγηθὼς ἐπέσπευδεν.
256 ὁ δ' υἱὸς ἀκούσας—σκοποὶ γὰρ καὶ φραστῆρες τῆς
ὁδοῦ πάντ' ἐδήλουν—οὐ μακρὰν τῶν ὁρίων ἀπ-
έχοντα[3] διὰ ταχέων ἀπήντα τῷ πατρί· καὶ κατὰ τὴν
καλουμένην Ἡρώων πόλιν ἐντυχόντες ἐπιπίπτουσιν

---

[1] My insertion. The sentence evidently needs correction,
which Cohn would make by expunging ἐπιτίθενται.
[2] Most mss. συνεξεληλυθότων or ἐξ-, one ἐξεληλυθότος.
[3] So mss., Cohn, and Mangey; but? ἀπέχοντι.

and that the lavish supplies of all that was needed agreed with the story they told him of his son, he praised God that He had filled the seeming gap in his house. But joy also straightway begat fear in his 254 soul at the thought of leaving his ancestral way of life. For he knew how natural it is for youth to lose its footing and what licence to sin belongs to the stranger's life, particularly in Egypt where things created and mortal are deified, and in consequence the land is blind to the true God. He knew what assaults wealth and renown make on minds of little sense, and that left to himself, since his father's house supplied no monitor to share his journey, alone and cut off from good teaching, he would be readily influenced to change to alien ways. Such were his 255 feelings when He Whose eye alone can see the invisible soul took pity, and in his sleep at night appeared to him and said, "Fear not to go to Egypt. I Myself will guide thee on the road and make the journey safe and to thy pleasure. Further, I will restore to thee the son for whom thou hast so greatly yearned,[a] who once was thought dead, but now, after many years, is found not only alive but a ruler of that great country." Then, filled with high hopes, he hastened at dawn to set forth rejoicing. But his son 256 when he heard it, informed of all by the scouts who watched the road, proceeded with all speed to meet his father when he was not far from the boundary. And when the two met at the place called the Heroes'

---

[a] Gen. xlvi. 4 " and Joseph shall put his hands upon thine eyes." Did Philo fail to understand this phrase, which does not occur again in the LXX? The idea of closing the eyes of the dead, otherwise expressed, was of course familiar to him in the classics, cf. § 23 above.

PHILO

ἀλλήλοις τὰς κεφαλὰς ἐπὶ τῶν αὐχένων ἐρείσαντες
καὶ τὰς ἐσθῆτας δάκρυσι φύροντες πολυχρονίων
ἀσπασμάτων ἀπλήστως ἐνεφοροῦντο καὶ μόλις
257 παυσάμενοι συνέτεινον ἄχρι τῶν βασιλείων. θεασάμενος δὲ ὁ βασιλεὺς καὶ τὴν ὄψιν καταπλαγεὶς τῆς
σεμνότητος ὡς οὐχ ὑπάρχου πατέρα ἀλλ' ἑαυτοῦ
μετὰ πάσης αἰδοῦς καὶ τιμῆς ἐδεξιοῦτο· καὶ μετὰ
τὰς ἐν ἔθει καὶ ἐξαιρέτους φιλοφροσύνας δίδωσιν
αὐτῷ γῆς ἀποτομὴν ἀρετῶσαν καὶ σφόδρα εὔκαρπον,
τούς τε υἱοὺς αὐτοῦ πυνθανόμενος εἶναι κτηνο-
τρόφους τὴν πολλὴν οὐσίαν ἔχοντας ἐν θρέμμασι
καθίστησιν ἐπιμελητὰς τῶν ἰδίων αἰπόλια καὶ βουκόλια καὶ ποίμνας καὶ μυρίας ὅσας ἀγέλας ἐγχειρίσας
αὐτοῖς.

258   XLIII. Ὁ δὲ νεανίας τοσαύτῃ πίστεως ἐχρήσατο
ὑπερβολῇ, ὥστε τῶν καιρῶν καὶ τῶν πραγμάτων
εἰς ἀργυρισμὸν παρεχόντων πλείστας ὅσας ἀφορμάς,
δυνηθεὶς δι' ὀλίγου πλουσιώτατος τῶν κατ' αὐτὸν
γενέσθαι, τὸν γνήσιον ὡς ἀληθῶς πρὸ τοῦ νόθου
πλοῦτον καὶ τὸν βλέποντα πρὸ τοῦ τυφλοῦ θαυμάσας
ἅπαντα τὸν ἄργυρον καὶ χρυσόν, ὅσον ἐκ τῆς τιμῆς
ἤθροισε τοῦ σίτου, ἐν τοῖς βασιλέως ἐθησαυρίζετο
ταμιείοις οὐδεμίαν δραχμὴν νοσφισάμενος, ἀλλὰ
μόναις ἀρκεσθεὶς ταῖς δωρεαῖς, αἷς ἀμειβόμενος
259 ἐκεῖνος ἀντεχαρίζετο. καθάπερ τε οἰκίαν μίαν

ᵃ So lxx.   E.V. Goshen.

ᵇ §§ 258-260 are a very free version of Gen. xlvii. 13-26.
Joseph's honesty is deduced from verse 14 " Joseph brought
264

City [a] they laid their heads upon each other's neck and while the tears smeared their raiment lingered long in embraces of which they could not take their fill, and, when at last they brought themselves to cease therefrom, pressed onwards to the king's court. When the king beheld him, overcome by his vener- 257 able appearance, he welcomed him with all modesty and respect, as though he were the father not of his viceroy but of himself. And, after the usual, and more than the usual, courtesies had passed, he gave him a portion of land, rich of soil and very fruitful. And, learning that the sons were graziers who had much substance of cattle, he appointed them keepers of his own, and put into their charge flocks and herds innumerable of goats and oxen and sheep.

XLIII. [b] Now the young man's honesty was ex- 258 ceedingly great, so much so that, though the times and state of affairs gave him very numerous oppor- tunities for gaining wealth, and he might have soon become the richest of his contemporaries, his rever- ence for the truly genuine riches rather than the spurious, the seeing rather than the blind, led him to store up in the king's treasuries all the silver and gold which he collected from the sale of corn and refuse to appropriate to himself a single drachma, contented with nothing more than the gifts with which the king repaid his services. The excellence 259

all the money into Pharaoh's house." Philo omits the stages by which the property and land of the Egyptians passed into the king's hand, and the tax of one-fifth of the produce imposed upon them. That the gift of seed was only made in the seventh year of the famine might be fairly inferred from the LXX in verse 24 "and the land shall have its produce" (ἔσται δὲ γεννήματα αὐτῆς). The appointment of overseers has no parallel in Genesis.

Αἴγυπτον καὶ σὺν αὐτῇ χώρας ἑτέρας καὶ ἔθνη
πιεσθέντα τῷ λιμῷ παντὸς λόγου κρεῖττον ἐπετρό-
πευσεν ὁ ἀνὴρ οὗτος κατὰ τὸ πρέπον διανέμων τὰς
τροφὰς καὶ ἀφορῶν οὐκ εἰς τὸ παρὸν μόνον λυσιτελὲς ἀλλὰ καὶ τὴν πρὸς τὸ μέλλον ὠφέλειαν.
260 ἡνίκα γοῦν ὁ ἕβδομος ἐνιαυτὸς τῆς ἐνδείας ἐνέστη,
[78] μεταπεμψάμενος τοὺς γεωργούς—ἤδη γὰρ | τῆς
εὐφορίας καὶ εὐθηνίας ἐλπὶς ἦν—ἐδίδου κριθάς τε
καὶ πυροὺς εἰς σπέρματα φροντίσας τοῦ μηδένα
νοσφίσασθαι καταθεῖναι δὲ[1] εἰς τὰς ἀρούρας ἃ
ἔλαβεν, ὀπτῆρας καὶ ἐφόρους ἐπιλέξας ἀριστίνδην,
οἳ τὴν σπορὰν παραφυλάξουσι.

261 Μετὰ δὲ τὸν λιμὸν χρόνοις μακροῖς ὕστερον
τελευτήσαντος τοῦ πατρός, ὑπονοίᾳ πληχθέντες
οἱ ἀδελφοὶ καὶ δείσαντες, μή τι χαλεπὸν πάθωσι
μνησικακίᾳ,[2] προσελθόντες ἐδέοντο λιπαρῶς ἐπ-
262 αγόμενοι γυναῖκας καὶ γενεάν. ὁ δ' ἐπιδακρύσας
φησίν· '' ὁ μὲν καιρὸς ἱκανὸς ὑπόνοιαν κατασκευά-
σαι τοῖς ἀφόρητα ἐργασαμένοις καὶ μὴ δι' ἑτέρου
μᾶλλον ἢ τοῦ συνειδότος ἐλεγχομένοις· ἡ γὰρ
τελευτὴ τοῦ πατρὸς τὸν ἀρχαῖον φόβον, ὃν πρὸ τῶν
καταλλαγῶν εἴχετε, κεκαίνωκεν, ὡς τοῦ μὴ λυπῆσαι
τὸν πατέρα χάριν τὴν ἀμνηστίαν ἐμοῦ παρασχόντος.
263 ἐγὼ δὲ τὸν τρόπον οὐ χρόνοις μεταβάλλομαι οὐδ'
ὁμολογήσας ἔνσπονδος εἶναι δράσω ποτὲ τὰ ἄ-
σπονδα· οὐ γὰρ ὑπερθέσεις ἀμύνης ἐκαιροφυλάκουν,
ἀλλὰ τὴν εἰς ἅπαν ἀπαλλαγὴν τῆς κολάσεως ἐχαρι-
ζόμην ἐπινέμων τὸ μέν τι τιμῇ τοῦ πατρός—δεῖ γὰρ
ἀψευδεῖν—, τὸ δέ τι εὐνοίᾳ τῇ πρὸς ὑμᾶς ἀναγκαίᾳ.

---

[1] So Mangey: Cohn and mss. καταθεῖναί τε.
[2] mss. μνησικακίας.

with which he managed Egypt, as though it were a single household, and also the other famine-stricken lands and nations was beyond all words, and he dispensed the lands and food as was suitable, looking not only to present profit but also to future advantage. Accordingly, when the seventh year of dearth came, 260 having now reason to hope for plentiful harvests, he sent for the farmers and gave them barley and wheat as seed, and at the same time, to ensure that no one should embezzle it instead of putting it in the fields, he appointed men of high merit as inspectors and supervisors to watch the sowing.

[a] Many years after the famine his father died, and 261 his brothers, attacked by misgivings and fears that he might still harbour malice and wreak his vengeance on them, approached him with their wives and families and made earnest supplication. But he, moved to 262 tears, said : " The occasion might well raise misgivings in those whom conscience rather than others convicts of intolerable misdoing. My father's death has awakened the old fear which you felt before our reconciliation, with the idea that I gave you my pardon only to save my father from sorrow. But time does not change my character, nor, after promising to keep the peace with you, will I ever violate it by my actions. I was not watching for the hour of vengeance 263 repeatedly delayed, but I freely granted you immunity from punishment once for all, partly no doubt influenced, for I must tell the truth, by respect for my father, but partly by the goodwill which I cannot but feel towards you. And, even if it were 264

[a] For §§ 261-268 see Gen. l. 15-end.

PHILO

264 εἰ δὲ καὶ πατρὸς ἔνεκα πάντ᾽ ἐποίουν τὰ χρηστὰ καὶ
φιλάνθρωπα, φυλάξω ταῦτα καὶ πατρὸς[1] τετελευ-
τηκότος· τέθνηκε δ᾽ οὐδεὶς παρ᾽ ἐμοὶ κριτῇ τῶν
ἀγαθῶν ἀνδρῶν, ἀλλὰ καὶ ζήσεται τὸν ἀεὶ χρόνον
ἀγήρως, ἀθανάτῳ φύσει ψυχῇ μηκέτι ταῖς σώματος
265 ἀνάγκαις ἐνδεδεμένῃ. τί δὲ δεῖ μόνου μεμνῆσθαι
τοῦ γενητοῦ πατρός; ἔχομεν τὸν ἀγένητον, τὸν
ἄφθαρτον, τὸν ἀίδιον, " ὃς ἐφορᾷ πάντα καὶ πάντων
ἐπακούει " καὶ τῶν ἡσυχαζόντων, τὸν ἀεὶ βλέποντα
καὶ τὰ ἐν μυχοῖς τῆς διανοίας, ὃν μάρτυρα καλῶ
266 τοῦ συνειδότος ἐπ᾽ ἀψευδέσι καταλλαγαῖς. ἐγὼ
γάρ, καὶ μὴ θαυμάσητέ μου τὸν λόγον, τοῦ θεοῦ
εἰμι τοῦ τὰ πονηρὰ βουλεύματα ὑμῶν εἰς ἀγαθῶν
περιουσίαν μεθαρμοσαμένου. γίνεσθε οὖν ἄφοβοι
καὶ πρὸς τὸ μέλλον χρησιμωτέρων μεθέξοντες ἢ
267 ζῶντος ἔτι τοῦ πατρὸς ἐκαρποῦσθε." XLIV. τοιούτοις θαρσύνας τοὺς ἀδελφοὺς λόγοις, ἔργοις τὰς
ὑποσχέσεις ἐβεβαίου μᾶλλον οὐδὲν παραλιπὼν τῶν
εἰς ἐπιμέλειαν. μετὰ δὲ τὸν λιμόν, ἐπ᾽
εὐθηνίᾳ καὶ εὐετηρίᾳ τῆς χώρας ἤδη γεγηθότων
τῶν οἰκητόρων, ἐτιμᾶτο πρὸς ἁπάντων ἀμοιβὰς
ἀντεκτινόντων ὑπὲρ ὧν εὖ πεπόνθεσαν ἐν καιροῖς
268 ἀβουλήτοις. ἡ δὲ φήμη ῥυεῖσα τὰς ἑξῆς πόλεις
κατέπλησε τῆς ἐπὶ τῷδε τῷ ἀνδρὶ εὐκλείας. ἔτη
δὲ βιώσας δέκα πρὸς τοῖς ἑκατὸν ἐτελεύτησεν
εὔγηρως ἐπ᾽ ἄκρον ἐλθὼν εὐμορφίας καὶ φρονή-
269 σεως καὶ λόγων δυνάμεως. μαρτυρεῖ δὲ τὸ μὲν

[1] mss. πρὸς (or omit): some have τετελευτηκότα for -ότος.

---

[a] Cohn places the comma after φύσει, "will live proof
against old age in an immortal existence with a soul," etc.

268

for my father's sake that I acted with this kindness
and humanity, I will continue in the same now that
he is gone. In my judgement, no good man is dead,
but will live for ever, proof against old age,[a] with a
soul immortal in its nature no longer fettered by the
restraints of the body. But why should I mention 265
that father who is but a creature ? We have the
uncreated Father, the Imperishable, the Eternal,
"Who surveys all things and hears all things," [b] even
when no word is spoken, He Who ever sees into the
recesses of the mind, Whom I call as witness to my
conscience, which affirms that that was no false
reconciliation. For I,—do not marvel at my words, 266
—belong to God [c] Who converted your evil schemes
into a superabundance of blessings. Rid yourselves,
then, of fear, since in the future greater advantage
will fall to your share than you enjoyed while our
father was still alive." XLIV. With such words he 267
encouraged his brothers, and by his actions he confirmed his promises, leaving nothing undone which
could shew his care for their interests.

But, after the famine, when the inhabitants were
now rejoicing in the prosperity and fertility of the
land, he was honoured by them all, who thus requited the benefits which they had received from
him in the times of adversity. And rumour, float- 268
ing into the neighbouring states, filled them with
his renown. He died in a goodly old age, having
lived 110 years, unsurpassed in comeliness, wisdom
and power of language. His personal beauty is 269

[b] *Il.* iii. 277, *Od.* xi. 109, xii. 323 ὃς πάντ᾽ ἐφορᾷ καὶ πάντ᾽
ἐπακούει (of the sun).

[c] So LXX. (Gen. l. 19). E.V. "Am I in the place of God
(to punish you) ? " Philo has made use of the text in the same
sense *De Mig.* 22 and 160. *De Som.* ii. 107.

PHILO

[79] κάλλος τοῦ σώματος ἔρως ὃς ἐξέμηνεν | ἐπ᾽ αὐτῷ
γυναῖκα, τὴν δὲ σύνεσιν ἡ ἐν ταῖς ἀμυθήτοις τῶν
κατὰ τὸν βίον ἀνωμαλίαις ὁμαλότης εὐαρμοστίαν
τοῖς ἀναρμόστοις καὶ συμφωνίαν τοῖς ἐξ αὐτῶν
ἀσυμφώνοις ἐργασαμένη, τὴν δὲ τῶν λόγων δύναμιν ἥ τε τῶν ὀνειράτων διάκρισις καὶ ἡ ἐν ταῖς
ὁμιλίαις εὐέπεια καὶ ἡ παρακολουθήσασα πειθώ, δι᾽
ἣν οὐδεὶς τῶν ἀρχομένων ἀνάγκῃ μᾶλλον ἢ ἑκὼν
270 ὑπήκουε. τούτων δὲ τῶν ἐνιαυτῶν ἑπτακαίδεκα
μὲν ἄχρι μειρακίου διέτριβεν ἐν τῇ πατρῴᾳ οἰκίᾳ,
τρισκαίδεκα δ᾽ ἐν ταῖς ἀβουλήτοις συντυχίαις, ἐπιβουλευόμενος, πιπρασκόμενος, δουλεύων, συκοφαν-
τούμενος, ἐν δεσμωτηρίῳ καταδούμενος, τοὺς δ᾽
ἄλλους ὀγδοήκοντα ἐν ἡγεμονίᾳ καὶ εὐπραγίᾳ τῇ
πάσῃ, λιμοῦ καὶ εὐθηνίας ἔφορος καὶ βραβευτὴς
ἄριστος, τὰ πρὸς ἑκάτερον καιρὸν πρυτανεύειν
ἱκανώτατος.

attested by the furious passion which a woman conceived for him ; his good sense by the equable temper he shewed amid the numberless inequalities of his life, a temper which created order in disorder and concord where all was naturally discordant ; his power of language by his interpretations of the dreams and the fluency of his addresses and the persuasiveness which accompanied them, which secured him the obedience, not forced but voluntary, of every one of his subjects.   Of these years he spent 270 seventeen up to adolescence in his father's house, thirteen in painful misfortunes, the victim of conspiracy, sold into slavery, falsely accused, chained in a prison, and the other eighty as a ruler and in complete prosperity, a most admirable supervisor and arbiter in times both of famine and plenty, and most capable of presiding over the requirements of both.

MOSES I

(DE VITA MOSIS)

INTRODUCTION TO *DE VITA MOSIS* I AND II

THE first of these two [a] treatises covers, as is stated at the beginning of the second, the early life and education of Moses and the main facts of his work as King; that is, as the leader of the Israelites in their escape from Egypt and adventures in the wilderness. It runs on very straightforwardly and does not call for any detailed analysis. There is only one attempt at allegory, viz. the reflections on the meaning of the vision of the Burning Bush.[b]

The second treatise is far more complicated. It treats the character of Moses under three heads, the legislative, the high-priestly and the prophetic, a method which necessarily precludes any chronological arrangement. The first division as it stands [c] begins with some general remarks on the need of these three qualifications as adjuncts to the ideal king (1-11), and proceeds to base the glory of Moses as a legislator first on the permanence of his laws (12-16), secondly on the respect paid to them by other nations (17-24) in support of which he adds an account of the making of the Septuagint (25-44). To these is to be added the greatness of the law-book itself, but this passes away into a justification of the scheme by which the

[a] Treated by all MSS. and all editions before Cohn as three; the second ending at § 65. This is almost certainly erroneous. Philo in *De Virt.* 52 speaks of two books, and the concluding words of ii. 1 ἦν δὲ νῦν συντάττομεν περὶ τῶν ἑπομένων καὶ ἀκολούθων, if considered in connexion with the sequel, clearly imply the same.

[b] This is hardly an allegory in the usual sense. The vision is interpreted not in any spiritual or theological way, but as a figure of the nation's condition at the time. Contrast with *De Fuga*, 161 ff.

[c] On the question whether something has been lost see App. p. 606.

legislative element is preceded by the historical, and this is followed by a dissertation on how the historical part records the punishment of the wicked and the salvation of the good, this last including a detailed account of Noah and the Ark (45-65).

In the second division the discussion of Moses as priest leads to a detailed description of the tabernacle and its appurtenances (66-108 and 136-140), the priest's vesture with its symbolism (109-135), the appointment of the priests and Levites (141-158) and this last to an account of the part played by the Levites in punishing the idolatry of the Golden Calf (159-173), and finally of the vindication of the superiority of the priests by the blossoming of Aaron's rod (174-186).

The third division treating of Moses as prophet is subdivided according as his pronouncements are made from an oracle given in answer to his question or from his own prophetic inspiration (181-191). Four examples are given of each : of the former, (a) the sentence on the blasphemer (192-208), (b) on the Sabbath-breaker (209-220), (c) special regulations as to the Passover (221-232), (d) the law of inheritance (233-245). As examples of the latter he gives Moses' prophecies (a) of the destruction of the Egyptians (246-257), (b) of the manna (258-269), (c) of the slaughter of the idolaters (270-274) [a] and (d) the destruction of Korah and his companions (275-287). The treatise ends with a few sections about the end of Moses. Altogether the two books, between them, cover most of the story of Moses as given in the Pentateuch, the only really serious omission being that of the theophany on Sinai.[b]

[a] Noted however by Philo himself as an exhortation rather than a prophecy.

[b] This would be more intelligible if one might suppose that the Life of Moses was, from the first, intended to be an integral part of the Exposition (see Gen. Introd. pp. xv f.), since the story of Sinai is treated at considerable length in De Decal. 32 ff.

Other omissions are Jethro's visit to Moses, the death of Aaron, and the appointment of Joshua as successor. Philo himself remarks on his omission of the last in De Virt. 52 ff.

ΠΕΡΙ ΤΟΥ ΒΙΟΥ ΜΩΥΣΕΩΣ
ΛΟΓΟΣ ΠΡΩΤΟΣ

[80]
1 I. Μωυσέως τοῦ κατὰ μέν τινας νομοθέτου τῶν
Ἰουδαίων, κατὰ δέ τινας ἑρμηνέως νόμων ἱερῶν,
τὸν βίον ἀναγράψαι διενοήθην, ἀνδρὸς τὰ πάντα
μεγίστου καὶ τελειοτάτου, καὶ γνώριμον τοῖς ἀξίοις
2 μὴ ἀγνοεῖν αὐτὸν ἀποφῆναι. τῶν μὲν γὰρ νόμων
τὸ κλέος, οὓς ἀπολέλοιπε, διὰ πάσης τῆς οἰκουμένης πεφοιτηκὸς ἄχρι καὶ τῶν τῆς γῆς τερμάτων
ἔφθακεν, αὐτὸν δὲ ὅστις ἦν ἐπ' ἀληθείας ἴσασιν οὐ
πολλοί, διὰ φθόνον ἴσως καὶ ἐν οὐκ ὀλίγοις τῶν διατεταγμένων ὑπὸ τῶν κατὰ πόλεις νομοθετῶν ἐναντίωσιν οὐκ ἐθελησάντων αὐτὸν μνήμης ἀξιῶσαι τῶν
3 παρ' Ἕλλησι λογίων· ὧν οἱ πλείους τὰς δυνάμεις
ἃς ἔσχον διὰ παιδείας ὕβρισαν ἔν τε ποιήμασι καὶ
[81] τοῖς καταλογάδην | συγγράμμασι κωμῳδίας καὶ
συβαριτικὰς ἀσελγείας συνθέντες, περιβόητον αἰσχύνην, οὓς ἔδει ταῖς φύσεσι καταχρήσασθαι πρὸς
τὴν τῶν ἀγαθῶν ἀνδρῶν τε καὶ βίων ὑφήγησιν, ἵνα
μήτε τι καλὸν ἡσυχίᾳ παραδοθὲν ἀρχαῖον ἢ νέον
ἀφανισθῇ λάμψαι δυνάμενον μήτ' αὖ τὰς ἀμείνους
ὑποθέσεις παρελθόντες τὰς ἀναξίους ἀκοῆς προ-
κρῖναι δοκῶσι σπουδάζοντες τὰ κακὰ καλῶς ἀπ-
4 αγγέλλειν εἰς ὀνειδῶν ἐπιφάνειαν. ἀλλ' ἔγωγε τὴν

ON THE LIFE OF MOSES, BOOK I

I. I purpose to write the life of Moses, whom some 1
describe as the legislator of the Jews, others as the
interpreter of the Holy Laws. I hope to bring the
story of this greatest and most perfect of men to
the knowledge of such as deserve not to remain in
ignorance of it; for, while the fame of the laws 2
which he left behind him has travelled throughout
the civilized world and reached the ends of the earth,
the man himself as he really was is known to few.
Greek men of letters have refused to treat him as
worthy of memory, possibly through envy, and also
because in many cases the ordinances of the legislators of the different states are opposed to his. Most 3
of these authors have abused the powers which education gave them, by composing in verse or prose
comedies and pieces of voluptuous licence, to their
widespread disgrace, when they should have used
their natural gifts to the full on the lessons taught
by good men and their lives. In this way they might
have ensured that nothing of excellence, old or new,
should be consigned to oblivion and to the extinction of the light which it could give, and also save
themselves from seeming to neglect the better
themes and prefer others unworthy of attention, in
which all their efforts to express bad matter in good
language served to confer distinction on shameful

τούτων βασκανίαν ὑπερβὰς τὰ περὶ τὸν ἄνδρα
μηνύσω μαθὼν αὐτὰ κἀκ βίβλων τῶν ἱερῶν, ἃς
θαυμάσια μνημεῖα τῆς αὐτοῦ σοφίας ἀπολέλοιπε,
καὶ παρά τινων ἀπὸ τοῦ ἔθνους πρεσβυτέρων·
τὰ γὰρ λεγόμενα τοῖς ἀναγινωσκομένοις ἀεὶ συνύφαινον καὶ διὰ τοῦτ᾽ ἔδοξα μᾶλλον ἑτέρων τὰ περὶ
τὸν βίον ἀκριβῶσαι.

5 II. Ἄρξομαι δ᾽ ἀφ᾽ οὗπερ ἀναγκαῖον ἄρξασθαι.
Μωυσῆς γένος μέν ἐστι Χαλδαῖος, ἐγεννήθη δ᾽ ἐν
Αἰγύπτῳ καὶ ἐτράφη, τῶν προγόνων αὐτοῦ διὰ
πολυχρόνιον λιμόν, ὃς Βαβυλῶνα καὶ τοὺς πλησιο-
χώρους ἐπίεζε, κατὰ ζήτησιν τροφῆς εἰς Αἴγυπτον
πανοικὶ μεταναστάντων, γῆν πεδιάδα καὶ βαθεῖαν
καὶ πρὸς πάντα γονιμωτάτην, ὧν ἡ ἀνθρωπίνη
φύσις δεῖται, καὶ μάλιστα τὸν τοῦ σίτου καρπόν.
6 ὁ γὰρ ταύτης ποταμὸς θέρους ἀκμάζοντος, ἡνίκα
τοὺς ἄλλους φασὶ μειοῦσθαι χειμάρρους τε καὶ
αὐθιγενεῖς, ἐπιβαίνων τε καὶ ἀναχεόμενος πλημ-
μυρεῖ καὶ λιμνάζει τὰς ἀρούρας, αἳ ὑετοῦ μὴ δεό-
μεναι φορᾶς ἀφθονίαν παντοίων ἀγαθῶν ἀνὰ πᾶν
ἔτος χορηγοῦσιν, εἰ μή που μεσολαβήσειεν ὀργὴ
θεοῦ δι᾽ ἐπιπολάζουσαν ἀσέβειαν τῶν οἰκητόρων.
7 πατρὸς δὲ καὶ μητρὸς ἔλαχε τῶν καθ᾽ ἑαυτοὺς
ἀρίστων, οὓς φυλέτας ὄντας ἡ ὁμοφροσύνη μᾶλλον
ᾠκείωσεν ἢ τὸ γένος. ἑβδόμη γενεὰ ⟨δ᾽⟩ οὗτός
ἐστιν ἀπὸ τοῦ πρώτου, ὃς ἐπηλύτης ὢν τοῦ σύμπαντος Ἰουδαίων ἔθνους ἀρχηγέτης ἐγένετο. III.
8 τροφῆς δ᾽ ἠξιώθη βασιλικῆς ἀπ᾽ αἰτίας τοιᾶσδε·

ᵃ For §§ 5–17 see Ex. ii. 1–10.

subjects. But I will disregard their malice, and tell 4
the story of Moses as I have learned it, both from
the sacred books, the wonderful monuments of his
wisdom which he has left behind him, and from some
of the elders of the nation ; for I always interwove
what I was told with what I read, and thus believed
myself to have a closer knowledge than others of
his life's history.

II. ᵃ I will begin with what is necessarily the right 5
place to begin. Moses was by race a Chaldean,
but was born and reared in Egypt, as his ancestors
had migrated thither to seek food with their whole
households, in consequence of the long famine under
which Babylon and the neighbouring populations
were suffering. Egypt is a land rich in plains, with
deep soil, and very productive of all that human
nature needs, and particularly of corn. For the river 6
of this country, in the height of summer, when other
streams, whether winter torrents or spring-fed, are
said to dwindle, rises and overflows, and its flood
makes a lake of the fields which need no rain but
every year bear a plentiful crop of good produce
of every kind, if not prevented by some visitation
of the wrath of God to punish the prevailing impiety of the inhabitants. He had for his father and 7
mother the best of their contemporaries, members
of the same tribe, though with them mutual affection was a stronger tie than family connexions. He
was seventh in descent from the first settler, who
became the founder of the whole Jewish nation.ᵇ
III. He was brought up as a prince, a promotion 8
due to the following cause. As the nation of the

ᵇ See Ex. vi. 16 ff., where Moses is given as fifth from Jacob
and therefore seventh from Abraham.

τῆς χώρας ὁ βασιλεύς, εἰς πολυανθρωπίαν ἐπιδιδόντος ἀεὶ τοῦ ἔθνους, δείσας μὴ οἱ ἔποικοι
πλείους γενόμενοι δυνατωτέρᾳ χειρὶ τοῖς αὐτόχθοσι
περὶ κράτους ἀρχῆς ἁμιλλῶνται, τὴν ἰσχὺν αὐτῶν
[82] ἀφαιρεῖν ἐπινοίαις ἀνοσιουργοῖς ἐμηχανᾶτο | καὶ
κελεύει τῶν γεννωμένων τὰ μὲν θήλεα τρέφειν—
ἐπεὶ γυνὴ διὰ φύσεως ἀσθένειαν ὀκνηρὸν εἰς πόλεμον—, τὰ δ' ἄρρενα διαφθείρειν, ἵνα μὴ αὐξηθῇ κατὰ
πόλεις· εὐανδροῦσα γὰρ δύναμις δυσάλωτον καὶ
9 δυσκαθαίρετον ἐπιτείχισμα. γεννηθεὶς οὖν ὁ παῖς
εὐθὺς ὄψιν ἐνέφαινεν ἀστειοτέραν ἢ κατ' ἰδιώτην,
ὡς καὶ τῶν τοῦ τυράννου κηρυγμάτων, ἐφ' ὅσον
οἷόν τε ἦν, τοὺς γονεῖς ἀλογῆσαι· τρεῖς γοῦν φασι
μῆνας ἐφεξῆς οἴκοι γαλακτοτροφηθῆναι λανθάνοντα
10 τοὺς πολλούς. ἐπεὶ δ', οἷα ἐν μοναρχίαις φιλεῖ, καὶ
τὰ ἐν μυχοῖς ἔνιοι διηρεύνων σπεύδοντες ἀεί τι
καινὸν ἄκουσμα προσφέρειν τῷ βασιλεῖ, φοβηθέντες μὴ σωτηρίαν ἑνὶ μνώμενοι πλείους ὄντες
αὐτοὶ σὺν ἐκείνῳ παραπόλωνται, δεδακρυμένοι τὸν
παῖδα ἐκτιθέασι παρὰ τὰς ὄχθας τοῦ ποταμοῦ καὶ
στένοντες ἀπῄεσαν, οἰκτιζόμενοι μὲν αὐτοὺς τῆς
ἀνάγκης αὐτόχειράς τε καὶ τεκνοκτόνους ἀπο-
καλοῦντες, οἰκτιζόμενοι δὲ καὶ τὸν παῖδα τῆς παρα-
11 λογωτάτης ἀπωλείας. εἶθ', ὡς εἰκὸς ἐν ἀλλοκότῳ
πράγματι, κατηγόρουν αὑτῶν ὡς μείζονος αἰτίων
συμφορᾶς· " τί γὰρ " ἔφασκον " εὐθὺς γεννώμενον
οὐκ ἐξεθήκαμεν; τὸν μὴ φθάσαντα τροφῆς ἡμέρου
μεταλαχεῖν οὐδ' ἄνθρωπον οἱ πολλοὶ νομίζουσιν·

---

^a Ex. ii. 2. The LXX word ἀστεῖος is quoted in Hebrews xi.
23 and Acts vii. 20.

newcomers was constantly growing more numerous,
the king of the country, fearing that the settlers,
thus increasing, might shew their superiority by con-
testing the chief power with the original inhabitants, contrived a most iniquitous scheme to deprive
them of their strength. He gave orders to rear the
female infants, since her natural weakness makes
a woman inactive in war, but to put the males to
death, to prevent their number increasing throughout the cities; for a flourishing male population
is a coign of vantage to an aggressor which cannot
easily be taken or destroyed. Now, the child from 9
his birth had an appearance of more than ordinary
goodliness,[a] so that his parents as long as they could
actually set at nought the proclamations of the despot. In fact we are told that, unknown to all but
few, he was kept at home and fed from his mother's
breast for three successive months. But, since, as is 10
often the case under a monarch, there were persons
prying into holes and corners, ever eager to carry
some new report to the king, his parents in their
fear that their efforts to save one would but cause
a larger number, namely themselves, to perish with
him, exposed him with tears on the banks of the
river, and departed groaning. They pitied themselves being forced, as they said in their self-re-
proach, to be the murderers of their own child, and
they pitied him too, left to perish in this unnatural
way. Then, as was natural in so strangely cruel a 11
situation, they began to accuse themselves of having
made bad worse. "Why did we not cast him away,"
they said, "directly he was born? The child who
has not survived to enjoy a kind nurture is not usually reckoned as a human being. But we meddlers

ἡμεῖς δ' οἱ περιττοὶ καὶ τρεῖς μῆνας ὅλους ἀνεθρέ-
ψαμεν, δαψιλεστέρας μὲν ἑαυτοῖς ἀνίας, τῷ δὲ
τιμωρίας ἐκπορίζοντες, ἵν' ἡδονῶν καὶ ἀλγηδόνων
ἐπὶ πλεῖστον ἀντιλαμβάνεσθαι δυνάμενος ἐν αἰσθήσει κακῶν ἀργαλεωτέρων διαφθείρηται."

12   IV. Καὶ οἱ μὲν ἀγνοίᾳ τοῦ μέλλοντος ἀπῆσαν
οἰκτρῷ κατεσχημένοι πένθει, ἀδελφὴ δὲ τοῦ ἐκτε-
θέντος βρέφους ἔτι παρθένος ὑπὸ φιλοικείου πάθους
μικρὸν ἄποθεν ἐκαραδόκει τὸ ἀποβησόμενον· ἃ μοι
δοκεῖ πάντα συμβῆναι κατὰ θεὸν προμηθούμενον
13 τοῦ παιδός. θυγάτηρ ἦν τῷ βασιλεῖ τῆς χώρας
ἀγαπητὴ καὶ μόνη· ταύτην φασὶ γημαμένην ἐκ
πολλοῦ χρόνου μὴ κυΐσκειν τέκνων ὡς εἰκὸς ἐπι-
θυμοῦσαν καὶ μάλιστα γενεᾶς ἄρρενος, ἣ τὸν εὐδαίμονα κλῆρον τῆς πατρῴας ἡγεμονίας διαδέξεται
κινδυνεύοντα ἐρημίᾳ θυγατριδῶν ἀλλοτριωθῆναι.
14 κατηφοῦσαν δὲ ἀεὶ καὶ στένουσαν ὡς μάλιστα
ἐκείνῃ τῇ ἡμέρᾳ τῷ βάρει τῶν φροντίδων ἀπαγο-
ρεῦσαι καὶ δι' ἔθους ἔχουσαν οἴκοι καταμένειν καὶ
μηδὲ τὰς κλισιάδας ὑπερβαίνειν ἐξορμῆσαι μετὰ
θεραπαινίδων ἐπὶ τὸν ποταμόν, ἔνθα ὁ παῖς ἐξ-
έκειτο· κἄπειτα λουτροῖς καὶ περιρραντηρίοις χρῆ-
[83] σθαι μέλλουσαν ἐν τῷ δασυτάτῳ τῶν ἑλῶν | αὐτὸν
15 θεάσασθαι καὶ κελεῦσαι προσφέρειν. εἶτα ἀπὸ
κεφαλῆς ἄχρι ποδῶν καταθεωμένην τήν τε εὐ-
μορφίαν καὶ εὐεξίαν ἀποδέχεσθαι καὶ δεδακρυμένον
ὁρῶσαν ἐλεῖν, ἤδη τῆς ψυχῆς τετραμμένης αὐτῇ
πρὸς μητρῷον πάθος ὡς ἐπὶ γνησίῳ παιδί· γνοῦσαν

———————————
ᵃ See App. p. 603.
ᵇ The statements (1) that Pharaoh's daughter was the only
child of her father, (2) that she had no child of her own, so

actually nurtured him for three whole months, thus procuring more abundant affliction for ourselves and torture for him, only that when he was fully capable of feeling pleasure and pain he should perish conscious of the increased misery of his sufferings." [a]

IV. While they departed ignorant of the future, 12 overcome by grief and sorrow, the sister of the infant castaway, a girl still unmarried, moved by family affection, remained at a little distance, waiting to see what would happen, all this being brought about, in my opinion, by the providence of God watching over the child. The king of the country had but 13 one cherished daughter, who, we are told, had been married for a considerable time but had never conceived a child, though she naturally desired one, particularly of the male sex, to succeed to the magnificent inheritance of her father's kingdom, which threatened to go to strangers if his daughter gave him no grandson. [b] Depressed and loud in lamenta- 14 tion she always was, but on this particular day she broke down under the weight of cares ; and, though her custom was to remain at home and never even cross the threshold, she set off with her maids to the river, where the child was exposed. Then, as she was preparing to make her ablutions in the purifying water, she saw him lying where the marshland growth was thickest, and bade him be brought to her. There- 15 upon, surveying him from head to foot, she approved of his beauty and fine condition, and seeing him weeping took pity on him, for her heart was now moved to feel for him as a mother for her own child.

that Moses was heir presumptive to the throne, are additions to Exodus also either given or implied by Josephus, who adds much other legendary matter, *Ant.* ii. 232 ff.

PHILO

δ' ὅτι τῶν Ἑβραίων ἐστὶ καταδεισάντων τοῦ βασιλέως τὸ πρόσταγμα βουλεύεσθαι περὶ τῆς τροφῆς αὐτοῦ· μὴ γὰρ ἀσφαλὲς εὐθὺς εἶναι νομίζειν εἰς τὰ 16 βασίλεια ἄγειν. διαπορούσης δ' ἔτι, τὴν ἀδελφὴν τοῦ παιδὸς καθάπερ ἀπὸ σκοπῆς τὸν ἐνδοιασμὸν στοχασαμένην πυνθάνεσθαι προσδραμοῦσαν, εἰ βουλήσεται γαλακτοτροφηθῆναι τοῦτον¹ παρὰ γυναίῳ 17 τῶν Ἑβραϊκῶν οὐ πρὸ πολλοῦ κυήσαντι· τῆς δὲ βούλεσθαι φαμένης, τὴν αὑτῆς καὶ τοῦ βρέφους μητέρα παραγαγεῖν ὡς ἀλλοτρίαν, ἣν ἑτοιμότερον ἀσμένην ὑπισχνεῖσθαι πρόφασιν ὡς ἐπὶ μισθῷ τροφεύσειν, ἐπινοίᾳ θεοῦ τοῦ τὰς πρώτας τροφὰς τῷ παιδὶ γνησίας εὐτρεπίζοντος· εἶτα δίδωσιν ὄνομα θεμένη Μωυσῆν ἐτύμως διὰ τὸ ἐκ τοῦ ὕδατος αὐτὸν ἀνελέσθαι· τὸ γὰρ ὕδωρ μῶυ ὀνομάζουσιν Αἰγύπτιοι.

18 V. Ἐπεὶ δ' ἀθρόας ἐπιδόσεις καὶ παραυξήσεις λαμβάνων οὐ σὺν λόγῳ τῷ κατὰ χρόνον θᾶττον δ' ἀπότιτθος γίνεται, παρῆν ἡ μήτηρ ἅμα καὶ τροφὸς κομίζουσα τῇ δούσῃ μηκέτι γαλακτοτροφίας δεό-19 μενον, εὐγενῆ καὶ ἀστεῖον ὀφθῆναι. τελειότερον δὲ τῆς ἡλικίας ἰδοῦσα κἀκ τῆς ὄψεως ἔτι μᾶλλον ἢ πρότερον σπάσασα εὐνοίας υἱὸν ποιεῖται τὰ περὶ τὸν ὄγκον τῆς γαστρὸς τεχνάσασα πρότερον, ἵνα γνήσιος ἀλλὰ μὴ ὑποβολιμαῖος νομισθῇ· πάντα δ' ἐξευμαρίζει θεὸς ἃ ἂν ἐθελήσῃ καὶ τὰ δυσκατ-20 όρθωτα. τροφῆς οὖν ἤδη βασιλικῆς καὶ θεραπείας ἀξιούμενος οὐχ οἷα κομιδῇ νήπιος ἥδετο τωθασμοῖς

¹ MSS. τοῦτο (sc. βρέφος?).

284

And, recognizing that he belonged to the Hebrews, who were intimidated by the king's orders, she considered how to have him nursed, for at present it was not safe to take him to the palace. While 16 she was still thus debating, the child's sister, who guessed her difficulty, ran up from where she stood like a scout, and asked whether she would like to take for his foster-mother a Hebrew woman who had lately been with child. When the princess agreed, 17 she brought her own and the babe's mother in the guise of a stranger, who readily and gladly promised to nurse him, ostensibly for wages. Thus, by God's disposing, it was provided that the child's first nursing should come from the natural source. Since he had been taken up from the water, the princess gave him a name derived from this,[a] and called him Moses, for *Möu* is the Egyptian word for water.

V. As he grew and thrived without a break, and 18 was weaned at an earlier date than they had reckoned, his mother and nurse in one brought him to her from whom she had received him, since he had ceased to need an infant's milk. He was noble and goodly to look upon ; and the princess, seeing him so advanced 19 beyond his age, conceived for him an even greater fondness than before, and took him for her son, having at an earlier time artificially enlarged the figure of her womb to make him pass as her real and not a supposititious child. God makes all that He wills easy, however difficult be the accomplishment. So now he received as his right the nurture and 20 service due to a prince. Yet he did not bear himself

---

[a] ἐτύμως as regularly in Philo used with reference to the "etymology" of the word, see note on *De Conf.* 137. So again § 130 below.

PHILO

καὶ γέλωσι καὶ παιδιαῖς, καίτοι τῶν τὴν ἐπιμέλειαν
αὐτοῦ παρειληφότων ἀνέσεις ἔχειν ἐπιτρεπόντων
καὶ μηδὲν ἐπιδεικνυμένων σκυθρωπόν, ἀλλ᾽ αἰδῶ
καὶ σεμνότητα παραφαίνων ἀκούσμασι καὶ θεάμασιν, ἃ τὴν ψυχὴν ἔμελλεν ὠφελήσειν, προσεῖχε.

21 διδάσκαλοι δ᾽ εὐθὺς ἀλλαχόθεν ἄλλοι παρῆσαν, οἱ
μὲν ἀπὸ τῶν πλησιοχώρων καὶ τῶν κατ᾽ Αἴγυπτον
νομῶν αὐτοκέλευστοι, οἱ δ᾽ ἀπὸ τῆς Ἑλλάδος ἐπὶ
[84] μεγάλαις δωρεαῖς μεταπεμφθέντες· ὧν | ἐν οὐ
μακρῷ χρόνῳ τὰς δυνάμεις ὑπερέβαλεν εὐμοιρίᾳ
φύσεως φθάνων τὰς ὑφηγήσεις, ὡς ἀνάμνησιν εἶναι
δοκεῖν, οὐ μάθησιν, ἔτι καὶ προσεπινοῶν αὐτὸς τὰ
22 δυσθεώρητα. πολλὰ γὰρ αἱ μεγάλαι φύσεις καινο-
τομοῦσι τῶν εἰς ἐπιστήμην· καὶ καθάπερ τὰ εὐεκ-
τικὰ τῶν σωμάτων καὶ πᾶσι τοῖς μέρεσιν εὐκίνητα
φροντίδων ἀπαλλάττει τοὺς ἀλείπτας οὐδὲν ἢ
βραχέα παρέχοντας τῶν εἰς ἐπιμέλειαν, ὥσπερ καὶ
γεωργοὺς τὰ εὔβλαστα καὶ εὐγενῆ δένδρα βελτιού-
μενα δι᾽ ἑαυτῶν, τὸν αὐτὸν τρόπον εὐφυὴς ψυχὴ
προαπαντῶσα τοῖς λεγομένοις ὑφ᾽ αὑτῆς μᾶλλον ἢ
τῶν διδασκόντων ὠφελεῖται καὶ λαβομένη τινὸς
ἐπιστημονικῆς ἀρχῆς κατὰ τὴν παροιμίαν "ἵππος
23 εἰς πεδίον" ὁρμᾷ. ἀριθμοὺς μὲν οὖν καὶ γεω-
μετρίαν τήν τε ῥυθμικὴν καὶ ἁρμονικὴν καὶ με-
τρικὴν θεωρίαν καὶ μουσικὴν τὴν σύμπασαν διά τε
χρήσεως ὀργάνων καὶ λόγων τῶν ἐν ταῖς τέχναις
καὶ διεξόδοις τοπικωτέραις Αἰγυπτίων οἱ λόγιοι

---

[a] Josephus on the other hand makes him shew his superiority in his games, *Ant.* ii. 230.

[b] See App. p. 603.

[c] Philo may have derived this from his own knowledge of
the scope of education in Egypt in the present and past, but
perhaps also from Plato, *Laws* 656 D, 799 A, 819 A, where

like the mere infant that he was, nor delight in fun and laughter and sport, though those who had the charge of him did not grudge him relaxation or shew him any strictness; [a] but with a modest and serious bearing he applied himself to hearing and seeing what was sure to profit the soul. Teachers at once 21 arrived from different parts, some unbidden from the neighbouring countries and the provinces of Egypt, others summoned from Greece under promise of high reward. But in a short time he advanced beyond their capacities; his gifted nature fore-stalled their instruction, so that his seemed a case rather of recollection than of learning, and indeed he himself devised and propounded problems which they could not easily solve. For great natures carve 22 out much that is new in the way of knowledge; and, just as bodies, robust and agile in every part, free their trainers from care, and receive little or none of their usual attention, and in the same way well-grown and naturally healthy trees, which improve of themselves, give the husbandmen no trouble, so the gifted soul takes the lead in meeting the lessons given by itself rather than the teacher and is profited thereby, and as soon as it has a grasp of some of the first principles of knowledge presses forward like the horse to the meadow, [b] as the proverb goes. Arith- 23 metic, geometry, the lore of metre, rhythm and harmony, and the whole subject of music as shown by the use of instruments or in textbooks and treatises of a more special character, were imparted to him by learned Egyptians. [c] These further in-

mathematics, music, and dancing are said to be the subjects most stressed by Egyptians. *Cf.*, as a summary of all that is said here, Acts vii. 22 " he was instructed in all the wisdom of the Egyptians."

παρεδίδοσαν καὶ προσέτι τὴν διὰ συμβόλων φιλοσοφίαν, ἣν ἐν τοῖς λεγομένοις ἱεροῖς γράμμασιν
ἐπιδείκνυνται καὶ διὰ τῆς τῶν ζῴων ἀποδοχῆς, ἃ
καὶ θεῶν τιμαῖς γεραίρουσι· τὴν δ' ἄλλην ἐγκύκλιον
παιδείαν Ἕλληνες ἐδίδασκον, οἱ δ' ἐκ τῶν πλησιοχώρων τά τε Ἀσσύρια γράμματα καὶ τὴν τῶν
24 οὐρανίων Χαλδαϊκὴν ἐπιστήμην. ταύτην καὶ παρ'
Αἰγυπτίων ἀνελάμβανε μαθηματικὴν ἐν τοῖς μάλιστα ἐπιτηδευόντων· καὶ τὰ παρ' ἀμφοτέροις
ἀκριβῶς ἐν οἷς τε συμφωνοῦσι καὶ διαφέρονται
καταμαθών, ἀφιλονείκως τὰς ἔριδας ὑπερβάς, τὴν
ἀλήθειαν ἐζήτει, μηδὲν ψεῦδος τῆς διανοίας αὐτοῦ
παραδέχεσθαι δυναμένης, ὡς ἔθος τοῖς αἱρεσιο-
μάχοις, οἳ τοῖς προτεθεῖσι δόγμασιν ὁποῖα ἂν τύχῃ
βοηθοῦσιν οὐκ ἐξετάζοντες, εἰ δόκιμα, τὸ δ' αὐτὸ
δρῶντες τοῖς ἐπὶ μισθῷ συναγορεύουσι καὶ μηδὲν
25 τοῦ δικαίου πεφροντικόσιν.   VI. ἤδη δὲ
τοὺς ὅρους τῆς παιδικῆς ἡλικίας ὑπερβαίνων ἐπ-
έτεινε τὴν φρόνησιν, οὐχ ὡς ἔνιοι τὰς μειρακιώδεις
ἐπιθυμίας ἀχαλινώτους ἐῶν καίτοι μυρία ἐχούσας
ὑπεκκαύματα διὰ παρασκευὰς ἀφθόνους, ἃς αἱ
βασιλεῖαι χορηγοῦσιν, ἀλλὰ σωφροσύνῃ καὶ καρ-
τερίᾳ ὥσπερ τισὶν ἡνίαις ἐνδησάμενος αὐτὰς τὴν εἰς
26 τὸ πρόσω φορὰν ἀνεχαίτιζε βίᾳ. καὶ τῶν ἄλλων
μέντοι παθῶν ἕκαστον ἐξ ἑαυτοῦ μεμηνὸς καὶ
λελυττηκὸς φύσει τιθασεύων κἀξημερῶν ἐπράυνεν·
εἰ δέ που διακινηθείη μόνον ἡσυχῇ καὶ πτερύξαιτο,
κολάσεις ἐμβριθεστέρας παρείχετο ἢ διὰ λόγων |

---

[a] This would normally be grammar or literature, rhetoric,
logic and perhaps astronomy as distinguished from astrology.
See *De Cong.* 11 and note; also *De Som.* i. 205 and note, with
other references. Clement, *Strom.* i. 23, adds ἰατρική.

structed him in the philosophy conveyed in symbols,
as displayed in the so-called holy inscriptions and
in the regard paid to animals, to which they even
pay divine honours. He had Greeks to teach him
the rest of the regular school course,[a] and the inhabitants of the neighbouring countries for Assyrian
letters [b] and the Chaldean science of the heavenly
bodies. This he also acquired from Egyptians,[c] who 24
give special attention to astrology. And, when he
had mastered the lore of both nations, both where
they agree and where they differ, he eschewed all
strife and contention and sought only for truth. His
mind was incapable of accepting any falsehood, as is
the way with the sectarians, who defend the doctrines
they have propounded, whatever they may be, without examining whether they can stand scrutiny, and
thus put themselves on a par with hired advocates
who have no thought nor care for justice.

VI. When he was now passing beyond the term of 25
boyhood, his good sense became more active. He
did not, as some, allow the lusts of adolescence
to go unbridled, though the abundant resources
which palaces provide supply numberless incentives
to foster their flame. But he kept a tight hold on
them with the reins, as it were, of temperance and
self-control, and forcibly pulled them back from their
forward course. And each of the other passions, 26
which rage so furiously if left to themselves, he tamed
and assuaged and reduced to mildness ; and if they
did but gently stir or flutter he provided for them
heavier chastisement than any rebuke of words

[b] See App. p. 603.

[c] This seems to suggest that in Philo's time astrology, as
taught on Chaldaean (*i.e.* the generally accepted) principles,
differed somewhat from the form current in Egypt.

289

PHILO

[85] ἐπιπλήξεις· καὶ συνόλως τὰς πρώτας τῆς ψυχῆς
ἐπιβολάς τε καὶ ὁρμὰς ὡς ἀφηνιαστὴν ἵππον ἐπ-
ετήρει δεδιώς, μὴ προεκδραμοῦσαι τοῦ ἡνιοχεῖν
ὀφείλοντος λογισμοῦ πάντα διὰ πάντων συγχέωσιν·
αὗται γάρ εἰσιν αἱ ἀγαθῶν αἴτιαι καὶ κακῶν, ἀγαθῶν μέν, ὅταν ἡγεμόνι λόγῳ πειθαρχῶσι, τῶν δ'
27 ἐναντίων, ὅταν εἰς ἀναρχίαν ἐκδιαιτῶνται. κατὰ
τὸ εἰκὸς οὖν οἵ τε συνδιατρίβοντες καὶ οἱ ἄλλοι
πάντες ἐτεθήπεσαν, ὡς ἐπὶ καινῷ θεάματι κατα-
πληττόμενοι καὶ τίς ἄρα ὁ ἐνοικῶν αὐτοῦ τῷ
σώματι καὶ ἀγαλματοφορούμενος νοῦς ἐστι, πότερον
ἀνθρώπειος ἢ θεῖος ἢ μικτὸς ἐξ ἀμφοῖν, διερευνώ-
μενοι, τῷ μηδὲν ἔχειν τοῖς πολλοῖς ὅμοιον, ἀλλ'
ὑπερκύπτειν καὶ πρὸς τὸ μεγαλειότερον ἐξῆρθαι.
28 γαστρί τε γὰρ ἔξω τῶν ἀναγκαίων δασμῶν, οὓς ἡ
φύσις ἔταξεν, οὐδὲν πλέον ἐχορήγει, τῶν τε ὑπο-
γαστρίων ἡδονῶν εἰ μὴ μέχρι σπορᾶς παίδων
29 γνησίων οὐδὲ ἐμέμνητο. γενόμενός τε διαφερόντως
ἀσκητὴς ὀλιγοδεείας καὶ τὸν ἁβροδίαιτον βίον ὡς
οὐδεὶς ἕτερος χλευάσας—ψυχῇ γὰρ ἐπόθει μόνῃ
ζῆν, οὐ σώματι—τὰ φιλοσοφίας δόγματα διὰ τῶν
καθ' ἑκάστην ἡμέραν ἔργων ἐπεδείκνυτο, λέγων μὲν
οἷα ἐφρόνει, πράττων δὲ ἀκόλουθα τοῖς λεγομένοις
εἰς ἁρμονίαν λόγου καὶ βίου, ἵν' οἷος ὁ λόγος τοιοῦτος ὁ βίος καὶ οἷος ὁ βίος τοιοῦτος ὁ λόγος ἐξετά-
ζωνται καθάπερ ἐν ὀργάνῳ μουσικῷ συνηχοῦντες.
30 οἱ μὲν οὖν πολλοί, κἂν αὐτὸ μόνον αὔρα
βραχεῖά τινος εὐτυχίας προσπέσῃ, φυσῶσι καὶ
πνέουσι μεγάλα καὶ καταλαζονευόμενοι τῶν ἀφανε-
τέρων καθάρματα καὶ παρενοχλήματα καὶ γῆς ἄχθη
καὶ ὅσα τοιαῦτα ἀποκαλοῦσιν, ὥσπερ τὸ ἀκλινὲς

could give ; and in general he watched the first
directions and impulses of the soul as one would a
restive horse, in fear lest they should run away with
the reason which ought to rein them in, and thus
cause universal chaos. For it is these impulses which
cause both good and bad—good when they obey
the guidance of reason, bad when they turn from
their regular course into anarchy.   Naturally, there- 27
fore, his associates and everyone else, struck with
amazement at what they felt was a novel spectacle,
considered earnestly what the mind which dwelt
in his body like an image in its shrine could be,
whether it was human or divine or a mixture of both,
so utterly unlike was it to the majority, soaring above
them and exalted to a grander height.   For on his 28
belly he bestowed no more than the necessary
tributes which nature has appointed, and as for the
pleasures that have their seat below, save for the
lawful begetting of children, they passed altogether
even out of his memory.   And, in his desire to live 29
to the soul alone and not to the body, he made a
special practice of frugal contentment, and had an
unparalleled scorn for a life of luxury. He ex-
emplified his philosophical creed by his daily actions.
His words expressed his feelings, and his actions ac-
corded with his words, so that speech and life were
in harmony, and thus through their mutual agreement were found to make melody together as on
a musical intrument.   Now, most men, 30
if they feel a breath of prosperity ever so small upon
them, make much ado of puffing and blowing, and
boast themselves as bigger than meaner men, and
miscall them offscourings and nuisances and cum-
berers of the earth and other suchlike names, as if

τῆς εὐπραγίας ἐν βεβαίῳ παρ' ἑαυτοῖς εὖ μάλα
σφραγισάμενοι μηδὲ μέχρι τῆς ὑστεραίας ἴσως δια-
31 μενοῦντες ἐν ὁμοίῳ. τύχης γὰρ ἀσταθμητότερον
οὐδὲν ἄνω καὶ κάτω τὰ ἀνθρώπεια πεττευούσης, ἣ
μιᾷ πολλάκις ἡμέρᾳ τὸν μὲν ὑψηλὸν καθαιρεῖ, τὸν
δὲ ταπεινὸν μετέωρον ἐξαίρει· καὶ ταῦτα ὁρῶντες
ἀεὶ γινόμενα καὶ σαφῶς εἰδότες ὅμως ὑπερόπται μὲν
οἰκείων καὶ φίλων εἰσί, νόμους δὲ παραβαίνουσι,
καθ' οὓς ἐγενήθησαν καὶ ἐτράφησαν, ἔθη δὲ πάτρια,
οἷς μέμψις οὐδεμία πρόσεστι δικαία, κινοῦσιν
ἐκδεδιῃτημένοι καὶ διὰ τὴν τῶν παρόντων ἀποδοχὴν
οὐδενὸς ἔτι τῶν ἀρχαίων μνήμην λαμβάνουσιν.
32 VII. ὁ δὲ ἐπ' αὐτὸν φθάσας τὸν ὅρον τῆς ἀνθρωπίνης εὐτυχίας καὶ θυγατριδοῦς μὲν τοῦ τοσούτου
βασιλέως νομισθείς, τῆς δὲ παππῴας ἀρχῆς ὅσον
[86] οὐδέπω γεγονὼς ἐλπίσι | ταῖς ἁπάντων διάδοχος
καὶ τί γὰρ ἄλλ' ἢ ὁ νέος βασιλεὺς προσαγορευό-
μενος, τὴν συγγενικὴν καὶ προγονικὴν ἐζήλωσε
παιδείαν, τὰ μὲν τῶν εἰσποιησαμένων ἀγαθά, καὶ εἰ
λαμπρότερα καιροῖς, νόθα εἶναι ὑπολαβών, τὰ δὲ
τῶν φύσει γονέων, εἰ καὶ πρὸς ὀλίγον ἀφανέστερα,
33 οἰκεῖα γοῦν καὶ γνήσια· καθάπερ τε κριτὴς ἀδέκαστος τῶν γεννησάντων καὶ τῶν εἰσποιησαμένων
τοὺς μὲν εὐνοίᾳ καὶ τῷ φιλεῖν ἐκθύμως τοὺς δ'
εὐχαριστίαις ἀνθ' ὧν εὖ ἔπαθεν ἠμείβετο καὶ μέχρι
παντὸς ἠμείψατ' ἄν, εἰ μὴ κατεῖδεν ἐν τῇ χώρᾳ
μέγα καινουργηθὲν ὑπὸ τοῦ βασιλέως ἀσέβημα.

ᵃ A paraphrase of the fragment of Euripides quoted *De
Som.* i. 154:

ἡ μία γὰρ ἡμέρα
τὸν μὲν καθεῖλεν ὑψόθεν, τὸν δ' ἦρ' ἄνω.

they themselves had the permanence of their prosperity securely sealed in their possession, though even the morrow may find them no longer where they are. For nothing is more unstable than Fortune, 31 who moves human affairs up and down on the draughtboard of life, and in a single day pulls down the lofty and exalts the lowly on high;[a] and though they see and know full well that this is always happening, they nevertheless look down on their relations and friends and set at naught the laws under which they were born and bred, and subvert the ancestral customs to which no blame can justly attach, by adopting different modes of life, and, in their contentment with the present, lose all memory of the past. VII. But Moses, having 32 reached the very pinnacle of human prosperity, regarded as the son of the king's daughter, and in general expectation almost the successor to his grandfather's sovereignty, and indeed regularly called the young king, was zealous for the discipline and culture of his kinsmen and ancestors. The good fortune of his adopters, he held, was a spurious one, even though the circumstances gave it greater lustre; that of his natural parents, though less distinguished for the nonce, was at any rate his own and genuine; and so, 33 estimating the claims of his real and his adopted parents like an impartial judge, he requited the former with good feeling and profound affection, the latter with gratitude for their kind treatment of him. And he would have continued to do so throughout had he not found the king adopting in the country a new and highly impious course of action.

34 ξένοι γὰρ ἦσαν, ὡς ἔφην πρότερον, οἱ
Ἰουδαῖοι, τῶν τοῦ ἔθνους ἀρχηγετῶν διὰ λιμὸν
ἀπορίᾳ τροφῆς ἐκ Βαβυλῶνος καὶ τῶν ἄνω σατρα-
πειῶν εἰς Αἴγυπτον μεταναστάντων, καὶ τρόπον
τινὰ ἱκέται καταπεφευγότες ὡς ἐπ' ἄσυλον ἱερὸν
τήν τε βασιλέως πίστιν καὶ τὸν ἀπὸ τῶν οἰκητόρων
35 ἔλεον. οἱ γὰρ ξένοι παρ' ἐμοὶ κριτῇ τῶν ὑποδεξα-
μένων ἱκέται γραφέσθωσαν, μέτοικοι δὲ πρὸς ἱκέταις καὶ φίλοι, σπεύδοντες εἰς ἀστῶν ἰσοτιμίαν καὶ
γειτνιῶντες ἤδη πολίταις, ὀλίγῳ τῶν αὐτοχθόνων
36 διαφέροντες. τούτους οὖν, οἳ τὴν μὲν οἰκείαν
ἀπέλιπον, εἰς δ' Αἴγυπτον ἧκον ὡς ἐν δευτέρᾳ
πατρίδι μετ' ἀσφαλείας οἰκήσοντες, ὁ τῆς χώρας
ἡγεμὼν ἠνδραποδίζετο καὶ ὡς πολέμου νόμῳ λαβὼν
αἰχμαλώτους ἢ πριάμενος παρὰ δεσποτῶν, οἷς ἦσαν
οἰκότριβες, ὑπήγετο καὶ δούλους ἀπέφαινε τοὺς οὐκ
ἐλευθέρους μόνον ἀλλὰ καὶ ξένους καὶ ἱκέτας καὶ
μετοίκους οὔτε αἰδεσθεὶς οὔτε δείσας τὸν ἐλευ-
θέριον καὶ ξένιον καὶ ἱκέσιον καὶ ἐφέστιον θεόν, ὃς
37 τῶν τοιούτων ἐστὶν ἔφορος. εἶτ' ἐπιτάγματα ἐπ-
έταττε βαρύτερα τῆς δυνάμεως ἄλλους ἐπ' ἄλλοις
πόνους προστιθείς, καὶ τοῖς ἀπαγορεύουσιν ὑπ'
ἀσθενείας ὁ σίδηρος εἵπετο· ἐπιστάτας ⟨γὰρ⟩ τῶν
ἔργων ἀνηλεεστάτους καὶ ὠμοθύμους οὐδενὶ συγγνώμης μεταδιδόντας ᾑρεῖτο, οὓς " ἐργοδιώκτας "
38 ἀπὸ τοῦ συμβεβηκότος ὠνόμαζον. εἰργάζοντο δ'
οἱ μὲν πηλὸν εἰς πλίνθον σχηματίζοντες, οἱ δὲ
πανταχόθεν ἄχυρα συγκομίζοντες—πλίνθου γὰρ

---

a §§ 19-33 cannot be said to have any basis at all in the
biblical narrative, though they give a reasonable sketch of
what Moses might be expected to have felt and done in such

294

a The Jews, as I have said before, were 34
strangers, since famine had driven the founders of
the nation, through lack of food, to migrate to Egypt
from Babylon and the inland satrapies. They were,
in a sense, suppliants, who had found a sanctuary
in the pledged faith of the king and the pity felt
for them by the inhabitants. For strangers, in my 35
judgement, must be regarded as suppliants of those
who receive them, and not only suppliants but
settlers and friends who are anxious to obtain equal
rights with the burgesses and are near to being
citizens because they differ little from the original
inhabitants. So, then, these strangers, who had left 36
their own country and come to Egypt hoping to live
there in safety as in a second fatherland, were made
slaves by the ruler of the country and reduced to the
condition of captives taken by the custom of war,
or persons purchased from the masters in whose
household they had been bred. And in thus making
serfs of men who were not only free but guests,
suppliants and settlers, he showed no shame or fear
of the God of liberty and hospitality and of justice
to guests and suppliants, Who watches over such as
these. Then he laid commands upon them, severe 37
beyond their capacity, and added labour to labour ;
and, when they failed through weakness, the iron
hand was upon them ; for he chose as superintendents
of the works men of the most cruel and savage
temper who showed no mercy to anyone, men whose
name of "task-pursuer" well described the facts.
Some of the workers wrought clay into brick, while 38
others fetched from every quarter straw which served

a situation. From §§ 34-59 we have an amplification of Ex.
ii. 14 end.

ἄχυρα δεσμός—, οἱ δ' ἦσαν ἀποτεταγμένοι πρὸς
οἰκιῶν καὶ τειχῶν καὶ πόλεων κατασκευὰς καὶ διω-
ρύχων ἀνατομάς, ὑλοφοροῦντες αὐτοὶ μεθ' ἡμέραν
καὶ νύκτωρ ἄνευ διαδοχῆς, οὐδεμίαν ἔχοντες ἀνά-
παυλαν, ἀλλ' οὐδ' ὅσον καταδαρθεῖν αὐτὸ μόνον
[87] ἐώμενοι, | πάντα καὶ τὰ τῶν δημιουργῶν καὶ τὰ
τῶν ὑπουργῶν δρᾶν ἀναγκαζόμενοι, ὡς ἐν βραχεῖ
τὰ σώματα αὐτοῖς ἀπαγορεύειν, ἅτε καὶ τῆς ψυχῆς
39 προαναπιπτούσης. ἄλλοι γοῦν ἐπ' ἄλλοις ἐξ-
έθνησκον ὡς ὑπὸ λοιμώδους φθορᾶς, οὓς ἀτάφους
ἔξω τῶν ὁρίων ἀπερρίπτουν οὐδὲ κόνιν ἐπαμήσασθαι τοῖς σώμασιν ἐῶντες ἀλλ' οὐδὲ δακρῦσαι
συγγενεῖς ἢ φίλους οὕτως οἰκτρῶς διαφθαρέντας·
ἀλλὰ καὶ τοῖς ἀδουλώτοις πάθεσι τῆς ψυχῆς, ἃ μόνα
σχεδὸν ἐξ ἁπάντων ἐλεύθερα ἡ φύσις ἀνῆκε, δεσποτείαν ἐπηπείλουν οἱ ἀσεβεῖς ἀνάγκης ἀνυποίστῳ
βάρει δυνατωτέρας πιέζοντες.

40 VIII. Ἐπὶ δὴ τούτοις ἀθυμῶν καὶ δυσχεραίνων
διετέλει μήτ' ἀμύνασθαι τοὺς ἀδικοῦντας μήτε
βοηθεῖν τοῖς ἀδικουμένοις ἱκανὸς ὤν· ἃ δ' οἷός τε
ἦν, διὰ λόγων ὠφέλει παραινῶν τοῖς μὲν ἐφεστῶσι
μετριάζειν καὶ τὸ σφοδρὸν τῶν ἐπιταγμάτων ὑπ-
ανιέναι καὶ χαλᾶν, τοῖς δ' ἐργαζομένοις φέρειν τὰ
παρόντα γενναίως ἄνδρας τε εἶναι τὰ φρονήματα
καὶ μὴ συγκάμνειν τὰς ψυχὰς τοῖς σώμασιν, ἀλλὰ
41 χρηστὰ προσδοκᾶν ἐκ πονηρῶν· πάντα γὰρ μετα-
βάλλειν τὰ ἐν κόσμῳ πρὸς τἀναντία, νέφωσιν εἰς
αἰθρίαν, πνευμάτων βίας εἰς ἀέρα νήνεμον, κλύ-
δωνα θαλάττης εἰς ἡσυχίαν καὶ γαλήνην, τὰ δ'

to bind the brick. Others were appointed to build houses and walls and cities or to cut canals. They carried the materials themselves day and night, with no shifts to relieve them, no period of rest, not even suffered just to sleep for a bit and then resume their work. In fact, they were compelled to do all the work, both of the artisan and his assistants, so that in a short time loss of heart was followed necessarily by bodily exhaustion. This was shown by the way 39 in which they died one after the other, as though they were the victims of a pestilence, to be flung unburied outside the borders by their masters, who did not allow the survivors even to collect dust to throw upon the corpses or even to shed tears for their kinsfolk or friends thus pitifully done to death. And, though nature has given to the untrammelled feelings of the soul a liberty which she has denied to almost everything else, they impiously threatened to exert their despotism over these also and suppressed them with the intolerable weight of a constraint more powerful than nature.

VIII. All this continued to depress and anger 40 Moses, who had no power either to punish those who did the wrong or help those who suffered it. What he could he did. He assisted with his words, exhorting the overseers to show clemency and relax and alleviate the stringency of their orders, and the workers to bear their present condition bravely, to display a manly spirit and not let their souls share the weariness of their bodies, but look for good to take the place of evil. All things in the world, he told 41 them, change to their opposites : clouds to open sky, violent winds to tranquil weather, stormy seas to calm and peaceful, and human affairs still more so,

ἀνθρώπεια καὶ μᾶλλον, ὅσῳ καὶ ἀσταθμητότερα.
42 τοιούτοις κατεπᾴδων ὥσπερ ἀγαθὸς ἰατρὸς ᾤετο
τὰς νόσους καίτοι βαρυτάτας οὔσας ἐπικουφιεῖν·
αἱ δ᾽ ὁπότε λωφήσειαν, αὖθις ἐκ περιτροπῆς ἐπετί-
θεντο φέρουσαί τι πάντως ἐκ τοῦ διαπνεῦσαι καινὸν
43 κακὸν ἀργαλεώτερον τῶν προτέρων. ἦσαν γάρ
τινες τῶν ἐφεστηκότων ἀτίθασοι σφόδρα καὶ λελυτ-
τηκότες, μηδὲν εἰς ἀγριότητα τῶν ἰοβόλων καὶ
σαρκοβόρων διαφέροντες, ἀνθρωποειδῆ θηρία, τὴν
τοῦ σώματος μορφὴν εἰς δόκησιν ἡμερότητος ἐπὶ
θήρᾳ καὶ ἀπάτῃ προβεβλημένοι, σιδήρου καὶ ἀδά-
44 μαντος ἀπειθέστεροι. τούτων ἕνα τὸν βιαιότατον,
ἐπειδὴ πρὸς τῷ μηδὲν ἐνδιδόναι καὶ ταῖς παρακλή-
σεσιν ἔτι μᾶλλον ἐξετραχύνετο, τοὺς τὸ προσταχθὲν
μὴ ἀπνευστὶ καὶ ὀξυχειρίᾳ δρῶντας τύπτων, προπη-
λακίζων ἄχρι θανάτου, πάσας αἰκιζόμενος αἰκίας,
ἀναιρεῖ δικαιώσας εὐαγὲς εἶναι τὸ ἔργον· καὶ ἦν
εὐαγὲς τὸν ἐπ᾽ ὀλέθρῳ ζῶντα ἀνθρώπων ἀπόλ-
λυσθαι.
45 Ταῦτ᾽ ἀκούσας ὁ βασιλεὺς ἠγανάκτει δεινὸν
ἡγούμενος, οὐκ εἴ τις τέθνηκεν ἢ ἀνῄρηκεν ἀδίκως ἢ
δικαίως, ἀλλ᾽ εἰ ὁ θυγατριδοῦς αὐτῷ μὴ συμφρονεῖ
μηδὲ τοὺς αὐτοὺς ἐχθροὺς καὶ φίλους ὑπείληφεν,
ἀλλὰ μισεῖ μὲν οὓς αὐτὸς στέργει, φιλεῖ δὲ οὓς
προβέβληται καὶ ἐλεεῖ πρὸς οὓς ἀτρέπτως καὶ
46 ἀπαραιτήτως ἔχει. IX. | λαβόμενοι δ᾽ ἅπαξ
[88] ἀφορμῆς οἱ ἐν τέλει καὶ τὸν νεανίαν ὑφορώμενοι—
ᾔδεσαν γὰρ μνησικακήσοντα τῶν ἀνοσιουργημάτων

even as they are more unstable. With such soothing 42
words, like a good physician, he thought to relieve
the sickness of their plight, terrible as it was. But,
when it abated, it did but turn and make a fresh
attack and gather from the breathing-space some
new misery more powerful than its predecessors.
For some of the overseers were exceedingly harsh 43
and ferocious, in savageness differing nothing from
venomous and carnivorous animals, wild beasts in
human shape who assumed in outward form the
semblance of civilized beings only to beguile and
catch their prey, in reality more unyielding than iron
or adamant. One of these, the cruellest of all, was 44
killed by Moses, because he not only made no con-
cession but was rendered harsher than ever by his
exhortations, beating those who did not execute his
orders with breathless promptness, persecuting them
to the point of death and subjecting them to every
outrage. Moses considered that his action in killing
him was a righteous action. And righteous it was
that one who only lived to destroy men should
himself be destroyed.

When the king heard this, he was very indignant. 45
What he felt so strongly was not that one man
had been killed by another whether justly or unjustly, but that his own daughter's son did not
think with him, and had not considered the king's
friends and enemies to be his own friends and
enemies, but hated those of whom he was fond, and
loved those whom he rejected, and pitied those to
whom he was relentless and inexorable. IX. When 46
those in authority who suspected the youth's intentions, knowing that he would remember their
wicked actions against them and take vengeance

αὐτοῖς καὶ ἐπὶ καιρῶν ἀμυνούμενον—ἀναπεπτα-
μένοις ὠσὶ τοῦ πάππου μυρίας διαβολὰς ἐπήντλουν,
οἱ μὲν ἔνθεν, οἱ δ' ἔνθεν, ὡς καὶ περὶ ἀφαιρέσεως
τῆς ἀρχῆς ἐμποιῆσαι δέος, " ἐπιθήσεται " λέγοντες,
" οὐδὲν φρονεῖ μικρόν, ἀεί τι προσπεριεργάζεται,
πρὸ καιροῦ βασιλείας ἐρᾷ, θωπεύει τινάς, ἑτέροις
ἀπειλεῖ, κτείνει χωρὶς δίκης, τοὺς μάλιστ' εὔνους
σοι προβέβληται. τί δὴ μέλλεις, ἀλλ' οὐχ ἃ δια-
νοεῖται δρᾶν ὑποτέμνεις; μέγα τοῖς ἐπιθεμένοις αἱ
τῶν ἐπιβουλευομένων ἀναβολαί."

47   Τοιαῦτα διεξιόντων, ὑπανεχώρησεν εἰς τὴν ὅμο-
ρον Ἀραβίαν, ἔνθα διατρίβειν ἦν ἀσφαλές, ἅμα καὶ
τὸν θεὸν ποτνιώμενος, ἵνα τοὺς μὲν ἐξ ἀμηχάνων
ῥύσηται συμφορῶν, τοὺς δὲ μηδὲν παραλιπόντας
τῶν εἰς ἐπήρειαν ἀξίως τίσηται, παράσχῃ δ' αὐτῷ
ταῦτ' ἐπιδεῖν ἀμφότερα διπλασιάσας τὴν χάριν.
ὁ δὲ ἐπακούει τῶν εὐχῶν ἀγάμενος αὐτοῦ τὸ φιλό-
καλον ἦθος καὶ μισοπόνηρον, οὐκ εἰς μακρὰν τὰ
48 κατὰ τὴν χώραν, ὡς θεῷ πρέπον, δικάσας. ἐν ᾧ
δὲ ἔμελλε δικάζειν, τοὺς ἀρετῆς ἄθλους Μωυσῆς
διήθλει τὸν ἀλείπτην ἔχων ἐν ἑαυτῷ λογισμὸν
ἀστεῖον, ὑφ' οὗ γυμναζόμενος πρὸς τοὺς ἀρίστους
βίους, τόν τε θεωρητικὸν καὶ πρακτικόν, ἐπονεῖτο
φιλοσοφίας ἀνελίττων ἀεὶ δόγματα καὶ τῇ ψυχῇ
διαγινώσκων εὐτρόχως καὶ μνήμῃ παρακατατι-
θέμενος εἰς τὸ ἄληστον αὐτὰ καὶ τὰς οἰκείας αὐτίκα
300

when the opportunity came, had thus once got a handle, they poured malicious suggestions by the thousand from every side into the open ears of his grandfather, so as to instil the fear that his sovereignty might be taken from him. "He will attack you," they said, "he is highly ambitious. He is always busy with some further project. He is eager to get the kingship before the time comes. He flatters some, threatens others, slays without trial and treats as outcasts those who are most loyal to you. Why do you hesitate, instead of cutting short his projected undertakings? The aggressor is greatly served by delay on the part of his proposed victim."

While such talk was in circulation, Moses retired 47 into the neighbouring country of Arabia, where it was safe for him to stay, at the same time beseeching God to save the oppressed from their helpless, miserable plight, and to punish as they deserved the oppressors who had left no form of maltreatment untried, and to double the gift by granting to himself that he should see both these accomplished. God, in high approval of his spirit, which loved the good and hated evil, listened to his prayers, and very shortly judged the land and its doings as became His nature. But, while the divine judgement was still waiting, 48 Moses was carrying out the exercises of virtue with an admirable trainer, the reason within him, under whose discipline he laboured to fit himself for life in its highest forms, the theoretical and the practical. He was ever opening the scroll of philosophical doctrines, digested them inwardly with quick understanding, committed them to memory never to be forgotten, and straightway brought his personal conduct,

πράξεις ἐφαρμόττων ἐπαινετὰς πάσας, ἐφιέμενος
οὐ τοῦ δοκεῖν ἀλλὰ τῆς ἀληθείας, διὰ τὸ προκεῖσθαι
σκοπὸν ἕνα τὸν ὀρθὸν τῆς φύσεως λόγον, ὃς μόνος
49 ἐστὶν ἀρετῶν ἀρχή τε καὶ πηγή.   ἕτερος
μὲν οὖν ὀργὴν ἀμείλικτον βασιλέως ἀποδιδράσκων
καὶ ἄρτι πρῶτον εἰς ἀλλοδαπὴν ἀφιγμένος, μήπω
τοῖς τῶν ἐπιχωρίων ἔθεσιν ἐνωμιληκὼς μηδὲ
ἀκριβῶς ἐπιστάμενος οἷς χαίρουσιν ἢ ἀλλοτριοῦνται,
κἂν ἐσπούδασεν ἡσυχίᾳ χρώμενος ἀφανέστερον ζῆν
τοὺς πολλοὺς λανθάνων ἢ βουληθεὶς εἰς μέσον
παρέρχεσθαι τοὺς γοῦν δυνατοὺς καὶ τοὺς πλεῖστον
ἰσχύοντας λιπαρέσι θεραπείαις ἐξευμενίζεσθαι, παρ'
ὧν τις ὠφέλεια προσεδοκᾶτο καὶ βοήθεια, εἴ τινες
50 ἐπελθόντες ἀπάγειν πρὸς βίαν ἐπειρῶντο. ὁ δὲ τὴν
ἐναντίαν τοῦ εἰκότος ἀτραπὸν ἤλαυνε ταῖς τῆς
ψυχῆς ὑγιαινούσαις ὁρμαῖς ἑπόμενος καὶ μηδεμίαν
ἐῶν ὑποσκελίζεσθαι· διὸ καὶ τῆς ὑπούσης δυνάμεως
[89] ἔστιν ὅτε πλέον ἐνεανιεύετο | δύναμιν ἀκαθαίρετον
τὸ δίκαιον ἡγούμενος, ὑφ' οὗ προτραπεὶς αὐτο-
κέλευστος ἐπὶ τὴν τῶν ἀσθενεστέρων συμμαχίαν
ἵετο.
51   X. Λέξω δὲ καὶ τὸ κατ' ἐκεῖνον αὐτῷ τὸν χρόνον
πραχθέν, εἰ καὶ μικρὸν ὅσα γε τῷ δοκεῖν, ἀλλ' οὐκ
ἀπὸ φρονήματος μικροῦ. κτηνοτροφοῦσιν Ἄραβες
καὶ νέμουσι τὰ θρέμματα οὐκ ἄνδρες μόνον ἀλλὰ
καὶ γυναῖκες νέοι τε καὶ παρθένοι παρ' αὐτοῖς, οὐχὶ
τῶν ἠμελημένων καὶ ἀδόξων μόνον ἀλλὰ καὶ τῶν
52 ἄγαν ἐπιφανῶν. ἑπτὰ δὴ κόραι πατρὸς ἱερέως
ποίμνην ἄγουσαι παρῆσαν ἐπί τινα πηγὴν καὶ τῶν
ἱμονιῶν ἐκδησάμενοι τοὺς καδίσκους ἄλλη διαδεχο-
μένη παρ' ἄλλης ὑπὲρ τῆς ἐν τῷ πονεῖν ἰσομοιρίας

praiseworthy in all respects, into conformity with them; for he desired truth rather than seeming, because the one mark he set before him was nature's right reason, the sole source and fountain of virtues.

Now, any other who was fleeing from 49 the king's relentless wrath, and had just arrived for the first time in a foreign land, who had not yet become familiar with the customs of the natives nor gained exact knowledge of what pleases or offends them, might well have been eager to keep quiet and live in obscurity unnoticed by the multitude; or else he might have wished to come forward in public, and by obsequious persistence court the favour of men of highest authority and power, if none others, men who might be expected to give help and succour should some come and attempt to carry him off by force. But the path which he took was the opposite of what 50 we should expect. He followed the wholesome impulses of his soul, and suffered none of them to be brought to the ground. And, therefore, at times he showed a gallant temper beyond his fund of strength, for he regarded justice as strength invincible, which urged him on his self-appointed task to champion the weaker.

X. I will describe an action of his at this time, 51 which, though it may seem a petty matter, argues a spirit of no petty kind. The Arabs are breeders of cattle, and they employ for tending them not only men but women, youths and maidens alike, and not only those of insignificant and humble families but those of the highest position. Seven maidens, 52 daughters of the priest, had come to a well, and, after attaching the buckets to the ropes, drew water, taking turns with each to share the labour equally. They

PHILO

μάλα προθύμως τὰς δεξαμενάς, αἳ πλησίον ἔκειντο,
53 πληροῦσιν. ἐπιφοιτήσαντες δ᾽ ἕτεροι ποιμένες καὶ
τῆς τῶν παρθένων ἀσθενείας ὑπεριδόντες τὰς μὲν
ἐπεχείρουν μετὰ τῆς ποίμνης ἐλαύνειν, τὰ δ᾽ οἰκεῖα
θρέμματα προσῆγον ἐπὶ τὸ εὐτρεπισθὲν ποτὸν
54 ἀλλότριον καρπωσόμενοι πόνον. ἰδὼν δὲ Μωυσῆς
τὸ γενόμενον—οὐ γὰρ ἦν πόρρω—συντείνας ἔθει καὶ
πλησίον στὰς " οὐ παύσεσθε " εἶπεν " ἀδικοῦντες,
τὴν ἐρημίαν νομίζοντες εἶναι πλεονεξίαν; βραχίο-
νας καὶ πήχεις ἀργοὺς τρέφοντες οὐκ ἐρυθριᾶτε;
χαῖται βαθεῖαι καὶ σάρκες ὑμεῖς ἐστε, οὐκ ἄνδρες·
αἱ μὲν κόραι νεανιεύονται μηδὲν ὀκνοῦσαι τῶν
55 πρακτέων, οἱ δὲ νεανίαι κορικῶς ἤδη τρυφᾶτε. οὐ
βαδιεῖσθε; οὐχ ὑπεκστήσεσθε ταῖς πρότερον ἡκού-
σαις, ὧν καὶ τὸ ποτόν ἐστι; δικαίως ἂν αὐταῖς
ἐπαντλήσαντες, ἵν᾽ ἀφθονώτερον ὕδωρ εἴη, καὶ τὸ
εὐτρεπισθὲν ἀφελέσθαι σπεύδετε; ἀλλὰ μὰ τὸν
οὐράνιον τῆς δίκης ὀφθαλμὸν οὐκ ἀφελεῖσθε βλέ-
56 ποντα καὶ τὰ ἐν τοῖς ἐρημοτάτοις. ἐμὲ γοῦν
ἐχειροτόνησε βοηθὸν οὐ προσδοκηθέντα· καὶ γάρ
εἰμι σύμμαχος ταῖς ἀδικουμέναις μετὰ μεγάλης
χειρός, ἣν οὐ θέμις πλεονέκταις ὁρᾶν· αἰσθήσεσθε
δὲ αὐτῆς ἐκ τοῦ ἀφανοῦς τιτρωσκούσης, εἰ μὴ
57 μεταβάλοιτε." ταῦτα διεξιόντος, φοβηθέντες, ἐπεὶ
καὶ λέγων ἅμα ἐνθουσίᾳ μεταμορφούμενος εἰς
προφήτην, μὴ χρησμοὺς καὶ λόγια θεσπίζει, καταπειθεῖς τε γίνονται καὶ τὴν ποίμνην τῶν παρθένων
ἐπὶ τὰς δεξαμενὰς ἄγονται πρότερον μεταστησά-
58 μενοι τὰς ἑαυτῶν. XI. αἱ δ᾽ ἐπανῄεσαν
οἴκαδε σφόδρα γεγηθυῖαι καὶ τὰ συμβάντα παρ᾽
ἐλπίδας ἐκδιηγοῦντο, ὡς πολὺν ἵμερον ἐνεργάσα-

304

had with great industry filled the troughs which lay near, when some other shepherds appeared on the spot who, disdaining the weakness of the girls, tried to drive them and their flock away, and proceeded to bring their own animals to the place where the water lay ready, and thus appropriate the labours of others. But Moses, who was not far off, seeing what had happened, quickly ran up and, standing near by, said : "Stop this injustice. You think you can take advantage of the loneliness of the place. Are you not ashamed to let your arms and elbows live an idle life ? You are masses of long hair and lumps of flesh, not men. The girls are working like youths, and shirk none of their duties, while you young men go daintily like girls. Away with you : give place to those who were here before you, to whom the water belongs. Properly, you should have drawn for them, to make the supply more abundant ; instead, you are all agog to take from them what they have provided. Nay, by the heavenly eye of justice, you shall not take it ; for that eye sees even what is done in the greatest solitude. In me at least it has appointed a champion whom you did not expect, for I fight to succour these injured maidens, allied to a mighty arm which the rapacious may not see, but you shall feel its invisible power to wound if you do not change your ways." As he proceeded thus, they were seized with fear that they were listening to some oracular utterance, for as he spoke he grew inspired and was transfigured into a prophet. They became submissive, and led the maidens' flock to the troughs, after removing their own.   XI. The girls went home in high glee, and told the story of the unexpected event to their father, who thence conceived a strong desire to

305

σθαι τοῦ ξένου τῷ πατρί. κατεμέμφετο γοῦν αὐτὰς
ἐπ᾽ ἀχαριστίᾳ τοιαῦτα λέγων· "τί παθοῦσαι μεθ-
ίετε, δέον ἄγειν εὐθὺς καὶ εἴπερ ἀνεδύετο λιπαρεῖν;
ἢ τινα μισανθρωπίαν μου κατέγνωτε; ἢ δεύτερον
[90] περιπεσεῖν ἀδίκοις οὐ | προσδοκᾶτε; βοηθῶν ἀπο-
ρεῖν ἀνάγκη τοὺς ἐπιλήσμονας χαρίτων. ἀλλ᾽ ὅμως
ἀναδραμοῦσαι (τὸ γὰρ ἁμάρτημα μέχρι νῦν ἐστιν
ἰάσιμον) ἴτε μετὰ σπουδῆς καὶ καλεῖτε ξενίων μὲν
πρότερον αὖθις δὲ καὶ ἀμοιβῆς (ὀφείλεται γὰρ αὐτῷ
59 χάρις) μεθέξοντα." συντείνασαι δὲ καταλαμβά-
νουσιν αὐτὸν οὐ πόρρω τῆς πηγῆς καὶ δηλώσασαι
τὰ ἀπὸ τοῦ πατρὸς οἴκαδε συμπείθουσιν ἥκειν. ὁ
δὲ πατὴρ τὴν μὲν ὄψιν εὐθὺς τὸ δὲ βούλημα ὀλίγον
ὕστερον καταπλαγείς—ἀρίδηλοι γὰρ αἱ μεγάλαι
φύσεις καὶ οὐ μήκει χρόνου γνωριζόμεναι—δίδωσι
τὴν καλλιστεύουσαν αὐτῷ τῶν θυγατέρων γυναῖκα,
δι᾽ ἑνὸς ἔργου πάνθ᾽ ὅσα τῶν εἰς καλοκἀγαθίαν
μαρτυρήσας καὶ ὡς ἀξιέραστον μόνον τὸ καλόν
ἐστι τῆς ἀφ᾽ ἑτέρου συστάσεως οὐ δεόμενον, ἀλλ᾽
ἐν ἑαυτῷ περιφέρον τὰ γνωρίσματα.

60 μετὰ δὲ τὸν γάμον παραλαβὼν τὰς ἀγέλας ἐποί-
μαινε προδιδασκόμενος εἰς ἡγεμονίαν· ποιμενικὴ
γὰρ μελέτη καὶ προγυμνασία βασιλείας τῷ μέλλοντι
τῆς ἡμερωτάτης τῶν ἀνθρώπων ἐπιστατεῖν ἀγέλης,
καθάπερ καὶ τοῖς πολεμικοῖς τὰς φύσεις τὰ κυνηγέσια—θήραις γὰρ ἐμπρομελετῶσιν οἱ πρὸς τὰς
στραταρχίας ἀλειφόμενοι—[1] τῶν ἀλόγων οἷά τινος
ὕλης ὑποβεβλημένων πρὸς ἄσκησιν τῆς καθ᾽ ἑκά-

---

[1] Cohn's punctuation (colon after κυνηγέσια, comma after
ἀλειφόμενοι) is faulty here. τῶν ἀλόγων κτλ. is common to
both shepherding and hunting.

---

[a] Cf. De Ios. 2 f.

see the stranger, which he showed by censuring them
for their ingratitude. " What possessed you," he
said, " to let him depart ? You should have brought
him straight along, and pressed him if he showed
reluctance. Did you ever have to charge me with
unsociable ways ? Do you not expect that you may
again fall in with those who would wrong you ?
Those who forget kindness are sure to lack defenders.
Still, your error is not yet past cure. Run back with
all speed, and invite him to receive from me first
the entertainment due to him as a stranger, secondly
some requital of the favour which we owe to him."
They hurried back and found him not far from the 59
well, and, after explaining their father's message,
persuaded him to come home with them. Their
father was at once struck with admiration of his face,
and soon afterwards of his disposition, for great
natures are transparent and need no length of time
to be recognized. Accordingly, he gave him the
fairest of his daughters in marriage, and, by that one
action, attested all his noble qualities, and showed
that excellence standing alone deserves our love, and
needs no commendation from aught else, but carries
within itself the tokens by which it is known.

After the marriage, Moses took charge of the 60
sheep and tended them, thus receiving his first lesson
in command of others ; for the shepherd's business
is a training-ground and a preliminary exercise in
kingship for one who is destined to command the herd
of mankind, the most civilized of herds, just as also
hunting is for warlike natures, since those who are
trained to generalship practise themselves first in the
chase.[a] And thus unreasoning animals are made to
subserve as material wherewith to gain practice in

PHILO

τερον καιρὸν ἀρχῆς, τόν τε πολέμου καὶ τὸν εἰρήνης.
61 ἡ μὲν γὰρ τῶν ἀγρίων θήρα στρατηγικὸν κατ'
ἐχθρῶν ἐστι γύμνασμα, ἡ δὲ τῶν ἡμέρων ἐπιμέλεια
καὶ προστασία βασιλικὸν πρὸς ὑπηκόους ἀγώνισμα·
διὸ καὶ "ποιμένες λαῶν" οἱ βασιλεῖς, οὐχ ὡς
ὄνειδος ἀλλ' ὡς ὑπερβάλλουσα τιμή, προσαγορεύ-
62 ονται. καί μοι δοκεῖ μὴ πρὸς δόξας τῶν πολλῶν
ἀλλὰ πρὸς ἀλήθειαν ἐρευνωμένῳ τὸ πρᾶγμα—
γελάτω δ' ὁ βουλόμενος—μόνος ἂν γενέσθαι βασιλεὺς τέλειος ὁ τὴν ποιμενικὴν ἐπιστήμην ἀγαθός,
ἐν ἐλάττοσι ζῴοις παιδευθεὶς τὰ τῶν κρειττόνων·
ἀμήχανον γὰρ τὰ μεγάλα πρὸ τῶν μικρῶν τελεσθῆναι.

63 XII. Γενόμενος οὖν τῶν καθ' αὑτὸν ἀγελαρχῶν
ἄριστος καὶ ποριστὴς ⟨τῶν⟩ ὅσα πρὸς τὴν τῶν
θρεμμάτων συνέτεινεν ὠφέλειαν ἱκανὸς ἐκ τοῦ
μηδὲν ἀποκνεῖν ἀλλ' ἐθελουργῷ καὶ αὐτοκελεύστῳ
προθυμίᾳ[1] εἰς δέον τῇ προστασίᾳ χρῆσθαι μετὰ |
[91] καθαρᾶς[2] καὶ ἀδόλου πίστεως ηὔξησε τὰς ἀγέλας·
64 ὡς ὑπὸ τῶν ἄλλων νομέων ἤδη καὶ φθονεῖσθαι
μηδὲν ὁμοιότροπον ἐν ταῖς ἰδίαις ποίμναις ὁρώντων,
αἷς εὐτυχὲς εἶναι ἐδόκει ἡ ἐν ὁμοίῳ μονή, ταῖς δὲ
τὸ μὴ βελτιοῦσθαι καθ' ἑκάστην ἡμέραν ἐλάττωσις
διὰ τὸ μεγάλας εἰωθέναι λαμβάνειν ἐπιδόσεις ἐκ μὲν

---

[1] MSS. προστασία.　　　　[2] MSS. χαρᾶς.

---

a Possibly, as the German translation takes it, τελεσθῆναι
may mean simply "accomplished," "consummated." But
De Sac. 62 οἱ πρὸ τῶν μεγάλων τούτων τὰ μικρὰ μυστήρια
μυηθέντες, cf. De Cher. 49, and other allusions to the
"great" mysteries seem to make it much more probable
that the more picturesque meaning is intended. So Mangey,
who on the strength of these two passages, and the adaptation

308

government in the emergencies of both peace and
war ; for the chase of wild animals is a drilling- 61
ground for the general in fighting the enemy, and the
care and supervision of tame animals is a schooling
for the king in dealing with his subjects, and therefore kings are called "shepherds of their people,"
not as a term of reproach but as the highest honour.
And my opinion, based not on the opinions of the 62
multitude but on my own inquiry into the truth of
the matter, is that the only perfect king (let him
laugh who will) is one who is skilled in the knowledge
of shepherding, one who has been trained by management of the inferior creatures to manage the superior.
For initiation in the lesser mysteries must precede
initiation in the greater.[a]

XII. [b] To return to Moses, he became more skilled 63
than any of his time in managing flocks and providing
what tended to the benefit of his charges. His
capacity was due to his never shirking any duty, but
showing an eager and unprompted zeal wherever it
was needed, and maintaining a pure and guileless
honesty in the conduct of his office. Consequently 64
the flocks increased under him, and this roused
the envy of the other graziers, who did not see
anything of the sort happening in their own flocks.
In their case it was felt to be a piece of luck if
they remained as they had been, but with the flocks
of Moses any failure to make daily improvement was
a set-back, so great was the progress regularly made,
both in fine quality, through increased fatness and firm-

given of them by Clement, would correct τελεῖσθαι to μυεῖσθαι.
But this sense of τελεῖσθαι is quite common in Philo, *cf.*
De Abr. 122.
  [b] For §§ 63-84 see Ex. iii. 1–iv. 17.

εὐσαρκίας καὶ πιότητος εἰς κάλλος, εἰς δὲ πλῆθος
ἐξ εὐτοκίας καὶ τῶν περὶ δίαιταν ὑγιεινῶν.

65 ἄγων δὲ[1] τὴν ποίμνην εἰς τόπον εὔυδρόν τε καὶ
εὔχορτον, ἔνθα συνέβαινε καὶ πολλὴν πόαν προ-
βατεύσιμον ἀναδίδοσθαι, γενόμενος πρός τινι νάπει
θέαμα ἐκπληκτικώτατον ὁρᾷ. βάτος ἦν, ἀκανθῶδές
τι φυτὸν καὶ ἀσθενέστατον· οὗτος, οὐδενὸς πῦρ
προσενεγκόντος, ἐξαίφνης ἀνακαίεται καὶ περι-
σχεθεὶς ὅλος ἐκ ῥίζης εἰς ἀκρέμονα πολλῇ φλογὶ
καθάπερ ἀπό τινος πηγῆς ἀνομβρούσης διέμενε
σῶος, οὐ κατακαιόμενος, οἷά τις ἀπαθὴς οὐσία
καὶ οὐχ ὕλη πυρὸς αὐτὸς ὤν, ἀλλὰ τροφῇ χρώμενος
66 τῷ πυρί. κατὰ δὲ μέσην τὴν φλόγα μορφή τις
ἦν περικαλλεστάτη, τῶν ὁρατῶν ἐμφερὴς οὐδενί,
θεοειδέστατον ἄγαλμα, φῶς αὐγοειδέστερον τοῦ
πυρὸς ἀπαστράπτουσα, ἣν ἄν τις ὑπετόπησεν
εἰκόνα τοῦ ὄντος εἶναι· καλείσθω δὲ ἄγγελος, ὅτι
σχεδὸν τὰ μέλλοντα γενήσεσθαι διήγγελλε τρανο-
τέρᾳ φωνῆς ἡσυχίᾳ διὰ τῆς μεγαλουργηθείσης
67 ὄψεως.   σύμβολον γὰρ ὁ μὲν καιόμενος
βάτος τῶν ἀδικουμένων, τὸ δὲ φλέγον πῦρ τῶν
ἀδικούντων, τὸ δὲ μὴ κατακαίεσθαι τὸ καιόμενον
τοῦ μὴ πρὸς τῶν ἐπιτιθεμένων φθαρήσεσθαι τοὺς
ἀδικουμένους, ἀλλὰ τοῖς μὲν ἄπρακτον καὶ ἀνωφελῆ
γενέσθαι τὴν ἐπίθεσιν, τοῖς δὲ τὴν ἐπιβουλὴν
ἀζήμιον, ὁ δὲ ἄγγελος προνοίας τῆς ἐκ θεοῦ τὰ
λίαν φοβερὰ παρὰ τὰς ἁπάντων ἐλπίδας κατὰ
68 πολλὴν ἡσυχίαν ἐξευμαρίζοντος. XIII. τὴν δὲ
εἰκασίαν ἀκριβῶς ἐπισκεπτέον. ὁ βάτος, ὡς ἐλέ-

---

[1] MSS. τε.

ness of flesh, and in number through their fecundity and the wholesomeness of their food.

Now, as he was leading the flock to a place where the 65 water and the grass were abundant, and where there happened to be plentiful growth of herbage for the sheep, he found himself at a glen where he saw a most astonishing sight. There was a bramble-bush, a thorny sort of plant, and of the most weakly kind, which, without anyone's setting it alight, suddenly took fire ; and, though enveloped from root to twigs in a mass of fire, which looked as though it were spouted up from a fountain, yet remained whole, and, instead of being consumed, seemed to be a substance impervious to attack, and, instead of serving as fuel to the fire, actually fed on it. In the midst of the 66 flame was a form of the fairest beauty, unlike any visible object, an image supremely divine in appearance, refulgent with a light brighter than the light of fire. It might be supposed that this was the image of Him that is ; but let us rather call it an angel or herald, since, with a silence that spoke more clearly than speech, it employed as it were the miracle of sight to herald future events.   For the 67 burning bramble was a symbol of those who suffered wrong, as the flaming fire of those who did it. Yet that which burned was not burnt up, and this was a sign that the sufferers would not be destroyed by their aggressors, who would find that the aggression was vain and profitless while the victims of malice escaped unharmed. The angel was a symbol of God's providence, which all silently brings relief to the greatest dangers, exceeding every hope. XIII. But the details of the comparison must be con- 68 sidered. The bramble, as I have said, is a very

χθη, φυτὸν ἀσθενέστατον ἀλλ' οὐδὲ ἄκεντρον, ὡς
εἰ καὶ μόνον ἐπιψαύσειέ τις τιτρώσκειν, οὔτ' ἐξαναλώθη τῷ φύσει δαπανηρῷ πυρί, τοὐναντίον δὲ
ἐφυλάχθη πρὸς αὐτοῦ καὶ διαμένων ὁποῖος ἦν πρὶν
ἀνακαίεσθαι μηδὲν ἀποβαλὼν τὸ παράπαν αὐγὴν
[92] προσέλαβε. | τοῦθ' ἅπαν ὑπογραφή τίς ἐστι τῆς
69 ἐθνικῆς ὑποθέσεως,[1] ἢ κατ' ἐκεῖνον τὸν χρόνον
ἐπεῖχε, μόνον οὐ βοῶσα τοῖς ἐν συμφοραῖς· "μὴ
ἀναπίπτετε, τὸ ἀσθενὲς ὑμῶν δύναμίς ἐστιν, ἢ καὶ
κεντεῖ καὶ κατατρώσει μυρίους. ὑπὸ τῶν ἐξαναλῶ-
σαι γλιχομένων τὸ γένος ἀκόντων διασωθήσεσθε
μᾶλλον ἢ ἀπολεῖσθε, τοῖς κακοῖς οὐ κακωθήσεσθε,
ἀλλ' ὅταν μάλιστα πορθεῖν νομίσῃ τις ὑμᾶς, τότε
70 μάλιστα πρὸς εὔκλειαν ἐκλάμψετε." πάλιν τὸ πῦρ
φθοροποιὸς[2] οὐσία διελέγχουσα τοὺς ὠμοθύμους·
"μὴ ταῖς ἰδίαις ἀλκαῖς ἐπαίρεσθε, τὰς ἀμάχους
ῥώμας ἰδόντες καθαιρουμένας σωφρονίσθητε· ἡ μὲν
καυστικὴ δύναμις τῆς φλογὸς ὡς ξύλον καίεται, τὸ
δὲ φύσει καυστὸν ξύλον οἷα πῦρ ἐμφανῶς καίει."
71 XIV. Τὸ τεράστιον τοῦτο καὶ τεθαυματουργη-
μένον δείξας ὁ θεὸς τῷ Μωυσεῖ, παραίνεσιν ἐναργεστάτην τῶν μελλόντων ἀποτελεῖσθαι, καὶ διὰ
χρησμῶν ἄρχεται προτρέπειν αὐτὸν ἐπὶ τὴν τοῦ
ἔθνους σπεύδειν ἐπιμέλειαν, ὡς οὐ μόνον ἐλευθερίας
παραίτιον ἀλλὰ καὶ ἡγεμόνα τῆς ἐνθένδε ἀποικίας
οὐκ εἰς μακρὰν γενησόμενον, ὁμολογῶν ἐν ἅπασι
72 συλλήψεσθαι. "κακουμένων γὰρ ἐκ πολλοῦ καὶ

---

[1] A strange use of the word. Cohn suggests διαθέσεως.
[2] I suggest φθοροποιὸς ⟨φθοροποιεῖται⟩. See note a.

---

[a] The absence of a finite verb, for οὐσία can hardly be
predicate, is curious. Also the sense is not brought out,
for the sequel shows that the point is that the fire ultimately

weakly plant, yet it is prickly and will wound if one
do but touch it. Again, though fire is naturally
destructive, the bramble was not devoured thereby,
but on the contrary was guarded by it, and remained
just as it was before it took fire, lost nothing at all but
gained an additional brightness. All this is a descrip 69
tion of the nation's condition as it then stood, and we
may think of it as a voice proclaiming to the sufferers:
" Do not lose heart ; your weakness is your strength,
which can prick, and thousands will suffer from its
wounds. Those who desire to consume you will be
your unwilling saviours instead of your destroyers.
Your ills will work you no ill. Nay, just when the
enemy is surest of ravaging you, your fame will shine
forth most gloriously." Again fire, the element 70
which works destruction, convicts the cruel-hearted.[a]
" Exult not in your own strength " it says. " Behold
your invincible might brought low, and learn wisdom.
The property of flame is to consume, yet it is consumed, like wood. The nature of wood is to be
consumed yet it is manifested as the consumer, as
though it were the fire."

XIV. After showing to Moses this miraculous 71
portent, so clearly warning him of the events that
were to be, God begins in oracular speech to urge
him to take charge of the nation with all speed, in
the capacity not merely of an assistant to their
liberation, but of the leader who would shortly take
them from Egypt to another home. He promised
to help him in everything: " For," he said, " suffering, 72

goes out and leaves the bramble victorious. I strongly
suspect that " is destroyed " has been lost and if so φθορο-
ποιεῖται in juxtaposition to φθοροποιός would be preferable to
φθείρεται. No such word is quoted in the lexica, but Philo
is quite capable of coining it.

PHILO

δυσανασχέτους ὕβρεις ὑπομενόντων, οὐδενὸς ἀνθρώπων οὔτ' ἐπικουφίζοντος οὔτ' ἐλεοῦντος τὰς
συμφοράς, οἶκτον" φησίν " αὐτὸς ἔλαβον. καὶ
γὰρ ⟨οἶδ'⟩ ἰδίᾳ ἕκαστον καὶ πάντας ὁμοθυμαδὸν
ἐφ' ἱκετείας καὶ λιτὰς τραπομένους ἐλπίζειν τὴν
ἐξ ἐμοῦ βοήθειαν· εἰμὶ δὲ τὴν φύσιν ἤπιος καὶ
73 γνησίοις ἱκέταις ἵλεως. ἴθι δὴ πρὸς τὸν βασιλέα
τῆς χώρας μηδὲν εὐλαβηθεὶς τὸ παράπαν—ὁ μὲν
γὰρ πρότερος τέθνηκεν, ὃν ἀπεδίδρασκες διὰ φόβον
ἐπιβουλῆς, ἕτερος δὲ τὴν χώραν ἐπιτέτραπται μηδενὸς τῶν πραγμάτων σοι μνησικακῶν—καὶ τὴν τοῦ
ἔθνους γερουσίαν προσπαραλαβὼν εἰπὲ χρησμῷ
προσκεκλῆσθαι ὑπ' ἐμοῦ τὸ ἔθνος, ἵνα κατὰ τὰ
πάτρια θύσῃ τριῶν ἡμερῶν ὁδὸν ἔξω τῶν ὅρων τῆς
74 χώρας προελθόν." ὁ δὲ οὐκ ἀγνοῶν ἐπὶ τοῖς λεγομένοις ἀπιστήσοντας τούς τε ὁμοφύλους καὶ τοὺς
ἄλλους ἅπαντας " ἐὰν οὖν " φησί " πυνθάνωνται, τί
τὸ ὄνομα τῷ πέμψαντι, μηδ' αὐτὸς εἰπεῖν ἔχων ἆρ'
75 οὐ δόξω διαπατᾶν; " ὁ δὲ " τὸ μὲν πρῶτον λέγε "
φησίν " αὐτοῖς, ὅτι ἐγώ εἰμι ὁ ὤν, ἵνα μαθόντες
διαφορὰν ὄντος τε καὶ μὴ ὄντος προσαναδιδαχθῶσιν,
ὡς οὐδὲν ὄνομα τὸ παράπαν ἐπ' ἐμοῦ κυριολογεῖται,
76 ᾧ μόνῳ πρόσεστι τὸ εἶναι. ἐὰν δ' ἀσθενέστεροι
τὰς φύσεις ὄντες ἐπιζητῶσι πρόσρησιν, δήλωσον
[93] αὐτοῖς μὴ μόνον τοῦθ' ὅτι | θεός εἰμι, ἀλλ' ὅτι καὶ
τριῶν τῶν ἐπωνύμων ἀνδρῶν ἀρετῆς, θεὸς Ἀβραὰμ
καὶ θεὸς Ἰσαὰκ καὶ θεὸς Ἰακώβ, ὧν ὁ μὲν τῆς
διδακτῆς, ὁ δὲ τῆς φυσικῆς, ὁ δὲ τῆς ἀσκητικῆς
σοφίας κανών ἐστιν. ἐὰν δὲ ἔτι ἀπιστῶσι, τρισὶ
σημείοις ἀναδιδαχθέντες μεταβαλοῦσιν, ἃ πρότερον
77 οὔτε τις εἶδεν οὔτε ἤκουσεν ἀνθρώπων." ἦν δὲ τὰ

as they do, prolonged ill-treatment, and subjected
to intolerable outrages, with no relief or pity for
their miseries from men, I have taken compassion
on them Myself. For I know that each severally,
and all unitedly, have betaken themselves to prayers
and supplications in hope to gain help from Me, and
I am of a kindly nature and gracious to true suppliants. Now go to the king of the land, and fear 73
not at all, for the former king from whom you fled
in fear that he meant mischief is dead, and the land
is in the hands of another who does not remember
any of your actions against you. Take with you also
the elders of the nation, and tell him that the people
has received a command from Me to make a three-
days' journey beyond the bounds of the country,
and there sacrifice according to the rites of their
fathers." Moses knew well that his own nation 74
and all the others would disbelieve his words, and
said : " If they ask the name of him who sent me,
and I cannot myself tell them, will they not think
me a deceiver?" God replied: "First tell them that 75
I am He Who is, that they may learn the difference
between what is and what is not, and also the further
lesson that no name at all can properly be used of
Me, to Whom alone existence belongs. And, if, 76
in their natural weakness, they seek some title to
use, tell them not only that I am God, but also the
God of the three men whose names express their
virtue, each of them the exemplar of the wisdom
they have gained—Abraham by teaching, Isaac by
nature, Jacob by practice.[a] And, if they still disbelieve, three signs which no man has ever before
seen or heard of will be sufficient lesson to convert

---

[a] For §§ 75-76 cf. De Mut. 11 ff.

σημεῖα τοιάδε· ῥάβδον, ἣν εἶχεν, εἰς τοὖδαφος ῥῖψαι
κελεύει· ἡ δ' αὐτίκα ψυχωθεῖσα εἷρπε καὶ τῶν
ἀπόδων τὸ ἡγεμονικώτατον ὑπερμεγέθης δράκων
γίνεται τελειότατος· ταχέως δ' ἀποχωρήσας ἀπὸ
τοῦ ζῴου καὶ διὰ δέος ἤδη πρὸς φυγὴν ὁρμῶν
μετακαλεῖται καὶ θεοῦ προστάξαντος ἅμα τε θάρσος
78 ἐμποιήσαντος ἐπιδράττεται τῆς οὐρᾶς. ὁ δὲ ἰλυ-
σπώμενος ἔτι κατὰ τὴν ἐπαφὴν ἵσταται καὶ πρὸς
μῆκος εὖ μάλα ταθεὶς εὐθὺς εἰς βακτηρίαν μετ-
εστοιχειοῦτο τὴν αὐτήν, ὡς θαυμάζειν μὲν τὰς μεταβολὰς ἀμφοτέρας, ποτέρα δὲ καταπληκτικωτέρα,
μὴ δύνασθαι διακρίνειν, τῆς ψυχῆς ἰσορρόπῳ
79 πληχθείσης φαντασίᾳ. τοῦτο μὲν δὴ πρῶτον,
ἕτερον δ' οὐκ εἰς μακρὰν ἐθαυματουργεῖτο· τῶν
χειρῶν τὴν ἑτέραν προστάττει τοῖς κόλποις ἐπι-
κρύψαντα μικρὸν ὕστερον προενεγκεῖν· δράσαντος
δὲ τὸ κελευσθέν, ἡ χεὶρ λευκοτέρα χιόνος ἐξαπιναίως ἀναφαίνεται· πάλιν δὲ καθέντος εἰς τοὺς
κόλπους καὶ ἀνενεγκόντος, εἰς τὴν αὐτὴν χρόαν
80 τρέπεται τὸ οἰκεῖον ἀπολαβοῦσα εἶδος. ταῦτα μὲν
οὖν ὑπὸ μόνου μόνος ἐπαιδεύετο, ὡς παρὰ διδα-
σκάλῳ γνώριμος, ἔχων παρ' ἑαυτῷ τὰ τῶν τεράτων
ὄργανα, τήν τε χεῖρα καὶ τὴν βακτηρίαν, οἷς
81 προεφωδιάσθη. τρίτον δ' ἐπιφέρεσθαι μὲν οὐκ ἦν
οὐδὲ προδιδάσκεσθαι, ἔμελλε δ' ἐκπλήττειν οὐκ
ἔλαττον τὴν ἀρχὴν τοῦ γίνεσθαι λαβὸν ἐν Αἰγύπτῳ.
ἦν δὲ τοιοῦτο· " τοῦ ποταμίου" φησίν " ὕδατος
ὅσον ἂν ἀρυσάμενος ἐπὶ τὴν γῆν ἐκχέῃς, αἷμα
ξανθότατον ἔσται πρὸς τῇ χρόᾳ καὶ τὴν δύναμιν
82 ἑτεροιωθὲν εἰς ἀλλαγὴν παντελῆ." πιστὸν δ' ὡς

them." The signs were such as these. He bade **77**
him cast on the ground the rod which he carried, and
this at once took life and began to creep, and became that high chief of the reptile kingdom, a huge
serpent grown to full strength. Moses quickly
leaped away from the creature, and, in his fright, was
starting to fly, when he was recalled by God, and,
at His bidding and inspired by Him with courage,
grasped its tail. It was still wriggling, but stopped **78**
at his touch, and, stretching itself to its full length,
was metamorphosed at once into the rod which it
had been before, so that Moses marvelled at the
double change, unable to decide which was the more
astonishing, so evenly balanced was the profound
impression which each made upon his soul. This **79**
was the first miracle, and a second followed soon.
God bade him conceal one of his hands in his bosom,
and, after a little while, draw it out. And when
he did as he was bid, the hand suddenly appeared
whiter than snow. He did the same again, put it in
his bosom and then brought it out, when it turned
to its original colour and recovered its proper appearance. These lessons he received when he and God **80**
were alone together, like pupil and master, and while
the instruments of the miracles, the hand and the staff,
with which he was equipped for his mission were both
in his own possession. But the third had its birth- **81**
place in Egypt. It was one which he could not carry
with him or rehearse beforehand, yet the amazement which it was sure to cause was quite as great.
It was this: "The water," God said, "which thou
dost draw from the river and pour on the land will
be blood quite ruddy, and not only its colour but its
properties will be completely changed." Moses evi- **82**

ἔοικε καὶ τοῦτ' ἀνεφαίνετο, οὐ μόνον διὰ τὸ τοῦ
λέγοντος ἀψευδές, ἀλλὰ καὶ διὰ τὰ ἤδη προεπιδει-
χθέντα ἐπί τε τῆς χειρὸς καὶ τῆς βακτηρίας θαυ-
83 ματουργήματα.   πιστεύων δ' ὅμως παρ-
ῃτεῖτο τὴν χειροτονίαν ἰσχνόφωνον καὶ βραδύγ-
λωσσον, οὐκ εὔλογον, αὑτὸν εἶναι φάσκων καὶ
μάλιστ' ἀφ' οὗ λέγοντος ἤκουε θεοῦ· νομίσας γὰρ
τὴν ἀνθρωπίνην λογιότητα κατὰ σύγκρισιν τῆς
θείας¹ ἀφωνίαν εἶναι καὶ ἅμα τὴν φύσιν εὐλαβὴς ὢν
[94] ὑπεστέλλετο | τοῖς ὑπερόγκοις, τὰ λίαν μεγάλα
κρίνων οὐ καθ' αὑτόν, καὶ παρεκάλει ἕτερον ἑλέσθαι
τὸν εὐμαρῶς ἕκαστα τῶν ἐπισταλέντων διαπράξα-
84 σθαι δυνησόμενον. ὁ δ' ἀποδεξάμενος αὐτὸν τῆς
αἰδοῦς "ἆρά γε ἀγνοεῖς" εἶπε "τὸν δόντα ἀνθρώπῳ στόμα καὶ κατασκευάσαντα γλῶτταν καὶ
ἀρτηρίαν καὶ τὴν ἅπασαν λογικῆς φωνῆς ὀργανο-
ποιίαν; αὐτός εἰμι ἐγώ. μηδὲν οὖν δείσῃς· ἐμοῦ
γὰρ ἐπινεύσαντος ἀρθρωθήσεται πάντα καὶ μετα-
βαλεῖ πρὸς τὸ μέτριον, ὡς μηδενὸς ἔτι ἐμποδίζοντος
ῥεῖν εὔτροχον καὶ λεῖον ἀπὸ καθαρᾶς πηγῆς τὸ τῶν
λόγων νᾶμα. χρεία δ' εἰ γένοιτο ἑρμηνέως, ὑπο-
διακονικὸν στόμα τὸν ἀδελφὸν ἕξεις, ἵν' ὁ μὲν τῷ
πλήθει ἀπαγγέλλῃ τὰ ἀπὸ σοῦ, σὺ δ' ἐκείνῳ τὰ
θεῖα."

85   XV. Ταῦτ' ἀκούσας—οὐ γὰρ ἦν εἰς ἅπαν ἀντι-
λέγειν ἀσφαλὲς οὐδ' ἀκίνδυνον—ἄρας ἐβάδιζε μετὰ
γυναικὸς καὶ τέκνων ὁδὸν τὴν ἐπ' Αἴγυπτον, καθ'
ἣν ὑπαντήσαντα τὸν ἀδελφὸν πείθει συνακολουθεῖν
ὑπειπὼν τὰ θεῖα λόγια· τῷ δ' ἄρα προϋπείργαστο ἡ

¹ MSS. ἀληθείας.

dently felt that this too was credible, not only because
of the infallibility of the Speaker, but through the
proofs he had already been shewn in the miracles of
the hand and the staff.   But, though he 83
believed, he tried to refuse the mission, declaring that
he was not eloquent, but feeble of voice and slow of
tongue, especially ever since he heard God speaking
to him ; for he considered that human eloquence
compared with God's was dumbness, and also,
cautious as he was by nature, he shrank from things
sublime and judged that matters of such magnitude
were not for him. And therefore he begged Him
to choose another, who would prove able to execute
with ease all that was committed to him. But God, 84
though approving his modesty, answered : " Dost
thou not know who it is that gave man a mouth, and
formed his tongue and throat and all the organism
of reasonable speech ? It is I Myself : therefore, fear
not, for at a sign from Me all will become articulate
and be brought over to method and order, so that
none can hinder the stream of words from flowing
easily and smoothly from a fountain undefiled. And,
if thou shouldst have need of an interpreter, thou
wilt have in thy brother a mouth to assist thy service,
to report to the people thy words, as thou reportest
those of God to him."

XV. ª Moses, hearing this, and knowing how un- 85
safe and hazardous it was to persist in gainsaying,
took his departure, and travelled with his wife and
children on the road to Egypt. During the journey
he met his brother, to whom he declared the divine
message, and persuaded him to accompany him.
His brother's soul, in fact, had already, through the

ª For §§ 85-95 see Ex. iv. 27, v. 22, vii. 8-13.

ψυχὴ κατ' ἐπιφροσύνην θεοῦ πρὸς πειθαρχίαν, ὡς
ἀνενδοιάστως συναινεῖν καὶ ἑτοίμως ἕπεσθαι.
86 παραγενόμενοι δ' εἰς Αἴγυπτον γνώμῃ καὶ ψυχῇ
μιᾷ τὸ μὲν πρῶτον τοὺς δημογέροντας τοῦ ἔθνους
συναγαγόντες ἐν ἀπορρήτῳ μηνύουσι τοὺς χρησμοὺς
καὶ ὡς ἔλεον καὶ οἶκτον λαβὼν αὐτῶν ὁ θεὸς ἐλευ-
θερίαν καὶ τὴν ἐνθένδε μετανάστασιν εἰς ἀμείνω
χώραν ὁμολογῶν αὐτὸς ἔσεσθαι τῆς ὁδοῦ ἡγεμὼν
87 ὑπισχνεῖται. μετὰ δὲ ταῦτα καὶ τῷ βασιλεῖ θαρ-
ροῦσιν ἤδη διαλέγεσθαι περὶ τοῦ τὸν λεὼν ἱερουρ-
γήσοντα ἐκπέμψαι τῶν ὅρων· δεῖν γὰρ ἔφασκον ἐν
ἐρήμῳ τὰς πατρίους θυσίας ἐπιτελεσθῆναι, μὴ κατὰ
τὰ αὐτὰ ταῖς τῶν ἄλλων ἀνθρώπων γινομένας,
ἀλλὰ τρόπῳ καὶ νόμῳ διαφεύγοντι τὴν κοινότητα
88 διὰ τὰς τῶν ἐθῶν ἐξαιρέτους ἰδιότητας. ὁ δ' ἐξ
ἔτι σπαργάνων προγονικῷ τύφῳ τὴν ψυχὴν πεπιεσμένος καὶ μηδένα τὸ παράπαν νοητὸν θεὸν ἔξω τῶν
ὁρατῶν νομίζων ἀποκρίνεται πρὸς ὕβριν εἰπών·
" τίς ἐστιν οὗ χρή με ὑπακούειν; οὐκ οἶδα τὸν
λεγόμενον τοῦτον καινὸν κύριον· οὐκ ἐξαποστέλλω
τὸ ἔθνος ἐπὶ προφάσει ἑορτῆς καὶ θυσιῶν ἀφη-
89 νιάσον." εἶθ' ἅτε χαλεπὸς καὶ βαρύμηνις καὶ
ἀπαραίτητος τὴν ὀργὴν κελεύει τοὺς τοῖς ἔργοις
ἐφεστῶτας προπηλακίζεσθαι ὡς ἀνέσεις καὶ σχολὴν
ἐνδιδόντας, ἀνέσεως καὶ σχολῆς εἶναι λέγων τὸ
βουλεύεσθαι περὶ θυσιῶν καὶ ἑορτῶν· τοὺς γὰρ ἐν
ἀνάγκαις τούτων οὐδὲ μεμνῆσθαι, ἀλλ' οἷς ὁ βίος
90 ἐν εὐπαθείᾳ πολλῇ καὶ τρυφῇ. βαρυτέρας οὖν ἢ
πρότερον συμφορὰς ὑπομενόντων καὶ ἐπὶ τοῖς ἀμφὶ

ᵃ Or perhaps "shrank from publicity." Like mysteries
in general, they had to be performed in secrecy.

watchful working of God, been predisposed to obedience, so that without hesitation he assented and
readily followed. When they had arrived in Egypt, 86
one in mind and heart, they first summoned the
senators of the nation secretly, and informed them
of the oracles, and how God had, in pity and compassion for them, assured them liberty and departure
from their present to a better country, and promised
to be Himself their leader. After this they were now 87
emboldened to talk to the king, and lay before him
their request that he should send the people out of
his boundaries to sacrifice. They told him that their
ancestral sacrifices must be performed in the desert,
as they did not conform with those of the rest of
mankind, but so exceptional were the customs
peculiar to the Hebrews that their rule and method
of sacrifices ran counter to the common course.[a] The 88
king, whose soul from his earliest years was weighed
down with the pride of many generations, did not
accept a God discernible only by the mind, or any
at all beyond those whom his eyes beheld ; and
therefore he answered insolently : "Who is he
whom I must obey ? I know not this new Lord of
whom you speak. I refuse to send the nation forth
to run loose under pretext of festival and sacrifices."
Then, in the harshness and ferocity and obstinacy 89
of his temper, he bade the overseers of the tasks
treat the people with contumely, for showing slack-
ness and laziness. "For just this," he said, " was
what was meant by the proposal to hold festival and
sacrifice—things the very memory of which was lost
by the hard pressed, and retained only by those
whose life was spent in much comfort and luxury."
Thus they endured woes more grievous than ever, 90

PHILO

[95] Μωυσῆν δυσχεραινόντων ὡς | ἀπατεῶσι καὶ τὰ μὲν λάθρα τὰ δὲ φανερῶς κακηγορούντων καὶ ἀσεβείας[1] αἰτιωμένων ἐπὶ τῷ δοκεῖν θεοῦ κατεψεῦσθαι, δεικνύειν ἄρχεται Μωυσῆς ἃ προὐδιδάχθη τέρατα, νομίσας τοὺς θεασομένους ἐκ τῆς ἐπεχούσης ἀπιστίας εἰς πίστιν τῶν λεγομένων μεταβαλεῖν.

91 ἡ δὲ τῶν τεράτων ἐπίδειξις ἐγένετο καὶ τῷ βασιλεῖ διὰ σπουδῆς καὶ τοῖς ἐν τέλει τῶν Αἰγυπτίων. XVI. πάντων οὖν τῶν δυνατῶν συρρυέντων εἰς τὰ βασίλεια, λαβὼν τὴν βακτηρίαν ὁ Μωυσέως ἀδελφὸς καὶ κατασείσας μάλα ἐπιδεικτικῶς εἰς τοὔδαφος ῥίπτει· καὶ ἡ μὲν δράκων αὐτίκα γίνεται, οἱ δ' ἐν κύκλῳ κατεθεῶντο καὶ ἅμα θαυμαστικῶς ἔχοντες 92 ὑπὸ δέους ἐξαναχωροῦντες ἀπέφευγον. σοφισταὶ δ' ὅσοι καὶ μάγοι παρετύγχανον "τί καταπλήττεσθε;" εἶπον· "οὐδ' ἡμεῖς τῶν τοιούτων ἀμελετήτως ἔχομεν, ἀλλὰ χρώμεθα τέχνῃ δημιουργῷ τῶν ὁμοίων." εἶθ' ἑκάστου βακτηρίαν ἣν εἶχε ῥίψαντος, δρακόντων πλῆθος ἦν καὶ περὶ ἕνα τὸν 93 πρῶτον εἰλοῦντο. ὁ δ' ἐκ πολλοῦ τοῦ περιόντος διαναστὰς πρὸς ὕψος τὰ μὲν στέρνα εὐρύνει, τὸ δὲ στόμα διοίξας ὁλκοῦ πνεύματος ῥύμῃ βιαιοτάτῃ καθάπερ βόλον ἰχθύων πάντας ἐν κύκλῳ σαγηνεύσας ἐπισπᾶται καὶ καταπιὼν εἰς τὴν ἀρχαίαν φύσιν τῆς 94 βακτηρίας μετέβαλεν. ἤδη μὲν οὖν ἐν ἑκάστου τῇ ψυχῇ τῶν ἐθελοκακούντων τὸ ὕποπτον διήλεγξεν ἡ μεγαλουργηθεῖσα ὄψις, ὡς μηκέτι νομίζειν ἀνθρώπων σοφίσματα καὶ τέχνας εἶναι τὰ γινόμενα πεπλασμένας πρὸς ἀπάτην, ἀλλὰ δύναμιν θειοτέραν 95 τὴν τούτων αἰτίαν, ᾗ πάντα δρᾶν εὐμαρές. ἐπεὶ δὲ

---

[1] MSS. ἀσέβειαν.

and were enraged against Moses and his companion as deceivers, abusing them, sometimes secretly, sometimes openly, and accusing them of impiety in that they appeared to have spoken falsely of God. Whereupon Moses began to show the wonders which he had been previously taught to perform, thinking that the sight would convert them from the prevailing unbelief to belief in his words. 91 The exhibition of these wonders to the king and the Egyptian nobles followed very quickly; (XVI.) so, when all the magnates had collected at the palace, the brother of Moses took his staff, and, after waving it in a very conspicuous manner, flung it on the ground, where it immediately turned into a serpent, while the onlookers standing round were filled with wonder, fell back in fear, and were on the point of running away. 92 But all the wizards and magicians who were present said: "Why are you terrified? We, too, are practised in such matters, and we use our skill to produce similar results." Then, as each of them threw down the staff which he held, there appeared a multitude of serpents writhing round a single one; 93 that one, the first, showed its great superiority by rising high, widening its chest and opening its mouth, when with the suction of its breath it swept the others in with irresistible force, like a whole draught of fishes encircled by the net, and, after swallowing them up, changed to its original nature, and became a staff. 94 By this time, the marvellous spectacle had refuted the scepticism in every ill-disposed person's soul, and they now regarded these events not as the works of human cunning or artifices fabricated to deceive, but as brought about by some diviner power to which every feat is easy.

καὶ ὁμολογεῖν ἀναγκασθέντες ὑπὸ τῆς τῶν γινομένων ἐμφανοῦς ἐναργείας οὐδὲν ἧττον ἐθρασύνοντο,
τῆς αὐτῆς ἀπανθρωπίας καὶ ἀσεβείας ὥσπερ ἀγαθοῦ
τινος ἐπειλημμένοι βεβαιοτάτου, μήτε τοὺς κατα-
δουλωθέντας ἀδίκως ἐλεοῦντες μήτε τὰ διὰ τῶν
λόγων[1] προσταττόμενα δρῶντες, ἅτε δὴ τοῦ θεοῦ
τρανοτέραις χρησμῶν ἀποδείξεσι ταῖς διὰ σημείων
καὶ τεράτων τὸ βούλημα δεδηλωκότος, ἐμβριθε-
στέρας ἐπανατάσεως[2] ἐδέησε καὶ πληγῶν ἐσμοῦ, αἷς
οἱ ἄφρονες νουθετοῦνται, οὓς λόγος οὐκ ἐπαίδευσε.

96 Δέκα δὲ ἐπάγονται τῇ χώρᾳ τιμωρίαι, κατὰ τῶν
τέλεια ἡμαρτηκότων τέλειος ἀριθμὸς κολάσεως· ἦν[3]
δὲ κόλασις παρηλλαχυῖα τὰς ἐν ἔθει. XVII. τὰ
γὰρ στοιχεῖα τοῦ παντός, γῆ καὶ ὕδωρ καὶ ἀὴρ καὶ
[96] πῦρ, ἐπιτίθενται, | δικαιώσαντος θεοῦ, οἷς ἀπετε-
λέσθη ὁ κόσμος, τὴν ἀσεβῶν χώραν φθαρῆναι, πρὸς
ἔνδειξιν κράτους ἀρχῆς ᾗ κέχρηται, τὰ αὐτὰ καὶ
σωτηρίως ἐπὶ γενέσει τῶν ὅλων σχηματίζοντος καὶ
τρέποντος ὁπότε βουληθείη πρὸς τὴν κατὰ τῶν
97 ἀσεβῶν ἀπώλειαν. διανέμει δὲ τὰς κολάσεις, τρεῖς
μὲν τὰς ἐκ τῶν παχυμερεστέρων στοιχείων γῆς καὶ
ὕδατος, ἐξ ὧν ἀπετελέσθησαν αἱ σωματικαὶ ποιό-
τητες, ἐφεὶς τῷ Μωυσέως ἀδελφῷ, τὰς δ' ἴσας ἐξ
ἀέρος καὶ πυρὸς τῶν ψυχογονιμωτάτων μόνῳ

---

[1] Perhaps read λογίων, as Mangey according to Cohn
suggested, though I cannot find it in his foot-notes or addenda.
On λόγου (?) see note a.
[2] MSS. ἐπαναστάσεως.   [3] MSS. ἦ.

---

[a] This seems to be the sense required, and so Mangey
"divinitus imperata." But it is difficult to extract this from
λόγων. λόγου "reason" will make good sense, correspond-

But, though they were compelled by the clear evi- 95
dence of the facts to admit the truth, they did not
abate their audacity, but clung to their old inhumanity and impiety as though it were the surest of
blessings. They did not show mercy to those who
were unjustly enslaved, nor carry out the orders
which had divine authority,[a] since God had shown
His will by the proofs of signs and wonders, which
are clearer than oracles. And therefore a severer
visitation was needed, and volley of those blows
whereby fools whom reason has not disciplined are
brought to their senses.

The punishments inflicted on the land were ten— 96
a perfect number for the chastisement of those who
brought sin to perfection. The chastisement was
different from the usual kind, (XVII.) for the elements
of the universe—earth, fire, air, water—carried out
the assault. God's judgement was that the materials
which had served to produce the world should serve
also to destroy the land of the impious; and to show the
mightiness of the sovereignty which He holds, what
He shaped in His saving goodness to create the universe He turned into instruments for the perdition
of the impious whenever He would. He distributed 97
the punishments in this wise : three belonging to the
denser elements, earth and water, which have gone
to make our bodily qualities what they are, He committed to the brother of Moses ; another set of three,
belonging to air and fire, the two most productive

ing to ὁ λόγος below, but in this sense the word does not seem
to be used in the plural. If λογίων is read, we must
suppose that it is contrasted with χρησμῶν as covering all
divine intimations, whereas χρησμῶν is confined to the spoken
oracle. But this also lacks authority.

Μωυσεῖ, μίαν δὲ κοινὴν ἀμφοτέροις ἑβδόμην ἐπι
τρέπει, τρεῖς δὲ τὰς ἄλλας εἰς συμπλήρωσιν δεκάδος
98 ἀνατίθησιν αὐτῷ.   καὶ πρώτας ἐπιφέρειν
ἄρχεται τὰς ἀφ᾽ ὕδατος· ἐπειδὴ γὰρ τὸ ὕδωρ
Αἰγύπτιοι διαφερόντως ἐκτετιμήκασιν ἀρχὴν τῆς
τῶν ὅλων γενέσεως τοῦτ᾽ εἶναι νομίζοντες, αὐτὸ
πρῶτον ἠξίωσε καλέσαι πρὸς τὴν τῶν ἀποδεχο
99 μένων ἐπίπληξίν τε καὶ νουθεσίαν. τί οὖν οὐκ εἰς
μακρὰ νσυνέβη;   τοῦ Μωυσέως ἀδελφοῦ προσ
τάξει θείᾳ κατενεγκόντος τὴν βακτηρίαν ἐπὶ τὸν
ποταμόν, ὁ μὲν εὐθὺς ἀπ᾽ Αἰθιοπίας ἄχρι θαλάσσης
εἰς αἷμα τρέπεται, συνεξαιματοῦνται δ᾽ αὐτῷ
λίμναι, διώρυχες, κρῆναι, φρέατα, πηγαί, σύμπασα
ἡ κατ᾽ Αἴγυπτον οὐσία ὕδατος, ὡς ἀπορίᾳ ποτοῦ
τὰ παρὰ ταῖς ὄχθαις ἀναστέλλειν, τὰς δ᾽ ἀνατεμνο
μένας φλέβας καθάπερ ἐν ταῖς αἱμορραγίαις κρου
νηδὸν αὐλοὺς ἀκοντίζειν αἵματος, μηδεμιᾶς ἐνορω
100 μένης διαυγοῦς λιβάδος. ἐναπέθνησκε δὲ καὶ τὰ
γένη τῶν ἰχθύων ἅπαντα, ἅτε τῆς ζωτικῆς δυνά
μεως εἰς φθοροποιὸν μεταβαλούσης, ὡς δυσωδίας
πάντα διὰ πάντων ἀναπεπλῆσθαι, τοσούτων σηπο
μένων ἀθρόον σωμάτων· πολὺς δὲ καὶ ἀνθρώπων
ὄχλος ὑπὸ δίψους διαφθαρεὶς ἔκειτο σωρηδὸν ἐπὶ
τῶν τριόδων, οὐ σθενόντων ἐπὶ τὰ μνήματα τῶν
101 οἰκείων τοὺς τετελευτηκότας ἐκκομίζειν. ἐπὶ γὰρ
ἡμέρας ἑπτὰ τὸ δεινὸν ἐκράτησεν, ἕως οἱ μὲν
Αἰγύπτιοι τοὺς ἀμφὶ Μωυσῆν, οὗτοι δὲ τὸν θεὸν
ἱκέτευσαν, οἶκτον λαβεῖν τῶν ἀπολλυμένων· ὁ δὲ
τὴν φύσιν ἵλεως μεταβάλλει τὸ αἷμα εἰς ὕδωρ
πότιμον ἀποδοὺς τῷ ποταμῷ καθαρὰ τὰ ἀρχαῖα

---

[a] The above grouping of the ten plagues compels Philo
to depart from the order of Exodus, as will appear in the

of life, He gave to Moses alone ; one, the seventh,
He committed to both in common ; and the other
three which go to complete the ten He reserved to
Himself.[a]   He began by bringing into 98
play first the plagues of water ; for, since the Egyptians had paid a specially high homage to water,
which they believed to be the original source of the
creation of the All, He thought well to summon
water first to reprove and admonish its votaries.
What, then, was the event which so soon came to 99
pass ? The brother of Moses, at the command of
God, smote the river with his staff, and at once, from
Ethiopia to the sea, it turned into blood, and so did
also the lakes, canals, springs, wells and fountains
and all the existing water-supply of Egypt. Consequently, having nothing to drink, they dug up the
ground along the banks ; but the veins thus opened
spouted up squirts of blood, which shot up as in
haemorrhages, and not a drop of clear liquid was
anywhere to be seen. Every kind of fish died 100
therein, since its life-giving properties had become
a means of destruction, so that a general stench
pervaded everything from all these bodies rotting
together. Also a great multitude of men, killed
by thirst, lay in heaps at the cross-roads, since their
relatives had not the strength to carry the dead to
the tombs. For seven days the terror reigned, until 101
the Egyptians besought Moses and his brother, and
they besought God, to take pity on the perishing.
And He Whose nature is to show mercy changed
the blood into water fit for drinking, and restored to
the river its old health-giving flood free from im-

sequel. The first three, however, are in the same order. See
Ex. vii. 14–viii. 19.

102 ῥεῖθρα καὶ σωτήρια. XVIII. μικρὸν δὲ ὅσον
ἀνεθέντες ἐπὶ τὴν αὐτὴν ὠμότητα καὶ παρανομίαν
ἵεντο, | ὡς ἢ τοῦ δικαίου παντάπασιν ἐξ ἀνθρώπων
ἀφανισθέντος ἢ τῶν ὑπομεινάντων μίαν τιμωρίαν
δεύτερον οὐκ εἰωθότων ἐπιπλήττεσθαι· παθόντες δ᾽
ἀνεδιδάσκοντο νηπίων παίδων τρόπον μὴ κατα-
φρονεῖν· ἡ γὰρ κόλασις ἑπομένη κατ᾽ ἴχνος μελλόντων μὲν ἐβράδυνε, πρὸς δὲ τὰ ἀδικήματα θέοντας
[97] ἐπιδραμοῦσα κατελάμβανε.

103 Πάλιν γὰρ ὁ Μωυσέως | ἀδελφὸς κελευσθεὶς
διώρυξι καὶ λίμναις καὶ ἕλεσι τὴν ῥάβδον ἐκτείνας
ἐπιφέρει· πρὸς δὲ τὴν ἔκτασιν βατράχων πληθὺς
ἀνέρπει τοσαύτη, ὡς μὴ μόνον ἀγορὰς καὶ πᾶσαν
τὴν ὕπαιθρον, ἀλλὰ πρὸς τούτοις ἐπαύλεις, οἰκίας,
ἱερά, πάντα ἰδιωτικὸν καὶ δημόσιον τόπον πεπλη-
ρῶσθαι, καθάπερ εἰς ἀποικίαν ἓν γένος τῶν ἐν-
ύδρων τῆς φύσεως ἐκπέμψαι διανοηθείσης πρὸς τὴν
104 ἐναντίαν χώραν· ἐναντία γὰρ χέρσος ὕδατι. μήτ᾽
οὖν ἔξω προελθεῖν ἕνεκα τοῦ προκατέχεσθαι τοὺς
στενωποὺς μήτ᾽ ἔνδον δυνάμενοι μένειν—καὶ γὰρ
τὰ ἐν μυχοῖς ἤδη προκατειλήφεσαν ἄχρι καὶ τῶν
ὑψηλοτάτων ἀνέρποντες—ἐν ἐσχάταις ἦσαν συμ-
105 φοραῖς καὶ σωτηρίας ἀπογνώσει. πάλιν οὖν κατα-
φεύγουσιν ἐπὶ τοὺς αὐτούς, ὑποσχομένου τοῦ βασιλέως ἐπιτρέψαι τὴν ἔξοδον Ἑβραίοις· οἱ δὲ λιταῖς
τὸν θεὸν ἐξευμενίζονται· καὶ ἐπινεύσαντος, τῶν
φρύνων οἱ μὲν εἰς τὸν ποταμὸν ἀναχωροῦσι, τῶν
δ᾽ εὐθὺς διαφθαρέντων κατὰ τὰς τριόδους θημῶνες
ἦσαν, σωρηδὸν ἐπιφερόντων καὶ τοὺς οἴκοθεν διὰ

purity. XVIII. For a very short time they relaxed, 102
but soon betook themselves to the same cruelty and
lawlessness as before, and seemed to think that either
justice had disappeared utterly from amongst men,
or that those who had suffered one punishment could
not be expected to receive a second blow. But, like
foolish children, they were taught once more by
experience not to despise the warning. For chastisement, dogging their steps, slowed down when they
tarried, but when they hastened to deeds of wickedness quickened its pace and overtook them.

For once more the brother of Moses, at God's com- 103
mand, stretched forth and brought his rod upon the
canals and lakes and fens ; and, as he stretched it, a
multitude of frogs crept up, so numerous that not only
the market-places and all the open spaces, but all the
farm-buildings as well, and houses and temples and
every place, public or private, was filled with them,
as though it were nature's purpose to send one kind
of the aquatic animals to colonize the opposite region,
since land is the opposite of water. The people, who 104
could neither go out into the streets, because the
passages were occupied by the frogs, nor yet stay
indoors, because they had already crept up even to
the tops of the houses and taken up the inmost recesses, were in the most unhappy and desperate
straits. So, after the king had promised them to 105
permit the Hebrews to leave the land, they fled for
refuge to those who had helped them before ; and
they made intercession with God, and when their
prayer was granted some of the frogs went back into
the river, and others died at once and lay in heaps at
the cross-roads, to which the Egyptians added the
piles of those which they brought out of their houses,

τὰς ἀνυποίστους ὀσμάς, αἳ ἐκ νεκρῶν σωμάτων καὶ
τοιούτων ἀνεφέροντο, ἃ καὶ ἔμψυχα ὄντα πολλὴν
ἀηδίαν παρέχεται ταῖς αἰσθήσεσι.

106 XIX. Διαπνεύσαντες δὲ τῆς τιμωρίας ἐπ᾽ ὀλίγον
ὥσπερ ἐν τοῖς ἀγῶσιν ἀθληταὶ συλλεξάμενοι δύναμιν, ἵν᾽ ἀπ᾽ ἐρρωμενεστέρας ἰσχύος ἀδικῶσι, πάλιν
εἰς τὴν συνήθη κακίαν ἀνέδραμον ἐκλαθόμενοι ὧν
107 τέως ὑπέμειναν κακῶν. ἐπισχὼν δὲ τὰς ἐκ τοῦ
ὕδατος τιμωρίας ὁ θεὸς τὰς ἐκ γῆς ἐπέφερε τὸν
αὐτὸν ἐπιστήσας κολαστήν, οὗ πάλιν κατὰ τὸ
προσταχθὲν τῇ βακτηρίᾳ τοὔδαφος παίσαντος φορὰ
σκνιπῶν ἐχύθη καὶ ταθεῖσα καθάπερ νέφος ἅπασαν
108 ἐπέσχεν Αἴγυπτον. τὸ δὲ ζῷον, εἰ καὶ βραχύτατον,
ὅμως ἀργαλεώτατον· οὐ γὰρ μόνον λυμαίνεται τὴν
ἐπιφάνειαν κνησμοὺς ἐμποιοῦν ἀηδεῖς καὶ βλαβερω-
τάτους, ἀλλὰ καὶ εἰς τἀντὸς βιάζεται διὰ μυκτήρων
καὶ ὤτων· σίνεται δὲ καὶ κόρας ὀφθαλμῶν εἰσπετό-
μενον, εἰ μὴ φυλάξαιτό τις· φυλακὴ δὲ τίς ἔμελλε
πρὸς τοσαύτην ἔσεσθαι φοράν, καὶ μάλιστα θεοῦ
109 κολάζοντος; ἴσως ἄν τις ἐπιζητήσειε, διὰ τί τοῖς
οὕτως ἀφανέσι καὶ ἠμελημένοις ζῴοις ἐτιμωρεῖτο
τὴν χώραν παρεὶς ἄρκτους καὶ λέοντας καὶ παρδά-
λεις καὶ τὰ ἄλλα γένη τῶν ἀτιθάσων θηρίων, ἃ
σαρκῶν ἀνθρωπείων ἅπτεται, καὶ εἰ μὴ ταῦτα, τὰς
γοῦν Αἰγυπτίας ἀσπίδας, ὧν τὰ δήγματα πέφυκεν
110 ἀνυπερθέτως ἀναιρεῖν. εἰ δ᾽ ὄντως ἀγνοεῖ, μαθέτω
πρῶτον μὲν ὅτι τοὺς οἰκήτορας τῆς χώρας ὁ θεὸς
νουθετῆσαι μᾶλλον ἐβούλετο ἢ διαφθεῖραι· βουλη-

---

[a] Or " hitherto."

[b] E.V. "lice"; R.V. in margin " or *sand-flies* or *fleas*."
Josephus (*Ant.* 300) has φθεῖρες, "lice." "Most moderns
330

because of the intolerable stench arising from the dead bodies, and bodies of a kind which, even when alive, is highly displeasing to the senses.

XIX. But, having thus obtained a short breathing- 106 space from punishment, and, like athletes in the arena, rallied their forces, only to gain fresh strength for evil-doing, they quickly returned to their familiar wickedness, forgetful of the evils which they had suffered so long.[a] Then God stayed from using water 107 to afflict them, and used the earth instead ; but appointed the same minister of chastisement, who once more, when bidden, struck the ground with his staff, when a stream of gnats[b] poured forth, and spread like a cloud over the whole extent of Egypt. Now the 108 gnat is a very small creature, but exceedingly troublesome, for it not only causes mischief to the surface of the body, and produces an unpleasant and very noxious itching, but it forces its way inside through the nostrils and ears, and also flies into and damages the pupils of the eyes, if one does not take precautions. And what precautions would be possible against such a stream, especially when it is a chastisement sent by God ? Someone perhaps may ask why 109 He punished the land through such petty and insignificant creatures, and refrained from using bears and lions and panthers and the other kinds of savage beasts which feed on human flesh ; and, if not these, at any rate the asps of Egypt, whose bites are such as to cause immediate death. If such a person really 110 does not know the answer, let him learn it : first, God wished to admonish the inhabitants of the land rather than to destroy them, for had He wished to annihilate

agree that *gnats* is the most probable rendering " (of the Hebrew word).—Driver.

PHILO

[98] θεὶς γὰρ ἀφανίζειν εἰς | ἄπαν οὐκ ἂν ζώοις ἐχρῆτο
πρὸς τὰς ἐπιθέσεις ὥσπερ συνεργοῖς, ἀλλὰ τοῖς
111 θεηλάτοις κακοῖς, λιμῷ τε καὶ λοιμῷ. μετὰ δὲ
ταῦτα κἀκεῖνο προσδιδασκέσθω μάθημα πρὸς
ἅπαντα τὸν βίον ἀναγκαῖον· τί δὲ τοῦτ' ἐστίν;
ἄνθρωποι μὲν γὰρ ὅταν πολεμῶσι, τὸ δυνατώτατον
εἰς συμμαχίαν ἐπικουρικὸν ἐξετάζουσιν, ὃ τὴν
αὑτῶν ἀσθένειαν ἐκπλήσει· θεὸς δ' ἡ ἀνωτάτω καὶ
μεγίστη δύναμις ὢν οὐδενός ἐστι χρεῖος· ἐὰν δέ που
βουληθῇ καθάπερ ὀργάνοις τισὶ χρήσασθαι πρὸς
τὰς τιμωρίας, οὐ τὰ ἐρρωμενέστατα καὶ μέγιστα
αἱρεῖται, τῆς τούτων ἀλκῆς ἥκιστα φροντίζων, ἀλλὰ
τοῖς εὐτελέσι καὶ μικροῖς ἀμάχους καὶ ἀηττήτους
δυνάμεις ἐγκατασκευάσας ἀμύνεται δι' αὐτῶν τοὺς
112 ἀδικοῦντας, καθὰ καὶ νῦν. τί γὰρ εὐτελέστερον
σκνιπός; ἀλλ' ὅμως τοσοῦτον ἴσχυσεν, ὡς ἀπ-
αγορεῦσαι πᾶσαν Αἴγυπτον καὶ ἐκβοᾶν ἀναγκα-
σθῆναι, ὅτι '' δάκτυλος θεοῦ τοῦτ' ἐστί ''· χεῖρα γὰρ
θεοῦ μηδὲ τὴν σύμπασαν οἰκουμένην ὑποστῆναι
ἂν ἀπὸ περάτων ἐπὶ πέρατα, μᾶλλον δ' οὐδὲ τὸν
σύμπαντα κόσμον.

113 XX. Τοιαῦται μὲν αἱ διὰ τοῦ Μωυσέως ἀδελφοῦ
τιμωρίαι· ἃς δὲ αὐτὸς Μωυσῆς ὑπηρέτησε καὶ ἐξ
οἵων τῆς φύσεως συνέστησαν μερῶν, κατὰ τὸ
ἀκόλουθον ἐπισκεπτέον. ἀὴρ μὲν οὖν καὶ οὐρανός,
αἱ καθαρώταται μοῖραι τῆς τῶν ὅλων οὐσίας, παρ'
ὕδατος καὶ γῆς διαδέχονται τὴν ἐπ' Αἰγύπτῳ
νουθεσίαν, ἧς ἐπίτροπος ἐχειροτονήθη Μωυσῆς.
114 ἤρξατο δὲ πρότερον τὸν ἀέρα διακινεῖν·
Αἴγυπτος γὰρ μόνη σχεδόν τι παρὰ τὰς ἐν τῷ νοτίῳ

---

[a] *i.e.* the phrase "finger of God" is interpreted as an
intervention in which only a small part of God's power is
332

them altogether He would not have taken animals to co-operate in His visitation, but calamities sent direct from heaven—pestilence and famine. And 111 after this the inquirer should be taught a further lesson, and one that is needed throughout life. What is this? When men make war, they look round to find the most powerful auxiliaries to fight beside them, and so compensate for their own weakness; but God, the highest and greatest power, needs no one. But if, at any time, He wills to use any as instruments for His vengeance, He does not choose the strongest and the greatest, of whose might He takes no account, but provides the slightest and the smallest with irresistible and invincible powers, and through them wreaks vengeance on the evil-doers. So it was in this case. For what is slighter than a 112 gnat? Yet so great was its power that all Egypt lost heart, and was forced to cry aloud: "This is the finger of God"; for as for His hand not all the habitable world from end to end could stand against it, or rather not even the whole universe.[a]

XX. Such, then, were the punishments in which 113 the brother of Moses was the agent. We have now, in due course, to examine those which were administered by Moses himself, and to shew what were the parts of nature which went to their making. We find that air and heaven, the purest portions of the universe, took on the succession to earth and water in that admonition of Egypt which Moses was appointed to superintend. First, he began 114 to cause disturbance in the air. We must remember that Egypt is almost the only country, apart from

used. For a somewhat different interpretation of the phrase see *De Mig.* 85.

κλίματι χώρας τῶν ἐτησίων ὡρῶν μίαν τὴν χει
μερινὴν οὐ παραδέχεται, τάχα μέν, ὡς λόγος, διὰ
τὸ μὴ πόρρω ζώνης διακεκαυμένης εἶναι, ῥέοντος
τοῦ πυρώδους ἐκεῖθεν ἀφανῶς καὶ τἀν κύκλῳ πάντα
ἀλεαίνοντος, τάχα δὲ ἐπεὶ καὶ ταῖς θεριναῖς τροπαῖς
πλημμυρῶν ὁ ποταμὸς προαναλίσκει τὰς νεφώσεις
115 —ἄρχεται μὲν γὰρ ἐπιβαίνειν θέρους ἐνισταμένου,
λήγει δὲ λήγοντος, ἐν ᾧ χρόνῳ καὶ οἱ ἐτησίαι
καταράττουσιν ἐξ ἐναντίας τῶν τοῦ Νείλου στο
μάτων, δι᾽ ὧν ἔτι κωλυόμενος ἐκχεῖσθαι, τῆς θα
λάσσης ὑπὸ βίας τῶν ἀνέμων πρὸς ὕψος αἰρομένης
καὶ τὰς τρικυμίας ὥσπερ μακρὸν τεῖχος ἀποτει
νούσης, ἐντὸς εἰλεῖται, κἄπειτα τῶν ῥείθρων ὑπαν
τιαζόντων τοῦ τε κατιόντος ἄνωθεν ἀπὸ τῶν πηγῶν
καὶ τοῦ θύραζε χωρεῖν ὀφείλοντος ταῖς ἀνακοπαῖς
ἀνατρέχοντος εὐρύνεσθαί τε μὴ δυναμένων (αἱ γὰρ
παρ᾽ ἑκάτερα ἐκθλίβουσιν ὄχθαι), μετεωριζόμενος
116 ὡς εἰκὸς ἐπιβαίνει—, τάχα δ᾽ ἐπεὶ καὶ περιττὸν ἦν
ἐν Αἰγύπτῳ χειμῶνα γενέσθαι· πρὸς ὃ γὰρ αἱ τῶν
ὄμβρων φοραὶ χρήσιμοι, καὶ ὁ ποταμὸς λιμνάζων
117 τὰς ἀρούρας εἰς καρπῶν ἐτησίων γένεσιν. ἡ δὲ
φύσις οὐ ματαιουργός, ὡς ὑετὸν χορηγεῖν μὴ
[99] δεομένῃ γῇ, καὶ | ἅμα χαίρει τῷ πολυτρόπῳ
καὶ πολυσχιδεῖ τῶν ἐπιστημονικῶν ἔργων τὴν συμ
φωνίαν τοῦ παντὸς ἐξ ἐναντιοτήτων ἐναρμοσαμένη·
καὶ διὰ τοῦτο τοῖς μὲν ἄνωθεν ἐξ οὐρανοῦ τοῖς δὲ
κάτωθεν ἐκ πηγῶν τε καὶ ποταμῶν παρέχει τὴν ἐξ
118 ὕδατος ὠφέλειαν.   οὕτως οὖν τῆς χώρας
διακειμένης καὶ ταῖς χειμεριναῖς ἐαριζούσης τρο
παῖς καὶ τῶν μὲν πρὸς θαλάττῃ μόναις ψεκάσιν

---

* At this point Philo's order begins to depart from that of

334

those in southern latitudes, which is unvisited by one
of the year's seasons—winter. The reason may be,
some say, that it is not far from the torrid zone, and
that the fiery heat which insensibly emanates thence
warms all its surroundings. It may be, again, that
the clouds are used up beforehand by the flooding of
the river at the summer solstice. The river begins to 115
rise as the summer opens, and ceases when it ceases,
and during that time the Etesian winds sweep down
opposite to the mouths of the Nile and put a stop to
its outflow through them. For, as the sea rises to a
great height through the violence of the winds, ex-
tending its huge billows like a long wall, it coops the
river up within ; and then as the stream which flows
from the upland springs, and the other which should
find its way out but is driven inland by the obstacles
which face it, meet each other, prevented as they
are from expanding by the banks which compress
them on either side, the river naturally rises aloft.
Another possible reason is that winter is unneeded 116
in Egypt. For the river, by making a lake of the
fields, and thus producing the yearly crops, serves
the purpose of rainfall. And, indeed, nature is no 117
wastrel in her work, to provide rain for a land which
does not want it. At the same time she rejoices to
employ her science in works of manifold variety, and
thus out of contrarieties form the harmony of the
universe. And therefore she supplies the benefit
of water to some from heaven above, to others from
the springs and rivers below. [a] Such was 118
the condition of the land, enjoying springtime at
mid-winter, the seaboard enriched by only slight

Exodus. His fourth plague, that of hail, is seventh in
Exodus (ix. 22-35).

PHILO

ἀραιαῖς λιπαινομένων, τῶν δ' ὑπὲρ Μέμφιν, τὸ
βασίλειον Αἰγύπτου, μηδὲ νιφομένων τὸ παράπαν,
ἐξαίφνης οὕτως ἐνεωτέρισεν ὁ ἀήρ, ὥσθ' ὅσα ἐν
τοῖς δυσχειμέροις ἀθρόα κατασκῆψαι, φορὰς ὑετῶν,
χάλαζαν πολλὴν καὶ βαρεῖαν, ἀνέμων συμπιπτόντων
καὶ ἀντιπαταγούντων βίας, νεφῶν ῥήξεις, ἐπαλλήλους ἀστραπὰς καὶ βροντάς, κεραυνοὺς συνεχεῖς,
οἳ τερατωδεστάτην ὄψιν παρείχοντο· θέοντες γὰρ
διὰ τῆς χαλάζης, μαχομένης οὐσίας, οὔτε ἔτηκον
αὐτὴν οὔτε ἐσβέννυντο, μένοντες δ' ἐν ὁμοίῳ καὶ
δολιχεύοντες ἄνω καὶ κάτω διετήρουν τὴν χάλαζαν.
119 ἀλλ' οὐ μόνον ἡ ἐξαίσιος φορὰ πάντων τοὺς οἰκήτορας εἰς ὑπερβαλλούσας δυσθυμίας ἤγαγεν, ἀλλὰ
καὶ τὸ τοῦ πράγματος ἄηθες· ὑπέλαβον γάρ, ὅπερ
καὶ ἦν, ἐκ μηνιμάτων θείων κεκαινουργῆσθαι τὰ
συμβάντα, νεωτερίσαντος ὡς οὔπω πρότερον τοῦ
ἀέρος ἐπὶ λύμῃ καὶ φθορᾷ δένδρων τε καὶ καρπῶν,
οἷς συνεφθάρη ζῷα οὐκ ὀλίγα, τὰ μὲν περιψύξει,
τὰ δὲ βάρει τῆς ἐπιπιπτούσης χαλάζης ὥσπερ
καταλευσθέντα, τὰ δ' ὑπὸ τοῦ πυρὸς ἐξαναλω-
θέντα· ἔνια δ' ἡμίφλεκτα διέμενε τοὺς τύπους τῶν
κεραυνίων τραυμάτων εἰς νουθεσίαν τῶν ὁρώντων
ἐπιφερόμενα.
120 XXI. Λωφήσαντος δὲ τοῦ κακοῦ καὶ πάλιν τοῦ
βασιλέως καὶ τῶν περὶ αὐτὸν θρασυνομένων, εἰς
τὸν ἀέρα Μωυσῆς τὴν ῥάβδον ἐκτείνει, κελεύσαντος
τοῦ θεοῦ. κἄπειτ' ἄνεμος καταράττει, νότος βιαιότατος, ὅλην τὴν ἡμέραν καὶ νύκτα προσεπι-
τεινόμενος καὶ σφοδρυνόμενος, αὐτὸς καθ' αὐτὸν ὢν

ᵃ Philo's fifth plague, the locusts, is eighth in Exodus
(x. 12-10).

showers, while the parts above Memphis, where the royal palace of Egypt was, experienced no rainfall at all, when suddenly a complete change came over the air, and all the visitations which belong to severe winter fell upon it in a body : rainstorms, a great quantity of heavy hail, violent winds, clashing and roaring against each other, cloudbursts, continuous claps of thunder and flashes of lightning and constant thunderbolts. These last provided a most marvellous spectacle, for they ran through the hail, their natural antagonist, and yet did not melt it nor were quenched by it, but unchanged coursed up and down and kept guard over the hail. Intense was the despondency 119 to which the inhabitants were reduced, not only by the disastrous onset of all these things, but by the strangeness of the event. For they thought, as indeed was the case, that divine wrath had brought about these novel happenings ; that the air in a way unknown before had conspired to ruin and destroy the trees and fruits, while at the same time many animals perished, some through excessive cold, others stoned to death, as it were, through the weight of the falling hail, others consumed by the fire, while some survived half-burnt and bore the marks of the wounds inflicted by the thunderbolts as a warning to the beholders.

XXI. When the plague abated, and the king and 120 his surroundings recovered their courage, Moses, at God's command,[a] stretched his rod into the air, and then a violent south [b] wind swooped down, gaining force and intensity throughout the day and night. This in itself was a source of much mischief, for the

[b] E.V. east wind (including winds at least from the south-east.—Driver).

μεγάλη ζημία· ξηρός τε γάρ ἐστι καὶ κεφαλαλγὴς
καὶ βαρυήκοος, ἄσας τε καὶ ἀδημονίας ἐμποιεῖν
ἱκανός, καὶ μάλιστ᾽ ἐν Αἰγύπτῳ κειμένῃ κατὰ τὰ
νότια, δι᾽ ὧν αἱ περιπολήσεις τῶν φωσφόρων
ἀστέρων, ὡς ἅμα τῷ διακινηθῆναι τὸν ἀφ᾽ ἡλίου
121 φλογμὸν συνεπωθεῖσθαι καὶ πάντα καίειν. ἀλλὰ
γὰρ ἅμ᾽ αὐτῷ καὶ πλῆθος ἀμήχανον ζῴων ἐπ-
εφέρετο φθοροποιὸν φυτῶν, ἀκρίδες, αἳ ῥεύματος
τρόπον ἀπαύστως ἐκχεόμεναι καὶ πάντα πληρώ-
σασαι τὸν ἀέρα διέφαγον ὅσα οἱ κεραυνοὶ ὑπ-
[100] ελίποντο καὶ ἡ χάλαζα, ὡς | μηδὲν ἐν τῇ τοσαύ-
122 τῃ χώρᾳ βλαστάνον ἔτι θεωρεῖσθαι. τότε μόλις εἰς
ἀκριβεστάτην ἔννοιαν τῶν οἰκείων ἐλθόντες οἱ
ἐν τέλει κακῶν προσελθόντες ἔλεγον τῷ βασιλεῖ·
" μέχρι τίνος οὐκ ἐπιτρέπεις τὴν ἔξοδον τοῖς ἀνδράσιν; ἢ οὔπω μανθάνεις ἐκ τῶν γινομένων,
ὅτι ἀπόλωλεν Αἴγυπτος;" ὁ δ᾽ ὅσα τῷ δοκεῖν
ἐφιεὶς ὡμολόγει, χαλάσαντος τοῦ δεινοῦ. πάλιν δ᾽
εὐξαμένου Μωυσέως, ὑπολαβὼν ἐκ τῆς θαλάττης
ἄνεμος ἀποσκίδνησι τὰς ἀκρίδας.

123 Ἀνασκεδασθεισῶν δὲ καὶ τοῦ βασιλέως περὶ τὴν
τοῦ ἔθνους ἄφεσιν δυσθανατοῦντος, ἐπιγίνεται τῶν
πρότερον κακῶν μεῖζον· λαμπρᾶς γὰρ ἡμέρας οὔσης,
ἐξαπιναίως ἀναχεῖται σκότος, ἴσως μὲν καὶ ἡλίου
γενομένης ἐκλείψεως τῶν ἐν ἔθει τελειοτέρας, ἴσως
δὲ καὶ συνεχείαις νεφῶν καὶ πυκνότησιν ἀδια-
στάτοις καὶ πιλήσει βιαιοτάτῃ τῆς τῶν ἀκτίνων
φορᾶς ἀνακοπείσης, ὡς ἀδιαφορεῖν ἡμέραν νυκτὸς
καὶ τί γὰρ ἄλλ᾽ ἢ μίαν νύκτα νομίζεσθαι μακρο-

south wind is dry and produces headache and makes hearing difficult, and thus is fitted to cause distress and suffering, particularly in Egypt which lies well to the south, where the sun and the planets have their orbits, so that when the wind sets it in motion the scorching of the sun is pushed forward with it, and burns up everything. But it also brought with 121 it a huge multitude of creatures which destroyed the plants, locusts that is, who poured forth ceaselessly like a stream, and filling the whole air devoured whatever the lightnings and hail had left, so that nothing any longer could be seen growing in all that great country. Then those in authority, reluctantly 122 brought to a full realization of their own evil plight, approached the king and said : " How long will you refuse to grant these men leave to depart ? Do you not yet understand that Egypt is destroyed ? " The king yielded, or appeared to do so, and promised to comply if he were relieved from the dire scourge. And when Moses prayed again, a wind from the sea caught and scattered the locusts.

But, when they were scattered, and the king was 123 sick to death at the thought of releasing the people, a plague [a] arose greater than all that had gone before ; for, in bright daylight, darkness was suddenly overspread, possibly because there was an eclipse of the sun more complete than the ordinary, or perhaps because the stream of rays was cut off by continuous clouds, compressed with great force into masses of unbroken density. The result was that night and day were the same, and indeed what else could it seem but a single night of great length, equivalent to three

[a] Philo's sixth plague, the darkness, is ninth in Exodus (x. 21-29).

τάτην τρισὶν ἢ μέραις ἴσην καὶ ταῖς ἰσαρίθμοις νυξί.
124 τότε δή φασι τοὺς μὲν ἐρριμμένους ἐν ταῖς εὐναῖς
μὴ τολμᾶν ἐξανίστασθαι, τοὺς δ' ὁπότε κατεπείγοι
τι τῶν τῆς φύσεως ἀναγκαίων ἐπαφωμένους τοίχων
ἢ τινος ἑτέρου καθάπερ τυφλοὺς μόλις προέρχεσθαι·
καὶ γὰρ τοῦ χρειώδους πυρὸς τὸ φέγγος τὸ μὲν ὑπὸ
τῆς κατεχούσης ζάλης ἐσβέννυτο, τὸ δὲ τῷ βάθει
τοῦ σκότους ἀμαυρούμενον ἐνηφανίζετο, ὡς τὴν
ἀναγκαιοτάτην ὄψιν τῶν αἰσθήσεων ὑγιαίνουσαν
πηρὸν εἶναι μηδὲν ὁρᾶν δυναμένην, τετράφθαι δὲ καὶ
τὰς ἄλλας οἷα ὑπηκόους πεσούσης τῆς ἡγεμονίδος·
125 οὔτε γὰρ λέγειν τις οὔτ' ἀκούειν οὔτε προσενέγκα-
σθαι τροφὰς ὑπέμενεν, ἀλλ' ἡσυχίᾳ καὶ λιμῷ παρ-
έτεινον αὐτοὺς οὐδεμιᾷ τῶν αἰσθήσεων σχολάζοντες,
ἀλλ' ὑπὸ τοῦ πάθους ὅλοι συνηρπασμένοι, μέχρι
πάλιν Μωυσῆς λαβὼν οἶκτον ἱκετεύει τὸν θεόν· ὁ
δὲ φῶς ἀντὶ σκότους καὶ ἡμέραν ἀντὶ νυκτὸς ἐργάζεται σὺν αἰθρίᾳ πολλῇ.
126 XXII. Τοιαύτας φασὶ γενέσθαι καὶ τὰς διὰ
μόνου Μωυσέως ἐπιπλήξεις, τὴν διὰ χαλάζης καὶ
κεραυνῶν, τὴν διὰ τῆς ἀκρίδος, τὴν διὰ σκότους, ὃ
πᾶσαν ἰδέαν φωτὸς οὐ παρεδέχετο· κοινῇ δ' αὐτός
τε καὶ ὁ ἀδελφὸς μίαν ἐπετράπησαν, ἣν αὐτίκα
127 σημανῶ. κελεύσαντος τοῦ θεοῦ, τέφραν ἀπὸ κα-
μίνου λαμβάνουσι ταῖς χερσίν, ἣν Μωυσῆς κατὰ
μέρος εἰς τὸν ἀέρα διέπαττεν· ἔπειτα κονιορτὸς
αἰφνίδιον ἐπενεχθεὶς ἀνθρώποις τε καὶ ἀλόγοις
ζῴοις ἀγρίαν καὶ δυσαλγῆ κατὰ τῆς δορᾶς ἁπάσης
[101] ἕλκωσιν εἰργάζετο καὶ τὰ σώματα εὐθὺς | συνῴδει

ᵃ Or "fire of common use," cf. De Abr. 157, Quis
Rerum 136.

days and the same number of nights? Then, in- 124
deed, as we are told, some who had thrown themselves on their beds did not dare to rise from them,
while others, when any of the needs of nature pressed,
felt their way along the walls or any other object,
proceeding with difficulty as though they were blind.
For the light of artificial fire *a* was partly quenched
by the prevailing storm wind, partly dimmed to the
point of disappearance by the depth of the darkness,
so that sight, the most indispensable of the senses,
though sound in itself, was helpless and unable to see
anything; and the other senses were discomfited,
like subjects when their queen has fallen. For men 125
could not bring themselves to speak or hear or take
food, but lay tortured in silence and famine with no
heart to use any of the senses, so entirely overwhelmed were they by the disaster, until Moses
again took pity and besought God, Who made light
to take the place of darkness, and day of night, with
bright open sky all around.

XXII. Such, we are told, were the plagues *b* in- 126
flicted through the agency of Moses alone, namely
the plague of hail and lightning, the plague of the
locusts, and that of the darkness which was proof
against every form of light. One was committed
to him and his brother together, which I will at once
proceed to describe. They took in their hands, at 127
God's bidding, ashes from a furnace, which Moses
scattered in the air, and then dust suddenly fell
upon men and the lower animals alike. It produced
an angry, painful ulceration over the whole skin,
and, simultaneously with this eruption, their bodies

b Philo's seventh plague, boils, is sixth in Exodus (ix.
8-12).

ταῖς ἐξανθήσεσιν ὑποπύους ἔχοντα φλυκταίνας,
ἃς ἐτόπασεν ἄν τις ἀφανῶς ὑποκαιομένας ἀναζεῖν.
128 ἀλγηδόσι τε καὶ περιωδυνίαις κατὰ τὸ εἰκὸς ἐκ τῆς
ἑλκώσεως καὶ φλογώσεως πιεζόμενοι μᾶλλον ἢ οὐχ
ἧττον τῶν σωμάτων τὰς ψυχὰς ἔκαμνον ἐκτετρυχω-
μένοι ταῖς ἀνίαις—ἓν γὰρ ἄν τις ἀπὸ κεφαλῆς ἄχρι
ποδῶν συνεχὲς ἕλκος ἐθεάσατο, τῶν κατὰ μέλος καὶ
μέρος διεσπαρμένων εἰς μίαν καὶ τὴν αὐτὴν ἰδέαν
ἀποκριθέντων—, ἕως πάλιν ἱκεσίαις τοῦ νομοθέτου,
ἃς ὑπὲρ τῶν πασχόντων ἐποιήσατο, ἡ νόσος ῥᾴων
129 ἐγένετο. κοινῇ μέντοι τὴν νουθεσίαν ταύτην ἐπετράπησαν δεόντως, ὁ μὲν ἀδελφὸς διὰ τὸν ἐπενε-
χθέντα κονιορτόν, ἐπεὶ τῶν ἀπὸ γῆς συμβαινόντων
τὴν ἐπιμέλειαν ἔλαχε, Μωυσῆς δὲ διὰ τὸν ἀέρα
μεταβαλόντα πρὸς κάκωσιν τῶν οἰκητόρων· ταῖς δ'
ἀπ' ἀέρος καὶ οὐρανοῦ πληγαῖς οὗτος ὑπηρέτει.
130   XXIII. Λοιπαὶ δὲ τιμωρίαι τρεῖς εἰσιν αὐτουρ-
γηθεῖσαι δίχα τῆς ἀνθρώπων ὑπηρεσίας, ὧν κατὰ
μίαν ἑκάστην, ὡς ἂν οἷόν τε ᾖ, δηλώσω. πρώτη δ'
ἐστὶν ἡ γενομένη διὰ ζῴου τῶν ἐν τῇ φύσει πάντων
θρασυτάτου, κυνομυίας, ἣν ἐτύμως ἐκάλεσαν οἱ
θετικοὶ τῶν ὀνομάτων—σοφοὶ γὰρ ἦσαν—ἐκ τῶν
ἀναιδεστάτων ζῴων συνθέντες τοὔνομα, μυίας καὶ
κυνός, τοῦ μὲν τῶν χερσαίων θρασυτάτου, τῆς
δὲ τῶν πτηνῶν· ἐπιφοιτῶσι γὰρ καὶ ἐπιτρέχουσιν
ἀδεῶς, κἂν ἀνείργῃ τις, εἰς τὸ ἀήττητον ἀντιφιλο-
νεικοῦσιν, ἄχρις ἂν αἵματος καὶ σαρκῶν κορε-
131 σθῶσιν. ἡ δὲ κυνόμυια τὴν ἀφ' ἑκατέρου τόλμαν

ᵃ Philo's eighth plague, dog-flies (E.V. flies), is fourth in
Exodus (viii. 20-30).

swelled with suppurated blisters, which might be supposed to be extravasations from inflammation lurking beneath. Oppressed as they naturally were 128 by the extreme painfulness and soreness of the ulceration and inflammation, they suffered in spirit more or no less than in body from the exhaustion which their miseries produced. For one continuous ulcer was to be seen stretching from head to foot, the sores scattered over every particular limb and part of the body being concentrated into a single form of the same appearance throughout. So it was until, again by the intercessions which the lawgiver made on behalf of the sufferers, the distemper was lightened. Rightly indeed was this chastisement 129 committed to the two in common : to the brother because the dust which came down upon the people was from the earth, and what was of earth was under his charge ; to Moses because the air was changed to afflict them, and plagues of heaven and air belonged to his ministration.

XXIII. The three remaining chastisements were 130 self-wrought, without any human agent, each of which I will proceed to describe as well as possible. In the first, a creature is employed whose ferocity is unequalled in all nature—the dog-fly.[a] This name, which the coiners of words in their wisdom have given it, well expresses its character, for it is a compound formed from the two most shameless animals of the land and the air—the dog and the fly. Both these are persistent and fearless in their assaults, and if one attempts to ward them off meet him with a perseverance which refuses to be beaten, until they have got their fill of flesh and blood. The dog-fly 131 has acquired the audacity of both, and is a creature

343

προσειληφυῖα δηκτικὸν καὶ ἐπίβουλον ζῷόν ἐστι·
καὶ γὰρ πόρρωθεν μετὰ ῥοίζου καθάπερ βέλος
εἰσακοντίζεται καὶ ἐπεμπίπτουσα βιαίως εὖ μάλα
132 ἐγχρίμπτεται. τότε δὲ καὶ θεήλατος ἦν ἡ προσ-
βολή, ὡς δεδιπλασιάσθαι τὴν ἐξ αὐτῆς ἐπιβουλὴν
οὐκέτι μόνον τοῖς φυσικοῖς κεχρημένης πλεονεκτή-
μασιν, ἀλλὰ καὶ τοῖς ἐκ θείας ἐπιφροσύνης, ἢ τὸ
ζῷον ὥπλιζε καὶ πρὸς ἀλκὴν ἀνήγειρε κατὰ τῶν
133 ἐγχωρίων.   μετὰ τὴν κυνόμυιαν εἵπετο
τιμωρία πάλιν ἄνευ συμπράξεως ἀνθρωπίνης, βοσκημάτων θάνατος· βουκόλια γὰρ καὶ αἰπόλια καὶ
ποίμνια μεγάλα καὶ ὅσαι ὑποζυγίων καὶ ἄλλων
θρεμμάτων ἰδέαι πᾶσαι μιᾷ ἡμέρᾳ, ὡς ἀφ' ἑνὸς
συνθήματος, ἀγεληδὸν διεφθείροντο, τὴν ἀνθρώπων
[102] | ἀπώλειαν, ἢ μικρὸν ὕστερον ἔμελλε γίνεσθαι,
προμηνύουσαι καθάπερ ἐν ταῖς λοιμώδεσι νόσοις·
λέγεται γὰρ προάγων τις εἶναι λοιμικῶν ἀρρωστη-
μάτων ἡ ζῴων ἀλόγων αἰφνίδιος φθορά.
134   XXIV. Μεθ' ἣν ἡ δεκάτη καὶ τελευταία δίκη
πάσας ὑπερβάλλουσα τὰς προτέρας ἐπεγένετο, θάνατος Αἰγυπτίων οὔτε πάντων—οὐ γὰρ ἐρημῶσαι
τὴν χώραν προῃρεῖτο ὁ θεὸς ἀλλὰ νουθετῆσαι μόνον
—οὔτε τῶν πλείστων ἀνδρῶν ὁμοῦ καὶ γυναικῶν ἐξ
ἁπάσης ἡλικίας, ἀλλὰ τοῖς ἄλλοις ζῆν ἐφιεὶς μόνων
τῶν πρωτοτόκων καταψηφίζεται θάνατον ἀρξάμενος ἀπὸ τοῦ πρεσβυτάτου τῶν βασιλέως παίδων
καὶ λήξας εἰς τὸν τῆς ἀφανεστάτης ἀλετρίδος.
135 περὶ γὰρ μέσας νύκτας οἱ πρῶτοι πατέρας καὶ
μητέρας προσειπόντες καὶ ὑπ' ἐκείνων υἱοὶ πάλιν

venomous and vicious, which comes with a whirr
from a distance, hurls itself like a javelin, and, with
a violent onrush, fastens itself firmly on its victim.
On this occasion the assault was also divinely im- 132
pelled, so that its viciousness was doubled, prompted
by avidity due not only to nature but to divine providence, which armed the creature and roused it to
use its force against the population.

After the dog-fly there followed again a chastise- 133
ment brought about without human co-operation,
the death of the live-stock *a*; for great herds of oxen
and sheep and goats, and every kind of beast of
burden and other cattle, perished as by a single agreed
signal in a single day, whole droves at a time, thus
presaging the destruction of men which was about
to follow, just as we find in epidemics. For pestilential disorders are said to be preluded by a sudden
murrain among the lower animals.

XXIV. After this came the tenth and final judge- 134
ment, transcending all its predecessors.*b* This was
the death of the Egyptians, not of the whole population, since God's purpose was not to make a complete
desert of the country, but only to teach them a lesson,
nor yet of the great majority of the men and women
of every age. Instead, He permitted the rest to live,
but sentenced the first-born only to death, beginning
with the king and ending with the meanest woman
who grinds at the mill, in each case their eldest male
child. For, about midnight, those who had been the 135
first to call their parents father and mother, first to

a Philo's ninth plague, the murrain, is fifth in Exodus
(ix. 1-7).
b For the tenth plague, and its sequel §§ 134-142, see
Ex. xii. 29-36.

πρῶτον ὀνομασθέντες ὑγιαίνοντες καὶ τὰ σώματα
ἐρρωμένοι πάντες ἀπ' οὐδεμιᾶς προφάσεως ἡβηδὸν
ἐξαπιναίως ἀνήρηντο καὶ οὐδεμίαν οἰκίαν ἀμοιρῆσαί
136 φασι τότε τῆς συμφορᾶς. ἅμα δὲ τῇ ἕῳ κατὰ τὸ
εἰκὸς ἕκαστοι θεασάμενοι τοὺς φιλτάτους ἀπροσ-
δοκήτως τετελευτηκότας, οἷς ὁμοδίαιτοι καὶ ὁμο-
τράπεζοι μέχρι τῆς ἑσπέρας ἐγεγένητο, βαρυτάτῳ
πένθει κατασχεθέντες οἰμωγῆς πάντα ἐνέπλησαν,
ὥστε συνέβη καὶ διὰ τὴν κοινοπραγίαν τοῦ πάθους
ἁπάντων ἀθρόως ὁμοθυμαδὸν ἐκβοησάντων ἕνα
θρῆνον ἀπὸ περάτων ἐπὶ πέρατα κατὰ πάσης τῆς
137 χώρας συνηχῆσαι. καὶ μέχρι μὲν ἐν ταῖς οἰκίαις
διέτριβον, ἀγνῶν ἕκαστος τὸ τοῦ πλησίον κακὸν
ἐπὶ τῷ ἑαυτοῦ μόνον ἔστενε, προελθὼν δὲ καὶ γνοὺς
τὰ τῶν ἄλλων διπλοῦν πένθος πρὸς τῷ ἰδίῳ καὶ τὸ
κοινὸν εὐθὺς ἐλάμβανεν, ἐπ' ἐλάττονι καὶ κουφοτέρῳ
μεῖζον καὶ βαρύτερον, ἅτε καὶ τὴν ἐλπίδα τῆς παραμυθίας ἀφῃρημένος· τίς γὰρ ἔμελλε παρηγορεῖν
138 ἕτερον αὐτὸς ὢν τοῦδε χρεῖος; ὅπερ δ' ἐν τοῖς
τοιούτοις φιλεῖ, τὰ παρόντα νομίσαντες ἀρχὴν εἶναι
μειζόνων καὶ περὶ τῆς τῶν ἔτι ζώντων ἀπωλείας
καταδείσαντες συνέδραμον εἰς τὰ βασίλεια δεδακρυμένοι καὶ τὰς ἐσθῆτας περιερρηγμένοι κατεβόων τε
τοῦ βασιλέως ὡς πάντων αἰτίου τῶν συμβεβηκότων
139 δεινῶν. εἰ γάρ, ἔλεγον, εὐθὺς ἐν ἀρχῇ Μωυσέως
ἐντυχόντος εἴασεν ἐξελθεῖν τὸ ἔθνος, οὐδενὸς ἂν
τῶν γεγονότων πειραθῆναι τὸ παράπαν· εἴξαντος
δ' αὐθαδείᾳ τῇ συνήθει, τὰ ἐπίχειρα τῆς ἀκαίρου
φιλονεικίας ἐξ ἑτοίμου λαβεῖν. εἶτ' ἄλλος ἄλλον
παρεκάλει τὸν λεὼν μετὰ πάσης σπουδῆς ἐξ ἁπάσης

─────────────────────────

ᵃ Cf. πρώτη σ' ἐκάλεσα πατέρα καὶ σὺ παῖδ' ἐμέ, Eur. Iph.
Aul. 122.

be called sons by them,[a] all in full health and robust of body, were suddenly cut off wholesale without apparent cause, and no household, as we are told, was spared this calamity. When dawn came, every 136 family, seeing their dearest thus unexpectedly dead, who, up till the evening, had shared their home and board, were naturally struck with profound grief and filled the whole place with their lamentations. And so, since in this general disaster the same emotion drew from all a united outcry, one single dirge of wailing resounded from end to end of the whole land. And, 137 as long as they stayed in their houses, everyone, ignorant of his neighbour's evil plight, bewailed his own only; but, when they came forth and learned what had befallen the rest, their grief was straightway doubled. To the personal sorrow, the lighter and lesser, was added the public, greater and heavier, since they lost even the hope of consolation. For who could be expected to comfort another if he needs consolation himself? And, as so often happens in 138 such circumstances, they thought that their present condition was but the beginning of greater evils, and were filled with fear of the destruction of those who still lived. Consequently, bathed in tears and with garments rent, they rushed together to the palace and cried out against the king as the cause of all the dire events that had befallen them. If, they said, 139 at the very beginning, when Moses first entreated him, he had suffered the people to go forth, they would have experienced none at all of these happenings; but, as he indulged his usual self-will, the rewards of his contentiousness had been promptly reaped by themselves. Then they exhorted each other to use all speed in driving the people from the

τῆς χώρας ἐξελαύνειν, καὶ τὸ μίαν ἡμέραν μᾶλλον
δὲ ὥραν αὐτὸ μόνον κατασχεῖν πρὸς ἀνήκεστον
τιμωρίαν τιθέμενοι.   XXV. | οἱ δ᾽ ἐλαυ-
νόμενοι καὶ διωκόμενοι τῆς αὐτῶν εὐγενείας εἰς
ἔννοιαν ἐλθόντες τόλμημα τολμῶσιν, ὁποῖον εἰκὸς
ἦν τοὺς ἐλευθέρους καὶ μὴ ἀμνήμονας ὧν ἐπεβου-
λεύθησαν ἀδίκως. πολλὴν γὰρ λείαν ἐκφορήσαντες
τὴν μὲν αὐτοὶ διεκόμιζον ἐπηχθισμένοι, τὴν δὲ τοῖς
ὑποζυγίοις ἐπέθεσαν, οὐ διὰ φιλοχρηματίαν ἤ, ὡς
ἄν τις κατηγορῶν εἴποι, τὴν τῶν ἀλλοτρίων ἐπιθυμίαν—πόθεν;—ἀλλὰ πρῶτον μὲν ὧν παρὰ πάντα
τὸν χρόνον ὑπηρέτησαν ἀναγκαῖον μισθὸν κομιζό-
μενοι, εἶτα δὲ ὑπὲρ ὧν κατεδουλώθησαν ἐν ἐλάττοσι
καὶ οὐχὶ τοῖς ἴσοις ἀντιλυποῦντες· ποῦ γὰρ ἐσθ᾽
ὅμοιον ζημία χρημάτων καὶ στέρησις ἐλευθερίας,
ὑπὲρ ἧς οὐ μόνον προΐεσθαι τὰς οὐσίας οἱ νοῦν
ἔχοντες ἀλλὰ καὶ ἀποθνῄσκειν ἐθέλουσιν; ἐν ἑκατέρῳ δὴ κατώρθουν, εἴθ᾽ ὡς ἐν εἰρήνῃ μισθὸν
λαμβάνοντες, ὃν παρ᾽ ἀκόντων[1] πολὺν χρόνον οὐκ
ἀποδιδόντων ἀπεστεροῦντο, εἴθ᾽ ὡς ἐν πολέμῳ τὰ
τῶν ἐχθρῶν φέρειν ἀξιοῦντες νόμῳ τῶν κεκρα-
τηκότων· οἱ μὲν γὰρ χειρῶν ἦρξαν ἀδίκων, ξένους
καὶ ἱκέτας, ὡς ἔφην πρότερον, καταδουλωσάμενοι
τρόπον αἰχμαλώτων, οἱ δὲ καιροῦ παραπεσόντος
ἠμύναντο δίχα τῆς ἐν ὅπλοις παρασκευῆς, προασπί-
ζοντος καὶ τὴν χεῖρα ὑπερέχοντος τοῦ δικαίου.

143   XXVI. Τοσαύταις μὲν δὴ πληγαῖς καὶ τιμωρίαις
Αἴγυπτος ἐνουθετεῖτο, ὧν οὐδεμία τῶν Ἑβραίων

___
[1] The mss. vary here considerably and the construction in
the text as here printed is difficult. A simple emendation
would be λαμβάνοντες παρ᾽ ἀκόντων ὄν, and so, except that ἃ
appears instead of ὄν, it is in the paraphrase of Procopius
quoted in Cohn, p. 153.

whole country, and declared that to detain them even
for a single day, or rather only for an hour, would bring
upon them a deadly vengeance.   XXV.
The Hebrews, thus hunted as outcasts from the land, 140
and conscious of their own high lineage, were emboldened to act as was natural to them, as freemen
and men who were not oblivious of the injustices
which malice had inflicted on them ; for they took 141
out with them much spoil, which they carried partly
on their backs, partly laid on their beasts of burden.
And they did this not in avarice, or, as their accusers
might say, in covetousness of what belonged to
others. No, indeed. In the first place, they were
but receiving a bare wage for all their time of service ;
secondly, they were retaliating, not on an equal but
on a lesser scale, for their enslavement. For what
resemblance is there between forfeiture of money and
deprivation of liberty, for which men of sense are
willing to sacrifice not only their substance but their
life ? In either case, their action was right, whether 142
one regard it as an act of peace, the acceptance of
payment long kept back through reluctance to pay
what was due, or as an act of war, the claim under
the law of the victors to take their enemies' goods.
For the Egyptians began the wrongdoing by reducing
guests and suppliants to slavery like captives, as I
said before. The Hebrews, when the opportunity
came, avenged themselves without warlike preparations, shielded by justice whose arm was extended
to defend them.

    XXVI. With all these plagues and punishments 143
was Egypt admonished, none of which touched the

καίτοι γε ἐν ταῖς αὐταῖς πόλεσι καὶ κώμαις καὶ
οἰκίαις συνδιατριβόντων ἥψατο, γῆς ὕδατος ἀέρος
πυρός, ἃ μέρη τῆς φύσεώς ἐστιν, ἣν ἀμήχανον
ἐκφυγεῖν, ἐπιθεμένων· ὃ δὴ καὶ παραδοξότατον ἦν,
ὑπὸ τῶν αὐτῶν κατὰ τὸν αὐτὸν τόπον καὶ χρόνον
144 τοὺς μὲν διαφθείρεσθαι, τοὺς δὲ σῴζεσθαι. ὁ
ποταμὸς εἰς αἷμα μετέβαλεν, ἀλλ᾽ οὐχ Ἑβραίοις·
ἡνίκα γὰρ βουληθεῖεν ἀρύσασθαι, τροπὴν ἐλάμβανεν
εἰς πότιμον. βάτραχος ἐκ τῶν ὑδάτων ἐπὶ τὴν
χέρσον ἀνερπύσας ἀγορὰς καὶ ἐπαύλεις καὶ οἰκίας
ἐπλήρωσεν, ἀλλ᾽ ἀπὸ τῶν Ἑβραίων ἐξανεχώρει
μόνων καθάπερ διακρίνειν ἐπιστάμενος, οὕς τε χρὴ
145 κολάζεσθαι καὶ τοὐναντίον. οὐ σκνῖπες, οὐ κυνόμυια, οὐκ ἀκρίς, ἣ καὶ φυτὰ καὶ καρποὺς καὶ
ζῷα καὶ ἀνθρώπους μεγάλα ἔβλαψε, τούτοις προσ-
έπτησαν· οὐχ ὑετῶν, οὐ χαλάζης, οὐ κεραυνῶν αἱ
[104] γενόμεναι | συνεχεῖς φοραὶ μέχρι τούτων ἔφθασαν·
ἑλκώσεως τῆς ἀργαλεωτάτης εἰς τὸ παθεῖν οὐδ᾽
ὄναρ ἐπῄσθοντο· βαθυτάτου σκότους τοῖς ἄλλοις
ἀναχυθέντος, ἐν αὐγῇ καθαρᾷ διήγαγον, τοῦ ἡμε-
ρησίου φωτὸς ἐπιλάμποντος· ἀναιρουμένων τῶν
παρ᾽ Αἰγυπτίοις πρωτοτόκων, ἐτελεύτησεν Ἑβραῖος
οὐδείς· οὐδὲ γὰρ εἰκὸς ἦν, ὁπότε καὶ ἡ τῶν ἀμυ-
θήτων φθορὰ θρεμμάτων οὐδεμίαν τῶν παρὰ τούτοις
146 ἀγέλην συνεπεσπάσατο πρὸς ἀπώλειαν. καί μοί τις
δοκεῖ παρατυχὼν τοῖς γενομένοις κατ᾽ ἐκεῖνον τὸν
καιρὸν μηδὲν ἂν ἄλλο νομίσαι τοὺς Ἑβραίους ἢ
θεατὰς ὧν ἕτεροι κακῶν ὑπέμενον καὶ οὐ μόνον[1]

---

[1] Cohn, following Clem. Al. *Strom.* i. 23 θεαταὶ δὲ Ἑβραῖοι
ἐγένοντο ὧν ἕτεροι κακῶν ὑπέμενον ἀκινδύνως ἐκμανθάνοντες τὴν
δύναμιν τοῦ θεοῦ, proposed to fill the lacuna with the last five

Hebrews, though they dwelt in the same cities and villages and houses, and though earth, water, air, fire, the constituent parts of that nature which it is impossible to escape, joined in the attack. And the strangest thing of all was that the same elements in the same place and at the same time brought destruction to one people and safety to the other. The river 144 changed to blood, but not for the Hebrews; for, when they wished to draw from it, it turned into good drinking-water. The frog tribe crept from the water on to the land, and filled the market-places, the farm buildings and houses, but held aloof from the Hebrews alone, as though it knew how to distinguish who should be punished and who should not. Neither the gnats, nor the dog-flies nor the 145 locusts, which did so great damage to plants and fruits and animals and men, winged their way to them; neither the rainstorm nor the hail nor the thunderbolts which fell continuously reached as far as them. That most painful ulceration was not felt, or even imagined, by them. When the others were wrapped in profound darkness, they lived in clear radiance with the light of day shining upon them. When the first-born of the Egyptians was slain, no Hebrew died, nor was it likely that they should, when even the murrain, by which numberless cattle perished, did not involve a single herd of theirs in the destruction. Indeed, I think that everyone 146 who witnessed the events of that time could not but have thought of the Hebrews as spectators of the sufferings of others, and not merely spectators

---

words of the quotation. Mangey was content with τοῦτο only. Perhaps ἀκινδύνους alone would be enough, Clement's remaining five words representing εὐσέβειαν.

. . ., ἀλλὰ καὶ μαθημάτων τὸ κάλλιστον καὶ ὠφελιμώτατον ἀναδιδασκομένους, εὐσέβειαν· οὐ γάρ ποθ' οὕτως ἡ τῶν ἀγαθῶν καὶ κακῶν κρίσις ἐμφανῶς ἦλθε τοῖς μὲν φθορὰν τοῖς δὲ σωτηρίαν παρασχοῦσα.

147 XXVII. Τῶν δ' ἐξιόντων καὶ μετανισταμένων οἱ μὲν ἀνδρὸς ἔχοντες ἡλικίαν ὑπὲρ ἑξήκοντα μυριάδας ἦσαν, ὁ δ' ἄλλος ὅμιλος πρεσβυτῶν, παίδων, γυναικῶν οὐ ῥᾴδιος ἀριθμηθῆναι· μιγάδων δὲ καὶ συγκλύδων καὶ θεραπείας ὄχλος συνεξῆλθεν ὡσανεὶ νόθον μετὰ γνησίου πλήθους· οὗτοι δ' ἦσαν οἱ ἐκ γυναικῶν γεννηθέντες Αἰγυπτίων τοῖς Ἑβραίοις καὶ τῷ πατρῴῳ γένει προσνεμηθέντες καὶ ὅσοι τὸ θεοφιλὲς ἀγάμενοι τῶν ἀνδρῶν ἐπηλύται ἐγένοντο καὶ εἰ δή τινες τῷ μεγέθει καὶ πλήθει τῶν ἐπαλλήλων κολάσεων μετεβάλοντο σωφρονισθέντες.

148 τούτων ἁπάντων ἡγεμὼν ἐχειροτονεῖτο Μωυσῆς τὴν ἀρχὴν καὶ βασιλείαν λαβὼν οὐχ ὥσπερ ἔνιοι τῶν ἐπὶ τὰς δυναστείας ὠθουμένων ὅπλοις καὶ μηχανήμασιν ἱππικαῖς τε καὶ πεζικαῖς καὶ ναυτικαῖς δυνάμεσιν, ἀλλ' ἀρετῆς ἕνεκα καὶ καλοκἀγαθίας καὶ τῆς πρὸς ἅπαντας εὐνοίας, ᾗ χρώμενος ἀεὶ διετέλει, καὶ προσέτι καὶ τοῦ φιλαρέτου καὶ φιλοκάλου θεοῦ

149 γέρας ἄξιον αὐτῷ παρασχόντος. ἐπειδὴ γὰρ τὴν Αἰγύπτου κατέλιπεν ἡγεμονίαν, θυγατριδοῦς τοῦ τότε βασιλεύοντος ὤν, ἕνεκα τῶν κατὰ τὴν χώραν γινομένων ἀδικημάτων πολλὰ χαίρειν φράσας ταῖς ἀπὸ τῶν θεμένων ἐλπίσι διὰ ψυχῆς εὐγένειαν καὶ φρονήματος μέγεθος καὶ τὸ μισοπόνηρον φύσει, τῷ

───────

ᵃ See Ex. xii. 27, 37 f.

in safety, but learners thereby of the finest and most profitable of lessons—piety. For never was judgement so clearly passed on good and bad, a judgement which brought perdition to the latter and salvation to the former.

XXVII. The departing emigrants had among them 147 over six hundred thousand men of military age, while the rest of the multitude, consisting of old men, women-folk and children, could not easily be counted. They were accompanied by a promiscuous, nondescript and menial crowd, a bastard host, so to speak, associated with the true-born. These were the children of Egyptian women by Hebrew fathers into whose families they had been adopted, also those who, rever-encing the divine favour shewn to the people, had come over to them, and such as were converted and brought to a wiser mind by the magnitude and the number of the successive punishments.[a]

The appointed leader of all these was Moses, invested 148 with this office and kingship, not like some of those who thrust themselves into positions of power by means of arms and engines of war and strength of infantry, cavalry and navy, but on account of his goodness and his nobility of conduct and the universal benevolence which he never failed to shew. Further, his office was bestowed upon him by God, the lover of virtue and nobility, as the reward due to him. For, when he gave up the lordship of Egypt, which 149 he held as son to the daughter of the then reigning king, because the sight of the iniquities committed in the land and his own nobility of soul and mag-nanimity of spirit and inborn hatred of evil led him to renounce completely his expected inheritance from the kinsfolk of his adoption, He Who presides

πρυτανεύοντι καὶ ἐπιμελουμένῳ τῶν ὅλων ἔδοξεν
αὐτὸν ἀμείψασθαι βασιλείᾳ πολυανθρωποτέρου καὶ
κρείττονος ἔθνους, ὅπερ ἔμελλεν ἐξ ἁπάντων τῶν
ἄλλων ἱερᾶσθαι τὰς ὑπὲρ τοῦ γένους τῶν ἀνθρώπων
αἰεὶ ποιησόμενον εὐχὰς ὑπέρ τε κακῶν ἀποτροπῆς
150 καὶ μετουσίας ἀγαθῶν. παραλαβὼν δὲ τὴν ἀρχὴν
οὐχ ὥσπερ ἔνιοι τὸν ἴδιον αὔξειν οἶκον καὶ τοὺς
υἱοὺς—δύο γὰρ ἦσαν αὐτῷ—προάγειν ἐπὶ μέγα
δυνάμεως ἐσπούδασεν, ὡς ἐν μὲν τῷ παρόντι
κοινωνοὺς αὖθις δὲ καὶ διαδόχους ἀποφῆναι· |
[105] γνώμῃ γὰρ ἀδόλῳ καὶ καθαρᾷ πρὸς πάντα μικρά
τε αὖ καὶ μεγάλα χρώμενος τὴν φυσικὴν πρὸς
τὰ τέκνα φιλοστοργίαν οἷα κριτὴς ἀγαθὸς ἐνίκα τῷ
151 περὶ τὸν λογισμὸν ἀδεκάστῳ. προὔκειτο γὰρ ἐν
αὐτῷ τέλος ἀναγκαιότατον, ὀνῆσαι τοὺς ἀρχομένους
καὶ πάνθ᾽ ὑπὲρ τῆς τούτων ὠφελείας ἔργῳ καὶ λόγῳ
πραγματεύεσθαι, μηδένα παραλιπόντι καιρὸν τῶν
152 συντεινόντων εἰς κοινὴν κατόρθωσιν. μόνος οὗτος
τῶν πώποθ᾽ ἡγεμονευσάντων οὐ χρυσὸν οὐκ ἄργυρον ἐθησαυρίσατο, οὐ δασμοὺς ἐξέλεξεν, οὐκ οἰκίας,
οὐ κτήματα, οὐ θρέμματα, οὐ θεραπείαν οἰκετικήν,
οὐ προσόδους, οὐκ ἄλλο τῶν εἰς πολυτέλειαν καὶ
περιουσίαν οὐδὲν ἐκτήσατο, καίτοι πάντων ἔχειν
153 ἀφθονίαν δυνάμενος· ἀλλ᾽ ὑπολαβὼν πενίας ψυχικῆς
ἔργον εἶναι τὸν ἐν ταῖς ὕλαις ἀποδέχεσθαι πλοῦτον
τοῦ μὲν ὡς τυφλοῦ κατεφρόνησε, τὸν δὲ βλέποντα
τῆς φύσεως ἐξετίμησε καὶ ζηλωτὴς ὡς οὐκ οἶδ᾽ εἴ
τις ἕτερος αὐτοῦ γενόμενος ἐν μὲν ἐσθῆσι καὶ
τροφαῖς καὶ τοῖς ἄλλοις τοῖς περὶ δίαιταν οὐδὲν
ἐπιτραγῳδῶν πρὸς σεμνότερον ὄγκον εὐτέλειαν καὶ
εὐκολίαν ἐπετήδευεν ἰδιώτου, πολυτέλειαν δὲ τῷ
ὄντι βασιλικὴν ἐν οἷς καλὸν ἦν πλεονεκτεῖν τὸν
354

over and takes charge of all things thought good
to requite him with the kingship of a nation more
populous and mightier, a nation destined to be consecrated above all others to offer prayers for ever on
behalf of the human race that it may be delivered from
evil and participate in what is good. Having received 150
this office, he did not, like some, take pains to exalt
his own house, and promote his sons, of whom he had
two, to great power and make them his consorts for
the present and his successors for the hereafter. For
in all things great and small he followed a pure and
guileless policy, and, like a good judge, allowed the
incorruptibility of reason to subdue his natural affection for his children. For he had set before him one 151
essential aim, to benefit his subjects ; and, in all that
he said or did, to further their interests and neglect
no opportunity which would forward the common
well-being. In solitary contrast to those who had 152
hitherto held the same authority, he did not treasure
up gold and silver, did not levy tributes, did not
possess houses or chattels or livestock or a staff of
slaves or revenues or any other accompaniment of
costly and opulent living, though he might have had
all in abundance. He held that to prize material 153
wealth shews poverty of soul, and despised such
wealth as blind ; but the wealth of nature which has
eyes to see he highly honoured and zealously pursued,
more perhaps than any other man. In dress and
food and the other sides of life, he made no arrogant
parade to increase his pomp and grandeur. But,
while in these he practised the economy and unassum-
ing ways of a private citizen, he was liberal in the
truly royal expenditure of those treasures which
the ruler may well desire to have in abundance.

154 ἄρχοντα· ταῦτα δ' ἦσαν ἐγκράτειαι, καρτερίαι, σω-
φροσύναι, ἀγχίνοιαι, συνέσεις, ἐπιστῆμαι, πόνοι,
κακοπάθειαι, ἡδονῶν ὑπεροψίαι, δικαιοσύναι, προ-
τροπαὶ πρὸς τὰ βέλτιστα, ψόγοι καὶ κολάσεις ἁμαρ-
τανόντων νόμιμοι, ἔπαινοι καὶ τιμαὶ κατορθούντων

155 πάλιν σὺν νόμῳ. XXVIII. τοιγαροῦν πολλὰ χαίρειν φράσαντα πολυχρηματίᾳ καὶ τῷ παρ' ἀνθρώποις μέγα πνέοντι πλούτῳ γεραίρει θεὸς τὸν μέγιστον καὶ τελεώτατον ἀντιδοὺς πλοῦτον αὐτῷ· οὗτος
δ' ἐστὶν ὁ τῆς συμπάσης γῆς καὶ θαλάττης καὶ
ποταμῶν καὶ τῶν ἄλλων ὅσα στοιχεῖα καὶ συγ-
κρίματα· κοινωνὸν γὰρ ἀξιώσας ἀναφανῆναι τῆς
ἑαυτοῦ λήξεως ἀνῆκε πάντα τὸν κόσμον ὡς κληρο-

156 νόμῳ κτῆσιν ἁρμόζουσαν. τοιγαροῦν ὑπήκουεν ὡς
δεσπότῃ τῶν στοιχείων ἕκαστον ἀλλάττον ἣν
εἶχε δύναμιν καὶ ταῖς προστάξεσιν ὑπεῖκον· καὶ
θαυμαστὸν ἴσως οὐδέν· εἰ γὰρ κατὰ τὴν παροιμίαν
" κοινὰ τὰ φίλων,'' φίλος δὲ ὁ προφήτης ἀνείρηται
θεοῦ, κατὰ τὸ ἀκόλουθον μετέχοι ἂν αὐτοῦ καὶ τῆς

157 κτήσεως, καθ' ὃ χρειῶδες. ὁ μὲν γὰρ θεὸς πάντα
κεκτημένος οὐδενὸς δεῖται, ὁ δὲ σπουδαῖος ἄνθρωπος
κέκτηται μὲν οὐδὲν κυρίως ἀλλ' οὐδ' ἑαυτόν, τῶν δὲ
τοῦ θεοῦ κειμηλίων, καθ' ὅσον ἂν οἷός τε ᾖ, μετα-
[106] λαγχάνει. | καὶ μήποτ' εἰκότως· κοσμοπολίτης
γάρ ἐστιν, ἧς χάριν αἰτίας οὐδεμιᾷ τῶν κατὰ τὴν
οἰκουμένην πόλεων ἐνεγράφη, δεόντως, οὐ μέρος

158 χώρας ἀλλ' ὅλον τὸν κόσμον κλῆρον λαβών. τί δ';
οὐχὶ καὶ μείζονος τῆς πρὸς τὸν πατέρα τῶν ὅλων
καὶ ποιητὴν κοινωνίας ἀπέλαυσε προσρήσεως τῆς
αὐτῆς ἀξιωθείς; ὠνομάσθη γὰρ ὅλου τοῦ ἔθνους

ᵃ Cf. De Abr. 235.　　　ᵇ Ex. xxxiii. 11.

These treasures were the repeated exhibition of self- 154
restraint, continence, temperance, shrewdness, good
sense, knowledge, endurance of toil and hardships,
contempt of pleasures, justice, advocacy of excellence,
censure and chastisement according to law for wrongdoers, praise and honour for well-doers, again as the
law directs. XXVIII. And so, as he abjured the 155
accumulation of lucre, and the wealth whose influence is mighty among men, God rewarded him
by giving him instead the greatest and most
perfect wealth. That is the wealth of the whole
earth and sea and rivers, and of all the other
elements and the combinations which they form.
For, since God judged him worthy to appear as a
partner of His own possessions, He gave into his
hands the whole world as a portion well fitted for His
heir. Therefore, each element obeyed him as its 156
master, changed its natural properties and submitted
to his command, and this perhaps is no wonder. For
if, as the proverb says, what belongs to friends is
common,[a] and the prophet is called the friend of God,[b]
it would follow that he shares also God's possessions,
so far as it is serviceable. For God possesses all 157
things, but needs nothing ; while the good man,
though he possesses nothing in the proper sense, not
even himself, partakes of the precious things of God
so far as he is capable. And that is but natural, for
he is a world citizen, and therefore not on the roll of
any city of men's habitation, rightly so because he has
received no mere piece of land but the whole world
as his portion. Again, was not the joy of his partner- 158
ship with the Father and Maker of all magnified
also by the honour of being deemed worthy to
bear the same title ? For he was named god and

PHILO

θεὸς καὶ βασιλεύς· εἴς τε τὸν γνόφον, ἔνθα ἦν ὁ
θεός, εἰσελθεῖν λέγεται, τουτέστιν εἰς τὴν ἀειδῆ καὶ
ἀόρατον καὶ ἀσώματον τῶν ὄντων παραδειγματικὴν
οὐσίαν, τὰ ἀθέατα φύσει θνητῇ κατανοῶν· καθάπερ
τε γραφὴν εὖ δεδημιουργημένην ἑαυτὸν καὶ τὸν
ἑαυτοῦ βίον εἰς μέσον προαγαγὼν πάγκαλον καὶ
θεοειδὲς ἔργον ἔστησε παράδειγμα τοῖς ἐθέλουσι
159 μιμεῖσθαι. εὐδαίμονες δ᾽ ὅσοι τὸν τύπον ταῖς
ἑαυτῶν ψυχαῖς ἐναπεμάξαντο ἢ ἐσπούδασαν ἐναπο-
μάξασθαι· φερέτω γὰρ ἡ διάνοια μάλιστα μὲν τὸ
εἶδος τέλειον ἀρετῆς, εἰ δὲ μή, τὸν γοῦν ὑπὲρ τοῦ
κτήσασθαι τὸ εἶδος ἀνενδοίαστον πόθον.

160 καὶ μὴν οὐδ᾽ ἐκεῖνό τις ἀγνοεῖ, ὅτι ζηλωταὶ τῶν
ἐνδόξων οἱ ἀφανεῖς εἰσι καί, ὧν ἂν ἐκεῖνοι μάλιστ᾽
ὀρέγεσθαι δοκῶσι, πρὸς ταῦτα τὰς αὑτῶν ἀποτεί-
νουσιν ὁρμάς· ἐπειδὰν γοῦν ἡγεμὼν ἄρξηται καθ-
ηδυπαθεῖν καὶ πρὸς τὸν ἁβροδίαιτον ἀποκλίνειν
βίον, σύμπαν ὀλίγου δεῖν τὸ ὑπήκοον τὰς γαστρὸς
καὶ τῶν μετὰ γαστέρα προσαναρρήγνυσιν ἔξω τῶν
ἀναγκαίων ἐπιθυμίας, εἰ μή τινες εὐμοιρίᾳ χρή-
σαιντο φύσεως ψυχὴν οὐκ ἐπίβουλον ἀλλ᾽ εὐμενῆ
161 καὶ ἵλεω κτησάμενοι· ἐὰν δ᾽ αὐστηροτέραν καὶ
σεμνοτέραν ἕληται προαίρεσιν, καὶ οἱ λίαν αὐτῶν
ἀκράτορες μεταβάλλουσι πρὸς ἐγκράτειαν ἢ φόβῳ
ἢ αἰδοῖ σπουδάζοντες ὑπόληψιν ἐμποιεῖν, ὅτι ἄρα
ζηλωταὶ τῶν ὁμοίων εἰσί· καὶ οὐκ ἄν ποθ᾽ οἱ χείρους
τὰ τῶν κρειττόνων ἀλλ᾽ οὐδὲ μανέντες ἀποδοκιμά-
162 ζοιεν. τάχα δ᾽, ἐπεὶ καὶ νομοθέτης ἔμελλεν ἔσεσθαι, πολὺ πρότερον αὐτὸς ἐγίνετο νόμος ἔμψυχός
τε καὶ λογικὸς θείᾳ προνοίᾳ, ἥτις ἀγνοοῦντα αὐτὸν
εἰς νομοθέτην ἐχειροτόνησεν αὖθις

king of the whole nation, and entered, we are told, into the darkness where God was,[a] that is into the unseen, invisible, incorporeal and archetypal essence of existing things. Thus he beheld what is hidden from the sight of mortal nature, and, in himself and his life displayed for all to see, he has set before us, like some well-wrought picture, a piece of work beautiful and godlike, a model for those who are willing to copy it. Happy are they who imprint, or 159 strive to imprint, that image in their souls. For it were best that the mind should carry the form of virtue in perfection, but, failing this, let it at least have the unflinching desire to possess that form.

And, indeed, we all know this, that 160 meaner men emulate men of distinction, and set their inclinations in the direction of what *they* seem to desire. Thus, when a ruler begins to shew profligacy and turn to a life of luxury, the whole body almost of his subjects gives full vent to the appetites of belly and sex beyond their actual needs, save in the case of some who, blessed by the gifts of nature, possess a soul kindly and propitious and free from viciousness; whereas, if that ruler adopt a more severe 161 and more serious rule of life, even the very licentious are converted to continence and are eager, either through fear or shame, to create the impression that, after all, their aims are like to his. In fact the worse, even in madness, will never be found to condemn the ways of the better. Perhaps, too, since he was 162 destined to be a legislator, the providence of God which afterwards appointed him without his knowledge to that work, caused him long before that day to be the reasonable and living impersonation of law.

[a] Ex. xx. 21, *cf. De Mut.* 7.

163 XXIX. Ἐπειδὴ τοίνυν παρ' ἑκόντων ἔλαβε τὴν ἀρχήν, βραβεύοντος καὶ ἐπινεύοντος θεοῦ, τὴν ἀποικίαν ἔστελλεν εἰς Φοινίκην καὶ Συρίαν τὴν κοίλην καὶ Παλαιστίνην, ἣ τότε προσηγορεύετο Χαναναίων, ἧς οἱ ὅροι τριῶν ἡμερῶν ὁδὸν διειστή-
164 κεσαν ἀπ' Αἰγύπτου. εἶτ' ἦγεν αὐτοὺς οὐ | τὴν
[107] ἐπίτομον, ἅμα μὲν εὐλαβηθείς, μή ποθ', ὑπαντια-σάντων τῶν οἰκητόρων διὰ φόβον ἀναστάσεως καὶ ἀνδραποδισμοῦ καὶ γενομένου πολέμου, πάλιν τὴν αὐτὴν ὁδὸν ὑποστρέψωσιν εἰς Αἴγυπτον, ἀπ' ἐχθρῶν ἐπ' ἐχθρούς, νέων ἐπ' ἀρχαίους, γέλως καὶ χλεύη γενησόμενοι καὶ χείρω καὶ ἀργαλεώτερα τῶν προτέρων ὑπομενοῦντες, ἅμα δὲ καὶ βουλόμενος αὐτοὺς δι' ἐρήμης ἄγων καὶ μακρᾶς δοκιμάσαι, πῶς ἔχουσι πειθαρχίας ἐν οὐκ ἀφθόνοις χορηγίαις ἀλλ'
165 ἐκ τοῦ κατ' ὀλίγον ὑποσπανιζούσαις. ἐκτραπό-μενος οὖν τὴν ἐπ' εὐθείας, ἐγκάρσιον ἀτραπὸν εὑ-ρὼν καὶ νομίσας κατατείνειν ἄχρι τῆς ἐρυθρᾶς θαλάττης ὁδοιπορεῖν ἤρχετο. τεράστιον δέ φασι συμβῆναι κατ' ἐκεῖνον τὸν χρόνον μεγαλούργημα τῆς φύσεως, ὃ μηδείς πω μέμνηται πάλαι γεγονός.
166 νεφέλη γὰρ εἰς εὐμεγέθη κίονα σχηματισθεῖσα προ-ῄει τῆς πληθύος, ἡμέρας μὲν ἡλιοειδὲς ἐκλάμπουσα φέγγος, νύκτωρ δὲ φλογοειδές, ὑπὲρ τοῦ μὴ πλάζεσθαι κατὰ τὴν πορείαν, ἀλλ' ἀπλανεστάτῳ ἕπεσθαι ἡγεμόνι ὁδοῦ. τάχα μέντοι καὶ τῶν ὑπ-άρχων τις ἦν τοῦ μεγάλου βασιλέως, ἀφανὴς ἄγγε-λος, ἐγκατειλημμένος τῇ νεφέλῃ προηγητήρ, ὃν οὐ θέμις σώματος ὀφθαλμοῖς ὁρᾶσθαι.
167 XXX. Θεασάμενος δ' ὁ τῆς Αἰγύπτου βασιλεὺς ἀνοδίᾳ χρωμένους, ὡς ᾤετο, καὶ διὰ τραχείας καὶ

―――――――――――

XXIX. *a* So, having received the authority which 163
they willingly gave him, with the sanction and
assent of God, he proposed to lead them to settle in
Phoenicia and Coelesyria and Palestine, then called
the land of the Canaanites, the boundaries of which
were three days' journey from Egypt. The course by 164
which he then led them was not the straight road.
He avoided this, partly because he was apprehensive
that if the inhabitants, fearing to lose their homes
and personal liberty, offered them opposition, and
war ensued, they might return by the same road to
Egypt, and thus, exchanging one enemy for another,
the new for the old, might be mocked, derided and
subjected to hardships worse and more painful than
what they underwent before. Partly, too, he wished
by leading them through a long stretch of desert
country to test the extent of their loyalty when supplies were not abundant but gradually grew scarcer
and scarcer. Therefore, leaving the straight road, 165
he found one at an angle to it, and, thinking that it
extended to the Red Sea, began the journey. It was
then, we are told, that there occurred a prodigy, a
mighty work of nature, the like of which none can
remember to have been seen in the past. A cloud 166
shaped like a tall pillar, the light of which in the day-
time was as the sun and in night as flame, went before
the host, so that they should not stray in their journey,
but follow in the steps of a guide who could never err.
Perhaps indeed there was enclosed within the cloud
one of the lieutenants of the great King, an unseen
angel, a forerunner on whom the eyes of the body
were not permitted to look.

XXX. But the king of Egypt, seeing, as he thought, 167
that they had lost their way and were traversing a

ἀτριβοῦς ἐρήμης βαδίζοντας ἤσθη μὲν ἐπὶ τῷ κατὰ
τὴν πορείαν σφάλματι, νομίσας συγκεκλεῖσθαι δι-
έξοδον οὐκ ἔχοντας, ἐπὶ δὲ τῷ μεθέσθαι μετανοῶν
ἐπεχείρει διώκειν, ὡς ἢ φόβῳ τὴν πληθὺν ὑπο-
στρέψων καὶ δουλωσόμενος αὖθις ἢ ἀποκτενῶν
168 ἡβηδὸν ἀφηνιάζουσαν. εἶθ᾽ ἅπασαν τὴν ἱππικὴν
δύναμιν παραλαβὼν ἀκοντιστάς τε καὶ σφενδονήτας
καὶ ἱπποτοξότας καὶ τοὺς ἄλλους ὅσοι τῆς κούφης
ὁπλίσεως καὶ τὰ κάλλιστα τῶν δρεπανηφόρων ἁρμάτων ἑξακόσια τοῖς ἐν τέλει δούς, ἵνα μετὰ τοῦ
πρέποντος ἀξιώματος ἐπακολουθήσωσι καὶ τῆς
στρατείας μετάσχωσιν, οὐδὲν τάχους ἀνεὶς ἐπεξέθει
καὶ συντείνων ἔσπευδε βουλόμενος ἐξαπιναίως οὐ
προϊδομένοις ἐπιστῆναι· τὸ γὰρ ἀνέλπιστον κακὸν
ἀργαλεώτερον αἰεὶ τοῦ προσδοκηθέντος, ὅσῳ καὶ
τὸ ὀλιγωρηθὲν εὐεπιχειρητότερον τοῦ σὺν φροντίδι.
169 καὶ ὁ μὲν ταῦτα διανοηθεὶς ἐπηκολούθει νομίζων αὐτοβοεὶ περιέσεσθαι, οἱ δ᾽ ἔτυχον ἤδη
παρὰ ταῖς ἠόσι τῆς θαλάττης στρατοπεδεύοντες·
μελλόντων δ᾽ ἀριστοποιεῖσθαι, τὸ μὲν πρῶτον
πάταγος ἐξηχεῖτο πολύς, ἅτε τοσούτων ἀνθρώπων
ὁμοῦ καὶ ὑποζυγίων μετὰ σπουδῆς ἐλαυνόντων, ὡς
ἐκχυθέντας[1] τῶν σκηνῶν περιβλέπεσθαι καὶ ὠτ-
[108] ακουστεῖν | ἀκροβατοῦντας· εἶτ᾽ ὀλίγῳ ὕστερον ἐπὶ
λόφου μετέωρος ἡ ἀντίπαλος καταφαίνεται δύναμις
170 ἐν τοῖς ὅπλοις ἐκτεταγμένη πρὸς μάχην. XXXI. ἐπὶ
δὲ τῷ παραλόγῳ καὶ ἀπροσδοκήτῳ καταπλαγέντες
καὶ μήτε πρὸς ἄμυναν εὐτρεπεῖς ὄντες διὰ σπάνιν
ἀμυντηρίων—οὐ γὰρ ἐπὶ πόλεμον ἀλλ᾽ εἰς ἀποικίαν
ἐξήεσαν—μήτε φυγεῖν δυνάμενοι—κατόπιν μὲν γὰρ
πέλαγος, ἐχθροὶ δ᾽ ἀντικρύ, τὰ δὲ παρ᾽ ἑκάτερα

---

[1] mss. ἐκλυθέντας et alia.

rough and pathless desert, was pleased to find that
disaster had befallen their journey, since he judged
them to be shut in without an outlet. And, repent-
ing that he had let them go, he essayed to pursue,
expecting that he would make the multitude return
in fear to renewed slavery, or massacre them wholesale if they proved refractory. Then he took with 168
him all his cavalry, javelineers, slingers, mounted
archers, and all his other light-armed troops, and
gave the six hundred finest of his scythed chariots
to the men of rank that they might follow in suitable
state and take part in the campaign. With unabated
rapidity he rushed to the attack, and pushed on
eagerly, wishing to come upon them suddenly and
unforeseen. For the unexpected ill is ever more
troublesome than the expected, since a negligently,
compared with a carefully, guarded force is more
liable to be successfully attacked. While he 169
pursued them with these intentions, hoping to win
an uncontested victory, they, as it happened, were
already encamped on the shores of the sea. And,
just as they were preparing to take their early meal,
first a mighty din was heard, caused by the host of
men and beasts coming on at full speed ; and, at the
sound, they poured out of their tents, standing on
tiptoe to look around and listen with both ears. Then,
shortly afterwards, high on the hill, appeared the
enemy's forces, armed and drawn up for battle.
XXXI. At this strange, unexpected sight, they were 170
panic-stricken. They were not ready to defend themselves, for lack of the necessary weapons, for their
expedition was not for war but for colonization. They
could not fly, for the sea was behind them, the enemy
in front, and on either side the depths of the trackless

βαθεῖα καὶ ἀτριβὴς ἐρήμη—σφαδάζοντες καὶ τῷ
μεγέθει τῶν κακῶν ἀπειρηκότες, οἷα παρὰ τὰς
τοιαύτας φιλεῖ συμφοράς, τὸν ἄρχοντα ᾐτιῶντο
171 φάσκοντες· " διὰ τὸ μὴ εἶναι μνήματα ἐν Αἰγύπτῳ,
οἷς ἀποθανόντες ἐνταφησόμεθα, ἐξήγαγες ἡμᾶς, ἵν'
ἐνταῦθα κηδεύσῃς ἀποκτείνας; ἢ οὐ πᾶσα δουλεία
κουφότερον κακὸν θανάτου; δελεάσας ἐλευθερίας ἐλπίδι τὸ πλῆθος τὸν χαλεπώτερον περὶ τοῦ
172 ζῆν ἐπεκρέμασας κίνδυνον. ἠγνόεις τὴν ἡμετέραν
ἀ⟨ο⟩πλότητα[1] καὶ τὴν Αἰγυπτίων πικρίαν καὶ τὸ
βαρύμηνι; τὸ μέγεθος τῶν ἀφύκτων κακῶν οὐχ
ὁρᾷς; τί πρακτέον; πολεμῶμεν ἄοπλοι πρὸς ὡπλι-
σμένους; ἀλλὰ φεύγωμεν καθάπερ ἄρκυσι κυκλω-
θέντες ἀνηλεέσιν ἐχθροῖς, ἐρημίαις ἀβάτοις, ἀπλώ-
τοις πελάγεσιν; εἰ δὲ δὴ καὶ πλωτά, τίς εὐπορία
173 σκαφῶν εἰς περαίωσιν; " ὁ δὲ ταῦτα ἀκούων τοῖς
μὲν συνεγίνωσκε, τῶν δὲ χρησμῶν ἐμέμνητο· καὶ
διανείμας τὸν νοῦν καὶ τὸν λόγον κατὰ τὸν αὐτὸν
χρόνον τῷ μὲν ἐνετύγχανεν ἀφανῶς τῷ θεῷ, ἵν' ἐξ
ἀμηχάνων ῥύσηται συμφορῶν, δι' οὗ δ' ἐθάρσυνε
καὶ παρηγόρει τοὺς καταβοῶντας " μὴ ἀναπίπτετε " λέγων· " οὐχ ὁμοίως ἄνθρωπος ἀμύνεται
174 καὶ θεός. τί μόνοις τοῖς εὐλόγοις καὶ πιθανοῖς προ-
πιστεύετε; παρασκευῆς οὐδεμιᾶς ἐστι χρεῖος ὁ
θεὸς βοηθός· ἐν ἀπόροις πόρον εὑρεῖν ἴδιον θεοῦ·
τὰ ἀδύνατα παντὶ γενητῷ μόνῳ δυνατὰ καὶ κατὰ
175 χειρός." καὶ ταῦτα μὲν ἔτι καθεστὼς διεξῄει·

---

[1] mss. ἁπλότητα, which all editors hitherto appear to have
accepted. But what sense has "simplicity," or any other
shade of meaning which the word can bear, in this context?
The correction here printed, suggested to me by Dr. Rouse,
appears certain. It is true that ἀοπλότης is not found in the
lexicon, nor is "unarmedness," by which I have translated

desert. So, in the bitterness of their hearts, broken
down by the greatness of their misfortune, they acted
as men often act in such troubles, and began to accuse
their ruler. "Was it because there were no tombs in **171**
Egypt where our dead bodies could be laid that you
brought us out to kill and bury us here ? Is not any
slavery a lighter ill than death ? You enticed this
multitude with the hope of liberty, and then have
saddled it with the greater danger which threatens
its life. Did you not know our unarmedness, and **172**
the bitterness and savage temper of the Egyptians ?
Do you not see how great are our troubles, how
impossible to escape ? What must we do ? Can we
fight unarmed against the armed ? Can we fly, surrounded as in a net by merciless enemies, pathless
deserts, seas impassable to ships, or, if indeed they
are passable, what supply of boats have we to enable
us to cross ? " Moses, when he heard these words, **173**
pardoned them, but remembered the divine messages,
and, using his mind and speech simultaneously for
different purposes, with the former silently interceded with God to save them from their desperate
afflictions, with the latter encouraged and comforted
the loud-voiced malcontents. " Do not lose heart,"
he said, " God's way of defence is not as that of men.
Why are you quick to trust in the specious and plaus- **174**
ible and that only ? When God gives help He needs
no armament. It is His special property to find a
way where no way is. What is impossible to all
created being is possible to Him only, ready to His
hand." Thus he discoursed, still calm and composed ; **175**

---

it, found in the abridged *N.E.D.* But both are natural and
possible formations.

μικρὸν δ' ἐπισχὼν ἔνθους γίνεται καταπνευσθεὶς
ὑπὸ τοῦ εἰωθότος ἐπιφοιτᾶν αὐτῷ πνεύματος καὶ
θεσπίζει προφητεύων τάδε· '' ἣν ὁρᾶτε στρατιὰν
εὐοπλοῦσαν, οὐκέτ' ἀντιτεταγμένην ὄψεσθε· πεσεῖ-
ται γὰρ προτροπάδην πᾶσα καὶ βύθιος ἀφανι-
σθήσεται, ὡς μηδὲ λείψανον αὐτῆς ὑπὲρ γῆς ἔτι
φανῆναι, καὶ οὐ μήκει χρόνου, ἀλλὰ τῇ ἐπιούσῃ
νυκτί.''

176 XXXII. Καὶ ὁ μὲν ταῦτ' ἀπεφθέγγετο. κατα-
δύντος δ' ἡλίου, νότος εὐθὺς ἤρξατο κατασκήπτειν
βιαιότατος, ὑφ' οὗ τὸ πέλαγος ἐξανεχώρησεν,
εἰωθὸς μὲν ἀμπωτίζειν, τότε δὲ καὶ μᾶλλον ὠθού-
[109] μενον τὸ πρὸς | αἰγιαλοῖς ὑπεσύρη καθάπερ εἰς
χαράδραν ἢ χάρυβδιν· ἀστήρ τε προὔφαινετ' οὐδείς,
ἀλλὰ πυκνὸν καὶ μέλαν νέφος ἅπαντα τὸν οὐρανὸν
ἐπεῖχε, γνοφώδους τῆς νυκτὸς οὔσης εἰς κατάπληξιν
177 τῶν διωκόντων. προσταχθεὶς δὲ Μωυσῆς τῇ
βακτηρίᾳ παίει τὴν θάλασσαν· ἡ δὲ ῥαγεῖσα δι-
ίσταται καὶ τῶν τμημάτων τὰ μὲν πρὸς¹ τῷ ῥαγέντι
μέρει μετέωρα πρὸς ὕψος ἐξαίρεται καὶ παγέντα
τρόπον τείχους κραταιῶς ἠρέμει καὶ ἡσύχαζε, τὰ δ'
ὀπίσω σταλέντα καὶ χαλινωθέντα τὴν εἰς τὸ πρόσω
φορὰν καθάπερ ἡνίαις ἀφανέσιν ἀνεχαίτιζε, τὸ δὲ
μεσαίτατον, καθ' ὃ ἐγένετο ἡ ῥῆξις, ἀναξηρανθὲν
ὁδὸς εὐρεῖα καὶ λεωφόρος γίνεται. τοῦτο ἰδὼν
Μωυσῆς καὶ θαυμάσας ἐγεγήθει καὶ πληρωθεὶς
χαρᾶς ἐθάρσυνε τοὺς ἰδίους καὶ ᾗ τάχιστα προὔ-
178 τρεπεν ἀναζευγνύναι. περαιοῦσθαι δὲ
μελλόντων, σημεῖον ἐπιγίνεται τερατωδέστατον· ἡ
γὰρ ὁδηγὸς νεφέλη πρωτοστατοῦσα τὸν ἄλλον
χρόνον ἀνακάμπτει πρὸς τὰ οὐραῖα τοῦ πλήθους,
ὅπως ὀπισθοφυλακῇ, καὶ ταχθεῖσα μεθόριος τῶν διω-

but, after a little, he became possessed, and, filled with the spirit which was wont to visit him, uttered these oracular words of prophecy : " The host which you see armed to the teeth you shall see no more arrayed against you. It shall all fall in utter ruin and disappear in the depths, so that no remnant may be seen above the earth. And this shall be at no distant time, but in the coming night."

XXXII. Such was his prediction. But at sunset 176 a south wind of tremendous violence arose, and, as it rushed down, the sea under it was driven back, and, though regularly tidal, was on this occasion more so than usually, and swept as into a chasm or whirlpool, when driven against the shore. No star appeared, but a thick black cloud covered the whole heaven, and the murkiness of the night struck terror into the pursuers. Moses now, at God's command, smote 177 the sea with his staff, and as he did so it broke and parted into two. Of the waters thus divided, one part rose up to a vast height, where the break was made, and stood quite firmly, motionless and still like a wall ; those behind were held back and bridled in their forward course, and reared as though pulled back by invisible reins ; while the intervening part, which was the scene of the breaking, dried up and became a broad highway. Moses, seeing this, marvelled and was glad, and in the fullness of his joy encouraged his men and bade them move on with all speed. And, when they were about to 178 begin the passage, a most extraordinary sign occurred. The guiding cloud, which at other times stood in front, turned round to the back of the multitude to form its rearguard, and thus posted between the pur-

---

¹ Perhaps τὰ μὲν ⟨πρόσω⟩ πρὸς.

κόντων καὶ τῶν διωκομένων τοὺς μὲν ἡνιοχοῦσα
σωτηρίως καὶ ἀσφαλῶς ἐπήλαυνε, τοὺς δὲ ἀνεῖργε
καὶ ἀνέκρουεν ἐφορμᾶν ἐπειγομένους· ἅπερ ὁρῶντες
οἱ Αἰγύπτιοι θορύβου καὶ ταραχῆς πάντ᾽ ἐπλήρουν
τάς τε τάξεις ὑπὸ δέους συνέχεον ἐπεμπίπτοντες
ἀλλήλοις καὶ ζητοῦντες ἤδη φυγεῖν, ὅτ᾽ οὐδὲν ἦν
179 ὄφελος. οἱ μὲν γὰρ Ἑβραῖοι διὰ ξηρᾶς ἀτραποῦ
περὶ βαθὺν ὄρθρον μετὰ γυναικῶν καὶ παίδων ἔτι
κομιδῇ νηπίων περαιοῦνται· τοὺς δὲ τὰ τμήματα
τοῦ πελάγους ἑκατέρωθεν ἐπικυλισθέντα καὶ ἑνω-
θέντα αὐτοῖς ἅρμασι καὶ ἵπποις καταποντοῖ, βορείοις πνεύμασι τῆς παλιρροίας ἀναχυθείσης καὶ
μετεώροις τρικυμίαις ἐπιδραμούσης, ὡς μηδὲ
πυρφόρον ὑπολειφθῆναι τὸν ἀπαγγελοῦντα τοῖς ἐν
180 Αἰγύπτῳ τὰς αἰφνιδίους συμφοράς. τὸ μέγα τοῦτο
καὶ θαυμαστὸν ἔργον Ἑβραῖοι καταπλαγέντες
ἀναιμωτὶ νίκην οὐκ ἐλπισθεῖσαν ἤραντο καὶ κατιδόντες ἐν ἀκαρεῖ φθορὰν ἀθρόαν πολεμίων δύο
χορούς, τὸν μὲν ἀνδρῶν, τὸν δὲ γυναικῶν, ἐπὶ τῆς
ἠϊόνος στήσαντες εὐχαριστικοὺς ὕμνους εἰς τὸν θεὸν
ᾖδον, ἐξάρχοντος Μωυσέως μὲν τοῖς ἀνδράσιν,
ἀδελφῆς δὲ τούτου ταῖς γυναιξίν· ἡγεμόνες γὰρ οὗτοι
τῶν χορῶν ἐγεγένηντο.

181 XXXIII. Ἄραντες δ᾽ ἀπὸ θαλάττης μέχρι μέν
τινος ὡδοιπόρουν μηκέτι τὸν ἀπὸ τῶν ἐχθρῶν
ὀρρωδοῦντες φόβον. ἐπιλιπόντος δὲ τοῦ ποτοῦ
τρισὶν ἡμέραις, αὖθις ἐν ἀθυμίαις ἦσαν ὑπὸ δίψους

ᵃ Or simply a " survivor," the phrase having passed into
a proverb without consideration of its origin, of which

368

suers and pursued regulated the course of the latter
and drove them before it under safe protection, but
checked and repelled the former when they strove
to advance. When the Egyptians saw this, tumult
and confusion prevailed everywhere among them.
In their terror their ranks fell into disorder. They
tumbled over each other, and sought to escape, but
it was of no avail; for, while the Hebrews with their 179
women and children, still mere infants, crossed on a
dry road in the early dawn, it was otherwise with the
Egyptians. Under the north wind the returning tide
was swept back, and hurled its lofty billows upon
them. The two sections of the sea rolled upon them
from either side, united and submerged them, horses,
chariots and all, with not even a torchbearer [a] left to
announce to the people of Egypt the sudden disaster.
This great and marvellous work struck the Hebrews 180
with amazement, and, finding themselves unexpectedly victorious in a bloodless conflict, and seeing
their enemies, one and all, destroyed in a moment,
they set up two choirs, one of men and one of women,
on the beach, and sang hymns of thanksgiving to
God. Over these choirs Moses and his sister pre-
sided, and led the hymns, the former for the men
and the latter for the women.

XXXIII. [b] They set out from the sea coast, and 181
travelled for some time, no longer in any fear of
danger from the enemy. But after three days the
water failed, and thirst once more reduced them

---

indeed there are other accounts besides that given in L. & S.,
viz. that it properly applied to the priest in the Spartan
army who carried the sacred fire, which was not allowed to
go out. So apparently even in the LXX Obadiah 18 οὐκ ἔσται
πυρφόρος τῷ οἴκῳ Ἠσαῦ.
  [b] For §§ 181–187 see Ex. xv. 22–26.

καὶ πάλιν ἤρξαντο μεμψιμοιρεῖν ὡς μηδὲν εὖ
προπεπονθότες· ἀεὶ γὰρ ἡ τοῦ παρόντος προσβολὴ
δεινοῦ τὰς ἐπὶ τοῖς προτέροις ἀγαθοῖς ἡδονὰς ἀφ-
182 αιρεῖται.   θεασάμενοι δὲ πηγὰς ἐπιτρέχουσιν |
[110] ὡς ἀρυσόμενοι χαρᾶς ὑπόπλεῳ, δι' ἄγνοιαν τἀληθοῦς
ἀπατηθέντες· πικραὶ γὰρ ἦσαν· εἶτα γευσάμενοι
γναμφθέντες τῷ παρ' ἐλπίδα τά τε σώματα
παρεῖντο καὶ τὰς ψυχὰς ἀναπεπτώκεσαν, οὐχ οὕτως
ἐφ' ἑαυτοῖς ὡς ἐπὶ τοῖς νηπίοις παισὶ στένοντες,
οὓς ἀδακρυτὶ ποτὸν αἰτοῦντας ὁρᾶν οὐχ ὑπέμενον.
183 ἔνιοι δὲ τῶν ὀλιγωροτέρων καὶ πρὸς εὐσέβειαν
ἀβεβαίων καὶ τὰ προγεγονότα ᾐτιῶντο ὡς οὐκ ἐπ'
εὐεργεσίᾳ συμβάντα μᾶλλον ἢ διὰ μετουσίαν ἀργαλεωτέρων συμφορῶν, ἄμεινον εἶναι λέγοντες τρίς,
οὐχ ἅπαξ, ὑπ' ἐχθρῶν ἀποθανεῖν ἢ δίψει παρ-
απολέσθαι· τὴν μὲν γὰρ ἄπονον καὶ ταχεῖαν τοῦ
βίου μετάστασιν οὐδὲν ἀθανασίας διαφέρειν τοῖς εὖ
φρονοῦσι, θάνατον δ' ὡς ἀληθῶς εἶναι τὸν βραδὺν
καὶ μετ' ἀλγηδόνων, οὐκ ἐν τῷ τεθνάναι τὸ φοβερὸν
ἀλλ' ἐν μόνῳ τῷ ἀποθνήσκειν ἐπιδεικνύμενον.
184   τοιαύταις χρωμένων ὀλοφύρσεσι, πάλιν
ἱκετεύει τὸν θεὸν Μωυσῆς ἐπιστάμενον τὴν ζῴων
καὶ μάλιστα τὴν ἀνθρώπων ἀσθένειαν καὶ τὰς
τοῦ σώματος ἀνάγκας ἐκ τροφῆς ἠρτημένου καὶ
δεσποίναις χαλεπαῖς συνεζευγμένου, βρώσει καὶ
πόσει, συγγνῶναι μὲν τοῖς ἀθυμοῦσι, τὴν δὲ πάντων ἔνδειαν ἐκπλῆσαι, μὴ χρόνου μήκει, δωρεᾷ δ'
ἀνυπερθέτῳ καὶ ταχείᾳ, διὰ τὴν τοῦ θνητοῦ φυσικὴν
ὀλιγωρίαν ὀξὺν καιρὸν τῆς βοηθείας ἐπιποθοῦντος.
370

to despondency. Again they began to grumble
at their lot, as though nothing good had befallen
them hitherto. For, under the onset of the present
terror, we always lose sense of the pleasantness of
past blessings. Then they saw some springs and 182
ran to draw from them, full of joy, but in their ignorance of the truth were deceived. For the water was
bitter, and, when they had tasted it, the disappoint-
ment broke them down. Their bodies were exhausted and their souls dejected, not so much for
themselves as for their infant children, the sight of
whom, as they cried for something to drink, was
more than they could face without tears. Some of 183
the more thoughtless, men of feeble piety, even de-
nounced the past events as not having been intended
for their benefit, but rather to bring them into worse
misfortunes. It were better, they said, to die thrice,
not merely once, at the hands of enemies, than to
perish, or worse than perish, by thirst. To depart
from life swiftly and easily is, in the eyes of the wise,
the same thing as never dying, and death in the true
sense is that which comes slowly and painfully, whose
terrors appear not in the state of death, but only in
the process of dying. While they were 184
engaged in such lamentations, Moses again addressed
his supplications to God, that, knowing the weakness
of His creatures, and particularly of mankind, and the
necessities of the body, which depends on food, and
is tied to those stern mistresses, meat and drink, He
should pardon the despondent and also satisfy the
needs of all, not at some distant time but with a boon
bestowed promptly and swiftly, considering the inborn short-sightedness of mortality, which desires that
assistance should be rendered quickly and at the

185 ὁ δὲ τὴν ἵλεων αὐτοῦ δύναμιν φθάνει προεκπέμψας
καὶ διοίξας τὸ τοῦ ἱκέτου τῆς ψυχῆς ἀκοίμητον
ὄμμα ξύλον δείκνυσιν, ὃ προσέταξεν ἀράμενον εἰς
τὰς πηγὰς καθεῖναι, τάχα μὲν κατεσκευασμένον ἐκ
φύσεως ποιοῦν δύναμιν, ἢ τάχα¹ ἠγνόητο, τάχα δὲ
καὶ τότε πρῶτον ποιηθὲν εἰς ἣν ἔμελλεν ὑπηρετεῖν
186 χρείαν. γενομένου δὲ τοῦ κελευσθέντος, αἱ μὲν
πηγαὶ γλυκαίνονται μεταβαλοῦσαι πρὸς τὸ πότιμον, ὡς μηδ' εἰ τὴν ἀρχὴν ἐγένοντό ποτε πικραὶ
δύνασθαι διαγνῶναι, διὰ τὸ μηδὲ ἴχνος ἢ ζώπυρον
τῆς ἀρχαίας κακίας εἰς μνήμην ὑπολελεῖφθαι.
187 XXXIV. τὸ δὲ δίψος ἀκεσάμενοι μεθ' ἡδονῆς δι-
πλασίας, ἐπειδὴ τῆς ἀπολαύσεως τὸ παρ' ἐλπίδα
συμβεβηκὸς ἀγαθὸν εὐφραίνει μᾶλλον, ἔτι καὶ τὰς
ὑδρίας πληρώσαντες ἀνεζεύγνυσαν, ὥσπερ ἀπὸ
θοίνης καὶ ἱλαρᾶς εὐωχίας ἑστιαθέντες καὶ μεθύον-
τες οὐ τὴν ἐν οἴνῳ μέθην ἀλλὰ τὴν νηφάλιον, ἣν
ᾐκρατίσαντο τὰς προπόσεις λαβόντες παρὰ τῆς
εὐσεβείας τοῦ προεστῶτος ἄρχοντος.

188 Ἀφικνοῦνται δ' εἰς σταθμὸν δεύτερον, εὔυδρόν τε
καὶ εὔδενδρον—Αἰλεὶμ ὠνομάζετο—, πηγαῖς καταρ-
ρεόμενον δώδεκα, παρ' αἷς στελέχη νέα φοινίκων
εὐερνέστατα ἦν τὸν ἀριθμὸν ἑβδομήκοντα, τοῖς ὀξὺ
[111] τῇ | διανοίᾳ βλέπειν δυναμένοις ἀγαθῶν τῶν
189 ἐθνικῶν ἐναργῆ σημεῖα καὶ δείγματα· φυλαί τε γάρ
εἰσι τοῦ ἔθνους δώδεκα, ὧν ἑκάστη πηγῆς ἕξει
λόγον εὐσεβοῦσα, χορηγούσης εὐσεβείας ἀενάους
καὶ ἀνελλιπεῖς καλὰς πράξεις, γενάρχαι δὲ τοῦ
σύμπαντος ἔθνους ἑβδομήκοντα γεγόνασι φοίνικι

---

¹ Clearly a mistake: ? τέως.

moment. Hardly had he so prayed, when God sent 185
in advance the power of His grace, and, opening the
vigilant eye of the suppliant's soul, bade him lift and
throw into the spring a tree which he shewed him,
possibly formed by nature to exercise a virtue which
had hitherto remained unknown, or possibly created
on this occasion for the service which it was destined
to perform. Moses did as he was bid, whereupon the 186
springs became sweet, and were converted into drink-
able water, so that no one could even guess that they
had originally been bitter, since no trace or tang remained to remind one of its former badness. XXXIV.
When they had relieved their thirst with double 187
pleasure, since the unexpectedness of the event gave
a delight beyond the actual enjoyment, they filled
their water-vessels and then resumed their journey,
feeling as though they had risen from a banquet and
merry-making, and elated, with the intoxication not
of wine, but of the sober carousal which the piety of
the ruler who led them had invited them to enjoy.[a]

[b] They then arrived at a second halting-place, one 188
well wooded and well watered, called Elim, irrigated
by twelve springs beside which rose young palm-
trees, fine and luxuriant, to the number of seventy.
Anyone who has the gift of keen mental sight may
see in this clear signs and tokens of the national blessings. For the nation has twelve tribes, each of 189
which, in virtue of its piety, will be represented by the
well which supplies piety in perennial streams and
noble actions unceasingly, while the heads of the
whole nation are seventy, who may properly be com-

[a] Or more literally " the sober intoxication in which they
indulged having first been pledged " etc.
[b] For §§ 188-190 see Ex. xv. 27 and cf. De Fuga 183 ff.

τῷ τῶν δένδρων ἀρίστῳ προσηκόντως παρεικα-
σθέντες, ὃ καὶ ὀφθῆναι καὶ καρπὸν ἐνεγκεῖν ἐστι
κάλλιστον, ὅπερ καὶ τὴν ζωτικὴν ἔχει δύναμιν οὐκ
ἐν ῥίζαις ὥσπερ τὰ ἄλλα κατορωρυγμένην ἀλλ᾽
ἀνώφοιτον, καρδίας τρόπον ἐν τῷ μεσαιτάτῳ τῶν
ἀκρεμόνων ἱδρυμένην, ὑφ᾽ ὧν οἷα ἡγεμονὶς ὄντως
190 ἐν κύκλῳ δορυφορεῖται. τοιαύτην δ᾽ ἔχει φύσιν καὶ
ἡ διάνοια τῶν γευσαμένων ὁσιότητος· ἄνω γὰρ
μεμάθηκε βλέπειν τε καὶ φοιτᾶν καὶ μετεωροπο-
λοῦσα ἀεὶ καὶ τὰ θεῖα διερευνωμένη κάλλη χλεύην
τίθεται τὰ ἐπίγεια, ταῦτα μὲν παιδιάν, ἐκεῖνα δὲ
σπουδὴν ὡς ἀληθῶς νομίζουσα.

191 XXXV. Μετὰ δὲ ταῦτ᾽ οὐ πολὺς διῆλθε χρόνος
καὶ ἀπορίᾳ σιτίων ἐλίμωττον, ὥσπερ ἐκ διαδοχῆς
ἀντεπιτιθεμένων τῶν ἀναγκαίων· δέσποινα γὰρ
χαλεπαὶ καὶ βαρεῖαι, πεῖνα καὶ δίψα, διακληρωσά-
μεναι τὰς κακώσεις ἐν μέρει προσέκειντο καὶ
συνέβαινε κατὰ τὴν τῆς ἑτέρας ἄνεσιν ἐπιγίνεσθαι
τὴν ἑτέραν, ὅπερ ἦν τοῖς πάσχουσιν ἀφορητότατον,
εἴ γε πρὸ μικροῦ δόξαντες ἀπαλλαγῆναι δίψους
192 ἐφεδρεῦον κακὸν πεῖναν εὕρισκον. ἦν δ᾽ οὐ μόνον
ἡ παροῦσα σπάνις χαλεπόν, ἀλλὰ καὶ ἡ πρὸς
τὸν μέλλοντα χρόνον τῶν ἐπιτηδείων ἀπόγνωσις·
ὁρῶντες γὰρ βαθεῖαν καὶ πολλὴν ἔρημον καὶ καρπῶν ἀγονωτάτην σφόδρα ἠθύμουν· πάντα γὰρ ἦσαν
ἢ τραχεῖαι καὶ ἀπορρῶγες πέτραι ἢ ἁλμυρόγεως
πεδιὰς ἢ ὄρη λιθωδέστατα ἢ ψάμμοι βαθεῖαι πρὸς
ἠλίβατον ὕψος ἀνατείνουσαι, καὶ προσέτι ποταμὸς
οὐδείς, οὐκ αὐθιγενής, οὐ χείμαρρους, οὐδεμία
πηγή, σπαρτὸν οὐδὲν οὐδὲ δένδρον, οὐχ ἥμερον, οὐ
τῆς ἀγρίας ὕλης, οὐ ζῷον πτηνὸν ἢ χερσαῖον, ὅτι

pared to the palm, the noblest of trees, excellent both in its appearance and in the fruit which it bears. Also it has its life-giving principle, not, like the others, buried in its roots, but mounted aloft, seated like a heart in the very centre of the branches which stand around to guard it as their very queen. Such, too, 190 is the nature of the mind of those who have tasted of holiness. Such a mind has learned to gaze and soar upwards, and, as it ever ranges the heights and searches into divine beauties, it makes a mock of earthly things, counting them to be but child's-play, and those to be truly matters for earnest care.

XXXV. [a] After this no long time had elapsed when 191 they were famished for want of food. It seemed as though the forces of necessity were taking turns to attack them. For those stern mistresses, hunger and thirst, had parcelled out their inflictions and plied them with these successively, with the result that when one was relaxed the other was upon them. This was most intolerable to the victims, since, often when they thought they had got free of thirst, they soon found the scourge of hunger waiting to take its place. And the presence of the dearth was not their 192 only hardship ; there was also the despair of obtaining provisions in the future. The sight of the deep, wide desert, utterly barren of fruits, filled them with despondency. All around there was nothing but rough, broken rocks, or plains where the soil was full of salt, or very stony mountains, or depths of sand stretching upwards steep and high, and again no rivers, spring-fed or winter torrent, no well, no tilth, no woodland of trees, either cultivated or wild, no living creature either of the air or of the land, save reptiles

[a] For §§ 191–208 see Ex. xvi.

μὴ τῶν ἑρπετῶν τὰ ἰοβόλα πρὸς ὄλεθρον ἀνθρώ-
193 πων, ὄφεις καὶ σκορπίοι. εἶθ' ὑπομιμνησκόμενοι τῆς
κατ' Αἴγυπτον εὐθηνίας καὶ εὐετηρίας καὶ τὴν
τῶν ἐκεῖ πάντων ἀφθονίαν ἀντιτιθέντες τῇ πάντων
ἐνταῦθα ἐνδείᾳ χαλεπῶς ἔφερον καὶ πρὸς ἑτέρους
ἕτεροι τοιαῦτ' ἐλογοποίουν· " ἐπ' ἐλευθερίας ἐλπίδι
μεταναστάντες οὐδὲ τοῦ ζῆν ἄδειαν ἔχομεν οἱ ταῖς
μὲν ὑποσχέσεσι τοῦ ἡγεμόνος εὐδαίμονες, ἐν δὲ τοῖς
194 ἔργοις ἀνθρώπων ἁπάντων κακοδαιμονέστατοι. τί
[112] τέλος ἔσται τῆς | ἀνηνύτου καὶ μακρᾶς οὕτως ὁδοῦ;
πᾶσι καὶ τοῖς πλέουσι καὶ τοῖς πεζεύουσιν ὅρος
εἰς ὃν ἀφίξονται πρόκειται, τοῖς μὲν ἐμπόρια καὶ
λιμένες, τοῖς δὲ πόλις τις ἢ χώρα, μόνοις δ' ἡμῖν
ἄβατος ἐρημία καὶ δυσοδία καὶ χαλεπαὶ δυσελ-
πιστίαι· προϊόντων γάρ, ὥσπερ ἀχανὲς καὶ βαθὺ
πέλαγος ἀπόρευτον ἀναφαίνεται καθ' ἑκάστην ἡμέ-
195 ραν εὐρυνόμενον. μετεωρίσας καὶ φυσήσας ἡμᾶς
τῷ λόγῳ καὶ κενῶν ἐλπίδων τὰ ὦτα πληρώσας
παρατείνει λιμῷ τὰς γαστέρας οὐδὲ τὰς ἀναγκαίας
ἐκπορίζων τροφάς· ἀποικίας ὀνόματι τοσαύτην
πληθὺν ἠπάτησεν ἐξ οἰκουμένης τὸ πρῶτον εἰς
ἀοίκητον ἀγαγών, εἶτα καὶ εἰς ᾅδου προπέμπων,
τὴν τοῦ βίου τελευταίαν ὁδόν."

196   XXXVI. Τοιαῦτ' ὀνειδιζόμενος οὐχ οὕτως ἐπὶ
ταῖς εἰς αὐτὸν κακηγορίαις ἐδυσχέραινεν, ὡς ἐπὶ
τῷ τῆς γνώμης αὐτῶν ἀνιδρύτῳ· πεπειραμένοι
γὰρ μυρίων ὅσων ἐκ τοῦ παραλόγου συμβεβηκότων
πραγμάτων παρὰ τὸ καθεστὸς ἔθος ὤφειλον ὑπὸ
μηδενὸς ἔτι τῶν εὐλόγων καὶ πιθανῶν ἄγεσθαι,
πεπιστευκέναι δ' αὐτῷ λαβόντες ἀποδείξεις ἐναρ-
197 γεστάτας τοῦ περὶ ἁπάντων ἀψευδεῖν. πάλιν δ'
ὅτε εἰς ἔννοιαν ἦλθε τῆς ἐνδείας, ἧς μεῖζον οὐδὲν
376

that vent poison for the destruction of mankind,
such as snakes and scorpions. Then, remembering 193
the teeming fertility of Egypt, and contrasting the
abundance of everything there with the lack of everything here, they were roused to anger, and expressed
their feelings to each other in such words as these :
" We left the country in the hope of freedom, and
yet we have no security even of life. Our leader
promised us happiness; in actual fact, we are the
most miserable of men. What will be the end of this 194
long, interminable journey ? Every traveller by sea
or land has set before him some goal to come to,
market or harbour for the one, city or country for the
other; we alone have before us a pathless wilderness, painful journeying, desperate straits. For, as
we proceed, there opens out before us, as it were, an
ocean, vast, deep, impassable, ever wider day by day.
He exhorted and puffed us up with his words, and 195
filled our ears with empty hopes, and then tortures
our bellies with hunger, not providing even the barest
nourishment. With the name of colonization he has
deceived this great multitude, and first carried us
from an inhabited to an uninhabited world, then led
us on to the grave along the road which brings life
to its end."

XXXVI. Moses, when reviled in this way, was 196
indignant not so much at their denunciations of himself as at their instability of judgement. For, after
experiencing strange events outside the customary
without number, they should have ceased to be guided
by anything that is specious and plausible, but should
have put their trust in him of whose unfailing truthfulness they had received the clearest proofs. But, 197
on the other hand, when he considered the want of

κακὸν ἀνθρώποις ἐστί, συνεγίνωσκεν ὄχλον εἰδὼς
ἀβέβαιον φύσει πρᾶγμα καὶ ὑπὸ τῶν ἐν χερσὶ
διακινούμενον, ἃ λήθην μὲν τῶν προγεγονότων
198 ἐργάζεται, δυσελπιστίαν δ' εἰς τὰ μέλλοντα. πάντων οὖν ἐν ἀσχέτοις ὄντων ἀνίαις καὶ τὰς ἀνωτάτω
προσδοκώντων συμφοράς, ἃς ἐνόμιζον ἐφεδρεύειν
καὶ ἐγγυτάτω παρεῖναι, τοῦτο μὲν διὰ τὴν σύμφυτον
ἐπιείκειαν καὶ φιλανθρωπίαν, τοῦτο δὲ βουλόμενος
ὃν ἐχειροτόνησεν ἡγεμόνα τιμῆσαι καὶ ἔτι μᾶλλον
ὡς εὐσεβείας ἔχει καὶ ὁσιότητος ἔν τε τοῖς φανεροῖς
κἂν τοῖς ἀδήλοις ἅπασι διασυστῆσαι ὁ θεὸς ἐλεήσας
199 τὸ πάθος ἰᾶται. ξένας οὖν εὐεργεσίας ἐκαινοτόμει,
τρανοτέραις ὅπως ἐμφάσεσι παιδευθῶσιν[1] ἤδη μὴ
δυσανασχετεῖν, εἴ τι μὴ κατὰ γνώμην εὐθὺς ἀπο-
βαίη, τλητικῶς δ' ὑπομένειν χρηστὰ περὶ τῶν
200 μελλόντων προσδοκῶντες. τί οὖν συνέβη; τῇ
ὑστεραίᾳ περὶ τὴν ἕω δρόσος βαθεῖα καὶ πολλὴ
περὶ σύμπαν ἦν ἐν κύκλῳ τὸ στρατόπεδον, ἣν
ἐπένιφεν ἡσυχῇ, ἀήθη ὑετὸν καὶ παρηλλαγμένον,
οὐχ ὕδωρ, οὐ χάλαζαν, οὐ χιόνα, οὐ κρύσταλλον—
ταῦτα γὰρ αἱ τῶν νεφῶν ἀπεργάζονται μεταβολαὶ
ταῖς χειμεριναῖς τροπαῖς—, ἀλλὰ κέγχρον βραχυ-
τάτην καὶ λευκοτάτην, ἣ διὰ τὴν ἐπάλληλον φορὰν
σωρηδὸν προὐκέχυτο τῶν σκηνῶν, ἄπιστος ὄψις·
ἦν καταπλαγέντες ἐπυνθάνοντο τοῦ ἡγεμόνος, τίς
τε ὁ ὑετὸς οὗτός ἐστιν, ὃν οὐδείς πω πρότερον
[113] εἶδεν | ἀνθρώπων, καὶ πρὸς τί γέγονεν. ὁ δὲ κατα-
201 πνευσθεὶς ἔνθους γίνεται καὶ θεσπίζει τάδε· " θνητοῖς μὲν ἀνεῖται πεδιὰς ἡ βαθύγειος, ἣν ἀνατέμοντες

---

[1] MSS. ἐμφάσεσιν αἰδεσθῶσιν.

food, as great a misfortune as any that can befall
mankind, he forgave them, knowing that the multitude by its very nature is an unstable thing, shaken
by the circumstances of the moment, which produce
oblivion of the past and despondency of the future.
So, while they were all thus overwhelmed by affliction, 198
and expecting the extreme misfortunes which they
believed to be close at hand, ready to attack them,
God, moved partly by the clemency and benevolence
to man which belongs to His nature, partly too by His
wish to honour the ruler whom He had appointed, and
still more to bring home to them the greatness of that
ruler's piety and holiness as shewn in matters both
clear and obscure, took pity on them and healed their
sufferings. He, therefore, devised new and strange 199
forms of benefaction, that by clearer manifestations
they might now be schooled not to shew bitter resentment if something did not at once turn out as they
would have it, but bear it patiently in expectation of
good to come. What, then, did happen ? On the 200
morrow about daybreak, a great quantity of dew lay
deep around the whole camp, showered noiselessly by
God ; a strange, extraordinary rain, not water, nor
hail, nor snow, nor ice, such as are produced by the
changes in the clouds at the winter solstice, but of
grains exceedingly small and white, which, poured
down in a continuous flow, lay in heaps in front of the
tents. It was an incredible sight ; and, in astonishment thereat, they asked their leader, " What is this
rain, which no man ever saw before, and for what
purpose has it come ? " Moses, in answer, possessed 201
by divine inspiration, spoke these oracular words :
" Mortals have the deep-soiled plainland given over
to them, which they cut into furrows with the plough,

εἰς αὔλακας ἀροῦσι καὶ σπείρουσι καὶ τὰ ἄλλα τὰ
κατὰ γεωργίαν δρῶσι καρποὺς ἐτησίους ἐκπορίζοντες εἰς ἀφθονίαν τῶν ἀναγκαίων· θεῷ δ' οὐ μία
μοῖρα τοῦ παντὸς ἀλλ' ὁ σύμπας κόσμος ὑπο-
βέβληται καὶ τὰ τούτου μέρη πρὸς ἅπασαν χρείαν
202 ὧν ἂν θέλῃ ὡς δεσπότῃ δοῦλα ὑπηρετήσοντα. νῦν
οὖν ἔδοξεν αὐτῷ, τὸν ἀέρα τροφὴν ἐνεγκεῖν ἀνθ'
ὕδατος, ἐπεὶ καὶ γῆ πολλάκις ὑετὸν ἤνεγκεν· ὁ γὰρ
ἐν Αἰγύπτῳ ποταμὸς καθ' ἕκαστον ἐνιαυτὸν ταῖς
ἐπιβάσεσι πλημμυρῶν ὅταν ἄρδῃ τὰς ἀρούρας, τί
ἕτερον ἢ ὑετός ἐστι κάτωθεν ἐπινίφων;"
203 παράδοξον μὲν δὴ τὸ ἔργον, εἰ καὶ ἐνταῦθα ἔστη·
νυνὶ δὲ καὶ παραδοξοτέροις ἄλλοις ἐθαυματουργεῖτο.
ἐπενεγκάμενοι γὰρ ἄλλος ἀλλαχόθεν ἀγγεῖα συν-
εκόμιζον, οἱ μὲν ἐπὶ τῶν ὑποζυγίων, οἱ δὲ κατὰ τῶν
ὤμων ἐπηχθισμένοι, προνοίᾳ τοῦ πρὸς πλείω χρόνον
204 ταμιεύεσθαι τὰ ἐπιτήδεια. ἦν δ' ἄρα ἀταμίευτα
καὶ ἀθησαύριστα, δωρεὰς ἀεὶ νέας ἐγνωκότος τοῦ
θεοῦ χαρίζεσθαι· τὰ μὲν γὰρ πρὸς τὴν τότε χρῆσιν
αὐτάρκη σκευάσαντες μεθ' ἡδονῆς προσηνέγκαντο,
τῶν δ' ἀπολειφθέντων εἰς τὴν ὑστεραίαν οὐδὲν
ἔτι σῶον εὕρισκον, ἀλλὰ μεταβεβληκότα καὶ δυσ-
ώδη καὶ μεστὰ τοιουτοτρόπων ζῴων, ἃ κατὰ σῆψιν
εἴωθε γεννᾶσθαι· ταῦτα μὲν οὖν ἀπερρίπτουν κατὰ
τὸ εἰκός, ἑτέρας δ' εὐτρεπεῖς τροφὰς ἀνεύρισκον,
ἃς ἅμα τῇ δρόσῳ καθ' ἑκάστην ἡμέραν συνέβαινε
205 νίφεσθαι.   γέρας δ' ἐξαίρετον ἡ ἱερὰ
ἑβδομὰς εἶχεν· ἐπειδὴ γὰρ οὐδὲν ἐφεῖται δρᾶν ἐν
αὐτῇ, πάντων δὲ μικρῶν καὶ μεγάλων ἔργων ἀνέχειν διείρηται, συγκομίζειν οὐ δυναμένοις τότε τὰ
ἐπιτήδεια πρὸ μιᾶς ὁ θεὸς ὕει διπλᾶ καὶ κελεύει

and there sow their seed, and perform the other tasks
of the husbandman, thus providing the yearly fruits,
and through them abundance of the necessaries of
life. But God has subject to Him not one portion
of the universe, but the whole world and its parts, to
minister as slaves to their master for every service
that He wills. So now it has seemed good to Him 202
that the air should bring food instead of water, for
the earth too often brings rain. What is the river of
Egypt, when every year it overflows and waters the
fields with its inroads, but a rainpour from beneath ? "

This work of God was strange enough 203
even if it had stopped at this point, but actually there
were other facts still stronger enhancing its marvels.
For the men brought vessels from every quarter, and
collected the grains, some on their beasts, others in
burdens on their shoulders, thinking thus to store up
provisions to last for later use. But, as it turned out, 204
it was impossible to store or hoard them, since it was
God's purpose to bestow gifts ever new. For when
they took a sufficient stock for their needs at the time,
they consumed it with pleasure, but anything they
left for the morrow they found did not keep, but
changed and stank and was full of such life as is
regularly bred in putrescence. This they naturally
threw away, but found other food prepared for them,
rained upon them with the dew every day.

A special distinction was given to the sacred seventh 205
day,[a] for, since it was not permitted to do anything
on that day, abstinence from works great or small
being expressly enjoined, and therefore they could
not then gather what was necessary, God rained a
double supply the day before, and bade them bring

---

[a] ἑβδομάς here is used for ἑβδόμη; cf. *Quis Rerum* 170 and note.

φέρειν εἰς δύο ἡμέρας αὐτάρκη τροφὴν ἐσομένην·
τὰ δὲ συγκομισθέντα σῷα διέμενεν, οὐδενὸς ἢ
πρότερον φθαρέντος τὸ παράπαν.

206 XXXVII. λέξω δὲ καὶ τὸ ἔτι τούτου θαυμασιώ-
τερον· ἐπὶ γὰρ ἔτη τεσσαράκοντα, τοσοῦτον μῆκος
αἰῶνος, ὁδοιποροῦσιν αὐτοῖς αἱ χορηγίαι τῶν ἀναγκαίων ἐν τάξεσι ταῖς εἰρημέναις ἐγίνοντο καθάπερ
ἐν σιταρχίαις μεμετρημέναις πρὸς τὰς ἐπιβαλλούσας
207 ἑκάστοις διανομάς. ἅμα μέντοι καὶ τὴν τριπόθητον
ἡμέραν ἀνεδιδάσκοντο—ζητοῦντες γὰρ ἐκ πολλοῦ,
τίς ἄρ᾽ ἐστὶν ἡ τοῦ κόσμου γενέθλιος, ἐν ᾗ τόδε τὸ
πᾶν ἀπετελέσθη, καὶ παρὰ πατέρων καὶ προγόνων
τὴν ζήτησιν ἄλυτον διαδεξάμενοι μόλις ἐδυνήθησαν
[114] εὑρεῖν—οὐ μόνον | χρησμοῖς ἀναδιδαχθέντες, ἀλλὰ
καὶ τεκμηρίῳ πάνυ σαφεῖ· τοῦ γὰρ πλεονάζοντος ἐν
ταῖς ἄλλαις ἡμέραις, ὡς ἐλέχθη, φθειρομένου, τὸ
πρὸ τῆς ἑβδόμης ὑόμενον οὐ μόνον οὐ μετέβαλεν,
208 ἀλλὰ καὶ μέτρον εἶχε διπλάσιον.   ἡ δὲ
χρῆσις ἦν τοιάδε· συλλέγοντες ἅμα τῇ ἕῳ τὸ νιφό-
μενον ἤλουν ἢ ἔτριβον, εἶθ᾽ ἕψοντες ἡδεῖαν πάνυ
τροφὴν οἷα μελίπηκτον προσεφέροντο μὴ δεόμενοι
209 σιτοπόνων περιεργίας.   ἀλλὰ γὰρ καὶ
τῶν εἰς ἁβροδίαιτον βίον οὐκ εἰς μακρὰν εὐπόρουν,
ὅσαπερ ἐν οἰκουμένῃ χώρᾳ καὶ εὐδαίμονι βουληθέντος τοῦ θεοῦ κατὰ πολλὴν περιουσίαν ἄφθονα
χορηγεῖν ἐν ἐρημίᾳ· ταῖς γὰρ ἑσπέραις ὀρτυγο-
μητρῶν νέφος συνεχὲς ἐκ θαλάττης ἐπιφερόμε-

---

[a] The meaning is that the seventh day was known to be
the birthday of the world (cf. De Op. 89), but the people had
lost count (see Mos. ii. 263). Philo probably noticed that
while it was hallowed in Gen. ii., no sign of observation of
it occurred in the narrative till this point. That the seventh
is the " birthday " rather than the sixth, because, though all

in what would be sufficient for two days. And what
was thus collected kept sound, nor did any of it decay
at all as in the previous case. XXXVII.
There is something still more wonderful to be told. 206
During all that long period of forty years in which
they journeyed, the food required was supplied
according to the rules just mentioned, like rations
measured out to provide the allotment needed for
each. At the same time, they learned to date aright 207
the day of which they had dearly longed to have
knowledge.[a] For, long before, they had asked what
was the birthday of the world on which this universe
was completed, and to this question, which had been
passed down unsolved from generation to generation,
they now at long last found the answer, learnt not
only through divine pronouncements but by a perfectly certain proof. For, as we have said, while the
surplus of the downpour decayed on the other days,
on the day before the seventh it not only did not
change, but was actually supplied in double measure.

The method they employed with the 208
food was as follows : At dawn they collected what
fell, ground or crunched it and then boiled it, when
they found it a very pleasant form of food, like a
honey-cake, and felt no need of elaborate cookery.

But in fact, not long after, they were 209
well supplied with the means of luxurious living, since
God was pleased to provide to them abundantly, and
more than abundantly, in the wilderness all the viands
which are found in a rich and well-inhabited country.
For in the evenings a continuous cloud of quails
appeared from the sea and overshadowed the whole

was completed on the sixth, it was seen in its perfection on
the seventh, is stated in *De Spec. Leg.* ii. 59.

νον ἅπαν τὸ στρατόπεδον ἐπεσκίαζε τὰς πτήσεις
προσγειοτάτας ποιουμένων εἰς τὸ εὔθηρον· συλ-
λαμβάνοντες οὖν καὶ σκευάζοντες ὡς φίλον ἑκάστοις
κρεῶν ἀπέλαυον ἡδίστων ἅμα καὶ τὴν τροφὴν
παρηγοροῦντες ἀναγκαίῳ προσοψήματι.

210 XXXVIII. Τούτων μὲν οὖν πολλὴν ἦγον ἀ-
φθονίαν οὐκ ἐπιλειπόντων, ὕδατος δὲ καὶ πάλιν
πιέσασα δεινὴ σπάνις ἐπιγίνεται· καὶ πρὸς ἀπό-
γνωσιν ἤδη τραπομένων σωτηρίας, λαβὼν Μωυσῆς
τὴν ἱερὰν βακτηρίαν ἐκείνην, δι' ἧς τὰ κατ'
Αἴγυπτον ἀπετέλεσε σημεῖα, θεοφορηθεὶς τὴν ἀκρό-
211 τομον πέτραν παίει. ἡ δ', εἴτε προϋποκειμένης
πηγῆς φλέβα καίριον διακοπεῖσα εἴτε καὶ τότε
πρῶτον ὕδατος ἀφανέσιν ὑπονόμοις εἰς αὐτὴν
ἀθρόου συρρυέντος καὶ σφόδρα ἐκθλιβέντος, ἀναστο-
μωθεῖσα τῇ βίᾳ τῆς φορᾶς κρουνηδὸν ἐκχεῖται, ὡς
μὴ τότε μόνον παρασχεῖν ἄκος δίψους ἀλλὰ καὶ
πρὸς πλείω χρόνον τοσαύταις μυριάσιν ἀφθονίαν
ποτοῦ· τὰ γὰρ ὑδρία πάντ' ἐπλήρωσαν, ὡς καὶ
πρότερον ἐκ τῶν πηγῶν, αἳ πικραὶ μὲν ἦσαν φύσει,
μετέβαλον δ' ἐπιφροσύνῃ θείᾳ πρὸς τὸ γλύκιον.

212 εἰ δέ τις τούτοις ἀπιστεῖ, θεὸν οὔτ'
οἶδεν οὔτ' ἐζήτησέ ποτε· ἔγνω γὰρ ἂν εὐθέως, ἔγνω
παγίως καταλαβών, ὅτι τὰ παράδοξα δὴ ταῦτα καὶ
παράλογα θεοῦ παίγνιά ἐστιν, ἀπιδὼν εἰς τὰ τῷ

ᵃ In § 209 Philo combines the account of the sending of
quails in Ex. xvi. 13 with that in Num. xi. 31-33. There, as
in Philo, the quails come later than the manna, not, as in
Exodus, before. On the other hand he ignores the statement
in Numbers, that the demand for flesh was punished with a
plague.

ᵇ For §§ 210-211 see Ex. xvii. 1-7 and Num. xx. 1-13.

camp, flying close to the land, so as to be an easy prey.[a]
So they caught and dressed them, each according to
his tastes, and feasted on flesh of the most delicious
kind, thus obtaining the relish required to make their
food more palatable.

XXXVIII. [b] Though this supply of food never failed 210
and continued to be enjoyed in abundance, a serious
scarcity of water again occurred. Sore pressed by
this, their mood turned to desperation, whereupon
Moses, taking that sacred staff with which he accomplished the signs in Egypt, under inspiration smote
the steep [c] rock with it. It may be that the rock con- 211
tained originally a spring and now had its artery clean
severed, or perhaps that then for the first time a body
of water collected in it through hidden channels was
forced out by the impact. Whichever is the case, it
opened under the violence of the stream and spouted
out its contents, so that not only then did it provide
a remedy for their thirst but also abundance of drink
for a longer time for all these thousands. For they
filled all their water vessels, as they had done on the
former occasion, from the springs that were naturally
bitter but were changed and sweetened by God's
directing care. If anyone disbelieves these 212
things, he neither knows God nor has ever sought
to know Him ; for if he did he would at once have
perceived—aye, perceived with a firm apprehension
—that these extraordinary and seemingly incredible
events are but child's-play to God. He has but to
turn his eyes to things which are really great and

[c] The epithet is taken from the allusion to the story in
Deut. viii. 15. Philo has made use of it in *Leg. All.* ii. 84,
and *De Som.* ii. 222. It might be translated "flinty" or
"hard," as in E.V., but in both these cases Philo stresses
its connexion with ἄκρος.

PHILO

ὄντι μεγάλα καὶ σπουδῆς ἄξια, γένεσιν οὐρανοῦ
καὶ πλανήτων καὶ ἀπλανῶν ἀστέρων χορείας καὶ
φωτὸς ἀνάλαμψιν, ἡμέρας μὲν ἡλιακοῦ, νύκτωρ δὲ
τοῦ διὰ σελήνης, καὶ γῆς ἵδρυσιν ἐν τῷ μεσαιτάτῳ
τοῦ παντός, ἠπείρων τε καὶ νήσων ὑπερβάλλοντα
μεγέθη καὶ ζῴων καὶ φυτῶν ἀμυθήτους ἰδέας, ἔτι
δὲ πελαγῶν ἀναχύσεις, ποταμῶν αὐθιγενῶν καὶ
χειμάρρων φοράς, ἀενάων ῥεῖθρα πηγῶν, ὧν αἱ |
[115] μὲν ψυχρὸν αἱ δὲ θερμὸν ὕδωρ ἀνομβροῦσιν, ἀέρος
παντοίας τροπάς, ἐτησίων ὡρῶν διακρίσεις, ἄλλα
213 κάλλη μυρία. ἐπιλίποι ἂν ὁ βίος τοῦ βουλομένου
διηγεῖσθαι τὰ καθ᾽ ἕκαστα, μᾶλλον δ᾽ ἕν τι τῶν
ὁλοσχερεστέρων τοῦ κόσμου μερῶν, κἂν εἰ μέλλοι
πάντων ἀνθρώπων ἔσεσθαι μακροβιώτατος. ἀλλὰ
ταῦτα μὲν πρὸς ἀλήθειαν ὄντα θαυμάσια κατα-
πεφρόνηται τῷ συνήθει· τὰ δὲ μὴ ἐν ἔθει, κἂν
μικρὰ ᾖ, ξέναις φαντασίαις ἐνδιδόντες καταπλητ-
τόμεθα τῷ φιλοκαίνῳ.

214 XXXIX. Ἤδη δὲ πολλὴν καὶ ἀπόρευτον δι-
εξεληλυθότων, ὅροι τινὲς ἀνεφαίνοντο γῆς οἰκουμένης καὶ προάστεια χώρας, εἰς ἣν μεθωρμίζοντο·
νέμονται δ᾽ αὐτὴν Φοίνικες. ἐλπίσαντες δὲ βίον
εὔδιον καὶ γαληνὸν αὑτοῖς ἀπαντήσεσθαι γνώμης
215 ἐσφάλησαν. ὁ γὰρ προκαθήμενος βασιλεὺς πόρ-
θησιν εὐλαβηθείς, ἀναστήσας τὴν ἐκ τῶν πόλεων
νεότητα, μάλιστα μὲν ἀνείρξων ὑπηντίαζεν, εἰ
δὲ βιάζοιτο, διὰ χειρῶν ἀμυνούμενος ἀκμῆσι καὶ

─────

[a] For §§ 214-219 see Ex. xvii. 8-16 (cf. Deut. xxv. 17-19).
Philo ignores the part taken by Aaron and Hur in holding
up Moses' hands.

[b] Presumably this refers to the inhabitants of Canaan in
general, not specially to Amalek, whose defeat is described
in the sequel.

386

worthy of his earnest contemplation, the creation of heaven and the rhythmic movements of the planets and fixed stars, the light that shines upon us from the sun by day and from the moon by night, the establishment of the earth in the very centre of the universe, the vast expanses of continents and islands and the numberless species of animals and plants, and again the widespreading seas, the rushing rivers, spring-fed and winter torrents, the fountains with their perennial streams, some sending forth cold, other warm, water, the air with its changes of every sort, the yearly seasons with their well-marked diversities and other beauties innumerable. He who 213 should wish to describe the several parts, or rather any one of the cardinal parts of the universe, would find life too short, even if his years were prolonged beyond those of all other men. But these things, though truly marvellous, are held in little account because they are familiar. Not so with the unfamiliar; though they be but small matters, we give way before what appears so strange, and, drawn by their novelty, regard them with amazement.

XXXIX. [a]After traversing a long and pathless 214 expanse, they came within sight of the confines of habitable land, and the outlying districts of the country in which they proposed to settle. This country was occupied by Phoenicians.[b] Here they had thought to find a life of peace and quiet, but their hopes were disappointed. For the king who ruled there, 215 fearing pillage and rapine, called up the youth of his cities and came to meet them, hoping to bar their way, or, if that were not feasible and they attempted violence, to discomfit them by force

ἄρτι πρῶτον καθισταμένοις εἰς ἀγῶνα κεκμηκότας
ὁδοιπορίαις καὶ ἐνδείαις σιτίων καὶ ποτῶν, ἃ κατὰ
216 μέρος ἀντεπετίθετο. Μωυσῆς δὲ παρὰ τῶν σκοπῶν
γνοὺς οὐ μακρὰν διεστηκότα τὸν ἐχθρὸν στρατόν,
καταλέξας τοὺς ἡβῶντας καὶ στρατηγὸν ἑλόμενος
ἕνα τῶν ὑπάρχων Ἰησοῦν, πρὸς τὴν μείζονα συμμαχίαν αὐτὸς ἠπείγετο· περιρρανάμενος γὰρ τοῖς
εἰωθόσι καθαρμοῖς ἐπὶ κολωνὸν τὸν πλησίον μετὰ
σπουδῆς ἀναδραμὼν ἱκέτευε τὸν θεὸν ὑπερασπίσαι
καὶ νίκην καὶ κράτος περιποιῆσαι τοῖς Ἑβραίοις,
οὓς ἐκ χαλεπωτέρων πολέμων καὶ κακῶν ἄλλων
ἐρρύσατο μὴ μόνον τὰς ἐξ ἀνθρώπων ἐπικρεμα-
σθείσας συμφορὰς ἀποσκεδάσας, ἀλλὰ καὶ ὅσας ὅ
τε τῶν στοιχείων νεωτερισμὸς ἐκαινούργησε κατ'
Αἴγυπτον καὶ ὁ ἐν ταῖς ὁδοιπορίαις ἀνήνυτος λιμός.
217 ἤδη δὲ μελλόντων εἰς μάχην καθίστασθαι, τερατωδέστατόν τι συμβαίνει πάθος περὶ τὰς χεῖρας αὐτοῦ·
κουφόταται γὰρ ἐγίνοντο ἐν μέρει καὶ βαρύταται·
εἶθ' ὁπότε μὲν ἐπελαφρίζοιτο πρὸς ὕψος αἰρόμεναι,
τὸ συμμαχικὸν ἐρρώννυτο καὶ ἀνδραγαθιζόμενον
ἐπικυδέστερον ἐγίνετο, ὁπότε δὲ κάτω βρίσειαν,
ἴσχυον οἱ ἀντίπαλοι, μηνύοντος διὰ συμβόλων τοῦ
θεοῦ, ὅτι τῶν μέν ἐστι γῆ καὶ αἱ τοῦ παντὸς ἐσ-
χατιαὶ κλῆρος οἰκεῖος, τῶν δ' αἰθὴρ ὁ ἱερώτατος,
καὶ ὥσπερ ἐν τῷ παντὶ βασιλεύει καὶ κρατεῖ γῆς
οὐρανός, οὕτω καὶ τὸ ἔθνος περιέσται τῶν ἀντι-
218 πολεμούντων. ἄχρι μὲν οὖν τινος¹ αἱ χεῖρες οἷα

---

¹ This, though accepted without objection by editors, can
hardly be right. A conjunction is clearly required, and
ἄχρι τινὸς should be the adverb, "for a time." Perhaps
ἄχρι μὲν οὗτινος (W.H.D.R.). Stephanus cites ἄχρις ὅτου from
Hippocrates.

of arms, seeing that his men were unwearied and fresh for the contest, while the others were exhausted with much journeying and by the famine and drought which had alternately attacked them. Moses, learning from his scouts that the enemy was 216 not far distant, mustered his men of military age, and, choosing as their general one of his lieutenants named Joshua, hastened himself to take a more important part in the fight.[a] Having purified himself according to the customary ritual, he ran without delay to the neighbouring hill and besought God to shield the Hebrews and give a triumphant victory to the people whom He had saved from wars and other troubles still more grievous than this, dispersing not only the misfortunes with which men had menaced them but also those so miraculously brought about in Egypt by the upheaval of the elements and by the continual dearth which beset them in their journeying. But, when they were 217 about to engage in the fight, his hands were affected in the most marvellous way. They became very light and very heavy in turns, and, whenever they were in the former condition and rose aloft, his side of the combatants was strong and distinguished itself the more by its valour, but whenever his hands were weighed down the enemy prevailed. Thus, by symbols, God shewed that earth and the lowest regions of the universe were the portion assigned as their own to the one party, and the ethereal, the holiest region, to the other; and that, just as heaven holds kingship in the universe and is superior to earth, so this nation should be victorious over its opponents in war. While, then, his hands became 218

---

[a] Or perhaps " to gain the mightier alliance," *i.e.* of God.

PHILO

[116] πλάστιγγες ἐν μέρει μὲν | ἐπεκουφίζοντο, ἐν μέρει δ' ἐπέρρεπον, τηνικαῦτα καὶ ὁ ἀγὼν ἀμφήριστος ἦν· ἐξαπιναίως δ' ἀβαρεῖς γενόμεναι, δακτύλοις ἀντὶ ταρσῶν χρώμεναι, μετέωροι πρὸς ὕψος ἤρθησαν, καθάπερ αἱ πτηναὶ φύσεις ἀεροπορ'οῦσαι, καὶ διέμενον ἀνώφοιτοι μέχρι τοῦ τὴν νίκην Ἑβραίους ἀνανταγώνιστον ἄρασθαι, τῶν ἐχθρῶν ἡβηδὸν ἀναιρεθέντων ἅπερ τε διαθεῖναι παρὰ τὸ προσῆκον
219 ἐσπούδαζον παθόντων μετὰ δίκης. τότε καὶ Μωυσῆς ἱδρύεται βωμόν, ὃν ἀπὸ τοῦ συμβεβηκότος ὠνόμασε " θεοῦ καταφυγήν,"ᵃ ἐφ' οὗ τὰ ἐπινίκια ἔθυε χαριστηρίους εὐχὰς ἀποδιδούς.

220 XL. Μετὰ τὴν μάχην ταύτην ἔγνω δεῖν τὴν χώραν, εἰς ἣν ἀπῳκίζετο τὸ ἔθνος, κατασκέψασθαι —δεύτερον δ' ὁδοιποροῦσιν ἔτος ἐνειστήκει—βουλόμενος μή, οἷα φιλεῖ, γνωσιμαχεῖν οὐκ εἰδότας, ἀλλ' ἀκοῇ προμαθόντας αὐτήν, ἐπιστήμῃ τῶν ἐκεῖ βεβαίᾳ χρωμένους, τὸ πρακτέον ἐκλογίζεσθαι.
221 δώδεκα δ' ἰσαρίθμους ταῖς φυλαῖς ἄνδρας, ἐξ ἑκάστης ἕνα φύλαρχον, αἱρεῖται τοὺς δοκιμωτάτους ἀριστίνδην προκρίνας, ἵνα μηδεμία μοῖρα πλέον ἢ ἔλαττον ἐνεγκαμένη διαφέρηται, πᾶσαι δ' ἐξ ἴσου διὰ τῶν ἐν τέλει τὰ παρὰ τοῖς κατοίκοις, εἰ βουλη-
222 θεῖεν οἱ πεμφθέντες ἀψευδεῖν, ἐπιγνῶσιν. ἑλόμενος δ' αὐτούς φησι τάδε· " τῶν ἀγώνων καὶ κινδύνων, οὓς ὑπέστημεν καὶ μέχρι νῦν ὑπομένομεν, ἆθλόν εἰσιν αἱ κληρουχίαι, ὧν τῆς ἐλπίδος μὴ διαμάρτοι-

---

ᵃ Or "taking refuge in God." LXX. "the Lord is my refuge." E.V. Jehovah-Nissi, "the Lord is my banner."
ᵇ For §§ 220-236 see Num. xiii., xiv.

390

successively lighter and weightier, like scales in the balance, the fight, too, continued to be doubtful ; but, when they suddenly lost all weight, the fingers serving them as pinions, they were lifted on high like the tribe that wings its way through the air, and remained thus soaring until the Hebrews won an undisputed victory and their enemies were slaughtered wholesale, thus justly suffering the punishment which they wrongly strove to deal to others. Then, 219 too, Moses set up an altar, and called it from the event " Refuge of God," [a] and on this, with prayers of thanksgiving, he offered sacrifices in celebration of the victory.

XL. [b]After this battle he came to the conclusion 220 that, since it was now the second year of their travels, he ought to inspect the land in which the nation proposed to settle. He wished them, instead of arguing ignorantly in the usual way, to obtain a good idea of the country by first-hand report, and with this solid knowledge of the conditions to calculate the proper course of action. He chose twelve 221 men corresponding to the number of the tribes, one headman from each, selecting the most approved for their high merit, in order that no part of the nation might be set at variance with the others through receiving either more or less than they, but all might get to know through their chieftains the conditions in which the inhabitants lived, as they would do if the emissaries were willing to report the full truth. When he had chosen them, he spoke as 222 follows : " The conflicts and dangers which we have undergone and still endure, have for their prize the lands which we hope to apportion, a hope which we trust may not be disappointed, since the nation

μεν ἔθνος πολυανθρωπότατον εἰς ἀποικίαν παρα-
πέμποντες. ἔστι δ᾽ ὠφελιμώτατον ἡ τόπων καὶ
ἀνθρώπων καὶ πραγμάτων ἐπιστήμη, ὥσπερ ἡ
223 ἄγνοια βλαβερόν. ὑμᾶς οὖν ἐχειροτονήσαμεν, ἵνα
ταῖς ὑμετέραις ὄψεσί τε καὶ διανοίαις τἀκεῖ θεασώ-
μεθα· γίνεσθε δὴ τῶν τοσούτων μυριάδων ὦτα καὶ
ὀφθαλμοὶ πρὸς τὴν ὧν ἀναγκαῖον εἰδέναι σαφῆ κατά-
224 ληψιν. ἃ δὲ γνῶναι ποθοῦμεν, τρία ταῦτ᾽ ἐστίν·
οἰκητόρων πλῆθός τε καὶ δύναμιν, πόλεων τὴν ἐν
εὐκαιρίᾳ θέσιν καὶ ἐν οἰκοδομίαις ἐχυρότητα ἢ
τοὐναντίον, χώραν εἰ βαθύγειός ἐστι καὶ πίων,
ἀγαθὴ παντοίους καρποὺς ἐνεγκεῖν σπαρτῶν τε καὶ
δένδρων, ἢ λεπτόγεως ἔμπαλιν, ἵνα πρὸς μὲν ἰσχὺν
καὶ πλῆθος οἰκητόρων ἰσορρόποις δυνάμεσι φραξώ-
μεθα, πρὸς δὲ τὴν ἐν τοῖς τόποις ἐρυμνότητα μη-
χανήμασι καὶ ταῖς ἑλεπόλεσιν· ἀναγκαῖον δὲ καὶ τὴν
χώραν εἰδέναι, εἰ ἀρετῶσα ἢ μή· περὶ γὰρ λυπρᾶς
225 ἑκουσίους κινδύνους ὑπομένειν ἠλιθιότητος. τὰ δ᾽
ὅπλα καὶ μηχανήματα ἡμῶν καὶ πᾶσα ἡ δύναμις ἐν
μόνῳ τῷ πιστεύειν θεῷ κεῖται· ταύτην ἔχοντες τὴν
παρασκευὴν οὐδενὶ τῶν φοβερῶν εἴξομεν· ἱκανὴ
γὰρ ἀμάχους ῥώμας εὐεξίαις, τόλμαις, ἐμπειρίαις,
[117] πλήθεσιν ἐκ πολλοῦ τοῦ | περιόντος κατακρατεῖν,
δι᾽ ἣν καὶ ἐν ἐρήμῃ βαθείᾳ χορηγίᾳ πάντων εἰσὶν
226 ὅσα ἐν εὐετηρίᾳ πόλεων. ὁ δὲ καιρός, ἐν ᾧ μάλιστα
χώρας ἀρετὴν δοκιμάζεσθαι συμβέβηκεν, ἔαρ ἐστίν,
ὃ νῦν ἐφέστηκεν· ὥρᾳ γὰρ ἔαρος τὰ μὲν σπαρέντα
τελεσφορεῖται γένη, αἱ δὲ τῶν δένδρων φύσεις ἀρχὴν λαμβάνουσιν. ἄμεινον δ᾽ ἂν εἴη καὶ ἐπιμεῖναι
μέχρι θέρους ἀκμάζοντος καὶ διακομίσαι καρποὺς
οἱονεὶ δείγματα χώρας εὐδαίμονος."

which we are bringing to settle there is so populous.
To know the places, the men and their circumstances, is as useful as the ignorance of them is mischievous. So we have appointed you that with 223 the aid of your sight and intelligence we may be able to survey the state of the country. Become, then, the ears and eyes of all this great multitude, to give them a clear apprehension of what they require to know. There are three things which we 224 desire to learn : the size and strength of the population, whether the cities are favourably situated and strongly built, or the contrary, and whether the land has a deep, rich soil, well-adapted to produce every kind of fruits from cornfields and orchards, or on the other hand is thin and poor. Thus shall we counter the number and power of the inhabitants with equal forces, and the strength of their position with machines and siege engines. Knowledge of the fertility or unfertility of the land is also indispensable, for if it is poor it would be folly to court danger to win it. Our arms and engines and all our power 225 consist solely in faith in God. Equipped with this, we shall defy every terror. Faith is able to overpower, and more than overpower, forces the most invincible, in physique, courage, experience and number, and by it we are supplied in the depths of the desert with all that the rich resources of cities can give. Now the season which has been found to be 226 best for testing the goodness of a land is spring, which is now present ; for in springtime the different crops come to their fullness and the fruit-trees begin to shew their natural growth. Yet it might be better to wait till summer is at its height, and bring back fruits as samples of the wealth of the land."

227 XLI. Ταῦτ᾽ ἀκούσαντες ἐπὶ τὴν κατασκοπὴν
ἐξῄεσαν ὑπὸ παντὸς τοῦ πλήθους προπεμπόμενοι
δεδιότος, μὴ συλληφθέντες ἀπόλωνται καὶ συμβῇ
δύο τὰ χαλεπώτατα, ἀνδρῶν τε, οἳ φυλῆς ἑκάστης
ὄψις ἦσαν, σφαγαὶ καὶ ἄγνοια τῶν παρὰ τοῖς
ἐφεδρεύουσιν ἐχθροῖς ὧν ὠφέλιμος ἡ ἐπιστήμη.

228 παραλαβόντες δ᾽ ὀπτῆρας καὶ ἡγεμόνας τῆς ὁδοῦ
προερχομένοις ἐφείποντο· καὶ γενόμενοι πλησίον,
ἐφ᾽ ὑψηλότατον ὄρος τῶν περὶ τὸν τόπον ἀνα-
δραμόντες, κατεθεῶντο τὴν χώραν, ἧς πεδιὰς μὲν
ἦν πολλὴ κριθοφόρος, πυροφόρος, εὔχορτος, ὀρεινὴ
δ᾽ οὐκ ἔλαττον ἀμπέλων καὶ στελεχῶν ἄλλων κατά-
πλεως, εὔδενδρος ἅπασα, λάσιος, ποταμοῖς καὶ
πηγαῖς διεζωσμένη πρὸς ἄφθονον ὑδρείαν, ὡς ἐκ
τῶν προπόδων ἄχρι τῶν κορυφῶν ὅλα τῶν ὀρῶν
τὰ κλίματα δένδρεσι κατασκίοις συνυφάνθαι, διαφερόντως δὲ τοὺς αὐχένας καὶ ὅσαι βαθεῖαι διαφύσεις.

229 κατεθεῶντο δὲ καὶ τὰς πόλεις ἐρυμνοτάτας διχόθεν,
ἔκ τε τοπικῆς περὶ τὴν θέσιν εὐκαιρίας καὶ περιβόλων ἐχυρότητος. ἐξετάζοντες δὲ καὶ τοὺς οἰκήτορας ἑώρων ἀπείρους τὸ πλῆθος, περιμηκεστάτους
γίγαντας ἢ γιγαντώδεις τὰς τῶν σωμάτων ὑπερ-

230 βολὰς ἔν τε μεγέθεσι καὶ ῥώμαις. ταῦτα κατιδόντες εἰς ἀκριβεστέραν κατάληψιν ἐπέμενον—
ὀλισθηρὸν γὰρ αἱ πρῶται φαντασίαι χρόνῳ μόλις
ἐνσφραγίζομεναι—καὶ ἅμα σπουδὴν ἐποιοῦντο δρε-
ψάμενοι τῶν ἀκροδρύων, μὴ ἄρτι πρῶτον στερι-
φουμένων ἀλλ᾽ ἤδη ὑποπερκαζόντων, ἐπιδείξασθαι

394

XLI. When the spies heard this, they set out on 227
their errand, escorted by the whole multitude, who
feared that they might be taken and slain, thus
entailing two heavy misfortunes, the death of the
men who were as eyesight to their particular tribe,
and concerning the foe that lay ready to attack them
ignorance of the facts which it would be useful to
know. The men took with them scouts and guides 228
to the road, and followed behind them. And, when
they came near to their destination, they quickly
ascended the highest of the mountains in the neighbourhood and surveyed the country. Much of it
was plainland bearing barley, wheat and grass,
while the uplands were equally full of vines and
other trees, all of it well timbered and thickly over-
grown and intersected with springs and rivers which
gave it abundance of water, so that from the lowest
part to the summits the whole of the hill country,
particularly the ridges and the deep clefts, formed a
close texture of umbrageous trees. They observed 229
also that the cities were strongly fortified, in two
ways, through the favourable nature of their situation and the solidity of their walls. And, on scrutin-
izing the inhabitants, they saw that they were countless in number and giants of huge stature, or at
least giant-like in their physical superiority both
in size and strength. Having marked these things, 230
they stayed on to get a more accurate apprehension,
for first impressions are treacherous and only slowly
in time get the seal of reality. And, at the same
time, they were at pains to pluck some of the fruits
of the trees, not those in the first stage of hardening,
but fruits darkening to ripeness, and thus have

παντὶ τῷ πλήθει τὰ μὴ ῥᾳδίως φθαρησόμενα.
231 μάλιστα δ' αὐτοὺς κατέπληττεν ὁ τῆς ἀμπέλου
καρπός· οἱ γὰρ βότρυες ὑπερμεγέθεις ἦσαν, ἀντι-
παρεκτεινόμενοι ταῖς κληματίσι καὶ μοσχεύμασιν,
ἄπιστος θέα· ἕνα γοῦν ἐκτεμόντες καὶ δοκίδος ἐκ
μέσων ἀπαιωρήσαντες, ἧς τὰς ἀρχὰς δυσὶ νέοις, τῷ
μὲν ἔνθεν τῷ δ' ἔνθεν, ἐπετίθεσαν,[1] ἐκ διαδοχῆς,
πιεζομένων αἰεὶ τῶν προτέρων—βαρύτατον γὰρ ἦν
ἄχθος—, ἐκόμιζον, περὶ τῶν ἀναγκαίων οὐχ ὁμο-
232 φρονοῦντες.   XLII. ἐγένοντο μὲν οὖν αὐτοῖς ἅμιλλαι μυρίαι καὶ πρὶν ἐπανήκειν κατὰ τὴν
ὁδόν, ἀλλὰ κουφότεραι, ὑπὲρ τοῦ μὴ γνωσιμα-
[118] χούντων μηδ' | ἄλλα ἄλλων ἀπαγγελλόντων στά-
σιν ἐν τῷ πλήθει γενέσθαι, χαλεπώτεραι δὲ μετὰ
233 τὴν ἐπάνοδον. οἱ μὲν γὰρ περὶ τῆς τῶν πόλεων
ἐχυρότητος καὶ ὡς ἑκάστη πολυάνθρωπός ἐστι
διεξιόντες καὶ πάντα αἴροντες τῷ λόγῳ πρὸς τὸ
μεγαλεῖον φόβον ἐνειργάζοντο τοῖς ἀκούουσιν, οἱ
δὲ τὸν ἁπάντων ὧν εἶδον ὑφαιροῦντες ὄγκον παρεκάλουν μὴ ἀναπίπτειν, ἀλλ' ἔχεσθαι τῆς ἀποικίας
ὡς αὐτοβοεὶ περιεσομένους· οὐδεμίαν γὰρ ἀνθέξειν
πόλιν πρὸς τοσαύτης δυνάμεως ἔφοδον ἀθρόως ἐπι-
στάσης, ἀλλὰ τῷ βάρει πιεσθεῖσαν πίπτειν· προσ-
ετίθεσαν δὲ καὶ τὰ ἐκ τῶν ἰδίων παθῶν ἑκά-
τεροι ταῖς ψυχαῖς τῶν ἀκουόντων, οἱ μὲν ἄνανδροι
δειλίαν, οἱ δ' ἀκατάπληκτοι θάρσος μετ' εὐελ-
234 πιστίας. ἀλλ' οὗτοι μὲν πέμπτη μοῖρα τῶν ἀπο-
δεδειλιακότων ἦσαν, οἱ δ' ἔμπαλιν τῶν γενναίων

---

[1] mss. ἐπιθέντες. The anacoluthon might perhaps be cured more simply by the omission of ἧς.

something which would naturally keep in good
condition to exhibit to the whole multitude. They 231
were especially amazed by the fruit of the vine, for
the bunches were of huge size, stretching right
along the branches and shoots and presenting an
incredible spectacle. One, indeed, they cut off,
and carried it suspended from the middle part of
a beam, the ends of which were laid on two youths,
one in front and another behind, a fresh pair at
intervals relieving its predecessors, as they continually were wearied by the great weight of the burden.

   On vital matters, the envoys were not
of one mind. XLII. Indeed, there were numberless 232
contentions among them, even during the journey
before they arrived back, though of a lighter kind,
as they did not wish that their disputes or conflicting
reports should produce faction in the mass of the
people. But, when they had returned, these contentions became more severe. For, while one party, 233
by dilating upon the fortifications of the cities and
the great population of each and by magnifying
everything in their description, created fear in their
hearers, the others belittled the gravity of all that
they had seen, and bade them not be faint-hearted
but persist in founding their settlement in the cer-
tainty that they would succeed without striking a
blow. No city, they said, could resist the combined
onset of so great a power, but would fall overwhelmed by its weight. Both parties transmitted
the results of their own feelings to the souls of their
hearers, the unmanly their cowardice, the undismayed their courage and hopefulness. But these 234
last numbered but a fifth part of the craven-hearted,
who were five times as many as the better spirited.

πενταπλάσιοι· τὸ δ' ὀλίγον θάρσος ἀτολμίας ἐν-
αφανίζεται περιουσίᾳ, ὃ δὴ καὶ τότε φασὶ συμ-
βῆναι· τῶν γὰρ τὰ βέλτιστα διεξιόντων δυοῖν οἱ
τἀναντία φάσκοντες δέκα περιῆσαν οὕτως, ὥστε
καὶ σύμπασαν ὑπηγάγοντο τὴν πληθὺν ἐκείνων μὲν
ἀλλοτριώσαντες, ἑαυτοῖς δ' οἰκειωσάμενοι.

235 περὶ δὲ τῆς χώρας ταὐτὰ πάντες ἀπεφαίνοντο
γνώμῃ μιᾷ τὸ κάλλος καὶ τῆς πεδιάδος καὶ τῆς
ὀρεινῆς ἐκδιηγούμενοι· "τί δ' ὄφελος" εὐθὺς
ἀνεβόησαν "ἡμῖν ἀλλοτρίων ἀγαθῶν καὶ ταῦτα
πεφρουρημένων κραταιᾷ χειρὶ πρὸς τὸ ἀναφ-
αίρετον;" καὶ τοῖς δυσὶν ἐπιδραμόντες μικροῦ
καταλεύουσιν αὐτοὺς ἡδονὴν ἀκοῆς τοῦ συμφέρον-
236 τος καὶ ἀπάτην ἀληθείας προκρίναντες. ἐφ' οἷς
ὁ ἡγεμὼν ἠγανάκτει καὶ ἅμα ηὐλαβεῖτο, μή τι
θεήλατον κατασκήψῃ κακὸν οὕτως ἐκθύμως ἀ-
πιστοῦσι τοῖς χρησμοῖς· ὅπερ καὶ ἐγένετο· τῶν γὰρ
κατασκόπων οἱ μὲν δειλοὶ δέκα λοιμώδει νόσῳ
διαφθείρονται μετὰ τῶν ἐκ τοῦ πλήθους συναπονοηθέντων, μόνοι δ' οἱ συμβουλεύσαντες δύο μὴ
ὀρρωδεῖν ἀλλ' ἐφίεσθαι τῆς ἀποικίας ἐσώθησαν, ὅτι
καταπειθεῖς ἐγένοντο τοῖς λογίοις, γέρας ἐξαίρετον
λαβόντες τὸ μὴ παραπολέσθαι.

237 XLIII. Τοῦτ' αἴτιον ἐγένετο τοῦ μὴ θᾶττον
ἥκειν εἰς ἣν ἀπῳκίζοντο γῆν. δυνάμενοι γὰρ ἔτει
δευτέρῳ μετὰ τὴν ἀπ' Αἰγύπτου μετανάστασιν τὰς
ἐν Συρίᾳ πόλεις καὶ τὰς κληρουχίας ἐννέμεσθαι,[1] τὴν
ἄγουσαν καὶ ἐπίτομον ἐκτραπόμενοι ὁδὸν ἐπλάζοντο, δυσαναπορεύτους καὶ μακρὰς ἀνοδίας ἄλλας

---

[1] MSS. ἐκνέμεσθαι.

Courage confined to few is lost to sight, when timidity has the superiority of numbers : and that, we are told, happened on this occasion ; for the two who gave a highly favourable account were so out-weighed by the ten who said the opposite that the latter brought over the whole multitude into dissent from the others and agreement with themselves.

With regard to the country, they all 235 stated the same, unanimously extolling the beauty of both the plain and hill country. "But of what use to us," at once cried out the people, " are good things which belong to others, and moreover are strongly guarded so that none can take them away ? " And they set upon the two, and nearly stoned them in their preference of the pleasant-sounding to the profitable, and of deceit to truth. This roused their 236 ruler's indignation, who, at the same time, feared lest some scourge should descend upon them from God for their senseless disbelief in His utterances. This actually happened. For the ten cowardly spies perished in a pestilence with those of the people who had shared their foolish despondency, while the two who alone had advised them not to be terrified, but hold to their plan of settlement, were saved, because they had been obedient to the oracles, and received the special privilege that they did not perish with the others.

XLIII. This event was the reason why they did 237 not come sooner to the land where they proposed to settle. For, though they could have occupied the cities of Syria and their portions of land in the second year after leaving Egypt, they turned away from the road which led directly thither and wandered about, travelling with difficulty, through long, pathless

PHILO

ἐπ' ἄλλαις ἀνευρίσκοντες εἰς ἀνήνυτον ψυχῆς τε
καὶ σώματος κάματον, δίκας ἀναγκαίας τῆς ἄγαν
238 ἀσεβείας ὑπομένοντες. ὀκτὼ γοῦν ἐνιαυτοὺς πρὸς
[119] τοῖς τριάκοντα δίχα τοῦ | παρεληλυθότος χρόνου,
γενεᾶς βίον ἀνθρωπίνης, ἄνω κάτω τριβόμενοι καὶ
τὰς ἀβάτους ἐρημίας ἀναμετροῦντες ἔτει τεσσαρα-
κοστῷ μόλις ἐπὶ τοὺς τῆς χώρας ὅρους παρ-
εγένοντο, ἐφ' οὓς καὶ πρότερον ἦλθον.
239 πρὸς δὲ ταῖς εἰσβολαῖς ᾤκουν ἕτεροί τε καὶ δὴ
καὶ συγγενεῖς αὐτῶν, οὓς ᾤοντο μάλιστα μὲν συν-
εκπολεμήσειν τὸν πρὸς τοὺς ἀστυγείτονας πόλεμον καὶ πρὸς τὴν ἀποικίαν ἅπαντα συμπράξειν,
εἰ δ' ἀποκνοῖεν, μετὰ μηδετέρων γοῦν τετάξεσθαι
240 χεῖρας ἀνέχοντας. οἱ γὰρ ἀμφοτέρων τῶν ἐθνῶν
πρόγονοι, τοῦ τε Ἑβραϊκοῦ καὶ τοῦ τὰ προάστεια
κατοικοῦντος, ἀδελφοὶ δύο ἦσαν ὁμοπάτριοι καὶ
ὁμομήτριοι, πρὸς δὲ καὶ δίδυμοι, ἀφ' ὧν εἰς πολυ-
παιδίαν ἐπιδιδόντων καὶ τῶν ἀπογόνων εὐφορίᾳ τινὶ
χρωμένων εἰς μέγα καὶ πολυάνθρωπον ἔθνος ἑκατέρα τῶν οἰκιῶν ἀνεχύθη· ἀλλ' ἡ μὲν ἐφιλοχώρησεν,
ἡ δ', ὡς ἐλέχθη πρότερον, εἰς Αἴγυπτον μετανα-
241 στᾶσα διὰ λιμὸν χρόνοις ὕστερον ἐπανῄει. τὴν δ'
οἰκειότητα ἡ μὲν διεφύλαττε, καίτοι πολὺν χρόνον
διαζευχθεῖσα, πρὸς τοὺς μηδὲν ἔτι τῶν πατρίων
φυλάττοντας, ἀλλὰ πάντα τὰ τῆς ἀρχαίας πολιτείας
ἐκδεδιητημένους, ὑπολαβοῦσα τοῖς ἡμέροις τὰς
φύσεις ἁρμόττον εἶναι διδόναι τι καὶ χαρίζεσθαι
242 συγγενείας ὀνόματι· ἡ δ' ἔμπαλιν τὰ φιλικὰ πάντα
ἔτρεψεν ἤθεσι καὶ λόγοις βουλαῖς τε καὶ πράξεσιν
ἀσπόνδοις καὶ ἀσυμβάτοις χρωμένη, πατρικὴν
ἔχθραν ζωπυροῦσα—ὁ γὰρ τοῦ ἔθνους ἀρχηγέτης

<hr>

ᵃ For §§ 239-249 see Num. xx. 14-21.

tracts, which appeared one after the other, bringing endless weariness of soul and body, the punishment they needs must endure for their great impiety. For thirty-eight years in addition to the time already 238 spent, the span of a generation of human life, they went wayworn up and down, tracing and retracing the trackless wilds till at last in the fortieth year they succeeded in reaching those boundaries of the country to which they had come before. *a* Near the 239 entrances there dwelt, among others, some kinsfolk of their own, who, they quite thought, would join in the war against their neighbours and assist the new settlement in every way, or, if they shrank from this, would at the worst abstain from force and remain neutral. For the ancestors of both nations, the Hebrews and 240 the inhabitants of the outlying districts, were two brothers with the same father and mother, and twins to boot. Both had become the parents of an increasing family and, as their descendants were by no means unfruitful, both households had spread into great and populous nations. One of these had clung to the homeland, the other, as has been said, migrated to Egypt on account of the famine, and was returning after many years. The latter in spite of its long 241 separation maintained the tie of relationship, and though it had to deal with men who retained none of their ancestral customs, but had abandoned all the old ways of communal life, considered that it was proper for humane natures to pay some tribute of goodwill to the name of kinship. The other, on the contrary, 242 had upset all that made for friendship. In its customs and language, its policy and actions, it shewed implacable enmity and kept alive the fire of an ancestral feud. For the founder of the nation,

αὐτὸς ἀποδόμενος τῷ ἀδελφῷ τὰ πρεσβεῖα μικρὸν
ὕστερον ὧν ἐξέστη μετεποιεῖτο παραβαίνων τὰς
ὁμολογίας καὶ ἐφόνα θάνατον ἀπειλῶν, εἰ μὴ
ἀποδοίη—· ταύτην τὴν παλαιὰν ἀνδρὸς ἑνὸς πρὸς
ἕνα ἔχθραν ἔθνος τοσαύταις ὕστερον γενεαῖς ἐκαί-
243 νωσεν.   ὁ μὲν οὖν ἡγεμὼν τῶν Ἑβραίων
Μωυσῆς, καίτοι γ' αὐτοβοεὶ δυνάμενος ἑλεῖν ἐξ
ἐπιδρομῆς, οὐκ ἐδικαίωσε διὰ τὴν εἰρημένην συγγένειαν, ἀλλ' ὁδῷ χρήσασθαι μόνον ἠξίου τῇ διὰ
τῆς χώρας πάνθ' ὑπισχνούμενος πράξειν τὰ ἔν-
σπονδα, μὴ τεμεῖν¹ χωρίον, μὴ θρέμματα, μὴ λείαν
ἀπάξειν, ὕδατος, εἰ ποτοῦ γένοιτο σπάνις, τιμὴν
παρέξειν καὶ τῶν ἄλλων τοῖς ἀχορηγήτοις ὠνίων·
οἱ δ' εἰρηνικαῖς οὕτω προκλήσεσιν ἀνὰ κράτος
ἠναντιοῦντο πόλεμον ἀπειλοῦντες, εἰ τῶν ὅρων
ἐπιβάντας ἢ ψαύσαντας αὐτὸ μόνον αἴσθοιντο.
244 XLIV. χαλεπῶς δὲ τὰς ἀποκρίσεις ἐνηνοχότων καὶ
ἤδη πρὸς ἄμυναν ὁρμώντων, ἐν ἐπηκόῳ στὰς
"ἄνδρες" εἶπεν, "ἡ μὲν ἀγανάκτησις ὑμῶν
εὔλογος καὶ δικαία· χρηστὰ γὰρ ἀφ' ἡμέρου γνώμης
προτειναμένων, πονηρὰ ἀπὸ διανοίας ἀπεκρίναντο
245 κακοήθους. ἀλλ' οὐχ ὅτι | τῆς ὠμότητος ἐκεῖνοι
[120] δίκας ἐπάξιοι τίνειν εἰσί, διὰ τοῦθ' ἡμῖν ἐπὶ τὰς
κατ' αὐτῶν τιμωρίας ἁρμόττον ἵεσθαι, ἕνεκα τῆς
πρὸς τὸ ἔθνος τιμῆς, ἵνα καὶ ταύτῃ μοχθηρῶν
ἀγαθοὶ διαφέρωμεν, ἐξετάζοντες οὐ μόνον, εἰ
κολαστέοι τινές εἰσιν, ἀλλ' εἰ καὶ ὑφ' ἡμῶν

¹ MSS. μήτε μήν.

after having of his own accord sold his birthright as the elder to his brother, had later reclaimed what he had surrendered, in violation of their agreement, and had sought his blood, threatening him with death if he did not make restitution ; and this old feud between two individual men was renewed by the nation so many generations after.   Now the 243 leader of the Hebrews, Moses, though an attack might have won him an uncontested victory, did not feel justified in taking this course because of the above-mentioned kinship.   Instead, he merely asked for the right of passage through the country, and promised to carry out all that he agreed to do, not to ravage any estate, not to carry off cattle or spoil of any kind, to pay a price for water if drink were scarce and for anything else which their wants caused them to purchase.   But they refused these very peaceful overtures with all their might, and threatened war if they found them overstepping their frontiers, or even merely on the threshold.   XLIV. The 244 Hebrews were incensed at the answer, and were now starting to take up arms when Moses, standing where he could be heard, said : " My men, your indignation is just and reasonable.   We made friendly proposals in the kindest spirit.   In the malice of their hearts, they have answered us with evil.   But the 245 fact that they deserve to be punished for their brutality does not make it right for us to proceed to take vengeance on them.   The honour of our nation forbids it, and demands that here too we should mark the contrast between our goodness and their unworthiness by inquiring not only whether some particular persons deserve to be punished, but

246 ἐπιτήδειοι τοῦτο πάσχειν." εἶτ᾽ ἐκτραπόμενος ἦγε
δι᾽ ἑτέρας τὴν πληθύν, ἐπειδὴ τὰς κατὰ τὴν χώραν
ὁδοὺς ἁπάσας φρουραῖς διεζωσμένας εἶδεν ὑπὸ τῶν
βλάβην μὲν οὐδεμίαν ἐνδεξομένων, φθόνῳ δὲ καὶ
βασκανίᾳ τὴν ἐπίτομον οὐκ ἐώντων προέρχεσθαι.
247 ταῦτα δὲ σαφεστάτη πίστις ἦν ἀνίας, ἣν ἐπὶ τῷ
τὸ ἔθνος ἐλευθερίας τυχεῖν ἠνιῶντο, δηλονότι
χαίροντες, ἡνίκα τὴν ἐν Αἰγύπτῳ πικρὰν δουλείαν
ὑπέμενον· ἀνάγκη γὰρ οἷς φέρει λύπην τἀγαθὰ τῶν
πλησίον ἐπὶ τοῖς τούτων εὐφραίνεσθαι κακοῖς, κἂν
248 μὴ ὁμολογῶσιν. ἔτυχον γὰρ ὡς πρὸς ὁμογνώμονας
καὶ τὰ αὐτὰ βουλομένους ἀνενεγκόντες τὰ συμβάντα
λυπηρά τε αὖ καὶ ὅσα καθ᾽ ἡδονήν, οὐκ εἰδότες ὅτι
πόρρω προεληλύθασι μοχθηρίας καὶ ἐθελέχθρως
καὶ φιλαπεχθημόνως ἔχοντες στένειν μὲν ἐπὶ τοῖς
ἀγαθοῖς, ἥδεσθαι δὲ ἐπὶ τοῖς ἐναντίοις ἔμελλον.
249 τῆς δὲ κακονοίας ἀνακαλυφθείσης ἐκείνων, ἐκωλύ-
θησαν εἰς χεῖρας ἐλθεῖν ὑπὸ τοῦ προεστῶτος ἐπι-
δειξαμένου δύο τὰ κάλλιστα, φρόνησιν ἐν ταὐτῷ
καὶ χρηστότητα· τὸ μὲν γὰρ μηδὲν παθεῖν φυλά-
ξασθαι συνέσεως, τὸ δὲ μηδ᾽ ἀμύνασθαι συγγενεῖς
ὄντας ἐθελῆσαι φιλανθρωπίας ἔργον.

250 XLV. Τὰς μὲν οὖν τούτων πόλεις παρημείψατο.
βασιλεὺς δέ τις τῆς ὁμόρου Χανάνης ὄνομα, τῶν
σκοπῶν ἀπαγγειλάντων τὸν ὁδοιποροῦντα στρατὸν
οὐ πάνυ μακρὰν ἀφεστηκότα, νομίσας ἀσύντακτόν
τε εἶναι καὶ ῥᾳδίως εἰ προεπίθοιτο νικήσειν, ἄρας

ᵃ For §§ 250-254 see Num. xxi. 1-3.

also whether the punishment can properly be carried out by us." He then turned aside and led the 246 multitude by another way, since he saw that all the roads of that country were barricaded by watches set by those who had no cause to expect injury but through envy and malice refused to grant a passage along the direct road. This was the clearest proof 247 of the vexation which these persons felt at the nation's liberation, just as doubtless they rejoiced at the bitter slavery which it endured in Egypt. For those who are grieved at the welfare of their neighbours are sure to enjoy their misfortunes, though they may not confess it. As it happened, the Hebrews, believing 248 that their feelings and wishes were the same as their own, had communicated to them all their experiences, painful and pleasant, and did not know that they were far advanced in depravity and with their spiteful and quarrelsome disposition were sure to mourn their good fortune and take pleasure in the opposite. But, when their malevolence was exposed, the 249 Hebrews were prevented from using force against them by their commander, who displayed two of the finest qualities—good sense, and at the same time good feeling. His sense was shown in guarding against the possibility of disaster, his humanity in that on kinsmen he had not even the will to take his revenge.

XLV. *a* So, then, he passed by the cities of this 250 nation; but the king of the adjoining country Chananes *b* by name, having received a report from his scouts that the host of wayfarers was at no great distance, supposed that they were disorganized and would be an easy conquest if he attacked them first.

---

b lxx The Canaanite king Arad (or of Arad), E.V. the Canaanite, the king of Arad.

μετὰ τῆς οἰκείας νεότητος εὐοπλούσης ἐπεξέθει καὶ
τοὺς πρώτους ὑπαντιάσαντας ἅτε μὴ παρεσκευα-
σμένους εἰς μάχην τρέπεται· καὶ λαβὼν αἰχμαλώτους
ἐπὶ τῷ παρ' ἐλπίδα εὐημερήματι φυσηθεὶς προῄει,
251 καὶ τοὺς ἄλλους ἅπαντας χειρώσεσθαι νομίζων. οἱ
δὲ—οὐ γὰρ ἐγνάμφθησαν ἥττῃ τῆς προερχομένης
τάξεως—ἀλλ' ἔτι μᾶλλον ἢ πρότερον σπάσαντες
εὐτολμίας καὶ τὴν ἔνδειαν τῶν ἑαλωκότων ἐκπλῆσαι
ταῖς προθυμίαις ἐπειγόμενοι συνεκρότουν ἄλλος
ἄλλον μὴ ἀποκάμνειν "ἀνεγειρώμεθα" λέγοντες,
"ἄρτι τῆς χώρας ἐπιβαίνομεν· ἀκατάπληκτοι μετὰ
τῆς ἐν τῷ θαρρεῖν ἐχυρότητος γινώμεθα· τὰ τέλη
ταῖς ἀρχαῖς πολλάκις κρίνεται· ἐπὶ τῶν εἰσβολῶν
ὄντες καταπληξώμεθα τοὺς οἰκήτορας, ὡς ἔχοντες
[121] μὲν τὴν ἐκ τῶν πόλεων εὐετηρίαν, | ἀντιδεδωκότες
δ' ἣν ἐκ τῆς ἐρημίας ἐπαγόμεθα σπάνιν τῶν ἀναγ-
252 καίων.'' καὶ ἅμα διὰ τούτων προτρέποντες αὐτοὺς
ηὔξαντο τῆς χώρας ἀπαρχὰς ἀναθήσειν τῷ θεῷ τὰς
πόλεις τοῦ βασιλέως καὶ τοὺς ἐν ἑκάστῃ πολίτας·
ὁ δ' ἐπινεύει ταῖς εὐχαῖς καὶ θάρσος ἐμπνεύσας
τοῖς Ἑβραίοις τὴν ἀντίπαλον στρατιὰν ἁλῶναι παρ-
253 εσκεύασεν. οἱ δ' ἀνὰ κράτος ἑλόντες τὰς χαριστηρίους ὁμολογίας ἐπετέλουν, οὐδὲν ἐκ τῆς λείας
νοσφισάμενοι, τὰς δὲ πόλεις αὐτοῖς ἀνδράσι καὶ
κειμηλίοις ἀνιερώσαντες, καὶ ἀπὸ τοῦ συμβεβηκότος
254 ὅλην τὴν βασιλείαν ὠνόμασαν "ἀνάθεμα.'' καθάπερ γὰρ εἷς ἕκαστος τῶν εὐσεβούντων ἀπὸ τῶν
ἐτησίων ἀπάρχεται καρπῶν, οὓς ἂν ἐκ τῶν ἰδίων
συγκομίζῃ κτημάτων, τὸν αὐτὸν τρόπον καὶ ὅλον

He, therefore, started with a strongly armed force of such younger men as he had around him, and by a rapid attack routed those who first met him, unprepared as they were for battle; and, having taken them captive, elated at the unexpected success he advanced further, expecting to overpower all the rest. But they, not 251 a whit daunted by the defeat of the vanguard, but infused with courage greater even than before, and eager to supply by their zealousness the deficiency caused by the capture of their comrades, worked upon each other not to be faint-hearted. "Let us be up and doing," they cried. "We are are now setting foot in the country. Let us shew ourselves undismayed and possessed of the security which courage gives. The end is often determined by the beginning. Here, at the entrance of the land, let us strike terror into the inhabitants, and feel that ours is the wealth of their cities, theirs the lack of necessities which we bring with us from the desert and have given them in exchange." While 252 they thus exhorted each other, they vowed to devote to God the cities of the king and the citizens in each as firstfruits of the land, and God, assenting to their prayers, and inspiring courage into the Hebrews, caused the army of the enemy to fall into their hands. Having thus captured them by the might of 253 their assault, in fulfilment of their vows of thank-offering, they took none of the spoil for themselves, but dedicated the cities, men and treasures alike, and marked the fact by naming the whole kingdom "Devoted." For, just as every pious person gives 254 firstfruits of the year's produce, whatever he reaps from his own possessions, so too the whole nation set

PHILO

τὸ ἔθνος μεγάλης χώρας, εἰς ἣν μετανίστατο, μέγα τμῆμα, τὴν εὐθὺς αἱρεθεῖσαν βασιλείαν, ἀνέθηκεν ἀπαρχήν τινα τῆς ἀποικίας· οὐ γὰρ ἐνόμιζεν ὅσιον εἶναι διανείμασθαι γῆν ἢ πόλεις κατοικῆσαι, πρὶν καὶ τῆς χώρας καὶ τῶν πόλεων ἀπάρξασθαι.

255 XLVI. Μικρὸν δ' ὕστερον καὶ πηγὴν εὔυδρον ἀνευρόντες, ἣ παντὶ τῷ πλήθει ποτὸν ἐχορήγησεν— ἐν φρέατι δ' ἦν ἡ πηγὴ καὶ ἐπὶ τῶν τῆς χώρας ὅρων—, ὥσπερ οὐχ ὕδατος ἀλλ' ἀκράτου σπάσαντες τὰς ψυχὰς ἀνεχύθησαν· ὑπό τε εὐφροσύνης καὶ χαρᾶς ᾆσμα καινὸν οἱ θεοφιλεῖς χοροὺς περὶ τὸ φρέαρ ἐν κύκλῳ στήσαντες ᾖδον εἰς τὸν κληροῦχον θεὸν καὶ τὸν ἀληθῶς ἡγεμόνα τῆς ἀποικίας, ὅτι πρῶτον ἐπιβάντες ἐξ ἐρημίας μακρᾶς τῆς οἰκουμένης καὶ ἣν ἔμελλον καθέξειν ποτὸν ἄφθονον ἀνεῦρον, ἁρμόττον ἡγησάμενοι μὴ ἀσημείωτον τὴν
256 πηγὴν παρελθεῖν. καὶ γὰρ ἔτυχεν οὐ χερσὶν ἰδιωτῶν ἀλλὰ βασιλέων ἀνατετμῆσθαι φιλοτιμηθέντων, ὡς λόγος, οὐ μόνον περὶ τὴν εὕρεσιν τοῦ ὕδατος ἀλλὰ καὶ περὶ τὴν τοῦ φρέατος κατασκευήν, ἵν' ἐκ τῆς πολυτελείας βασιλικὸν φαίνηται τὸ ἔργον καὶ ἡ τῶν κατασκευασάντων ἀρχὴ καὶ μεγαλόνοια.
257 γεγηθὼς δ' ἐπὶ τοῖς αἰεὶ συμβαίνουσιν ἀπροσδοκήτοις ἀγαθοῖς ὁ Μωυσῆς ἐχώρει προσωτέρω, τὴν μὲν νεότητα διανείμας εἴς τε πρωτοστάτας καὶ ὀπισθοφύλακας, γηραιοὺς δὲ καὶ γύναια καὶ παῖδας ἐν μέσοις τάξας, ἵνα διὰ τῶν παρ' ἑκάτερα φρουρὰν

---

[a] For §§ 255-256 see Num. xxi. 16-18.
[b] Or " as we are told " (in the song).
[c] Philo interprets the words " the rulers dug it " of the

408

apart the kingdom which they took at the outset, and thus gave a great slice of the great country into which they were migrating as the firstfruits of their settlement. For they judged it irreligious to distribute the land until they had made a firstfruit offering of the land and the cities.

XLVI. [a]Shortly afterwards they also found a 255 spring of good water in a well situated on the borders of the land. This supplied the whole multitude with drink, and their spirits were enlivened thereby, as though the draught were strong wine rather than water. In their joy and gladness, the people of God's choice set up choirs around the well, and sang a new song to the Deity, Who gave them the land as their portion and had, in truth, led them in their migration. They did so at this point because here, for the first time, when they passed from the long expanse of desert to set foot in a habitable land, and one which they were to possess, they had found water in abundance, and therefore they judged it fitting not to leave the well uncelebrated. For, as they were told,[b] it had 256 been dug by the hands of no common men, but of kings, whose ambition was not only to find the water but so to build the well that the wealth lavished upon it should shew the royal character of the work and the sovereignty and lofty spirit of the builders.[c] Moses, rejoicing at the succession of unexpected 257 happinesses, proceeded further, after distributing his younger men into vanguard and rearguard and placing the old men, womenfolk and children in the centre, so as to be protected by those on either side

act of finding the water, and " kings hewed it " ($\epsilon\lambda\alpha\tau\delta\mu\eta\sigma\alpha\nu$) of building up the sides of the well. Cf. De Ebr. 113, where the spiritual meaning of the song is given.

ἔχωσιν, ἐάν τε ἀντικρὺ ἐάν τε κατόπιν ἐχθρὸς ὅμιλος ἐπίῃ.

258 XLVII. Ὀλίγαις δ' ὕστερον ἡμέραις εἰς τὴν τῶν Ἀμορραίων χώραν ἐμβαλὼν πρέσβεις ἐξέπεμπε πρὸς τὸν βασιλέα—Σηὼν δ' ὠνομάζετο—προτρέπων ἐφ' ἃ καὶ τὸν συγγενῆ πρότερον· ὁ δ' οὐ μόνον πρὸς ὕβριν ἀπεκρίνατο τοῖς ἥκουσι μικροῦ καὶ ἀνελὼν αὐτούς, εἰ μὴ νόμος ὁ πρεσβευτικὸς ἐμποδὼν ἐγένετο, ἀλλὰ καὶ πάντα τὸν στρατὸν συναγαγὼν [122] ἐφώρμα | νομίζων αὐτίκα τῷ πολέμῳ περιέσεσθαι.

259 συμπλακεὶς δὲ οὐ πρὸς ἀμελετήτους καὶ ἀνασκήτους ἔγνω τὴν μάχην οὖσαν ἀλλ' ἀθλητὰς τῷ ὄντι πολέμων ἀηττήτους, οἳ πρὸ μικροῦ πολλὰ καὶ μεγάλα ἠνδραγαθίσαντο σωμάτων ἀλκὴν καὶ φρόνημα διανοίας καὶ ἀρετῆς ὕψος ἐπιδειξάμενοι, δι' ὧν τοὺς μὲν ἐναντιωθέντας ἐκ πολλοῦ τοῦ περιόντος εἷλον, ἔψαυσαν δὲ τῶν ἀπὸ τῆς λείας οὐδενὸς τὰ πρῶτα τῶν ἄθλων ἀναθεῖναι τῷ θεῷ σπουδάσαντες·

260 οἳ καὶ τότε φραξάμενοι καρτερῶς ἀπὸ τῶν αὐτῶν βουλευμάτων καὶ παρασκευῶν ἀντεφώρμησαν ἅμα καὶ τῇ ἀκαθαιρέτῳ τοῦ δικαίου χρώμενοι συμμαχίᾳ, δι' ἣν εὐτολμότεροί τε ἦσαν καὶ ἀγωνισταὶ πρόθυ-

261 μοι. σαφὴς δὲ πίστις· δευτέρας οὐκ ἐδέησε μάχης, ἀλλ' ἡ πρώτη καὶ μόνη ἐγένετο, καθ' ἣν πᾶσα ἡ ἀντίπαλος ἐκλίθη δύναμις καὶ ἀνατραπεῖσα ἡβηδὸν

262 αὐτίκα ἠφανίσθη. αἱ δὲ πόλεις ὑπὸ τὸν αὐτὸν χρόνον κεναί τε καὶ πλήρεις ἐγεγένηντο, κεναὶ μὲν τῶν ἀρχαίων οἰκητόρων, πλήρεις δὲ τῶν κεκρατη-κότων· τὸν αὐτὸν μέντοι τρόπον καὶ αἱ κατ' ἀγροὺς ἐπαύλεις ἐρημωθεῖσαι τῶν ἐν αὐταῖς ἀντέλαβον ἄνδρας βελτίους τὰ πάντα.

ᵃ For §§ 258-262 see Num. xxi. 20-25.

if any enemy host should attack either in front or behind.

XLVII. *A few days after, he entered the land of 258 the Amorites, and sent ambassadors to the king, Sihon by name, with the same demands as he had made to his kinsman before. But Sihon not merely answered the envoys insolently, and came nigh to putting them to death, had he not been prevented by the law of embassies, but also mustered his whole army, and went to the attack thinking to win an immediate victory. But, when he engaged, he per- 259 ceived that he had no untrained or unpractised fighters to deal with, but men who were truly masters in warfare and invincible, men who had shortly before performed many great feats of bravery and shown themselves strong in body, mettlesome in spirit, and lofty in virtue, and through these qualities had captured their enemies with abundant ease, while they left the spoil untouched in their eagerness to dedicate the first prizes to God. So, too, on this 260 occasion, mightily fortified by the same resolutions and armoury, they went out to meet the foe, taking with them that irresistible ally, justice, whereby also they became bolder in courage and champions full of zeal. The proof of this was clearly shewn. No 261 second battle was needed, but this first fight was the only one, and in it the whole opposing force was turned to flight, then overthrown and straightway annihilated in wholesale slaughter. Their cities 262 were at once both emptied and filled—emptied of their old inhabitants, filled with the victors. And, in the same way, the farm-houses in the country were deserted by the occupants, but received others superior in every way.

PHILO

263 XLVIII. Οὗτος ὁ πόλεμος ἅπασι μὲν τοῖς
Ἀσιανοῖς ἔθνεσι φοβερὸν δέος ἐνειργάσατο, διαφερόντως δὲ τοῖς ὁμόροις, ὅσῳ καὶ τὰ δεινὰ ἐγ-
γυτέρῳ προσεδοκᾶτο. εἰς δὲ δὴ ἐκ τῶν ἀστυ-
γειτόνων βασιλέων ὄνομα Βαλάκης, μεγάλην καὶ
πολυάνθρωπον τῆς ἑῴας μοῖραν ὑπηγμένος, πρὶν
εἰς χεῖρας ἐλθεῖν ἀπειπών, ἄντικρυς μὲν ὑπαντᾶν
οὐκ ἐδοκίμαζε τὸν ἐκπορθήσεως δι' ὅπλων ἐλεύθερον
πόλεμον διαδιδράσκων, ἐπ' οἰωνοὺς δὲ καὶ μαντείας
ἐτράπετο νομίζων ἀραῖς τισι δυνήσεσθαι τὴν ἄμαχον
264 ῥώμην τῶν Ἑβραίων καθελεῖν. ἀνὴρ δ' ἦν κατ'
ἐκεῖνον τὸν χρόνον ἐπὶ μαντείᾳ περιβόητος Μεσο-
ποταμίαν οἰκῶν, ὃς ἅπαντα μὲν ἐμεμύητο τὰ
μαντικῆς εἴδη, οἰωνοσκοπίαν δ' ἐν τοῖς μάλιστα
συγκεκροτηκὼς ἐθαυμάζετο, πολλοῖς καὶ πολλάκις
265 ἐπιδειξάμενος ἄπιστα καὶ μεγάλα. προεῖπε γὰρ
τοῖς μὲν ἐπομβρίας θέρους ἀκμάζοντος, τοῖς δ'
αὐχμόν τε καὶ φλογμὸν ἐν μέσῳ χειμῶνι, τοῖς δ'
ἐξ εὐετηρίας ἀφορίαν καὶ ἔμπαλιν ἐκ λιμοῦ φοράν,
ἐνίοις δὲ πλημμύρας ποταμῶν καὶ κενώσεις καὶ
θεραπείας λοιμικῶν νοσημάτων καὶ ἄλλων μυρίων,
ὧν ἕκαστον ὁ προθεσπίζειν δοκῶν ὀνομαστότατος
ἦν ἐπὶ μέγα εὐκλείας προερχόμενος διὰ τὴν ἐπι-
βαίνουσιν ἀεὶ καὶ φθάνουσαν πανταχόσε φήμην.
266 ἐπὶ τοῦτον ἐξέπεμπε τῶν ἑταίρων τινὰς παρακαλῶν
ἥκειν καὶ δωρεὰς τὰς μὲν ἤδη παρεῖχε, τὰς δὲ
δώσειν ὡμολόγει τὴν χρείαν ἧς ἕνεκα μεταπέμποιτο

ᵃ For §§ 263-293, the story of Balaam, see Num. xxii.–xxiv.
Philo treats it in a curiously rationalistic way. The divinely
sent dreams of Balaam in ch. xxii. are said to be fictions of

412

XLVIII. ^aThis war caused terrible alarm among all 263
the nations of Asia, particularly among those of the
adjoining territories, since the expectation of danger
was nearer. But one of the neighbouring kings,
named Balak, who had brought under his sway a
great and populous portion of the East, lost heart
before the contest began. As he had no mind to
meet the enemy face to face, and shrank from a war
of destruction waged freely and openly with arms,
he had recourse to augury and soothsaying, and
thought that, if the power of the Hebrews was invincible in battle, he might be able to overthrow
it by imprecations of some kind. Now, there was 264
at that time a man living in Mesopotamia far-famed
as a soothsayer, who had learned the secrets of
that art in its every form, but was particularly
admired for his high proficiency in augury, so
great and incredible were the things which he had
revealed to many persons and on many occasions.
To some he had foretold rainstorms in summer, 265
to others drought and great heat in mid-winter,
to some barrenness to follow fertility, or again plenty
to follow dearth, to some rivers full or empty, ways
of dealing with pestilences, and other things without
number. In every one of these his reputation for
prediction made his name well known and was
advancing him to great fame, since the report of
him was continually spreading and reaching to every
part. To him Balak sent some of his courtiers, and 266
invited him to come, offering him gifts at once and
promising others to follow, at the same time explaining the purpose for which his presence was

---

his, and, though the appearance of the Angel to the ass is admitted, nothing is said of the animal speaking. See App. p. 603.

PHILO

δηλῶν· ὁ δ' οὐκ ἀπὸ φρονήματος εὐγενοῦς καὶ
[123] βεβαίου, | ἀλλὰ τὸ πλέον ἀστεϊζόμενος[1] ὡς δὴ τῶν
ἐλλογίμων προφητῶν γεγονὼς καὶ μηδὲν ἄνευ
χρησμῶν εἰωθὼς πράττειν τὸ παράπαν, ὑπανεδύετο
267 λέγων οὐκ ἐπιτρέπειν αὐτῷ βαδίζειν τὸ θεῖον. καὶ
οἱ μὲν ἥκοντες ἐπανῄεσαν ἄπρακτοι πρὸς τὸν
βασιλέα, ἕτεροι δ' εὐθὺς ἐπὶ τὴν αὐτὴν χρείαν
ἐχειροτονοῦντο τῶν δοκιμωτέρων, πλείω μὲν ἐπι-
φερόμενοι χρήματα, περιττοτέρας δὲ δωρεὰς ὑπ-
268 ισχνούμενοι. δελεασθεὶς δὲ καὶ τοῖς ἤδη προτει-
νομένοις καὶ ταῖς μελλούσαις ἐλπίσι καὶ τὸ ἀξίωμα
τῶν παρακαλούντων καταιδεσθεὶς ἐνεδίδου, πάλιν
προφασιζόμενος τὸ θεῖον οὐκ ἐφ' ὑγιεῖ· τῇ γοῦν
ὑστεραίᾳ παρεσκευάζετο τὴν ἔξοδον ὀνείρατα
διηγούμενος, ὑφ' ὧν ἔλεγε πληχθεὶς ἐναργέσι
φαντασίαις ἀναγκάζεσθαι μηκέτι μένειν, ἀλλὰ τοῖς
269 πρέσβεσιν ἀκολουθεῖν. XLIX. ἤδη δὲ
αὐτῷ προερχομένῳ γίνεται κατὰ τὴν ὁδὸν σημεῖον
ἀρίδηλον περὶ τοῦ τὴν χρείαν ἐφ' ἣν συνέτεινεν
εἶναι παλίμφημον· τὸ γὰρ ὑποζύγιον, ᾧ συνέβαινεν
αὐτὸν ἐποχεῖσθαι, προερχόμενον ἐπ' εὐθείας ἐξ-
270 απιναίως ἵσταται τὸ πρῶτον· εἶθ', ὥσπερ ἐξ ἐναντίας
βίᾳ τινὸς ἀνωθοῦντος ἢ ἀναχαιτίζοντος, ὑπὸ πόδας
ἐχώρει καὶ πάλιν ἐπὶ δεξιὰ καὶ εὐώνυμα ἐπιφερό-
μενον καὶ ὧδε κἀκεῖσε πλαζόμενον οὐκ ἠρέμει,
καθάπερ ἐν οἴνῳ καὶ μέθῃ καρηβαροῦν, καὶ πολλάκις τυπτόμενον ἠλόγει τῶν πληγῶν, ὥστε καὶ

---

[1] Cohn suggests ἀκκιζόμενος and points out that in § 297, where
ἀκκισμός is clearly right, the majority of mss. have ἀστεϊσμός.

---

[a] Or "cleverly posing." If ἀστεϊζόμενος is kept we must
suppose that the word, which regularly applies to witty or
ironical talk, is extended to any kind of dissimulation. But
ἀκκιζόμενος, "feigning reluctance," is easier.

required. But the seer, actuated not by any honourable or sincere feelings, but rather by a wish to pose [a] as a distinguished prophet whose custom was to do nothing without the sanction of an oracle, declined, saying that the Deity did not permit him to go. The envoys then returned to the king without 267 success, but others, selected from the more highly reputed courtiers, were at once appointed for the same purpose who brought more money and promised more abundant gifts. Enticed by those 268 offers present and prospective, and in deference to the dignity of the ambassadors, he gave way, again dishonestly alleging a divine command. And so on the morrow he made his preparations for the journey, and talked of dreams in which he said he had been beset by visions so clear that they compelled him to stay no longer but follow the envoys. XLIX. But, as he proceeded 269 there was given to him on the road an unmistakable sign that the purpose which he was so eager to serve was one of evil omen. For the beast on which he happened to be riding, while proceeding along the straight road, first came to a sudden stop, then, as 270 though someone opposite was thrusting it by force or causing it to rear, it fell back [b] and then again swerved to right and left and floundered hither and thither unable to keep still, as though heady with wine or drink; and, while repeatedly beaten, it paid no regard to the blows, so that it almost

[b] The Greek is odd. L. & S. give οἱ ὑπὸ πόδα as "those in the rear" and ὑπὸ πόδα χωρεῖν = "recede," "decline" (of strength), but these are hardly parallels. On the other hand ἐπὶ πόδα (or πόδας) χωρεῖν is a recognized phrase for "retreat" and should perhaps be read here.

415

τὸν ἐποχούμενον μικροῦ καταβαλεῖν καὶ καθεζό-
271 μενον ὅμως ἀντιλυπῆσαι. τῶν ⟨γὰρ⟩ παρ' ἑκάτερα χωρίων ἦσαν αἱμασιαὶ καὶ φραγμοὶ πλησίον·
ὁπότ' οὖν τούτοις προσηράχθη φερόμενον, γόνυ καὶ
κνήμας καὶ πόδας ὁ δεσπότης θλιβόμενος καὶ
272 πιεζόμενος ἀπεδρύπτετο. ἦν δ', ὡς ἔοικε, θεία τις
ὄψις, ἣν τὸ μὲν ζῷον ἐπιφοιτῶσαν ἐκ πολλοῦ
θεασάμενον ὑπέπτηξεν, ὁ δ' ἄνθρωπος οὐκ εἶδεν,
εἰς ἔλεγχον ἀναισθησίας· ὑπὸ γὰρ ἀλόγου ζῴου
παρευημερεῖτο τὰς ὄψεις ὁ μὴ μόνον τὸν κόσμον
273 ἀλλὰ καὶ τὸν κοσμοποιὸν αὐχῶν ὁρᾶν. μόλις γοῦν
τὸν ἀνθεστηκότα ἰδὼν ἄγγελον, οὐκ ἐπειδὴ τοιαύτης
θέας ἦν ἄξιος, ἀλλ' ἵνα τὴν ἀτιμίαν καὶ οὐδένειαν
ἑαυτοῦ καταλάβῃ, πρὸς ἱκεσίας καὶ λιτὰς ἐτράπετο
συγγνῶναι δεόμενος ὑπ' ἀγνοίας ἀλλ' οὐ καθ'
274 ἑκούσιον γνώμην ἁμαρτόντι. τότε μὲν οὖν ὑπο-
στρέφειν δέον, ἐπυνθάνετο τῆς φανείσης ὄψεως, εἰ
ἀνακάμπτοι πάλιν τὴν ἐπ' οἴκου· ἡ δὲ συνιδοῦσα
τὴν εἰρωνείαν καὶ σχετλιάσασα—τί γὰρ ἔδει πυνθάνεσθαι περὶ πράγματος οὕτως ἐμφανοῦς, ὃ τὰς
ἀποδείξεις εἶχεν ἐξ ἑαυτοῦ μὴ δεόμενον τῆς ἐκ
[124] λόγων πίστεως, εἰ μὴ | ἄρα ὀφθαλμῶν ὦτα ἀλη-
θέστερα καὶ πραγμάτων ῥήματα;—" βάδιζε " εἶπεν
" ἐφ' ἣν σπεύδεις ὁδόν· ὀνήσεις γὰρ οὐδέν, ἐμοῦ τὰ
λεκτέα ὑπηχοῦντος ἄνευ τῆς σῆς διανοίας καὶ τὰ
φωνῆς ὄργανα τρέποντος, ᾗ δίκαιον καὶ συμφέρον·
ἡνιοχήσω γὰρ ἐγὼ τὸν λόγον θεσπίζων ἕκαστα διὰ
τῆς σῆς γλώττης οὐ συνιέντος."
275 L. Ἀκούσας δ' ὁ βασιλεὺς ἐγγὺς ἤδη γεγονότα
μετὰ τῶν δορυφόρων ὑπαντησόμενος ἐξῄει, καὶ

threw its rider, and, even though he kept his seat, caused him as much pain as he gave. For the 271 estates on either side had walls and hedges close by, so that when the beast in its movements dashed against these, the feet, knees and shins of its master were crushed and lacerated by the pressure. It was 272 evidently a divine vision, whose haunting presence had for a considerable time been seen by the terrified animal, though invisible to the man, thus proving his insensibility. For the unreasoning animal showed a superior power of sight to him who claimed to see not only the world but the world's Maker. When, 273 at last, he did discern the angel standing in his way, not because he was worthy of such a sight, but that he might perceive his own baseness and nothingness, he betook himself to prayers and supplications, begging pardon for an error committed in ignorance and not through voluntary intention. Yet even 274 then, when he should have returned, he asked of the apparition whether he should retrace his steps home-wards. But the angel perceived his dissimulation, for why should he ask about a matter so evident, which in itself provided its own demonstration and needed no confirmation by word, as though ears could be more truthful than eyes or speech than facts? And so in displeasure he answered : " Pursue your journey. Your hurrying will avail you nought. I shall prompt the needful words without your mind's consent, and direct your organs of speech as justice and convenience require. I shall guide the reins of speech, and, though you understand it not, employ your tongue for each prophetic utterance."

L. When the king heard that he was now near 275 at hand, he came forth with his guards to meet him.

ἐντυχόντων, οἷα εἰκός, τὸ μὲν πρῶτον ἦσαν φιλοφροσύναι καὶ δεξιώσεις, εἶτα βραχεῖα κατάμεμψις
περὶ τῆς βραδυτῆτος καὶ τοῦ μὴ ἑτοιμοτέρου ἥκειν·
μετὰ δὲ ταῦτ᾽ εὐωχίαι ἦσαν καὶ πολυτελεῖς ἑστιά-
σεις καὶ ὅσα ἄλλα πρὸς ὑποδοχὴν ξένων ἔθος εὐτρεπίζεσθαι, φιλοτιμίαις βασιλικαῖς πάντα πρὸς
τὸ μεγαλειότερον ἐπιδιδόντα καὶ σεμνότερον ὄγκον.
276 τῇ δ᾽ ὑστεραίᾳ ἅμα τῇ ἕῳ τὸν μάντιν ὁ Βαλάκης
παραλαβὼν ἐπὶ γεώλοφον ἀνήγαγεν, ἔνθα καὶ
στήλην συνέβαινεν ἱδρῦσθαι δαιμονίου τινός, ἣν οἱ
ἐγχώριοι προσεκύνουν· μέρος δ᾽ ἐνθένδε καθεωρᾶτο
τῆς τῶν Ἑβραίων στρατοπεδείας, ὃ καθάπερ ἀπὸ
277 σκοπιᾶς ἐπεδείκνυτο τῷ μάγῳ. ὁ δὲ θεασάμενός
φησι· " σὺ μέν, ὦ βασιλεῦ, βωμοὺς ἑπτὰ δειμά-
μενος μόσχον ἐφ᾽ ἑκάστου καὶ κριὸν ἱέρευσον· ἐγὼ
δ᾽ ἐκτραπόμενος πεύσομαι τοῦ θεοῦ, τί λεκτέον."
ἔξω δὲ προελθὼν ἔνθους αὐτίκα γίνεται, προφητικοῦ
πνεύματος ἐπιφοιτήσαντος, ὃ πᾶσαν αὐτοῦ τὴν
ἔντεχνον μαντικὴν ὑπερόριον τῆς ψυχῆς ἤλασε·
θέμις γὰρ οὐκ ἦν ἱερωτάτῃ κατοκωχῇ συνδιαιτᾶσθαι
μαγικὴν σοφιστείαν. εἶθ᾽ ὑποστρέψας καὶ τάς τε
θυσίας ἰδὼν καὶ τοὺς βωμοὺς φλέγοντας ὥσπερ
278 ἑρμηνεὺς ὑποβάλλοντος ἑτέρου θεσπίζει τάδε· " ἐκ
Μεσοποταμίας μετεπέμψατό με Βαλάκης μακρὰν
τὴν ἀπ᾽ ἀνατολῶν στειλάμενον ἀποδημίαν, ἵνα
τίσηται τοὺς Ἑβραίους ἀραῖς. ἐγὼ δὲ τίνα τρόπον
ἀράσομαι τοῖς μὴ καταράτοις ὑπὸ θεοῦ; θεάσομαι
μὲν αὐτοὺς ὀφθαλμοῖς ἀφ᾽ ὑψηλοτάτων ὀρῶν καὶ τῇ
διανοίᾳ καταλήψομαι, βλάψαι δ᾽ οὐκ ἂν δυναίμην
λαόν, ὃς μόνος κατοικήσει, μὴ συναριθμούμενος

The interview naturally began with friendly greetings, which were followed by a few words of censure for his slowness and failing to come more readily. Then came high feasting and sumptuous banquets, and the other usual forms of provision for the reception of guests, each through the king's ambition of more magnificence and more imposing pomp than the last. The next day at dawn Balak took the 276 prophet to a hill, where it chanced that in honour of some deity a pillar^a had been set up which the natives worshipped. From thence a part of the Hebrew encampment was visible, which he shewed as a watchman from his tower to the wizard. He 277 looked and said : " King, do you build seven altars, and sacrifice a calf and a ram on each, and I will go aside and inquire of God what I should say." He advanced outside, and straightway became possessed, and there fell upon him the truly prophetic spirit which banished utterly from his soul his art of wizardry. For the craft of the sorcerer and the inspiration of the Holiest might not live together. Then he returned, and, seeing the sacrifices and the altars flaming, he spake these oracles as one repeating the words which another had put into his mouth. " From Mesopotamia hath Balak called me, 278 a far journey from the East, that he may avenge him on the Hebrews through my cursing. But I, how shall I curse them whom God hath not cursed ? I shall behold them with my eyes from the highest mountains, and perceive them with my mind. But I shall not be able to harm the people, which shall dwell alone, not reckoned among other nations ; and

---

^a So LXX " Pillar of Baal." E.V. " high places of Baal," xxii. 41.

PHILO

ἑτέροις ἔθνεσιν, οὐ κατὰ τόπων ἀποκλήρωσιν καὶ χώρας ἀποτομήν, ἀλλὰ κατὰ τὴν τῶν ἐξαιρέτων ἐθῶν ἰδιότητα, μὴ συναναμιγνύμενος¹ ἄλλοις εἰς
279 τὴν τῶν πατρίων ἐκδιαίτησιν. τίς ἐπ' ἀκριβείας εὗρε τὴν πρώτην καταβολὴν τῆς τούτων γενέσεως; τὰ μὲν σώματ' αὐτοῖς ἐξ ἀνθρωπίνων διεπλάσθη σπερμάτων, ἐκ δὲ θείων ἔφυσαν αἱ ψυχαί· διὸ καὶ γεγόνασιν ἀγχίσποροι θεοῦ. ἀποθάνοι μου ἡ ψυχὴ
[125] τὸν | σωματικὸν βίον, ἵν' ἐν ψυχαῖς δικαίων καταριθμηθῇ, οἵας εἶναι συμβέβηκε τὰς τούτων."
280 LI. Ταῦτ' ἀκούων ὁ Βαλάκης ὤδινεν ἐν ἑαυτῷ. παυσαμένου δέ, τὸ πάθος οὐ χωρήσας "ἐπὶ κατάραις" εἶπεν "ἐχθρῶν μετακληθεὶς εὐχὰς τιθέμενος ἐκείνοις οὐκ ἐρυθριᾷς; ἐλελήθειν ἄρ' ἐμαυτὸν ἀπατῶν ὡς ἐπὶ φίλῳ σοι τὴν ὑπὲρ τῶν πολεμίων ἀφανῶς τεταγμένῳ τάξιν, ἢ νῦν γέγονε δήλη. μήποτε καὶ τὰς ὑπερθέσεις τῆς ἐνθάδε ἀφίξεως ἐποιοῦ διὰ τὴν ὑποικουροῦσαν ἐν τῇ ψυχῇ πρὸς μὲν ἐκείνους οἰκειότητα πρὸς δ' ἐμὲ καὶ τοὺς ἐμοὺς ἀλλοτρίωσιν· πίστις γάρ, ὡς ὁ παλαιὸς λόγος, τῶν
281 ἀδήλων τὰ ἐμφανῆ." ὁ δὲ τῆς κατοκωχῆς ἀνεθεὶς "ἀδικωτάτην" εἶπεν "αἰτίαν ὑπομένω συκοφαντούμενος· λέγω γὰρ ἴδιον οὐδέν, ἀλλ' ἅττ' ἂν

¹ MSS. συναναμιγνυμένων.

ᵃ Or "foundation" (?). But both καταβάλλω and καταβολή are frequently used of sowing and this meaning fits better the corresponding verse of LXX (xxiii. 10) τίς ἐξηκριβάσατο τὸ σπέρμα Ἰακώβ;

ᵇ Cf. the fragment of Aeschylus's Niobe quoted by Plato, Rep. iii. 391ᴇ:

οἱ θεῶν ἀγχίσποροι

οἱ Ζηνὸς ἐγγύς,

. . . .

καὶ οὔ πώ σφιν ἐξίτηλον αἷμα δαιμόνων.

that, not because their dwelling-place is set apart
and their land severed from others, but because
in virtue of the distinction of their peculiar customs
they do not mix with others to depart from the
ways of their fathers. Who has made accurate dis- 279
covery of how the sowing *a* of their generation was
first made ? Their bodies have been moulded from
human seeds, but their souls are sprung from divine
seeds, and therefore their stock is akin to God.*b*
May my soul die to the life of the body *c* that it
may be reckoned among the souls of the just, even
such as are the souls of these men."

LI. Balak suffered tortures inwardly as he listened 280
to these words, and, when the speaker ceased, he could
not contain his passion. " Are you not ashamed," he
cried, " that, summoned to curse the enemy, you have
prayed for them ? It seems that all unconsciously
I was deceiving myself in treating you as a friend,
who were secretly ranged on the side of the enemy,
as has now become plain. Doubtless also your delay
in coming here was due to your secretly harbouring
a feeling of attachment to them and aversion for me
and mine. For, as the old saying goes, the certain
proves the uncertain." The other, now liberated 281
from the possession, replied : " I suffer under a most
unjust charge and calumny, for I say nothing that is

As there is nothing corresponding to this sentence in the
LXX, it may be assumed that this is a conscious quotation.

c The LXX (v. 10) is ἀποθάνοι ἡ ψυχή μοῦ ἐν ψυχαῖς δικαίων
καὶ γένοιτο τὸ σπέρμα μοῦ ὡς τὸ σπέρμα τούτων. E.V. " Let me
die the death of the righteous, and let my last end be like
his." Philo's idea presumably is that the souls of the
righteous cannot die in the ordinary sense. For the construction *cf. De Gig.* 14 ψυχαὶ . . . μελετῶσαι τὸν μετὰ σωμάτων
ἀποθνῇσκειν βίον.

ὑπηχήσῃ τὸ θεῖον, ὅπερ οὐχὶ νῦν πρῶτον ἐγὼ μὲν
εἶπον, σὺ δ᾽ ἤκουσας, ἀλλὰ καὶ πρόσθεν, ἡνίκα τοὺς
282 πρέσβεις ἔπεμψας, οἷς ἀπεκρινάμην ταὐτά.᾽᾽ νομίσας δ᾽ ὁ βασιλεὺς ἢ τὸν μάντιν ἀπατᾶν ἢ τὸ θεῖον
τρέπεσθαι καὶ ταῖς τῶν τόπων μεταβολαῖς τὸ τῆς
γνώμης ἐχυρὸν ἀλλάττειν, εἰς ἕτερον ἀπαγαγὼν
χωρίον ἐκ λόφου πάνυ περιμήκους ἐπεδείκνυτο
μέρος τι τῆς ἀντιπάλου στρατιᾶς· εἶτα πάλιν ἑπτὰ
βωμοὺς ἱδρυσάμενος καὶ τὰ ἴσα τοῖς πρόσθεν ἱερεῖα
καταθύσας ἐξέπεμπε τὸν μάντιν ἐπ᾽ οἰωνοὺς καὶ
283 φήμας αἰσίους. ὁ δὲ μονωθεὶς ἐξαίφνης θεοφορεῖται καὶ μηδὲν συνιείς, ὥσπερ μετανισταμένου
τοῦ λογισμοῦ, τὰ ὑποβαλλόμενα ἐξελάλει προφητεύων τάδε· ῾῾ ἀναστὰς ἄκουε, βασιλεῦ, τὰ ὦτα
ἐπουρίσας.[1]   οὐχ ὡς ἄνθρωπος ὁ θεὸς διαψευσθῆναι
δύναται οὐδ᾽ ὡς υἱὸς ἀνθρώπου μετανοεῖ καὶ ἅπαξ
εἰπὼν οὐκ ἐμμένει. φθέγξεται τὸ παράπαν οὐδέν,
ὃ μὴ τελειωθήσεται βεβαίως, ἐπεὶ ὁ λόγος ἔργον
ἐστὶν αὐτῷ. παρελήφθην δ᾽ ἐπ᾽ εὐλογίαις, οὐ
284 κατάραις, ἐγώ. οὐκ ἔσται πόνος ἢ μόχθος ἐν
Ἑβραίοις. ὁ θεὸς αὐτῶν προασπίζει περιφανῶς,
ὃς καὶ τὴν τῶν Αἰγυπτιακῶν ῥύμην κακῶν ἀπεσκέ-
δασεν ὡς ἕνα ἄνδρα τὰς τοσαύτας μυριάδας ἀν-
αγαγών. τοιγαροῦν οἰωνῶν ἀλογοῦσι καὶ πάντων
τῶν κατὰ μαντικὴν ἑνὶ τῷ τοῦ κόσμου ἡγεμόνι

---

[1] See on *De Abr.* 20. Here as in *De Decal.* 148, the word
is fairly well suited to the context. The best mss. have
ἐπαιωρήσας, which does not seem altogether impossible, for
though no similar use of the compound verb is quoted, the
simple verb is found in this sense, *e.g.* αἰωρεῖν τὰς ὀφρῦς.

---

[a] Or "sounds and voices"=κληδόνας § 287. In Numbers
Balaam goes to "meet the Lord," but the account of his

422

my own, but only what is prompted by God, and this I do not say or you hear now for the first time, but I said it before when you sent the ambassadors to whom I gave the same answer." But the king, 282 thinking either to deceive the seer or to move the Deity and draw Him from His firm purpose by a change of place, led the way to another spot, and from an exceedingly high hill shewed the seer a part of the enemy's host. Then again he set up seven altars, and, after sacrificing the same number of victims as before, sent him away to seek good omens through birds or voices.[a] In this solitude, he was suddenly possessed, 283 and, understanding nothing, his reason as it were roaming, uttered these prophetic words which were put into his mouth.[b] "Arise, O King, and listen. Lend me a ready ear. God cannot be deceived [c] as a man, nor as the son of man does He repent [d] or fail to abide by what He has once said. He will utter nothing at all which shall not certainly be performed, for His word is His deed. As for me, I was summoned to bless, not to curse. There shall be no 284 trouble or labour among the Hebrews. Their God is their shield for all to see, He Who also scattered the fierce onset of the ills of Egypt, and brought up all these myriads as a single man. Therefore, they care nothing for omens and all the lore of the soothsayer, because they trust in One Who is the ruler of

purpose given here might be justified from xxiv. 1 "he went not, as at the other times, to meet with enchantments."

[b] This is curiously expressed. We expect "returned and uttered" as in Num. xxiii. 17.

[c] So LXX (διαρτηθῆναι). E.V. "lie" (xxiii. 19).

[d] Here Philo whether accidentally or not agrees with the Hebrew against the LXX, which has ἀπειληθῆναι ("be threatened").

πιστεύοντες. ὁρῶ λαὸν ὡς σκύμνον ἀνιστάμενον καὶ ὡς λέοντα γαυρούμενον. εὐωχηθήσεται θήρας καὶ ποτῷ χρήσεται τραυματιῶν αἵματι καὶ κορεσθεὶς [126] οὐ τρέψεται πρὸς ὕπνον, ἀλλ' | ἐγρηγορὼς τὸν ἐπινίκιον ᾄσεται ὕμνον."

285   LII. Χαλεπῶς δ' ἐνεγκὼν ἐπὶ τῷ παρ' ἐλπίδας αὐτῷ τὰ τῆς μαντικῆς ἀπαντᾶσθαι[a] " ἄνθρωπε " εἶπε, " μήτε ἀρὰς τίθεσο μήτ' εὐχὰς ποιοῦ· βελτίων γὰρ τῶν μὴ καθ' ἡδονὴν λόγων ἢ ἀκίνδυνος ἡσυχία." καὶ ταῦτ' εἰπὼν ὥσπερ ἐκλαθόμενος ὧν εἶπε διὰ τὸ τῆς γνώμης ἀβέβαιον εἰς ἄλλον τόπον ἀπῆγε τὸν μάντιν, ἀφ' οὗ δείξας μέρος τι τῆς Ἑβραϊκῆς
286 στρατιᾶς καταρᾶσθαι παρεκάλει.   ὁ δ' ἅτε χείρων ἐκείνου, καίτοι πρὸς τὰς ἐπιφερομένας κατηγορίας ἀπολογίᾳ μιᾷ χρώμενος ἀληθεῖ, ὡς οὐδὲν ἴδιον λέγοι, κατεχόμενος δὲ καὶ ἐνθουσιῶν διερμηνεύοι τὰ ἑτέρου, δέον μηκέτ' ἐπακολουθεῖν ἀλλ' οἴκαδε ἀπαίρειν, ἑτοιμότερον τοῦ παραπέμποντος προεξέτρεχεν, ἅμα μὲν οἰήσει, κακῷ μεγάλῳ, πεπιεσμένος, ἅμα δὲ καὶ τῇ διανοίᾳ καταρᾶσθαι γλιχό-
287 μενος, εἰ καὶ τῇ φωνῇ διεκωλύετο.   παραγενόμενος δ' εἰς ὄρος μεῖζον τῶν προτέρων ἄχρι πολλοῦ κατατεῖνον κελεύει μὲν τὴν αὐτὴν ἐπιτελεῖν θυσίαν βωμοὺς πάλιν ἑπτὰ κατασκευάσαντας καὶ ἱερεῖα τεσσαρεσκαίδεκα προσαγαγόντας ἑκάστῳ βωμῷ δύο, μόσχον τε καὶ κριόν.   αὐτὸς δὲ οὐκέτι κατὰ τὸ εἰκὸς ἐπὶ κληδόνας καὶ οἰωνοὺς ᾔετο πολλὰ τὴν

---

[a] ἀπαντᾶσθαι is apparently used in the middle here. The usage is found occasionally, but censured by Lucian, *Lexiphanes* 25 as non-Attic.

424

the world. I see the people rising up as a lion's cub, and exulting as a lion. He shall feast upon the prey, and take for his drink the blood of the wounded, and, when he has had his fill, he shall not betake himself to slumber, but unsleeping sing the song of the victorious."

LII. Highly indignant at finding the soothsayer's 285 powers thus unexpectedly hostile,[a] Balak said : "Sirrah, do not either curse or bless, for the silence which avoids danger is better than words which displease." And, having said this, as though in the inconstancy of his judgement he had forgotten what he said, he led the seer away to another place from which he shewed him a part of the Hebrew host and begged him to curse them. Here the seer proved 286 himself to be even worse than the king ; for, though he had met the charges brought against him solely by the true plea that nothing which he said was his own but the divinely inspired version of the promptings of another, and therefore ought to have ceased to follow, and departed home, instead, he pressed forward even more readily than his conductor, partly because he was dominated by the worst of vices, conceit, partly because in his heart he longed to curse, even if he were prevented from doing so with his voice. And, having arrived at a mountain higher 287 than those where he had stood before, and of great extent, he bade them perform the same sacrifice after again erecting seven altars, and bringing fourteen victims, two for each altar, a ram and a calf. But he himself did not go again, as was to be expected, to seek for omens from birds or voices, for he had conceived a great contempt for his

αὐτοῦ τέχνην κακίσας ὡς χρόνῳ καθάπερ γραφὴν
ἐξίτηλον γενομένην καὶ τοὺς εὐθυβόλους στο
χασμοὺς ἐξαμαυρωθεῖσαν· ἄλλως δὲ καὶ μόλις
ἐνενόησεν, ὅτι οὐ συνᾴδει τῷ τοῦ θεοῦ βουλήματι
ἡ τοῦ μισθωσαμένου προαίρεσις αὐτὸν βασιλέως.

288 τραπόμενος οὖν κατὰ τὴν ἐρήμην ὁρᾷ κατὰ φυλὰς
ἐστρατοπεδευκότας Ἑβραίους καὶ τό τε πλῆθος καὶ
τὴν τάξιν ὡς πόλεως ἀλλ' οὐ στρατοπέδου κατα
πλαγεὶς ἔνθους γενόμενος ἀναφθέγγεται τάδε·

289 " φησὶν ὁ ἄνθρωπος ὁ ἀληθινῶς ὁρῶν, ὅστις καθ'
ὕπνον ἐναργῆ φαντασίαν εἶδε θεοῦ τοῖς τῆς ψυχῆς
ἀκοιμήτοις ὄμμασιν. ὡς καλοί σου οἱ οἶκοι,
στρατιὰ Ἑβραίων, αἱ σκηναί σου ὡς νάπαι σκιά
ζουσαι, ὡς παράδεισος ἐπὶ ποταμοῦ, ὡς κέδρος

290 παρ' ὕδατα. ἐξελεύσεταί ποτε ἄνθρωπος ἐξ ὑμῶν
καὶ ἐπικρατήσει πολλῶν ἐθνῶν καὶ ἐπιβαίνουσα
ἡ τοῦδε βασιλεία καθ' ἑκάστην ἡμέραν πρὸς ὕψος
ἀρθήσεται. ὁ λαὸς οὗτος ἡγεμόνι τῆς ἀπ' Αἰγύπτου
πάσης ὁδοῦ κέχρηται θεῷ καθ' ἓν κέρας ἄγοντι τὴν

291 πληθύν. τοιγαροῦν ἔδεται | ἔθνη πολλὰ ἐχθρῶν
[127] καὶ ὅσον ἐν αὐτοῖς πῖον ἄχρι μυελοῦ λήψεται καὶ
ταῖς ἐκηβολίαις ἀπολεῖ τοὺς δυσμενεῖς. ἀνα
παύσεται κατακλινεὶς ὡς λέων ἢ σκύμνος λέοντος,
μάλα καταφρονητικῶς δεδιὼς οὐδένα, φόβον τοῖς
ἄλλοις ἐνειργασμένος· ἄθλιος ὃς ἂν αὐτὸν παρα
κινήσας ἐγείρῃ. οἱ μὲν εὐλογοῦντές σε εὐφημίας
ἄξιοι, κατάρας δ' οἱ καταρώμενοι."

292 LIII. Σφόδρα δ' ἐπὶ τούτοις ἀγανακτήσας ὁ
βασιλεὺς " ἐπ' ἀραῖς " εἶπεν " ἐχθρῶν μετακληθεὶς

---

[a] LXX " The kingdom of Gog shall be exalted (E.V. his
king shall be higher than Agag) and his kingdom shall
be increased."

own art, feeling that, as a picture fades in the course
of years, its gift of happy conjecture had lost all
its brilliance. Besides, he at last realized that the
purpose of the king who had hired him was not in
harmony with the will of God. So, setting his face 288
to the wilderness, he looked upon the Hebrews
encamped in their tribes, and, astounded at their
number and order, which resembled a city rather
than a camp, he was filled with the spirit, and spoke
as follows : " Thus saith the man who truly sees, who 289
in slumber saw the clear vision of God with the unsleeping eyes of the soul. How goodly are thy dwell-
ings, thou host of the Hebrews ! Thy tents are as
shady dells, as a garden by the riverside, as a cedar
beside the waters. There shall come forth from you 290
one day a man and he shall rule over many nations,
and his kingdom spreading every day shall be exalted
on high.*ᵃ* This people, throughout its journey from
Egypt, has had God as its guide, Who leads the multitude in a single column.*ᵇ* Therefore, it shall eat up 291
many nations of its enemies, and take all the fatness
of them right up to the marrow, and destroy its foes
with its far-reaching bolts. It shall lie down and
rest as a lion, or a lion's cub, full of scorn, fearing
none but putting fear in all others. Woe to him
who stirs up and rouses it. Worthy of benediction
are those who bless thee, worthy of cursing those
who curse thee."

LIII. Greatly incensed by this, the king said : 292
" Thou wast summoned to curse the enemy, and hast

> *ᵇ* Philo is evidently interpreting Num. xxiv. 8 ὡς δόξα
μονοκέρωτος αὐτῷ, " he has as it were the glory of the unicorn "
(R.V. " wild ox "). The mistake is strange, since the word
occurs frequently in the LXX, and even in the Pentateuch
(Deut. xxxiii. 17).

427

PHILO

εὐχὰς ἤδη τρεῖς τὰς ὑπὲρ ἐκείνων πεποίησαι· φεῦγε
δὴ θᾶττον—ὀξὺ πάθος ἐστὶ θυμός—, μή τι καὶ
293 νεώτερον ἐργάσασθαι βιασθῶ. πόσον πλῆθος χρημάτων, ἀνοητότατε, καὶ δωρεῶν, πόσην δ' εὐφημίαν
καὶ δόξαν ἀφῄρησαι σεαυτὸν φρενοβλαβὴς ὤν·
ἐπανελεύσῃ φέρων ἀπὸ τῆς ξένης εἰς τὴν οἰκείαν
ἀγαθὸν μὲν οὐδέν, ὀνείδη δὲ καὶ πολλὴν ὡς ἔοικεν
αἰσχύνην, οὕτως σοι τῶν κατὰ τὴν ἐπιστήμην, ἐφ'
294 οἷς πρότερον ἐσεμνύνου, γελασθέντων." ὁ δὲ " τὰ
μὲν πρότερα " εἶπε " πάντ' ἐστὶ λόγια καὶ χρησμοί,
τὰ δὲ μέλλοντα λέγεσθαι γνώμης τῆς ἐμῆς
εἰκασίαι." καὶ τῆς δεξιᾶς λαβόμενος μόνος μόνῳ
συνεβούλευε, δι' ὧν, ὡς ἂν οἷόν τε ᾖ, φυλάξεται
τὸν ἀντίπαλον στρατόν, ἀσέβημα κατηγορῶν αὐτοῦ
μέγιστον· τί γάρ, εἴποι τις ἄν, ἰδιάζεις καὶ συμ-
βουλεύεις τὰ ἐναντία τοῖς χρησμοῖς ὑποτιθέμενος, εἰ
μὴ ἄρα τῶν λογίων αἱ σαὶ βουλαὶ δυνατώτεραι;
295 LIV. φέρε δ' οὖν καὶ τὰς καλὰς αὐτοῦ παραινέσεις
ἐξετάσωμεν, ὡς τετεχνιτευμέναι πρὸς ὁμολογου-
μένην ἧτταν τῶν ἀεὶ νικᾶν δυναμένων. εἰδὼς γὰρ
Ἑβραίοις μίαν ὁδὸν ἁλώσεως παρανομίαν, διὰ
λαγνείας καὶ ἀκολασίας, μεγάλου κακοῦ, πρὸς
μεῖζον κακόν, ἀσέβειαν, ἄγειν αὐτοὺς ἐσπούδασεν
296 ἡδονὴν δέλεαρ προθείς. " εἰσὶ " γὰρ εἶπεν " αἱ
ἐγχώριοι γυναῖκες, ὦ βασιλεῦ, διαφέρουσαι τὴν
ὄψιν ἑτέρων· ἀνὴρ δ' οὐδενὶ μᾶλλον εὐάλωτος ἢ
γυναικὸς εὐμορφίᾳ. ταῖς οὖν περικαλλεστάταις ἐὰν

ᵃ §§ 294-299 are based on Num. xxxi. 16, where the sin of
Israel is ascribed to the counsels of Balaam.

now thrice invoked blessings on them. Flee quickly, for fierce is the passion of wrath, lest I be forced to do thee some mischief. Most foolish of men, of what 293 a store of wealth and presents, of what fame and glory, hast thou robbed thyself by thy madness. Thou wilt return from the stranger's land to thy own with nothing good in thy hand, but with reproaches and deep disgrace, as all may see, having merely brought such ridicule on the lore of the knowledge on which thou didst pride thyself before." *ª* The other 294 replied : " All that has been said hitherto was oracles from above. What I have now to say is suggestions of my own designing." And, taking him by the right hand, he counselled him in strict privacy as to the means by which, as far as might be, he should defend himself against the army of the enemy. Hereby he convicted himself of the utmost impiety ; for, " Why," we might ask him, " do you put forth your own personal counsels in opposition to the oracles of God ? That were to hold that your projects are more powerful than the divine utterances." LIV. Well, then, let us examine these fine injunctions of 295 his, and see how they were contrived to gain an unquestioned victory over the truths which have ever the power to prevail. His advice was this. Knowing that the one way by which the Hebrews could be overthrown was disobedience, he set himself to lead them, through wantonness and licentiousness, to impiety, through a great sin to a still greater, and put before them the bait of pleasure. " You 296 have in your countrywomen, king," he said, " persons of pre-eminent beauty. And there is nothing to which a man more easily falls a captive than women's comeliness. If, then, you permit the fairest among

ἐπιτρέψῃς μισθαρνεῖν καὶ δημοσιεύειν, ἀγκιστρεύ-
297 σονται τὴν νεότητα τῶν ἀντιπάλων. ὑφηγητέον δὲ
αὐταῖς, μὴ εὐθὺς ἐμπαρέχεσθαι τοῖς ἐθέλουσι τὴν
ὥραν· ὁ γὰρ ἀκκισμὸς ὑποκνίζων τὰς ὁρμὰς ἐπ-
εγείρει μᾶλλον καὶ τοὺς ἔρωτας ἀναφλέγει· τραχηλι-
ζόμενοι δὲ ταῖς ἐπιθυμίαις πάνθ' ὑπομενοῦσι δρᾶν
298 τε καὶ πάσχειν. πρὸς δὲ τὸν οὕτω διακείμενον
[128] ἐραστὴν λεγέτω | φρυαττομένη τις τῶν ἐπὶ τὴν
θήραν ἀλειφομένων· 'οὐ θέμις ὁμιλίας σοι τῆς
ἐμῆς ἀπολαῦσαι, πρὶν ἂν ἐκδιαιτηθῇς μὲν τὰ πάτρια,
μεταβαλὼν δὲ τιμήσῃς ἅπερ ἐγώ. πίστις δέ μοι
τῆς βεβαίου μεταβολῆς γένοιτ' ἂν ἀρίδηλος, ἢν
ἐθελήσῃς μετασχεῖν τῶν αὐτῶν σπονδῶν τε καὶ
θυσιῶν, ἃς ἀγάλμασι καὶ ξοάνοις καὶ τοῖς λοιποῖς
299 ἀφιδρύμασιν ἐπιτελοῦμεν.' ὁ δ' ἅτε σαγηνευθεὶς
πάγαις πολυειδέσι, κάλλει καὶ στωμυλίας χειρ-
αγωγίαις, οὐδὲν ἀντειπών, ἐξηγκωνισμένος τὸν
λογισμόν, ἄθλιος ὑπηρετήσει τοῖς προσταττομένοις,
ἀναγραφεὶς τοῦ πάθους δοῦλος.''

300 LV. Ὁ μὲν δὴ τοιαῦτα συνεβούλευεν. ὁ δ' οὐκ
ἀπὸ σκοποῦ νομίσας εἶναι τὰ λεχθέντα, τὸν κατὰ
μοιχῶν νόμον παρακαλυψάμενος καὶ τοὺς ἐπὶ φθορᾷ
καὶ πορνείᾳ κειμένους ἀνελών, ὡς εἰ μηδὲ τὴν
ἀρχὴν ἐγράφησαν, ἀνέδην ἐπιτρέπει ταῖς γυναιξὶ
301 τὰς ὁμιλίας πρὸς οὓς ἂν ἐθέλωσι ποιεῖσθαι. δο-
θείσης δὲ ἀδείας, τὴν πληθὺν τῶν μειρακίων
ἐπήγοντο πολὺ πρότερον τὴν διάνοιαν αὐτῶν
ἀπατῶσαι καὶ τρέπουσαι ταῖς γοητείαις πρὸς
ἀσέβειαν, ἕως υἱὸς τοῦ ἀρχιερέως Φινεὲς ἐπὶ τοῖς
γινομένοις σφόδρα χαλεπήνας—δεινότατον γὰρ αὐτῷ

ᵃ For §§ 300-304 see Num. xxv.

them to prostitute themselves for hire, they will en-
snare the younger of their enemies. But you must 297
instruct them not to allow their wooers to enjoy
their charms at once. For coyness titillates, and
thereby makes the appetites more active, and in-
flames the passions. And, when their lust has them
in its grip, there is nothing which they will shrink
from doing or suffering. Then, when the lover is in 298
this condition, one of those who are arming to take
their prey should say, with a saucy air : ' You must
not be permitted to enjoy my favours until you have
left the ways of your fathers and become a convert
to honouring what I honour. That your conversion
is sincere will be clearly proved to me if you are
willing to take part in the libations and sacrifices
which we offer to idols of stone and wood and
the other images.' Then the lover, caught in the 299
meshes of her multiform lures, her beauty and the
enticements of her wheedling talk, will not gainsay
her, but, with his reason trussed and pinioned, will
subserve her orders to his sorrow, and be enrolled
as a slave of passion."

LV. *a* Such was his advice. And the king, thinking 300
that the proposal was good, ignoring the law against
adultery, and annulling those which prohibited seduc-
tion and fornication as though they had never been
enacted at all, permitted the women, without re-
striction, to have intercourse with whom they would.
Having thus received immunity, so greatly did they 301
mislead the minds of most of the young men, and
pervert them by their arts to impiety, that they soon *b*
made a conquest of them. And this continued until
Phinehas, the son of the high priest, greatly angered

---

b Lit. "*First* greatly deceiving . . . they made a conquest."

κατεφαίνετο, εἰ ὑφ' ἕνα καιρὸν ἄμφω τά τε σώματα
καὶ τὰς ψυχὰς ἐπιδεδώκασι, τὰ μὲν ἡδοναῖς, τὰς
δὲ τῷ παρανομεῖν καὶ ἀνοσιουργεῖν—ἐνεανιεύσατο
νεανείαν ἀνδρὶ καλῷ καὶ ἀγαθῷ προσήκουσαν.
302 ἰδὼν γάρ τινα τῶν ἀπὸ τοῦ γένους θύοντα καὶ
εἰσιόντα πρὸς πόρνην, μήτε κεκυφότα εἰς τοὔδαφος
μήτε λανθάνειν τοὺς πολλοὺς πειρώμενον μήθ' οἷα
φιλεῖ κλέπτοντα τὴν εἴσοδον, ἀλλὰ μετ' ἀναισχύντου
θράσους τὴν ἀκοσμίαν ἐπιδεικνύμενον καὶ φρυατ-
τόμενον ὡς ἐπὶ σεμνῷ πράγματι τῷ καταγελάστῳ,
πάνυ πικρανθεὶς καὶ πληρωθεὶς ὀργῆς δικαίας
ἐπεισδραμὼν ἔτι κατ' εὐνὴν κειμένους ἀμφοτέρους
τόν τ' ἐραστὴν καὶ τὴν ἑταίραν ἀναιρεῖ προσανα-
τεμὼν καὶ τὰ γεννητικά, διότι σποραῖς ὑπηρέτησαν
303 ἐκθέσμοις. τοῦτο θεασάμενοί τινες τὸ παράδειγμα
τῶν τὴν ἐγκράτειαν καὶ θεοσέβειαν ἐζηλωκότων
προστάξαντος Μωυσέως ἐμιμήσαντο καὶ πάντας
τοὺς τελεσθέντας τοῖς χειροποιήτοις συγγενεῖς καὶ
φίλους ἡβηδὸν ἀνελόντες τὸ μὲν μίασμα τοῦ ἔθνους
ἐκκαθαίρουσι διὰ τῆς τῶν προηδικηκότων ἀπαρ-
αιτήτου τιμωρίας, τοὺς δ' ἄλλους παρασχόντας ἀπο-
λογίαν ἐναργεστάτην ὑπὲρ τῆς αὐτῶν εὐσεβείας
περιεποιήσαντο, μηδένα τῶν ἀφ' αἵματος κατα-
κρίτων οἰκτισάμενοι μηδ' ἐλέῳ τἀδικήματα αὐτῶν
παρελθόντες, ἀλλὰ καθαροὺς νομίσαντες τοὺς αὐτό-
χειρας· ὅθεν οὐδενὶ παρεχώρησαν τὴν ἐπέξοδον
φέρουσαν τοῖς δρῶσιν ἀψευδέστατον ἔπαινον.
304 τετρακισχιλίους δέ φασι πρὸς τοῖς δισμυρίοις |
[129] ἀναιρεθῆναι μιᾷ ἡμέρᾳ, συναναιρεθέντος εὐθὺς τοῦ
κοινοῦ μιάσματος, ὃ πᾶσαν τὴν στρατιὰν ἐκηλίδου.

at what he saw, and horrified at the thought that his people had at the same moment surrendered their bodies to pleasure and their souls to lawlessness and unholiness, shewed the young, gallant spirit which befitted a man of true excellence. For, seeing one 302 of his race offering sacrifice and visiting a harlot, not with his head bowed down towards the ground, nor trying in the usual way to make a stealthy entrance unobserved by the public, but flaunting his licentiousness boldly and shamelessly, and pluming himself as though his conduct called for honour instead of scorn,[a] he was filled with bitterness and righteous anger, and attacking the pair whilst they still lay together he slew both the lover and his concubine, ripping up also her parts of generation because they had served to receive the illicit seed. This example 303 being observed by some of those who were zealous for continence and godliness they copied it at the command of Moses, and massacred all their friends and kinsfolk who had taken part in the rites of these idols made by men's hands. And thus they purged the defilement of the nation, by relentlessly punishing the actual sinners, while they spared the rest who gave clear proof of their piety. To none of their convicted blood-relations did they shew pity, or mercifully condone their crimes, but held that their slayers were free from guilt. And, therefore, they kept in their own hand the act of vengeance, which in the truest sense was laudable to its executors. Twenty-four thousand, we are told, perished in one 304 day. And with them perished, at the same moment, the common pollution which was defiling the whole

---

[a] *Cf.* xxv. 6, "in the sight of Moses, and all the congregation."

τῶν δὲ καθαρσίων ἐπιτελεσθέντων, ὡς ἀριστεῖ
γέρας ἐπάξιον τῷ υἱῷ τοῦ ἀρχιερέως, ὃς πρῶτος
ἐπὶ τὴν ἄμυναν ὥρμησεν, ἐζήτει παρασχεῖν Μωυσῆς.
φθάνει δὲ χρησμοῖς δωρησάμενος ὁ θεὸς Φινεεῖ
τὸ μέγιστον ἀγαθόν, εἰρήνην, ὃ μηδεὶς ἱκανὸς ἀνθρώπων παρασχεῖν, πρὸς δὲ τῇ εἰρήνῃ καὶ παγ-
κρατησίαν ἱερωσύνης, αὐτῷ καὶ γένει κλῆρον ἀν-
αφαίρετον.

305 LVI. Ἐπεὶ δὲ τῶν ἐμφυλίων οὐδὲν ἔτ᾽ ἦν
ὑπόλοιπον κακῶν, ἀλλὰ καὶ ὅσοι πρὸς αὐτομολίαν
ἢ προδοσίαν ὑπωπτεύοντο πάντες ἀπωλώλεσαν,
ἔδοξεν εἶναι καιρὸς ἐπιτηδειότατος τῆς ἐπὶ τὸν
Βαλάκην στρατείας, ἄνδρα μυρία καὶ βεβουλευμένον
ἐργάσασθαι κακὰ καὶ δεδρακότα, βεβουλευμένον
μὲν διὰ τοῦ μάντεως, ὃν ἤλπισεν ἀραῖς τισι δυνήσεσθαι καθελεῖν τὴν δύναμιν τῶν Ἑβραίων, δεδρακότα δὲ διὰ τῆς τῶν γυναικῶν ἀσελγείας καὶ
ἀκολασίας, αἳ τὰ μὲν σώματα λαγνείαις τὰς δὲ
306 ψυχὰς ἀσεβείᾳ τῶν χρωμένων διέφθειραν. παντὶ
μὲν οὖν τῷ στρατῷ πολεμεῖν οὐκ ἐδοκίμαζεν, εἰδὼς
τὰ ὑπέρογκα[1] πλήθη πταίοντα περὶ αὐτοῖς καὶ ἅμα
λυσιτελὲς ἡγούμενος ἐφεδρείας εἶναι συμμάχων τοῖς
προκαμοῦσι βοηθούς, ἀριστίνδην δὲ τοὺς ἡβῶντας
ἐπιλέξας, χιλίους ἐκ φυλῆς ἑκάστης, δώδεκα χιλιά-
δας—τοσαῦται γὰρ ἦσαν αἱ φυλαί—καὶ στρατηγὸν ἑλόμενος τοῦ πολέμου Φινεὲς πεῖραν ἤδη δεδω-

---

[1] mss. ὑπερόρια.

---

a Philo understands the " plague " of xxv. 8, 9, lxx πληγή,
to refer not to a pestilence sent by God, but to the slaughter
of the guilty. The mistake, if it is a mistake, is not unnatural. Not only has the mention of the " plague " been
introduced so abruptly that probably something has been lost,
but the coupling of πεπληγυῖα, referring to the slain woman,

host.[a] When the purging was completed, Moses
sought how to give to the high priest's son, who had
been the first to rush to the defence, such reward
as he deserved for his heroism. But he was fore-
stalled by God, Whose voice granted to Phinehas the
highest of blessings, peace—a gift which no human
being can bestow—and, besides peace, full possession
of the priesthood, a heritage to himself and his
family which none should take from them.[b]

LVI. [c] Since, now, their internal troubles were en- 305
tirely at an end, and, further, all those who were
suspected of desertion or treachery had perished, it
seemed to be a very suitable opportunity for waging
war against Balak who had both plotted and executed
mischief on so vast a scale. In the plotting he had
been served by the soothsayer, who, he hoped, would
be able by his curses to destroy the power of the
Hebrews ; in the execution by the licentiousness
and wantonness of the women, who had caused the
ruin of their paramours, of their bodies through lust,
of their souls through impiety. However, Moses did 306
not think well to employ his whole army, knowing
that over-large multitudes fall through their own
unwieldiness, and, at the same time, he thought it
was an advantage to have reserves to reinforce those
who bore the first brunt. He accordingly selected
the flower of his men of military age, one thousand
from each tribe, twelve thousand, that is, corresponding to the number of the tribes, and chose as com-
mander-in-chief Phinehas, who had already given

with πληγή in verse 18 (*cf.* also vv. 14, 15), would lend itself
to his interpretation. See further App. pp. 603-604.

[b] The rewards of Phinehas have been treated in their
allegorical sense, *De Ebr.* 75 f., *De Post.* 183 f., *De Conf.* 57.

[c] For §§ 305-318 see Num. xxxi.

κότα στρατηγικῆς εὐτολμίας ἐπὶ καλοῖς ἱερείοις
ἐξέπεμπε τοὺς ὁπλίτας καὶ θαρσύνων τοιάδε διεξ-
307 ῄει· "οὐχ ὑπὲρ κράτους ἀρχῆς ὁ παρὼν ἀγών
ἐστιν οὐδ' ὑπὲρ τοῦ κτήσασθαι τὰ ἑτέρων, περὶ ὧν
ἢ μόνων ἢ μάλιστα οἱ πόλεμοι, ἀλλ' ὑπὲρ εὐσεβείας
καὶ ὁσιότητος, ὧν τοὺς ἡμετέρους συγγενεῖς καὶ
φίλους ἠλλοτρίωσαν οἱ ἐχθροὶ παραίτιοι γενόμενοι
308 τοῖς ὑπαχθεῖσι χαλεπῆς ἀπωλείας. ἔστιν οὖν
ἄτοπον οἰκείων μὲν αὐτόχειρας γεγενῆσθαι παρα-
νομησάντων, ἐχθρῶν δὲ χαλεπώτερα ἠδικηκότων
ἀποσχέσθαι, καὶ τοὺς μὲν μαθόντας ἀδικεῖν ἀν-
ῃρηκέναι, τοὺς δὲ βιασαμένους καὶ διδάξαντας ἀ-
τιμωρήτους καταλιπεῖν, οὓς ἁπάντων αἰτίους εἶναι
συμβέβηκεν, ὧν ἢ δεδράκασιν ἢ πεπόνθασιν ἐκεῖ-
309 νοι." LVII. νευρωθέντες οὖν ταῖς παραινέσεσιν
ἐκεῖνοι καὶ ὅσον ἐν ταῖς ψυχαῖς προϋπῆρχε γεν-
ναιότητος ζωπυρήσαντες ὡς ἐφ' ὁμολογουμένῃ νίκῃ
πρὸς τὸν ἀγῶνα ἵεντο φρονήμασιν ἀηττήτοις· καὶ
συμπλακέντες τοσαύτῃ περιουσίᾳ ῥώμης καὶ τόλμης
ἐχρήσαντο, ὡς ἱερεῦσαι μὲν τοὺς ἀντιπάλους, αὐτοὶ
δὲ πάντες σῷοι ἐπανελθεῖν, οὐδενὸς ἀποθανόντος
310 ἀλλ' οὐδὲ τρωθέντος. | ὑπέλαβεν ἄν τις τῶν
[130] ἀγνοούντων τὸ συμβεβηκὸς ἰδὼν αὐτοὺς ἐπανιόντας
οὐκ ἀπὸ πολέμου καὶ παρατάξεως ἀφικνεῖσθαι
μᾶλλον ἢ τῶν ἐν ταῖς ὁπλοσκοπίαις ἐπιδείξεων, ἃς
ἔθος ἐν εἰρήνῃ ποιεῖσθαι, γυμνάσματα δ' εἰσὶ καὶ
μελέται συγκροτουμένων[1] τὰ κατ' ἐχθρῶν ἐν φίλοις.
311 τὰς μὲν οὖν πόλεις ἢ κατασκάπτοντες ἢ ἐμπιπράν-
τες, ἠφάνισαν, ὡς μηδ' εἰ τὴν ἀρχὴν ᾠκίσθησαν

---

[1] Mangey wished to read συγκροτούντων, a very common
usage no doubt with πόλεμον and the like, cf. e.g. De Abr. 29,
but in a somewhat different sense. Here the passive=

436

proof of his courage in that capacity; and after favourable sacrifices he dispatched his armed men, with words of encouragement to the following effect: " The contest before you is not to win dominion, nor 307 to appropriate the possessions of others, which is the sole or principal object of other wars, but to defend piety and holiness, from which our kinsfolk and friends have been perverted by the enemies who have indirectly caused their victims to perish miserably. It would be absurd, then, if, after having 308 slain with our own hands those who transgressed the law, we should spare the enemies who committed the graver wrong; if, after putting to death those who learned the lesson of wrongdoing, we should leave unpunished the teachers who forced them to it, and are responsible for all they did or suffered." LVII. So, braced by these exhortations, with the 309 native gallantry of their souls kindled to a flame, they went forth to the contest as to certain victory with indomitable resolution, and in the engagement shewed such a wealth of strength and boldness, that they made a slaughter of their opponents, and returned themselves all safe and sound without a single one killed or even wounded. Indeed, any spectator 310 who did not know the facts would have supposed that they were returning not from a war or pitched battle but from those military reviews and displays of arms so frequently made in peace-time, which serve as drilling and practising grounds, where training for hostilities is carried on among friends. They 311 proceeded to destroy the cities utterly by demolition or fire, so that no one could have told that

---

"trained in" followed by the acc. of respect is more appropriate.

εἰπεῖν ἔχειν· αἰχμαλώτων δὲ σωμάτων ἀπερίληπτον
ἀριθμὸν ἀπαγαγόντες ἄνδρας μὲν καὶ γυναῖκας
κτείνειν ἐδικαίωσαν, τοὺς μὲν ὅτι βουλευμάτων καὶ
χειρῶν ἦρξαν ἀδίκων, τὰς δ' ἐπεὶ κατεγοήτευσαν
τὴν Ἑβραίων νεότητα, παραιτίας γενομένας αὐτοῖς
ἀκολασίας καὶ ἀσεβείας καὶ τὰ τελευταῖα θανάτου·
νέοις δὲ κομιδῇ παισὶ καὶ παρθένοις συνέγνωσαν,
ἀμνηστίαν τῆς ἡλικίας ἐφελκομένης.

312   Λείας δὲ πολλῆς ἄγαν εὐπορήσαντες ἔκ τε τῶν
βασιλείων κἀκ τῶν ἰδιωτικῶν οἰκιῶν, ἔτι δὲ τῶν
κατ' ἀγροὺς ἐπαύλεων—ἦν γὰρ ἐν τοῖς χωρίοις οὐκ
ἐλάττων τῆς ἐν τοῖς ἄστεσιν—, ἧκον εἰς τὸ στρατόπεδον ἐπηχθισμένοι τὸν παρὰ τῶν ἐχθρῶν πάντα
313 πλοῦτον. ἐπαινέσας δὲ Μωυσῆς τόν τε στρατηγὸν
Φινεὲς καὶ τοὺς παραταξαμένους ἐπί τε τοῖς κατορθώμασι καὶ ὅτι ταῖς ὠφελείαις οὐκ ἐπέδραμον τὴν
λείαν μόνοι σφετερίσασθαι διανοηθέντες, ἀλλ' εἰς
μέσον προύθεσαν, ἵνα καὶ οἱ καταμείναντες ἐν ταῖς
σκηναῖς μετάσχωσι, προστάττει τοὺς μὲν ἔξω τοῦ
στρατοπέδου καταμένειν τινὰς ἡμέρας, τῷ δὲ
μεγάλῳ ἱερεῖ καθᾶραι τοῦ φόνου τοὺς ἀπὸ τῆς
314 παρατάξεως ἥκοντας τῶν συμμάχων. καὶ γὰρ εἰ
νόμιμοι αἱ κατ' ἐχθρῶν σφαγαί, ἀλλ' ὅ γε κτείνων
ἄνθρωπον, εἰ καὶ δικαίως καὶ ἀμυνόμενος καὶ
βιασθείς, ὑπαίτιος εἶναι δοκεῖ διὰ τὴν ἀνωτάτω καὶ
κοινὴν συγγένειαν· οὗ χάριν καθαρσίων ἐδέησε τοῖς
κτείνασι πρὸς ἀπαλλαγὴν τοῦ νομισθέντος ἄγους
315 γεγενῆσθαι.   LVIII. μετ' οὐ πολὺν μέντοι χρόνον καὶ τὴν λείαν διένειμε, τοῖς μὲν στρατευ-
438

they had ever been inhabited. And, having carried off prisoners more than they could count, they felt justified in putting the men and women to death, the former because these iniquitous designs and actions had been begun by them, the women because they had bewitched the younger Hebrews and thus led them into licentiousness and impiety and finally to death ; but to the boys who were quite young and the maidens they shewed the mercy which their tender age secured for them.

Having greatly enriched themselves with much 312 booty from the palaces and private houses, and also from the country homesteads, since there was as much to be got from the estates as from the cities, they returned to the camp laden with all the wealth obtained from their enemies. Moses praised the 313 general, Phinehas, and the combatants for their exploits, and also because they had not rushed to gain the prizes, nor thought of taking the spoil for themselves alone, but put it into a common stock, that those who had stayed behind in the tents might have their share. But he gave orders that they should stay outside the camp for some days, and that the high priest should purge from bloodshed those members of the united army who returned after being actually engaged. For, though the 314 slaughter of enemies is lawful, yet one who kills a man, even if he does so justly and in self-defence and under compulsion, has something to answer for, in view of the primal common kinship of mankind. And therefore purification was needed for the slayers, to absolve them from what was held to have been a pollution.   LVIII. However, after 315 a short time, he went on to distribute the spoil,

σαμένοις—ὀλίγος δ' ἀριθμὸς ἦσαν παρὰ τοὺς
ἡσυχάσαντας—διδοὺς ἥμισυ μέρος, θάτερον δὲ τοῖς
καταμείνασιν ἐν τῷ στρατοπέδῳ· δίκαιον γὰρ
ὑπέλαβεν εἶναι καὶ τούτοις μεταδοῦναι τῆς ὠφελείας,
εἰ καὶ μὴ τοῖς σώμασι, ταῖς γοῦν ψυχαῖς δι-
αγωνισαμένοις· οἱ γὰρ ἔφεδροι τῶν ἀγωνιστῶν οὐκ
ἐλαττούμενοι ταῖς προθυμίαις χρόνῳ καὶ τῷ φθα-
316 σθῆναι μόνον ὑστερίζουσι. λαβόντων δὲ τῶν μὲν
ὀλίγων πλείω διὰ τὸ προκινδυνεῦσαι, τῶν δὲ
[131] πλειόνων ἐλάττω διὰ | τὴν ἔνδον μονήν, ἔδοξεν
ἀναγκαῖον εἶναι πάσης τῆς λείας τὰς ἀπαρχὰς
καθιερῶσαι· τὸ μὲν οὖν πεντηκοστὸν οἱ ἐφεδρεύ-
σαντες, πεντακοσιοστὴν δὲ μοῖραν οἱ προπολεμή-
σαντες εἰσήνεγκαν· τῶν δ' ἀπαρχῶν τὰς μὲν παρὰ
τῶν στρατευσαμένων τῷ μεγάλῳ ἱερεῖ προστάττει
δοθῆναι, τὰς δὲ παρὰ τῶν καταμεινάντων ἐν τῷ
στρατοπέδῳ τοῖς νεωκόροις, οἷς ὄνομα Λευῖται.
317 χιλίαρχοι δὲ καὶ ἑκατόνταρχοι καὶ ὁ ἄλλος ὅμιλος
λοχαγῶν καὶ ταξιαρχῶν ὑπέρ τε τῆς αὐτῶν σωτηρίας καὶ τῶν συστρατευσαμένων καὶ τῆς παντὸς
λόγου κρείττονος νίκης ἐθελονταὶ κομίζουσιν ἐξαιρέτους ἀπαρχάς, κόσμον τε χρυσοῦν ὅσον ἕκαστος
ἐκ τῆς λείας ἀνεῦρε καὶ σκεύη πολυτελέστατα, ὧν
πάλιν ὕλη χρυσὸς ἦν· ἃ Μωυσῆς λαβὼν καὶ τὴν
εὐσέβειαν τῶν φερόντων ἀγάμενος ἀνατίθησιν ἐν τῇ
καθιερωμένῃ σκηνῇ τῆς εὐχαριστίας τῶν ἀνδρῶν
318 ὑπόμνημα. παγκάλη δὲ ἡ διανομὴ τῶν ἀπαρχῶν·
τὰς μὲν τῶν μὴ πεπολεμηκότων, ἡμίσειαν ἀρετῆς

giving half to the campaigners, who were a small
number compared with those who had remained inactive, while the other half he gave to those who
had stayed in the camp. For he considered that it
was just to give them a part of the prizes, seeing
that their souls at least, if not their bodies, had
taken part in the conflict. For reserve troops are
not inferior in spirit to the actual fighters, but take
a second place only in time and because the first
place is preoccupied by others. And, now that the 316
few had taken more, because they were in the fore-
front of danger, and the many less, because they
had remained in the camp, he thought it necessary
to dedicate the firstfruits of all the spoil. So the
reserves contributed a fiftieth, and those who had
led the advance a five-hundredth. The offerings of
the latter class he ordered to be given to the high
priest, and those of the former class to the temple
servants, who were called Levites. But the com- 317
manders of hundreds and thousands, and the rest of
the company of officers who led the various divisions,[a]
voluntarily made a special offering of firstfruits in
acknowledgement of the preservation of themselves
and their fellow-combatants, and of the victory whose
glory no words could describe. These offerings were
all the golden ornaments which each of them obtained
from the spoil, and very costly vessels also made of
gold ; all of which Moses took, and, honouring the
piety of the donors, laid them up in the consecrated
tabernacle as a memorial of their thankfulness. Admirable indeed was the system of distributing the
firstfruits. The tribute of the non-combatants, who 318

[a] More literally "captain of regiments and brigades."
The "taxiarch" is the higher of the two.

τὴν χωρὶς ἔργου προθυμίαν αὐτὸ μόνον ἐπιδειξα-
μένων, τοῖς νεωκόροις ἀπένειμε, τὰς δὲ τῶν ἀγωνι-
σαμένων, οἳ σώμασι καὶ ψυχαῖς ἐκινδύνευσαν ὁλόκληρον ἀνδραγαθίαν παρασχόμενοι, τῷ προεστηκότι
τῶν νεωκόρων ἱερεῖ τῷ μεγάλῳ, τὰς δὲ τῶν ταξιαρχῶν ἅτε ἡγεμονικὰς τῷ συμπάντων ἡγεμόνι θεῷ.

319 LIX. Πάντες οὗτοι διεπολεμήθησαν οἱ πόλεμοι,
μήπω διαβεβηκότων Ἰορδάνην τὸν ἐγχώριον ποταμόν, πρὸς τοὺς τῆς ἀντιπέρας γῆς οἰκήτορας εὐδαίμονος καὶ βαθείας, ἐν ᾗ πολλὴ πεδιὰς σιτο-
320 φόρος καὶ χιλὸν κτήνεσιν ἐνεγκεῖν ἀγαθή. ταύτην
ὡς ἐθεάσαντο τὴν χώραν αἱ κτηνοτρόφοι δύο φυλαί,
μοῖρα τοῦ σύμπαντος ἕκτη στρατοῦ, Μωυσῆν ἱκέτευον ἐπιτρέψαι τὰς κληρουχίας ἐνταυθοῖ λαβεῖν
αὐτὰς ἤδη ποτὲ ἱδρυθείσας·[1] ἐπιτηδειότατον γὰρ
ἔφασκον εἶναι τὸν τόπον ἐννέμεσθαί τε καὶ ἐμ-
βόσκεσθαι θρέμμασιν εὔυδρον ὄντα καὶ εὔχορτον καὶ
321 προβατευσίμην ἄφθονον πόαν ἀπαυτοματίζοντα. ὁ
δὲ νομίσας αὐτοὺς ἢ προεδρίᾳ τὴν διανομὴν τά τε
γέρα πρὸ καιροῦ λαμβάνειν ἀξιοῦν ἢ πρὸς τοὺς
μέλλοντας πολέμους ἀποκνεῖν, ἐφεδρευόντων ἔτι
πλειόνων βασιλέων, οἳ τὴν εἴσω τοῦ ποταμοῦ χώραν
διεκεκλήρωντο, πάνυ δυσχεράνας πρὸς ὀργὴν
322 ἀποκρίνεται καί φησιν· " ὑμεῖς μὲν οὖν ἐνταυθοῖ
καθεδεῖσθε σχολὴν ἐν οὐ δέοντι καὶ ἀργίαν ἕξοντες,
τοὺς δ' ὑμετέρους συγγενεῖς καὶ φίλους οἱ λειπό-
μενοι τραχηλιοῦσι πόλεμοι, καὶ τὰ μὲν ἆθλα μόνοις
ὑμῖν ὡς ἐπὶ κατωρθωμένοις πᾶσι δοθήσεται, μάχαι
[132] δὲ καὶ πόνοι καὶ | ταλαιπωρίαι καὶ οἱ ἀνωτάτω

---

[1] The text has not been questioned, but seems to me
difficult. Presumably αὐτὰς . . . ἱδρυθείσας refers to φυλαί, not
to κληρουχίας, but no example is given of this construction
with ἐπιτρέπω. I should like to read αὐταῖς . . ἱδρυθείσαις.

had shewn a half-excellence by a zeal unaccompanied by action, he assigned to the temple servants; that of the fighters, who had hasarded bodies and souls, and thus displayed a complete measure of manly worth, he gave to the high priest, the president of the temple servants, that of the commanders of divisions, being the gift of captains, to the captain all, even God.

LIX. [a] All these wars were fought and won without 319 crossing the river of the land, the Jordan, against the inhabitants of the rich and deep-soiled country on the outer side, where there was much expanse of plain fit for growing corn and providing excellent fodder for cattle. When the two cattle-breeding 320 tribes, who were a sixth part of the whole host, surveyed this country, they besought Moses to let them take their allotments there and settle down at once ; for the region, they said, was very well suited to give pasturage and grazing to cattle, being well supplied with water and grassland and producing of itself abundance of herbage for maintaining sheep. Moses, 321 however, considered that they were either claiming to have precedence in the distribution and to take their prizes before they were due, or else were shirking the wars which awaited them, where more kings, whose possessions were situated on the inner side of the river, were still lying ready to resist them. Consequently, he was greatly incensed, and answered them angrily in these words : " Are you, then, to 322 settle down here to enjoy an undeserved leisure and idleness, leaving your kinsfolk and friends to the agony of the wars which still remain ? And are the prizes to be given to you alone, as though success was complete, while battles and labours and tribula-

[a] For §§ 319-333 see Num. xxxii.

PHILO

323 κίνδυνοι ἑτέρους ἀναμενοῦσιν; ἀλλ' οὐ δίκαιον
ὑμᾶς μὲν εἰρήνην καὶ τὰ ἐκ τῆς εἰρήνης ἀγαθὰ
καρποῦσθαι, τοὺς δ' ἄλλους πολέμοις καὶ κακοῖς
ἀμυθήτοις ἐναθλεῖν, οὐδὲ προσθήκην τὸ ὅλον μέρους
εἶναι· τοὐναντίον γὰρ ἕνεκα τῶν ὅλων τὰ μέρη
324 κληρονομίας ἀξιοῦται. πάντες ἐστὲ ἰσότιμοι, γένος
ἕν, οἱ αὐτοὶ πατέρες, οἰκία μία, ἔθη τὰ αὐτά,
κοινωνία νόμων, ἄλλα μυρία, ὧν ἕκαστον τὴν
οἰκειότητα συνδεῖ καὶ πρὸς εὔνοιαν ἁρμόζεται. διὰ
τί δὴ τῶν ἴσων ἐν τοῖς μεγίστοις καὶ ἀναγκαιοτάτοις ἀξιωθέντες ἐν ταῖς διανομαῖς πλεονεκτήσετε, ὡς
ἢ ἄρχοντες ὑπηκόων ἢ δεσπόται δούλων κατα-
325 φρονήσαντες; ἔδει μὲν ὑμᾶς ταῖς ἑτέρων πληγαῖς
πεπαιδεῦσθαι· φρονίμων γὰρ ἀνδρῶν μὴ ἀναμένειν,
ἄχρις ἂν ἐπ' αὐτοὺς ἔλθῃ τὰ δεινά· νυνὶ δὲ παρα-
δείγματ' ἔχοντες οἰκεῖα τοὺς πατέρας, οἳ κατ-
εσκέψαντο τήνδε τὴν χώραν, καὶ τὰς ἐκείνων
συμφορὰς καὶ τῶν συναπονοηθέντων—ἅπαντες γὰρ
ἔξω δυοῖν ἀπώλοντο—, δέον μηδενὶ τῶν ὁμοίων
συνεπιγράφεσθαι, δειλίαν, ὦ κενοὶ φρενῶν, ζηλοῦτε
ὡς οὐκ εὐαλωτότεροι γενησόμενοι καὶ τὰς προθυμίας ὑποσκελίζετε τῶν ἀνδραγαθίζεσθαι προ-
αιρουμένων ἐκλύοντες καὶ παριέντες αὐτῶν τὰ
326 φρονήματα. τοιγάρτοι σπεύδοντες ἁμαρτάνειν σπεύ-
σετε καὶ πρὸς τιμωρίας· ἡ γὰρ δίκη μόλις μὲν
εἴωθε κινεῖσθαι, κινηθεῖσα δ' ἅπαξ φθάνει προ-
327 καταλαμβάνουσα τοὺς ἀποδιδράσκοντας. ὅταν οὖν

---

[a] Lit. "and is fitted to goodwill," *i.e.* fitted to take part
in producing goodwill.

[b] The thought is taken from v. 23 (in Moses' second

tion and supreme dangers await the others? Nay, **323**
it is not just that you should reap peace and its blessings, while the others are struggling with wars and
countless ills, or that the whole should be a mere
appendage to the parts, whereas, on the contrary, it
is only on the merits of the whole that the parts are
held deserving of their portion. You have all equal **324**
rights with us ; one race, the same fathers, one house,
the same customs, community of laws, and other
things innumerable, each of which strengthens the
tie of kinship and the harmony of goodwill.[a] Why,
then, when you have been adjudged an equal share
in the greatest and most vital matters, should you
seek an unfair preference in the distribution, with
the arrogance which a ruler might shew to his subjects or a master to his slaves? You ought, indeed, **325**
to have learnt a lesson from the blows which others
have suffered ; for wise men do not wait till the
calamity is upon them. As it is, though your own kin
supplies you with examples of warning in your fathers
who inspected this land, and in the misfortune of
them and those who shared their craven-heartedness,
all of whom perished save two, though you should not
let your name be associated with any such as these,
so senseless are you that you follow after cowardice
and forget that it will make you an easier prey. And
you upset the ardent resolution of those who are fully
disposed to manliness, whose spirits you paralyse and
unnerve. Therefore, in hastening to sin, you will be **326**
hastening to punishment also ;[b] for it is the way of
justice to be slow to move, but, when it is once moved,
it overtakes and seizes the fugitives. When all the **327**

speech). LXX " you shall know your sin, when evils overtake
you." E.V. " and be sure your sin will find you out."

ἅπαντες μὲν οἱ ἐχθροὶ καθαιρεθῶσιν, ἔφεδρος δὲ
μηδεὶς ἔτι προσδοκᾶται πόλεμος, ἐν δὲ ταῖς εὐ-
θύναις ἀνεπίληπτοι δοκιμασθῶσιν οἱ σύμμαχοι, μὴ
λιποτάξιον, μὴ λιποστράτιον, μηδὲν ἄλλο τῶν
ἐφ' ἥττῃ διαπεπραγμένοι, παραμεμενηκότες δ' ἐξ
ἀρχῆς ἄχρι τέλους φαίνωνται καὶ τοῖς σώμασι καὶ
ταῖς προθυμίαις, ἐρημωθῇ δὲ πᾶσα ἡ χώρα τῶν
προενῳκηκότων, τηνικαῦτα δοθήσεται τὰ γέρα καὶ
τὰ ἀριστεῖα ταῖς φυλαῖς ἐξ ἴσου."

328 LX. Τὴν δὲ νουθεσίαν πράως ἐνεγκόντες ὡς
υἱοὶ γνήσιοι σφόδρα εὔνου πατρὸς—ᾔδεσαν γὰρ
αὐτὸν οὐ καταλαζονευόμενον ἀρχῆς ἐξουσίᾳ, προ-
κηδόμενον δὲ πάντων καὶ δικαιοσύνην καὶ ἰσότητα
τιμῶντα καὶ τὸ μισοπόνηρον οὐκ ἐπ' ὀνείδει σωφρο-
νισμῷ δὲ τῶν βελτιοῦσθαι δυναμένων ἀεὶ ποιούμενον[1]—" εἰκότως μὲν" ἔφασαν " ἀγανακτεῖς, εἰ
τοῦθ' ὑπείληφας, ὅτι τὴν συμμαχίαν ἀπολιπόντες
329 πρὸ καιροῦ τὰς λήξεις λαβεῖν ἐπειγόμεθα. χρὴ δὲ
σαφῶς εἰδέναι, ὅτι οὐδὲν ἡμᾶς φοβεῖ τῶν σὺν
ἀρετῇ, κἂν ἐπιπονώτατον τυγχάνῃ. κρίνομεν δ'
[133] ἀρετῆς ἔργα, πειθαρχεῖν τέ | σοι τοιῷδε ἡγεμόνι
καὶ τῶν δεινῶν μὴ ὑστερίζειν καὶ ἐν ἁπάσαις
ἐξετάζεσθαι ταῖς μελλούσαις στρατείαις, ἄχρις ἂν
330 τὰ πράγματα λάβῃ τέλος αἴσιον. ἡμεῖς μὲν οὖν
καθὰ καὶ πρότερον συνταξάμενοι διαβησόμεθα τὸν
Ἰορδάνην ἐν ταῖς παντευχίαις, οὐδενὶ τῶν ὁπλιτῶν
πρόφασιν παρασχόντες μονῆς· υἱοὶ δὲ κομιδῇ νήπιοι
καὶ θυγατέρες καὶ γυναῖκες καὶ τὸ πλῆθος τῶν

---

[1] Cohn and Mangey both question this use of ποιούμενον,
but do not propose any satisfactory emendation. Perhaps

enemies are destroyed, and there is no prospect of
war still awaiting us ; when all the confederates have
on scrutiny been found guiltless of desertion from
the ranks or from the army, or of any other action
which is the sequel of defeat, but have proved their
constancy both of body and spirit from first to last ;
when finally the whole country has been cleared of
its former inhabitants, then will the prizes and rewards for valour be given to the tribes on equal
terms."

LX. The two tribes listened to this admonition 328
meekly, as true-born sons to a very kindly father.
For they knew that he did not speak with an arrogance
founded on official authority, but out of solicitude
for them all and respect for justice and equality, and
that his detestation of evil was never meant to cast
reproach but always to bring those capable of improvement to a better mind. " You are naturally
indignant," they replied, " if you have got the idea
that we are eager to leave the confederacy and take
our portions before they are due. But you must 329
clearly understand that no form of virtuous conduct,
however toilsome it may be, alarms us. And by
virtuous conduct we understand that we should obey
you, great leader as you are, and be backward in no
danger, and take our place in all the coming campaigns until the happy consummation is reached.
We will, therefore, as before, take our place in the 330
ranks, and cross Jordan with our full equipment, and
give none of our armed men any excuse to stay behind ; but our sons who are mere children and our
daughters and our wives and our great stock of cattle

τὸ μισοπόνηρον ⟨ὡς ὄν⟩ . . . ποιούμενον (" deeming to be ")
would accord with the ordinary usage of the middle.

βοσκημάτων, ἐὰν ἐπιτρέπῃς, ὑπολελείψονται, παισὶ
μὲν καὶ γυναιξὶν οἰκίας ἐπαύλεις δὲ θρέμμασι
κατασκευασάντων ἡμῶν, ἵνα μηδὲν ἐξ ἐπιδρομῆς
δεινὸν πάθωσιν ἐν ἀτειχίστοις καὶ ἀφρουρήτοις προ-
καταληφθέντες.''

331 Ὁ δ' ἵλεῳ τῷ βλέμματι καὶ πρᾳοτέρᾳ τῇ φωνῇ
'' ἀψευδοῦσιν ὑμῖν '' ἔφη '' βέβαιοι μενοῦσιν ἃς
ᾐτήσασθε λήξεις. ὑπολείπεσθε μὲν ὡς ἀξιοῦτε
γυναῖκας καὶ παῖδας καὶ βοσκήματα, κατὰ λόχους
δ' αὐτοὶ διαβαίνετε μετὰ τῶν ἄλλων ὡπλισμένοι
καὶ ἐκτεταγμένοι πρὸς μάχην ὡς αὐτίκα, ἢν δέῃ,
332 πολεμήσοντες. αὖθις δ' ὅταν ἅπαντες οἱ ἐχθροὶ
καθαιρεθῶσι καὶ γενομένης εἰρήνης τὴν χώραν οἱ
κεκρατηκότες διανείμωνται, καὶ ὑμεῖς ἐπανελεύ-
σεσθε πρὸς τοὺς οἰκείους τῶν ἐπιβαλλόντων ἀπο-
λαύσοντες ἀγαθῶν καὶ καρπωσόμενοι ἣν εἵλεσθε
333 μοῖραν.'' ταῦτ' εἰπόντος καὶ ὑποσχομένου, πληρω-
θέντες εὐθυμίας καὶ χαρᾶς τοὺς μὲν οἰκείους μετὰ
τῶν θρεμμάτων ἀσφαλῶς ἐν ἐρύμασι δυσαλώτοις,
ὧν τὰ πλεῖστα χειροποίητα ἦν, ἱδρύονται, τὰ δ'
ὅπλα ἀναλαβόντες ἐξέθεον τῶν ἄλλων συμμάχων
προθυμότερον ὡς ἢ μόνοι πολεμήσοντες ἢ προαγω-
νιούμενοι πάντων[1]· ὁ γὰρ προλαβών τινα δωρεὰν
προθυμότερος εἰς συμμαχίαν, ἀποτίνειν ἀναγκαῖον
ὄφλημα νομίζων, οὐ χαρίζεσθαι.

334 Τὰ μὲν δὴ κατὰ τὴν βασιλείαν πεπραγμένα αὐτῷ
μεμήνυται· λεκτέον δ' ἑξῆς καὶ ὅσα διὰ τῆς ἀρχ-
ιερωσύνης καὶ νομοθετικῆς κατώρθωσε· καὶ γὰρ
ταύτας περιεποιήσατο τὰς δυνάμεις ὡς ἁρμοττούσας μάλιστα βασιλείᾳ.

[1] MSS. πάντως.

will be left behind, if you permit, after we have built houses for the women and children and sheds for the animals, since otherwise, caught before we return, in a position unfortified and unprotected, they might meet with disaster at the hands of raiders."

Moses' face was kindly and his tones milder, as he 331 replied as follows : " If you are true to your words, the apportionments which you have asked shall remain secure to you. Leave your women and children and cattle, as you demand, and cross the river yourselves in your battalions with the rest, fully armed and arrayed for the fight, ready to engage at once if necessary. Later, when all the enemy are destroyed, 332 and, peace having been made, the victors divide the land, you too will return to your people to enjoy the good things that fall to your share and reap the fruits of the lot that you have chosen." When they heard 333 these promises from his lips, filled with joy and courage, they settled their people and cattle safely in positions strongly protected against assault, in most cases by artificial fortifications. Then, taking up their arms, they rushed to the field more eagerly than the other confederates, as though they would wage the war alone or at any rate be the first of all to enter the conflict. For the acceptance of a gift beforehand increases a man's readiness to support his comrades. He feels that he is not a free giver, but is repaying a debt which he cannot escape.

We have now told the story of Moses' actions in his 334 capacity of king. We must next deal with all that he achieved by his powers as high priest and legislator, powers which he possessed as the most fitting accompaniments of kingship.

ΠΕΡΙ ΤΟΥ ΒΙΟΥ ΜΩΥΣΕΩΣ ΛΟΓΟΣ
ΔΕΥΤΕΡΟΣ

[134]

1   I. Ἡ μὲν προτέρα σύνταξίς ἐστι περὶ γενέσεως
τῆς Μωυσέως καὶ τροφῆς, ἔτι δὲ παιδείας καὶ
ἀρχῆς, ἣν οὐ μόνον ἀνεπιλήπτως ἀλλὰ καὶ σφόδρα
ἐπαινετῶς ἦρξε, καὶ τῶν ἔν τε Αἰγύπτῳ καὶ ταῖς
ὁδοιπορίαις ἐπί τε τῆς ἐρυθρᾶς θαλάσσης καὶ κατὰ
τὴν ἔρημην πεπραγμένων, ἃ δύναμιν πᾶσαν λόγων
ὑπερβάλλει, καὶ προσέτι πόνων οὓς κατώρθωσε καὶ
κληρουχιῶν ἃς ἐκ μέρους ἀπένειμε τοῖς στρατευσα-
μένοις· ἣν δὲ νυνὶ συντάττομεν, περὶ τῶν ἑπομένων
2   καὶ ἀκολούθων. φασὶ γάρ τινες οὐκ ἀπὸ σκοποῦ,
μόνως ἂν οὕτω τὰς πόλεις ἐπιδοῦναι πρὸς τὸ
βέλτιον, ἐὰν ⟨ἢ⟩ οἱ βασιλεῖς φιλοσοφήσωσιν ἢ οἱ
φιλόσοφοι βασιλεύσωσιν. ὁ δ' ἐκ περιττοῦ φανεῖται
μὴ μόνον ταύτας ἐπιδεδειγμένος τὰς δυνάμεις ἐν
ταὐτῷ, τήν τε βασιλικὴν καὶ φιλόσοφον, ἀλλὰ καὶ
τρεῖς ἑτέρας, ὧν ἡ μὲν πραγματεύεται περὶ νομο-
[135] θεσίαν, ἡ | δὲ περὶ ἀρχιερωσύνην, ἡ δὲ τελευταία
3   περὶ προφητείαν. περὶ ὧν νυνὶ λέγειν εἱλόμην
ἀναγκαίως ὑπολαβὼν τῷ αὐτῷ πάντ' ἐφαρμόττειν·
ἐγένετο γὰρ προνοίᾳ θεοῦ βασιλεύς τε καὶ νομοθέτης καὶ ἀρχιερεὺς καὶ προφήτης καὶ ἐν ἑκάστῳ

ᵃ Plato, *Rep.* v. 473 D.

ON THE LIFE OF MOSES, BOOK II

I. The former treatise dealt with the birth and **1**
nurture of Moses ; also with his education and career
as a ruler, in which capacity his conduct was not
merely blameless but highly praiseworthy ; also
with the works which he performed in Egypt and
during the journeys both at the Red Sea and in the
wilderness—works which no words can adequately
describe ; further, with the troubles which he successfully surmounted, and with his partial distribution of territories to the combatants. The present
treatise is concerned with matters allied and conse-
quent to these. For it has been said, not without **2**
good reason, that states can only make progress in
well-being if either kings are philosophers or philosophers are kings.[a] But Moses will be found to
have displayed, and more than displayed, combined in his single person, not only these two faculties
—the kingly and the philosophical—but also three
others, one of which is concerned with law-giving,
the second with the high priest's office, and the last
with prophecy. On these three I have now elected **3**
to write, being forced to the conviction that it is
fitting that they should be combined in the same
person. For Moses, through God's providence,
became king and lawgiver and high priest and
prophet ; and in each function he won the highest

451

τὰ πρωτεῖα ἠνέγκατο· διὰ τί δὲ τῷ αὐτῷ πάντ᾽ ἐφ-
4 αρμόττει, δηλωτέον. βασιλεῖ προσήκει προστάττειν
ἃ χρὴ καὶ ἀπαγορεύειν ἃ μὴ χρή· πρόσταξις δὲ
τῶν πρακτέων καὶ ἀπαγόρευσις τῶν οὐ πρακτέων
ἴδιον νόμου, ὡς εὐθὺς εἶναι τὸν μὲν βασιλέα νόμον
5 ἔμψυχον, τὸν δὲ νόμον βασιλέα δίκαιον. βασιλεὺς
δὲ καὶ νομοθέτης ὀφείλει μὴ τἀνθρώπεια μόνον
ἀλλὰ καὶ τὰ θεῖα συνεπισκοπεῖν· οὐ γὰρ ἄνευ θείας
ἐπιφροσύνης κατορθοῦται τὰ βασιλέων καὶ ὑπηκόων
πράγματα· δι᾽ ἣν αἰτίαν ἐδέησε τῷ τοιούτῳ τῆς
πρώτης ἱερωσύνης, ἵν᾽ ἐπὶ τελείοις ἱεροῖς καὶ
ἐπιστήμῃ τελείᾳ τῆς τοῦ θεοῦ θεραπείας ἀποτροπὴν
μὲν κακῶν μετουσίαν δ᾽ ἀγαθῶν αὑτῷ τε καὶ τοῖς
ἀρχομένοις αἰτῆται παρὰ τοῦ ἵλεω καὶ ταῖς εὐχαῖς
συνεπινεύοντος· πῶς γὰρ οὐ τελεσφορήσει τὰς εὐχὰς ὁ καὶ ἐκ φύσεως εὐμενὴς καὶ τοὺς γνησίως
θεραπεύοντας αὐτὸν προνομίας ἀξιῶν;
6 ἀλλ᾽ ἐπειδὴ μυρία καὶ βασιλεῖ καὶ νομοθέτῃ καὶ
ἀρχιερεῖ τῶν ἀνθρωπείων καὶ θείων ἄδηλα—γε-
νητὸς γὰρ οὐδὲν ἧττον καὶ θνητός ἐστιν, εἰ καὶ
τοσοῦτον καὶ οὕτως ἄφθονον περιβέβληται κλῆρον
εὐπραγιῶν—, ἀναγκαίως καὶ προφητείας ἔτυχεν, ἵν᾽
ὅσα μὴ λογισμῷ δύναται καταλαμβάνειν, ταῦτα
προνοίᾳ θεοῦ εὕροι· ὧν γὰρ ὁ νοῦς ἀπολείπεται,
7 πρὸς ταῦθ᾽ ἡ προφητεία φθάνει. καλή γε ἡ συζυγία
καὶ παναρμόνιος τῶν τεττάρων δυνάμεων· ἐμ-
πλεκόμεναι γὰρ καὶ ἀλλήλων ἐχόμεναι συγχορεύουσι
τὰς ὠφελείας ἀντιλαμβάνουσαί τε καὶ ἀντεκ-
τίνουσαι, μιμούμεναι τὰς παρθένους Χάριτας, αἷς
μὴ διαζεύγνυσθαι νόμος φύσεως ἀκίνητος· ἐφ᾽ ὧν

---

[a] Cf. De Abr. 5 and note, and see App. p. 605.

place. But why it is fitting that they should all be
combined in the same person needs explanation.
It is a king's duty to command what is right 4
and forbid what is wrong. But to command what
should be done and to forbid what should not be
done is the peculiar function of law ; so that it
follows at once that the king is a living law, and the
law a just king.[a] But a king and lawgiver ought to 5
have under his purview not only human but divine
things ; for, without God's directing care, the affairs
of kings and subjects cannot go aright. And therefore such as he needs the chief priest-hood, so that,
fortified with perfect rites and the perfect knowledge
of the service of God, he may ask that he and those
whom he rules may receive prevention of evil and
participation in good from the gracious Being Who
assents to prayers. For surely that Being will grant
fulfilment to prayers, seeing that He is kindly by
nature and deems worthy of His special favour those
who give Him genuine service. But, since 6
to this king, lawgiver and high priest who, though
possessed of so generous a heritage of fortune's gifts,
is after all but a mortal creature, countless things
both human and divine are wrapped in obscurity,
Moses necessarily obtained prophecy also, in order
that through the providence of God he might discover
what by reasoning he could not grasp. For prophecy
finds its way to what the mind fails to reach. Beauti- 7
ful and all-harmonious is the union of these four
faculties ; for, intertwined and clinging to each
other, they move in rhythmic concord, mutually receiving and repaying benefits, and thus imitate the
virgin Graces whom an immutable law of nature forbids to be separated. And of them it may be justly

δεόντως εἴποι τις ἄν, ὃ καὶ ἐπὶ τῶν ἀρετῶν εἴωθε
λέγεσθαι, ὅτι ὁ μίαν ἔχων καὶ πάσας ἔχει.

8 II. Ῥητέον δὲ πρῶτον περὶ τῶν κατὰ τὴν νομοθετικὴν ἕξιν. οὐκ ἀγνοῶ μὲν οὖν, ὅτι τῷ μέλλοντι
ἀρίστῳ γενήσεσθαι νομοθέτῃ προσήκει παντελέσι
καὶ ὁλοκλήροις κεχρῆσθαι ταῖς ἀρεταῖς πάσαις·
ἐπεὶ δὲ κἀν ταῖς οἰκίαις οἱ μὲν ἐγγυτάτω γένους
εἰσίν, οἱ δὲ πόρρω, συγγενεῖς δὲ πάντες ἀλλήλων,
καὶ τῶν ἀρετῶν τὰς μὲν προσπεφυκέναι νομιστέον
9 μᾶλλον ἐνίοις πράγμασι, τὰς δ' ἧττον ᾠκειῶσθαι.
[136] | νομοθετικῇ δ' ἀδελφὰ καὶ συγγενῆ τέτταρα ταυτὶ
διαφερόντως ἐστί· τὸ φιλάνθρωπον, τὸ φιλοδίκαιον,
τὸ φιλάγαθον, τὸ μισοπόνηρον· ὑπὸ γὰρ τούτων
ἑκάστου παρακαλεῖται πᾶς, ὅτῳ ζῆλος εἰσέρχεται
τοῦ νομοθετεῖν, φιλανθρωπίας μὲν εἰς μέσον προ-
τιθέναι τὰς κοινωφελεῖς γνώμας ἀναδιδασκούσης,
δικαιοσύνης δὲ ὡς ἰσότητα τιμητέον καὶ ὡς τὸ
κατ' ἀξίαν ἀπονεμητέον ἑκάστοις, φιλαγαθίας δ'
ἀποδέχεσθαι τὰ φύσει καλὰ καὶ παρέχειν ἅπασι
τοῖς ἀξίοις ἀταμίευτα πρὸς ἀφθονωτάτην χρῆσιν,
μισοπονηρίας δὲ προβεβλῆσθαι τοὺς ἀτιμάζοντας
ἀρετὴν καὶ ὡς κοινοὺς δυσμενεῖς τοῦ τῶν ἀνθρώπων
10 γένους ὑποβλέπεσθαι. μέγα μὲν οὖν, εἴ τῳ καὶ ἕν
τι τῶν λεχθέντων λαβεῖν ἐγένετο, θαυμαστὸν δ' ὡς
ἔοικε τούτων ἀθρόων περιδράξασθαι δυνηθῆναι, οὗ
μόνος Μωυσῆς ἐφικέσθαι δοκεῖ τρανώσας εὖ μάλα
11 τὰς εἰρημένας ἀρετὰς ἐν οἷς διετάξατο. συνίσασι
δ' οἱ ταῖς ἱεραῖς βίβλοις ἐντυγχάνοντες, ἃς οὐκ ἄν,
εἰ μὴ τοιοῦτος ἐπεφύκει, συνέγραψεν ὑφηγησαμένου
θεοῦ καὶ παρέδωκε τοῖς ἀξίοις χρῆσθαι, κτημάτων

ᵃ Cf. Diog. Laert. vii. 125.

said, what is often said of the virtues, that to have one is to have all.[a]

II. First, we must speak of the legislative condi- 8 tion of mind. I know, indeed, that he who is to obtain excellence as a legislator should possess all the virtues fully and completely. But, since also in households there are some very nearly and others only distantly connected with the family, though all are akin to each other, so too we must suppose that some virtues are more closely associated with some situations, while others have less affinity. The 9 legislative faculty has for its brothers and close kins-folk these four in particular : love of humanity, of justice, of goodness, and hatred of evil. Each of these has its message of encouragement for everyone who is inspired with a zeal for law-making. By love of humanity he is bidden to produce for public use his thoughts for the common weal ; by justice to honour equality and to render to every man his due ; by love of goodness to approve of things naturally ex-cellent, and to supply them without reserve to all who are worthy of them for their unstinted use ; by hatred of evil to spurn the dishonourers of virtue, and frown upon them as the common enemies of the human race. It is no small thing if it is given to any- 10 one to acquire even one of these—a marvel surely that he should be able to grasp them all together. And to this Moses alone appears to have attained, who shews distinctly these aforesaid virtues in his ordinances. They know this well who read the 11 sacred books, which, unless he was such as we have said, he would never have composed under God's guidance and handed on for the use of those who are worthy to use them, to be their fairest pos-

τὸ κάλλιστον, τῶν ἀγαλματοφορουμένων ἐν τῇ
ψυχῇ παραδειγμάτων ἀπεικονίσματα καὶ μιμήματα,
ἃ καὶ οἱ δηλωθέντες νόμοι γεγόνασι σαφέστατα τὰς
λεχθείσας ἐμφαίνοντες ἀρετάς.

12 III. Ὅτι δ' αὐτός τε νομοθετῶν ἄριστος τῶν
πανταχοῦ πάντων, ὅσοι παρ' Ἕλλησιν ἢ βαρβάροις
ἐγένοντο, καὶ οἱ νόμοι κάλλιστοι καὶ ὡς ἀληθῶς
θεῖοι μηδὲν ὧν χρὴ παραλιπόντες, ἐναργεστάτη
13 πίστις ἥδε· τὰ μὲν τῶν ἄλλων νόμιμα εἴ τις ἐπίοι
τῷ λογισμῷ, διὰ μυρίας προφάσεις εὑρήσει κεκινη-
μένα, πολέμοις ἢ τυραννίσιν ἤ τισιν ἄλλοις ἀβουλήτοις, ἃ νεωτερισμῷ τύχης κατασκήπτει· πολλάκις
δὲ καὶ τρυφὴ πλεονάσασα χορηγίαις καὶ περι-
ουσίαις ἀφθόνοις καθεῖλε νόμους, "τὰ λίαν ἀγαθὰ"
τῶν πολλῶν φέρειν οὐ δυναμένων, ἀλλὰ διὰ κόρον
14 ἐξυβριζόντων· ὕβρις δ' ἀντίπαλον νόμῳ. τὰ δὲ
τούτου μόνου βέβαια, ἀσάλευτα, ἀκράδαντα, καθάπερ σφραγῖσι φύσεως αὐτῆς σεσημασμένα, μένει
παγίως ἀφ' ἧς ἡμέρας ἐγράφη μέχρι νῦν καὶ πρὸς
τὸν ἔπειτα πάντα διαμενεῖν ἐλπὶς αὐτὰ αἰῶνα ὥσπερ
ἀθάνατα, ἕως ἂν ἥλιος καὶ σελήνη καὶ ὁ σύμπας
15 οὐρανός τε καὶ κόσμος ᾖ. τοσαύταις γοῦν χρησαμένου τοῦ ἔθνους μεταβολαῖς κατά τε εὐπραγίας
καὶ τοὐναντίον, οὐδὲν ἀλλ' οὐδὲ τὸ μικρότατον
[137] τῶν | διατεταγμένων ἐκινήθη, πάντων ὡς ἔοικε τὸ
16 σεμνὸν καὶ θεοπρεπὲς αὐτῶν ἐκτετιμηκότων. ἃ δὲ
μὴ λιμὸς ἢ λοιμὸς ἢ πόλεμος ἢ βασιλεὺς ἢ τύραννος
ἢ ψυχῆς ἢ σώματος ἢ παθῶν ἢ κακιῶν ἐπανάστασις
ἤ τι ἄλλο θεήλατον ἢ ἀνθρώπειον κακὸν ἔλυσε, πῶς
οὐ περιμάχητα καὶ παντὸς λόγου κρείττονα καθ-

ᵃ See *De Abr.* 134 and note.

session, likenesses and copies of the patterns enshrined in the soul, as also are the laws set before us
in these books, which shew so clearly the said virtues.

III. That Moses himself was the best of all law- 12
givers in all countries, better in fact than any that
have ever arisen among either the Greeks or the
barbarians, and that his laws are most excellent and
truly come from God, since they omit nothing that is
needful, is shewn most clearly by the following proof.
Anyone who takes a considered view of the institu- 13
tions of other peoples will find that they have been
unsettled by numberless causes—wars, tyrannies or
other mishaps—which the revolutions of fortune have
launched upon them. Often, too, luxury, growing
to excess by lavish supplies of superfluities, has upset
the laws ; because the mass of people, being unable
to bear " good things in excess," *a* becomes surfeited
and consequently violent : and violence is the enemy
of law. But Moses is alone in this, that his laws, 14
firm, unshaken, immovable, stamped, as it were, with
the seals of nature herself, remain secure from the day
when they were first enacted to now, and we may
hope that they will remain for all future ages as
though immortal, so long as the sun and moon and
the whole heaven and universe exist. Thus, though 15
the nation has undergone so many changes, both to
increased prosperity and the reverse, nothing—not
even the smallest part of the ordinances—has been
disturbed ; because all have clearly paid high honour
to their venerable and godlike character. But that 16
which no famine nor pestilence nor war nor king nor
tyrant, no rebel assault of soul or body or passion
or vice, nor any other evil whether of God's sending
or man's making, could undo, must surely be precious

17 ἕστηκεν;   IV. ἀλλ' οὔπω τοῦτο θαυμαστόν, καίτοι μέγα καθ' αὑτὸ δεόντως ἂν νομισθέν,
τὸ ἐξ ἅπαντος τοῦ χρόνου πεφυλάχθαι τοὺς νόμους
ἐν βεβαίῳ· ἀλλ' ἐκεῖνο θαυμασιώτερον, ὡς ἔοικε,
τὸ μὴ μόνον Ἰουδαίους ἀλλὰ καὶ τοὺς ἄλλους
σχεδὸν ἅπαντας καὶ μάλιστα οἷς ἀρετῆς πλείων
λόγος πρὸς τὴν ἀποδοχὴν αὐτῶν καὶ τιμὴν ὡσιώ-
σθαι· γέρας γὰρ τοῦτ' ἔλαχον ἐξαίρετον, ὃ μηδενὶ
18 πρόσεστιν ἑτέρῳ. σημεῖον δέ· τῶν κατὰ τὴν
Ἑλλάδα καὶ βάρβαρον, ὡς ἔπος εἰπεῖν, οὐδεμία
πόλις ἐστίν, ἣ τὰ ἑτέρας νόμιμα τιμᾷ, μόλις δὲ καὶ
τῶν αὑτῆς εἰς ἀεὶ περιέχεται, πρὸς τὰς τῶν καιρῶν
καὶ τῶν πραγμάτων μεθαρμοζομένη τροπάς.
19 Ἀθηναῖοι τὰ Λακεδαιμονίων ἔθη καὶ νόμιμα
προβέβληνται καὶ Λακεδαιμόνιοι τὰ Ἀθηναίων·
ἀλλ' οὐδὲ κατὰ τὴν βάρβαρον Αἰγύπτιοι τοὺς
Σκυθῶν νόμους φυλάττουσιν ἢ Σκύθαι τοὺς Αἰγυπτίων ἢ συνελόντι φράσαι τοὺς τῶν κατ' Εὐρώπην
οἱ τὴν Ἀσίαν οἰκοῦντες ἢ τοὺς τῶν Ἀσιανῶν
ἐθνῶν οἱ ἐν Εὐρώπῃ· ἀλλὰ σχεδὸν οἱ ἀφ' ἡλίου
ἀνιόντος ἄχρι δυομένου, πᾶσα χώρα καὶ ἔθνος καὶ
πόλις, τῶν ξενικῶν νομίμων ἀλλοτριοῦνται καὶ
οἴονται τὴν τῶν οἰκείων ἀποδοχήν, εἰ τὰ παρὰ τοῖς
20 ἄλλοις ἀτιμάζοιεν, συναυξήσειν. ἀλλ' οὐχ ὧδ'
ἔχει τὰ ἡμέτερα· πάντας γὰρ ἐπάγεται καὶ συν-
επιστρέφει, βαρβάρους, Ἕλληνας, ἠπειρώτας, νησιώ-
τας, ἔθνη τὰ ἑῷα, τὰ ἑσπέρια, Εὐρώπην, Ἀσίαν,
ἅπασαν τὴν οἰκουμένην ἀπὸ περάτων ἐπὶ πέρατα.
21   τίς γὰρ τὴν ἱερὰν ἐκείνην ἑβδόμην οὐκ
ἐκτετίμηκεν, ἄνεσιν πόνων καὶ ῥᾳστώνην αὐτῷ τε

beyond what words can describe.   IV.
Yet, though it may be rightly thought a great 17
matter in itself that the laws should have been
guarded securely through all time, we have not
reached the true marvel.   There is something surely
still more wonderful—even this : not only Jews but
almost every other people, particularly those which
take more account of virtue, have so far grown in
holiness as to value and honour our laws.   In this
they have received a special distinction which belongs
to no other code.   Here is the proof.   Throughout 18
the world of Greeks and barbarians, there is practically no state which honours the institutions of any
other.   Indeed, they can scarcely be said to retain
their own perpetually, as they adapt them to meet
the vicissitudes of times and circumstances.   The 19
Athenians reject the customs and institutions of the
Lacedaemonians, and the Lacedaemonians those of
the Athenians ; nor, in the world of the barbarians,
do the Egyptians maintain the laws of the Scythians
nor the Scythians those of the Egyptians—nor, to put
it generally, Europeans those of Asiatics nor Asiatics
those of Europeans.   We may fairly say that mankind from east to west, every country and nation and
state, shew aversion to foreign institutions, and think
that they will enhance the respect for their own by
shewing disrespect for those of other countries.   It 20
is not so with ours.   They attract and win the attention of all, of barbarians, of Greeks, of dwellers on the
mainland and islands, of nations of the east and the
west, of Europe and Asia, of the whole inhabited
world from end to end.   For, who has not 21
shewn his high respect for that sacred seventh day,
by giving rest and relaxation from labour to himself

καὶ τοῖς πλησιάζουσιν, οὐκ ἐλευθέροις μόνον ἀλλὰ
καὶ δούλοις, μᾶλλον δὲ καὶ ὑποζυγίοις διδούς;
22 φθάνει γὰρ ἡ ἐκεχειρία καὶ πρὸς πᾶσαν ἀγέλην καὶ
ὅσα πρὸς ὑπηρεσίαν γέγονεν ἀνθρώπου καθάπερ
δοῦλα θεραπεύοντα τὸν φύσει δεσπότην, φθάνει καὶ
πρὸς δένδρων καὶ φυτῶν ἅπασαν ἰδέαν· οὐ γὰρ
ἔρνος, οὐ κλάδον, ἀλλ' οὐδὲ πέταλον ἐφεῖται τεμεῖν
ἢ καρπὸν ὁντινοῦν δρέψασθαι, πάντων διαφειμένων
[138] κατ' ἐκείνην | τὴν ἡμέραν καὶ ὥσπερ ἐλευθερίαν
ἀγόντων, κοινῷ κηρύγματι μηδενὸς ἐπιψαύοντος.
23   τίς δὲ τὴν λεγομένην νηστείαν
οὐ τέθηπε καὶ προσκυνεῖ δι' ἔτους ἀγομένην τῆς
ἱερομηνίας αὐστηρότερον καὶ σεμνότερον τρόπον;
ἐν ᾗ μὲν γὰρ πολὺς ἄκρατος καὶ τράπεζαι πολυτελεῖς καὶ ὅσα περὶ ἐδωδὴν καὶ πόσιν ἄφθονα
πάντα, δι' ὧν αἱ ἀκόρεστοι γαστρὸς ἡδοναὶ συν-
αὔξονται προσαναρρηγνῦσαι καὶ τὰς ὑπογαστρίους
24 ἐπιθυμίας· ἐν ᾗ δ' οὐ σιτίον, οὐ ποτὸν ἔξεστι προσ-
ενέγκασθαι, καθαραῖς ὅπως διανοίαις, μηδενὸς ἐν-
οχλοῦντος μηδ' ἐμποδίζοντος σωματικοῦ πάθους,
ὁποῖα φιλεῖ συμβαίνειν ἐκ πλησμονῆς, ἑορτάζωσιν
ἱλασκόμενοι τὸν πατέρα τοῦ παντὸς αἰσίοις εὐχαῖς,
δι' ὧν ἀμνηστίαν μὲν παλαιῶν ἁμαρτημάτων, κτῆσιν
δὲ καὶ ἀπόλαυσιν νέων ἀγαθῶν εἰώθασιν αἰτεῖσθαι.
25   V. Τὸ δὲ τῆς νομοθεσίας ἱεροπρεπὲς ὡς οὐ παρ'
Ἰουδαίοις μόνον ἀλλὰ καὶ παρὰ πᾶσι τοῖς ἄλλοις
τεθαύμασται, δῆλον ἔκ τε τῶν εἰρημένων ἤδη κἀκ
26 τῶν μελλόντων λέγεσθαι. τὸ παλαιὸν ἐγράφησαν

---

^a *i.e.* the Day of Atonement. For the term "the fast"
cf. Acts xxvii. 9.
^b Or "holy season." A vague term (not indicating
necessarily a whole month) for the periods varying with

and his neighbours, freemen and slaves alike, and
beyond these to his beasts? For the holiday ex- 22
tends also to every herd, and to all creatures made to
minister to man, who serve like slaves their natural
master. It extends also to every kind of trees and
plants; for it is not permitted to cut any shoot or
branch, or even a leaf, or to pluck any fruit whatsoever.
All such are set at liberty on that day, and live as
it were in freedom, under the general edict that
proclaims that none should touch them.

Again, who does not every year shew awe and rever- 23
ence for the fast, as it is called,[a] which is kept more
strictly and solemnly than the "holy month"[b] of
the Greeks? For in this last the untempered wine
flows freely, and the board is spread sumptuously,
and all manner of food and drink are lavishly provided, whereby the insatiable pleasures of the belly
are enhanced, and further cause the outburst of the
lusts that lie below it. But in our fast men may not 24
put food and drink to their lips, in order that with
pure hearts, untroubled and untrammelled by any
bodily passion, such as is the common outcome of
repletion, they may keep the holy-day, propitiating
the Father of All with fitting prayers, in which they
are wont to ask that their old sins may be forgiven
and new blessings gained and enjoyed.

V. That the sanctity of our legislation has been a 25
source of wonder not only to the Jews but also to all
other nations, is clear both from the facts already
mentioned and those which I proceed to state.[c] In 26

different Greek states, in which hostilities or legal processes
were forbidden.

[c] For the relation of this remarkable account (§§ 26-44) of
the making of the Septuagint to other traditions see
App. pp. 605-606.

PHILO

οἱ νόμοι γλώσσῃ Χαλδαϊκῇ καὶ μέχρι πολλοῦ
διέμειναν ἐν ὁμοίῳ τὴν διάλεκτον οὐ μεταβάλ-
λοντες, ἕως μήπω τὸ κάλλος εἰς τοὺς ἄλλους
27 ἀνθρώπους ἀνέφηναν αὐτῶν. ἐπεὶ δὲ ἐκ τῆς καθ᾽
ἑκάστην ἡμέραν συνεχοῦς μελέτης καὶ ἀσκήσεως
τῶν χρωμένων αἴσθησις ἐγένετο καὶ ἑτέροις καὶ
τὸ κλέος ἐφοίτα πανταχόσε—τὰ γὰρ καλὰ κἂν
φθόνῳ πρὸς ὀλίγον ἐπισκιασθῇ χρόνον, ἐπὶ καιρῶν
αὖθις ἀναλάμπει φύσεως εὐμενείᾳ—, δεινὸν ἡγησά-
μενοί τινες, εἰ οἱ νόμοι παρὰ τῷ ἡμίσει τμήματι
τοῦ γένους ἀνθρώπων ἐξετασθήσονται μόνῳ τῷ
βαρβαρικῷ, τὸ δ᾽ Ἑλληνικὸν εἰς ἅπαν ἀμοιρή-
28 σει, πρὸς ἑρμηνείαν τὴν τούτων ἐτράποντο. τὸ δ᾽
ἔργον ἐπεὶ καὶ μέγα ἦν καὶ κοινωφελές, οὐκ ἰδιώταις οὐδ᾽ ἄρχουσιν, ὧν πολὺς ἀριθμός, ἀλλὰ βασι-
λεῦσι καὶ βασιλέων ἀνετέθη τῷ δοκιμωτάτῳ.
29 Πτολεμαῖος ὁ Φιλάδελφος ἐπικληθεὶς τρίτος μὲν
ἦν ἀπ᾽ Ἀλεξάνδρου τοῦ τὴν Αἴγυπτον παραλαβόν-
τος, ἀρεταῖς δὲ ταῖς ἐν ἡγεμονίᾳ πάντων, οὐχὶ
[139] τῶν καθ᾽ αὑτὸν μόνον, | ἀλλὰ καὶ τῶν πάλαι πώποτε
γεγενημένων ἄριστος, οὗ καὶ μέχρι νῦν τοσαύταις
ὕστερον γενεαῖς ᾄδεται τὸ κλέος πολλὰ δείγματα
καὶ μνημεῖα τῆς μεγαλοφροσύνης κατὰ πόλεις καὶ
χώρας ἀπολιπόντος, ὡς ἤδη καὶ ἐν παροιμίας εἴδει
τὰς ὑπερόγκους φιλοτιμίας καὶ μεγάλας κατασκευὰς Φιλαδελφείους ἀπ᾽ ἐκείνου καλεῖσθαι.
30 συνόλως μὲν οὖν ἡ τῶν Πτολεμαίων οἰκία διαφερόντως παρὰ τὰς ἄλλας βασιλείας ἤκμασεν,
ἐν δὲ τοῖς Πτολεμαίοις ὁ Φιλάδελφος—ὅσα γὰρ
εἷς ἔδρασεν οὗτος ἐπαινετά, μόλις ἐκεῖνοι πάντες

ancient times the laws were written in the Chaldean tongue, and remained in that form for many years, without any change of language, so long as they had not yet revealed their beauty to the rest of mankind. But, in course of time, the daily, unbroken regularity 27 of practice exercised by those who observed them brought them to the knowledge of others, and their fame began to spread on every side. For things excellent, even if they are beclouded for a short time through envy, shine out again under the benign operation of nature when their time comes. Then it was that some people, thinking it a shame that the laws should be found in one half only of the human race, the barbarians, and denied altogether to the Greeks, took steps to have them translated. In 28 view of the importance and public utility of the task, it was referred not to private persons or magistrates, who were very numerous, but to kings, and amongst them to the king of highest repute. Ptolemy, sur- 29 named Philadelphus, was the third in succession to Alexander, the conqueror of Egypt. In all the qualities which make a good ruler, he excelled not only his contemporaries, but all who have arisen in the past ; and even till to-day, after so many generations, his praises are sung for the many evidences and monuments of his greatness of mind which he left behind him in different cities and countries, so that, even now, acts of more than ordinary munificence or buildings on a specially great scale are proverbially called Philadelphian after him. To put it shortly, 30 as the house of the Ptolemies was highly distinguished, compared with other dynasties, so was Philadelphus among the Ptolemies. The creditable achievements of this one man almost outnumbered

ἀθρόοι διεπράξαντο[1]—γενόμενος καθάπερ ἐν ζῴῳ
τὸ ἡγεμονεῦον κεφαλὴ τρόπον τινὰ τῶν βασιλέων.

31   VI. ὁ δὴ τοιοῦτος ζῆλον καὶ πόθον
λαβὼν τῆς νομοθεσίας ἡμῶν εἰς Ἑλλάδα γλῶτταν
τὴν Χαλδαϊκὴν μεθαρμόζεσθαι διενοεῖτο καὶ πρέσβεις εὐθὺς ἐξέπεμπε πρὸς τὸν τῆς Ἰουδαίας ἀρχιερέα καὶ βασιλέα—ὁ γὰρ αὐτὸς ἦν—τό τε βούλημα
δηλῶν καὶ προτρέπων ἀριστίνδην ἑλέσθαι τοὺς
32 τὸν νόμον διερμηνεύσοντας. ὁ δ' οἷα εἰκὸς ἡσθεὶς
καὶ νομίσας οὐκ ἄνευ θείας ἐπιφροσύνης περὶ τὸ
τοιοῦτον ἔργον ἐσπουδακέναι τὸν βασιλέα, σκεψά-
μενος τοὺς παρ' αὐτῷ δοκιμωτάτους Ἑβραίων, οἳ
πρὸς τῇ πατρίῳ καὶ τὴν Ἑλληνικὴν ἐπεπαίδευντο
33 παιδείαν, ἄσμενος ἀποστέλλει. ὡς δ' ἧκον, ἐπὶ
ξενίαν κληθέντες λόγοις ἀστείοις καὶ σπουδαίοις
τὸν ἑστιάτορα εὐώχουν ἀντεφεστιῶντες· ὁ μὲν γὰρ
ἀπεπειρᾶτο τῆς ἑκάστου σοφίας καινὰς ἀλλ' οὐ
τὰς ἐν ἔθει ζητήσεις προτείνων, οἱ δ' εὐστόχως
καὶ εὐθυβόλως, οὐκ ἐπιτρέποντος μακρηγορεῖν τοῦ
καιροῦ καθάπερ ἀποφθεγγόμενοι τὰ προταθέντα δι-
34 ελύοντο.   δοκιμασθέντες δ' εὐθὺς ἦρ-
ξαντο τὰ τῆς καλῆς πρεσβείας ἀποτελεῖν καὶ
λογισάμενοι παρ' αὐτοῖς, ὅσον εἴη τὸ πρᾶγμα
θεσπισθέντας νόμους χρησμοῖς διερμηνεύειν, μήτ'
ἀφελεῖν τι μήτε προσθεῖναι ἢ μεταθεῖναι δυναμένους, ἀλλὰ τὴν ἐξ ἀρχῆς ἰδέαν καὶ τὸν τύπον
αὐτῶν διαφυλάττοντας, ἐσκόπουν τὸ καθαρώτατον
τῶν περὶ τὸν τόπον χωρίων ἔξω πόλεως· τὰ γὰρ
ἐντὸς τείχους ἅτε παντοδαπῶν πεπληθότα ζῴων

----

[1] Cohn punctuates with a colon before ὅσα, and comma
before γενόμενος.

those of all the others put together, and, as the head
takes the highest place in the living body, so he may
be said to head the kings.   **VI.** This great 31
man, having conceived an ardent affection for our
laws, determined to have the Chaldean translated
into Greek, and at once dispatched envoys to the
high priest and king of Judaea, both offices being
held by the same person, explaining his wishes and
urging him to choose by merit persons to make a full
rendering of the Law into Greek. The high priest 32
was naturally pleased, and, thinking that God's
guiding care must have led the king to busy himself
in such an undertaking, sought out such Hebrews
as he had of the highest reputation, who had received
an education in Greek as well as in their native lore,
and joyfully sent them to Ptolemy. When they 33
arrived, they were offered hospitality, and, having
been sumptuously entertained, requited their entertainer with a feast of words full of wit and weight.
For he tested the wisdom of each by propounding
for discussion new instead of the ordinary questions,
which problems they solved with happy and well-
pointed answers in the form of apophthegms, as the
occasion did not allow of lengthy speaking.
After standing this test, they at once began to fulfil 34
the duties of their high errand. Reflecting how great
an undertaking it was to make a full version of the
laws given by the Voice of God, where they could not
add or take away or transfer anything, but must keep
the original form and shape, they proceeded to look
for the most open and unoccupied *a* spot in the neighbourhood outside the city. For, within the walls,
it was full of every kind of living creatures, and

---

a Or " the most cleanly," but see on § 72.

διὰ νόσους καὶ τελευτὰς καὶ τὰς ὑγιαινόντων οὐκ
35 εὐαγεῖς πράξεις ἦν ὕποπτα.   νῆσος ἡ Φάρος
προκεῖται τῆς Ἀλεξανδρείας, ἧς αὐχὴν ὑποταίνιος
[140] τέταται πρὸς τὴν πόλιν περικλειόμενος | οὐκ ἀγχι-
βαθεῖ τὰ δὲ πολλὰ τεναγῶδει θαλάττῃ, ὡς καὶ τῆς
τῶν κυμάτων φορᾶς τὸν πολὺν ἦχον καὶ πάταγον
26 ἐκ πάνυ μακροῦ διαστήματος προεκλύεσθαι. τοῦτον ἐξ ἁπάντων τῶν ἐν κύκλῳ κρίναντες ἐπιτηδειότατον εἶναι τὸν τόπον ἐνησυχάσαι καὶ ἐνηρεμῆσαι
καὶ μόνῃ τῇ ψυχῇ πρὸς μόνους ὁμιλῆσαι τοὺς νόμους, ἐνταυθοῖ κατέμειναν καὶ τὰς ἱερὰς βίβλους
λαβόντες ἀνατείνουσιν ἅμ' αὐταῖς καὶ τὰς χεῖρας
εἰς οὐρανόν, αἰτούμενοι τὸν θεὸν μὴ διαμαρτεῖν τῆς
προθέσεως· ὁ δ' ἐπινεύει ταῖς εὐχαῖς, ἵνα τὸ πλεῖστον ἢ καὶ τὸ σύμπαν γένος ἀνθρώπων ὠφεληθῇ
χρησόμενον εἰς ἐπανόρθωσιν βίου φιλοσόφοις καὶ
37 παγκάλοις διατάγμασι.   VII. καθίσαντες
δ' ἐν ἀποκρύφῳ καὶ μηδενὸς παρόντος ὅτι μὴ τῶν
τῆς φύσεως μερῶν, γῆς ὕδατος ἀέρος οὐρανοῦ, περὶ
ὧν πρῶτον τῆς γενέσεως ἔμελλον ἱεροφαντήσειν—
κοσμοποιία γὰρ ἡ τῶν νόμων ἐστὶν ἀρχή—, καθάπερ
ἐνθουσιῶντες προεφήτευον οὐκ ἄλλα ἄλλοι, τὰ δ'
αὐτὰ πάντες ὀνόματα καὶ ῥήματα, ὥσπερ ὑπο-
38 βολέως ἑκάστοις ἀοράτως ἐνηχοῦντος.   καίτοι τίς
οὐκ οἶδεν, ὅτι πᾶσα μὲν διάλεκτος, ἡ δ' Ἑλληνικὴ
διαφερόντως, ὀνομάτων πλουτεῖ, καὶ ταὐτὸν ἐν-
θύμημα οἷόν τε μεταφράζοντα καὶ παραφράζοντα
σχηματίσαι πολλαχῶς, ἄλλοτε ἄλλας ἐφαρμόζοντα

---

[a] For Philo's use of ἐνηχεῖν see note on *De Mut.* 57.
[b] Or " by paraphrasing more or less freely." The general
distinction between μετάφρασις and παράφρασις is that the
former sticks more closely than the latter to the material on
which it is exercised. See Ernesti, *Lex. tech. s.v.* μετάφρασις.

consequently the prevalence of diseases and deaths, and the impure conduct of the healthy inhabitants, made them suspicious of it. In front of Alexandria 35 lies the island of Pharos, stretching with its narrow strip of land towards the city, and enclosed by a sea not deep but mostly consisting of shoals, so that the loud din and booming of the surging waves grows faint through the long distance before it reaches the land. Judging this to be the most suit- 36 able place in the district, where they might find peace and tranquillity and the soul could commune with the laws with none to disturb its privacy, they fixed their abode there ; and, taking the sacred books, stretched them out towards heaven with the hands that held them, asking of God that they might not fail in their purpose. And He assented to their prayers, to the end that the greater part, or even the whole, of the human race might be profited and led to a better life by continuing to observe such wise and truly admirable ordinances.

VII. Sitting here in seclusion with none present save 37 the elements of nature, earth, water, air, heaven, the genesis of which was to be the first theme of their sacred revelation, for the laws begin with the story of the world's creation, they became as it were possessed, and, under inspiration, wrote, not each several scribe something different, but the same word for word, as though dictated [a] to each by an invisible prompter. Yet who does not know that 38 every language, and Greek especially, abounds in terms, and that the same thought can be put in many shapes by changing single words and whole phrases [b] and suiting the expression to the occasion ?

λέξεις; ὅπερ ἐπὶ ταύτης τῆς νομοθεσίας οὔ φασι
συμβῆναι, συνενεχθῆναι δ' εἰς ταὐτὸν κύρια κυρίοις
ὀνόμασι, τὰ Ἑλληνικὰ τοῖς Χαλδαϊκοῖς, ἐναρμο-
39 σθέντα εὖ μάλα τοῖς δηλουμένοις πράγμασιν. ὃν
γὰρ τρόπον, οἶμαι, ἐν γεωμετρίᾳ καὶ διαλεκτικῇ
τὰ σημαινόμενα ποικιλίαν ἑρμηνείας οὐκ ἀνέχεται,
μένει δ' ἀμετάβλητος ἡ ἐξ ἀρχῆς τεθεῖσα, τὸν αὐτὸν
ὡς ἔοικε τρόπον καὶ οὗτοι συντρέχοντα τοῖς πράγμασιν ὀνόματα ἐξεῦρον, ἅπερ δὴ μόνα ἢ μάλιστα
τρανώσειν ἔμελλεν ἐμφαντικῶς τὰ δηλούμενα.
40 σαφεστάτη δὲ τοῦδε πίστις· ἐάν τε Χαλδαῖοι τὴν
Ἑλληνικὴν γλῶτταν ἐάν τε Ἕλληνες τὴν Χαλδαίων ἀναδιδαχθῶσι καὶ ἀμφοτέραις ταῖς γραφαῖς
ἐντύχωσι, τῇ τε Χαλδαϊκῇ καὶ τῇ ἑρμηνευθείσῃ,
καθάπερ ἀδελφὰς μᾶλλον δ' ὡς μίαν καὶ τὴν αὐτὴν
ἔν τε τοῖς πράγμασι καὶ τοῖς ὀνόμασι τεθήπασι καὶ
προσκυνοῦσιν, οὐχ ἑρμηνέας ἐκείνους ἀλλ' ἱερο-
φάντας καὶ προφήτας προσαγορεύοντες, οἷς ἐξεγένετο συνδραμεῖν λογισμοῖς εἰλικρινέσι τῷ Μω-
41 σέως καθαρωτάτῳ πνεύματι.   διὸ καὶ μέχρι
νῦν ἀνὰ πᾶν ἔτος ἑορτὴ καὶ πανήγυρις ἄγεται κατὰ
τὴν Φάρον νῆσον, εἰς ἣν οὐκ Ἰουδαῖοι μόνον ἀλλὰ
[141] καὶ παμπληθεῖς ἕτεροι διαπλέουσι τό τε | χωρίον
σεμνυνοῦντες, ἐν ᾧ πρῶτον τὰ τῆς ἑρμηνείας ἐξ-
έλαμψε, καὶ παλαιᾶς ἕνεκεν εὐεργεσίας ἀεὶ νεαζού-
42 σης εὐχαριστήσοντες τῷ θεῷ.   μετὰ δὲ τὰς εὐχὰς
καὶ τὰς εὐχαριστίας οἱ μὲν πηξάμενοι σκηνὰς ἐπὶ
τῶν αἰγιαλῶν οἱ δ' ἐπὶ τῆς αἰγιαλίτιδος ψάμμου
κατακλινέντες ἐν ὑπαίθρῳ μετ' οἰκείων καὶ φίλων
ἑστιῶνται, πολυτελεστέραν τῆς ἐν βασιλείοις κατα-
43 σκευῆς τότε τὴν ἀκτὴν νομίζοντες.   οὕτω μὲν οἱ
νόμοι ζηλωτοὶ καὶ περιμάχητοι πᾶσιν ἰδιώταις τε

468

This was not the case, we are told, with this law of ours, but the Greek words used corresponded literally[a] with the Chaldean, exactly suited to the things they indicated. For, just as in geometry and logic, 39 so it seems to me, the sense indicated does not admit of variety in the expression which remains unchanged in its original form, so these writers, as it clearly appears, arrived at a wording which corresponded with the matter, and alone, or better than any other, would bring out clearly what was meant. The clearest proof of this is that, if Chaldeans have 40 learned Greek, or Greeks Chaldean, and read both versions, the Chaldean and the translation, they regard them with awe and reverence as sisters, or rather one and the same, both in matter and words, and speak of the authors not as translators but as prophets and priests of the mysteries, whose sincerity and singleness of thought has enabled them to go hand in hand with the purest of spirits, the spirit of Moses. Therefore, even to the 41 present day, there is held every year a feast and general assembly in the island of Pharos, whither not only Jews but multitudes of others cross the water, both to do honour to the place in which the light of that version first shone out, and also to thank God for the good gift so old yet ever young. But, after the prayers and thanksgivings, some 42 fixing tents on the seaside and others reclining on the sandy beach in the open air feast with their relations and friends, counting that shore for the time a more magnificent lodging than the fine mansions in the royal precincts. Thus the laws are 43 shewn to be desirable and precious in the eyes of all,

[a] See App. p. 606.

καὶ ἡγεμόσιν ἐπιδείκνυνται, καὶ ταῦτ' ἐκ πολλῶν
χρόνων τοῦ ἔθνους οὐκ εὐτυχοῦντος—τὰ δὲ τῶν
44 μὴ ἐν ἀκμαῖς πέφυκέ πως ἐπισκιάζεσθαι—· εἰ δὲ
γένοιτό τις ἀφορμὴ πρὸς τὸ λαμπρότερον, πόσην
εἰκὸς ἐπίδοσιν γενήσεσθαι; καταλιπόντας ἂν οἶμαι
τὰ ἴδια καὶ πολλὰ χαίρειν φράσαντας τοῖς πατρίοις
ἑκάστους μεταβαλεῖν ἐπὶ τὴν τούτων μόνων τιμήν·
εὐτυχίᾳ γὰρ τοῦ ἔθνους οἱ νόμοι συναναλάμψαντες
ἀμαυρώσουσι τοὺς ἄλλους καθάπερ ἀνατείλας ἥλιος
τοὺς ἀστέρας.

45 VIII. Ἀπόχρη μὲν οὖν καὶ τὰ λεχθέντα πολὺς
ἔπαινος εἶναι τοῦ νομοθέτου. πλείων δ' ἐστὶν
ἕτερος, ὃν αὐταὶ περιέχουσιν αἱ ἱερώταται βίβλοι,
πρὸς ἃς ἤδη τρεπτέον, εἰς ἔνδειξιν τῆς τοῦ συγ-
46 γράψαντος ἀρετῆς. τούτων τοίνυν τὸ μέν ἐστιν
ἱστορικὸν μέρος, τὸ δὲ περὶ τὰς προστάξεις καὶ
ἀπαγορεύσεις, ὑπὲρ οὗ δεύτερον λέξομεν τὸ πρότερον
47 τῇ τάξει πρότερον ἀκριβώσαντες. ἔστιν οὖν τοῦ
ἱστορικοῦ τὸ μὲν περὶ τῆς τοῦ κόσμου γενέσεως, τὸ
δὲ γενεαλογικόν, τοῦ δὲ γενεαλογικοῦ τὸ μὲν περὶ
κολάσεως ἀσεβῶν, τὸ δ' αὖ περὶ τιμῆς δικαίων.
οὗ δὲ χάριν ἐνθένδε τῆς νομοθεσίας ἤρξατο τὰ
περὶ τὰς προστάξεις καὶ ἀπαγορεύσεις ἐν δευτέρῳ
48 θείς, λεκτέον. οὐ γὰρ οἷά τις συγγραφεὺς ἐπετή-
δευσε παλαιῶν πράξεων καταλιπεῖν ὑπομνήματα
τοῖς ἔπειτα τοῦ ψυχαγωγῆσαι χάριν ἀνωφελῶς,
ἀλλ' ἠρχαιολόγησεν ἄνωθεν ἀρξάμενος ἀπὸ τῆς τοῦ

---

[a] Though of course genealogies play a great part in the
Pentateuch, γενεαλογικός if used in the strict sense is a very
inadequate term to describe the historical part of the books,
as distinct from the creation story. The wider sense, as
given in the translation, appears to have been in use in the

ordinary citizens and rulers alike, and that too though
our nation has not prospered for many a year. It
is but natural that when people are not flourishing
their belongings to some degree are under a cloud.
But, if a fresh start should be made to brighter 44
prospects, how great a change for the better might
we expect to see! I believe that each nation would
abandon its peculiar ways, and, throwing overboard
their ancestral customs, turn to honouring our laws
alone. For, when the brightness of their shining is
accompanied by national prosperity, it will darken the
light of the others as the risen sun darkens the stars.

VIII. The above is sufficient in itself as a high com- 45
mendation to the lawgiver; but there is another still
greater contained in the sacred books themselves,
and to these we must now turn to shew the great
qualities of the writer. They consist of two parts : 46
one the historical, the other concerned with commands and prohibitions, and of this we will speak
later, after first treating fully what comes first in
order. One division of the historical side deals with 47
the creation of the world, the other with particular
persons,[a] and this last partly with the punishment of
the impious, partly with the honouring of the just.
We must now give the reason why he began his law-
book with the history, and put the commands and
prohibitions in the second place. He did not, like 48
any historian, make it his business to leave behind
for posterity records of ancient deeds for the pleasant
but unimproving entertainment which they give;
but, in relating the history of early times, and going
for its beginning right to the creation of the universe,

grammatical schools, whose language Philo often adopts.
For the evidence for this see App. p.606.

471

παντὸς γενέσεως, ἵν' ἐπιδείξῃ δύο τὰ ἀναγκαιότατα·
ἓν μὲν τὸν αὐτὸν πατέρα καὶ ποιητὴν τοῦ κόσμου
καὶ ἀληθείᾳ νομοθέτην, ἕτερον δὲ τὸν χρησόμενον
τοῖς νόμοις ἀκολουθίαν φύσεως ἀσπασόμενον καὶ
βιωσόμενον κατὰ τὴν τοῦ ὅλου διάταξιν ἁρμονίᾳ
καὶ συμφωνίᾳ πρὸς ἔργα λόγων καὶ πρὸς λόγους
49 ἔργων. IX. τῶν μὲν οὖν ἄλλων νομοθετῶν οἱ μὲν
εὐθὺς ἅ τε χρὴ πράττειν καὶ ἃ μὴ διαταξάμενοι
τιμωρίας κατὰ τῶν παραβαινόντων ὥρισαν, οἱ δ' |
[142] ἀμείνους δόξαντες εἶναι τὴν ἀρχὴν οὐκ ἐνθένδε
ἐποιήσαντο, πόλιν δὲ τῷ λόγῳ κτίσαντες καὶ
ἱδρυσάμενοι πρότερον ἣν ἐνόμιζον οἰκειοτάτην καὶ
πρεπωδεστάτην εἶναι τῇ κτισθείσῃ πολιτείαν διὰ
50 τῆς τῶν νόμων θέσεως ἐφήρμοζον. ὁ δὲ τὸ μὲν
πρότερον ὑπολαβὼν (ὅπερ ἦν) τυραννικόν τε καὶ
δεσποτικόν, ἄνευ παραμυθίας προστάττειν ὡς οὐκ
ἐλευθέροις ἀλλὰ δούλοις, τὸ δ' ὕστερον ἐμμελὲς
μέν, οὐ μὴν τελείως ἐπαινετὸν ἅπασι τοῖς κριταῖς,
ὡς ἔοικεν, ἐν ἑκατέρῳ τῶν λεχθέντων διήνεγκεν.
51 ἔν τε γὰρ ταῖς προστάξεσι καὶ ἀπαγορεύσεσιν
ὑποτίθεται καὶ παρηγορεῖ τὸ πλέον ἢ κελεύει, μετὰ
προοιμίων καὶ ἐπιλόγων τὰ πλεῖστα καὶ ἀναγ-
καιότατα πειρώμενος ὑφηγεῖσθαι, τοῦ προτρέψασθαι χάριν μᾶλλον ἢ βιάσασθαι· πόλεώς τε χειρο-
ποιήτου κτίσιν ἀρχὴν ποιήσασθαι τῆς γραφῆς
ταπεινότερον ἢ κατὰ τὴν ἀξίαν τῶν νόμων ὑπολαβὼν
εἶναι, πρὸς τὸ μέγεθος καὶ κάλλος τῆς ὅλης νομο-

---

a Compare the beginning of *De Op.*, especially § 3.
b The allusion is, of course, primarily to Plato's *Laws* and
Republic. Perhaps also to Zeno, whose Πολιτεία is said to
have been written in opposition to Plato's (*S.V.F.* i. 260,

he wished to shew two most essential things : first
that the Father and Maker of the world was in the
truest sense also its Lawgiver, secondly that he who
would observe the laws will accept gladly the duty
of following nature and live in accordance with the
ordering of the universe, so that his deeds are attuned
to harmony with his words and his words with his
deeds.[a] IX. Now, other legislators are divided into 49
those who set out by ordering what should or should
not be done, and laying down penalties for disobedience, and those who, thinking themselves
superior, did not begin with this, but first founded
and established their state as they conceived it, and
then, by framing laws, attached to it the constitution
which they thought most agreeable and suitable to
the form in which they had founded it.[b] But Moses, 50
thinking that the former course, namely issuing
orders without words of exhortation, as though to
slaves instead of free men, savoured of tyranny and
despotism, as indeed it did, and that the second,
though aptly conceived, was evidently not entirely
satisfactory in the judgement of all, took a different
line in both departments. In his commands and 51
prohibitions he suggests and admonishes rather than
commands, and the very numerous and necessary
instructions which he essays to give are accompanied
by forewords and after-words, in order to exhort
rather than to enforce. Again, he considered that
to begin his writings with the foundation of a man-
made city was below the dignity of the laws, and,
surveying the greatness and beauty of the whole

cf. 262). Aristotle's *Politics* hardly fits the case. Josephus,
Apion ii. 222, makes the same point, but adds that passing
over the other philosophers he will only name Plato.

θεσίας ἀκριβεστάτῃ ὄψει τῇ κατὰ διάνοιαν ἀπιδὼν
καὶ νομίσας αὐτὴν κρείττονα καὶ θειοτέραν ἢ ὥστε
κύκλῳ τινὶ τῶν ἐπὶ γῆς ὁρισθῆναι, τῆς μεγαλο
πόλεως τὴν γένεσιν εἰσηγήσατο, τοὺς νόμους
ἐμφερεστάτην εἰκόνα τῆς τοῦ κόσμου πολιτείας
52 ἡγησάμενος εἶναι.   X. τῶν γοῦν ἐν
μέρει διατεταγμένων τὰς δυνάμεις εἴ τις ἀκριβῶς
ἐξετάζειν ἐθελήσειεν, εὑρήσει τῆς τοῦ παντὸς
ἁρμονίας ἐφιεμένας καὶ τῷ λόγῳ τῆς ἀιδίου φύσεως
53 συναδούσας. διὸ καὶ τοὺς ἀφθόνων μὲν ἀγαθῶν
ἀξιωθέντας ὅσα κατ᾽ εὐεξίαν σωμάτων καὶ τὰς
περὶ πλοῦτον καὶ δόξαν καὶ τὰ ἄλλα ἐκτὸς εὐτυχίας,
ἀρετῆς δ᾽ ἀφηνιάσαντας καὶ οὐκ ἀνάγκῃ γνώμῃ
δ᾽ ἑκουσίῳ πανουργίαν καὶ ἀδικίαν καὶ τὰς ἄλλας
κακίας, ὡς μέγα ὄφελος τὴν μεγίστην ζημίαν, ἐπι
τηδεύσαντας καθάπερ οὐκ ἀνθρώπων ἐχθροὺς ἀλλὰ
τοῦ σύμπαντος οὐρανοῦ τε καὶ κόσμου τὰς ἐν ἔθει
τιμωρίας οὔ φησιν ὑπομεῖναι, ἀλλὰ καινοτάτας καὶ
παρηλλαγμένας, ἃς ἐμεγαλούργησεν ἡ πάρεδρος τῷ
θεῷ μισοπόνηρος δίκη, τῶν τοῦ παντὸς δραστικω
τάτων στοιχείων ἐπιθεμένων ὕδατος καὶ πυρός,
ὡς καιρῶν περιόδοις τοὺς μὲν κατακλυσμοῖς
φθαρῆναι, τοὺς δὲ καταφλεχθέντας ἀπολέσθαι.
54 πελάγη μὲν ἀρθέντα καὶ ποταμοὶ μετεωρισθέντες
αὐθιγενεῖς τε καὶ χείμαρροι τὰς ἐν τῇ πεδιάδι
πόλεις ἁπάσας ἐπέκλυσαν καὶ κατέσυραν, τὰς
δὲ κατὰ τὴν ὀρεινὴν αἱ μεθ᾽ ἡμέραν καὶ νύκτωρ
55 συνεχεῖς καὶ ἀδιάστατοι ὄμβρων φοραί. χρόνῳ δ᾽
ὕστερον ἐκ τῶν ὑπολειφθέντων πάλιν τοῦ γένους
συναυξηθέντος καὶ εἰς πολυανθρωπίαν ἐπιδόντος,
[143] ἐπειδὴ τὸ περὶ τοὺς προγόνους πάθος οἱ | ἀπόγονοι
μάθημα σωφροσύνης οὐκ ἐποιήσαντο, πρὸς δ᾽

code with the accurate discernment of his mind's eye, and thinking it too good and godlike to be confined within any earthly walls, he inserted the story of the genesis of the " Great City," holding that the laws were the most faithful picture of the world-polity.   X. Thus whoever will care- 52 fully examine the nature of the particular enactments will find that they seek to attain to the harmony of the universe and are in agreement with the principles of eternal nature.   Therefore all those to whom God 53 thought fit to grant abundance of the good gifts of bodily well-being and of good fortune in the shape of wealth and other externals—who then rebelled against virtue, and, freely and intentionally under no compulsion, practised knavery, injustice and the other vices, thinking to gain much by losing all, were counted, Moses tells us, as enemies not of men but of the whole heaven and universe, and suffered not the ordinary, but strange and unexampled punishments wrought by the might of justice, the hater of evil and assessor of God.   For the most forceful elements of the universe, fire and water, fell upon them, so that, as the times revolved, some perished by deluge, others were consumed by conflagration.[a] The seas lifted up their waters, and the rivers, spring- 54 fed and winter torrents, rose on high and flooded and swept away all the cities of the plain, while the continuous and ceaseless streams of rain by night and day did the same for the cities of the uplands.   At a 55 later time, when the race sprung from the remnant had again increased and become very populous, since the descendants did not take the fate of their forefathers as a lesson in wisdom, but turned to deeds

[a] See note on *De Abr.* 1.

ἀκολασίας ἐτράποντο ζηλωταὶ χαλεπωτέρων ἐπιτηδευμάτων γενόμενοι, πυρὶ τούτους ἀναλῶσαι δι-
56 ενοήθη. τότ' οὖν, ὡς μηνύει τὰ λόγια, κεραυνοὶ
ῥυέντες ἐξ οὐρανοῦ τούς τε ἀσεβεῖς κατέπρησαν
καὶ τὰς πόλεις αὐτῶν· καὶ μέχρι τοῦ νῦν μνημεῖα
τοῦ συμβεβηκότος ἀλέκτου πάθους δείκνυται κατὰ
Συρίαν, ἐρείπια καὶ τέφρα καὶ θεῖον καὶ καπνὸς καὶ
ἡ ἔτι ἀναδιδομένη φλὸξ ἀμαυρὰ καθάπερ δια-
σμυχομένου πυρός.

57 Ἐν δὲ τούτῳ συνέβαινε τούς τε ἀσεβεῖς ταῖς
εἰρημέναις τιμωρίαις κολάζεσθαι καὶ τοὺς καλο-
κἀγαθίᾳ διενηνοχότας εὖ πάσχειν ἀρετῆς ἐπαξίων
58 ἄθλων τυγχάνοντας. ἐν μέν γε τῇ φορᾷ τοῦ
κεραυνίου πυρὸς οἰκήτορσιν αὐτοῖς ὅλης χώρας
ἐμπιπραμένης, εἷς μόνος ἀνὴρ μέτοικος ἐπιφροσύνῃ
θείᾳ σῴζεται, διότι τῶν ἐγχωρίων παρανομημάτων
οὐδὲν ἠσπάσατο, τῶν μετοίκων εἰωθότων ἀσφαλείας
ἕνεκα τὰ ξενικὰ τιμᾶν, ἐπεὶ τοῖς ἀτιμάζουσι κίν-
δυνος ἐκ τῶν αὐτοχθόνων ἕπεται· καίτοι γ' οὐκ ἐπ'
ἄκρον ἦλθε σοφίας, ὡς διὰ τελειότητα τῆς ἐν αὐτῷ
φύσεως τοσούτου γέρως ἀξιωθῆναι, ἀλλ' ὅτι μόνος[1]
τοῖς πολλοῖς οὐ συνηνέχθη πρὸς τὸ ἁβροδίαιτον
ἀποκλίνασι καὶ πάσας μὲν ἡδονὰς πάσας δ' ἐπιθυμίας χορηγίαις ἀφθόνοις ἀνάψασιν ὥσπερ φλόγα
59 λασίῳ ὕλῃ κεχυμένῃ.   XI. κατὰ δὲ τὸν
μέγαν κατακλυσμὸν ὀλίγου δέω φάναι τοῦ σύμπαντος ἀνθρώπων γένους φθειρομένου, ἕνα οἶκον ἀπαθῆ
γενέσθαι παντὸς κακοῦ λόγος ἔχει, τὸν πρεσβύτατον
καὶ ἡγεμόνα τῆς οἰκίας ἐπειδὴ συνέβαινε μηδενὸς
ἀδικήματος ἑκουσίου προσάψασθαι. τὸν δὲ τρόπον
τῆς σωτηρίας, ὡς αἱ ἱεραὶ βίβλοι περιέχουσιν, ἄξιον

[1] MSS. μόνον.

476

of licence and followed eagerly still more grievous
practices, He determined to destroy them with fire.
Then, as the oracles declare, the lightnings poured 56
from heaven and consumed the impious and their
cities, and to the present day the memorials to the
awful disaster are shewn in Syria, ruins and cinders
and brimstone and smoke, and the dusky flame
still arises as though fire were smouldering within.

But while in these disasters the impious were 57
chastised with the said punishments, it was also the
case that those who stood out in excellence of conduct fared well and received the rewards which their
virtue deserved. While the rush of the flaming 58
thunderbolts consumed the whole land, and the inhabitants to boot, one man alone, an immigrant, was
saved by God's protecting care, because he had shewn
no liking for any of the misdeeds of the country,
though immigrants, to secure themselves, usually
shew respect for the customs of their hosts, knowing
that disrespect for these entails danger at the hands
of the original inhabitants. Yet he did not reach
the summit of wisdom, nor was it because of the
perfection of his nature that he was deemed worthy
of this great privilege, but because he alone
did not fall in with the multitude, when they
turned aside to licentious living and fed every
pleasure and every lust with lavish supplies of fuel
like a flame when the brushwood is piled upon it.

XI. So, too, in the great deluge when 59
all but the whole human race perished, one house,
we are told, suffered no harm because the most
venerable member and head of the household had
committed no deliberate wrong. The manner of his
preservation is a story worth recording, both as a

ἱστορηθῆναι διά τε μεγαλουργίαν καὶ ἅμα βελτίωσιν
60 ἠθῶν. νομισθεὶς γὰρ ἐπιτήδειος εἶναι μὴ μόνον
ἀμοιρῆσαι τῆς κοινῆς συμφορᾶς, ἀλλὰ καὶ δευτέρας
γενέσεως ἀνθρώπων αὐτὸς ἀρχὴ γενέσθαι, θείαις
προστάξεσιν, ἃς ὑφηγοῦντο οἱ χρησμοί, ξύλινον
δημιουργήσας ἔργον μέγιστον εἰς πήχεις τριακο-
σίους μῆκος καὶ πεντήκοντα εὖρος καὶ τριάκοντα
ὕψος καὶ συνεχῆ κατασκευασάμενος ἔνδον οἰκήματα
ἐπίπεδα καὶ ὑπερῷα, τριώροφα καὶ τετρώροφα, καὶ
τροφὰς ἑτοιμασάμενος, ἀφ' ἑκάστου γένους ζῴων
ὅσα χερσαῖα καὶ πτηνὰ εἰσήγαγεν ἄρρεν τε καὶ
θῆλυ σπέρματα ὑπολειπόμενος πρὸς καταλλαγὴν
61 καιρῶν¹ τῶν αὖθίς ποτε γενησομένων· ᾔδει γὰρ τὴν
τοῦ θεοῦ φύσιν ἵλεω, κἂν εἰ τὰ εἴδη φθείροιτο, ἀλλά
τοι τὴν ἐν τοῖς γένεσιν ἀφθαρσίαν ἕνεκα τῆς πρὸς
[144] αὐτὸν ὁμοιότητος | καὶ τοῦ μηδὲν τῶν κατὰ πρό-
θεσιν φύντων ποτὲ λυθῆναι διαμένουσαν· XII. οὗ
χάριν πάντα ἐπειθάρχει καὶ τὰ τέως ἐξηγριωμένα
ἡμεροῦτο καὶ οἷα νομεῖ καὶ ἀγελάρχῃ τιθασευθέντα
62 ἐπηκολούθει. μετὰ δὲ τὴν εἴσοδον ἁπάντων εἴ τις
ἐθεάσατο τὸ πλήρωμα, οὐκ ἂν διήμαρτεν εἰπών,
ἀντίμιμον εἶναι γῆς ἁπάσης ἐν ἑαυτῷ φέρον τὰ
ζῴων γένη, ὧν καὶ ἡ σύμπασα γῆ τὰ ἀμύθητα εἴδη
63 καὶ πρότερον ἤνεγκε καὶ ἴσως αὖθις οἴσει. τὰ δ'
εἰκασθέντα χρόνοις ὕστερον οὐ μακροῖς ἀπέβαινε·
τὸ μὲν γὰρ πάθος ἐλώφα καὶ ἡ τοῦ κατακλυσμοῦ
φορὰ καθ' ἑκάστην ἡμέραν ἐμειοῦτο, τῶν τε ὄμβρων
ἐπισχεθέντων καὶ τοῦ κατὰ πᾶσαν γῆν ἀναχυθέντος

---

¹ Cohn somewhat arbitrarily declares καταλλαγὴν καιρῶν
corrupt and suggests καταγωγὴν γενῶν. The translation does
perhaps require an unusual sense for καταλλαγή. If this is

marvel and as a means of edification. Being judged 60
a fit person not only to be exempted from the common
fate, but also to be himself the beginner of a second
generation of mankind, by God's commands enjoined by the oracular voice, he built a huge structure
of wood, three hundred cubits in length, fifty in
breadth and thirty in height. Inside this, he framed
a series of rooms, on the ground floor and second,
third and fourth stories. Then, having laid up provisions, he introduced a male and female specimen
of every kind of living creature both of the land
and the air, thus reserving seeds in expectation
of the better times *a* that were once more to come.
For he knew that the nature of God was gracious, 61
and that, though the individuals perished, the race
would be preserved indestructible because of its
likeness to Himself, and that nothing whose being
He had willed would ever be brought to nought.
XII. In consequence, all the creatures obeyed him,
and the erstwhile savage grew gentle, and in
their new tameness followed him as a flock follows
its leader. When they had all entered, anyone 62
who surveyed the crew might fairly have said
that it was a miniature of earth in its entirety, com-
prising the races of living creatures, of which the
world had carried before innumerable specimens,
and perhaps would carry them again. What he had 63
surmised came to pass not long afterwards, for the
trouble abated, and the force of the deluge diminished
every day, as the rain ceased and the water that had

a Lit. "for change brought about by (or 'into') the
seasons," etc. See note 1.

---

fatal, I should suggest πρὸς ⟨καταβολὴν⟩ κατ' ἀλλαγὴν καιρῶν,
i.e. "to be sown when the times change."

ὕδατος τῇ μὲν ἀναλισκομένου τῷ ἀφ' ἡλίου φλογμῷ
τῇ δὲ ὑπονοστοῦντος εἰς χαράδρας καὶ φάραγγας
καὶ τὰς ἄλλας τῆς γῆς κοιλότητας· ὥσπερ γὰρ
θεοῦ προστάξαντος, ἑκάστη φύσις ὅπερ ἔχρησεν οἷα
δάνειον ἀναγκαῖον ἀπελάμβανε, θάλαττα καὶ πηγαὶ
καὶ ποταμοί· πρὸς γὰρ τοὺς οἰκείους τόπους ἕκα-
64 στον ῥεῖθρον ὑπενόστει. μετὰ δὲ τὴν κάθαρσιν τῶν
ὑπὸ σελήνην, ἀπολουσαμένης τῆς γῆς καὶ νέας ἀνα-
φανείσης καὶ τοιαύτης, οἵαν εἰκὸς εἶναι ὅτε τὴν
ἀρχὴν μετὰ τοῦ κόσμου παντὸς ἐκτίζετο, πρόεισιν
ἐκ τοῦ ξυλίνου κατασκευάσματος αὐτὸς καὶ γυνὴ
καὶ υἱοὶ καὶ τούτων γυναῖκες καὶ μετὰ τῆς οἰκίας
ἀγεληδὸν τὰ συνεληλυθότα τῶν ζῴων γένη πρὸς
τὴν τῶν ὁμοίων σποράν τε καὶ γένεσιν.

65 ταῦτα τῶν ἀγαθῶν ἀνδρῶν ἐστιν ἀριστεῖα καὶ ἆθλα,
δι' ὧν οὐ μόνον αὐτοὶ καὶ γένη σωτηρίας ἔτυχον
τοὺς μεγίστους κινδύνους ἐκφυγόντες, οἳ κατὰ τὸν
τῶν στοιχείων νεωτερισμὸν τοῖς πανταχοῦ πᾶσιν
ἐπετειχίσθησαν, ἀλλὰ καὶ παλιγγενεσίας ἐγένοντο
ἡγεμόνες καὶ δευτέρας ἀρχηγέται περιόδου, καθάπερ
ἐμπυρεύματα τοῦ ζῴων ἀρίστου γένους ἀνθρώπων
ὑπολειφθέντες, ὃ τὴν ἡγεμονίαν τῶν περιγείων ἅπαξ
ἁπάντων ἔλαχεν ἀντίμιμον γεγονὸς θεοῦ δυνάμεως,
εἰκὼν τῆς ἀοράτου φύσεως ἐμφανής, ἀιδίου γενητή.

66
[145]
*   *   *   *   *

XIII. | Δύο μὲν ἤδη μέρη τοῦ βίου Μωυσέως
διεξεληλύθαμεν, τό τε περὶ βασιλείας καὶ νομο-
θετικῆς· τρίτον δὲ προσαποδοτέον τὸ περὶ ἱερωσύνης. ὃ τοίνυν μέγιστον καὶ ἀναγκαιότατον
ἀρχιερεῖ προσεῖναι δεῖ, τὴν εὐσέβειαν, ἐν τοῖς

---

^a On the question of a considerable lacuna at this point
see App. pp. 606-607.

covered every land partly disappeared under the heat of the sun, partly subsided into the beds of water torrents and into chasms and the other hollows in the earth. For, as though by God's command, every form of nature, sea, springs and rivers, received back what it had lent as a debt which must be repaid ; for each stream subsided into its proper place. But 64 when the sublunary world had been purged, when earth rising from its ablutions shewed itself renewed with the likeness which we may suppose it to have worn when originally it was created with the universe, there issued from the wooden structure himself and his wife and his sons and his sons' wives, and with the household, moving like a herd, the various animals which had been assembled there came forth to beget and reproduce their kind.   These are the 65 guerdons and the prizes of the good, by which not only they themselves and their families won safety and escaped the greatest dangers, which, with the wild uprising of the elements as their weapon, stood menacingly over all and everywhere, but also became leaders of the regeneration, inaugurators of a second cycle, spared as embers to rekindle mankind, that highest form of life, which has received dominion over everything whatsoever upon earth, born to be the likeness of God's power and image of His nature, the visible of the Invisible, the created of the Eternal.[a]

*   *   *   *   *

XIII. We have now fully treated of two sides of 66 the life of Moses, the royal and the legislative. We must proceed to give account of the third, which concerns his priesthood. The chief and most essential quality required by a priest is piety, and

PHILO

μάλιστα οὗτος ἤσκησεν ἅμα καὶ φύσεως εὐμοιρίᾳ
χρησάμενος, ἣν ὥσπερ ἀγαθὴν ἄρουραν φιλοσοφία
παραλαβοῦσα δογμάτων θεωρίᾳ παγκάλων ἐβελ-
τίωσε καὶ οὐ πρότερον ἀνῆκεν ἢ τελειογονηθῆναι
τοὺς ἀρετῆς καρποὺς διά τε λόγων καὶ πράξεων.
67 τοιγαροῦν μετ' ὀλίγων ἄλλων φιλόθεός τε καὶ
θεοφιλὴς ἐγένετο, καταπνευσθεὶς ὑπ' ἔρωτος οὐρανίου καὶ διαφερόντως τιμήσας τὸν ἡγεμόνα τοῦ
παντὸς καὶ ἀντιτιμηθεὶς ὑπ' αὐτοῦ· τιμὴ δ' ἁρ-
μόττουσα σοφῷ θεραπεύειν τὸ πρὸς ἀλήθειαν ὄν·
ἱερωσύνη δὲ θεραπείαν ἐπιτετήδευκε θεοῦ. τούτου
τοῦ γέρως, οὗ μεῖζον ἀγαθὸν ἐν τοῖς οὖσιν οὐκ
ἔστιν, ἠξιοῦτο χρησμοῖς ἕκαστα τῶν εἰς τὰς λειτουργίας καὶ ἱερὰς ὑπηρεσίας ἀναδιδασκόμενος.
68 XIV. ἔδει δὲ πρότερον ὥσπερ τὴν ψυχὴν καὶ τὸ
σῶμα καθαρεῦσαι, μηδενὸς πάθους προσαψάμενον,
ἀλλ' ἀγνεύσαντα ἀπὸ πάντων ὅσα τῆς θνητῆς ἐστι
φύσεως, σιτίων καὶ ποτῶν καὶ τῆς πρὸς γυναῖκας
69 ὁμιλίας. ἀλλὰ ταύτης μὲν ἐκ πολλῶν χρόνων κατεφρόνησε καὶ σχεδὸν ἀφ' οὗ τὸ πρῶτον ἤρξατο
[146] | προφητεύειν καὶ θεοφορεῖσθαι, προσῆκον ἡγού-
μενος ἕτοιμον ἐμπαρέχειν ἀεὶ τοῖς χρησμοῖς ἑαυτόν·
σιτίων δὲ καὶ ποτῶν ἐπὶ ἡμέρας τεσσαράκοντα ἑξῆς
ἠλόγησε, δηλονότι τροφὰς ἔχων ἀμείνους τὰς διὰ
θεωρίας, αἷς ἄνωθεν ἀπ' οὐρανοῦ καταπνεόμενος
τὴν μὲν διάνοιαν τὸ πρῶτον, ἔπειτα δὲ καὶ τὸ σῶμα
διὰ τῆς ψυχῆς ἐβελτιοῦτο, καθ' ἑκάτερον πρός
τε ἰσχὺν καὶ εὐεξίαν ἐπιδιδούς, ὡς τοὺς ἰδόντας
70 ὕστερον ἀπιστεῖν. εἰς γὰρ ὄρος ὑψηλότατον καὶ
ἱερώτατον τῶν περὶ τὸν τόπον ἀνελθὼν προστάξεσι

this he practised in a very high degree, and at the
same time made use of his great natural gifts.
In these, philosophy found a good soil, which she
improved still further by the admirable truths which
she brought before his eyes, nor did she cease until
the fruits of virtue shewn in word and deed were
brought to perfection. Thus he came to love God 67
and be loved by Him as have been few others. A
heaven-sent rapture inspired him, so markedly did he
honour the Ruler of the All and was honoured in
return by Him. An honour well-becoming the wise
is to serve the Being Who truly is, and the service
of God is ever the business of the priesthood. This
privilege, a blessing which nothing in the world can
surpass, was given to him as his due, and oracles
instructed him in all that pertains to rites of worship
and the sacred tasks of his ministry. XIV. But first 68
he had to be clean, as in soul so also in body, to have
no dealings with any passion, purifying himself from
all the calls of mortal nature, food and drink and
intercourse with women. This last he had disdained 69
for many a day, almost from the time when, possessed
by the spirit, he entered on his work as prophet,
since he held it fitting to hold himself always in
readiness to receive the oracular messages. As for
eating and drinking, he had no thought of them
for forty successive days, doubtless because he had
the better food of contemplation, through whose inspiration, sent from heaven above, he grew in grace,
first of mind, then of body also through the soul, and
in both so advanced in strength and well-being that
those who saw him afterwards could not believe
their eyes. For we read that by God's command 70
he ascended an inaccessible and pathless mountain,

θείαις, ὅπερ ἀπρόσιτον καὶ ἄβατον ἦν, εἰς ἐκεῖνον
λέγεται διαμεῖναι τὸν χρόνον οὐδὲν ἐπιφερόμενος
τῶν εἰς ἀναγκαίας ἀπόλαυσιν τροφῆς ⟨καὶ⟩[1] ἡμέραις
ὕστερον, ὡς ἐλέχθη, τεσσαράκοντα κατέβαινε πολὺ
καλλίων τὴν ὄψιν ἢ ὅτε ἀνῄει, ὡς τοὺς ὁρῶντας
τεθηπέναι καὶ καταπεπλῆχθαι καὶ μηδ' ἐπὶ πλέον
ἀντέχειν τοῖς ὀφθαλμοῖς δύνασθαι κατὰ τὴν προσ-
βολὴν ἡλιοειδοῦς φέγγους ἀπαστράπτοντος.

71   XV. Ἔτι δ' ἄνω διατρίβων ἐμυσταγωγεῖτο παιδευόμενος τὰ κατὰ τὴν ἱερωσύνην πάντα καὶ
πρῶτα, ἃ δὴ καὶ πρῶτα τῇ τάξει, τὰ περὶ τὴν τοῦ
72 ἱεροῦ καὶ τῶν ἐν αὐτῷ κατασκευήν. εἰ μὲν οὖν
τὴν χώραν, εἰς ἣν μετανίσταντο, ἤδη παρειλήφεσαν,
ἀναγκαῖον ἦν ἱδρύσασθαι περισημότατον νεὼν ἐν
τῷ καθαρωτάτῳ λίθων πολυτελῶν ὕλης καὶ περὶ
αὐτὸν τείχη μεγάλα δείμασθαι καὶ νεωκόροις
παμπληθεῖς οἰκίας, ὀνομάσαντας ἱερόπολιν τὸν
73 τόπον. ἐπεὶ δ' ἔτι κατὰ τὴν ἐρήμην ἐπλάζοντο,
τοῖς μήπω παγίως ἱδρυθεῖσιν ἥρμοττε φορητὸν
ἔχειν ἱερόν, ἵν' ἐν ταῖς ὁδοιπορίαις καὶ στρατοπε-
δείαις ἀνάγωσι θυσίας καὶ τὰ ἄλλα ὅσα κατὰ τὰς
ἱερουργίας δρῶσι μηδενὸς ἀμοιρούντες ὧν χρὴ τοὺς
74 ἐν πόλεσιν οἰκοῦντας. σκηνὴν οὖν, ἔργον ἱερώτατον, δημιουργεῖν ἔδοξεν, ἧς τὴν κατασκευὴν
θεσφάτοις λογίοις ἐπὶ τοῦ ὄρους Μωυσῆς ἀν-
εδιδάσκετο, τῶν μελλόντων ἀποτελεῖσθαι σωμάτων
ἀσωμάτους ἰδέας τῇ ψυχῇ θεωρῶν, πρὸς ἃς ἔδει

[1] ⟨καὶ⟩ : so Cohn emends this defective sentence. I suggest
as an alternative to insert ᾗ (="where") before εἰς ἐκεῖνον.

---

[a] See Ex. xxiv. 18, xxxiv. 28 ff.

the highest and most sacred in the region, and remained for the period named, taking nothing that is needed to satisfy the requirements of bare sustenance. Then, after the said forty days had passed, he descended with a countenance far more beautiful than when he ascended, so that those who saw him were filled with awe and amazement; nor even could their eyes continue to stand the dazzling brightness that flashed from him like the rays of the sun.[a]

XV. While he was still staying on the mount, he was 71 being instructed in all the mysteries of his priestly duties : and first in those which stood first in order, namely the building and furnishing of the sanctuary. Now, if they had already occupied the land into which 72 they were removing, they would necessarily have had to erect a magnificent temple on the most open and conspicuous site,[b] with costly stones for its material, and build great walls around it, with plenty of houses for the attendants, and call the place the holy city. But, as they were still wandering in the desert and 73 had as yet no settled habitation, it suited them to have a portable sanctuary, so that during their journeys and encampment they might bring their sacrifices to it and perform all their other religious duties, not lacking anything which dwellers in cities should have. It was determined, therefore, to fashion a tabernacle, 74 a work of the highest sanctity, the construction of which was set forth to Moses on the mount by divine pronouncements. He saw with the soul's eye the immaterial forms of the material objects about to be

[b] Mangey "augustissima sede," the German translation "geweihter Stätte," but the sense given above seems more probable. Cf. §§ 34 and 214, also In Flaccum 122 ἐπὶ τοὺς πλησίον αἰγιαλοὺς ἀφικνοῦνται κἂν τῷ καθαρωτάτῳ στάντες ἀνεβόησαν.

καθάπερ ἀπ' ἀρχετύπου γραφῆς καὶ νοητῶν παραδειγμάτων αἰσθητὰ μιμήματα ἀπεικονισθῆναι.
75 προσῆκον γὰρ ἦν τῷ ὡς ἀληθῶς ἀρχιερεῖ καὶ τὴν
τοῦ ἱεροῦ κατασκευὴν ἐπιτραπῆναι, ἵν' ἐκ πολλοῦ
τοῦ περιόντος ἡρμοσμένας καὶ συμφώνους τοῖς
δημιουργηθεῖσι ποιῆται τὰς ἐν τῷ ἱερᾶσθαι λει-
76 τουργίας. XVI. ὁ μὲν οὖν τύπος τοῦ παραδείγ-
ματος ἐνεσφραγίζετο τῇ διανοίᾳ τοῦ προφήτου
διαζωγραφούμενος καὶ προδιαπλαττόμενος ἀφανῶς
ἄνευ ὕλης ἀοράτοις εἴδεσι· τὸ δ' ἀποτέλεσμα πρὸς
τὸν τύπον ἐδημιουργεῖτο, ἐναποματτομένου τὰς
σφραγῖδας τοῦ τεχνίτου ταῖς προσφόροις ἑκάστων
77 ὑλικαῖς οὐσίαις. ἦν δ' ἡ κατασκευὴ τοιάδε· ὀκτὼ
[147] καὶ τεσσαράκοντα κίονες κέδρου | τῆς ἀσηπτοτάτης
ἀπὸ στελεχῶν κοπέντες εὐερνεστάτων περιεβάλλον-
το χρυσῷ βαθεῖ· κἄπειθ' ἑκάστῳ δύο ἀργυραῖ
βάσεις ὑπηρείδοντο καὶ κατὰ τὸ ἀκροκιόνιον ἐφ-
78 ηρμόζετο χρυσῆ κεφαλίς. εἰς μὲν οὖν τὸ μῆκος
τεσσαράκοντα κίονας διέταττεν ὁ τεχνίτης, ἑκατέρωθεν τοὺς ἡμίσεις εἴκοσι, μηδὲν ἐν μέσῳ διάστημα
ποιούμενος, ἀλλ' ἑξῆς ἐφαρμόζων καὶ συνάπτων,
ἵν' οἷα τείχους ὄψις μία προφαίνηται· εἰς δὲ τὸ
πλάτος ἐσώτατον τοὺς λοιποὺς ὀκτώ, ἐξ μὲν κατὰ
τὴν μέσην χώραν, δύο δ' ἐν ταῖς παρ' ἑκάτερα τῆς
μέσης γωνίαις, τὸν μὲν ἐπὶ δεξιά, τὸν δ' ἐπ' εὐ-
ώνυμα· κατὰ δὲ τὴν εἴσοδον ἄλλους τέσσαρας, τὰ
μὲν ἄλλα ὁμοίους, μίαν δ' ἀντὶ δυοῖν ἔχοντας βάσιν
τῶν ἐξ ἀντικρύ, μεθ' οὓς ἐξωτάτω πέντε μόναις
79 ταῖς βάσεσι διαφέροντας, χαλκαῖ γὰρ ἦσαν· ὥστε
τῆς σκηνῆς τοὺς σύμπαντας εἶναι, δίχα τῶν ἐν ταῖς

---

[a] For §§ 77-83 see Ex. xxvi. 18 ff.
[b] LXX στῦλοι ("posts"?).   E.V. "boards."

made, and these forms had to be reproduced in copies
perceived by the senses, taken from the original
draught, so to speak, and from patterns conceived
in the mind.   For it was fitting that the construction 75
of the sanctuary should be committed to him who was
truly high priest, in order that his performance of
the rites belonging to his sacred office might be in
more than full accordance and harmony with the
fabric.   XVI. So the shape of the model was stamped 76
upon the mind of the prophet, a secretly painted or
moulded prototype, produced by immaterial and invisible forms ; and then the resulting work was built
in accordance with that shape by the artist impressing
the stampings upon the material substances required
in each case.   *a*The actual construction was as follows. 77
Forty-eight pillars *b* of the most durable cedar wood,
hewn out of the finest trunks, were encased in a deep
layer of gold, and each of these had two silver bases *c*
set to support it and a golden capital fixed on the top.
For the length of the building, the craftsman put 78
forty pillars, half of them—that is a row of twenty—
on each side, with no interval left between them, but
each joined and fitted on to the next, so as to present
the appearance of a single wall.   For the breadth he
set right inside the remaining eight, six in the central
space and two in the corners on either side of the
centre, one on the right and one on the left ; also four
others at the entrance, like the rest in everything else,
except that they had one base instead of the two of
the pillars opposite, and after these, at the very outside, five, differing only in their bases, which were of
brass.   Thus the whole number of pillars visible in 79
the tabernacle, leaving out the two in the corners,

c Or "sockets."

487

γωνίαις δυοῖν ἀφανῶν, πέντε καὶ πεντήκοντα
ἐμφανεῖς, τὸν ἀπὸ μονάδος ἄχρι δεκάδος τῆς
80 παντελείας συμπληρούμενον ἀριθμόν. εἰ δὲ βουληθείη τις τοὺς ἐν τῷ προπυλαίῳ πέντε τῷ ὑπαίθρῳ
συνάπτοντας, ὃ κέκληκεν αὐλήν, τιθέναι χωρίς,
ἀπολειφθήσεται ὁ ἁγιώτατος πεντηκοντάδος ἀριθμός, δύναμις ὢν τοῦ ὀρθογωνίου τριγώνου, ὅπερ
ἐστὶ τῆς τῶν ὅλων γενέσεως ἀρχή, συμπληρωθεὶς
ἐκ τῶν ἐντὸς κιόνων, τεσσαράκοντα μὲν τῶν καθ'
ἑκατέραν πλευρὰν εἴκοσιν, ἓξ δὲ τῶν ἐν μέσῳ δίχα
τῶν παρὰ ταῖς γωνίαις ἀποκεκρυμμένων, τεσσάρων
81 δὲ τῶν ἀντικρύ, ἐφ' ὧν τὸ καταπέτασμα. τὴν δ'
αἰτίαν, ἧς ἕνεκα[1] τοὺς πέντε τοῖς πεντήκοντα συγ-
κατατάττω καὶ χωρὶς αὐτῶν τίθημι, δηλώσω. ἡ
πεντὰς αἰσθήσεων ἀριθμός ἐστιν, αἴσθησις δ' ἐν
ἀνθρώπῳ τῇ μὲν νεύει πρὸς τὰ ἐκτός, τῇ δὲ ἀνακάμπτει πρὸς νοῦν ὑπηρέτις οὖσα φύσεως νόμοις
82 αὐτοῦ. διὸ καὶ τὴν μεθόριον χώραν ἀπένειμε τοῖς
πέντε· τὰ μὲν γὰρ ἐντὸς αὐτῶν ἐκνένευκε πρὸς τὰ
ἄδυτα τῆς σκηνῆς, ἅπερ ἐστὶ συμβολικῶς νοητά,
τὰ δ' ἐκτὸς πρὸς τὸ ὕπαιθρον καὶ τὴν αὐλήν, ἅπερ
ἐστὶν αἰσθητά· παρὸ καὶ ταῖς βάσεσι διήνεγκαν,
χαλκαῖ γάρ εἰσιν· ἐπεὶ δὲ τῆς ἐν ἡμῖν αἰσθήσεως
κεφαλὴ μὲν καὶ ἡγεμονικὸν ὁ νοῦς, ἐσχατιὰ δὲ καὶ
ὡσανεὶ βάσις τὸ αἰσθητόν, εἴκασε δὴ τὸν μὲν νοῦν
83 χρυσῷ, χαλκῷ δὲ τὸ αἰσθητόν. μέτρα δὲ τῶν
κιόνων ταῦτα· δέκα μὲν πήχεις τὸ μῆκος, εἰς δὲ

---

[1] Perhaps καί has fallen out after ἕνεκα.

[a] See App. pp. 607-608, and for παντελεια note on *De Abr.* 244.

[b] *i.e.* $50 = 3^2 + 4^2 + 5^2$, and 3, 4, 5 are the sides of the primary form of the right-angled triangle, which in *De Op.* 97

hidden from view, amounted to fifty-five, that is to the sum of successive numbers from one to the supremely perfect ten.[a] But if you choose to exclude 80 the five in the propylaeum adjoining the open-air space which he has called the court, there will be left the most sacred number, fifty, the square of the sides of the right-angled triangle, the original source from which the universe springs.[b] This fifty is obtained by adding together the inside pillars, namely the forty made up by the twenties on each side, then the six in the middle, leaving out the two hidden away in the corners, and then the four opposite which support the veil. I will now give my reason for first 81 counting the five with the fifty and then separately. Five is the number of the senses, and sense in mankind inclines on one side to things external, while on the other its trend is towards mind, whose handmaiden it is by the laws of nature. And therefore he assigned the position on the border to the five pillars, for what lies inside them verges on the inmost sanctuary of the tabernacle, which symbolically represents the realm of mind, while what lies outside them verges on the open-air space and court which represent the realm of sense. And therefore the five differ from the rest 82 also in their bases which are of brass. Since the mind is head and ruler of the sense-faculty in us, and the world which sense apprehends is the extremity and, as it were, the base of mind, he symbolized the mind by the gold and the sense-objects by the brass. The 83 dimensions of the pillars were as follows : the height,

is said to be the σχημάτων καὶ ποιοτήτων ἀρχή. The virtues of fifty are described more fully in *De Spec. Leg.* ii. 176, when it is said to be στοιχειωδέστατον καὶ πρεσβύτατον τῶν ἐν οὐσίαις περιλαμβανομένων.

καὶ ἥμισυς τὸ εὖρος, ἵν' ἡ σκηνὴ πᾶσι τοῖς μέρεσιν
ἴση προφαίνηται.

XVII. | Παγκάλοις δὲ καὶ ποικίλοις ὑφάσμασιν
αὐτὴν περιέβαλεν, ὑακίνθῳ καὶ πορφύρᾳ καὶ κοκκίνῳ καὶ βύσσῳ καταχρώμενος εἰς τὴν ὑφήν. δέκα
γὰρ ἃς διὰ τῆς ἱερᾶς γραφῆς ὠνόμασεν αὐλαίας ἐκ
τῶν ἀρτίως λεχθέντων γενῶν ἐδημιούργει, μήκει
μὲν ὀκτὼ καὶ εἴκοσι πηχῶν ἑκάστην, εἰς δὲ τέσσαρας πήχεις πρὸς εὖρος ἀποτείνων, ἵνα καὶ δεκάδα
ἔχωσι τὴν παντέλειαν καὶ τετράδα τὴν δεκάδος
οὐσίαν καὶ τὸν ὀκτὼ καὶ εἴκοσι ἀριθμὸν τέλειον
ἴσον τοῖς ἑαυτοῦ μέρεσι καὶ τεσσαρακοντάδα τὴν
ζῳογονικωτάτην, ἐν ᾗ διαπλάττεσθαί φασιν ἄν-
85 θρωπον ἐν τῷ τῆς φύσεως ἐργαστηρίῳ. οἱ μὲν οὖν
ὀκτὼ καὶ εἴκοσι πήχεις τῶν αὐλαίων τοιαύτην
ἔχουσι τὴν διανομήν· δέκα μὲν κατὰ τὸν ὄροφον—
τοσοῦτον γάρ ἐστι τῆς σκηνῆς τὸ εὖρος—, οἱ δὲ
λοιποὶ κατὰ τὰς πλευράς, ἑκατέρωθεν ἐννέα, πρὸς
σκέπην ἀποτείνονται τῶν κιόνων, ὑπολειπομένου
πήχεως ἀπὸ τοῦ ἐδάφους, ἵνα μὴ ἐπισύρηται ⟨τὸ⟩
86 πάγκαλον καὶ ἱεροπρεπὲς ὕφασμα. τῶν δὲ τεσσαράκοντα, οἳ συναριθμοῦνται ἐκ τοῦ τῶν δέκα
αὐλαίων πλάτους, τριάκοντα μὲν ἀπολαμβάνει τὸ
μῆκος—τοσοῦτον γάρ ἐστι καὶ ⟨τὸ⟩ τῆς σκηνῆς[1]—,
ἐννέα δὲ ὁ ὀπισθόδομος, τὸν δὲ λοιπὸν τὸ κατὰ τὸ
προπύλαιον, ἵνα δεσμὸς ᾖ τοῦ ὅλου περιβλήματος·
87 ἐπὶ δὲ τοῦ προπυλαίου τὸ καταπέτασμα. σχεδὸν
δὲ καὶ αἱ αὐλαῖαι καταπετάσματ' εἰσίν, οὐ μόνον
τῷ τὸν ὄροφον καὶ τοὺς τοίχους καλύπτειν, ἀλλὰ
καὶ τῷ συνυφάνθαι γένεσι τοῖς αὐτοῖς, ὑακίνθῳ καὶ

---

[1] Or perhaps read τὸ μῆκος—τοσοῦτον γάρ ἐστι—τῆς σκηνῆς,
i.e. instead of adding τὸ as Cohn and Mangey, omit καὶ.

ten cubits, the breadth, one-and-a-half, so that the tabernacle might appear equal in all its parts.

XVII. [a] He also surrounded it with the most beauti- **84** ful pieces of woven work of various colours, using without stint materials of dark red and purple and scarlet and bright white, for the weaving. For he made ten curtains, as he calls them in the sacred writings, of the four kinds of material just mentioned, twenty-eight cubits in length and extended to four cubits in breadth. Thus we find in them ten, the supremely perfect number, four which contains the essence of ten, twenty-eight, a perfect number, equal to the sum of its factors,[b] and forty, the most prolific of life, which gives the time in which, as we are told, the man is fully formed in the laboratory of nature.[c] The twenty-eight cubits of the curtains were dis- **85** tributed as follows : ten along the roof, that being the breadth of the tabernacle, the rest extended along the sides, nine on each to cover the pillars, but leaving one cubit free from the floor, that this work so magnificent and worthily held sacred should not trail in the dust. Of the forty cubits which sum up the breadth **86** of the ten curtains, thirty are taken up by the length of the tabernacle itself, that being its extent, nine by the backyard, and the remaining one by the space at the propylaeum, thus forming a bond to make the enclosing complete.[d] On the propylaeum was set the veil. But in a sense the curtains also are veils, not **87** only because they cover the roof and the walls, but also because they are woven with the same kinds of

---

[a] For §§ 84-88 see Ex. xxvi. 1-14.

[b] *i.e.* $1+2+4+7+14=28$. See note on *De Op.* 101.

[c] *i.e.* forty weeks, or about ten months is supposed to be the period of gestation. *Cf. e.g.* Virg. *Ecl.* 4. 61.

[d] Lit. " to be a bond of all that was put round."

PHILO

πορφύρᾳ καὶ κοκκίνῳ καὶ βύσσῳ. ἐκ δὲ τῶν αὐτῶν
τό τε καταπέτασμα καὶ τὸ λεγόμενον κάλυμμα
κατεσκευάζετο, τὸ μὲν εἴσω κατὰ τοὺς τέσσαρας
κίονας, ἵν᾽ ἐπικρύπτηται τὸ ἄδυτον, τὸ δ᾽ ἔξω κατὰ
τοὺς πέντε, ὡς μηδεὶς ἐξ ἀπόπτου δύναιτο τῶν μὴ
88 ἱερωμένων καταθεάσασθαι τὰ ἅγια. XVIII. τὰς
δὲ τῶν ὑφασμάτων ὕλας ἀριστίνδην ἐπέκρινεν ἐκ
μυρίων ὅσων ἑλόμενος τοῖς στοιχείοις ἰσαρίθμους,
ἐξ ὧν ἀπετελέσθη ὁ κόσμος, καὶ πρὸς αὐτὰ λόγον
ἐχούσας, γῆν καὶ ὕδωρ καὶ ἀέρα καὶ πῦρ· ἡ μὲν
γὰρ βύσσος ἐκ γῆς, ἐξ ὕδατος δ᾽ ἡ πορφύρα, ἡ δ᾽
ὑάκινθος ἀέρι ὁμοιοῦται—φύσει γὰρ μέλας οὗτος—,
τὸ δὲ κόκκινον πυρί, διότι φοινικοῦν ἑκάτερον· ἦν
γὰρ ἀναγκαῖον ἱερὸν χειροποίητον κατασκευάζοντας
τῷ πατρὶ καὶ ἡγεμόνι τοῦ παντὸς τὰς ὁμοίας |
[149] λαβεῖν οὐσίας, αἷς τὸ ὅλον ἐδημιούργει.
89 Ἡ μὲν οὖν σκηνή, καθάπερ νεὼς ἅγιος, τὸν
εἰρημένον τρόπον κατεσκευάσθη. τέμενος δ᾽ αὐτῆς
ἐν κύκλῳ περιεβάλετο πηχῶν μῆκος ἑκατὸν καὶ
πλάτος πεντήκοντα, κίονας ἔχον ἀφεστῶτας ἴσον
ἀλλήλων διάστημα πέντε πήχεις, ὡς τοὺς μὲν
σύμπαντας ἑξήκοντα εἶναι, διανέμεσθαι δ᾽ εἰς μὲν
τὸ μῆκος τεσσαράκοντα, πρὸς δὲ τὸ εὖρος εἴκοσι,
90 καθ᾽ ἑκάτερα μέρη τοὺς ἡμίσεις. ὕλη δὲ τῶν
στύλων τὰ μὲν ἐντὸς κέδρος, τὰ δ᾽ ἐκ τῆς ἐπι-
φανείας ἄργυρος, ἁπάντων δ᾽ αἱ βάσεις χαλκαῖ, καὶ
τὸ ὕψος ἴσον πέντε πηχῶν· ἔδοξε γὰρ ἁρμόττον
εἶναι τῷ τεχνίτῃ συνελεῖν ὅλῳ ἡμίσει τὸ ὕψος τῆς

ᵃ Philo seems to have made a slip here. The screen for the
door of the tent (Ex. xxvi. 36) is in the LXX ἐπίσπαστρον,
while κάλυμμα is the name given (Ex. xxvii. 16) to the

material, dark red and purple and scarlet and bright white. And what he calls the " covering "[a] was also made with the same materials as the veil, that being placed inside along the four pillars to hide the inmost sanctuary, the " covering " outside along the five pillars, so that no unconsecrated person should get even a distant view of the holy precincts. XVIII. But, in choosing the materials for the woven work, 88 he selected as the best out of a vast number possible four, as equal in number to the elements—earth, water, air, fire—out of which the world was made, and with a definite relation to those elements ; the byssus, or bright white, coming from the earth, purple from the water, while dark red is like the air, which is naturally black, and scarlet like fire, since both are bright red. For it was necessary that in framing a temple of man's making, dedicated to the Father and Ruler of All, he should take substances like those with which that Ruler made the All.

[b] The tabernacle, then, was constructed to resemble 89 a sacred temple in the way described. Its precincts contained an area of a hundred cubits long by fifty broad, with pillars at equal intervals of five cubits from each other, so that the total number was sixty, with forty arranged on the long sides and twenty on the broad sides, in both cases half to each side. The 90 material of the columns was of cedar wood overlaid by silver. The bases in all cases were of brass, and the height was five cubits. For the master craftsman thought it proper to cut down the height of what he calls the court by a complete half, in order that the

screen at the gate of the court represented in Philo by the ὕφασμα of § 93.
[b] For §§ 89–93 see Ex. xxvii. 9–18.

PHILO

λεγομένης αὐλῆς, ἵν' ἡ σκηνὴ πρὸς τὸ διπλάσιον
μετέωρος ἀρθεῖσα προφαίνηται. λεπταὶ δ' ὀθόναι
κατὰ τοῦ μήκους καὶ πλάτους ἦσαν ἐφαρμοζόμεναι
τοῖς κίοσιν ἱστίοις ἐμφερεῖς, ὑπὲρ τοῦ μηδένα τῶν
91 μὴ καθαρῶν εἰσιέναι. XIX. ἡ δὲ θέσις τοιάδε ἦν·
μέση μὲν ἵδρυτο ἡ σκηνὴ μῆκος ἔχουσα τριάκοντα
πήχεις καὶ εὖρος δέκα σὺν τῷ βάθει τῶν κιόνων,
ἀφειστήκει δὲ τῆς αὐλῆς ἐκ τριῶν μερῶν ἴσῳ
διαστήματι, δυοῖν μὲν κατὰ τὰς πλευράς, ἑνὸς δὲ
κατὰ τὸν ὀπισθόδομον, τὸ δὲ διάστημα ἐξ εἴκοσι
πηχῶν ἀνεμετρεῖτο· κατὰ δὲ τὸ προπύλαιον, ὡς
εἰκός, ἕνεκα τοῦ πλήθους τῶν εἰσιόντων μεῖζον
ἐγίνετο διάστημα πεντήκοντα πηχῶν· οὕτως γὰρ
οἱ ἑκατὸν τῆς αὐλῆς ἔμελλον ἐκπληροῦσθαι, τῶν
κατὰ τὸν ὀπισθόδομον εἴκοσι καὶ οὓς ἀπελάμβανεν
ἡ σκηνὴ τριάκοντα συντεθέντων τοῖς κατὰ τὰς
92 εἰσόδους πεντήκοντα. τὰ γὰρ προπύλαια τῆς
σκηνῆς ὡσανεὶ μέσος ὅρος ἵδρυτο διττῆς πεντηκοντάδος, τῆς μὲν κατ' ἀνατολάς, ἔνθα αἱ εἴσοδοι,
τῆς δὲ πρὸς δυσμάς, ἔνθα τό τε μῆκος τῆς σκηνῆς
93 καὶ ὁ κατόπιν περίβολος. κάλλιστον δὲ καὶ μέγιστον ἄλλο προπύλαιον ἐν ἀρχῇ τῆς εἰς τὴν αὐλὴν
εἰσόδου κατεσκευάζετο διὰ τεττάρων κιόνων, καθ'
ὧν ἐτείνετο ποικίλον ὕφασμα τὸν αὐτὸν τρόπον τοῖς
εἴσω κατὰ τὴν σκηνὴν κἀκ τῆς ὁμοίας ὕλης
ἀπειργασμένον.
94 Ἅμα δὲ τούτοις ἐδημιουργεῖτο καὶ σκεύη ἱερά,
κιβωτός, λυχνία, τράπεζα, θυμιατήριον, βωμός.
ὁ μὲν οὖν βωμὸς ἱδρύετο ἐν ὑπαίθρῳ, τῶν εἰσόδων
τῆς σκηνῆς ἀντικρύ, ἀφεστὼς τοσοῦτον ὅσον ἱκανὸν

ᵃ Or "the frontage," the plural, which here as in § 136 is

tabernacle should be conspicuous by rising up to double the height. Five linen sheets like sails were attached to the pillars, both on the length and the breadth, so that no impure person could enter the place. XIX. The plan was as follows. The taber- 91 nacle itself was set in the midst, thirty cubits long and ten broad, including the thickness of the pillars. From three aspects, namely the two long sides and the space at the back, it was the same distance from the boundary of the court, reckoned at twenty cubits. But at the propylaeum there was naturally a greater interval of fifty cubits, on account of the number of people entering. This increase was required to make up the hundred cubits of the court ; the twenty of the back-space and the thirty taken up by the tabernacle being added to the fifty at the entrances. For 92 the propylaeum [a] of the tabernacle was set as the border-line between the two fifties, namely the fifty on the eastern half, where the entrance is, and the fifty on the western half, consisting of the tabernacle and the area behind it. At the beginning of the 93 entrance to the court was built another very fine and large propylaeum with four pillars, on which was stretched a piece of woven work of various colours, made in the same way as those within the tabernacle and of like materials.

With these were also made the sacred vessels and 94 furniture, the ark, candlestick, table and altars for incense and burnt offerings. The altar for burnt offerings was placed in the open air, opposite the entrance of the tabernacle,[b] at a distance sufficient to

applied to what is clearly a single " propylaeum," indicating that the line in which the portico stands is included.

[b] See Ex. xl. 6, 29.

λειτουργοῖς εἶναι διάστημα πρὸς τὰς καθ᾽ ἑκάστην
95 ἡμέραν ἐπιτελουμένας θυσίας. XX. ἡ δὲ κιβωτὸς
ἐν ἀδύτῳ καὶ ἀβάτῳ τῶν καταπετασμάτων εἴσω,
[150] κεχρυσωμένη πολυτελῶς ἔνδοθέν | τε καὶ ἔξωθεν,
ἧς ἐπίθεμα ὡσανεὶ πῶμα τὸ λεγόμενον ἐν ἱεραῖς
96 βίβλοις ἱλαστήριον. τούτου μῆκος μὲν καὶ πλάτος
μεμήνυται, βάθος δ᾽ οὐδέν, ἐπιφανείᾳ γεωμετρικῇ
μάλισθ᾽ ὡμοιωμένου, ὅπερ ἔοικεν εἶναι σύμβολον
φυσικώτερον μὲν τῆς ἵλεω τοῦ θεοῦ δυνάμεως,
ἠθικώτερον δὲ διανοίας πάλιν, ἵλεω δ᾽ ἑαυτῇ, τὴν
πρὸς ὕψος ἄλογον αἴρουσαν καὶ φυσῶσαν οἴησιν
ἀτυφίας ἔρωτι σὺν ἐπιστήμῃ στέλλειν καὶ καθαιρεῖν
97 ἀξιούσης. ἀλλ᾽ ἡ μὲν κιβωτὸς ἀγγεῖον νόμων
ἐστίν· εἰς γὰρ ταύτην κατατίθεται τὰ χρησθέντα
λόγια· τὸ δ᾽ ἐπίθεμα τὸ προσαγορευόμενον ἱλαστήριον βάσις ἐστὶ πτηνῶν δυοῖν, ἃ πατρίῳ μὲν γλώττῃ
προσαγορεύεται Χερουβίμ, ὡς δ᾽ ἂν Ἕλληνες
98 εἴποιεν, ἐπίγνωσις καὶ ἐπιστήμη πολλή. ταῦτα δέ
τινες μέν φασιν εἶναι σύμβολα τῶν ἡμισφαιρίων
ἀμφοῖν κατὰ τὴν ἀντιπρόσωπον θέσιν, τοῦ τε ὑπὸ
γῆν καὶ ὑπὲρ γῆν· πτηνὸν γὰρ ὁ σύμπας οὐρανός.
99 ἐγὼ δ᾽ ἂν εἴποιμι δηλοῦσθαι δι᾽ ὑπονοιῶν τὰς
πρεσβυτάτας καὶ ἀνωτάτω δύο τοῦ ὄντος δυνάμεις,
τήν τε ποιητικὴν καὶ βασιλικήν· ὀνομάζεται δ᾽ ἡ
μὲν ποιητικὴ δύναμις αὐτοῦ θεός, καθ᾽ ἣν ἔθηκε

ᵃ For §§ 95-97 see Ex. xxv. 10-22.
ᵇ Or place of grace.
ᶜ See note on *De Abr.* 99.
ᵈ Or "full knowledge and much science." These words
are not interpretations of the symbolical meaning of the two
cherubim, but the supposed meaning of the Hebrew word,
of which Philo gives two almost synonymous (and presumably
alternative) renderings. The statement is reproduced by

give the ministrants room for the daily performance of the sacrifices. XX. ^a The ark was placed on the 95 forbidden ground of the inner sanctuary, within the veils. It was coated with costly gilding within and without, and was covered by a sort of lid, which is called in the sacred books the mercy-seat.^b The 96 length and breadth of this are stated, but no depth, and thus it closely resembles the plane surface of geometry. It appears to be a symbol in a theological sense ^c of the gracious power of God; in the human sense, of a mind which is gracious to itself and feels the duty of repressing and destroying with the aid of knowledge the conceit which in its love of vanity uplifts it in unreasoning exaltation and puffs it with pride. The ark itself is the coffer of the laws, for in 97 it are deposited the oracles which have been delivered. But the cover, which is called the mercy-seat, serves to support the two winged creatures which in the Hebrew are called cherubim, but, as we should term them, recognition and full knowledge.^d Some hold 98 that, since they are set facing each other, they are symbols of the two hemispheres, one above the earth and one under it, for the whole heaven has wings. I 99 should myself say that they are allegorical representations of the two most august and highest potencies of Him that is, the creative and the kingly. His creative potency is called God, because through it He placed ^e

Clem. as ἐπίγνωσις πολλή, by Jerome as " multitudo scientiae," to which add Augustine's " plenitudo scientiae." All these are presumably dependent on Philo and no explanation of how he got this belief seems to be forthcoming.

The symbolical interpretations mentioned below have been given in *De Cher.* 21 ff, together with a third, that they represent the spheres of the planets and fixed stars. See notes *ad loc.*

^e θεός again associated with τίθημι, cf. *De Abr.* 122.

καὶ ἐποίησε καὶ διεκόσμησε τόδε τὸ πᾶν, ἡ δὲ
βασιλικὴ κύριος, ᾗ τῶν γενομένων ἄρχει καὶ σὺν
100 δίκῃ βεβαίως ἐπικρατεῖ. μόνος γὰρ πρὸς ἀλήθειαν
ὢν καὶ ποιητής ἐστιν ἀψευδῶς, ἐπειδὴ τὰ μὴ ὄντα
ἤγαγεν εἰς τὸ εἶναι, καὶ βασιλεὺς φύσει, διότι τῶν
γεγονότων οὐδεὶς ἂν ἄρχοι δικαιότερον τοῦ πεποιηκότος.

101   XXI. Ἐν δὲ τῷ μεθορίῳ τῶν τεσσάρων καὶ
πέντε κιόνων, ὅπερ ἐστὶ κυρίως εἰπεῖν πρόναον
εἰργόμενον δυσὶν ὑφάσμασι, τῷ μὲν ἔνδον ὃ καλεῖται
καταπέτασμα, τῷ δ' ἐκτὸς ὃ προσαγορεύεται
κάλυμμα, τὰ λοιπὰ τρία σκεύη τῶν προειρημένων
ἱδρύετο· μέσον μὲν τὸ θυμιατήριον, γῆς καὶ ὕδατος
σύμβολον εὐχαριστίας, ἣν ἕνεκα τῶν γινομένων ἀφ'
ἑκατέρου προσῆκε ποιεῖσθαι· τὸν γὰρ μέσον ταῦτα
102 τοῦ κόσμου τόπον κεκλήρωται· τὴν δὲ λυχνίαν ἐν
τοῖς νοτίοις, δι' ἧς αἰνίττεται τὰς τῶν φωσφόρων
κινήσεις ἀστέρων· ἥλιος γὰρ καὶ σελήνη καὶ οἱ
ἄλλοι πολὺ τῶν βορείων ἀφεστῶτες νοτίους ποιοῦνται τὰς περιπολήσεις· ὅθεν ἐξ μὲν κλάδοι, τρεῖς δ'
ἑκατέρωθεν, τῆς μέσης λυχνίας ἐκπεφύκασιν εἰς
103 ἀριθμὸν ἕβδομον· ἐπὶ δὲ πάντων λαμπάδιά τε καὶ
λύχνοι ἑπτά, σύμβολα τῶν λεγομένων παρὰ τοῖς
[151] φυσικοῖς ἀνδράσι πλανήτων· ὁ γὰρ ἥλιος, | ὥσπερ
ἡ λυχνία, μέσος τῶν ἐξ τεταγμένος ἐν τετάρτῃ
χώρᾳ φωσφορεῖ τοῖς ὑπεράνω τρισὶ καὶ τοῖς ὑπ'
αὐτὸν ἴσοις, ἁρμοζόμενος τὸ μουσικὸν καὶ θεῖον
104 ὡς ἀληθῶς ὄργανον. XXII. ἡ δὲ τράπεζα τίθεται
πρὸς τοῖς βορείοις, ἐφ' ἧς ἄρτοι καὶ ἅλες, ἐπειδὴ

and made and ordered this universe, and the kingly is called Lord, being that with which He governs what has come into being and rules it steadfastly with justice. For, as He alone really is, He is undoubtedly 100 also the Maker, since He brought into being what was not, and He is in the nature of things King, since none could more justly govern what has been made than the Maker.

XXI. In the space between the four and the five 101 pillars, which may properly be called the vestibule of the temple, and is shut off by two woven screens, the inner and the outer, called respectively the veil and the covering, he set the remaining three of the equipments mentioned above. [a] The altar of incense he placed in the middle, a symbol of the thankfulness for earth and water which should be rendered for the benefits derived from both these, since the mid-position in the universe has been assigned to them. [b] The candlestick he placed at the south, figuring 102 thereby the movements of the luminaries above; for the sun and the moon and the others run their courses in the south far away from the north. And therefore six branches, three on each side, issue from the central candlestick, bringing up the number to seven, and on all these are set seven lamps and candle- 103 bearers, symbols of what the men of science call planets. For the sun, like the candlestick, has the fourth place in the middle of the six and gives light to the three above and the three below it, so tuning to harmony an instrument of music truly divine. XXII. [c] The table is set at the north and has bread 104

---

[a] See Ex. xxx. 1 f.
[b] See Ex. xxv. 31 ff. *Cf. Quis Rerum*, 221-225.
[c] See Ex. xxv. 23 ff.

τῶν πνευμάτων τὰ βόρεια τροφιμώτατα καὶ διότι
ἐξ οὐρανοῦ καὶ γῆς αἱ τροφαί, τοῦ μὲν ὕοντος, τῆς
δὲ τὰ σπέρματα ταῖς τῶν ὑδάτων ἐπιρροίαις τελειο-
105 γονούσης. οὐρανοῦ δὲ[1] καὶ γῆς παρίδρυται τὰ
σύμβολα, καθάπερ ἔδειξεν ὁ λόγος, τοῦ μὲν οὐρανοῦ
ἡ λυχνία, τῶν δὲ περιγείων, ἐξ ὧν αἱ ἀναθυμιάσεις,
106 τὸ ἐτύμως προσαγορευόμενον θυμιατήριον. τὸν δ᾽
ἐν ὑπαίθρῳ βωμὸν εἴωθε καλεῖν θυσιαστήριον,
ὡσανεὶ τηρητικὸν καὶ φυλακτικὸν ὄντα θυσιῶν τὸν
ἀναλωτικὸν τούτων, αἰνιττόμενος οὐ τὰ μέλη καὶ
τὰ μέρη τῶν ἱερουργουμένων, ἅπερ δαπανᾶσθαι
πυρὶ πέφυκεν, ἀλλὰ τὴν προαίρεσιν τοῦ προσ-
107 φέροντος· εἰ μὲν γὰρ ἀγνώμων καὶ ἄδικος, ἄθυτοι
θυσίαι καὶ ἀνίεροι ἱερουργίαι καὶ εὐχαὶ παλίμφημοι
παντελῆ φθορὰν ἐνδεχόμεναι· καὶ γὰρ ὁπότε γίνεσθαι δοκοῦσιν, οὐ λύσιν ἁμαρτημάτων, ἀλλ᾽ ὑπό-
108 μνησιν ἐργάζονται· εἰ δ᾽ ὅσιος καὶ δίκαιος, μένει
βέβαιος ἡ θυσία, κἂν τὰ κρέα δαπανηθῇ, μᾶλλον
δὲ καὶ εἰ τὸ παράπαν μηδὲν προσάγοιτο ἱερεῖον·
ἡ γὰρ ἀληθὴς ἱερουργία τίς ἂν εἴη πλὴν ψυχῆς
θεοφιλοῦς εὐσέβεια; ἧς τὸ εὐχάριστον ἀθανατί-
ζεται καὶ ἀνάγραπτον στηλιτεύεται παρὰ θεῷ
συνδιαιωνίζον ἡλίῳ καὶ σελήνῃ καὶ τῷ παντὶ
κόσμῳ.

[1] Perhaps, as the German translator, omit δὲ, put a full
stop after τροφιμώτατα, and a comma after τελειογονούσης.
See note b.

[a] So LXX Lev. xxiv. 7—not in Hebrew.
[b] The punctuation and reading suggested in note 1 certainly
make the connexion of thought clearer. If the text is kept,
I take the meaning to be that the table with the food upon it
represents heaven and earth which send the food, and
therefore it is fitting that the other two symbols of heaven
and earth should be set beside it.

and salt[a] on it, as the north winds are those which most provide us with food, and food comes from heaven and earth, the one sending rain, the other bringing the seeds to their fullness when watered by the showers.[b] In a line with the table are set 105 the symbols of heaven and earth, as our account has shewn, heaven being signified by the candlestick, earth and its parts, from which rise the vapours, by what is appropriately called the vapour-keeper[c] or altar of incense. The great altar in the open court 106 he usually calls by a name which means sacrifice-keeper, and when he thus speaks of the altar which destroys sacrifices as their keeper and guardian he alludes not to the parts and limbs of the victims, whose nature is to be consumed by fire, but to the intention of the offerer. For, if the worshipper is 107 without kindly feeling or justice, the sacrifices are no sacrifices, the consecrated oblation is desecrated, the prayers are words of ill omen with utter destruction waiting upon them. For, when to outward appearance they are offered, it is not a remission but a reminder of past sins which they effect. But, if 108 he is pure of heart and just, the sacrifice stands firm, though the flesh is consumed, or rather, even if no victim at all is brought to the altar. For the true oblation, what else can it be but the devotion of a soul which is dear to God? The thank-offering of such a soul receives immortality, and is inscribed in the records of God, sharing the eternal life of the sun and moon and the whole universe.

---

[c] Philo does not expressly derive the -τηριον of θυμιατήριον from τηρεῖν. But as ἐτύμως implies etymological derivation, and in the next words he gives this derivation for θυσιαστήριον, it seems probable that he means it to apply to both words.

PHILO

109 XXIII. Τούτοις ἐξῆς ἱερὰν ἐσθῆτα κατεσκεύαζεν
ὁ τεχνίτης τῷ μέλλοντι ἀρχιερεῖ καθίστασθαι
παγκάλην καὶ θαυμασιωτάτην ἔχουσαν ἐν τοῖς
ὑφάσμασι πλοκήν. τὰ δ' ὕφη διττὰ ἦν, τὸ μὲν
110 ὑποδύτης, τὸ δὲ προσαγορευόμενον ἐπωμίς. ὁ μὲν
οὖν ὑποδύτης ἀμιγεστέρας ἰδέας· ὅλος γὰρ ὑακίνθινος, ἔξω τῶν κατωτάτω καὶ πρὸς ἐσχατιὰς
μερῶν, ταῦτα γὰρ ἐποικίλλετο χρυσοῖς ῥοΐσκοις καὶ
111 κώδωσι καὶ ἀνθίνοις πλέγμασιν. ἡ δ' ἐπωμίς,
ἐκπρεπέστατον ἔργον καὶ τεχνικώτατον, ἐπιστήμῃ
τελειοτάτῃ κατεσκευάζετο τοῖς προειρημένοις γένεσιν, ὑακίνθῳ καὶ πορφύρᾳ καὶ βύσσῳ καὶ κοκκίνῳ,
συγκαταπλεκομένου χρυσοῦ· πέταλα γὰρ εἰς λεπτὰς
τρίχας κατατμηθέντα πᾶσι τοῖς νήμασι συν-
112 υφαίνετο. λίθοι δ' ἐπὶ τῶν ἀκρωμίων ἐνηρμόζοντο
[152] σμαράγδου πολυτελοῦς δύο τιμαλφέσταται, | οἷς
τὰ ὀνόματα τῶν φυλάρχων ἐξ καθ' ἑκάτερον ἐν-
εχαράττετο, δώδεκα τὰ σύμπαντα· καὶ κατὰ τὸ
στῆθος ἄλλοι λίθοι πολυτελεῖς δώδεκα διαφέροντες
ταῖς χρόαις, σφραγῖσιν ἐοικότες, ἐκ τριῶν τετρα-
στοιχεί· οὗτοι δ' ἐνηρμόζοντο τῷ προσαγορευομένῳ
113 λογείῳ. τὸ δὲ λογεῖον τετράγωνον διπλοῦν κατεσκευάζετο ὡσανεὶ βάσις, ἵνα δύο ἀρετὰς ἀγαλ-
ματοφορῇ, δήλωσίν τε καὶ ἀλήθειαν· ὅλον δ'
ἀλυσειδίοις χρυσοῖς ἀνήρτητο πρὸς τὴν ἐπωμίδα,
σφιγγόμενον ἐξ αὐτῆς, ὑπὲρ τοῦ μὴ χαλᾶσθαι.
114 χρυσοῦν δὲ πέταλον ὡσανεὶ στέφανος ἐδημιουργεῖτο

ᵃ For §§ 109-116 see Ex. xxviii.
ᵇ Lit. "shoulder-covering." I have retained the familiar
and neutral word "ephod," by some supposed to be a kind
of waistcoat, by others an apron. See note in Driver's
Exodus, p. 312, or article in *Biblical Encyclopaedia*.
502

XXIII. *a* Next after these, the master prepared for 109
the future high priest a vesture, the fabric of which
had a texture of great and marvellous beauty. It
consisted of two garments, one of which he calls
the robe and the other the ephod.*b* The robe was 110
of a comparatively uniform make, for it was all of
the dark red colour, except at the lowest extremities,
where it was variegated with golden pomegranates
and bells and intertwined flowers. The ephod, a 111
work of special magnificence and artistry, was
wrought with perfect knowledge in the kinds of
materials mentioned above, namely dark red and
purple and bright white and scarlet, with gold thread
intertwined. For gold leaf cut into fine threads was
woven with all the yarn. On the shoulder-tops 112
were fitted two highly precious stones of the costly
emerald kind, and on them were graven the names of
the patriarchs, six for each shoulder, twelve in all.
On the breast were twelve other costly stones of
different colours, like seals, in four rows of three each.
These were fitted into what he calls the " place of
reason." *c* This was made four-square and doubled, 113
forming a ground to enshrine the two virtues, clear
showing and truth.*d* The whole was attached by
golden chainlets to the ephod, fastened strongly to
it so as not to come loose. A piece of gold plate, 114
too, was wrought into the form of a crown with four

c Or "oracle" (lxx λογεῖον τῶν κρίσεων, Ex. xxviii. 15).
But Philo clearly uses the word in the sense given in the
translation (see §§ 125 and 128), and the same meaning is
given to it *De Spec. Leg.* i. 87. The E.V. has " breastplate
of judgement" though the word translated "breastplate" is
said to be rather="pouch."

d The lxx translation of the mysterious words rendered
in E.V. as Urim and Thummim. *Cf. Leg. All.* iii. 142.

τέτταρας ἔχον γλυφὰς ὀνόματος, ὃ μόνοις τοῖς ὦτα
καὶ γλῶτταν σοφίᾳ κεκαθαρμένοις θέμις ἀκούειν
καὶ λέγειν ἐν ἁγίοις, ἄλλῳ δ᾽ οὐδενὶ τὸ παράπαν
115 οὐδαμοῦ. τετραγράμματον δὲ τοὔνομά φησιν ὁ
θεολόγος εἶναι, τάχα που σύμβολα τιθεὶς αὐτὰ τῶν
πρώτων ἀριθμῶν, μονάδος καὶ δυάδος καὶ τριάδος
καὶ τετράδος, ἐπειδὴ πάντα ἐν τετράδι, σημεῖον καὶ
γραμμὴ καὶ ἐπιφάνεια καὶ στερεόν, τὰ μέτρα τῶν
συμπάντων, καὶ αἱ κατὰ μουσικὴν ἄρισται συμ-
φωνίαι, ἥ τε διὰ τεσσάρων ἐν ἐπιτρίτῳ λόγῳ καὶ ἡ
διὰ πέντε ἐν ἡμιολίῳ καὶ ἡ διὰ πασῶν ἐν διπλασίῳ
καὶ ἡ δὶς διὰ πασῶν ἐν τετραπλασίῳ· ἔχει δὲ καὶ
τὰς ἄλλας ἀμυθήτους ἀρετὰς ἡ τετράς, ὧν τὰς
πλείστας ἠκριβώσαμεν ἐν τῇ περὶ ἀριθμῶν πραγ-
116 ματείᾳ. μίτρα δ᾽ ἦν ὑπ᾽ αὐτῷ, τοῦ μὴ ψαύειν τῆς
κεφαλῆς τὸ πέταλον. πρὸς δὲ καὶ κίδαρις κατ-
εσκευάζετο· κιδάρει γὰρ οἱ τῶν ἑῴων βασιλεῖς ἀντὶ
διαδήματος εἰώθασι χρῆσθαι.
117 XXIV. Τοιαύτη μὲν ἡ τοῦ ἀρχιερέως ἦν ἐσθής.
ὃν δ᾽ ἔχει λόγον οὐ παρασιωπητέον αὐτή τε καὶ
τὰ μέρη. ὅλη μὲν δὴ γέγονεν ἀπεικόνισμα καὶ
μίμημα τοῦ κόσμου, τὰ δὲ μέρη τῶν καθ᾽ ἕκαστον
118 μερῶν. ἀρκτέον δ᾽ ἀπὸ τοῦ ποδήρους. οὗτος ὁ |
[153] χιτὼν σύμπας ἐστὶν ὑακίνθινος, ἀέρος ἐκμαγεῖον·
φύσει γὰρ ὁ ἀὴρ μέλας καὶ τρόπον τινὰ ποδήρης,
ἄνωθεν ἀπὸ τῶν μετὰ σελήνην ἄχρι τῶν γῆς ταθεὶς
περάτων, πάντῃ κεχυμένος· ὅθεν καὶ ὁ χιτὼν ἀπὸ

ᵃ The apparently traditional idea, which appears again
in § 132, that the inscription on the πέταλον was the "tetragrammaton" YHVH is not borne out by the LXX ἁγίασμα
κυρίου, or the Hebrew and E.V. "Holy (holiness) to the Lord"
(Ex. xxviii. 32 (E.V. 36)). Philo has quoted it correctly *De
Mig.* 103.

incisions, showing a name which only those whose
ears and tongues are purified may hear or speak in
the holy place, and no other person, nor in any other
place at all. That name has four letters,[a] so says 115
that master learned in divine verities, who, it may
be, gives them as symbols of the first numbers, one,
two, three and four ; since the geometrical categories under which all things fall, point, line, super-
ficies, solid, are all embraced in four. So, too, with
the best harmonies in music, the fourth, fifth, octave
and double octave intervals, where the ratios are
respectively four to three, three to two, two to one
and four to one. Four, too, has countless other
virtues, most of which I have set forth in detail in
my treatise on numbers.[b] Under the crown, to prevent 116
the plate touching the head, was a headband. A
turban also was provided, for the turban is regularly
worn by eastern monarchs instead of a diadem.

XXIV. [c] Such was the vesture of the high priest. 117
But I must not leave untold its meaning and that of
its parts. We have in it as a whole and in its parts a
typical representation of the world and its particular
parts. Let us begin with the full-length robe. This 118
gown is all of violet, and is thus an image of the air ;
for the air is naturally black, and so to speak a robe
reaching to the feet, since it stretches down from
the region below the moon to the ends of the earth,
and spreads out everywhere. And, therefore, the

The statement given here is also made by Josephus *Bell.
Jud.* v. 235 (*cf. Ant.* iii. 178). See too App. pp. 608-609.

[b] Presumably the same as the "special treatise" mentioned
in *De Op.* 52, after enumerating many of the properties of
the number. He has also dealt with them in *De Plant.* 117 ff.

[c] For some notes on and illustration of the symbolism of
§§ 117-135 see App. p. 609.

στέρνων ἄχρι ποδῶν περὶ ὅλον τὸ σῶμα κέχυται.
119 ἐξ αὐτοῦ δὲ κατὰ τὰ σφυρὰ ῥοΐσκοι καὶ ἄνθινα καὶ
κώδωνές εἰσι· τὰ μὲν ἄνθινα σύμβολον γῆς, ἀνθεῖ
γὰρ καὶ βλαστάνει πάντα ἐκ ταύτης· οἱ δὲ ῥοΐσκοι
ὕδατος, παρὰ τὴν ῥύσιν λεχθέντες εὐθυβόλως· οἱ
δὲ κώδωνες τῆς ἁρμονίας καὶ συμφωνίας τούτων,
οὔτε γὰρ γῆ χωρὶς ὕδατος οὔθ᾽ ὕδωρ ἄνευ τῆς
γεώδους οὐσίας αὔταρκες εἰς γένεσιν, ἀλλ᾽ ἡ
120 σύνοδος καὶ κρᾶσις ἀμφοῖν. μάρτυς δὲ τοῦ δηλουμένου καὶ ὁ τόπος ἐναργέστατος· ὡς γὰρ ἐν ἐσχάτοις
τοῦ ποδήρους οἱ ῥοΐσκοι καὶ τὰ ἄνθινα καὶ οἱ
κώδωνές εἰσιν, οὕτως καὶ τὰ ὧν ἐστι σύμβολα τὴν
κατωτάτω χώραν ἔλαχεν ἐν κόσμῳ, γῆ καὶ ὕδωρ,
καὶ τῇ τοῦ παντὸς ἁρμονίᾳ συνηχοῦντα τὰς οἰκείας
ἐπιδείκνυται δυνάμεις ἐν ὡρισμέναις χρόνων περι-
121 όδοις καὶ τοῖς προσήκουσι καιροῖς. τριῶν μὲν δὴ
στοιχείων, ἐξ ὧν τε καὶ ἐν οἷς τὰ θνητὰ καὶ φθαρτὰ
γένη πάντα, ἀέρος, ὕδατος, γῆς, ὁ ποδήρης σὺν
τοῖς ἀπῃωρημένοις κατὰ τὰ σφυρὰ σύμβολον
ἐδείχθη προσηκόντως· ὡς γὰρ ὁ χιτὼν εἷς, καὶ τὰ
λεχθέντα τρία στοιχεῖα μιᾶς ἰδέας ἐστίν, ἐπειδὴ τὰ
κατωτέρω σελήνης ἅπαντα τροπὰς ἔχει καὶ μετα-
βολάς· καὶ καθάπερ ἐκ τοῦ χιτῶνος ἤρτηνται οἵ τε
ῥοΐσκοι καὶ τὰ ἄνθινα, καὶ ἀπ᾽ ἀέρος τρόπον τινὰ
γῆ καὶ ὕδωρ ἐκκρέμανται, τὸ γὰρ ὄχημα τούτων
ἐστὶν ἀήρ.
122 Τὴν δ᾽ ἐπωμίδα οὐρανοῦ σύμβολον ὁ λόγος εἰκόσι
στοχασμοῖς χρώμενος παραστήσει· πρῶτον μὲν γὰρ
οἱ ἐπὶ τῶν ἀκρωμίων σμαράγδου δύο λίθοι περι-

---

[a] The stress lies on προσηκόντως; we may see that the

gown, too, spreads out from the breast to the feet round the whole body. At the ankles there stand 119 out from it pomegranates and flower trimming and bells. The earth is represented by the flowers, for all that flowers and grows comes from the earth ; the water by the pomegranates or flowing fruit, so aptly called from their flowing juice ; while the bells represent the harmonious alliance of these two, since life cannot be produced by earth without water or by water without the substance of earth, but only by the union and combination of both. Their 120 position testifies most clearly to this explanation. For, just as the pomegranates, the flower trimming and the bells are at the extremities of the long robe, so too what these symbolize, namely earth and water, occupy the lowest place in the universe, and in unison with the harmony of the All display their several powers at fixed revolutions of time and at their proper seasons. This proof that the three 121 elements, earth, water and air, from which come and in which live all mortal and perishable forms of life, are symbolized by the long robe with the appendages at the ankles, is supported [a] by observing that as the gown is one, the three said elements are of a single kind, since all below the moon is alike in its liability to change and alteration, and that, as the pomegranates and flower patterns are fastened to the gown, so too in a sense earth and water are suspended on the air, which acts as their support.

As for the ephod, consideration following what 122 probability suggests will represent it as a symbol of heaven. For first the two circular emerald stones

symbolism described above is suitable by the other resemblances pointed out in the last part of the sentence.

507

φερεῖς μηνύουσιν, ὡς μὲν οἴονταί τινες, ἀστέρων
τοὺς ἡμέρας καὶ νυκτὸς ἡγεμόνας, ἥλιον καὶ
σελήνην, ὡς δ' ἂν ἐγγυτέρω τις τῆς ἀληθείας
προσερχόμενος εἴποι, τῶν ἡμισφαιρίων ἑκάτερον·
ἴσα τε γὰρ ὡς οἱ λίθοι τό τε ὑπὲρ γῆν καὶ ὑπὸ γῆν
καὶ οὐδέτερον πέφυκε μειοῦσθαι καὶ συναύξεσθαι
123 καθάπερ σελήνη. συνεπιμαρτυρεῖ δὲ καὶ ἡ χρόα·
σμαράγδῳ γὰρ ἔοικεν ἡ τοῦ παντὸς οὐρανοῦ φαντασία κατὰ τὴν τῆς ὄψεως προσβολήν. ἀναγκαίως
δὲ καὶ καθ' ἑκάτερον τῶν λίθων ἐξ ὀνόματα ἐγγλύ-
φεται, διότι καὶ τῶν ἡμισφαιρίων ἑκάτερον δίχα
τέμνον τὸν ζωοφόρον ἐξ ἐναπολαμβάνει ζῴδια.
124 ἔπειθ' οἱ κατὰ τὰ στέρνα δώδεκα λίθοι ταῖς χρόαις
οὐχ ὅμοιοι διανεμηθέντες εἰς τέσσαρας στοίχους
ἐκ τριῶν τίνος ἑτέρου δεῖγμα τ' εἰσὶν ἢ τοῦ ζωδιακοῦ
[154] κύκλου; καὶ γὰρ | οὗτος τετραχῇ διανεμηθεὶς ἐκ
τριῶν ζῳδίων τὰς ἐτησίους ὥρας ἀποτελεῖ, ἔαρ,
θέρος, μετόπωρον, χειμῶνα, τροπὰς τέσσαρας, ὦν
ἑκάστης ὅρος τρία ζῴδια, γνωριζόμενος ταῖς τοῦ
ἡλίου περιφοραῖς κατὰ τὸν ἐν ἀριθμοῖς ἀσάλευτον
125 καὶ βεβαιότατον καὶ θεῖον ὄντως λόγον. ὅθεν
ἐνηρμόζοντο καὶ τῷ προσαγορευθέντι δεόντως
λογείῳ· λόγῳ γὰρ αἱ τροπαὶ καὶ ἐτήσιοι ὦραι
τεταγμένῳ καὶ παγίῳ συνίστανται, τὸ παραδοξότατον, διὰ τῆς καιρίου μεταβολῆς ἐπιδεικνύμεναι
126 τὴν διαιωνίζουσαν αὐτῶν μονήν. εὖ δ' ἔχει καὶ
πάνυ καλῶς τὸ τοῖς χρώμασι τοὺς δώδεκα λίθους
διαλλάττειν καὶ μηδένα ὅμοιον εἶναι μηδενί· καὶ
γὰρ τῶν ἐν τῷ ζωοφόρῳ ἕκαστον ἀποτελεῖ τι
χρῶμα οἰκεῖον κατά τε ἀέρα καὶ γῆν καὶ ὕδωρ καὶ

on the shoulder-pieces indicate, as some think, those
heavenly bodies which rule the day and night, namely
the sun and moon, or, as may be said with a nearer
approach to truth, the two hemispheres of the sky.
For, just as the stones are equal to each other, so is
the hemisphere above to that below the earth, and
neither is so constituted as to increase and diminish
as does the moon. A similar testimony is given by 123
their colour, for the appearance of the whole heaven
as presented to our sight is like the emerald. Six
names, too, had to be engraved on each of the
stones, since each of the hemispheres also divides the
zodiac into two, and appropriates six of the signs.
Secondly, the stones at the breast, which are dis- 124
similar in colour, and are distributed into four rows
of threes, what else should they signify but the
zodiac circle ? For that circle, when divided into
four parts, constitutes by three signs in each case
the seasons of the year—spring, summer, autumn,
winter—those four, the transition in each of which
is determined by three signs and made known to us
by the revolutions of the sun, according to a mathematical law, unshaken, immutable and truly divine.
Therefore also they were fitted into what is rightly 125
called the place of reason, for a rational principle,
ordered and firmly established, creates the transi-
tions and seasons of the year. And the strangest
thing is that it is this seasonal change which demon-
strates their age-long permanence. It is an excellent 126
and indeed a splendid point that the twelve stones
are of different colours and none of them like to any
other. For each of the signs of the zodiac also produces its own particular colouring in the air and

τὰ τούτων παθήματα καὶ ἔτι κατὰ τὰ τῶν ζῴων
127 καὶ φυτῶν γένη πάντα. XXV. διπλοῦν
δὲ τὸ λογεῖον οὐκ ἀπὸ σκοποῦ· διττὸς γὰρ ὁ λόγος
ἔν τε τῷ παντὶ καὶ ἐν ἀνθρώπου φύσει· κατὰ μὲν
τὸ πᾶν ὅ τε περὶ τῶν ἀσωμάτων καὶ παραδειγ-
ματικῶν ἰδεῶν, ἐξ ὧν ὁ νοητὸς ἐπάγη κόσμος, καὶ
ὁ περὶ τῶν ὁρατῶν, ἃ δὴ μιμήματα καὶ ἀπεικονίσματα τῶν ἰδεῶν ἐκείνων ἐστίν, ἐξ ὧν ὁ αἰσθητὸς
οὗτος ἀπετελεῖτο· ἐν ἀνθρώπῳ δ' ὁ μέν ἐστιν
ἐνδιάθετος, ὁ δὲ προφορικός, ⟨καὶ ὁ μὲν⟩ οἷά τις
πηγή, ὁ δὲ γεγονὼς ἀπ' ἐκείνου ῥέων· καὶ τοῦ μέν
ἐστι χώρα τὸ ἡγεμονικόν, τοῦ δὲ κατὰ προφορὰν
γλῶττα καὶ στόμα καὶ ἡ ἄλλη πᾶσα φωνῆς ὀρ-
128 γανοποιία. σχῆμα δ' ἀπένειμεν ὁ τεχνίτης τετράγωνον τῷ λογείῳ πάνυ καλῶς αἰνιττόμενος, ὡς
χρὴ καὶ τὸν τῆς φύσεως λόγον καὶ τὸν τοῦ ἀνθρώπου βεβηκέναι πάντῃ καὶ κατὰ μηδ' ὁτιοῦν
κραδαίνεσθαι. παρὸ καὶ τὰς εἰρημένας δύο ἀρετὰς
προσεκλήρωσεν αὐτῷ, δήλωσίν τε καὶ ἀλήθειαν·
ὅ τε γὰρ τῆς φύσεως λόγος ἀληθὴς καὶ δηλωτικὸς
πάντων ὅ τε τοῦ σοφοῦ μιμούμενος ἐκεῖνον ὀφείλει
προσηκόντως ἀψευδέστατός τε εἶναι τιμῶν ἀλήθειαν καὶ μηδὲν φθόνῳ συσκιάζειν, ὧν ἡ μήνυσις
129 ὠφελήσει τοὺς ἀναδιδαχθέντας. οὐ μὴν ἀλλὰ καὶ
δυσὶ λόγοις τοῖς καθ' ἕκαστον ἡμῶν, τῷ τε προφορικῷ καὶ ἐνδιαθέτῳ, δύο ἀρετὰς ἀπένειμεν οἰκείας,
τῷ μὲν προφορικῷ δήλωσιν, τῷ δὲ κατὰ διάνοιαν
ἀλήθειαν· ἁρμόζει γὰρ διανοίᾳ μὲν μηδὲν παρα-

earth and water and their phases, and also in the different kinds of animals and plants.   XXV.
There is a point, too, in the reason-seat being doubled, 127
for the rational principle is twofold as well in the
universe as in human nature. In the universe we
find it in one form dealing with the incorporeal and
archetypal ideas from which the intelligible world
was framed, and in another with the visible objects
which are the copies and likenesses of those ideas
and out of which this sensible world was produced.
With man, in one form it resides within, in the other
it passes out from him in utterance. The former is
like a spring, and is the source from which the latter,
the spoken, flows. The inward is located in the
dominant mind, the outward in the tongue and
mouth and the rest of the vocal organism. The 128
master did well also in assigning a four-square shape
to the reason-seat, thereby shewing in a figure that
the rational principle, both in nature and in man,
must everywhere stand firm and never be shaken in
any respect at all; and, therefore, he allotted to it
the two above-named virtues, clear shewing and
truth. For the rational principle in nature is true,
and sets forth all things clearly, and, in the wise
man, being a copy of the other, has as its bounden
duty to honour truth with absolute freedom from
falsehood, and not keep dark through jealousy anything the disclosure of which will benefit those who
hear its lesson. At the same time, as in each of us, 129
reason has two forms, the outward of utterance and
the inward of thought, he gave them each one of the
two virtues as its special property; to utterance
clear shewing, to the thinking mind truth. For it is
the duty of the thinking faculty to admit no false-

δέχεσθαι ψεῦδος, ἑρμηνείᾳ δὲ μηδὲν ἐμποδίζειν τῶν
130 εἰς τὴν ἀκριβεστάτην δήλωσιν. λόγου δὲ οὐδὲν
ὄφελος τὰ καλὰ καὶ σπουδαῖα σεμνηγοροῦντος, ᾧ
μὴ πρόσεστιν οἰκείων ἀκολουθία πράξεων· ὅθεν τὸ
λογεῖον ἤρτησεν ἐκ τῆς ἐπωμίδος, ἵνα μὴ χαλᾶται,
[155] τὸν λόγον οὐ δικαιώσας | ἔργων ἀπεζεῦχθαι· τὸν
γὰρ ὦμον ἐνεργείας καὶ πράξεως ποιεῖται σύμβολον.

131 XXVI. Ἃ μὲν οὖν αἰνίττεται διὰ τῆς ἱερᾶς
ἐσθῆτος, ἐστὶ τοιαῦτα. κίδαριν δὲ ἀντὶ διαδήματος
ἐπιτίθησι τῇ κεφαλῇ δικαιῶν τὸν ἱερωμένον τῷ
θεῷ, καθ᾽ ὃν χρόνον ἱερᾶται, προφέρειν ἁπάντων
132 καὶ μὴ μόνον ἰδιωτῶν ἀλλὰ καὶ βασιλέων. ὑπεράνω
δὲ τὸ χρυσοῦν ἐστι πέταλον, ᾧ τῶν τεττάρων αἱ
γλυφαὶ γραμμάτων ἐνεσφραγίσθησαν, ἐξ ὧν ὄνομα
τοῦ ὄντος φασὶ μηνύεσθαι, ὡς οὐχ οἷόν τε ὂν ἄνευ
κατακλήσεως θεοῦ συστῆναί τι τῶν ὄντων· ἁρμονία
γὰρ πάντων ἐστὶν ἡ ἀγαθότης καὶ ἵλεως δύναμις
133 αὐτοῦ.   τοῦτον τὸν τρόπον ὁ ἀρχιερεὺς
διακοσμηθεὶς στέλλεται πρὸς τὰς ἱερουργίας, ἵν᾽,
ὅταν εἰσίῃ τὰς πατρίους εὐχάς τε καὶ θυσίας ποιη-
σόμενος, συνεισέρχηται πᾶς ὁ κόσμος αὐτῷ δι᾽ ὧν
ἐπιφέρεται μιμημάτων¹ ἀέρος τὸν ποδήρη, ὕδατος
τὸν ῥοῖσκον, γῆς τὸ ἄνθινον, πυρὸς τὸ κόκκινον,
οὐρανοῦ τὴν ἐπωμίδα, καὶ κατ᾽ εἶδος τοῖν δυοῖν
ἡμισφαιρίοιν τοὺς ἐπὶ τῶν ἀκρωμίων σμαράγδους
περιφερεῖς, ἐφ᾽ ὧν καθ᾽ ἑκάτερον γλυφαὶ ἕξ, τοῦ
ζῳοφόρου τοὺς ἐπὶ τῶν στέρνων δώδεκα λίθους ἐκ

---

¹ So mss. or μίμημα. Cohn corrects to μιμήματα, wrongly,
I think. The grammatical usage of relative attraction for
διὰ μιμημάτων ἃ ἐπιφέρεται justifies, if it does not require, the
attraction of the noun to the case of the relative.

hood, and of the language faculty to give free play
to all that helps to shew facts clearly with the utmost
exactness. Yet reason, as seen in either of these 130
faculties, is of no value, however admirable and
excellent are its lofty pronouncements, unless
followed by deeds in accordance with it. And, therefore, since in his judgement speech and thought
should never be separated from actions, he fastened
the reason-seat to the ephod or shoulder-piece so
that it should not come loose. For he regards the
shoulder as the symbol of deeds and activity.

XXVI. Such are the ideas which he suggests under 131
the figure of the sacred vesture ; but, in setting a
turban on the priest's head, instead of a diadem, he
expresses his judgement that he who is consecrated
to God is superior when he acts as a priest to all
others, not only the ordinary laymen, but even kings.
Above the turban is the golden plate on which the 132
graven shapes of four letters, indicating, as we are
told, the name of the Self-Existent, are impressed,
meaning that it is impossible for anything that is
to subsist without invocation of Him ; for it is His
goodness and gracious power which join and com-
pact all things.   Thus is the high priest 133
arrayed when he sets forth to his holy duties, in
order that when he enters to offer the ancestral
prayers and sacrifices there may enter with him the
whole universe, as signified in the types of it which
he brings upon his person, the long robe a copy of
the air, the pomegranate of water, the flower trimming of earth, the scarlet of fire, the ephod of heaven,
the circular emeralds on the shoulder-tops with the
six engravings in each of the two hemispheres which
they resemble in form, the twelve stones on the

τριῶν κατὰ τέτταρας στοίχους, τοῦ συνέχοντος καὶ
134 διοικοῦντος τὰ σύμπαντα τὸ λογεῖον. ἀναγκαῖον
γὰρ ἦν τὸν ἱερωμένον τῷ τοῦ κόσμου πατρὶ παρα-
κλήτῳ χρῆσθαι τελειοτάτῳ τὴν ἀρετὴν υἱῷ πρός τε
ἀμνηστίαν ἁμαρτημάτων καὶ χορηγίαν ἀφθονω-
135 τάτων ἀγαθῶν. ἴσως μέντοι καὶ προδιδάσκει τὸν
τοῦ θεοῦ θεραπευτήν, εἰ καὶ μὴ τοῦ κοσμοποιοῦ
δυνατόν, ἀλλὰ τοῦ γε κόσμου διηνεκῶς ἄξιον εἶναι
πειρᾶσθαι, οὗ τὸ μίμημα ἐνδυόμενος ὀφείλει τῇ
διανοίᾳ τὸ παράδειγμα εὐθὺς ἀγαλματοφορῶν αὐτὸς
τρόπον τινὰ πρὸς τὴν τοῦ κόσμου φύσιν ἐξ ἀνθρώπου μεθηρμόσθαι καί, εἰ θέμις εἰπεῖν—θέμις δὲ
ἀψευδεῖν περὶ ἀληθείας λέγοντα—, βραχὺς κόσμος
εἶναι.

136 XXVII. Τῶν δὲ προπυλαίων ἔξω παρὰ ταῖς
εἰσόδοις λουτήρ ἐστι χαλκοῦς, οὐκ ἀργὸν ὕλην
λαβόντος τοῦ τεχνίτου πρὸς τὴν κατασκευήν, ὅπερ
φιλεῖ γίνεσθαι, σκεύη δ' ἐπιμελῶς δημιουργηθέντα
πρὸς ἑτέραν χρείαν, ἃ μετὰ σπουδῆς καὶ φιλοτιμίας
πάσης αἱ γυναῖκες εἰσήνεγκαν ἁμιλλώμεναι τοῖς
ἀνδράσι πρὸς εὐσέβειαν, ἀγώνισμα καλὸν ἄρασθαι
διανοηθεῖσαι καὶ καθ' ὅσον δυνάμεως εἶχον σπου-
δάσασαι μὴ ἀπολειφθῆναι τῆς ἐκείνων ὁσιότητος·
137 κάτοπτρα γάρ, οἷς εὐμορφίαν | εἰώθασι δια-
[156] κοσμεῖσθαι, μηδενὸς προστάξαντος, αὐτοκελεύστῳ
προθυμίᾳ, σωφροσύνης καὶ τῆς περὶ γάμον ἁγνείας
καὶ τί γὰρ ἀλλ' ἢ ψυχικοῦ κάλλους ἀπαρχὴν πρε-
138 πωδεστάτην ἀπήρξαντο. ταῦτ' ἔδοξε τῷ τεχνίτῃ

ᵃ λόγου must be understood with τοῦ συνέχοντος, if indeed
it has not fallen out of the text.

breast in four rows of threes of the zodiac, the reason-
seat of that Reason [a] which holds together and ad-
ministers all things. For he who has been con- 134
secrated to the Father of the world must needs have
that Father's Son [b] with all His fullness of excellence
to plead his cause, that sins may be remembered no
more and good gifts showered in rich abundance.
Perhaps, too, he is preparing the servant of God to 135
learn the lesson, that, if it be beyond him to be
worthy of the world's Maker, he should try to be
throughout worthy of the world. For, as he wears a
vesture which represents the world, his first duty is
to carry the pattern enshrined in his heart, and so
be in a sense transformed from a man into the nature
of the world ; and, if one may dare to say so—and
in speaking of truth one may well dare to state the
truth—be himself a little world, a microcosm.

XXVII. [c] Outside the propylaeum, at the entrance, 136
there was a brazen laver, for the making of which the
master did not take unworked material, as is usually
done, but chattels already elaborately wrought for
another purpose. These the women brought, filled
with fervent zeal, rivalling the men in piety, resolved
to win the prize of high excellence, and eager to use
every power that they had that they might not be
outstripped by them in holiness. For, with spont- 137
aneous ardour at no other bidding than their own,
they gave the mirrors which they used in adorning
their comely persons, a truly fitting firstfruit offering
of their modesty and chastity in marriage, and in fact
of their beauty of soul. These the master thought 138

[b] The Son here is of course the World.
[c] For §§ 136-140 see Ex. xxxviii. 26, 27 (E.V. 8). The incident has been treated briefly in the same way *De Mig.* 98.

PHILO

λαβόντι χωνεῦσαι καὶ μηδὲν ἀπ' αὐτῶν ἕτερον
ἢ τὸν λουτῆρα κατασκευάσασθαι, περιρραντηρίοις
ὅπως οἱ μέλλοντες εἰς τὸν νεὼν εἰσιέναι ἱερεῖς ἐπὶ
τῷ τὰς διατεταγμένας ὑπουργεῖν λειτουργίας
χρῶνται πόδας μάλιστα καὶ χεῖρας ἀπονιπτόμενοι
—σύμβολον ἀνυπαιτίου ζωῆς καὶ βίου καθαρεύ-
οντος ἐν πράξεσιν ἐπαινεταῖς, οὐ τὴν τραχεῖαν
κακίας ὁδὸν ἢ κυριώτερον εἰπεῖν ἀνοδίαν ἀλλὰ
139 τὴν δι' ἀρετῆς λεωφόρον ἀπευθύνοντος—. "ὑπο-
μιμνησκέσθω μέντοι" φησί "καὶ ὁ μέλλων περιρ-
ραίνεσθαι, ὅτι τοῦδε τοῦ σκεύους ἡ ὕλη κάτοπτρα
ἦν, ἵνα καὶ αὐτὸς οἷα πρὸς κάτοπτρον αὐγάζῃ τὸν
ἴδιον νοῦν καί, εἴ τι ὑποφαίνοιτο αἶσχος ἐξ ἀλόγου
πάθους ἢ παρὰ φύσιν ἐπαιρούσης καὶ μετεωριζούσης
ἡδονῆς ἢ στελλούσης ἔμπαλιν λύπης καὶ καθ-
αιρούσης ἢ ἀποστρέφοντος καὶ ἀποκλίνοντος τὴν
ἐπ' εὐθείας ὁρμὴν φόβου ἢ τῆς ἐπιθυμίας πρὸς τὰ
μὴ παρόντα ἑλκούσης καὶ ἀποτεινούσης βίᾳ, τοῦτο
θεραπεύῃ τε καὶ ἰᾶται τοῦ γνησίου καὶ ἀνόθου
140 μεταποιούμενος κάλλους· τὸ μὲν γὰρ τοῦ σώματος
ἐν συμμετρίᾳ μερῶν εὐχροίᾳ τε καὶ εὐσαρκίᾳ κεῖται,
βραχὺν τῆς ἀκμῆς ἔχον καιρόν, τὸ δὲ τῆς διανοίας
ἐν ἁρμονίᾳ δογμάτων καὶ ἀρετῶν συμφωνίᾳ, μὴ
χρόνου μήκει μαραινόμενον, ἀλλ' ἐφ' ὅσον ἐγχρο-
νίζει καινούμενον καὶ νεάζον, χρώματι διαπρεπεῖ
κεκοσμημένον ἀληθείας καὶ ὁμολογίας ἔργων πρὸς
λόγους καὶ πρὸς ἔργα λόγων καὶ ἔτι βουλευμάτων
πρὸς ἑκάτερα."

141 XXVIII. Διδαχθέντι δ' αὐτῷ τὰ παραδείγματα
τῆς ἱερᾶς σκηνῆς καὶ ἀναδιδάξαντι τοὺς διανοίᾳ
ὀξεῖς καὶ εὐφυῶς ἔχοντας πρὸς ἀνάληψιν καὶ

good to take, and, after melting them down, construct therewith the laver and nothing else, to serve for lustration to priests who should enter the temple to perform the appointed rites, particularly for washing the hands and feet ; a symbol, this, of a blameless life, of years of cleanliness employed in laudable actions, and in straight travelling, not on the rough road or more properly pathless waste of vice, but on the smooth high road through virtue's land. Let him, 139 he means, who shall be purified with water, bethink him that the mirrors were the material of this vessel, to the end that he himself may behold his own mind as in a mirror ; and, if some ugly spot appear of unreasoning passion, either of pleasure, uplifting and raising him to heights which nature forbids, or of its converse pain, making him shrink and pulling him down, or of fear, diverting and distorting the straight course to which his face was set, or of desire, pulling and dragging him perforce to what he has not got, then he may salve and heal the sore and hope to gain the beauty which is genuine and unalloyed. For beauty of body 140 lies in well-proportioned parts, in a fine complexion and good condition of flesh, and short is the season of its bloom. But beauty of mind lies in harmony of creed, in concent of virtues. The passing of time cannot wither it, and, as its years lengthen, it ever renews its youth, adorned with the lustrous hue of truth and of consistency of deeds with words and words with deeds, and further of thoughts and intentions with both.

XXVIII. When he had been taught the patterns 141 of the holy tabernacle, and had passed on the lesson to those who were of quick understanding and happily gifted to undertake and complete the works in which

τελείωσιν ἔργων, ἅπερ ἀναγκαίως εἶχε δημιουρ-
γηθῆναι, κατὰ τὸ εἰκὸς ἱεροῦ κατασκευασθέντος
ἔδει καὶ ἱερεῖς τοὺς ἐπιτηδειοτάτους αἱρεθῆναί τε
καὶ προμαθεῖν, ὃν τρόπον τὰς θυσίας ἀνάγειν τε
142 καὶ ἱερουργεῖν προσῆκε.   τὸν μὲν οὖν ἀδελφὸν ἐξ
ἁπάντων ἐπικρίνας ἀριστίνδην ἀρχιερέα, τοὺς δ᾽
ἐκείνου παῖδας ἱερεῖς ἐχειροτόνει, προνομίαν οὐ τῷ
οἰκείῳ γένει διδούς, ἀλλ᾽ εὐσεβείᾳ καὶ ὁσιότητι, ἃς
ἐνεώρα τοῖς ἀνδράσιν ὑπούσας. σαφὴς δὲ πίστις·
οὐδέτερον υἱὸν—δύο γὰρ ἦσαν αὐτῷ—τούτου τοῦ
γέρως ἠξίωσεν, ἀναγκαίως ἂν ἀμφοτέρους ἑλό-
143 μενος, εἴ τινα τιμὴν ἔνεμε τῷ φιλοικείῳ. καθίστη
δὲ μετὰ τῆς ἅπαντος τοῦ ἔθνους γνώμης, ὡς τὰ
[157] λόγια ὑφηγεῖτο, καινότατον τρόπον καὶ | ἄξιον
ἱστορηθῆναι· λούει τὸ πρῶτον αὐτοὺς ὕδατι πηγῆς
τῷ καθαρωτάτῳ καὶ ζωτικωτάτῳ κἄπειτα τὰς
ἱερὰς ἀναδίδωσιν ἐσθῆτας, τῷ μὲν ἀδελφῷ τὸν
ποδήρη καὶ τὴν ἐπωμίδα οἱονεὶ θώρακα, τὸ παμ-
ποίκιλον ὕφασμα καὶ μίμημα τοῦ παντός, τοῖς δ᾽
ἀδελφιδοῖς χιτῶνας λινοῦς, ζώνας τε καὶ περισκελῆ
144 πᾶσι· τὰς μέν, ὅπως ἀνεμπόδιστοι καὶ ἑτοιμότεροι
πρὸς τὰς ἱερὰς ὑπουργίας ὦσι, σφιγγομένων τοὺς
ἀνειμένους κόλπους τῶν χιτώνων, τὰ δ᾽, ὅπως
μηδὲν ὧν κρύπτεσθαι θέμις προφαίνηται, καὶ
μάλιστ᾽ ἀνερχομένων ἐπὶ τὸν βωμὸν ἢ κατιόντων
ἄνωθεν καὶ πάντα δρώντων μετὰ σπουδῆς καὶ
145 τάχους· εἰ γὰρ μὴ οὕτως ἀκριβὴς γεγένητο ἡ
στόλισις διὰ τὴν τοῦ μέλλοντος ἀδήλου προφυλακήν,

---

their handicraft was necessary, the construction of the sacred fabric followed in natural course. The next step needed was that the most suitable persons should be chosen as priests, and learn in good time how they should proceed to bring the offerings to the altar and perform the holy rites. Accordingly, he selected 142 out of the whole number his brother as high priest on his merits, and appointed that brother's sons as priests, and in this he was not giving precedence to his own family but to the piety and holiness which he observed in their characters. This is clearly shewn by the following fact. Neither of his sons, of whom he had two, did he judge worthy of this distinction, though he would surely have chosen both if he had attributed any value to family affection. *a* The installation was made with the consent of the 143 whole nation, and, followed the directions laid down by the oracles, in a wholly new manner which deserves to be recorded. First he washed them with the purest and freshest spring water, then he put on them the sacred garments ; on his brother the vesture, woven with its manifold workmanship to represent the universe, that is the long robe and the ephod in the shape of a breastplate ; on his nephews linen tunics, and on all three girdles and breeches. The object of the girdles was to keep them 144 unhampered and readier for the holy ministry, by tightening the loose folds of the tunics ; of the breeches to prevent anything being visible which decency requires to be concealed, particularly when they were going up to the altar or coming down from above and moving quickly and rapidly in all their operations. For, if their dress had not been arranged so carefully, 145 as a precaution against unforseen events, they would

PHILO

κἂν ἕνεκα τῆς συντόνου περὶ τὰς λειτουργίας
ὀξύτητος ἀπεγυμνοῦτο τὸν προσήκοντα ἱεροῖς καὶ
ἱερωμένοις κόσμον φυλάττειν ἀδυνατοῦντες.

146 XXIX. ὡς δὲ ταῖς ἐσθήσεσιν ἤσκησεν αὐτούς,
χρίσματος εὐωδεστάτου λαβών, ὃ μυρεψικῇ τέχνῃ
κατειργάσθη, τὰ ἐν ὑπαίθρῳ πρῶτα, τόν τε βωμὸν
καὶ τὸν λουτῆρα, κατέχριεν ἐπιρραίνων ἑπτάκις,
ἔπειτα τὴν σκηνὴν καὶ τῶν ἱερῶν σκευῶν ἕκαστον,
τὴν κιβωτόν, τὴν λυχνίαν, τὸ θυμιατήριον, τὴν
τράπεζαν, τὰ σπονδεῖα, τὰς φιάλας, τὰ ἄλλα ὅσα
πρὸς θυσίας ἀναγκαῖα καὶ χρήσιμα, καὶ τελευταῖον
προσαγαγὼν τὸν ἀρχιερέα πολλῷ λίπει τὴν κεφαλὴν
147 ἀλείφει. ταῦτ' ἐπιτελέσας εὐαγῶς ἀχθῆναι κελεύει
μόσχον καὶ κριοὺς δύο· τὸν μέν, ἵνα θύσῃ περὶ
ἀφέσεως ἁμαρτημάτων, αἰνιττόμενος ὅτι παντὶ
γενητῷ, κἂν σπουδαῖον ᾖ, παρόσον ἦλθεν εἰς
γένεσιν, συμφυὲς τὸ ἁμαρτάνειν ἐστίν, ὑπὲρ οὗ τὸ
θεῖον εὐχαῖς καὶ θυσίαις ἀναγκαῖον ἐξευμενίζεσθαι,
148 μὴ διακινηθὲν ἐπιθεῖτο· τῶν δὲ κριῶν τὸν μὲν
ἕτερον εἰς ὁλοκαύτωμα εὐχαριστήριον τῆς τῶν
ὅλων διοικήσεως, ἧς κατὰ τὸ ἐπιβάλλον ἑκάστῳ
μέρος μέτεστι καρπουμένῳ τὴν ἀπὸ τῶν στοιχείων
ὠφέλειαν, γῆς πρὸς οἴκησιν καὶ τὰς ἐξ αὐτῆς
τροφάς, ὕδατος πρὸς ποτὸν καὶ λουτρὰ καὶ πλοῦν,
ἀέρος πρὸς ἀναπνοὴν καὶ τὰς διὰ τῶν αἰσθήσεων
ἀντιλήψεις—ἐπειδὴ πασῶν ἀὴρ ὄργανον—καὶ ἔτι
τὰς ἐτησίους ὥρας, πυρὸς τοῦ μὲν χρειώδους πρὸς
τὰ ἑψόμενα καὶ θερμαινόμενα, τοῦ δὲ οὐρανίου πρὸς
149 αὐγὴν καὶ τὰ ὁρατὰ πάντα· τὸν δ' ἕτερον εἰς τὴν
520

in their eagerness to carry out their duties with expedition reveal their nakedness and be unable to preserve the decency befitting consecrated places and persons. XXIX. When he had attired them in these 146 vestments, he took some very fragrant ointment which was compounded by the perfumer's art, and applied it first to what stood in the open court, namely the great altar and the laver, sprinkling it on them seven times, then to the tabernacle and each of the sacred chattels, the ark, the candlestick, the altar of incense, the table, the libation cups or bowls, the vials, and everything else which was necessary or useful in sacrifices ; and finally, coming to the high priest, he anointed him on his head plentifully with the unguent. Having performed all this religiously, he ordered a 147 calf and two rams to be brought. The calf he purposed to offer to gain remission of sins, showing by this figure that sin is congenital to every created being, even the best, just because they are created, and this sin requires prayers and sacrifices to propitiate the Deity, lest His wrath be roused and visited upon them. Of the rams, one he offered as a whole 148 burnt offering in thanksgiving for His ordering of the whole, that gift which each of us shares according to the part allotted through the benefits which he receives from the elements : from earth, for habitation and the food which it affords ; from water, for drinking and cleansing and voyaging ; from air, for breathing and perception through the senses, all of which operate by means of air, which also gives us the seasons of the year ; from the fire of common use, for cooking and heating, and from the heavenly variety for light-giving and all visibility. The other ram he 149

τῶν ἱερωμένων διὰ καθάρσεως ἁγνευτικῆς παντέλειαν, ὃν ἐτύμως " τελειώσεως " ἐκάλεσεν, ἐπειδὴ
τὰς ἁρμοττούσας θεραπευταῖς καὶ λειτουργοῖς θεοῦ
150 τελετὰς ἔμελλον ἱεροφαντεῖσθαι. τοῦ δ᾽ αἵματος
αὐτοῦ τὸ μὲν ἐν κύκλῳ τοῦ βωμοῦ σπένδει λαβών,
τὸ δὲ φιάλην ὑποσχὼν δέχεται καὶ ἀπὸ τούτου τρία
μέρη τοῦ σώματος χρίει τῶν τελουμένων ἱερέων,
[158] οὓς ἄκρον, ἄκραν χεῖρα, ποδὸς ἄκρον, | δεξιὰ τὰ
σύμπαντα, αἰνιττόμενος ὅτι δεῖ τὸν τέλειον καὶ
λόγῳ καὶ ἔργῳ καὶ βίῳ παντὶ καθαρεύειν· λόγον μὲν
γὰρ ἀκοὴ δικάζει, χεὶρ δ᾽ ἔργου σύμβολον, διεξόδου
151 δὲ τῆς περὶ τὸν βίον πούς. ἐπεὶ δ᾽ ἕκαστον αὐτῶν
ἄκρον τε καὶ δεξιόν, ὑπονοητέον δηλοῦσθαι τὴν ἐν
ἑκάστοις ἐπίδοσιν μετὰ δεξιότητος, ἐφιεμένην τῆς
ἄκρας εὐδαιμονίας καὶ τοῦ τέλους, ἐφ᾽ ὃ σπεύδειν
ἀναγκαῖον καὶ τὰς πράξεις ἁπάσας ἀναφέρειν
στοχαζομένους ὥσπερ ἐν ταῖς τοξείαις σκοποῦ τοῦ
152 περὶ τὸν βίον. XXX. πάλαι μὲν οὖν ἱερείου ἑνός,
ὃ προσηγορεύετο " τελειώσεως," ἀκράτῳ αἵματι τὰ
λεχθέντα τρία μέρη κατέχριε τῶν ἱερέων. αὖθις
δ᾽ ἐκ τοῦ παρὰ τῷ βωμῷ λαβών, ὅπερ ἐξ ἁπάντων ἦν τῶν τεθυμένων, καὶ τοῦ λεχθέντος χρίσματος,
ὃ μυρεψοὶ κατεσκεύασαν, ἀναμίξας τὸ ἔλαιον τῷ
αἵματι τοῦ κράματος τοῖς ἱερεῦσι καὶ ταῖς ἐσθήσεσιν αὐτῶν ἐπέρραινε, βουλόμενος αὐτοὺς μὴ
μόνον τῆς ἔξω καὶ ἐν ὑπαίθρῳ μεταλαχεῖν ἁγνείας,
ἀλλὰ καὶ τῆς ἐν ἀδύτοις, ἐπειδὴ καὶ ἔνδον

offered on behalf of those who were consecrated by
the sanctifying purification for their full perfection,
and accordingly called it the ram of " fulfilment," from
the full rites befitting the servants and ministers of
God into which they were to be initiated.   He then 150
took its blood and poured part of it round the altar.
The rest he received in a vial which he held under-
neath, and smeared it on three parts of the bodies
of those who were being admitted to the priesthood,
on the extremity of the ear, the extremity of the
hand, the extremity of the foot, in all these on the
right side.   In this figure, he indicated that the fully-
consecrated must be pure in words and actions and
in his whole life ; for words are judged by the hearing,
the hand is a symbol of action, and the foot of the
pilgrimage of life.   And, as in each case the part 151
smeared is the extreme end and on the right-hand
side, we must suppose the truth indicated to be that
improvement in all things needs a dexterous spirit,
and seeks to reach the extreme of happiness, and the
end to which we must press and refer all our actions,
aiming our shafts, like archers, at the target of life.
XXX. His first step, then, is to smear the unmixed 152
blood of the single victim called the ram of fulfilment
on the three parts of the priests' bodies named above.
After this, he took some of the blood at the altar, got
from all the victims, and also some of the unguent
already mentioned as compounded by the perfumers,
and mixed the oil with the blood.   He then used the
mixture to sprinkle the priests and their garments,
wishing to make them partakers not only of the
sanctity of the outer and open court but that of the
shrine within, since they were going to minister in the

λειτουργεῖν ἔμελλον· τὰ δ' εἴσω πάντα ἐλαίῳ
κατεκέχριστο.

153 Θυσίας δ' ἐπὶ ταῖς προτέραις ἄλλας ἀναγαγόντων,
τοῦτο μὲν τῶν ἱερέων ὑπὲρ αὐτῶν, τοῦτο δὲ τῆς
γερουσίας ὑπὲρ ἅπαντος τοῦ ἔθνους, Μωυσῆς μὲν
εἰς τὴν σκηνὴν εἰσέρχεται τὸν ἀδελφὸν ἐπαγόμενος
—ὀγδόη δ' ἦν τῆς τελετῆς ἡμέρα καὶ τελευταία,
ταῖς γὰρ πρότερον ἑπτὰ ἱεροφαντῶν αὐτόν τε
καὶ τοὺς ἀδελφιδοῦς ὠργίαζεν—, εἰσελθὼν δ' ἀν-
εδίδασκεν οἷα ὑφηγητὴς ἀγαθὸς εὐμαθῆ γνώριμον,
ὃν χρὴ τρόπον τὸν ἀρχιερέα τὰς εἴσω ποιεῖσθαι
154 λειτουργίας. εἶτ' ἐξελθόντες ἀμφότεροι καὶ τὰς
χεῖρας ἀνατείναντες πρὸ τῆς κεφαλῆς εὐχὰς τίθενται
τῷ ἔθνει τὰς προσηκούσας ἀπὸ καθαρᾶς καὶ ὁσιω-
τάτης γνώμης. ἔτι δ' εὐχομένων, τερατωδέστατόν
τι συμβαίνει· ἐκ γὰρ τῶν ἀδύτων, εἴτε αἰθέρος
ἀπόσπασμα τοῦ καθαρωτάτου, εἴτε ἀέρος κατὰ τὴν
τῶν στοιχείων φύσει μεταβολὴν ἀναλυθέντος εἰς
πῦρ, αἰφνίδιον ἀθρόα φλὸξ διεκπαίει καὶ συντόνῳ
ῥύμῃ φέρεται μὲν ἐπὶ τὸν βωμόν, τὰ δ' ἐπ' αὐτοῦ
πάντα ἐξαναλίσκει, πρὸς οἶμαι σαφεστάτην δήλωσιν, ὅτι οὐδὲν ἄνευ θείας ἐπιφροσύνης ἐπετελεῖτο.

155 δωρεὰν γὰρ ἐξαίρετον εἰκὸς ἦν τοῖς ἁγίοις προσ-
νεμηθῆναι, μὴ μόνον ἐν οἷς ἄνθρωποι δημιουργοί,
ἀλλὰ καὶ τῷ καθαρωτάτῳ τῆς οὐσίας πυρί, τὸ χρειῶδες καὶ παρ' ἡμῖν ὅπως μὴ προσάψαιτο τοῦ βωμοῦ,

156 διὰ τὸ μυρίας ἴσως ἀναμεμῖχθαι κῆρας· ἅπτεται γὰρ
οὐ μόνον ζώων ἀλόγων ὀπτωμένων ἢ ἑψομένων
[159] εἰς πλησμονὴν | ἄδικον γαστρὸς τῆς ταλαίνης, ἀλλὰ

---

a For §§ 153-158 see Lev. ix. (particularly verse 24).

inner part also, all of which had been anointed with oil.

a After other additional sacrifices had been brought, 153 some by the priests on behalf of themselves, and others by the body of elders on behalf of the whole nation, Moses entered the tabernacle, taking his brother with him. This was on the eighth and last day of the celebration, the seven preceding days having been spent by him in initiating his nephews and their father and in acting as their guide to the sacred mysteries. After entering, he gave such instruction as the good teacher gives to an apt pupil on the way in which the high priest should perform the rites of the inner shrine. Then they both came 154 out, and, stretching forth their hands in front of their faces, offered prayers which befitted the needs of the nation in all sincerity and purity of heart. And, while they were still praying, a great marvel happened. There issued suddenly from the shrine a mass of flame. Whether it was a fragment of ether, the purest of substances, or of air resolved into fire by a natural conversion of the elements, it suddenly burst right through, and, with a mighty rush, fell upon the altar and consumed all that was on it, thus giving, I hold, the clearest proof that none of these rites was without divine care and supervision. For it was natural that 155 the holy place should have a special gift attached to it, over and above what human handiwork had given, through the purest of elements, fire, and thus the altar be saved from contact with the familiar fire of common use, perhaps because such a multitude of evils are associated with it. For its activity is applied 156 not only to the lower animals when they are roasted or boiled, to satisfy the cruel cravings of the miserable

PHILO

καὶ ἀνθρώπων ἐξ ἐπιβουλῆς ἀναιρουμένων, οὐ
τριῶν ἢ τεττάρων, ἀλλὰ καὶ πολυανθρώπων ὁμίλων·
157 ἤδη γοῦν καὶ στόλους μεγάλους ἐπιβατικοῦ πλήρεις ὀϊστοὶ πυρφόροι κατέφλεξαν βληθέντες καὶ ὅλας
πόλεις ἐξανάλωσαν, αἳ σμυχόμεναι μέχρι θεμελίων
εἰς τέφραν ἐδαπανήθησαν, ὡς μηδ᾽ ἴχνος ὑπολε-
158 λεῖφθαι τοῦ πάλαι συνοικισμοῦ. ταύτης ἕνεκά μοι
δοκῶ τῆς αἰτίας ὡς μεμιασμένον ἤλασε τοῦ ἱερωτάτου καὶ καθαρωτάτου βωμοῦ πῦρ τὸ χρειῶδες,
ἀνθ᾽ οὗ φλόγα αἰθέριον ὤμβρησεν ἀπὸ τοῦ οὐρανοῦ
πρὸς διαστολὴν ἁγίων τε καὶ βεβήλων, ἀνθρωπείων
τε καὶ θείων· ἥρμοττε γὰρ ταῖς θυσίαις ἀφθαρτο-
τέραν οὐσίαν ἀπονενεμῆσθαι πυρὸς τῆς πρὸς τὰς
βιωτικὰς χρείας ὑπηρετούσης.

159 XXXI. Πολλῶν δὲ κατὰ τὸ ἀναγκαῖον ἀν-
αγομένων θυσιῶν καθ᾽ ἑκάστην ἡμέραν καὶ διαφερόντως ἐν πανηγύρεσι καὶ ἑορταῖς ὑπέρ τε ἰδίᾳ
ἑκάστου καὶ κοινῇ ὑπὲρ ἁπάντων, διὰ μυρίας καὶ
οὐχὶ τὰς αὐτὰς αἰτίας, ἅτε πολυανθρωποτάτου ἔθνους εὐσεβοῦντος, ἐδέησε καὶ νεωκόρων πλήθους εἰς
160 τὰς ἱερὰς ὑπηρεσίας. ἡ δ᾽ αἵρεσις ἐγίνετο πάλιν
καινότατον ἀλλ᾽ οὐ τὸν εἰωθότα τρόπον· μίαν τῶν
δώδεκα φυλῶν ἐπικρίνας ἀριστίνδην ἐχειροτόνει
161 θεοφιλοῦς ἔργου προθεὶς ἆθλα καὶ ἀριστεῖα. τὸ
δ᾽ ἔργον τοιόνδε ἦν· Μωυσέως ἀναβάντος εἰς τὸ
πλησίον ὄρος καὶ πλείους ἡμέρας ἰδιάζοντος τῷ
θεῷ, τὴν ἀπουσίαν αὐτοῦ καιρὸν ἐπιτήδειον εἶναι
νομίσαντες οἱ μὴ βέβαιοι τὰς φύσεις, ὥσπερ ἀναρ-
χίας γενομένης, ἄφετοι πρὸς ἀσέβειαν ὥρμησαν καὶ
ἐκλαθόμενοι τῆς πρὸς τὸ ὂν ὁσιότητος ζηλωταὶ τῶν

belly, but to the human beings slaughtered by the design of others, and that not in threes or fours but in assembled multitudes. Ere now we have known 157 the impact of fire-carrying arrows burn up great fully-manned fleets, and consume whole cities which have smouldered down to their very foundations and wasted away into ashes, leaving no trace to shew that they were populated in the past. This is the reason, 158 I imagine, why God expelled from His most pure and sacred altar the fire of common use and rained instead an ethereal flame from heaven, to distinguish between the holy and the profane, the human and the divine. For it was fitting that fire of a more incorruptible nature than that which subserves the needs of human life should be assigned to the sacrificial offerings.

XXXI. Many sacrifices were necessarily brought 159 every day, and particularly at general assemblies and feasts, on behalf both of individuals and all in common, and for a multitude of different reasons. This piety shewn by so populous a nation made it needful to have also a number of temple attendants to help in the sacred services. These, again, were 160 chosen in a very novel and unusual manner. He selected and appointed one of the twelve tribes as the most meritorious, giving them the office as the prize and reward of a deed well pleasing to God. *a* The story of that deed is as follows: When Moses 161 had gone up into the mountain, and was there several days communing privately with God, the men of unstable nature, thinking his absence a suitable opportunity, rushed into impious practices unrestrainedly, as though authority had ceased to be, and, forgetting the reverence they owed to the Self-Existent,

---

a For §§ 161-173 see Ex. xxxii.

162 Αἰγυπτιακῶν γίνονται πλασμάτων. εἶτα χρυσοῦν
ταῦρον κατασκευασάμενοι, μίμημα τοῦ κατὰ τὴν
χώραν ἱερωτάτου ζῴου δοκοῦντος εἶναι, θυσίας
ἀθύτους ἀνῆγον καὶ χοροὺς ἀχορεύτους ἵστασαν
ὕμνους τε ᾖδον θρήνων οὐδὲν διαφέροντας καὶ
ἐμφορηθέντες ἀκράτου διπλῇ μέθῃ κατίσχοντο, τῇ
μὲν ἐξ οἴνου, τῇ δὲ καὶ ἀφροσύνης, κωμάζοντές τε
καὶ παννυχίζοντες ἀπροόρατοι τοῦ μέλλοντος ἡδέσι
κακοῖς συνεβίουν, ἐφεδρευούσης δίκης, ἣ μὴ βλέ-
163 ποντας ἔβλεπε καὶ ὧν ἄξιοι τιμωριῶν εἰσιν. ἐπεὶ
δὲ αἱ ἐν τῷ στρατοπέδῳ συνεχεῖς ἐκβοήσεις κατὰ
πολυανθρώπους ὁμίλους ἀθροιζομένων ἄχρι πολλοῦ
διαστήματος ἐχώρουν, ὡς καὶ μέχρι τῆς ἀκρωρείας
τὴν περιήχησιν ἐλθεῖν, πληχθεὶς τὰ ὦτα Μωυσῆς
ἐν ἀμηχάνοις ἦν ἅτε θεοφιλὴς ὁμοῦ καὶ φιλάνθρωπος, μήτ' ἐκλιπεῖν ὑπομένων τὰς πρὸς θεὸν
ὁμιλίας, ἃς ἰδιάζων μόνος μόνῳ διελέγετο, μήθ'
ὑπεριδεῖν τοῦ πλήθους ἐμπιπλαμένου τῶν ἐξ ἀν-
164 αρχίας κακοπραγιῶν· ἔγνω γὰρ τὸν θροῦν δεινὸς
[160] | ὧν ἐκ φωνῆς ἀνάρθρου καὶ ἀσήμου στοχάσασθαι
ψυχῆς ἀδήλων καὶ ἀφανῶν τοῖς ἄλλοις παθῶν ἰδιότητας, ὅτι παροινίας ἐστὶν ἡ κατέχουσα ταραχή,
γεννώσης ἀκρασίας μὲν κόρον, κόρου δὲ ὕβριν.
165 ἀνθελκόμενος δὲ καὶ ἀντισπώμενος πρὸς ἑκατέρου
μέρους ὧδε κἀκεῖσε τί χρὴ δρᾶν ἠπόρει. σκοπου-
μένῳ δ' αὐτῷ θεσπίζεται τάδε· " βάδιζε ταχέως
ἐνθένδε, κατάβηθι· πρὸς ἀνομίαν ἔσπευσεν ὁ λεώς·
χειροποίητον κατασκευάσαντες ταυρόμορφον θεὸ·

ᵃ Here as elsewhere Philo assumes that the making of the
golden calf was an imitation of the worship of Apis (though,
as Driver points out, the Egyptian bull worship was given
to a living animal). See note on *De Ebr.* 95

became zealous devotees of Egyptian fables. Then, 162
having fashioned a golden bull, in imitation of the
animal held most sacred in that country,[a] they offered
sacrifices which were no sacrifices, set up choirs
which were no choirs, sang hymns which were very
funeral chants, and, filled with strong drink, were
overcome by the twofold intoxication of wine and
folly. And so, revelling and carousing the livelong
night, and unwary of the future, they lived wedded
to their pleasant vices, while justice, the unseen
watcher of them and the punishments they deserved, stood ready to strike.   But, since 163
the continuous shouting in the camp which arose
from the great masses of men gathered together
carried for a long distance, so that the echoes reached
even to the mountain-top, Moses, as they smote upon
his ear, was in a dilemma between God's love for
him and his love for man. He could not bear to
leave his converse with God, in which he talked with
Him as in private with none other present, nor yet
to disregard the multitude, brimful of the miseries
which anarchy creates. For, skilled as he was to 164
divine in an inarticulate and meaningless noise the
distinguishing marks of inward passions which to
others were obscure and invisible, he recognized the
tumult for what it was, saw that drunkenness caused
the ·prevailing confusion, since intemperance begets
satiety, and satiety riot. So, drawn backwards and 165
forwards, hither and thither, by the two sides of his
being, he was at a loss what he should do. And,
as he considered, this divine message came. " Go
quickly hence. Descend. The people have run after
lawlessness. They have fashioned a god, the work
of their hands, in the form of a bull, and to this

οὐ θεὸν προσκυνοῦσι καὶ θύουσιν, ὧν εἶδον καὶ ὧν
ἤκουσαν ἁπάντων ὅσα συντείνει πρὸς εὐσέβειαν
166 ἐκλαθόμενοι." καταπλαγεὶς δὲ καὶ ἀναγκασθεὶς
πιστεύειν ἀπίστοις πράξεσιν οἷα μεσίτης καὶ δι-
αλλακτὴς οὐκ εὐθὺς ἀπεπήδησεν, ἀλλὰ πρότερον
τὰς ὑπὲρ τοῦ ἔθνους ἱκεσίας καὶ λιτὰς ἐποιεῖτο
συγγνῶναι τῶν ἡμαρτημένων δεόμενος· εἶτ' ἐξ-
ευμενισάμενος ὁ κηδεμὼν καὶ παραιτητὴς τὸν ἡγεμόνα ἐπανῄει χαίρων ἅμα καὶ κατηφῶν· ἐγεγήθει
μὲν γὰρ τὴν ἱκεσίαν τοῦ θεοῦ προσιεμένου, συννοίας
δὲ καὶ κατηφείας μεστὸς ἦν οἰδῶν ἐπὶ τῇ τοῦ
167 πλήθους παρανομίᾳ.   XXXII. γενόμενος
δ' ἐν μέσῳ τοῦ στρατοπέδου καὶ τὴν ἐξαπίναιον
ἐκδιαίτησιν τοῦ πλήθους θαυμάσας καὶ ὅσον ψεῦδος
ἀνθ' ὅσης ἀληθείας ὑπηλλάξαντο, κατιδὼν οὐκ εἰς
ἅπαντας τὴν νόσον ἀφιγμένην, ἀλλά τινας ὑγιαίνοντας ἔτι καὶ μισοπονήρῳ πάθει χρωμένους,
βουλόμενος διαγνῶναι τούς τε ἀνιάτως ἔχοντας
καὶ τοὺς ἐπὶ τοῖς πεπραγμένοις δυσχεραίνοντας
καὶ εἰ δή τινες ἁμαρτόντες μετανοοῦσι, κήρυγμα
κηρύττει—τὸ δ' ἦν ἄρα βάσανος ἀκριβὴς τῆς
ἑκάστου διανοίας, ὡς ἔχοι πρός τε ὁσιότητα καὶ
168 τοὐναντίον—. " εἴ τις " γάρ φησι " πρὸς κύριον,
ἴτω πρός μέ." βραχὺ μὲν τὸ λεχθέν, μεγάλη δ'
ἡ ἔμφασις, ἔστι γὰρ τοιόνδε τὸ δηλούμενον· εἴ τις
μηδὲν τῶν χειροποιήτων μηδ' ὅσα γενητὰ νομίζει
θεούς, ἀλλ' ἕνα τὸν ἡγεμόνα τῶν ὅλων, ἐμοὶ προσ-
169 ίτω.   τῶν μὲν οὖν ἄλλων οἱ μὲν ἕνεκα τοῦ τὸν
Αἰγυπτιακὸν ἐζηλωκέναι τῦφον ἀφηνιάζοντες οὐ
προσεῖχον τοῖς λεγομένοις, οἱ δὲ φόβῳ κολάσεως

god, who is no god, they offer worship and sacrifice, and have forgotten all the influences to piety which they have seen and heard." Struck with dismay, 166 and compelled to believe the incredible tale, he yet took the part of mediator and reconciler and did not hurry away at once, but first made prayers and supplications, begging that their sins might be forgiven. Then, when this protector and intercessor had softened the wrath of the Ruler, he wended his way back in mingled joy and dejection. He rejoiced that God accepted his prayers, yet was ready to burst with the dejection and heaviness that filled him at the transgression of the multitude.

XXXII. When he arrived at the middle of the camp, 167 and marvelled at the sudden apostasy of the multitude and their delusion, so strongly contrasting with the truth which they had bartered for it, he observed that the contagion had not extended to all and that there were still some sound at heart and cherishing a feeling of hatred of evil. Wishing, therefore, to distinguish the incurable from those who were displeased to see such actions and from any who had sinned but repented, he made a proclamation, a touchstone calculated to test exactly the bias of each to godliness or its opposite. " If 168 any is on the Lord's side," he said, " let him come to me." Few words, indeed, but fraught with much meaning, for the purport was as follows: "Whoso holds that none of the works of men's hands, nor any created things, are gods, but that there is one God only, the Ruler of the universe, let him join me." Of the rest, some, whom devotion to the vanity of 169 Egypt had made rebellious, paid no heed to his words, while others, possibly in fear of chastisement,

531

PHILO

ἴσως ἐγγυτέρω προσελθεῖν οὐκ ἐθάρρουν ἢ τὴν ἐκ
Μωυσέως τίσιν δεδιότες ἢ τὴν ἐκ τοῦ πλήθους
ἐπανάστασιν· ἀεὶ γὰρ οἱ πολλοὶ τοῖς μὴ συν-
170 αποονουμένοις ἐπιτίθενται. μία δ' ἐξ ἁπάντων ἡ
λεγομένη Λευϊτικὴ φυλὴ τοῦ κηρύγματος ἐπ-
ακούσασα καθάπερ ἀφ' ἑνὸς συνθήματος ἔθει μετὰ
σπουδῆς, τῇ ποδωκείᾳ τὴν προθυμίαν ἐπιδεικνυμένη
[161] καὶ τὴν ὀξύτητα τῆς εἰς εὐσέβειαν ψυχικῆς | ὁρμῆς.
171 οὓς ἰδὼν Μωυσῆς ὥσπερ ἀπὸ βαλβῖδος ἁμιλλω-
μένους " εἰ μὴ μόνον τοῖς σώμασιν " εἶπεν " ἐπι-
σπεύδετε τὴν πρὸς ἡμᾶς ἄφιξιν ἀλλὰ καὶ ταῖς
διανοίαις, αὐτίκα μαρτυρηθήσεται· ξίφος ἀναλαβὼν
ἕκαστος τοὺς μυρίων ἄξια θανάτων εἰργασμένους,
οἳ τὸν ἀληθῆ θεὸν καταλιπόντες τοὺς ψευδωνύμους
ἐδημιούργησαν φθαρταῖς καὶ γενηταῖς οὐσίαις τὴν
τοῦ ἀφθάρτου καὶ ἀγενήτου πρόσρησιν ἐπιφημί-
σαντες, συγγενεῖς καὶ φίλους ἀποκτεινάτω φιλίαν
καὶ συγγένειαν ὑπολαβὼν εἶναι μόνην ἀνδρῶν
172 ἀγαθῶν ὁσιότητα." οἱ δὲ τὴν παραίνεσιν ἑτοι-
μότητι φθάσαντες, ἐπεὶ καὶ τὰς γνώμας ἔτυχον
ἠλλοτριωμένοι σχεδὸν ἀφ' οὗ τὸ παρανόμημα
γενόμενον εἶδον, ἀναιροῦσιν ἡβηδὸν εἰς τρισχιλίους
τῶν πρὸ μικροῦ φιλτάτων. κειμένων δ' ἐν ἀγορᾷ
μέσῃ τῶν σωμάτων, ἡ πληθὺς θεασαμένη τοὺς
μὲν ᾠκτίσατο, τὸ δὲ τῶν κτεινόντων ἔνθερμον ἔτι
καὶ μεστὸν ὀργῆς παράστημα καταδείσασα φόβῳ
173 νουθετεῖται. Μωυσῆς δὲ τὴν ἀριστείαν ἀποδεξάμενος γέρας ἐπενόησε καὶ ἐβεβαίωσε τῇ πράξει

had not the courage to take their place beside him, either because they feared the vengeance they might suffer at the hand of Moses or the onslaught of an insurgent mob. For the multitude always set upon those who refuse to share their madness. Among 170 them all one tribe alone, known as Levites, when they heard the proclamation, came running with all speed, like troops for whom one signal is enough, shewing by their swiftness their zeal and the keenness of the inward feelings which urged them to piety. Moses saw them coming like racers from 171 the starting-point, and cried : " Whether the speed which has brought you here exists not only in your bodies but in your minds shall at once be put to the proof. Take each of you his sword, and slay those whose deeds deserve a thousand deaths, who have left the true God, and wrought gods, falsely so called, from corruptible and created matter, and given them a title which belongs to the Incorruptible and Uncreated. Yea, slay them, though they be kinsmen and friends, believing that between the good there is no kinship and friendship but godliness." Their readiness anticipated his exhorta- 172 tions, for their sentiments had been hostile to the offenders almost from the first moment that they saw their misconduct, and they made a wholesale slaughter to the number of three thousand of those who but now had been their dearest. As their corpses lay in the middle of the market-place, the multitude as they gazed felt pity for them, but, terror-struck at the still heated and wrathful resolution of the slayers, learned wisdom from fear. But 173 Moses, in approval of this heroism, devised and confirmed a reward for the victors well suited to the

τὸ οἰκεῖον· ἔδει γὰρ τοὺς ὑπὲρ θεοῦ τιμῆς ἑκούσιον
πόλεμον ἀραμένους καὶ βραχεῖ καιρῷ κατωρθω-
κότας ἀξιωθῆναι τῆς θεραπείας αὐτοῦ λαχόντας
ἱερωσύνην.

174 XXXIII. Ἐπεὶ δ' οὐ μία τάξις τῶν ἱερωμένων,
ἀλλ' οἷς μὲν ἐπιτέτραπται τὰ περὶ τὰς εὐχὰς καὶ
θυσίας καὶ τὰς ἄλλας ἱερουργίας ἄχρι τῶν ἀδύτων
ἰοῦσιν, οἷς δὲ τούτων μὲν οὐδέν, ἐπιμέλειαι δὲ καὶ
φυλακαὶ μεθ' ἡμέραν καὶ νύκτωρ τοῦ τε ἱεροῦ
καὶ τῶν ἐν αὐτῷ, οὓς νεωκόρους ἔνιοι καλοῦσιν,
ἡ πολλοῖς πολλαχοῦ μυρίων αἰτία κακῶν γενομένη
περὶ πρωτείων στάσις ἐπεπόλασε κἀνταῦθα, τῶν
νεωκόρων ἐπιθεμένων τοῖς ἱερεῦσι καὶ τὴν ἐκείνων
τιμὴν παρασπάσασθαι διανοηθέντων· καὶ τοῦτ' εὐμαρῶς ἤλπισαν ἔσεσθαι πολλαπλασίους τὸν ἀρι-
175 θμὸν ὄντες. ὑπὲρ δὲ τοῦ μὴ δοκεῖν ἰδίᾳ γνώμῃ
νεωτερίζειν καὶ τὴν πρεσβυτάτην τῶν δώδεκα
φυλῶν συμφρονεῖν ἀναπείθουσιν, ᾗ πολλοὶ τῶν
εἰκαιοτέρων ἐπηκολούθησαν ὡς ἔχειν δυναμένῃ
176 πρεσβεῖον ἡγεμονίας. μέγαν τοῦτον ἐπιτειχισμὸν
ἔγνω Μωυσῆς φυόμενον καθ' αὑτοῦ· τὸν γὰρ
ἀδελφὸν ἀρχιερέα κατὰ τὰ χρησθέντα λόγια ᾕρητο,
διαβολαὶ δ' ἦσαν ὡς τοὺς μὲν χρησμοὺς ἐπιψευσαμένου, ποιησαμένου δὲ τὴν αἵρεσιν διὰ τὴν
177 οἰκειότητα καὶ τὴν πρὸς τὸν ἀδελφὸν εὔνοιαν. ἐφ'
οἷς εἰκότως ἀνιαθείς, εἰ μὴ μόνον ἀπιστεῖται διὰ
τοσούτων ἐλέγχων τὴν ἑαυτοῦ πίστιν ἐπιδειξάμε-
[162] νος, ἀλλὰ καὶ ἐπ' | ἔργοις ἅπερ ἀναφέρεται πρὸς

ᵃ For §§ 174-179 see Num. xvi. 1-3 and xvii.

534

deed. For it was right that those who had voluntarily taken up arms for the honour of God, and so
quickly achieved success, should receive the priesthood, and thus be worthily promoted to be His
ministers.

XXXIII. *a* Now the consecrated persons consisted 174
of more than one order. They included both those who
were commissioned to penetrate to the inner shrine
and offer the prayers and sacrifices and the other holy
rites, and those sometimes called temple attendants
who had none of these duties but had the care and
guarding of the sacred building and its contents by day
and night. Consequently, the strife for precedence,
the cause of innumerable troubles to many persons
and in many places, gained ground here also. The
temple attendants made headway against the priests,
and purposed to wrest their privileges from them,
and they hoped to accomplish this easily, since they
were many times the number of the others. To pre- 175
vent this sedition appearing to be their own particular
project, they persuaded the senior tribe of the twelve
to make common cause with them, and this tribe had
many adherents among the more thoughtless, who
supposed it capable of taking the supremacy as its
birthright. Moses recognized in this the rise of a 176
grave attack upon himself, for he had chosen his
brother as high priest in accordance with the oracles
vouchsafed to him. But there were spiteful rumours
that he had falsely invented the oracles, and had made
his choice through family feeling and affection for
his brother. He was naturally pained at this, not 177
merely that he was distrusted when he had shewn his
good faith by so many proofs, but that this distrust
extended to actions which concerned the honouring

θεοῦ τιμήν, δι' ἃ μόνα καὶ τὸν ἐν τοῖς ἄλλοις
τὸ ἦθος κατεψευσμένον ἀναγκαῖον ἦν ἀληθεύειν—
ἀλήθεια γὰρ ὀπαδὸς θεοῦ—, λόγοις μὲν ἀναδιδά-
σκειν περὶ τῆς ἑαυτοῦ προαιρέσεως οὐκ ἐδοκίμαζε,
τὸ μεταπείθειν ἐπιχειρεῖν τοὺς προκαταληφθέντας
ἐναντίαις δόξαις ἀργαλέον εἰδώς, ἱκετεύει δὲ τὸν
θεὸν ἐμφανεῖς ἀποδείξεις αὐτοῖς παρασχεῖν περὶ
τοῦ μηδὲν ἐψεῦσθαι κατὰ τὴν τῆς ἱερωσύνης αἵρεσιν.
178 ὁ δὲ κελεύει δώδεκα ῥάβδους λαβεῖν ταῖς φυλαῖς
ἰσαρίθμους καὶ τὰ μὲν τῶν ἄλλων ὀνόματα φυλάρχων ἐπιγράψαι ταῖς ἔνδεκα, τῇ δὲ λοιπῇ τὸ τοῦ
ἀδελφοῦ καὶ ἀρχιερέως, εἶτ' εἰς τὸν νεὼν ἄχρι τῶν
ἀδύτων εἰσενεγκεῖν· ὁ δὲ τὰ προσταχθέντα ποιήσας
179 ἐκαραδόκει τὸ ἀποβησόμενον. τῇ δ' ὑστεραίᾳ
λογίῳ πληχθείς, ἅπαντος τοῦ ἔθνους παρεστῶτος,
εἰσέρχεται καὶ τὰς ῥάβδους ἐκκομίζει, τὰς μὲν
ἄλλας οὐδὲν διάφορον ἐχούσας, μίαν δ' ἐφ' ᾗ
τοὔνομα ἐπεγέγραπτο τοῦ ἀδελφοῦ τεθαυματουργη-
μένην· οἷα γὰρ φυτὸν εὐγενὲς ἅπασα νέους βλαστοὺς
ἐξέφυσε καὶ ὑπ' εὐφορίας καρπῶν ἔβριθεν.
180 XXXIV. οἱ δὲ καρποὶ κάρυα ἦσαν, ἃ φύσιν
ἐναντίαν ἔχει τοῖς ἄλλοις· ἐπὶ γὰρ τῶν πλείστων,
σταφυλῆς, ἐλαίας, μήλων, διαφέρει τὸ σπέρμα καὶ
τὸ ἐδώδιμον, ἃ διαφέροντα τόποις χωρίζεται· τὸ
μὲν γὰρ ἐδώδιμον ἔξω, τὸ δὲ σπέρμα εἴσω κατα-
κέκλεισται· τοῦ δὲ καρύου ταὐτόν ἐστι τό τε σπέρμα
καὶ τὸ ἐδώδιμον, ἀμφοτέρων εἰς μίαν ἰδέαν ἀποκριθέντων, καὶ τόπος εἷς ὁ ἐντὸς ὠχυρωμένος καὶ
περιπεφρουρημένος ἕρκει διπλῷ, τῷ μὲν ἐκ φλοιοῦ
πάνυ βαθέος, τῷ δ' οὐδὲν ἀποδέοντι ξυλίνου κατα-

of God, actions which by themselves would necessarily ensure truthfulness even in one whose character was false in everything else, for truth is God's attendant. But he did not think good to use words to explain to them his motives, knowing that it is vain labour to try to change the convictions of those of whom the opposite opinions have already taken hold, but besought God to shew them by clear demonstration that there had been no dishonesty in his choice of persons for the priesthood. God commanded him 178 to take twelve rods, corresponding to the number of the tribes, and on eleven of them to inscribe the names of the other patriarchs, but on the twelfth that of his brother who was also high priest, and then to take them into the temple, right into the inner sanctuary. Moses did as he was bidden, and eagerly awaited the result. On the next day, under the impulse of a 179 divine intimation, with all the people standing near, he went in and brought out the rods. The others shewed no difference, but the one on which was inscribed the name of his brother had undergone a wonderful change. Like a goodly plant, it had young sprouts growing all over it, and was laden with abundance of fruits. XXXIV. Now, the fruits were 180 nuts, which in nature are the opposite of other fruits, for in most cases, the grape, the olive, the apple, there is a difference between the seed and the eatable part, and this difference extends to their situation, which is separate, for the edible part is outside, and the seed enclosed within. But, in the nut, seed and edible part are identical, merged in a single form, and their situation is the same inside, shielded and guarded on all sides by a double fence, composed partly of very thick shell and partly of a substance equivalent to a

181 σκευάσματος· ἀφ' οὗ τελείαν ἀρετὴν αἰνίττεται. ὥσπερ γὰρ ἐν καρύῳ ταὐτόν ἐστιν ἀρχὴ καὶ τέλος,
ἀρχὴ μὲν ᾖ σπέρμα, τέλος δὲ ᾖ καρπός, οὕτως ἔχει
καὶ ἐπὶ τῶν ἀρετῶν· ἑκάστῃ γὰρ συμβέβηκεν εἶναι
καὶ ἀρχὴν καὶ τέλος, ἀρχὴν μέν, ὅτι οὐκ ἐξ ἑτέρας
δυνάμεως ἀλλ' ἐξ ἑαυτῆς φύεται, τέλος δέ, ὅτι
πρὸς αὐτὴν ὁ κατὰ φύσιν βίος σπεύδει.

182 μία μὲν αἰτία ἥδε, λέγεται δὲ καὶ ἑτέρα τῆς προτέρας ἐμφαντικωτέρα· καρύου τὸ μὲν φλοιῶδές ἐστι
πικρόν, τὸ δ' εἴσω περικείμενον ὡσανεὶ ξύλινον
ἕρκος στιφρὸν εὖ μάλα καὶ κραταιόν, οἷς ἀμφοτέροις
ὁ καρπὸς ἐγκατακεκλεισμένος οὐκ ἔστιν εὔληπτος.

183 τοῦτο ποιεῖται σύμβολον ἀσκητικῆς ψυχῆς, ἀφ' οὗ
προτρέπειν αὐτὴν οἴεται δεῖν ἐπ' ἀρετὴν ἀναδιδά-
σκων, ὅτι πόνῳ προεντυχεῖν ἀναγκαῖον· πικρὸν δὲ
καὶ ἀντιτυπὲς καὶ σκληρὸν ὁ πόνος, ἐξ οὗ φύεται
184 τἀγαθόν, οὗ χάριν οὐ μαλακιστέον. ὁ | μὲν γὰρ
[163] τὸν πόνον φεύγων φεύγει καὶ τὰ ἀγαθά, ὁ δὲ
τλητικῶς καὶ ἀνδρείως ὑπομένων τὰ δυσκαρτέρητα
σπεύδει πρὸς μακαριότητα· οὐ γὰρ ἁβροδιαίτοις
καὶ τὴν ψυχὴν ἐκτεθηλυμμένοις καὶ τὸ σῶμα διαρ-
ρέουσιν ὑπὸ τῆς καθ' ἑκάστην ἡμέραν ἀδιαστάτου
θρύψεως ἀρετὴ πέφυκεν ἐνδιαιτᾶσθαι, κακουμένη
δὲ μετανίσταται πρότερον ἀπόλειψιν χρηματί-
185 σασα πρὸς τὸν ἄρχοντα τὸν ὀρθὸν λόγον.[a] ἀλλ' εἰ
δεῖ τἀληθὲς εἰπεῖν, ὁ φρονήσεως καὶ σωφροσύνης
ἀνδρείας τε καὶ δικαιοσύνης ἱερώτατος θίασος
ἀσκητὰς μετατρέχει καὶ ὅσοι τὸν αὐστηρὸν καὶ
σκληροδίαιτον βίον, ἐγκράτειαν καὶ καρτερίαν,

---

[a] Or "before right reason as Archon." See note on *De
Cher.* 115, where it is shewn that χρηματίζειν ἀπόλειψιν is a

538

wooden framework. In this way, it signifies perfect 181
virtue ; for, just as in a nut, beginning and end are
identical, beginning represented by seed and end by
fruit, so it is with the virtues. There, too, it is the
case that each is both a beginning and an end ; a
beginning in that it springs from no other power but
itself, an end in that it is the aspiration of the life
which follows nature.   This is one reason 182
why the nut is a type of virtue, but there is another
given which is even clearer than that. The shell-
formed part of the nut is bitter, and the inner layer
which surrounds the fruit like a wooden fence is exceedingly solid and hard ; and, as the fruit is enclosed
in both these, it is not easy to get at. In this Moses 183
finds the parable of the practising soul, which he
thinks he can rightly use to encourage that soul to
virtue and teach it that it must first encounter toil.
Toil is bitter and stiff and hard, yet from it springs
goodness, and therefore there must be no softening.
For he who flees from toil flees from the good also, 184
but he who patiently and manfully endures what is
hard to bear is pressing on to blessedness. For in
the voluptuous livers, whose souls are emasculated
and whose bodies run to waste with ceaseless luxury
prolonged from day to day, virtue cannot make its
lodging ; but it will first procure its divorce for mis-
usage in the court of right reason,[a] and then seek
another home. But in very truth that most holy 185
company, justice, temperance, courage, wisdom,
follow in the train of the practisers and all who devote
themselves to a life of austerity and hardship, that
is to continence and self-restraint, together with

regular phrase in Attic law, used of a wife who appeals to
the Archon for divorce or separation from her husband.

ζηλοῦσι σὺν εὐτελείᾳ καὶ ὀλιγοδείᾳ, δι' ὧν τὸ
κυριώτατον τῶν ἐν ἡμῖν, ὁ λογισμός, εἰς ὑγείαν
ἄνοσον καὶ εὐεξίαν ἐπιδίδωσι καθελὼν τὸν βαρὺν
τοῦ σώματος ἐπιτειχισμόν, ὃν οἰνοφλυγίαι καὶ
ὀψοφαγίαι καὶ λαγνεῖαι καὶ αἱ ἄλλαι ἀπλήρωτοι
ἐπιθυμίαι συνεκρότησαν γεννήσασαι τὴν ἀντίπαλον
186 ἀγχινοίας πολυσαρκίαν. λέγεται μέντοι καὶ τῶν
ἐν ἔαρι βλαστάνειν εἰωθότων δένδρων ἡ ἀμυγδαλῆ
καὶ πρῶτον ἀνθεῖν εὐαγγελιζομένη φορὰν ἀκροδρύων καὶ ὕστατον φυλλορροεῖν τὴν ἐπέτειον πρὸς
μήκιστον ἀποτείνουσα τῆς χλόης εὐγηρίαν· ὧν
ἑκάτερον ποιεῖται σύμβολον τῆς ἱερατικῆς φυλῆς,
αἰνιττόμενος ὅτι καὶ πρώτη καὶ ὑστάτη τοῦ
σύμπαντος ἀνθρώπων γένους ἀνθήσει, καθ' ὃν ἂν
χρόνον δόξῃ τῷ θεῷ ταῖς ἐαριναῖς τροπαῖς ἐξομοιῶσαι τὸν ἡμέτερον βίον ἀνελόντι τὴν ἐπίβουλον
καὶ τοῦ κακοδαιμονεῖν πηγὴν πλεονεξίαν.

187 XXXV. Ἐπειδὴ τοίνυν τῷ τελειοτάτῳ ἡγεμόνι
τέτταρα δεῖν ἔφαμεν προσεῖναι, βασιλείαν καὶ
νομοθετικὴν ἕξιν καὶ ἱερωσύνην καὶ προφητείαν,
ἵνα διὰ μὲν τῆς νομοθετικῆς προστάττῃ ἃ δεῖ καὶ
ἀπαγορεύῃ ἃ μὴ δεῖ πράττειν, διὰ δὲ τῆς ἱερωσύνης
μὴ μόνον τἀνθρώπεια ἀλλὰ καὶ τὰ θεῖα διέπῃ, διὰ
δὲ τῆς προφητείας ὅσα μὴ λογισμῷ καταλαμβάνεται θεσπίζῃ, διειλεγμένος περὶ τῶν πρώτων
τριῶν καὶ ἐπιδεδειχὼς Μωυσῆν ἄριστον βασιλέα

---

a The thought of this sentence seems confused. The
permanent triumph of Aaron's family over the lower Levites
assisted by Reuben was symbolized by the blossoming of the
most permanent of blossoms and so when the πλεονεξία
(" self-assertion ") of mankind as a whole is destroyed,
there will be a permanent blossoming. But of whom?
We expect of all mankind. Instead we have "the priestly

simplicity and frugal contentment. For by these the highest authority within us, reason, advances to sound health and well-being, and brings to nought the formidable menace to the body, engineered in many a scene of drunkenness and gluttony and lewdness and the other insatiable lusts, the parents of that grossness of flesh which is the enemy of quickness of mind. Further, they say, that of all the trees which 186 regularly bud in the spring the almond-tree is the first to blossom with a welcome promise of a plentiful crop of fruit, and the last to shed its leaves, year by year protracting the hale old age of its verdure to the longest span. Each of these facts he takes as a parable of the priestly tribe, intimating that it will be the first and last of all the human race to blossom, in that day, whenever it shall be, when it shall please God to make our life as a springtime by ridding it of covetousness, that insidious foe which is the source of our misery.[a]

XXXV. We said above that there are four adjuncts to the truly perfect ruler. He must have 187 kingship, the faculty of legislation, priesthood and prophecy, so that in his capacity of legislator he may command what should be done and forbid what should not be done, as priest dispose not only things human but things divine, as prophet declare by inspiration what cannot be apprehended by reason. I have discussed the first three, and shewn that Moses was the best of kings, of lawgivers and of

tribe." Is this to be taken literally, or does it stand for Israel, the nation of priests or even for the truly priestly soul? If we could insert ἡ εὐχὴ ὑπὲρ after ὑστάτη the thought would become clear. Philo often insists (e.g. De Spec. Leg. i. 97), that the prayers of the priests are for the whole human race.

PHILO

καὶ νομοθέτην καὶ ἀρχιερέα τὸ τελευταῖον ἔρχομαι
δηλώσων, ὅτι καὶ προφήτης γέγονε δοκιμώτατος.

188 οὐκ ἀγνοῶ μὲν οὖν, ὡς πάντ' εἰσὶ χρησμοί, ὅσα ἐν
ταῖς ἱεραῖς βίβλοις ἀναγέγραπται, χρησθέντες δι'
αὐτοῦ· λέξω δὲ τὰ ἰδιαίτερα, πρότερον εἰπὼν ἐκεῖνο·
τῶν λογίων τὰ μὲν ἐκ προσώπου τοῦ θεοῦ λέγεται
δι' ἑρμηνέως τοῦ θείου προφήτου, τὰ δ' ἐκ πεύσεως
καὶ ἀποκρίσεως ἐθεσπίσθη, τὰ δ' ἐκ προσώπου
Μωυσέως ἐπιθειάσαντος καὶ ἐξ αὐτοῦ κατασχε-

189 θέντος. τὰ μὲν οὖν πρῶτα ὅλα δι' ὅλων ἀρετῶν
[164] θείων δείγματά ἐστι, τῆς τε | ἵλεω καὶ εὐεργέτιδος,
δι' ὧν ἅπαντας μὲν ἀνθρώπους πρὸς καλοκἀγαθίαν
ἀλείφει, μάλιστα δὲ τὸ θεραπευτικὸν αὐτοῦ γένος,
ᾧ τὴν πρὸς εὐδαιμονίαν ἄγουσαν ἀνατέμνει ὁδόν·

190 τὰ δὲ δεύτερα μῖξιν ἔχει καὶ κοινωνίαν, πυνθανο-
μένου μὲν τοῦ προφήτου περὶ ὧν ἐπεζήτει, ἀπο-
κρινομένου δὲ τοῦ θεοῦ καὶ διδάσκοντος· τὰ δὲ
τρίτα ἀνατίθεται τῷ νομοθέτῃ, μεταδόντος αὐτῷ
τοῦ θεοῦ τῆς προγνωστικῆς δυνάμεως, ᾗ θεσπιεῖ

191 τὰ μέλλοντα. τὰ μὲν οὖν πρῶτα ὑπερθετέον, μείζω
γάρ ἐστιν ἢ ὡς ὑπ' ἀνθρώπου τινὸς ἐπαινεθῆναι,
μόλις ἂν ὑπ' οὐρανοῦ τε καὶ κόσμου καὶ τῆς τῶν
ὅλων φύσεως ἀξίως ἐγκωμιασθέντα, καὶ ἄλλως
λέγεται ὡσανεὶ δι' ἑρμηνέως· ἑρμηνεία δὲ καὶ
προφητεία διαφέρουσι. περὶ δὲ τῶν δευτέρων αὐτίκα πειράσομαι δηλοῦν συνυφήνας αὐτοῖς καὶ τὸ
τρίτον εἶδος, ἐν ᾧ τὸ τοῦ λέγοντος ἐνθουσιωδῶς
ἐμφαίνεται, καθ' ὃ μάλιστα καὶ κυρίως νενόμισται
προφήτης.

542

high priests, and will now go on to shew in conclusion that he was a prophet of the highest quality. Now I am fully aware that all things written in the 188 sacred books are oracles delivered through Moses ; but I will confine myself to those which are more especially his, with the following preliminary remarks. Of the divine utterances, some are spoken by God in His own Person with His prophet for interpreter, in some the revelation comes through question and answer, and others are spoken by Moses in his own person, when possessed by God and carried away out of himself. The first kind are 189 absolutely and entirely signs of the divine excellences, graciousness and beneficence, by which He incites all men to noble conduct, and particularly the nation of His worshippers, for whom He opens up the road which leads to happiness. In the second 190 kind we find combination and partnership : the prophet asks questions of God about matters on which he has been seeking knowledge, and God replies and instructs him. The third kind are assigned to the lawgiver himself : God has given to him of His own power of foreknowledge and by this he will reveal future events. Now, the first kind must be 191 left out of the discussion. They are too great to be lauded by human lips ; scarcely indeed could heaven and the world and the whole existing universe worthily sing their praises. Besides, they are delivered through an interpreter, and interpretation and prophecy are not the same thing. The second kind I will at once proceed to describe, interweaving with it the third kind, in which the speaker appears under that divine possession in virtue of which he is chiefly and in the strict sense considered a prophet.

192 XXXVI. Τῆς δ' ὑποσχέσεως ἀρκτέον ὧδε.
τέτταρές εἰσι τόποι διὰ πεύσεως καὶ ἀποκρίσεως
χρησμοῖς νομοθετηθέντες, μικτὴν ἔχοντες δύναμιν·
τῇ μὲν γὰρ ὁ προφήτης ἐνθουσιᾷ πυνθανόμενος,
τῇ δὲ ὁ πατὴρ θεσπίζει λόγου καὶ ἀποκρίσεως
μεταδιδούς. ἔστι δὲ πρῶτος, ὃς οὐχ ὅτι Μωυσῆν ὁσιώτατον τῶν πώποτε γενομένων ἀλλὰ καὶ
193 τὸν ἐπὶ βραχὺ γευσάμενον εὐσεβείας ὤργισεν.[1] ἐξ
ἀνομοίων τις γενόμενος ἄνθρωπος νόθος, Αἰγυπτίου
μὲν πατρός, μητρὸς δὲ Ἰουδαίας, τῶν μὲν ταύτης
πατρίων ἐθῶν ἠλόγησε, πρὸς δὲ τὴν Αἰγυπτιακήν,
ὡς λόγος, ἀπέκλινεν ἀσέβειαν τὴν τῶν ἀνδρῶν
194 ζηλώσας ἀθεότητα. μόνοι γὰρ σχεδὸν ἁπάντων
ἐθνῶν Αἰγύπτιοι γῆν ἐπετείχισαν οὐρανῷ, τὴν μὲν
ἰσοθέων τιμῶν ἀξιώσαντες, τῷ δ' οὐδὲν γέρας ἐξαίρετον ἀπονείμαντες, ὡς δέον πρὸ τῶν βασιλείων
τὰς ἐσχατιὰς περιέπειν—ἐν γὰρ κόσμῳ βασίλειον
μὲν ἱερώτατον οὐρανός, ἐσχατιὰ δὲ γῆ, καθ' ἑαυτὴν
μὲν ἀξιοσπούδαστος, εἰς δὲ σύγκρισιν ἰοῦσα αἰθέρος
ἀπολειπομένη τοσοῦτον ὅσον σκότος μὲν φωτός,
νὺξ δὲ ἡμέρας, φθορὰ δ' ἀφθαρσίας καὶ θνητὸς
195 θεοῦ—. τῆς γὰρ χώρας οὐχ ὑετῷ καθάπερ αἱ ἄλλαι
νιφομένης, ἀλλὰ ταῖς τοῦ ποταμοῦ πλημμύραις
εἰωθυίας ἀνὰ πᾶν ἔτος λιμνάζεσθαι, θεοπλαστοῦσι
τῷ λόγῳ τὸν Νεῖλον Αἰγύπτιοι ὡς ἀντίμιμον οὐ-

---

[1] ? ὤργισ' ἄν.

---

[a] Literally "giving him a share of speech and answer."
[b] For §§ 193-208 see Lev. xxiv. 10-16.
[c] Cf. De Fuga 180.

XXXVI. In fulfilment of my promise, I must 192
begin with the following examples. There are four
cases upon which the divine voice laid down the
law in the form of question and answer and which
therefore have a mixed character ; for, on the one
hand, the prophet asks a question under divine possession, and on the other hand the Father, in giving
the word of revelation, answers him and talks with
him as with a partner.[a] The first case is one which
would have enraged not only Moses, the holiest of
men ever yet born, but even one who knew but a little
of the flavour of godliness. [b] A certain base-born 193
man, the child of an unequal marriage, his father an
Egyptian, his mother a Jewess, had set at naught
the ancestral customs of his mother and turned aside,
as we are told, to the impiety of Egypt and embraced
the atheism of that people. For the Egyptians 194
almost alone among the nations have set up earth
as a power to challenge heaven.[c] Earth they held
to be worthy of the honours due to a god, and refused to render to heaven any special tribute of
reverence, acting as though it were right to shew
respect to the outermost regions rather than to the
royal palace. For in the universe heaven is a palace
of the highest sanctity, and earth is the outer region,
estimable indeed in itself, but when it comes into comparison with ether, as far inferior to it as darkness is to
light and night to day and corruption to incorruption
and mortal man to God. The Egyptians thought 195
otherwise ; for, since the land is not watered like other
countries by the downpour of rain but regularly every
year becomes a standing water through the flooding of
the river, they speak of the Nile as though it were
the counterpart of heaven and therefore to be deified,

545

ρανοῦ γεγονότα καὶ περὶ τῆς χώρας σεμνηγο-
196 ροῦσιν. XXXVII. ὁ δὴ μικτὸς οὗτος ἐκεῖνος
διενεχθείς τινι τῶν ἀπὸ τοῦ ὁρατικοῦ καὶ ἐπιστη-
μονικοῦ γένους, ἀκράτωρ ὑπ' ὀργῆς αὐτὸς αὑτοῦ
γενόμενος καὶ ἅμα τῆς Αἰγυπτιακῆς ἀθεότητος
ζηλωτὴς ὤν, ἀπὸ γῆς εἰς οὐρανὸν ἔτεινε τὴν ἀ-
[165] σέβειαν | ἐπαράτῳ καὶ ἐναγεῖ καὶ μεμιασμένῃ ψυχῇ
τε καὶ γλώττῃ καὶ πάσῃ τῇ φωνῆς ὀργανοποιίᾳ
καταρασάμενος δι' ὑπερβολὴν κακιῶν[1] ὃν οὐδ' ὑπὸ
πάντων ἀλλὰ μόνων τῶν ἀρίστων εὐλογεῖσθαι
197 θέμις, ὅσοι τὰς τελείας καθάρσεις ἐδέξαντο. διὸ
καὶ θαυμάσας τὴν φρενοβλάβειαν καὶ τὴν τοῦ
θράσους ὑπερβολήν, καίτοι γ' ὑπόπλεως ὢν παραστήματος εὐγενοῦς καὶ ἱέμενος αὐτοχειρίᾳ διαρτῆ-
σαι τὸν ἄνθρωπον, ἔδεισε μὴ κουφοτέραν ἀναπράξῃ
τιμωρίαν· ἰσόρροπον γὰρ ἐπινοῆσαι πρὸς τοσαύτην
198 ἀσέβειαν κόλασιν ἄνθρωπος οὐκ ἂν ἴσχυσεν. ἐπεὶ
δὲ καὶ τῷ μὴ σέβειν[2] θεὸν ἕπεται τὸ μήτε γονεῖς
μήτε πατρίδα μήτ' εὐεργέτας τιμᾶν, ὁ δὲ δὴ
πρὸς τῷ μὴ σέβειν καὶ κακηγορεῖν τολμῶν τίνα
μοχθηρίας ὑπερβολὴν ἀπολέλοιπε· καίτοι καὶ
τὸ κακηγορεῖν ἧττον ἐν συγκρίσει κατάρας· ἀλλὰ
γλωσσαλγία καὶ ἀχάλινον στόμα ὅταν ἐκνόμοις
ἀφροσύναις ὑπηρετῶσι, πάντως τι καινουργεῖται
199 τῶν ἀθέσμων. ὦ ἄνθρωπε, καταρᾶταί τις θεόν;
τίνα καλῶν ἕτερον θεὸν εἰς τὴν τῆς ἀρᾶς βεβαίωσιν; ἢ δῆλον ὅτι αὐτὸν κατ' αὑτοῦ; ἄπαγε βεβήλων καὶ ἀνοσίων ἐνθυμημάτων. καλὸν ἐκνίψασθαι
τὴν ἀθλίαν ψυχὴν ἐπηρεασθεῖσαν μὲν ὑπὸ φωνῆς,
διακόνοις δὲ τοῖς ὠσὶ χρησαμένην, αἰσθήσει τυφλῇ.

---

[1] MSS. κακῶν.   [2] MSS. σέβοντι.

and talk about the land in terms of high reverence. XXXVII. And, lo, this half-bred person, 196 having a quarrel with someone of the nation that has vision and knowledge, losing in his anger all control over himself, and also urged by fondness for Egyptian atheism, extended his impiety from earth to heaven, and with his soul and tongue and all the organism of speech alike accursed, foul, abominable, in the superabundance of his manifold wickedness cursed Him, Whom even to bless is a privilege not permitted to all but only to the best, even those who have received full and complete purification. Whereupon Moses, astonished at his madness and 197 the superabundance of his audacity, though the spirit of noble indignation was strong within him and he would fain have cut him off with his own hand, feared lest he might exact too light a penalty ; for to devise an adequate punishment for such impiety was beyond human powers. Refusal to reverence 198 God implies refusal to honour parents and country and benefactors. And, if so, what depths of depravity remain for him to reach who besides refusing reverence dares also to revile Him ? And yet even reviling is a lesser sin compared with cursing. But, when an idle tongue and an unbridled mouth put themselves at the service of lawless follies, some monstrous violation of the moral law is sure to be committed. Answer me, thou man, Does anyone 199 curse God ? Then what other god does he call on to make good the curse, or is it clear that he invokes the help of God against Himself ? Avaunt such profane and unholy thoughts ! Well may the unhappy soul purge itself, which through the ministry of that purblind sense, the ears, has been outraged

200 καὶ οὔτε ἡ γλῶττα τοῦ τοσοῦτον ἀσέβημα φθεγξα-
μένου παρείθη οὔτε τὰ τοῦ μέλλοντος ἀκούειν ὦτα
ἐπεφράχθη; εἰ μὴ ἄρα κατὰ πρόνοιαν τῆς δίκης,
ἥτις οὔτ' ἀγαθὸν ὑπερβάλλον οὔτε μέγιστον κακὸν
οἴεται δεῖν ἐπισκιάζεσθαι, πρὸς ἔλεγχον ἐναργέστατον ἀρετῆς ἢ κακίας, ἵνα τὴν μὲν ἀποδοχῆς τὴν
201 δὲ τιμωρίας ἀξιώσῃ. διὰ τοῦτο τὸν μὲν εἰς εἱρκτὴν
ἀπαχθέντα κελεύει δεθῆναι, ποτνιᾶται δὲ τὸν θεὸν
ἱλασάμενος ταῖς ἀνάγκαις τῶν αἰσθήσεων, δι' ὧν
καὶ βλέπομεν ἃ μὴ θέμις ὁρᾶν καὶ ἀκούομεν ὧν
μὴ θέμις ἀκούειν, ὅ τι χρὴ παθεῖν τὸν εὑρετὴν
ἀσεβήματος καὶ ἀνοσιουργήματος ἐκτόπου καὶ
202 ξένου δηλῶσαι. ὁ δὲ προστάττει καταλευσθῆναι,
προσήκουσαν οἶμαι δίκην ὑπολαβὼν τὴν διὰ λίθων
κατ' ἀνδρὸς λιθίνην καὶ ἀπόκροτον ψυχὴν ἔχοντος
καὶ ἅμα βουλόμενος πάντας τοὺς ἀπὸ τοῦ ἔθνους
συνεφάψασθαι τῆς κολάσεως, οὓς ᾔδει σφόδρα τρα-
χέως ἐνεγκόντας καὶ φονῶντας· μόνης δ' ὡς ἔοικε
τῆς διὰ βλημάτων ἔμελλον αἱ τοσαῦται μυριάδες
ἐφάπτεσθαι.

203 Μετὰ δὲ τὴν τοῦ ἀνοσίου καὶ παλαμναίου τίσιν
ἐγράφη διάταγμα καινόν, οὐκ ἄν ποτε προ-
ηγουμένης ἀξιωθὲν γραφῆς, ἀλλ' αἱ ἀπροσδόκητοι
[166] νεωτεροποιίαι καινοὺς νόμους εἰς ἀνακοπὴν | ἁμαρ-
τημάτων ἐπιζητοῦσιν. αὐτίκα γοῦν νομοθετεῖται
τάδε· ὃς ἂν καταράσηται θεόν, ἁμαρτίας ἔνοχος

ᵃ Or "immediately," as Mangey and others take it. But
the use of αὐτίκα = "for example" is common enough and

548

by listening to such words. And was not the tongue 200
of him who uttered such a blasphemy paralysed?
and the ears of him who was to hear it blocked?
Surely they would have been, were it not otherwise
provided by justice, who holds that over nothing
which is extremely good or exceedingly bad should
a veil be thrown, but would have them submitted
to the clearest test of their goodness or badness, that
it may award approval to the one and punishment to
the other. Moses, therefore, ordered the man to be 201
haled to prison and put in chains, and implored God,
to Whose mercy he appealed, pleading the enforce-
ment of the senses by which we see what by rights
we should not see and hear what we should not
hear, to shew what should be done to the author of
this impious and unholy crime, so monstrous and
unheard-of. God commanded that he should be 202
stoned, holding, I suppose, that stoning was the
fitting punishment for a man of a hard and stony soul,
and also desiring that the work of vengeance should
be shared by all the people, who, as He knew, were
deeply indignant and desired the death of the
offender. And execution by missiles appeared to
be the only mode in which so many thousands could
take part.

When this impious malefactor had paid the penalty, 203
a new ordinance was drawn up. Previous to this, no
such enactment would have seemed to be required.
But unexpected disorders demand new laws as a
check to offences. And so on this occasion[a] the
following law was promulgated: Whoever curses
god, let him bear the guilt of his sin, but he that

fits in well with the general statement in the preceding
sentence.

ἔστω, ὃς δ' ἂν ὀνομάσῃ τὸ ὄνομα κυρίου, θνησκέτω.

204 εὖ γ', ὦ πάνσοφε, μόνος ἀμιγοῦς ἠκρατίσω σοφίας·
τοῦ καταρᾶσθαι χεῖρον τὸ ὀνομάζειν ὑπείληφας·[1]
οὐ γὰρ ἂν τὸν μὲν βαρύτατον ἀσέβημα εἰργασμένον
ἐπεκούφιζες διημαρτηκόσιν ἐπιεικέστερον συν-
τάττων, κατὰ δὲ τοῦ βραχύτερον ἠδικηκέναι
δόξαντος τὴν ἀνωτάτω τιμωρίαν, θάνατον, ὥριζες.

205 XXXVIII. ἀλλ' ὡς ἔοικε " θεοῦ " τὰ νῦν οὐχὶ
τοῦ πρώτου καὶ γεννητοῦ τῶν ὅλων ἀλλὰ τῶν ἐν
ταῖς πόλεσι μέμνηται· ψευδώνυμοι δ' εἰσὶ γραφέων
καὶ πλαστῶν τέχναις δημιουργούμενοι· ξοάνων γὰρ
καὶ ἀγαλμάτων καὶ τοιουτοτρόπων ἀφιδρυμάτων
ἡ οἰκουμένη μεστὴ γέγονεν, ὧν τῆς βλασφημίας
ἀνέχειν ἀναγκαῖον, ἵνα μηδεὶς ἐθίζηται τῶν Μωυσέως γνωρίμων συνόλως θεοῦ προσρήσεως ἀλογεῖν·

206 ἀξιονικοτάτη γὰρ καὶ ἀξιέραστος ἡ κλῆσις. εἰ δέ
τις οὐ λέγω βλασφημήσειεν εἰς τὸν ἀνθρώπων καὶ
θεῶν κύριον, ἀλλὰ καὶ τολμήσειεν ἀκαίρως αὐτοῦ
φθέγξασθαι τοὔνομα, θάνατον ὑπομεινάτω τὴν δί-

207 κην. οὐδὲ γὰρ τῶν φυτευσάντων καίτοι θνητῶν
ὑπαρχόντων οἷς μέλει γονέων τιμῆς τὰ ὀνόματα
προφέρουσιν, ἀλλὰ τὰ κύρια διὰ τὸν ἐπ' αὐτοῖς
σεβασμὸν ἡσυχάζοντες τοῖς τῆς φύσεως ἀνακαλοῦσι
πατέρα καὶ μητέρα προσαγορεύοντες, δι' ὧν εὐθὺς
αἰνίττονται τὰς ἐξ ἐκείνων ἀνυπερβλήτους εὐερ-

---

[1] Cohn puts a note of interrogation here, which I do not
understand. Better perhaps, as two mss., ὑπειληφώς.

---

[a] So lxx Lev. xxiv. 15, 16. E.V. " Whosoever curseth his

nameth the name of the Lord let him die.[a] Well 204
hast thou said, thou wisest of men, who alone hast
drunk deep of the untempered wine of wisdom.
Thou hast held the naming to be worse than the
cursing, for thou couldst not be treating lightly one
guilty of the gravest impiety and ranking him with
the milder offenders while thou didst decree the
extreme penalty of death to one who was judged to
have committed the lesser iniquity. XXXVIII. No, 205
clearly by " god," he is not here alluding to the
Primal God, the Begetter of the Universe, but to
the gods of the different cities who are falsely so
called, being fashioned by the skill of painters and
sculptors. For the world as we know it is full of
idols of wood and stone, and suchlike images. We
must refrain from speaking insultingly of these, lest
any of Moses' disciples get into the habit of treating
lightly the name " god " in general, for it is a title
worthy of the highest respect and love. But if any- 206
one, I will not say blasphemes the Lord of gods and
men, but even ventures to utter His Name un-
seasonably, let him suffer the penalty of death. For, 207
even in the case of our own parents, though they
are but mortals, all who have regard for the honour
due to parentage abstain from using their personal
names, and, leaving these unsaid, call them instead
by the terms of natural relationship—father and
mother—and their so addressing them is seen at once
to be an indirect acknowledgement of unsurpassed
benefits conferred by them and an expression of

God shall bear his sin. And he that blasphemeth the name
of the Lord shall surely be put to death." Philo's explanation is repeated by Josephus, *Ant.* iv. 207, *Ap.* ii. 237,
with reference to Ex. xxii. 28, "Thou shalt not revile God,"
where the LXX has θεούς.

PHILO

208 γεσίας καὶ τὴν αὐτῶν εὐχάριστον διάθεσιν. ἔτι νῦν[1]
συγγνώμης ἀξιούσθωσαν οἱ κατ᾽ ἐπισυρμὸν γλώττης
ἀκαιρευόμενοι καὶ λόγων ἀναπλήρωμα ποιούμενοι
τὸ ἁγιώτατον καὶ θεῖον ὄνομα.

209 XXXIX. Μετὰ δὲ τὴν τοῦ γεννητοῦ τῶν ὅλων
τιμὴν τὴν ἱερὰν ἑβδόμην ἐσέμνυνεν ὁ προφήτης
ἰδὼν αὐτῆς ὀξυωπεστέροις ὄμμασι κάλλος ἐξαίσιον
ἐνεσφραγισμένον οὐρανῷ τε καὶ τῷ σύμπαντι
κόσμῳ καὶ ὑπὸ τῆς φύσεως αὐτῆς ἀγαλματοφορού-
210 μενον. εὕρισκε γὰρ αὐτὴν τὸ μὲν πρῶτον ἀμήτορα,
γενεᾶς τῆς θήλεος ἀμέτοχον, ἐκ μόνου πατρὸς
σπαρεῖσαν ἄνευ σπορᾶς καὶ γεννηθεῖσαν ἄνευ
κυήσεως· ἔπειτα δ᾽ οὐ ταῦτα μόνον κατεῖδεν, ὅτι
παγκάλη καὶ ἀμήτωρ, ἀλλ᾽ ὅτι καὶ ἀειπάρθενος,
[167] οὔτ᾽ ἐκ μητρὸς οὔτε μήτηρ οὔτ᾽ ἐκ | φθορᾶς οὔτε
φθαρησομένη· εἶτ᾽ ἐκ τρίτου κατενόησεν αὐτὴν ἐξετάζων καὶ κόσμου γενέθλιον, ἣν ἑορτάζει μὲν
οὐρανός, ἑορτάζει δὲ γῆ καὶ τὰ ἐν γῇ γανύμενα καὶ
211 ἐνευφραινόμενα τῇ παναρμονίῳ ἑβδομάδι. ταύτης
ἕνεκα τῆς αἰτίας ὁ πάντα μέγας Μωυσῆς ἐδικαίωσε
τοὺς ἐγγραφέντας αὐτοῦ τῇ ἱερᾷ πολιτείᾳ θεσμοῖς
φύσεως ἑπομένους πανηγυρίζειν, ἐν ἱλαραῖς δι-
άγοντας εὐθυμίαις, ἀνέχοντας μὲν ἔργων καὶ τεχνῶν
τῶν εἰς πορισμὸν καὶ πραγματειῶν ὅσαι κατὰ βίου
ζήτησιν, ἄγοντας δ᾽ ἐκεχειρίαν καὶ διαφειμένους
πάσης ἐπιπόνου καὶ καματηρᾶς φροντίδος, σχολά-

---

[1] Cohn would read ἔτι τοίνυν comparing *De Abr.* 158.
But ἐπιχειρῶμεν there is the interrogative subjunctive, ἀξιούσθωσαν here imperative, *i.e.* "let them still be thought worthy,
if it is possible" (which of course it is not). In this case it
seems to be better to retain νῦν, and to expunge the mark of
interrogation which Cohn places after ὄνομα.

their own standing gratitude. After this, can we 208
still think worthy of pardon those, who, with a reckless tongue, make unseasonable use of the most
holy name of the Deity and treat it as a mere ex-
pletive ?

XXXIX. After this honour paid to the Parent 209
of All, the prophet magnified the holy seventh day,
seeing with his keener vision its marvellous beauty
stamped upon heaven and the whole world and
enshrined in nature itself. For he found that she 210
was in the first place motherless, exempt from
female parentage, begotten by the Father alone,
without begetting, brought to the birth, yet not
carried in the womb. Secondly, he saw not only
these, that she was all lovely and motherless, but
that she was also ever virgin, neither born of a
mother nor a mother herself, neither bred from
corruption nor doomed to suffer corruption.[a] Thirdly,
as he scanned her, he recognized in her the birthday of the world,[b] a feast celebrated by heaven, celebrated by earth and things on earth as they rejoice
and exult in the full harmony of the sacred number.
For this cause, Moses, great in everything, determined 211
that all whose names were written on his holy
burgess-roll and who followed the laws of nature
should hold high festival through hours of cheerful
gaiety, abstaining from work and profit-making
crafts and professions [c] and business pursued to get a
livelihood, and enjoy a respite from labour released
from weary and painful care. But this leisure should

[a] Cf. De Op. 100 and Leg. All. i. 15, and further App.
p. 609.
[b] Cf. Mos. i. 207 and note.
[c] Both the mental and the manual arts are included under
τέχναι, cf. § 219.

PHILO

ζοντας οὐχ ὡς ἔνιοι γέλωσιν ἢ παιδιαῖς ἢ μίμων
ἢ ὀρχηστῶν ἐπιδείξεσι, περὶ ἃς κηραίνουσι καὶ
δυσθανατοῦσιν οἱ θεατρομανοῦντες καὶ διὰ τῶν
ἡγεμονικωτάτων αἰσθήσεων, ὁράσεως καὶ ἀκοῆς,
δούλην ἀπεργαζόμενοι τὴν φύσει βασιλίδα ψυχήν,
212 ἀλλὰ μόνῳ τῷ φιλοσοφεῖν· οὐχ ὅπερ μεθοδεύουσιν
οἱ λογοθῆραι καὶ σοφισταὶ πιπράσκοντες ὡς ἄλλο
τι τῶν ὠνίων ἐπ᾽ ἀγορᾶς δόγματα καὶ λόγους, οἳ
φιλοσοφίᾳ κατὰ φιλοσοφίας (ὦ γῆ καὶ ἥλιε!) χρώμενοι δι᾽ αἰῶνος οὐκ ἐρυθριῶσιν, ἀλλὰ τῷ τῷ ὄντι
φιλοσοφεῖν, ὅπερ ἐκ τριῶν συνύφανται, βουλευμάτων καὶ λόγων καὶ πράξεων, εἰς ἓν εἶδος ἡρμο-
σμένων πρὸς κτῆσιν καὶ ἀπόλαυσιν εὐδαιμονίας.
213   τούτου δή τις ἀλογήσας τοῦ διατάγ-
ματος, ἔτι τοὺς χρησμοὺς ἐναύλους ἔχων τοὺς περὶ
τῆς ἱερᾶς ἑβδόμης, οὓς ἐθέσπισεν ἄνευ προφήτου
ὁ θεὸς διὰ φωνῆς—τὸ παραδοξότατον—ὁρατῆς, ἢ
τῶν παρατυγχανόντων ὀφθαλμοὺς ὤτων ἐπήγειρε
μᾶλλον, ἐπὶ φρυγανισμὸν ἐξῄει διὰ μέσου τοῦ
στρατοπέδου πάντας εἰδὼς ἐν ταῖς σκηναῖς ἠρε-
μοῦντας, καὶ δρῶν ἔτι τἀδίκημα καταφανὴς ὑπὲρ
214 τοῦ μὴ λαθεῖν γίνεται. πυλῶν γὰρ ἔξω προελ-
θόντες τινὲς εἰς ἐρημίαν, ἵν᾽ ἐν τῷ καθαρωτάτῳ καὶ
ἡσυχάζοντι εὔξωνται, θέαν ἔκνομον ἰδόντες, ξύλων
ὕλην συγκομίζοντα, καὶ δυσανασχετήσαντες ἐμέλ-
λησαν μὲν αὐτὸν ἀνελεῖν, λογισμῷ δὲ τὸ παρα-
κεκινημένον τῆς ὀργῆς ἐπισχόντες, ἵνα μήτε ἰδιῶται

ᵃ For §§ 213-220 see Num. xv. 32-36.
ᵇ Referring to LXX Ex. xx. 18 "all the people *saw* the
voice," *cf. De Mig.* 47.
ᶜ *i.e.* providence to ensure his conviction caused this certain
evidence to be forthcoming.

be occupied, not as by some in bursts of laughter or sports or shows of mimes and dancers on which stage-struck fools waste away their strength almost to the point of death, and through the dominant senses of sight and hearing reduce to slavery their natural queen, the soul, but by the pursuit of wisdom only. And the wisdom must not be that of 212 the systems hatched by the word-catchers and sophists who sell their tenets and arguments like any bit of merchandise in the market, men who for ever pit philosophy against philosophy without a blush, O earth and sun, but the true philosophy which is woven from three strands—thoughts, words and deeds—united into a single piece for the attainment and enjoyment of happiness. [a] Now, a certain 213 man, setting at nought this ordinance, though the echoes of the divine commands about the sacredness of the seventh day were ringing in his ears, commands promulgated by God not through His prophet but by a voice which, strange paradox, was visible [b] and aroused the eyes rather than the ears of the bystanders, went forth through the midst of the camp to gather firewood, knowing that all were resting in their tents. But that his crime might not remain hidden,[c] he was observed while still engaged in the wicked deed. For some persons who had gone out of the gates into 214 the wilderness to pray in the quiet open solitude [d] saw this lawless sight, a man gathering sticks for fuel, and, hardly able to control themselves, they were minded to slay him. Reflection, however, caused them to restrain the fierceness of their anger. They

---

[d] lxx (xv. 32). "And the children of Israel were in the wilderness and they found," etc., E.V. "while they were . . . they found."

PHILO

πρὸ ἀρχόντων κολάζειν τινὰ δοκῶσι καὶ ταῦτ᾽
ἄκριτον, κἂν ἄλλως τὸ παρανόμημα ᾖ ἐμφανές,
μήτε τοῦ περὶ τὴν ἡμέραν εὐαγοῦς μίασμα φόνου,
κἂν δικαιότατος ᾖ, προσάψηται, συλλαβόντες
ἄγουσιν αὐτὸν ἐπὶ τὸν ἄρχοντα, ᾧ συνήδρευον μὲν
οἱ ἱερεῖς, παρειστήκει δὲ σύμπασα ἡ πληθὺς πρὸς
215 ἀκρόασιν. ἔθος γὰρ ἦν, ἀεὶ μὲν κατὰ τὸ παρεῖκον,
προηγουμένως δὲ ταῖς ἑβδόμαις, ὡς ἐδήλωσα καὶ
πρόσθεν, φιλοσοφεῖν, τοῦ μὲν ἡγεμόνος ὑφηγου-
[168] μένου καὶ διδάσκοντος ἅ τε | χρὴ πράττειν καὶ
λέγειν, τῶν δ᾽ εἰς καλοκἀγαθίαν ἐπιδιδόντων καὶ
216 βελτιουμένων τά τε ἤθη καὶ τὸν βίον. ἀφ᾽ οὗ καὶ
εἰσέτι νῦν φιλοσοφοῦσι ταῖς ἑβδόμαις Ἰουδαῖοι τὴν
πάτριον φιλοσοφίαν τὸν χρόνον ἐκεῖνον ἀναθέντες
ἐπιστήμῃ καὶ θεωρίᾳ τῶν περὶ φύσιν· τὰ γὰρ
κατὰ πόλεις προσευκτήρια τί ἕτερόν ἐστιν ἢ διδα-
σκαλεῖα φρονήσεως καὶ ἀνδρείας καὶ σωφροσύνης
καὶ δικαιοσύνης εὐσεβείας τε καὶ ὁσιότητος καὶ
συμπάσης ἀρετῆς, ᾗ κατανοεῖται καὶ κατορθοῦται
τά τε ἀνθρώπεια καὶ θεῖα;
217 XL. Τότε μὲν οὖν εἰς εἱρκτὴν ὁ τηλικοῦτον
ἀσέβημα δράσας ἀπάγεται. Μωυσῆς δὲ ἀπορῶν
ὅ τι χρὴ παθεῖν τὸν ἄνθρωπον—ᾔδει γὰρ ἄξια
θανάτου διαπεπραγμένον, ἀλλὰ τίς ἂν γένοιτο τρόπος ἁρμόζων τῆς τιμωρίας;—ἀφικνεῖται πρὸς τὸ
ἀόρατον ἀοράτῳ ψυχῇ δικαστήριον καὶ ἐπυνθάνετο
τοῦ καὶ πρὶν ἀκοῦσαι πάντ᾽ ἐπισταμένου δικα-
218 στοῦ, τί κέκρικεν. ὁ δ᾽ ἀποφαίνεται τὴν γνῶσιν,

---

^a Or " of theology." See on *De Abr.* 99.
^b According to the narrative as it stands, sabbath-break-
ing had already been declared a capital crime, Ex. xxxi. 14,
xxxv. 2.

did not wish to make it appear that they who were but private citizens took upon themselves the ruler's duty of punishment, and that too without a trial, however clear was the offence in other ways, or that the pollution of bloodshed, however justly deserved, should profane the sacredness of the day. Accordingly they arrested him, and took him before the ruler beside whom the priests were seated, while the whole multitude stood around to listen ; for it was 215 customary on every day when opportunity offered, and pre-eminently on the seventh day, as I have explained above, to pursue the study of wisdom with the ruler expounding and instructing the people what they should say and do, while they received edification and betterment in moral principles and conduct. Even now this practice is retained, and 216 the Jews every seventh day occupy themselves with the philosophy of their fathers, dedicating that time to the acquiring of knowledge and the study of the truths of nature.[a] For what are our places of prayer throughout the cities but schools of prudence and courage and temperance and justice and also of piety, holiness and every virtue by which duties to God and men are discerned and rightly performed?

XL. So, then, the perpetrator of this great sin 217 against God was for the time being taken into custody. But Moses was in doubt as to what should be done to him. He knew that the action deserved death,[b] but what would be the proper method of punishment? So, then, in spirit, he approached the judgement-seat, invisible even as the spirit which sought it, and asked of the Judge Who knows all before He hears it what His sentence was. That Judge declared His decision 218

ὅτι καὶ θνήσκειν ὀφείλει καὶ οὐχ ἑτέρως ἢ κατα-
λευσθείς, ἐπειδὴ καὶ τούτῳ καθάπερ καὶ τῷ προ-
τέρῳ μετέβαλεν ὁ νοῦς εἰς κωφὴν λίθον εἰργα-
σμένῳ τελεώτατον παρανόμημα, ᾧ σχεδὸν πάντα
τἆλλα ἐμφέρεται, ὅσα περὶ τοῦ σεβασμοῦ τῆς
219 ἑβδόμης νενομοθέτηται. διὰ τί; ὅτι οὐχ αἱ βά-
ναυσοι μόνον ἀλλὰ καὶ αἱ ἄλλαι τέχναι καὶ πραγ-
ματεῖαι καὶ μάλιστα αἱ περὶ πορισμὸν καὶ βίου
ζήτησιν ἢ διὰ πυρός εἰσιν ἢ οὐκ ἄνευ τῶν διὰ
πυρός· ὅθεν ἀπαγορεύει πολλάκις ἐν ταῖς ἑβδόμαις
πῦρ ἐναύειν ὡς ἀρχηγικώτατον αἴτιον καὶ πρεσβύτατον ἔργον, οὗ ἡσυχάσαντος ἐνενοήθη καὶ τὰ κατὰ
220 μέρος ὡς εἰκὸς συνησυχάσειν. ὕλη δὲ ξύλα πυρός,
ὡς τὸν ξυλιζόμενον ἀδελφὸν καὶ συγγενὲς ἁμάρτημα
τῷ καίοντι δρᾶν, τὸ παρανόμημα διπλασιάζοντα,
τῇ μὲν ὅτι προσταχθὲν ἠρεμεῖν συνεκόμιζε, τῇ δ'
ὅτι καὶ τοιαῦτα συνεκόμιζεν, ἃ πυρός ἐστιν ὕλη,
τῆς τῶν τεχνῶν ἀρχῆς.

221 XLI. Ἄμφω μὲν οὖν τὰ εἰρημένα τιμωρίας
ἀσεβῶν περιέχει διὰ πεύσεως καὶ ἀποκρίσεως
βεβαιουμένας. ἕτερα δὲ δύο ἐστὶν οὐχὶ τῆς αὐτῆς
ἀλλὰ διαφερούσης ἰδέας, ὧν τὸ μὲν περὶ κλήρου
[169] διαδοχῆς, τὸ δ' ὅσα τῷ δοκεῖν παρὰ καιρὸν | ἐπι-
τελουμένης ἱερουργίας, περὶ ἧς λεκτέον πρότερον.
222 τὴν ἀρχὴν τῆς ἐαρινῆς ἰσημερίας πρῶτον ἀναγράφει
μῆνα Μωυσῆς ἐν ταῖς τῶν ἐνιαυτῶν περιόδοις ἀναθεὶς οὐχ ὥσπερ ἔνιοι χρόνῳ τὰ πρεσβεῖα μᾶλλον
ἢ ταῖς τῆς φύσεως χάρισιν, ἃς ἀνέτειλεν ἀνθρώποις·

---

[a] Only found in Ex. xxxv. 3, though the command to bake
or boil the manna before the Sabbath, Ex. xvi. 23, may be
taken to imply it. (Driver.)

[b] For §§ 222-232 see Num. ix. 1-14.

that the man should die, and by no other death but stoning; since in him, as in the earlier culprit, the mind had been changed into a senseless stone by a deed which was the perfection of wickedness, and covered practically all the prohibitions enacted for the honouring of the seventh day. How is this? 219 Because not merely the mechanical but also the other arts and occupations, particularly those which are undertaken for profit and to get a livelihood, are carried on directly or indirectly by the instrumentality of fire. And, therefore, he often[a] forbids the lighting of a fire on the seventh day, regarding it as the cause which lay at the root of all and as the primary activity; and, if this ceased, he considered that other particular activities would naturally cease also. But 220 sticks are the material for fire, so that by picking them up he committed a sin which was brother to and of the same family as the sin of burning them. And his was a double crime; it lay first in the mere act of collecting, in defiance of the commandment to rest from work, secondly in the nature of what he collected, being materials for fire which is the basis of the arts.

XLI. Both the incidents mentioned above are con- 221 cerned with the punishment of impious persons, ratified by means of question and answer. There are two others of a different kind: one connected with the succession to an inheritance, the other with a rite performed at apparently a wrong season. It will be better to take the latter example before the other. [b] Moses dates the first month of the year's 222 revolution at the beginning of the spring equinox. And, in doing so, he is not like some giving the place of honour to the actual time but rather to the gifts of nature which she raises up for men. For at the equinox

PHILO

κατὰ γὰρ ταύτην τὰ μὲν σπαρτά, ἡ ἀναγκαία
τροφή, τελειογονεῖται, ὁ δὲ τῶν δένδρων καρπὸς
ἡβώντων ἄρτι γεννᾶται δευτέραν ἔχων τάξιν, ὅθεν
καὶ ὀψίγονός ἐστιν· ἀεὶ γὰρ ἐν τῇ φύσει τὰ μὴ λίαν
223 ἀναγκαῖα τῶν σφόδρα ἀναγκαίων δεύτερα. σφόδρα
μὲν οὖν ἀναγκαῖα πυροί τε καὶ κριθαὶ καὶ ὅσα
ἄλλα εἴδη τροφῆς, ὧν ἄνευ ζῆν οὐκ ἔστιν· ἔλαιον δὲ
καὶ οἶνος καὶ ἀκρόδρυα οὐχὶ τῶν ἀναγκαίων, ἐπεὶ
καὶ δίχα τούτων ἄχρι μακροτάτου γήρως παρα-
224 τείνοντες εἰς πολυετίαν βιοῦσιν ἄνθρωποι. τῷ
δὴ μηνὶ τούτῳ περὶ τεσσαρεσκαιδεκάτην ἡμέραν,
μέλλοντος τοῦ σεληνιακοῦ κύκλου γίνεσθαι πλησι-
φαοῦς, ἄγεται τὰ διαβατήρια, δημοφανὴς ἑορτή,
τὸ Χαλδαϊστὶ λεγόμενον Πάσχα, ἐν ᾗ οὐχ οἱ μὲν
ἰδιῶται προσάγουσι τῷ βωμῷ τὰ ἱερεῖα, θύουσι δ᾽
οἱ ἱερεῖς, ἀλλὰ νόμου προστάξει σύμπαν τὸ ἔθνος
ἱερᾶται, τῶν κατὰ μέρος ἑκάστου τὰς ὑπὲρ αὑτοῦ
225 θυσίας ἀνάγοντός τε καὶ χειρουργοῦντος. ὁ μὲν
οὖν ἄλλος ἅπας λεὼς ἐγεγήθει καὶ φαιδρὸς ἦν,
ἑκάστου νομίζοντος ἱερωσύνῃ τετιμῆσθαι· δεδακρυμένοι δ᾽ ἕτεροι καὶ στένοντες διῆγον, οἰκείων αὐτοῖς
ἔναγχος τετελευτηκότων, οὓς πενθοῦντες διπλῇ
κατείχοντο λύπῃ, προσειληφότες τῇ διὰ τοὺς
ἀποθανόντας συγγενεῖς καὶ τὴν ἐκ τοῦ στερηθῆναι
τῆς περὶ τὴν ἱερουργίαν ἡδονῆς τε καὶ τιμῆς, οἷς
οὐδὲ καθάρασθαι καὶ περιρράνασθαι κατ᾽ ἐκείνην
τὴν ἡμέραν ἐξεγένετο, μήπω τοῦ πένθους ὑπερ-
226 ημέρου καὶ ἐκπροθέσμου γεγονότος. οὗτοι μετὰ
τὴν πανήγυριν προσελθόντες τῷ ἄρχοντι συννοίας
μεστοὶ καὶ κατηφείας τὰ συμβεβηκότα διηγήσαντο,
τὴν ὑπόγυον τῶν συγγενῶν τελευτήν, τὸ πένθος ᾧ
κατ᾽ ἀναγκαῖον ἐχρήσαντο, τὸ μὴ δυνηθῆναι διὰ

560

the corn crops, our necessary food, become ripe, while on the trees, which are in full bloom, the fruit is just beginning to appear. This ranks second to the corn, and therefore is a later growth. For in nature what is a less pressing always comes after a really pressing necessity. Now, wheat and barley and the other 223 kinds of food without which life is impossible are pressing necessities, but wine and olive oil and tree fruits do not come under this head, as men continue their life for many years and reach extreme old age without them. In this month, about the fourteenth 224 day, when the disc of the moon is becoming full, is held the commemoration of the crossing, a public festival called in Hebrew Pasch, on which the victims are not brought to the altar by the laity and sacrificed by the priests, but, as commanded by the law, the whole nation acts as priest, each individual bringing what he offers on his own behalf and dealing with it with his own hands. Now, 225 while all the rest of the people were joyful and cheer-ful, each feeling that he had the honour of priesthood, there were others passing the time in tears and sorrow. They had lost relations lately by death, and in mourning them they suffered a double sorrow. Added to their grief for their dead kinsfolk was that which they felt at the loss of the pleasure and honour of the sacred rite. For they were not even allowed to purify or besprinkle themselves with holy water on that day, since their mourning had still some days to run and had not passed the appointed term. These 226 persons, after the festival, came to the ruler full of gloom and depression and put the case before him— the still recent death of their kinsfolk, the necessity of performing their duty as mourners and their con-

PHILO

227 τοῦτο μετασχεῖν τῆς τῶν διαβατηρίων θυσίας. εἶτ᾽
ἐδέοντο μὴ ἔλαττον τῶν ἄλλων ἐνέγκασθαι μηδὲ τὸ
ἐπὶ τοῖς ἀποθανοῦσιν οἰκείοις ἀτύχημα ἐν ἀδική
ματος μέρει καταριθμηθῆναι τιμωρίαν ἐργασάμενον
[170] πρὸ | ἐλέου· νομίσαι γὰρ ἂν χείρονα παθεῖν τῶν
ἀποθανόντων, εἴ γε τοῖς μὲν οὐδενός ἐστιν ἀντίληψις
ἔτι τῶν ἀβουλήτων, οἱ δὲ ζῶντες δόξουσι τεθνάναι
228 τὸν μετ᾽ αἰσθήσεως θάνατον. XLII. ταῦτ᾽ ἀκούσας
ἑώρα μὲν καὶ τὴν δικαιολογίαν οὐκ ἀπῳδὸν καὶ τὴν
τοῦ μὴ ἱερουργῆσαι πάλιν πρόφασιν ἀναγκαίαν καὶ
τὸ συμπαθὲς ἀνακεκραμένον τούτοις, ἐπαμφοτε-
ρίζων δὲ τὴν γνώμην καὶ ὥσπερ ἐπὶ πλάστιγγος
ἀντιρρέπων—τῇ μὲν γὰρ ἐταλάντευεν ὁ ἔλεος καὶ
τὰ δίκαια, τῇ δ᾽ ἀντέβριθεν ὁ νόμος τῆς τῶν διαβατηρίων θυσίας, ἐν ᾧ καὶ πρῶτος μὴν καὶ ἡμέρα
τεσσαρεσκαιδεκάτη δεδήλωται τῆς ἱερουργίας—,
ἀρνήσεως καὶ συγκαταθέσεως μεταξὺ φορούμενος
ἱκετεύει τὸν θεὸν δικαστὴν γενέσθαι καὶ χρησμῷ
229 τὴν κρίσιν ἀναφῆναι. ὁ δ᾽ ἐπακούσας θεσπίζει
λόγιον οὐ περὶ ὧν ἐνετεύχθη μόνον ἀλλὰ καὶ περὶ
τῶν αὖθίς ποτε γενησομένων, εἰ ταῖς αὐταῖς χρή-
σαιντο συντυχίαις· ἐπιδαψιλευόμενος δὲ καὶ περὶ
τῶν κατ᾽ ἄλλας αἰτίας οὐ δυνηθέντων ἱερουργῆσαι
230 μετὰ παντὸς τοῦ ἔθνους προσεπιθεσπίζει. τίνα οὖν
ἐστι τὰ περὶ τούτων χρησθέντα λόγια, μηνυτέον.
" συγγενικὸν " φησί " πένθος ἀναγκαία μὲν τοῖς
ἀφ᾽ αἵματος ἀνία, γράφεται δ᾽ οὐκ ἐν πλημμελείαις.
231 ἕως μὲν οὖν ἐμπρόθεσμόν ἐστιν, ἔξω περιβόλων
562

sequent inability to take part in the sacrifice of the
crossing-feast. Then they prayed that they might 227
not fare worse than the others, and that the misfortune which they had sustained in the death of
their relations might not be counted as misconduct
entailing punishment rather than pity. In that case
they considered that their fate would be worse than
that of the dead, for they have no longer any perception of their troubles, while they themselves
would be suffering a living death, in which they still
retained consciousness. XLII. Moses, hearing this, 228
recognized the reasonableness of their claim, and also
the cogency of their excuse for absenting themselves
from the sacrifice ; and with these was mingled a
feeling of sympathy. Yet he wavered in his judgement, and oscillated as on a balance : one scale was
weighed down by pity and justice, while in the other
lay as a counterpoise the law of the Paschal sacrifices
in which both the first month and the fourteenth day
were clearly appointed for the rite. So, vacillating
between refusal and assent, he besought God to act
as judge and to give an oracle declaring his decision.
And God hearkened to him and vouchsafed an answer 229
revealing His will, touching not only those for whom
the prophet interceded but those of future generations who might find themselves in the same case.
And, His grace abounding further, He included in
the divine edict those who for other reasons might
be unable to join the whole nation in a sacred service.
It is right to state what the pronouncements thus 230
given were. "Mourning for kinsfolk," He said, "is
an affliction which the family cannot avoid, but it
does not count as an offence. While it is still running 231
its appointed course, it should be banished from the

ἱερῶν ἐλαυνέσθω, οὓς ἀπὸ παντὸς ἁγνεύειν οὐχ
ἑκουσίου μόνον ἀλλὰ καὶ τοῦ μὴ κατὰ γνώμην
μιάσματος δεῖ· γενομένου δ' ἐκπροθέσμου, μὴ
στερέσθωσαν ἰσομοιρίας τῆς ἐν ταῖς ἱερουργίαις,
ἵνα μὴ προσθήκη τετελευτηκότων οἱ ζῶντες ὦσιν·
ἴτωσαν δὲ ἅτε δεύτεροι δευτέρῳ μηνί, πάλιν τεσ-
σαρεσκαιδεκάτῃ ἡμέρᾳ, καὶ θυέτωσαν κατὰ τὰ
αὐτὰ τοῖς προτέροις καὶ τῷ θύματι χρήσθωσαν ὡς
232 ἐκεῖνοι νόμῳ καὶ τρόπῳ τῷ παραπλησίῳ. τὰ δ'
αὐτὰ ἐπιτετράφθω καὶ τοῖς μὴ διὰ πένθος ἀλλὰ
μακρᾶς χάριν ἀποδημίας κωλυομένοις ἅμα τῷ
παντὶ ἔθνει συνιερουργεῖν· οὐ γὰρ οἱ ξενιτεύοντες
ἢ ἑτέρωθι οἰκοῦντες ἀδικοῦσιν, ὡς στέρεσθαι τῆς
ἴσης τιμῆς, καὶ ταῦτα μὴ χωρούσης διὰ πολυανθρωπίαν τὸ ἔθνος μιᾶς χώρας, ἀλλ' ἀποικίας
πανταχόσε διαπεμψαμένης."

233   XLIII. Τοσαῦτα διειλεγμένος περὶ τῶν ὑστερη-
σάντων μὲν ἅμα τῷ πλήθει θῦσαι τὰ διαβατήρια
κατὰ συντυχίας ἀβουλήτους, ἐκπλῆσαι δ' εἰ καὶ ὀψὲ
ἀλλ' οὖν ἀναγκαίως τὸ ἐλλειφθὲν σπουδασάντων,
ἐπὶ τελευταῖον μέτειμι διάταγμα τὸ περὶ τῆς τῶν
κλήρων διαδοχῆς, ὅπερ ὁμοίως μικτὸν ἦν ἐκ πεύ-
234 σεως καὶ ἀποκρίσεως λαβὸν τὴν σύστασιν. ἦν
τις ὄνομα Σαλπαάδ, ἀνὴρ δόκιμος καὶ φυλῆς οὐκ
ἀσήμου· τούτῳ πέντε μὲν γίνονται θυγατέρες, υἱὸς
[171] | δὲ οὐδείς· αἱ μετὰ τὴν τελευτὴν τοῦ πατρὸς
στέρησιν τῆς πατρῴας λήξεως ὑποτοπήσασαι διὰ
τὸ τὰς κληρουχίας ἄρρεσι δίδοσθαι προσίασι τῷ
ἡγεμόνι μετὰ τῆς ἁρμοττούσης κόραις αἰδοῦς, οὐ
θηρώμεναι πλοῦτον, ἀλλὰ τοὔνομα καὶ ἀξίωμα

---

[a] For this idiomatic use of ἀναγκαίως see note on *Quod
Det.* 160.

sacred precincts which must be kept pure from all pollution, not only that which is voluntary but also that which is unintentionally incurred. But when its term is finished let not the mourners be denied an equal share in the sacred services, and thus the living be made an appendage to the dead. Let them form a second set to come on the second month and also on the fourteenth day, and sacrifice just as the first set, and observe a similar rule and method in dealing with the victims. The same permission also must be 232 given to those who are prevented from joining the whole nation in worship not by mourning but by absence in a distant country. For settlers abroad and inhabitants of other regions are not wrongdoers who deserve to be deprived of equal privileges, particularly if the nation has grown so populous that a single country cannot contain it and has sent out colonies in all directions."

XLIII. Having thus discussed the case of those 233 who, through adverse circumstances, failed to make the Paschal sacrifice with the mass of the nation, but were set upon repairing the omission if late yet as best they could,[a] I will pass on to the final ordinance, which concerns the succession to an inheritance. This, like the others, originated in a question and answer and was thus of a mixed character. [b] There 234 was a man called Zelophehad, highly reputed and of no mean tribe, who had five daughters and no son. After the death of their father, the daughters, suspecting that they would be deprived of the property he had left, since inheritances went in the male line, approached the ruler in all maidenly modesty, not in pursuit of wealth but from a desire to preserve the

[b] For §§ 234-245 see Num. xxvii. 1-11.

235 γλιχόμεναι διασῶσαι τοῦ πατρὸς καί φασιν· " ὁ μὲν
πατὴρ ἡμῶν ἐτελεύτησεν, ἐτελεύτησε δ' ἐν οὐδεμιᾷ
στάσει γενόμενος, ἐφ' ὧν συνέβη διαφθαρῆναι μυρίους, ἀλλ' ἐζήλωσε βίον ἀπράγμονα καὶ ἰδιώτην,
εἰ μὴ ἄρα ἐν ἁμαρτίᾳ θετέον τὸ γενεᾶς ἄρρενος
ἀμοιρῆσαι.ᵃ πάρεσμεν δ' ἡμεῖς ὅσα μὲν τῷ δοκεῖν
ὀρφαναί, τὸ δ' ἀληθὲς σοὶ χρησόμεναι πατρί· τοῦ
γὰρ γεννήσαντος ὁ νόμιμος ἄρχων οἰκειότερος
236 ὑπηκόοις." ὁ δὲ θαυμάσας τὴν φρόνησιν τῶν
παρθένων καὶ τὴν πρὸς τὸν γεινάμενον εὔνοιαν
ἐπέσχεν ὑφ' ἑτέρας ἑλκόμενος φαντασίας, καθ' ἣν
τὰς κληρουχίας ἄνδρες ὤφειλον διανέμεσθαι γέρας
ληψόμενοι στρατείας καὶ πολέμων οὓς διήθλησαν,
γυναικὶ δ' ἡ φύσις ἀσυλίαν τῶν τοιούτων ἀγω-
νισμάτων παρέχουσα δηλονότι καὶ τῶν ἐπ' αὐτοῖς
237 τιθεμένων ἄθλων οὐ μεταδίδωσιν. ὅθεν εἰκότως
τῆς διανοίας ἀμφικλινῶς ἐχούσης καὶ ἀντισπω-
μένης, ἀναφέρει τῷ θεῷ τὴν διαπόρησιν, ὃν ᾔδει
μόνον ἀψευδέσι καὶ ἀπλανεστάτοις κριτηρίοις τὰς
κατὰ μικρὸν διαφορὰς διαστέλλοντα πρὸς ἐπίδειξιν
238 ἀληθείας καὶ δικαιοσύνης. ὁ δὲ ποιητὴς τῶν ὅλων,
ὁ τοῦ κόσμου πατήρ, γῆν καὶ οὐρανὸν ὕδωρ τε καὶ
ἀέρα καὶ ὅσα ἐκ τούτων ἑκάστου συνέχων καὶ
διακρατῶν, ὁ θεῶν καὶ ἀνθρώπων ἡγεμών, οὐκ
ἀπηξίωσε χρηματίσαι κόραις ὀρφαναῖς· χρηματίσας
δὲ καὶ πλέον τι παρέσχεν ἢ κατὰ δικαστὴν ὁ
εὐμενὴς καὶ ἵλεως, ὁ πάντα διὰ πάντων πεπληρωκὼς
τῆς εὐεργέτιδος ἑαυτοῦ δυνάμεως· ἔπαινον γὰρ δι-
239 εξῆλθε τῶν παρθένων. ὦ δέσποτα, πῶς ἄν σέ τις

ᵃ Philo is trying to interpret verse 3, E.V. " but he died in
his own sin " (*i.e.* in the ordinary sinfulness of a man). " and

566

name and reputation of their father. " Our father 235
died," they said, " but not in any of the risings in
which, as it fell out, multitudes perished, but followed
contentedly the quiet life of an ordinary citizen,
and surely it is not to be accounted as a sin that
he had no male issue.ᵃ We are here outwardly as
orphans, but in reality hoping to find a father in you ;
for a lawful ruler is closer akin to his subjects than he
who begat them." Moses admired the good sense 236
of the maidens and their loyalty to their parent, but
suspended his judgement, being influenced by another
view, which holds that men should divide inheritances
among themselves, to be taken as the reward for
military service and the wars of which they have
borne the brunt ; while nature, who grants to women
exemption from such conflicts, clearly also refuses
them a share in the prizes assigned thereto. Natur- 237
ally, therefore, in this wavering and undecided state
of mind, he referred the difficulty to God, Who alone,
as he knew, can distinguish by infallible and absolutely unerring tests the finest differences and thereby
shew His truth and justice. And He, the Maker of 238
All, the Father of the World, Who holds firmly knit
together heaven and earth and water and air and all
that each of them produces, the Ruler of men and
gods, did not disdain to give response to the petition
of some orphan girls. And, with that response, He
gave something more than a judge would give, so
kind and gracious was He, Who has filled the universe
through and through with His beneficent power ; for
He stated His full approval of the maidens. O 239
Lord and Master, how can one hymn Thee ? What

ᵃ he had no sons." The LXX is hardly intelligible " because
he died on account of his sin, and had no sons."

ὑμνήσειε, ποίῳ στόματι, τίνι γλώττῃ, ποίᾳ φωνῆς
ὀργανοποιίᾳ, ποίῳ ψυχῆς ἡγεμονικῷ; οἱ γὰρ
ἀστέρες εἷς γενόμενοι χορὸς ᾄσονταί τι μέλος
ἐπάξιον; ὁ δ᾽ οὐρανὸς ὅλος εἰς φωνὴν ἀναλυθεὶς
δυνήσεταί τι τῶν σῶν ἀρετῶν διηγήσασθαι μέρος;
" ὀρθῶς " φησίν " ἐλάλησαν αἱ θυγατέρες
240 Σαλπαάδ." τοῦθ᾽ ἡλίκον ἐστὶν ἐγκώμιον θεοῦ
μαρτυροῦντος, τίς οὐκ οἶδε; πάριτε νῦν, οἱ ἀλα-
ζόνες, οἱ μέγα πνέοντες ἐπὶ ταῖς εὐπραγίαις, οἱ τοὺς
αὐχένας πλέον τῆς φύσεως ἐπαίροντες καὶ τὰς
ὀφρῦς ἀνεσπακότες, παρ᾽ οἷς χηρεία μὲν γυναικῶν
γέλως, [καὶ] οἰκτρὸν κακόν, ἐρημία δὲ παίδων
[172] ὀρφανῶν, | οἰκτρότερον τοῦ προτέρου, χλευάζεται·
241 καὶ κατιδόντες ὅτι οὕτω ταπεινοὶ καὶ ἀτυχεῖς εἶναι
δοκοῦντες οὐκ ἐν ἐξουθενημένοις καὶ ἀφανέσι
τάττονται παρὰ τῷ θεῷ, οὗ τῆς ἀρχῆς τὸ ἀτιμό-
τατον μέρος εἰσὶν αἱ πανταχοῦ τῆς οἰκουμένης
βασιλεῖαι, διότι καὶ ὁ τῆς γῆς ἅπας ἐν κύκλῳ
περίβολος ἐσχατιὰ τῶν ἔργων ἐστὶν αὐτοῦ, δέξασθε
242 νουθεσίαν ἀναγκαίαν.   ἐπαινέσας δ᾽ ὅμως
τὴν ἔντευξιν τῶν παρθένων οὔτε ταύτας ἀγεράστους
κατέλιπεν οὔτ᾽ εἰς τὴν ἴσην τιμὴν τοῖς ἀγωνισταῖς
ἀνδράσι περιήγαγεν, ἀλλὰ τοῖς μὲν ὡς ἆθλα οἰκεῖα
ἀπένειμε τὰς κληρουχίας ἀνθ᾽ ὧν ἠνδραγαθίσαντο,
τὰς δὲ χάριτος καὶ φιλανθρωπίας, οὐ γέρως, ἠξίω-
σεν· ὃ ἐναργέστατα παρίστησι διὰ τῶν ὀνομάτων
" δόμα " λέγων καὶ " δώσεις," ἀλλ᾽ οὐκ " ἀπό-
δομα " οὐδ᾽ " ἀποδώσεις"· ταῦτα μὲν γὰρ ἴδια τῶν
568

mouth, what tongue, what else of the instruments of speech, what mind, soul's dominant part, is equal to the task? If the stars become a single choir, will their song be worthy of Thee? If all heaven be resolved into sound, will it be able to recount any part of Thy excellences? "The daughters of Zelophehad have spoken rightly," He said. Who 240 can fail to know how great a commendation is this testimony from God? Come now, you boasters, with your windy pride in your prosperity, and your pose of perked up necks and lifted eyebrows, who treat widowhood, that piteous calamity, as a joke, and the still more piteous desolation of orphanhood as a matter for mockery. Mark how the persons 241 who seem thus lonely and unfortunate are not treated as nothing worth and negligible in the judgement of God, of Whose empire the least honoured parts are the kingdoms found everywhere in the civilized world; for even the whole compass of the round earth is but the outermost fringe of His works—mark this, I say, and learn its much-needed lesson.   Still, 242 though he praised the petition of the maidens and refrained from leaving them empty-handed, he did not promote them to equal honour with the men who bore the brunt of conflict. To these he assigned the inheritances as prizes suitable to their feats of valour ; the women he judged worthy of charity and kindness, not of reward for services. He shows this clearly by the words He uses. He says : " Gift " and " thou shall give," *a* not " payment " and " thou shalt pay," for the latter pair are used when we receive what is

---

a Or " restore," " return."   *Cf. De Som.* i. 100.

PHILO

λαμβανόντων,¹ ἐκεῖνα δὲ τῶν χαριζομένων.

243 XLIV. θεσπίσας δὲ περὶ ὧν ἐνετύγχανον αἱ ὀρφαναὶ
παρθένοι καὶ καθολικώτερον τίθησι νόμον περὶ
κλήρων διαδοχῆς, πρώτους μὲν υἱοὺς ἐπὶ μετουσίαν
καλῶν τῶν πατρῴων, εἰ δὲ μὴ εἶεν υἱοί, δευτέρας
θυγατέρας, αἷς φησι δεῖν περιτιθέναι τὸν κλῆρον
ὡσανεὶ κόσμον ἔξωθεν, ἀλλ᾽ οὐχ ὡς ἴδιον καὶ
συγγενὲς κτῆμα· τὸ γὰρ περιτιθέμενον οὐδεμίαν
οἰκείωσιν ἔχει πρὸς τὸ διακοσμούμενον, ἁρμονίας
244 καὶ ἑνώσεως ἀλλοτριούμενον. μετὰ δὲ θυγατέρας
τρίτους ἀδελφοὺς καλεῖ, τετάρτην δὲ θείοις πρὸς
πατρὸς ἀπονέμει τάξιν, αἰνιττόμενος ὅτι καὶ
πατέρες γένοιντ᾽ ἂν υἱῶν κληρονόμοι· πάνυ γὰρ
εὔηθες ὑπολαβεῖν, ὅτι πατρὸς ἀδελφῷ νέμων κλῆρον
ἀδελφιδοῦ διὰ τὴν πρὸς πατέρα συγγένειαν αὐτὸν
245 ἀφείλετο τὸν πατέρα τῆς διαδοχῆς. ἀλλ᾽ ἐπειδὴ
νόμος φύσεώς ἐστι κληρονομεῖσθαι γονεῖς ὑπὸ
παίδων ἀλλὰ μὴ τούτους κληρονομεῖν, τὸ μὲν
ἀπευκτὸν καὶ παλίμφημον ἡσύχασεν, ἵνα μὴ πατὴρ
καὶ μήτηρ προσοδεύεσθαι δοκῶσι τὰ ἐπ᾽ ὠκυμόροις
τέκνοις ἀπαρηγόρητα πένθη, πλαγίως δ᾽ αὐτοὺς
ἐκάλεσε τοῖς θείοις ἐφείς, ἵν᾽ ἀμφοτέρων στοχά-
σηται καὶ τοῦ πρέποντος καὶ τοῦ μὴ τὴν οὐσίαν

---

¹ Corrupt? Perhaps read ὀφλισκανόντων = "debtors" or
ἀποτινόντων. See note a.

ᵃ This seems the only way of taking the passage as it
stands, but it is most unsatisfactory. For (1) we should
expect τὰ ἴδια, and ἴδια in this position strongly suggests that
it agrees with ταῦτα, and as often = "specially used of":
(2) The substitution of the payee for the payer is extra-
ordinarily awkward. The first difficulty might be surmounted

our own,[a] the former when we make a free gift.

XLIV. After signifying His will as to 243
the petition of the orphan maids, He lays down also
a more general law about succession to inheritances.
He names sons first for participation in their father's
property, and daughters second, if there are no sons.
In the case of the daughters His phrase is that
the inheritance should be "put round"[b] them, as
though it were an external ornament, not a possession
by right of kinship inalienable. For what is put
round does not have an intimate connexion with
what it adorns, and the ideas of close fitting and
union are quite foreign to it. After the daughters, 244
He names the brothers as standing third, and the
fourth place He assigns to uncles on the father's
side, thereby indirectly suggesting that fathers may
become the heirs of sons. For it would be foolish
to suppose that, while He assigns the inheritance
of a nephew to his paternal uncle, because of that
uncle's relation to the father, He withdraws from
the father himself the right of succession. But 245
since, in the natural order of things, sons are the
heirs of their fathers and not fathers of their
sons, He left unmentioned this deplorable and
sinister possibility, to avoid the idea of a father and
mother making profit out of their inconsolable sorrow
at the untimely death of their children. But He
does indirectly mention this by admitting the right
of the uncles; and thus He attains both ends,
the preservation of decency and the rule that the

by reading ἴδια τῶν ⟨τὰ ἴδια⟩ λαμβανόντων (W.H.D.R.), but
the second would remain. I believe that λαμβανόντων is
corrupt, though neither Cohn nor Mangey, who translates
"propria recuperantium," seem to have felt difficulty.

[b] So LXX; E.V. "cause to pass."

ἀλλοτριωθῆναι. μετὰ δὲ θείους πέμπτη τάξις
ἐστὶν οἱ ἔγγιστα γένους, ὧν ἀεὶ τοῖς πρώτοις
δίδωσι τοὺς κλήρους.

246 XLV. Ταῦτ᾽ ἀναγκαίως διεξεληλυθὼς περὶ τῶν
μικτὴν ἐχόντων κληρουχίαν[1] χρησμῶν, ἑξῆς δηλώσω
[173] | τὰ κατ᾽ ἐνθουσιασμὸν τοῦ προφήτου θεσπισθέντα
λόγια· τοῦτο γὰρ ὑπεσχόμην δείξειν. ἀρχὴ τοίνυν
ἐστὶν αὐτῷ τῆς θεοφορήτου κατοκωχῆς, ἥτις καὶ
τῷ ἔθνει γέγονεν εὐπραγίας ἀρχὴ στειλαμένῳ
τὴν ἀπ᾽ Αἰγύπτου πρὸς τὰς κατὰ Συρίαν πόλεις
247 ἀποικίαν μυριάσι πολλαῖς. ἄνδρες γὰρ ὁμοῦ καὶ
γυναῖκες ἀτριβῆ καὶ μακρὰν ἐρήμην ἅπασαν ἀνύ-
σαντες ἐπὶ θάλατταν ἀφικνοῦνται τὴν Ἐρυθρὰν
προσαγορευομένην· εἶθ᾽ ὡς εἰκὸς ἐν ἀμηχάνοις
ἦσαν οὔτε περαιοῦσθαι δυνάμενοι διὰ σκαφῶν
ἀπορίαν οὔτ᾽ ἐπιστρέφειν τὴν αὐτὴν ὁδὸν ἀσφαλὲς
248 ἡγούμενοι. διακειμένοις δ᾽ οὕτως μεῖζον ἐπιρ-
ράττει κακόν· ὁ γὰρ τῶν Αἰγυπτίων βασιλεὺς
δύναμιν παραλαβὼν οὐκ εὐκαταφρόνητον, ἱππότην
καὶ πεζὸν στρατόν, ἐπεξέθει διώκων καὶ σπεύδων
καταλαβεῖν, ἵνα τίσηται τῆς ἐξόδου, ἣν θεσφάτοις
ἀριδήλοις ἐπέτρεψε ποιήσασθαι. ἀλλ᾽ ὡς ἔοικεν
ἀβέβαιος ἡ μοχθηρῶν ἀνθρώπων διάθεσις ὡς ἐπὶ
πλάστιγγος μικρᾶς ἕνεκα προφάσεως ῥέπουσα πρὸς
249 τἀναντία. μέσοι δὴ ληφθέντες ἐχθρῶν καὶ θαλάττης ἀπέγνωσαν τὴν ἰδίαν σωτηρίαν, οἱ μὲν
εὐκτὸν ἀγαθὸν ἡγούμενοι τὸν οἴκτιστον ὄλεθρον, οἱ
δ᾽ ἄμεινον εἶναι νομίζοντες ὑπὸ τῶν τῆς φύσεως
ἀπολέσθαι μερῶν ἢ γέλως ἐχθροῖς γενέσθαι ῥίπτειν

---

[1] Clearly a mistake, induced by the subject of the
preceding sections. δύναμιν from § 192 is suggested. Perhaps
τὴν οὐσίαν.

property should not go out of the family. After the uncles comes the fifth class, the nearest relations. And in all such cases it is the first in succession to whom He gives the inheritances.

XLV. Having completed this necessary account 246 of the oracles of mixed character, I will proceed next to describe those delivered by the prophet himself under divine inspiration, for this was included in my promise. The examples of his possession by God's spirit begin with one which was also the beginning of the prosperity of the nation, when its many myriads set out as colonists from Egypt to the cities of Syria. ^a Men and women alike, they had traversed 247 a long and pathless wilderness, and arrived at the Red Sea, as it is called. They were then naturally in great difficulties, as they could not cross the sea for want of boats, and did not think it safe to retrace their steps. When they were in this state of mind, 248 a greater misfortune burst upon them. The king of Egypt, accompanied by a very formidable body of infantry and cavalry, came in hot pursuit, eager to overtake them and so chastise them for leaving the country. He had, indeed, permitted them to do so, induced by unmistakable warnings from God. But the disposition of the wicked is, as may be well seen, unstable, suspended as it were on a balance and swayed up and down by the slightest cause in opposite directions. Thus, caught between the enemy and 249 the sea, they despaired each of his own safety. Some thought that the most miserable death would be a welcome blessing, while others, believing it to be better to perish by the elements of nature than to become a laughing-stock to their enemies, purposed

---

^a For §§ 247-257 see Ex. xiv.

ἑαυτοὺς εἰς θάλασσαν διενοοῦντο καὶ τινα τῶν
βάρος ἐχόντων ἐπαχθισάμενοι παρὰ ταῖς ἠϊόσιν
ἐφήδρευον, ἵν', ὁπόταν θεάσωνται τοὺς πολεμίους
ἐγγὺς ὄντας, καθαλλόμενοι ῥᾷον εἰς βυθὸν ἐνε-
250 χθῶσιν. ἀλλὰ γὰρ οἱ μὲν πρὸς τὸ ἄπορον τῆς
ἀνάγκης διεπτόηντο δυσθανατοῦντες· XLVI. ὁ δὲ
προφήτης, ὑπ' ἐκπλήξεως ὁρῶν σεσαγηνευμένον
ὥσπερ βόλον ἰχθύων τὸ σύμπαν ἔθνος, οὐκέτ' ὢν
251 ἐν ἑαυτῷ θεοφορεῖται καὶ θεσπίζει τάδε· " τὸ μὲν
δέος ἀναγκαῖον, φόβος ἐγγὺς καὶ μέγας ὁ κίνδυνος·
ἐξ ἐναντίας ἀχανές ἐστι πέλαγος, ὑπόδρομος εἰς
καταφυγὴν οὐδείς, ἀπορία πλοίων, κατόπιν ἔφεδροι
φάλαγγες ἐχθρῶν, αἳ στείχουσιν ἀπνευστὶ διώ-
κουσαι. ποῖ τις τράπηται, ποῖ τις ἐκνεύσῃ; πάντα
πανταχόθεν ἐξαπιναίως ἐπέθετο, γῆ, θάλαττα,
252 ἄνθρωποι, στοιχεῖα φύσεως. ἀλλὰ θαρρεῖτε, μὴ
ἀποκάμητε, στῆτε ταῖς διανοίαις μὴ κραδαινόμενοι,
προσδοκᾶτε τὴν ἀήττητον ἐκ θεοῦ βοήθειαν· αὐτ-
επάγγελτος ἤδη παρέσται, μὴ ὁρωμένη προαγω-
νιεῖται· πεπείρασθε αὐτῆς ἤδη πολλάκις ἀμυνομένης
ἀφανῶς· βλέπω μέλλουσαν κονίεσθαι, βρόχους τοῖς
αὐχέσι περιβάλλουσαν τῶν ἀντιπάλων· ἕλκει κατὰ
τῆς θαλάττης· μολύβδου τρόπον εἰς βυθὸν χωροῦσιν.
ὑμεῖς μὲν ἔτι ζώντων αἰσθάνεσθε, τεθνεώτων δ'
ἐγὼ φαντασίαν λαμβάνω· τήμερον δὲ καὶ ὑμεῖς
νεκροὺς αὐτοὺς θεάσεσθε."

[174]
253 | Καὶ ὁ μὲν ταῦτ' ἀπεφθέγγετο μείζονα ὄντα
πάσης ἐλπίδος, οἱ δ' ἐπειρῶντο ἔργοις τῆς περὶ
τὸ λόγιον ἀληθείας. ἀπέβαινε γὰρ τὰ χρησθέντα

to throw themselves into the sea, and, loaded with some heavy substances, sat waiting by the shore, so that when they saw the foe near at hand they might leap down and easily sink into the depths. But, 250 while in these helpless straits, they were at death's door with consternation (XLVI.) the prophet, seeing the whole nation entangled in the meshes of panic, like a draught of fishes, was taken out of himself by divine possession and uttered these inspired words : " Alarm you needs must feel. Terror is near at 251 hand : the danger is great. In front is a vast expanse of sea ; no haven for a refuge, no boats at hand : behind, the menace of the enemy's troops, which march along in unresting pursuit. Whither can one turn or swim for safety ? Everything has attacked us suddenly from every side—earth, sea, man, the elements of nature. Yet be of good 252 courage, faint not. Stand with unshaken minds, look for the invincible help which God will send. Self-sent it will be with you anon, invisible it will fight before you. Ere now you have often experienced its unseen defence. I see it preparing for the contest and casting a noose round the necks of the enemy. It drags them down through the sea. They sink like lead into the depths.[a] You see them still alive : I have a vision of them dead, and to-day you too shall see their corpses."

So he spake with words of promise exceeding any- 253 thing they could hope for. But they began to find by the experience of facts the truth of the heavenly message. For what he prophesied came to pass

[a] Taken from the song, Ex. xv. 10 "they sank like lead in the mighty water" and 5, "they sank in the depth like a stone.

PHILO

θείαις δυνάμεσι μύθων ἀπιστότερα· ῥῆξις θαλάττης,
ἀναχώρησις ἑκατέρου τμήματος, πῆξις τῶν κατὰ
τὸ ῥαγὲν μέρος διὰ παντὸς τοῦ βάθους κυμά ων, ἵν᾽
ἀντὶ τειχῶν ᾖ κραταιοτάτων, εὐθυτενὴς ἀνατομὴ
τῆς μεγαλουργηθείσης ὁδοῦ, ᾗ τῶν κρυσταλλω-
254 θέντων μεθόριος ἦν, ὁδοιπορία τοῦ ἔθνους ἀκινδύνως
πεζεύοντος διὰ θαλάττης ὡς ἐπὶ ξηρᾶς ἀτραποῦ καὶ
λιθώδους ἐδάφους—ἐκραυρώθη γὰρ ἡ ψάμμος καὶ ἡ
σπορὰς αὐτῆς οὐσία συμφῦσα ἡνώθη—, ἐχθρῶν
ἀπνευστὶ διωκόντων ἐφόρμησις σπευδόντων ἐπ᾽
οἰκεῖον ὄλεθρον, νεφέλης ὀπισθοφυλακούσης ἡνιό-
χησις, ἐν ᾗ θεία τις ὄψις πυρὸς αὐγὴν ἀπαστράπτουσα ἦν, πελαγῶν ἃ τέως ἀνακοπέντα διειστήκει
παλίρροια, τοῦ διακοπέντος καὶ ἀναξηρανθέντος
255 μέρους αἰφνίδιος θαλάττωσις, πολεμίων φθορά, οὓς
τά τε κρυσταλλωθέντα τείχη καὶ ἀνατραπέντα
κατεύνασε[1] καὶ αἱ πλήμμυραι τοῦ πελάγους ὥσπερ
εἰς φάραγγα τὴν ὁδὸν ἐπενεχθεῖσαι κατέκλυσαν,
ἐπίδειξις τῆς φθορᾶς διὰ τῶν ἐπαναπλευσάντων
σωμάτων, ἃ τὴν ἐπιφάνειαν τοῦ πελάγους κατεστόρεσε, καὶ σφοδρὰ κυμάτωσις, ὑφ᾽ ἧς ἅπαντες οἱ
νεκροὶ σωρηδὸν ἀπεβράσθησαν εἰς τοὺς ἀντιπέραν
αἰγιαλούς, ἀναγκαία θέα γενησόμενοι τοῖς δια-
σωθεῖσιν, οἷς ἐξεγένετο μὴ μόνον τοὺς κινδύνους
διαφυγεῖν ἀλλὰ καὶ ἐπιδεῖν τοὺς ἐχθροὺς οὐκ
ἀνθρωπίναις ἀλλὰ θείαις δύναμεσι παντὸς λόγου
256 μεῖζον κολασθέντας. διόπερ εἰκότως εὐχαρίστοις
ὕμνοις γεραίρει τὸν εὐεργέτην· εἰς γὰρ δύο χοροὺς
διανείμας τὸ ἔθνος, τὸν μὲν ἀνδρῶν, τὸν δὲ
γυναικῶν, ἐξάρχει μὲν αὐτὸς τοῖς ἀνδράσιν, ἔξαρχον

---

[1] MSS. κατένευσε(αν) or κατέκλυσε. Κατευνάζω is a poetical
word used in this sense by Soph. *Ant.* 833.

through the might of God, though harder to credit
than any fable. Let us picture the scene. The
sea breaks in two, and each section retires. The
parts around the break, through the whole depth of
their waters, congeal to serve as walls of vast strength:
a path is drawn straight, a road of miracle between
the frozen walls on either side : the nation makes 254
its passage, marching safely through the sea, as on
a dry path or a stone-paved causeway ; for the sand
is crisped, and its scattered particles grow together
into a unity : the enemy advance in unresting pursuit, hastening to their own destruction : the cloud
goes behind the travellers' rear to guide them on
their way, and within is the vision of the Godhead,
flashing rays of fire. Then the waters which had
been stayed from their course and parted for a while
return to their place : the dried-up cleft between
the walls suddenly becomes a sea again : the enemy 255
meet their doom, sent to their last sleep by the fall
of the frozen walls, and overwhelmed by the tides,
as they rush down upon their path as into a ravine !
that doom is evidenced by the corpses which are
floated to the top and strew the surface of the sea :
last comes a mighty rushing wave, which flings the
corpses in heaps upon the opposite shore, a sight
inevitably to be seen by the saved, thus permitted
not only to escape their dangers, but also to behold
their enemies fallen under a chastisement which no
words can express, through the power of God and
not of man. After this, what should Moses do but 256
honour the Benefactor with hymns of thanksgiving ?
He divides the nation into two choirs, one of men,
the other of women, and himself leads the men while

δὲ καὶ τῶν γυναικῶν καθίστησι τὴν ἀδελφήν, ἵν'
ἄδωσιν ὕμνους εἰς τὸν πατέρα καὶ ποιητὴν ἀντι-
φθόγγοις ἁρμονίαις συνηχοῦντες, διά τε κράσεως
ἠθῶν καὶ μέλους, τῶν μὲν ἐπὶ τὴν αὐτὴν σπευδόντων
ἀμοιβήν, τοῦ δὲ συνισταμένου κατὰ τὴν βαρύτητος
πρὸς ὀξύτητα συμφωνίαν· φθόγγοι γὰρ οἱ μὲν
ἀνδρῶν βαρεῖς, ὀξεῖς δ' οἱ γυναικῶν, ἐξ ὧν, ὅταν
ἡ κρᾶσις γένηται σύμμετρος, ἥδιστον καὶ παν-
257 αρμόνιον ἀποτελεῖται μέλος. τὰς δὲ τοσαύτας
μυριάδας ἔπεισεν ὁμογνωμονῆσαι καὶ τὸν αὐτὸν
ὕμνον ἐν ταὐτῷ συνᾴδειν τὰ τεράστια ἐκεῖνα μεγα-
λουργήματα, περὶ ὧν ὀλίγῳ πρότερον διεξῆλθον·
ἐφ' οἷς ὁ προφήτης γεγηθώς, ὁρῶν καὶ τὴν τοῦ
ἔθνους περιχάρειαν, οὐδ' αὐτὸς ἔτι χωρῶν τὴν
ἡδονήν, κατῆρχε τῆς ᾠδῆς· οἱ δ' ἀκούοντες εἰς
δύο χοροὺς ἁλισθέντες τὰ λεχθέντα συνῇδον.

[175]
258   XLVII. | Τοῦτ' ἐστὶ τῆς κατ' ἐνθουσιασμὸν
προφητείας Μωυσέως ἀρχὴ καὶ προοίμιον. ἑξῆς δὲ
θεσπίζει περὶ τοῦ πρώτου καὶ ἀναγκαιοτάτου,
τροφῆς, ἣν γῆ μὲν οὐκ ἤνεγκε — καὶ γὰρ ἦν στεῖρα
καὶ ἄγονος—, ὤμβρησε δ' οὐρανὸς οὐχ ἅπαξ ἀλλ'
ἐπὶ τεσσαρακονταετίαν ἑκάστης ἡμέρας πρὸ τῆς ἕω
καρπὸν αἰθέριον ἐν δρόσῳ κέγχρῳ παραπλήσιον.
259 ὃν ἰδὼν Μωυσῆς συγκομίζειν κελεύει καὶ ἐπιθειάσας φησί· "πιστεύειν δεῖ τῷ θεῷ πεπειρα-
μένους αὐτοῦ τῶν εὐεργεσιῶν ἐν μείζοσιν ἐλπίδος
πράγμασιν· ἀθησαύριστα, ἀταμίευτα τὰ τῆς τροφῆς
ἔστω· μηδεὶς ἄχρι πρωίας ὑπολειπέσθω μηδὲν

---

a Or "feelings." The thought is that while men and
women have their different characteristics, here for the
578

he appoints his sister to lead the women, that the two in concert might sing hymns to the Father and Creator in tuneful response, with a blending both of temperaments [a] and melody—temperaments eager to render to each other like for like ; melody produced by the concord of treble and bass ; for the voices of men are bass and the women's treble, and when they are blended in due proportion the resulting melody is of the fullest and sweetest harmony. All these myriads were persuaded by Moses to sing 257 with hearts in accord the same song, telling of those mighty and marvellous works which I have recorded just above. And the prophet, rejoicing at this, seeing the people also overjoyed, and himself no longer able to contain his delight, led off the song, and his hearers massed in two choirs sang with him the story of these same deeds.[b]

XLVII. [c] It was thus that Moses began and opened 258 his work as a prophet possessed by God's spirit. His next utterance of this sort was concerned with that primary and most necessary matter, food ; and this food was not produced by the earth, which was barren and unfruitful, but heaven rained down before daybreak, not once only but every day for forty years, a celestial fruit in the form of dew, like millet grain. When Moses saw it, he bade them gather it, and 259 said under inspiration : " We must trust God as we have experienced His kindnesses in deeds greater than we could have hoped for. Do not treasure up or store the food He sends. Let none leave any

moment they are entirely united. The phrase is often used by Philo as a synonym for ὁμόνοια and the like.

   [b] *i.e.* " the above-mentioned." Others take it to mean the words which Moses said to them.

   [c] For §§ 258-269 see Ex. xvi. 4-30.

260 αὐτῆς μέρος." τοῦτ' ἀκούσαντες ἔνιοι τῶν πρὸς
εὐσέβειαν ἀνερματίστων, ὑπολαβόντες ἴσως οὐ
χρησμοὺς ἀλλὰ παραίνεσιν ἄρχοντος εἶναι τὰ
λεγόμενα, λείπουσιν εἰς τὴν ὑστεραίαν· τὸ δὲ
σηπόμενον τὸν κύκλον τοῦ στρατοπέδου δυσοδμίας
πληροῖ τὸ πρῶτον, εἶτ' εἰς σκώληκας, ὧν ἡ γένεσις
261 ἐκ φθορᾶς ἐστι, μετέβαλεν. ἅπερ ἰδὼν Μωυσῆς
εἰκότως ἐπὶ τοῖς ἀπειθέσι πικραίνεται· πῶς γὰρ
οὐκ ἔμελλεν, εἰ τοσαῦτα καὶ τηλικαῦτα θεασάμενοι,
πρὸς μὲν τὰς πιθανὰς καὶ εὐλόγους φαντασίας
ἀδύνατα πραχθῆναι, τελειωθέντα δὲ εὐμαρῶς ἐπι-
φροσύναις θείαις, οὐκ ἐνδοιάζουσι μόνον, ἀλλὰ καὶ
262 ἀπιστοῦσιν οἱ δυσμαθέστατοι πάντων; ἀλλ' ὅ γε
πατὴρ δυσὶν ἐναργεστάταις ἀποδείξεσι τὸ λόγιον
τοῦ προφήτου διασυνέστησεν, ὧν τὴν μὲν ἑτέραν
εὐθὺς ἀπεδείξατο φθορᾷ τοῦ ὑπολειφθέντος καὶ
δυσωδίᾳ καὶ τῇ πρὸς σκώληκας, τὸ φαυλότατον
ζῷον, μεταβολῇ, τὴν δ' ἑτέραν ὕστερον· ἀεὶ γὰρ τὸ
πλεονάζον τοῦ συγκομισθέντος ὑπὸ τῆς πληθύος
ταῖς ἡλιακαῖς ἀκτῖσι διελύετο καὶ τηκόμενον
ἐξανηλοῦτο.
263 XLVIII. Δεύτερον οὐκ εἰς μακρὰν ἐπιθειάσας
ἀποφθέγγεται λόγιον τὸ περὶ τῆς ἱερᾶς ἑβδόμης.
ἔχουσαν γὰρ αὐτὴν ἐν τῇ φύσει προνομίαν, οὐκ ἀφ'
οὗ μόνον ἐδημιουργήθη ὁ κόσμος, ἀλλὰ καὶ πρὸ τῆς
οὐρανοῦ καὶ παντὸς αἰσθητοῦ γενέσεως, ἠγνόησαν
ἄνθρωποι, τάχα που διὰ τὰς ἐν ὕδασι καὶ πυρὶ
γενομένας συνεχεῖς καὶ ἐπαλλήλους φθορὰς οὐ
δυνηθέντων παρὰ τῶν πρότερον διαδέξασθαι μνήμην
τῶν ἔπειτα τῆς κατὰ τὸν ἐν χρόνοις εἱρμὸν ἀκολου-
θίας καὶ τάξεως· ὅπερ ἀδηλούμενον ἐπιθειάσας

part of it over till the morrow." On hearing this, 260
some whose piety had little ballast, thinking perhaps
that the statement was no divine oracle but just the
exhortation of the ruler, left it to the next day ; but
it first rotted and filled the whole extent of the camp
with its stench, and then turned into worms which
are bred from corruption. Moses, seeing this, was 261
naturally and indeed inevitably indignant at their
disobedience—to think that after witnessing wonders
so many and so great, impossibilities no doubt as
judged by what to outward appearance is credible
and reasonable but easily accomplished by the
dispensations of God's providence, they not only
doubted, but in their utter incapacity for learning
actually disbelieved. But the Father confirmed the 262
utterance of the prophet with two most convincing
proofs. One proof He had given at the time, when
what was left over corrupted and stank and then was
changed into worms, the vilest of living creatures.
The other He gave later, for the unneeded surplus
over what was gathered by the multitude was
dissolved by the sun's rays, melted away and
disappeared.

XLVIII. Not long after, Moses delivered a second 263
inspired pronouncement concerning the sacred
seventh day. That day has held the place of honour
in nature, not merely from the time when the world
was framed, but even before the heaven and all that
sense perceives came into being. Yet men knew it
not, perhaps because by reason of the constant and
repeated destructions by water and fire the later
generations did not receive from the former the
memory of the order and sequence of events in the
series of years.[a] This hidden truth Moses, under

ἀνέφηνε λογίῳ μαρτυρηθέντι διὰ σημείου τινὸς
264 ἐναργοῦς. τὸ δὲ σημεῖον τοιοῦτον ἦν· ἐλάττων μὲν
ἀπ᾽ ἀέρος ἐγίνετο ἡ φορὰ ταῖς προτέραις ἡμέραις
τῆς τροφῆς, τότε δ᾽ αὖ διπλασίων· καὶ ταῖς μὲν
προτέραις εἴ τι κατελείφθη, λειβόμενον ἐτήκετο
μέχρι τοῦ παντελῶς εἰς νοτίδα μεταβαλὸν ἀναλωθῆναι, τότε δ᾽ οὐδεμίαν ἐνδεχόμενον τροπὴν ἐν
ὁμοίῳ διέμενεν· ἐφ᾽ οἷς ἀγγελλομένοις ἅμα καὶ
ὁρωμένοις καταπλαγεὶς Μωυσῆς οὐκ ἐστοχάσατο
[176] μᾶλλον ἢ θεοφορηθεὶς ἐθέσπισε τὴν ἑβδόμην. | ἐῶ
265 λέγειν, ὅτι καὶ αἱ τοιαῦται εἰκασίαι συγγενεῖς
προφητείας εἰσίν· ὁ γὰρ νοῦς οὐκ ἂν οὕτως εὐσκόπως εὐθυβόλησεν, εἰ μὴ καὶ θεῖον ἦν πνεῦμα τὸ
266 ποδηγετοῦν πρὸς αὐτὴν τὴν ἀλήθειαν. τὸ δὲ
τεράστιον οὐ μόνον ἐκ τοῦ διπλασιασθῆναι τὴν
τροφὴν ἐδηλοῦτο οὐδ᾽ ἐκ τοῦ διαμεῖναι σῶον παρὰ
τὸ καθεστὼς ἔθος, ἀλλὰ κἀκ τοῦ ἀμφότερα ταῦτα
συμβῆναι κατὰ τὴν ἕκτην ἡμέραν, ἀφ᾽ ἧς ἤρξατο
ἀπ᾽ ἀέρος ἡ τροφὴ χορηγεῖσθαι, μεθ᾽ ἣν ὁ ἱερώτατος τῆς ἑβδόμης ἀριθμὸς ἔμελλεν ἀνατέλλειν,
ὥστε λογιζόμενος ἄν τις εὕροι κατὰ τὴν ἀκολουθίαν
τῆς τοῦ κόσμου γενέσεως τὴν οὐράνιον δοθεῖσαν
τροφήν· ἤρξατο γὰρ καὶ τὸν κόσμον ἑξάδος τῇ
πρώτῃ δημιουργεῖν καὶ τὴν λεχθεῖσαν ὕειν τροφήν.
267 ἡ δ᾽ εἰκὼν ὁμοιοτάτη· καθάπερ γὰρ ἐκ τοῦ μὴ
ὄντος εἰς τὸ εἶναι τὸ τελειότατον ἔργον, τὸν κόσμον,
ἀνέφηνε, τὸν αὐτὸν τρόπον καὶ εὐθηνίαν ἐν ἐρήμῳ
μεταβαλὼν τὰ στοιχεῖα πρὸς τὸ κατεπεῖγον τῆς
χρείας, ἵν᾽ ἀντὶ γῆς ὁ ἀὴρ σιτία τροφὴν ἄπονον

inspiration, revealed in an announcement to which a manifest sign gave testimony. This sign was as follows : the shower of food from the air was less on the first days, but on a later day was doubled ; and on those first days anything left melted and was dissolved till, after turning completely into moisture, it disappeared ; but on that later day it admitted no change and remained just as it had been. Moses, when he heard of this and also actually saw it, was awestruck and, guided by what was not so much surmise as God-sent inspiration, made announcement of the sabbath. I need hardly say that conjectures of this kind are closely akin to prophecies. For the mind could not have made so straight an aim if there was not also the divine spirit guiding it to the truth itself. Now the greatness of the wonder was shown not only by the double supply of food and its remaining sound contrary to the usual happening, but by the combination of both these occurring on the sixth day, counting from the day on which the food began to be supplied from the air ; and that sixth day was to be followed by the dawning of the seventh which is the most sacred of numbers. And therefore consideration will show the inquirer that the food given from heaven followed the analogy of the birth of the world ; for both the creating of the world and also the raining of the said food were begun by God on the first day out of six. The copy reproduces the original very exactly : for, as God called up His most perfect work, the world, out of not being into being, so He called up plenty in the desert, changing round the elements to meet the pressing need of the occasion, so that instead of the earth the air bore food for their nourishment, and

φέρῃ καὶ ἀταλαίπωρον οἷς ἀναχώρησις οὐκ ἦν
εὐτρεπίζεσθαι κατὰ σχολὴν τἀπιτήδεια.

268 μετὰ ταῦτα τρίτον ἀναφθέγγεται χρησμὸν τερατωδέστατον, δηλῶν ὅτι τῇ ἑβδόμῃ τὴν εἰωθυῖαν
ὁ ἀὴρ οὐ παρέξει τροφὴν καὶ οὐδὲν ἐπὶ γῆν ἀλλ᾽
οὐδὲ τὸ βραχύτατον ὡς ἔθος ἐνεχθήσεται. τοῦτ᾽

269 ἀπέβαινεν ἔργοις· τῇ μὲν γὰρ προτεραίᾳ ταῦτα
θεσπίζει, τινὲς δὲ τῶν ἀβεβαίων τὸ ἦθος ὥρμησαν
ἐπὶ τὴν συγκομιδὴν καὶ σφαλέντες τῆς ἐλπίδος ἐπανῄεσαν ἄπρακτοι, κακίζοντες μὲν ἑαυτοὺς τῆς
ἀπιστίας, ἀληθόμαντιν δὲ καὶ θεοφράδμονα καὶ
μόνον προορατικὸν τῶν ἀδήλων ἀνακαλοῦντες τὸν
προφήτην.

270 XLIX. Τοιαῦτα μέν ἐστιν, ἃ περὶ τῆς οὐρανίου
τροφῆς κατεχόμενος ἐθέσπισεν. ἕτερα δ᾽ ἑξῆς
ἀναγκαῖα, καίτοι δόξαντα ἂν παραινέσεσιν ἐοικέναι
μᾶλλον ἢ χρησμοῖς, ὧν ἐστι καὶ τὸ χρησθὲν κατὰ
τὴν μεγίστην τῶν πατρίων ἐκδιαίτησιν, περὶ ἧς
καὶ πρόσθεν εἶπον, ἡνίκα τεκτηνάμενοι ταῦρον
χρυσοῦν, Αἰγυπτιακοῦ μίμημα τύφου, χοροὺς
ἵστασαν καὶ βωμοὺς κατεσκεύαζον καὶ θυσίας
ἀνῆγον ἐκλαθόμενοι τοῦ πρὸς ἀλήθειαν θεοῦ καὶ
τὴν προγονικὴν εὐγένειαν, ἣ δι᾽ εὐσεβείας καὶ

271 ὁσιότητος ηὐξήθη, καθαιροῦντες. ἐφ᾽ οἷς Μωυσῆς
περιπαθήσας, εἰ πρῶτον μὲν ὁ λαὸς πᾶς ἐξαίφνης
γεγένηται τυφλὸς ὁ ἄχρι πρὸ μικροῦ πάντων ἐθνῶν
[177] ὀξυωπέστατος, ἔπειτα δὲ εἰ πλάσμα | μύθου κατ-
εψευσμένον ἴσχυσε τοσαύτην αὐγὴν σβέσαι τῆς

---

[a] For §§ 270-274 see Ex. xxxii.
[b] See note on § 162 above.

that without labour or travail for those who had no chance of resorting to any deliberate process of providing sustenance.   After this, he uttered 268 a third prophetic saying of truly marvellous import. He declared that on the sabbath the air would not yield the accustomed food, and that nothing would come down to earth as it had done before, not even the smallest morsel. And this proved true in the 269 result, for it was on the day before the sabbath that he prophesied this, but on the morrow some of the weaker-minded set out to gather the food but were disappointed and returned baffled, reproaching themselves for their disbelief and hailing the prophet as a true seer, an interpreter of God, and alone gifted with foreknowledge of the hidden future.

XLIX. [a] Such was his pronouncement under divine 270 inspiration on the matter of the food which came from heaven, but there are examples to follow which must be noted, though perhaps they may be thought to resemble exhortations rather than oracular sayings. Among these is the command given at their great backsliding from the ways of their fathers, about which I have spoken above. This was when, after fashioning a golden bull in imitation of the vanity of Egypt,[b] they set up choirs and built altars and brought victims for sacrifice in forgetfulness of the true God and to the ruin of the high-born qualities inherited from their forefathers and fostered by piety and holiness. At this, Moses was cut to the heart to 271 think that in the first place the whole people had suddenly been blinded who a few hours ago had excelled every nation in clearness of vision, and secondly, that a fable falsely invented could quench the bright radiance of truth—truth on which no

ἀληθείας, ἣν οὔθ' ἥλιος ἐκλιπὼν οὔθ' ὁ σύμπας χορὸς τῶν ἀστέρων ἐπισκιάσει—περιλάμπεται γὰρ ἰδίῳ φέγγει νοητῷ καὶ ἀσωμάτῳ, πρὸς ὃ παραβαλλόμενον τὸ αἰσθητὸν νὺξ ἂν πρὸς ἡμέραν εἶναι 272 νομισθείη—, δι' ἣν αἰτίαν οὐκέτι μένων ὁ αὐτὸς ἐξαλλάττεται τό τε εἶδος καὶ τὴν διάνοιαν καὶ ἐπιθειάσας φησί· "τίς ἐστιν ὁ μὴ τῷ πλάνῳ συνενεχθεὶς μηδὲ τὸ κῦρος ἐπιφημίσας τοῖς ἀκύροις; 273 πᾶς ὁ τοιοῦτος ἐμοὶ προσίτω." μιᾶς δὲ φυλῆς προσελθούσης οὐχ ἧττον ταῖς διανοίαις ἢ τοῖς σώμασιν, οἳ πάλαι μὲν ἐφόνων κατὰ τῶν ἀθέων καὶ ἀνοσιουργῶν, ἡγεμόνα δ' ἐζήτουν καὶ στρατάρχην ἀνευρεῖν, ὃς ἐνδίκως ὑφηγήσεται καιρὸν καὶ τρόπον τῆς ἀμύνης,—οὓς ὀργῶντας εὑρὼν καὶ γέμοντας εὐτολμίας καὶ παραστήματος, ἔτι μᾶλλον ἢ πρότερον θεοφορηθείς, "ξίφος ἕκαστος ὑμῶν ἀναλαβὼν" φησίν "ἀττέτω διὰ παντὸς τοῦ στρατοπέδου καὶ κτεινέτω μὴ μόνον ἀλλοτρίους ἀλλὰ καὶ φίλων καὶ συγγενῶν τοὺς οἰκειοτάτους ἐπιστροφάδην, εὐαγέστατον κρίνων τὸ ἔργον ὑπὲρ ἀληθείας καὶ θεοῦ τιμῆς, ὧν ὑπερμαχεῖν καὶ προαγωνίζεσθαι κουφό- 274 τατος πόνος." οἱ δ' αὐτοβοεὶ τρισχιλίους κτείναντες τοὺς ἀρχηγέτας μάλιστα τῆς ἀσεβείας γενομένους οὐκ ἀπελογήσαντο μόνον περὶ τοῦ μὴ συνεφάψασθαι τοῦ τολμήματος, ἀλλὰ καὶ ἐν ἀριστέων τοῖς γενναιοτάτοις ἐνεγράφησαν καὶ γέρως ἠξιώθησαν οἰκειοτάτου ταῖς πράξεσιν, ἱερωσύνης· ἔδει γὰρ θεραπευτὰς ὁσιότητος γενέσθαι τοὺς ὑπὲρ αὐτῆς ἀνδραγαθισαμένους καὶ προπολεμήσαντας.

eclipse of the sun or of all the starry choir can cast
a shadow, since it is illumined by its own light, the
intelligible, the incorporeal, compared with which
the light of the senses would seem to be as night
compared with day. He therefore became another 272
man, changed both in outward appearance and mind ;
and, filled with the spirit, he cried : " Who is there
who has no part with this delusion nor has given to
no-lords the name of lordship ? Let all such come
to me." One tribe came at the call, bringing with 273
them their minds no less than their bodies, men who
for some time had been breathing slaughter against
the godless workers of unholiness, but sought to find
a leader and captain who would have the right to
tell them when and how to make this attack. When
Moses found them hot with rage and brimful of
courage and resolution, he was more than ever
possessed by the spirit and said : " Let each of you
take his sword and rush through the whole camp, and
slay not only those who are strangers to you but also
the very nearest of your friends and kinsfolk. Mow
them down, holding that to be a truly righteous deed
which is done for truth and God's honour, a cause
which to champion and defend is the lightest of
labours." So they slaughtered three thousand of the 274
principal leaders in godlessness, without meeting any
resistance, and thereby not only made good their
defence against the charge of having been party
to the shameless crime, but were accounted as the
noblest of heroes and awarded the prize most suitable
to their action, that is the priesthood. For it was
meet that the duty of ministering to holiness should
be given to those who had battled and acquitted
themselves bravely in its defence.

PHILO

275 L. Ἔχω δέ τι μηνῦσαι σημειωδέστερον λόγιον,
περὶ οὗ καὶ πάλαι διεξῆλθον, ὅτε τὰ τῆς ἀρχ-
ιερωσύνης ἐπῄειν τοῦ προφήτου, ὅπερ αὐτὸς πάλιν
κατασχεθεὶς ἀνεφθέγξατο, τελειωθὲν οὐ μακροῖς
276 χρόνοις ὕστερον, ἀλλ' εὐθὺς ὅτ' ἐχρησμῳδεῖτο. τῶν
περὶ τὸν νεὼν λειτουργῶν δύο τάξεις εἰσίν, ἡ μὲν
κρείσσων ἱερέων, ἡ δ' ἐλάττων νεωκόρων· ἦσαν δὲ
κατ' ἐκεῖνον τὸν χρόνον τρεῖς μὲν ἱερεῖς, νεωκόρων
277 δὲ πολλαὶ χιλιάδες. οὗτοι φυσηθέντες ἐπὶ τῇ τοῦ
οἰκείου πλήθους περιουσίᾳ τῆς τῶν ἱερέων κατ-
εφρόνουν ὀλιγότητος καὶ δύο ἐν ταὐτῷ παρανομή-
ματα συνύφαινον, ὧν τὸ μὲν ἦν καθαίρεσις τῶν
ὑπερεχόντων, τὸ δ' αὔξησις τῶν ἐλαττόνων, οἷα
ἡγεμόσιν ὑπηκόων ἐπιτιθεμένων ἐπὶ συγχύσει τοῦ
278 κρατίστου καὶ δημωφελεστάτου, τῆς τάξεως. εἶτ'
ἐπισυνιστάμενοι καὶ ἀθροιζόμενοι κατεβόων τοῦ
προφήτου, ὡς δι' οἰκειότητα τῷ τε ἀδελφῷ καὶ
[178] τοῖς | ἀδελφιδοῖς χαρισαμένου τὴν ἱερωσύνην καὶ
ἐπιψευσαμένου τὰ περὶ τὴν αἵρεσιν αὐτῶν, ὡς
ἐπιφροσύνῃ θείᾳ, καθάπερ διεξῄειμεν, μὴ γενόμενα.
279 ἐφ' οἷς ἀνιαθεὶς καὶ περιαλγήσας, καίτοι πρᾶότατος
ὢν καὶ ἡμερώτατος, οὕτως πρὸς δικαίαν ὀργὴν ὑπὸ
μισοπονήρου πάθους ἠκονήθη, ὡς ἱκετεῦσαι τὸν
θεὸν ἀποστραφῆναι τὴν θυσίαν αὐτῶν, οὐκ ἐπειδήπερ ἔμελλεν ὁ δικαιότατος κριτὴς ἱερουργίας
ἀσεβῶν παραδέχεσθαι, ἀλλ' ὅτι καὶ ἡ ψυχὴ τοῦ
θεοφιλοῦς τὸ κατ' αὐτὴν μέρος οὐχ ὑποσιωπᾷ,
σπεύδουσα μὴ εὐοδεῖν ἀνοσίους, ἀλλ' ἀεὶ τῆς

ᵃ For §§ 275-287 see Num. xvi.
ᵇ i.e. Aaron, Eleazar, and Ithamar. The death, or
according to Philo the translation, of Nadab and Abihu is
dated before this.

L. *a* There is another still more remarkable utter- 275
ance of this kind which I may mention. It is one
which I described some way back when I was speaking of the prophet in his capacity of high priest. This
again came from his own mouth when again under
possession, and it was fulfilled not long afterwards
but at the very time when the prediction was given.
The ministers of the temple are of two ranks, the 276
higher consisting of priests, the lower of temple
attendants; and at that time there were three priests *b*
but many thousand attendants. These last, puffed 277
with pride at their own numerical superiority over
the priests, despised their fewness, and combined in
the same deed two trespasses, by attempting on the
one hand to bring low the superior, on the other to
exalt the inferior. This is what happens when subjects attack their rulers to confound that most excellent promoter of the common weal, order. Then, 278
conspiring with each other, and collecting in great
numbers, they raised an outcry against the prophet,
declaring that he had bestowed the priesthood on his
brother and nephews because of their relation to him,
and had given a false account of their election, which
had not really been made under divine direction, as we
stated it above to be. Moses, greatly hurt and grieved 279
at this, though the mildest and meekest of men, was
so spurred to righteous anger by his passionate hatred
of evil that he besought God to turn His face from
their sacrifice ; not that the All-righteous Judge
would ever accept the ministries of the impious, but
because the soul of one whom God loves must also do
its part and not keep silence, so eagerly does it desire
that the unholy may not prosper but ever fail to

280 προθέσεως διαμαρτάνειν. ἔτι δὲ ζέων καὶ πεπυρω-
μένος ὑπὸ τῆς νομίμου διαγανακτήσεως ἐνθουσιᾷ
μεταβαλὼν εἰς προφήτην καὶ θεσπίζει τάδε· '' χαλεπὸν ἀπιστία πρᾶγμα τοῖς ἀπίστοις μόνοις· τούτους¹
οὐ λόγος ἀλλ' ἔργα παιδεύει· παθόντες εἴσονται τὸ
281 ἐμὸν ἀψευδές, ἐπεὶ μαθόντες οὐκ ἔγνωσαν. ἐπι-
κριθήσεται δὲ τοῦτο τῇ τοῦ βίου τελευτῇ· εἰ μὲν
γὰρ θάνατον ἐνδέξονται τὸν κατὰ φύσιν, πέπλασμαι
τὰ λόγια, εἰ δὲ καινόν τινα καὶ παρηλλαγμένον, τὸ
φιλάληθές μοι μαρτυρηθήσεται. χάσματα γῆς ὁρῶ
διηνοιγμένης ἐπὶ μήκιστον εὐρυνόμενα, πολυανθρώπους ἀπολλυμένας συγγενείας, αὐτάνδρους ὑπο-
συρομένας καὶ καταπινομένας οἰκίας, ζῶντας ἀν-
282 θρώπους εἰς ᾅδου κατερχομένους.'' ἐπεὶ δ' ἡσύ-
χασε, ῥήγνυται μὲν ἡ γῆ σεισμῷ τιναχθεῖσα,
ῥήγνυται δὲ καθ' ὃ μάλιστα μέρος αἱ σκηναὶ τῶν
ἀσεβῶν ἦσαν, ὡς ὑπενεχθείσας ἀθρόας ἐπικρυ-
φθῆναι· τὰ γὰρ διαστάντα μέρη πάλιν συνῆλθε, τῆς
283 χρείας ἀποτελεσθείσης, ἧς ἕνεκα διεζεύχθη. μικρὸν
δ' ὕστερον τοὺς τῆς στάσεως ἡγεμόνας πεντήκοντα
πρὸς τοῖς διακοσίοις ἄνδρας κεραυνοὶ κατασκή-
ψαντες αἰφνίδιον ἀθρόους ἐξανάλωσαν μηδὲν μέρος
ὑπολειπόμενοι τῶν σωμάτων, ὃ ταφῆς ἐπιμοιρά-
284 σεται. τὸ δὲ τῶν τιμωριῶν ἐπάλληλον καὶ τὸ
ἑκατέρας μέγεθος διάσημον καὶ περιβόητον ἀπέφηνε
τὴν εὐσέβειαν τοῦ προφήτου χρησαμένου θεῷ
285 μάρτυρι τῆς περὶ τοὺς χρησμοὺς ἀληθείας. ἄξιον
δὲ κἀκεῖνο μὴ παριδεῖν, ὅτι τὰς κατὰ τῶν ἀσεβῶν
κολάσεις διεκληρώσαντο γῆ καὶ οὐρανός, αἱ τοῦ
παντὸς ἀρχαί· τὴν γὰρ μοχθηρίαν ἐρρίζωσαν μὲν

---

¹ Mangey with some mss. reads χαλεπὸν ἀπιστία πρᾶγμα·
τοὺς ἀπίστους μόνους τούτους κτλ.

attain their purpose. While his heart was still hot 280
within him, burning with lawful indignation, inspiration came upon him, and, transformed into a prophet,
he pronounced these words : " Disbelief falls hardly
on the disbelievers only. Such are schooled by facts
alone, and not by words. Experience will show them
what teaching has failed to show that I do not lie.
This matter will be judged by the manner of their 281
latter end. If the death they meet is in the ordinary
course of nature, my oracles are a false invention ;
but, if it be of a new and different kind, my truthfulness will be attested. I see the earth opened and
vast chasms yawning wide. I see great bands of
kinsfolk perishing, houses dragged down and swallowed up with their inmates, and living men descend-
ing into Hades." As he ceased speaking, the earth 282
burst open under the shock of a convulsion, and the
bursting was just in that part where the tents of
the impious stood, so that they were borne below in
a mass and hidden from sight ; for the gaping sides
closed again when the object was accomplished for
which they had been split asunder. And, shortly 283
after, thunderbolts fell suddenly on two hundred and
fifty men who had led the sedition and destroyed
them in a mass, leaving no part of their bodies to
receive the tribute of burial. The quick succession 284
of these punishments and their magnitude in both
cases clearly and widely established the fame of the
prophet's godliness, to the truth of whose pronouncements God Himself had testified. This too we 285
should not fail to note, that the work of chastising
the impious was shared by earth and heaven, the
fundamental parts of the universe. For they had
set the roots of their wickedness on earth, but let it

ἐπὶ γῆς, ἐξέτειναν δ' εἰς αἰθέρα, τοσοῦτον ὕψος,
286 αὐτὴν διάραντες. ὅθεν καὶ τῶν στοιχείων ἑκάτερον
ἐχορήγησε τὰς τιμωρίας, ἡ μὲν ἵν' ὑποσύρῃ καὶ
καταπίῃ τοὺς τότε βαρύνοντας αὐτὴν ῥαγεῖσα καὶ
διαστᾶσα, ὁ δ' ἵνα καταφλέξῃ καὶ διαφθείρῃ πυρὸς
287 πολλοῦ φοράν, καινότατον ὑετόν, ὀμβρήσας. τὸ
δὲ τέλος καὶ τοῖς καταποθεῖσι καὶ τοῖς ὑπὸ
[179] τῶν κεραυνῶν | διεφθαρμένοις ταὐτὸν ἀπέβαινεν·
οὐδέτεροι γὰρ ἐφάνησαν, οἱ μὲν ἐπικρυφθέντες
γῇ τῇ τοῦ χάσματος συνόδῳ πρὸς τὸ ἰσόπεδον
ἑνωθείσῃ, οἱ δ' ὅλοι δι' ὅλων ἀναλωθέντες ὑπὸ τοῦ
κεραυνίου πυρός.
288 LI. Χρόνοις δ' ὕστερον, ἐπειδὴ τὴν ἐνθένδε ἀποικίαν ἔμελλεν εἰς οὐρανὸν στέλλεσθαι καὶ τὸν θνητὸν
ἀπολιπὼν βίον ἀπαθανατίζεσθαι μετακληθεὶς ὑπὸ
τοῦ πατρός, ὃς αὐτὸν δυάδα ὄντα, σῶμα καὶ ψυχήν,
εἰς μονάδος ἀνεστοιχείου φύσιν ὅλον δι' ὅλων
μεθαρμοζόμενος εἰς νοῦν ἡλιοειδέστατον, τότε δὴ
κατασχεθεὶς οὐκέτι συλλήβδην ἀθρόῳ παντὶ τῷ
ἔθνει θεσπίζειν ἔοικεν ἀλλὰ καὶ κατὰ μέρος ἑκάστῃ
φυλῇ τὰ μέλλοντα γενέσθαι καὶ αὖθις ἀποβησόμενα·
ὧν τὰ μὲν ἤδη συμβέβηκε, τὰ δὲ προσδοκᾶται,
διότι πίστις τῶν μελλόντων ἡ τῶν προγεγονότων
289 τελείωσις. ἥρμοττε γὰρ διαφέροντας καὶ ταῖς
σποραῖς, καὶ μάλιστα ἐν τοῖς μητρῴοις γένεσι, καὶ
βουλευμάτων πολυτρόποις ἰδέαις καὶ τῶν περὶ τὸν
βίον ἐπιτηδευμάτων ἀμυθήτοις διαφοραῖς ὥσπερ
τινὰ κλήρου διανομὴν λογίων καὶ χρησμῶν ἁρμό-
290 ζουσαν εὑρέσθαι. θαυμάσια μὲν οὖν ταῦτα· θαυ-
μασιώτατον δὲ καὶ τὸ τέλος τῶν ἱερῶν γραμμάτων,
ὃ καθάπερ ἐν τῷ ζῴῳ κεφαλὴ τῆς ὅλης νομοθεσίας

ᵃ For §§ 288-291 see Deut. xxxiii. and xxxiv.

grow so high that it mounted right up to ether above. Therefore each of the two elements supplied its punish- 286 ment: earth burst and parted asunder to drag down and swallow up those who had then become a burden to it; heaven poured down the strangest of rainstorms, a great stream of fire to blast them in its flames. Whether they were swallowed up or destroyed by 287 the thunderbolts, the result was the same : neither party was ever seen again, the former hidden in the earth by the closing of the chasm which united to form level ground again, the latter consumed absolutely and entirely by the flame of the thunderbolt.

LI. ᵃ Afterwards the time came when he had to 288 make his pilgrimage from earth to heaven, and leave this mortal life for immortality, summoned thither by the Father Who resolved his twofold nature of soul and body into a single unity, transforming his whole being into mind, pure as the sunlight. Then, indeed, we find him possessed by the spirit, no longer uttering general truths to the whole nation but prophesying to each tribe in particular the things which were to be and hereafter must come to pass. Some of these have already taken place, others are still looked for, since confidence in the future is assured by fulfilment in the past. It was very fitting that 289 persons so different in the history of their birth, particularly in their descent on the mother's side and in the manifold varieties of their thoughts and aims and the endless diversities of their practices and habits of life, should receive as a sort of legacy a suitable apportionment of oracles and inspired sayings. This was indeed wonderful : but most wonderful of 290 all is the conclusion of the Holy Scriptures, which stands to the whole law-book as the head to the living

291 ἐστίν. ἤδη γὰρ ἀναλαμβανόμενος καὶ ἐπ' αὐτῆς
βαλβῖδος ἑστώς, ἵνα τὸν εἰς οὐρανὸν δρόμον διπτά-
μενος εὐθύνῃ, καταπνευσθεὶς καὶ ἐπιθειάσας ζῶν
ἔτι τὰ ὡς ἐπὶ θανόντι ἑαυτῷ προφητεύει δεξιῶς,[1] ὡς
ἐτελεύτησε μήπω τελευτήσας, ὡς ἐτάφη μηδενὸς
παρόντος, δηλονότι χερσὶν οὐ θνηταῖς ἀλλ' ἀθανάτοις
δυνάμεσιν, ὡς οὐδ' ἐν τάφῳ τῶν προπατόρων
ἐκηδεύθη τυχὼν ἐξαιρέτου μνήματος, ὃ μηδεὶς εἶδεν
ἀνθρώπων, ὡς σύμπαν τὸ ἔθνος αὐτὸν ὅλον μῆνα
δακρυρροοῦν ἐπένθησεν ἴδιον καὶ κοινὸν πένθος
ἐπιδειξάμενον ἕνεκα τῆς ἀλέκτου καὶ πρὸς ἕνα
ἕκαστον καὶ πρὸς ἅπαντας εὐνοίας καὶ κηδεμονίας.

292 Τοιοῦτος μὲν ὁ βίος, τοιαύτη δὲ καὶ ἡ τελευτὴ
τοῦ βασιλέως καὶ νομοθέτου καὶ ἀρχιερέως καὶ
προφήτου Μωυσέως διὰ τῶν ἱερῶν γραμμάτων
μνημονεύεται.

[1] A rather strange use: Mangey διεξιών.

creature ; for when he was already being exalted and 291
stood at the very barrier, ready at the signal to direct
his upward flight to heaven, the divine spirit fell upon
him and he prophesied with discernment while still
alive the story of his own death ; told ere the end how
the end came ; told how he was buried with none
present, surely by no mortal hands but by immortal
powers ; how also he was not laid to rest in the tomb
of his forefathers but was given a monument of special
dignity which no man has ever seen ; how all the
nation wept and mourned for him a whole month and
made open display, private and public, of their sorrow,
in memory of his vast benevolence and watchful care
for each one of them and for all.

Such, as recorded in the Holy Scriptures, was the 292
life and such the end of Moses, king, lawgiver, high
priest, prophet.

APPENDIX TO *DE ABRAHAMO*

§ 5. *Laws endowed with life and reason.* Here we have the common idea that the *king* is a "living law" (given in that form in *Mos.* ii. 4, where see note) extended to the good and wise in general, *cf. De Virt.* 194 νόμοι δέ τινες ἄγραφοι καὶ οἱ βίοι τῶν ζηλωσάντων τὴν ἀρετήν.

§ 12. *Enos . . . is fourth.* That the number is obtained by the omission of Cain rather than Abel is suggested by *Quaest. in Gen.* i. 81 "quare neque terrigena patris successorem eum (*i.e.* Cain) indicat neque caput posteriorum generationum."

§ 17. *Transferred him.* In this passage Philo, to support his idea of Enoch as signifying repentance, takes μετετέθη as referring to a moral change in this life. The common view (*cf.* Hebrews xi. 5 "translated that he should not see death") is adopted in *Quaest. in Gen.* i. 86, and perhaps also in *De Mut.* 38.

§ 51. *Relative instead of absolute.* Philo, as often, shews his familiarity with grammatical terms. The distinction between relative nouns (πρός τι, Lat. *ad aliquid*) and absolute (usually ἀπολελυμένα, whence Lat. *absoluta*) is regularly given by Greek and Latin grammarians. θεός is usually an "absolute," but the addition "of Abraham," etc., makes it a "relative," as "father" or "king" always is. *Cf. De Mut.* 27 and note.

§ 99. *Natural philosophers.* The Stoic view of the higher study of nature is well illustrated by *S.V.F.* ii. 42 (from Chrysippus) τῶν δὲ φυσικῶν ἔσχατος εἶναι ὁ περὶ τῶν θεῶν λόγος, and *ibid.* 44 the study of φυσική comes later than λογική and ἠθική—θειοτέρα γάρ ἐστι καὶ βαθυτέρας δεῖται τῆς ἐπιστάσεως.

§§ 100-102. The thought of these sections is not quite clear and the translation might perhaps be improved. Philo seems to be criticizing an allegorization, which is not his own, on the ground that it reverses the spiritual connexion

597

PHILO

between the mind and virtue, though as a matter of fact
he adopts the same interpretation of Abraham's relation to
Sarah in *De Cher.* and elsewhere. The criticism begins with
ἐναντιώτατοι δέ (§ 100), where δέ = " but " rather than " now,"
and ends with σωτήριον (§ 102), so that ἅπαντες μὲν οὖν might be
translated " however that may be, all men . . ." In § 101
ἢ μήποτε, " or perhaps," is not very clear, nor is the " perhaps however " of the translation. One would like to read
καὶ μήποτε or μήποτε δὲ.

§ 118. *Gave the appearance of both eating and drinking.*
So Josephus, *Ant.* i. 197 οἱ δὲ δόξαν αὐτῷ πάρεσχον ἐσθιόντων,
and so later Rabbinical writers (references in Cohn's translation of this book, p. 121). This is a point sometimes supposed to shew Josephus's dependence on Philo. But the doubt
whether angels would really eat and drink would naturally
be felt and noted in any discussion of the story. The same
may be said of § 170, where the statement that Abraham told
no one in his household of the divine command to sacrifice,
is compared by commentators to a similar statement in
Joseph. *Ant.* i. 225.

§ 182. The practice of " Suttee " seems to have been well-
known from the time of Alexander. Strabo xv. 30 and 62
quotes Onesicritus and Aristobulus, both companions of
Alexander, as having reported the existence of the custom
in different tribes. Diodorus Siculus xix. 33 gives a long
account of the competition between the two wives of the
Indian prince Keteus, who was killed in the wars of Anti-
gonus 316 B.C., for the honour of dying on their husband's
pyre, and of the joy with which the one chosen went to her
death.

§ 244. *The supremely perfect number.* The term Panteleia
seems to have been rather a divine name for ten in Pythagorean use than a mere epithet. Stobaeus, *Ecl.* i. 1. 10
(p. 22 H.) says that Pythagoras gave the name of Apollo
to one, Artemis to two, Aphrodite to six, Athena to seven,
Poseidon to eight, and Panteleia to ten. The word is once
applied by Philo to seven, but to ten in the other five cases,
in which he uses it of a number.

§ 257. This passage is quoted by Wyttenbach in his note
on Plutarch, *Consolatio ad Apollonium* 102 D. Plutarch there
advocates μετριοπάθεια in bereavements in similar terms and
proceeds to quote Crantor the Academician Περὶ πένθους to
the same effect. The same passage from Crantor is quoted

APPENDICES

by Cic. *Tusc. Disp.* iii. 12, and his book may very possibly have been in Philo's mind.

§ 261. Here once more we have the Stoic paradox of the sage as king (see *S.V.F.* iii. 617). See note on *De Mut.* 152 (where the saying is founded on the same text as here) for other references in Philo.

APPENDIX TO *DE IOSEPHO*

§ 3. στρατηγίας. It should perhaps be noted that the papyri (see L. & S. 1935) shew that στρατηγός was in common use as the title of a civil as well as military governor of a nome in Ptolemaic and Roman Egypt. But this hardly justifies its use as an antithesis to στρατηγός in the military sense.

§ 20. *Less grievous to suffer wrong than to do it.* This thought, which is, of course, one of the leading ideas of the *Republic*, is expressed in almost the same words as here *Gorgias* 469 c ἑλοίμην ἂν μᾶλλον ἀδικεῖσθαι ἢ ἀδικεῖν, *ibid.* 508 B ἀληθῆ ἄρα ἦν τὸ εἶναι τὸ ἀδικεῖν τοῦ ἀδικεῖσθαι, ὅσῳπερ αἴσχιον, τοσούτῳ κάκιον, and so again 509 c.

§ 28. *Addition to nature.* This idea of the superfluousness of the laws of the different states, which follows naturally on the Stoic doctrine of the law of nature, is expressed in the view attributed to Zeno by Plutarch, ἵνα μὴ κατὰ πόλεις μηδὲ κατὰ δήμους οἰκῶμεν, ἰδίοις ἕκαστοι διωρισμένοι δικαίοις, ἀλλὰ πάντας ἀνθρώπους ἡγώμεθα δημότας καὶ πολίτας (*S.V.F.* i. 262). Compare also Chrysippus's exposure of the ridiculous varieties in laws and customs, *ibid.* iii. 322.

§ 38. *Statesmanship the household management of the general public.* Compare the opening of Plato's *Politicus*, particularly 259 c ἐπιστήμη μία περὶ πάντ᾽ ἐστὶ ταῦτα· ταύτην δὲ εἴτε βασιλικὴν εἴτε πολιτικὴν εἴτε οἰκονομικήν τις ὀνομάζοι μηδὲν αὐτῷ διαφερώμεθα. The idea is combated by Aristotle at the beginning of the *Politics*, but admitted by him of monarchy iii. 10.2 ὥσπερ γὰρ ἡ οἰκονομικὴ βασιλεία τις οἰκίας ἐστίν, οὕτως ἡ βασιλεία πόλεως . . . οἰκονομία.

§ 48. Seneca in his *Phaedra* has some fairly close parallels to these sections, put into the mouth of Hippolytus. Thus

APPENDICES

in 145 ff., supposing the crime remains undetected, "Quid ille qui mundum gerit?" Then 159 ff.:

> sed ut secundus numinum abscondat favor
> coitus nefandos utque contingat stupro
> negata magnis sceleribus semper fides,
> quid poena praesens, conscius mentis pavor
> animusque culpa plenus et semet timens?

Considering the likeness of the themes, Philo may very possibly have had in mind some similar passage in the earlier and lost *Hippolytus* of Euripides, or the lost play of Sophocles on the same subject, on which Seneca's play is based. It may be observed that the phrase ὀρθοῖς ὄμμασιν in 47 occurs in Sophocles, *Oed. Tyr.* 1385 in the same sort of context:

> τοιάνδ' ἐγὼ κηλῖδα μηνύσας ἐμὴν
> ὀρθοῖς ἔμελλον ὄμμασιν τούτους ὁρᾶν;

See on this subject Dr. Martin Braun, *Griechischer Roman und hellenische Geschichtsschreibung.*

§ 62. *Cooks and physicians.* Another reminiscence of the *Gorgias*, where medicine is shewn as standing in the same relation to cookery as justice and legislation bear to the "flattery" of rhetoric, 464 D ff., also 500 B and 501 A.

§§ 125-147. Arnim in his *Quellenstudien zu Philo von Alexandria* discusses these sections in a chapter headed "Philo und Aenesidem." In the first part of this chapter he deals with the reproduction of the "Tropes of Aenesidemus" in *De Ebr.* 171-205, and also with the close connexion of the philosophy of that sceptic with that of Heracleitus. His best, though not his only point, is the resemblance of the treatise of Plutarch *De E apud Delphos*, chap. xviii., a chapter in which Heracleitus is twice cited, and which is supposed to be Heracleitean throughout, to §§ 127-129 of *De Iosepho.* In both the same point is made that each successive stage of life from childhood to old age brings the death of the previous stage, and the same inference is drawn that we need not fear the final death.

However this may be, it should be noted that in the *De Iosepho* we do not find the same type of scepticism as in *De Ebr.*, if indeed it can be called scepticism at all. Human life is a "dream," it is "full of confusion, disorder, and uncertainty," and men, as a whole, are incapable of knowledge,

601

PHILO

but the dream is interpreted by the true statesman. The same interpreter can give adequate guidance on moral questions, and though this is not perhaps opposed to the principles of the sceptics, who admitted probability as supplying a rule of conduct, it is very different from the view expressed in *De Ebr.* 197, that only the foolish will assert positively that any particular thing is just or prudent or honourable.

§ 168. βαθεῖ ἤθει. The exact meaning of this phrase is obscure. Cohn translates *in tiefer Bewegung*, Mangey *profunda solertia*. But neither of these fits in well with any sense of ἤθος known to me. The combination occurs again in *Quod Omn. Prob.* 144, where to illustrate the advisability of answering threats mildly the story is told of the slave-musician Antigenidas that when one of his rivals in a rage threatened to buy him, he replied, βαθεῖ ἤθει, "then I shall be able to teach you to play the flute." There perhaps the phrase = "very wittily," a sense which ἤθει or ἐν ἤθει certainly sometimes bears; or it may mean "very mildly," *cf.* τοῖς ἐν ἤθει καὶ μετὰ παιδιᾶς λεγομένοις, Plutarch, *De Poet. Aud.* 20 E, and ἐν ἤθει καὶ μετ' εὐνοίας προσφέρεσθαι τοῖς ἁμαρτάνουσι, *ibid. De Adul.* 73 E. But this last does not suit our passage, for though Joseph's words are milder than in his first speech, they are described as angry threats in § 170. For the rendering suggested in the footnote, it may be argued that ἤθος in dramatic criticism often denotes the mood or air which the speaker or writer assumes. The fullest treatment known to me of the numerous shades of meaning which the word has is to be found in Rutherford's *Chapter in the History of Annotation*, see index, *s.v.* ἤθος.

§ 219. προβλήτους. The absence of any legal reference is not fatal to the suggestion made in the footnote, as if the owner's title was not disputed, there would be no need in law for differentiation according to the method in which it had been acquired.

I would suggest also for consideration προκλήτους, *i.e.* "who had been offered for examination by torture." No example of the word is cited, but it would be naturally formed from πρόκλησις, the regular term for an offer or challenge of the kind. It would not, however, so well account for the variants προσβλήτους and προσηλύτους.

APPENDIX TO *DE VITA MOSIS* I.

§ 11. *Conscious of the increased misery*, etc. This idea, which does not seem very applicable to a three-months-old infant, is mentioned as a common, though mistaken, feeling about the death of older children in *Tusc. Disp.* i. 93 " idem, si puer parvus occidit, aequo animo ferendum putant; si vero in cunis ne querendum quidem . . . ' Nondum gustaverat,' inquiunt, ' vitae suavitatem; hic autem iam sperabat magna, quibus frui coeperat.' "

§ 22. *Like the horse to the meadow.* The proverb appears with ἱππεύς instead of ἵππος in Plato, *Theaetetus* 183 D ἱππέας εἰς πεδίον προκαλεῖ Σωκράτη εἰς λόγους προκαλούμενος, and so in Lucian, *Pseudosophistes* 8. On the other hand ἵππος as here in Lucian, *Piscator* 9.

§ 23. *Assyrian letters.* Whatever Philo understood by this, he may have got the idea from Herodotus iv. 87, where Herodotus records the erection by Darius on the Bosporus of two *stelae*, one inscribed with Ἀσσύρια γράμματα, the other with Ἑλληνικά.

§ 263. Balaam's ass (see footnote). Philo's omission of any mention of the ass speaking may no doubt be due to the feeling that the story might seem ridiculous to the Gentile readers, whom he certainly has in view. But he quite possibly may have felt that it was one of the many passages which could only be accepted in a spiritual sense, like the mythical (μυθῶδες) account of the creation of Eve from the rib of Adam. In the one place where he mentions this part of the story, *De Cher.* 32-35, he gives the interpretation that the ass stands for the "unreasoning rule of life," *i.e.* ordinary life pursuits, which the fool unjustly blames when things go wrong.

§ 304. πληγή (in Num. xxv. 8, 9). Not only is Philo's mistake in taking this as="slaughter" very natural, but are we sure that the LXX did not intend it? The word does

603

not seem to be used in the LXX, in the historical books at least, of a pestilence as excluding other forms of divine visitation, except perhaps in 1 Chron. xxi. 22, and on the other hand is constantly used of a slaughter, *e.g.* 1 Sam. iv. 10. Psalm cvi. (cv.) 30 speaking of the incident takes it as a plague, but uses the θραῦσις of Num. xvi. 48, 49. Whether Paul understood it as a plague or a slaughter is not clear (1 Cor. x. 8).

APPENDIX TO *DE VITA MOSIS* II.

§ 4. *The king is a living law.* This application of the term νόμος ἔμψυχος to the ruler (rather than as in *De Abr.* 4 to an exemplary person) is often met with. *Cf.* especially Musonius, δεῖ αὐτὸν ὥσπερ ἐδόκει τοῖς παλαιοῖς νόμον ἔμψυχον εἶναι (Stobaeus, *Flor.* xlvii. 67, Meineke's edition, vol. ii. p. 274). Other examples are Archytas, νόμων δὲ ὁ μὲν ἔμψυχος, βασιλεύς, ὁ δὲ ἄψυχος, γράμμα (*ibid.* xliii. 132, Mein. *ibid.* p. 136), and Diotogenes, ὁ δὲ βασιλεὺς ἤτοι νόμος ἔμψυχος ἢ νόμιμος ἄρχων (*ibid.* xlvii. 61, Mein. *ibid.* p. 260). I owe these examples to an article by Professor Goodenough in *Yale Classical Studies*, vol. i. pp. 56-101, on " The Political Philosophy of Hellenistic Kingship." For the other part of the dictum, that the law is a just king, *cf. Quod Det.* 141 and note, where Plato, *Symposium* 196 c οἱ πόλεως βασιλῆς νόμοι, is quoted.

§ 26-44. Philo's story of the origin of the Septuagint is probably founded on and in the main agrees with the long and elaborate account in the so-called letter of Aristeas. This document is admittedly pseudonymous and not written as it claims to be by a contemporary Greek at the court of Ptolemy Philadelphus. Its probable date is a matter of dispute, opinions ranging from 200 to 80 B.C. The chief difference is that Aristeas represents the seventy-two translators as comparing their work as they write it and producing an agreed though not an inspired version. The feasting also is more elaborate than Philo suggests, and occupies seven days, during which some question bearing on morals, particularly on the duties of kingship, is propounded to each of the translators in turn, and each of the answers is recorded. The account of the annual festival at Pharos could not of course appear in Aristeas.

Aristeas like Philo, as also Josephus, who gives a free paraphrase of a large part of the letter (*Ant.* xii. 2. 1),

PHILO

confines the translation to the Pentateuch. Modern criticism tends to accept the view that the version was made in the time of Philadelphus and may well have had his approval, but doubts the official co-operation of the king with the high priest and the employment of Palestinian Jews.

(See Swete, *Introduction to the Old Testament in Greek*, or Thackeray's translation of the letter with appendices.)

§ 38. κύρια κυρίοις ὀνόμασι. Thackeray in his version of these sections in an appendix to his translation of the letter of Aristeas, p. 92, renders "the appropriate technical words in the translation corresponded with the technical words in the original." I do not think that κύριον ὄνομα, here at any rate, means a technical term. A κύριον ὄνομα is a word used in its literal and exact sense (without μετάφρασις or παράφρασις), and all that the phrase suggests is that each word is an exact rendering of the corresponding word in the original. The duplication serves to bring out more strongly the mutuality of the correspondence like μόνη . . . μόνους in § 36. See note on *De Mut.* 12.

§ 47. τὸ γενεαλογικόν. In the grammatical schools the ἐξήγησις ἱστοριῶν, *i.e.* the elucidation of allusions in literature, was classified according as they dealt with places (τοπικαί), dates (χρονικαί), events (πραγματικαί), and persons (γενεαλογικαί); see Usener, *Kleine Schriften* ii. p. 286. So in Polybius ix. 1 the γενεαλογικὸς τρόπος of historiography is opposed to ὁ περὶ τὰς ἀποικίας καὶ κτίσεις καὶ συγγενείας, *i.e.* the ethnological, and ὁ περὶ τὰς πράξεις τῶν ἐθνῶν καὶ πόλεων καὶ δυναστῶν, called afterwards ὁ πραγματικός, which Polybius himself adopts. No doubt the Pentateuch contains much of the "pragmatical," but Philo's preoccupation with character would lead him to regard it as "genealogical." (This use of the word is ignored in L. & S.)

§ 65. While I have followed Cohn's text in indicating a lacuna at this point, which is also the termination of the second book in those editions which divide the *De Vita Mosis* into three, the correctness of this should not, I think, be regarded as certain. The decision really depends on the interpretation put on § 46 ὑπὲρ οὗ (*i.e.* the legislative part of the Pentateuch) δεύτερον λέξομεν τὸ πρότερον τῇ τάξει (*i.e.* the historical part) πρότερον ἀκριβώσαντες. If these words, as has generally been thought and at first sight seems natural, refer to the plan of this treatise we should conclude that the following sections give the "full treatment" of the historical

606

part and that some similar discussion on the legislative part has been lost. [It does not, however, seem to me that this need have been of any great length, or much more than a general praise of the laws to the same effect as what we find in § 52.] But I am inclined to agree with the suggestion of Professor Goodenough that the reference is to the scheme of the whole Exposition. On this view the full treatment of the historical part is being carried out in the four treatises, and the discussion of the legislation relegated to books *De Specialibus Legibus*, and the sections 47-65 are merely a justification of Moses' plan of setting the historical before the legislative.

This will not, of course, seem convincing to those who regard the *De Vita Mosis* as a separate work entirely independent of the scheme of the Exposition (see General Introduction pp. xv f.). Also it may be argued that if there is no lacuna, or only a very small one, the length of the treatment of Moses as lawgiver is disproportionately short compared with what is given to him as high priest and prophet. Also it must be remembered that in the copies made by the scribes whose MSS. we possess, the book did end at § 65, and that a loss at the end of a book is more likely to occur than a lacuna in the middle.

§ 79. *The sum of successive numbers*, etc. Fifty-five is what in ancient arithmetic is called a "triangular" number being the sum of $1+2+3 \ldots 10$, and therefore $=\dfrac{10.11}{2}$ $\left(1+2 \ldots n.=\dfrac{n.\overline{n+1}}{2}\right)$. This name is given to these numbers because the units can be arranged in the form of an equilateral triangle. Thus *e.g.* 10 units can be arranged

so as to form an equilateral triangle
$$
\begin{array}{cccc}
 & & a & \\
 & a & & a \\
 a & & a & & a \\
a & a & a & a
\end{array}
$$
with

each side consisting of 4 units. This side, sometimes called the gnomon, is regarded as the base of the whole triangle, and thought to possess any allegorical virtues which belong to it. *Cf.* § 84, where four is said to be the essence of ten. Twenty-eight is also a triangular number, being the sum of $1+2 \ldots 7$, but any virtues which it possesses as such appear to be superseded by its being also the sum of its factors.

PHILO

The number of the Beast ($666 = 1 + 2 \ldots 36$) and the Fishes in John xxi. ($153 = 1 + 2 \ldots 17$) are also triangular, and attempts have been made to interpret them from this point of view.

§ 114. (The inscription on the πέταλον.) The footnote requires supplementing and perhaps correcting. Thackeray in his note to Joseph. *Bell. Iud.* v. 235 states positively that the inscription has been shewn to be the "tetragrammaton" rather than "Holiness to the Lord." He refers to a note in the *Journal of Theological Studies*, vol. xxvi. p. 72 by Mr. J. E. Hogg. I do not think this note does more than argue (with what success I cannot tell) that the Hebrew in Ex. xxviii. 36 (LXX 32) and in Ex. xxxix. 30 (LXX, xxxvi. 38)—though the *prima facie* meaning is "Holy to Jahve"—*may* mean "the sacred name Jahve," and also that the LXX in Ex. xxviii. does not assert more than that the thing engraved was a "holy thing belonging to the Lord." This last is true, but in the other passage, Ex. xxxix. (LXX, xxxvi.), the translators make it perfectly clear that the inscription was ἁγίασμα κυρίῳ.

As for Philo, in *De Mig.* 103, where he quotes Ex. xxviii. in the form πέταλον χρυσοῦν καθαρόν, ἔχον ἐκτύπωμα σφραγῖδος, ἁγίασμα κυρίῳ, it is quite possible that he takes ἁγίασμα in apposition to πέταλον or ἐκτύπωμα, and does not mention any inscription at all. The words then mean "a plate of pure gold, having the engraving (embossment?) of a signet, a sacred thing to the Lord"; not "*as* of a signet," for he goes on to explain that the signet represents the ἰδέα ἰδεῶν, a phrase which, I think, refers to the Logos rather than to the Self-existent. If so, in *Mos.* ii. 114 and 132 he is following quite another tradition. What authorities are there for this besides himself and Josephus? Prof. Burkitt in a supplementary note in *J.T.S.* xxvi. p. 180 remarks that the same is stated by Bar Hebraeus, "who must ultimately have derived it from Origen," and by Origen, who may "possibly" have derived it from Philo. Considering Origen's well-known acquaintance with Philo, "possibly" seems a weak word. Mangey also quotes Jerome to the same effect, but Jerome also makes frequent use of Philo. Is it a Rabbinic tradition? The German translators, generally well versed in such parallels, quote nothing from this source.

The question then suggests itself, "Did Josephus also merely follow Philo?" If so, though it is not given among

APPENDICES

Cohn's examples of coincidence between the two, it is the strongest evidence I have yet seen of Josephus's use of his predecessor.

A further question, to which I can give no answer, is what does Philo mean by saying that the "theologian," presumably Moses, declares that the name of the Self-existent has four letters. I do not think he anywhere shews any knowledge of the YHVH, or that it is represented by κύριος in the LXX.

§ 117-135. (Symbolism of the High Priest's vesture.) A much shorter account in *De Spec. Leg.* i. 85-95 agrees very closely with this in substance. The chief differences are that the bells there signify the harmony, not between merely earth and water, but between all the parts of the universe, and that "Clear-shewing" and "Truth" are given a somewhat different interpretation. There "Clear-shewing" is entirely confined to the "natures in heaven" (corresponding more or less to the "rational principle in nature" of this treatise), and "Truth" only concerns men as a qualification for the "heaven" which the breastplate in both passages represents, while in this treatise both are common to both forms of λόγος. In *De Mig.* 102 f. the only parts noticed are the gold-plate on the head, and the flowers and the bells at the feet (the pomegranates being left unnoticed). The treatment of these two (the flowers and bells) is altogether different. The two together represent the αἰσθητά, as opposed to the νοητά (the head-gear), the flowers being the things seen, and the bells the things heard, and, while in *De Vita Mosis* the harmony produced by the latter is that between earth and water, in *De Mig.* we have the profounder idea that it is the essential harmony between the world of sense and the world of thought.

In Josephus's short notice (*Ant.* ii. 184), besides other differences, the pomegranates signify the lightning, and the bells the thunder.

§ 210. *Ever virgin*, etc. In *De Op.* 100 Philo has ascribed these epithets to philosophers other than Pythagorean; in *Leg. All.* i. 15 to the Pythagoreans themselves. The second view is supported by the statement of Stobaeus, *Ecl.* i. 1. 10, that Pythagoras, likening the numbers to the Gods, called Seven Athena.

609

SUPPLEMENTARY LIST OF CASES WHERE THE TEXT PRINTED IS NOT VOUCHED FOR BY ANY MANUSCRIPT

De Abrahamo

§	TEXT	MSS.	§	TEXT	MSS.
111	οὐδ'	οὐχ	200	ἀποδόσεως	ὑποθέσεως [1]
185	ἐξευμαρίζον	ἐξευμαριζόν-των	235	ἐν τέλος	ἐντελὲς

De Josepho

§	TEXT	MSS.	§	TEXT	MSS.
132	τοσοῦτος	τοιοῦτος	156	ᾧ	ὧν
137	ἀπεράτους	ἀπειράτους or ἀπείρους			

De Vita Mosis I

§	TEXT	MSS.
44	δικαιώσας	δικάσας

De Vita Mosis II

§	TEXT	MSS.	§	TEXT	MSS.
179	παρεστῶτος	προεστῶτος	268	δηλῶν	δηλοῦντα or δῆλον
264	ἐνδεχόμενον	ἐκδεχόμενον or δεχόμενον			

[1] A doubtful correction. The senses in which ὑπόθεσις is used are very wide. *Cf. Mos.* i. 69.

Printed in Great Britain by R. & R. CLARK, LIMITED, Edinburgh.

THE LOEB CLASSICAL LIBRARY

VOLUMES ALREADY PUBLISHED

LATIN AUTHORS

AMMIANUS MARCELLINUS. ˙J. C. Rolfe. 3 Vols.

APULEIUS : THE GOLDEN ASS (METAMORPHOSES). W. Adlington (1566). Revised by S. Gaselee.

ST. AUGUSTINE : CITY OF GOD. 7 Vols. Vol. I. G. E. McCracken. Vol. II. W. M. Green. Vol. V. E. M. Sanford and W. M. Green. Vol. VI. W. C. Greene.

ST. AUGUSTINE, CONFESSIONS OF. W. Watts (1631). 2 Vols.

ST. AUGUSTINE : SELECT LETTERS. J. H. Baxter.

AUSONIUS. H. G. Evelyn White. 2 Vols.

BEDE. J. E. King. 2 Vols.

BOETHIUS : TRACTS AND DE CONSOLATIONE PHILOSOPHIAE. Rev. H. F. Stewart and E. K. Rand.

CAESAR : ALEXANDRIAN, AFRICAN AND SPANISH WARS. A. G. Way.

CAESAR : CIVIL WARS. A. G. Peskett.

CAESAR : GALLIC WAR. H. J. Edwards.

CATO AND VARRO : DE RE RUSTICA. H. B. Ash and W. D. Hooper.

CATULLUS. F. W. Cornish ; TIBULLUS. J. B. Postgate ; and PERVIGILIUM VENERIS. J. W. Mackail.

CELSUS : DE MEDICINA. W. G. Spencer. 3 Vols.

CICERO : BRUTUS AND ORATOR. G. L. Hendrickson and H. M. Hubbell.

CICERO : DE FINIBUS. H. Rackham.

CICERO : DE INVENTIONE, etc. H. M. Hubbell.

CICERO : DE NATURA DEORUM AND ACADEMICA. H. Rackham.

CICERO : DE OFFICIIS. Walter Miller.

CICERO : DE ORATORE, etc. 2 Vols. Vol. I : DE ORATORE, Books I and II. E. W. Sutton and H. Rackham. Vol. II : DE ORATORE, Book III ; DE FATO ; PARADOXA STOICORUM ; DE PARTITIONE ORATORIA. H. Rackham.

1

THE LOEB CLASSICAL LIBRARY

LUCRETIUS. W. H. D. Rouse.

MARTIAL. W. C. A. Ker. 2 Vols.

MINOR LATIN POETS: from PUBLILIUS SYRUS to RUTILIUS NAMATIANUS, including GRATTIUS, CALPURNIUS SICULUS, NEMESIANUS, AVIANUS, with "Aetna," "Phoenix" and other poems. J. Wight Duff and Arnold M. Duff.

OVID: THE ART OF LOVE AND OTHER POEMS. J. H. Mozley.

OVID: FASTI. Sir James G. Frazer.

OVID: HEROIDES AND AMORES. Grant Showerman.

OVID: METAMORPHOSES. F. J. Miller. 2 Vols.

OVID: TRISTIA AND EX PONTO. A. L. Wheeler.

PETRONIUS. M. Heseltine; SENECA: APOCOLOCYNTOSIS. W. H. D. Rouse.

PHAEDRUS AND BABRIUS (Greek). B. E. Perry.

PLAUTUS. Paul Nixon. 5 Vols.

PLINY: LETTERS. Melmoth's translation revised by W. M. L. Hutchinson. 2 Vols.

PLINY: NATURAL HISTORY. 10 Vols. Vols. I-V and IX. H. Rackham. Vols. VI-VIII. W. H. S. Jones. Vol. X. D. E. Eichholz.

PROPERTIUS. H. E. Butler.

PRUDENTIUS. H. J. Thomson. 2 Vols.

QUINTILIAN. H. E. Butler. 4 Vols.

REMAINS OF OLD LATIN. E. H. Warmington. 4 Vols. Vol. I (Ennius and Caecilius). Vol. II (Livius, Naevius, Pacuvius, Accius). Vol. III (Lucilius, Laws of the XII Tables). Vol. IV (Archaic Inscriptions).

SALLUST. J. C. Rolfe.

SCRIPTORES HISTORIAE AUGUSTAE. D. Magie. 3 Vols.

SENECA: APOCOLOCYNTOSIS. Cf. PETRONIUS.

SENECA: EPISTULAE MORALES. R. M. Gummere. 3 Vols.

SENECA: MORAL ESSAYS. J. W. Basore. 3 Vols.

SENECA: TRAGEDIES. F. J. Miller. 2 Vols.

SIDONIUS: POEMS AND LETTERS. W. B. Anderson. 2 Vols.

SILIUS ITALICUS. J. D. Duff. 2 Vols.

STATIUS. J. H. Mozley. 2 Vols.

SUETONIUS. J. C. Rolfe. 2 Vols.

TACITUS: DIALOGUS. Sir Wm. Peterson; and AGRICOLA AND GERMANIA. Maurice Hutton.

TACITUS: HISTORIES AND ANNALS. C. H. Moore and J. Jackson. 4 Vols.

TERENCE. John Sargeaunt. 2 Vols.

THE LOEB CLASSICAL LIBRARY

TERTULLIAN: APOLOGIA AND DE SPECTACULIS. T. R. Glover;
MINUCIUS FELIX. G. H. Rendall.
VALERIUS FLACCUS. J. H. Mozley.
VARRO: DE LINGUA LATINA. R. G. Kent. 2 Vols.
VELLEIUS PATERCULUS AND RES GESTAE DIVI AUGUSTI.
F. W. Shipley.
VIRGIL. H. R. Fairclough. 2 Vols.
VITRUVIUS: DE ARCHITECTURA. F. Granger. 2 Vols.

GREEK AUTHORS

ACHILLES TATIUS. S. Gaselee.
AELIAN: ON THE NATURE OF ANIMALS. A. F. Scholfield.
3 Vols.
AENEAS TACTICUS, ASCLEPIODOTUS AND ONASANDER. The
Illinois Greek Club.
AESCHINES. C. D. Adams.
AESCHYLUS. H. Weir Smyth. 2 Vols.
ALCIPHRON, AELIAN AND PHILOSTRATUS: LETTERS. A. R.
Benner and F. H. Fobes.
APOLLODORUS. Sir James G. Frazer. 2 Vols.
APOLLONIUS RHODIUS. R. C. Seaton.
THE APOSTOLIC FATHERS. Kirsopp Lake. 2 Vols.
APPIAN'S ROMAN HISTORY. Horace White. 4 Vols.
ARATUS. Cf. CALLIMACHUS.
ARISTOPHANES. Benjamin Bickley Rogers. 3 Vols. Verse
trans.
ARISTOTLE: ART OF RHETORIC. J. H. Freese.
ARISTOTLE: ATHENIAN CONSTITUTION, EUDEMIAN ETHICS,
VIRTUES AND VICES. H. Rackham.
ARISTOTLE: THE CATEGORIES. ON INTERPRETATION. H. P.
Cooke; PRIOR ANALYTICS. H. Tredennick.
ARISTOTLE: GENERATION OF ANIMALS. A. L. Peck.
ARISTOTLE: HISTORIA ANIMALIUM. A. L. Peck. 3 Vols. Vol. I.
ARISTOTLE: METAPHYSICS. H. Tredennick. 2 Vols.
ARISTOTLE: METEOROLOGICA. H. D. P. Lee.
ARISTOTLE: MINOR WORKS. W. S. Hett. "On Colours,"
"On Things Heard," "Physiognomics," "On Plants,"
"On Marvellous Things Heard," "Mechanical Problems,"
"On Indivisible Lines," "Situations and Names of
Winds," "On Melissus, Xenophanes, and Gorgias."

ARISTOTLE: NICOMACHEAN ETHICS. H. Rackham.

ARISTOTLE: OECONOMICA AND MAGNA MORALIA. G. C. Armstrong. (With Metaphysics, Vol. II.)

ARISTOTLE: ON THE HEAVENS. W. K. C. Guthrie.

ARISTOTLE: ON THE SOUL, PARVA NATURALIA, ON BREATH. W. S. Hett.

ARISTOTLE: PARTS OF ANIMALS. A. L. Peck; MOTION AND PROGRESSION OF ANIMALS. E. S. Forster.

ARISTOTLE: PHYSICS. Rev. P. Wicksteed and F. M. Cornford. 2 Vols.

ARISTOTLE: POETICS; LONGINUS ON THE SUBLIME. W. Hamilton Fyfe; DEMETRIUS ON STYLE. W. Rhys Roberts.

ARISTOTLE: POLITICS. H. Rackham.

ARISTOTLE: POSTERIOR ANALYTICS. H. Tredennick; TOPICS. E. S. Forster.

ARISTOTLE: PROBLEMS. W. S. Hett. 2 Vols.

ARISTOTLE: RHETORICA AD ALEXANDRUM. H. Rackham. (With Problems, Vol. II.)

ARISTOTLE: SOPHISTICAL REFUTATIONS. COMING-TO-BE AND PASSING-AWAY. E. S. Forster; ON THE COSMOS. D. J. Furley.

ARRIAN: HISTORY OF ALEXANDER AND INDICA. Rev. E. Iliffe Robson. 2 Vols.

ATHENAEUS: DEIPNOSOPHISTAE. C. B. Gulick. 7 Vols.

BABRIUS AND PHAEDRUS (Latin). B. E. Perry.

ST. BASIL: LETTERS. R. J. Deferrari. 4 Vols.

CALLIMACHUS: FRAGMENTS. C. A. Trypanis.

CALLIMACHUS: HYMNS AND EPIGRAMS, AND LYCOPHRON A. W. Mair; ARATUS. G. R. Mair.

CLEMENT OF ALEXANDRIA. Rev. G. W. Butterworth.

COLLUTHUS. *Cf.* OPPIAN.

DAPHNIS AND CHLOE. *Cf.* LONGUS.

DEMOSTHENES I: OLYNTHIACS, PHILIPPICS AND MINOR ORATIONS: I-XVII AND XX. J. H. Vince.

DEMOSTHENES II: DE CORONA AND DE FALSA LEGATIONE. C. A. Vince and J. H. Vince.

DEMOSTHENES III: MEIDIAS, ANDROTION, ARISTOCRATES, TIMOCRATES, ARISTOGEITON. J. H. Vince.

DEMOSTHENES IV-VI: PRIVATE ORATIONS AND IN NEAERAM. A. T. Murray.

DEMOSTHENES VII: FUNERAL SPEECH, EROTIC ESSAY, EXORDIA AND LETTERS. N. W. and N. J. DeWitt.

THE LOEB CLASSICAL LIBRARY

DIO CASSIUS : ROMAN HISTORY. E. Cary. 9 Vols.

DIO CHRYSOSTOM. 5 Vols. Vols. I and II. J. W. Cohoon. Vol. III. J. W. Cohoon and H. Lamar Crosby. Vols. IV and V. H. Lamar Crosby.

DIODORUS SICULUS. 12 Vols. Vols. I-VI. C. H. Oldfather. Vol. VII. C. L. Sherman. Vol. VIII. C. B. Welles. Vols. IX and X. Russel M. Geer. Vol. XI. F. R. Walton.

DIOGENES LAERTIUS. R. D. Hicks. 2 Vols.

DIONYSIUS OF HALICARNASSUS : ROMAN ANTIQUITIES. Spelman's translation revised by E. Cary. 7 Vols.

EPICTETUS. W. A. Oldfather. 2 Vols.

EURIPIDES. A. S. Way. 4 Vols. Verse trans.

EUSEBIUS : ECCLESIASTICAL HISTORY. Kirsopp Lake and J. E. L. Oulton. 2 Vols.

GALEN : ON THE NATURAL FACULTIES. A. J. Brock.

THE GREEK ANTHOLOGY. W R. Paton. 5 Vols.

THE GREEK BUCOLIC POETS (THEOCRITUS, BION, MOSCHUS). J. M. Edmonds.

GREEK ELEGY AND IAMBUS WITH THE ANACREONTEA. J. M. Edmonds. 2 Vols.

GREEK MATHEMATICAL WORKS. Ivor Thomas. 2 Vols.

HERODES. Cf. THEOPHRASTUS : CHARACTERS.

HERODOTUS. A. D. Godley. 4 Vols.

HESIOD AND THE HOMERIC HYMNS. H. G. Evelyn White.

HIPPOCRATES AND THE FRAGMENTS OF HERACLEITUS. W. H. S. Jones and E. T. Withington. 4 Vols.

HOMER : ILIAD. A. T. Murray. 2 Vols.

HOMER : ODYSSEY. A. T. Murray. 2 Vols.

ISAEUS. E. S. Forster.

ISOCRATES. George Norlin and LaRue Van Hook. 3 Vols.

ST. JOHN DAMASCENE : BARLAAM AND IOASAPH. Rev. G. R. Woodward and Harold Mattingly.

JOSEPHUS. 9 Vols. Vols. I-IV. H. St. J. Thackeray. Vol. V. H. St. J. Thackeray and Ralph Marcus. Vols. VI and VII. Ralph Marcus. Vol. VIII. Ralph Marcus and Allen Wikgren. Vol. IX. L. H. Feldman.

JULIAN. Wilmer Cave Wright. 3 Vols.

LONGUS : DAPHNIS AND CHLOE. Thornley's translation revised by J. M. Edmonds ; and PARTHENIUS. S. Gaselee.

LUCIAN. 8 Vols. Vols. I-V. A. M. Harmon. Vol. VI. K. Kilburn. Vol. VII. M. D. Macleod.

LIMACHUS.
Edmonds. 3 Vols.
amb.
ddell; PTOLEMY: TETRABIBLOS. F. E.

R. Haines.
inson.
s. 2 Vols. K. J. Maidment **and**

. W. H. D. Rouse. 3 Vols.
US, TRYPHIODORUS. A. W. Mair.
-LITERARY SELECTIONS. A. S. Hunt and C. C.
2 Vols. LITERARY SELECTIONS (Poetry). D. L.

ENIUS. *Cf.* LONGUS.
ANIAS: DESCRIPTION OF GREECE. W. H. S. Jones. **5**
ols. and Companion Vol. arranged by R. E. Wycherley.
ILO. 10 Vols. Vols. I-V. F. H. Colson and Rev. G. H.
Whitaker. Vols. VI-X. F. H. Colson. General Index.
Rev. J. W. Earp.
Two Supplementary Vols. Translation only from an
Armenian Text. Ralph Marcus.
PHILOSTRATUS: THE LIFE OF APOLLONIUS OF TYANA. F. C.
Conybeare. 2 Vols.
PHILOSTRATUS: IMAGINES; CALLISTRATUS: DESCRIPTIONS.
A. Fairbanks.
PHILOSTRATUS AND EUNAPIUS: LIVES OF THE SOPHISTS.
Wilmer Cave Wright.
PINDAR. Sir J. E. Sandys.
PLATO: CHARMIDES, ALCIBIADES, HIPPARCHUS, THE LOVERS,
THEAGES, MINOS AND EPINOMIS. W. R. M. Lamb.
PLATO: CRATYLUS, PARMENIDES, GREATER HIPPIAS, LESSER
HIPPIAS. H. N. Fowler.
PLATO: EUTHYPHRO, APOLOGY, CRITO, PHAEDO, PHAEDRUS.
H. N. Fowler.
PLATO: LACHES. PROTAGORAS, MENO. EUTHYDEMUS.
W. R. M. Lamb.
PLATO: LAWS. Rev. R. G. Bury. 2 Vols.
PLATO: LYSIS, SYMPOSIUM, GORGIAS. W. R. M. Lamb.
PLATO: REPUBLIC. Paul Shorey. 2 Vols.
PLATO: STATESMAN, PHILEBUS. H. N. Fowler: ION.
W. R. M. Lamb.

THE LOEB CLASSICAL

PLATO : THEAETETUS AND SOPHIST.
PLATO : TIMAEUS, CRITIAS, CLITOP
stulae. Rev. R. G. Bury.
PLUTARCH : MORALIA. 15 Vols. V
Vol. VI. W. C. Helmbold. Vol.
B. Einarson. Vol. IX. E. L. Mi
W. C. Helmbold. Vol. X. H. N
Pearson, F. H. Sandbach. Vol.
Helmbold.
PLUTARCH : THE PARALLEL LIVES. D.
POLYBIUS. W. R. Paton. 6 Vols.
PROCOPIUS : HISTORY OF THE WARS. H. B. De
PTOLEMY : TETRABIBLOS. Cf. MANETHO.
QUINTUS SMYRNAEUS. A. S. Way. Verse trans.
SEXTUS EMPIRICUS. Rev. R. G. Bury. 4 Vols.
SOPHOCLES. F. Storr. 2 Vols. Verse trans.
STRABO : GEOGRAPHY. Horace L. Jones. 8 Vols.
THEOPHRASTUS : CHARACTERS. J. M. Edmonds ; HERO
etc. A. D. Knox.
THEOPHRASTUS : ENQUIRY INTO PLANTS. Sir Arthur Ho
2 Vols.
THUCYDIDES. C. F. Smith. 4 Vols.
TRYPHIODORUS. Cf. OPPIAN.
XENOPHON : CYROPAEDIA. Walter Miller. 2 Vols.
XENOPHON : HELLENICA, ANABASIS, APOLOGY, AND SYMPO-
SIUM. C. L. Brownson and O. J. Todd. 3 Vols.
XENOPHON : MEMORABILIA AND OECONOMICUS. E. C. Mar-
chant.
XENOPHON : SCRIPTA MINORA. E. C. Marchant.

VOLUMES IN PREPARATION

GREEK AUTHORS

PLOTINUS. A. H. Armstrong.

DESCRIPTIVE PROSPECTUS ON APPLICATION

CAMBRIDGE, MASS.   LONDON
HARVARD UNIV. PRESS   WILLIAM HEINEMANN LTD

8

tt.
und
ach.
W. L.
W. C.

ols.

V ols.

rt.